# SPAIN:
## FROM DICTATORSHIP
## TO DEMOCRACY
### 1939 TO THE PRESENT

# A HISTORY OF SPAIN

## Published

Iberia in Prehistory[*]
*María Cruz Fernández Castro*

The Romans in Spain[†]
*John S. Richardson*

Visigothic Spain 409–711
*Roger Collins*

The Arab Conquest of Spain, 710–797
*Roger Collins*

The Contest of Christian and Muslim Spain 1031–1157[†]
*Bernard F. Reilly*

Spain's Centuries of Crisis: 1300–1474
*Teofilo Ruiz*

The Spain of the Catholic Monarchs 1474–1520
*John Edwards*

Spain 1516–1598: From Nation State to World Empire[*]
*John Lynch*

The Hispanic World in Crisis and Change, 1598–1700[*]
*John Lynch*

Bourbon Spain, 1700–1808[*]
*John Lynch*

Spain in the Liberal Age: From Constitution to Civil War, 1808–1939
*Charles J. Esdaile*

Spain: From Dictatorship to Democracy. 1939 to the Present
*Javier Tusell*

## Forthcoming

Caliphs and Kings 798–1033
*Roger Collins*

Spain 1157–1312
*Peter Linehan*

[*] Out of print
[†] Print on demand

# JAVIER TUSELL

# SPAIN:

## FROM DICTATORSHIP
## TO DEMOCRACY
## 1939 TO THE PRESENT

### TRANSLATED BY ROSEMARY CLARK

**WILEY-BLACKWELL**

A John Wiley & Sons, Ltd., Publication

# Contents

# Note on the Author

Javier Tusell (1945–2005) was Professor of Contemporary History in the Universidad Nacional de Educación a Distancia (Spain's Open University) and a leading figure among the intellectuals of post-Franco Spain. The author of many books on the history of modern Spain, he was held in high esteem for his scholarship and judgment and recognized as supreme in his access to contemporary sources. By the time he came to write the present work he had reached his prime, but was then cruelly cut down by terminal illness which afflicted him for the last years of his life. He completed the research and writing, and bequeathed the results in this masterly account of a people in transition from dictatorship to democracy, a book which is evidence too of his personal triumph over adversity.

John Lynch, Series Editor

# Introduction

On May 19, 1939, a hundred and twenty thousand soldiers paraded before Franco in Madrid. The press hailed the ceremony as the victory following a second reconquest of Spain's enemies. During the march-past, the general was awarded Spain's highest military honor, the Grand Cross Laureate of San Fernando. Although the public was not informed, Alfonso XIII himself had written to Franco pledging his support. The king was unaware that the general was no longer a monarchist and indeed was now playing absolute monarch himself.

The celebrations continued with a religious ceremony the following day. Franco entered the Church of Santa Barbara beneath a palium – a treatment reserved for the Blessed Sacrament and for ruling monarchs. Awaiting him in the church was a selection of artifacts that evoked Spain's past struggle against the Infidel. Every detail in the appearance of those present alluded to past tradition, not only the military uniforms and ecclesiastical robes but also the "Spanish *mantillas* worn with pride on tall combs" by the not very numerous women present. The climax of the religious ceremony was the moment at which Franco laid down his sword of victory before the Christ of Lepanto, brought all the way from Barcelona for the occasion. Everything combined to glorify the great leading figure of the entire ceremony. The Primate of Spain, Cardinal Gomá, prayed that God "in His mercy and in praise might look kindly upon you, forever protect you and protect the nation whose governance He has entrusted to your care."

The entire ceremonial, which more properly belonged to a medieval warrior society in which military, political, and religious life were bound together, largely explains what happened after 1939. If ever there has been a crucial break in continuity in Spanish history it was at that moment, at the end of the Civil War. If the war had never happened, if it had not lasted so long, or if there had been less bloodshed, continuity between the 1930s and 1940s would have been conceivable. Yet although there was a clear intention to make such a break, it was altogether less clear exactly what form it should take. The repression already exercised during the war years was a foretaste of the treatment that would be meted out to the vanquished, while friendship with Germany and Italy defined Spain's foreign policy; yet decisions still needed to be taken to determine whether Spain's dictatorship would be personal or fascist, how long it would last, and, above all, how it would function.

So far, circumstances and expediency rather than a political program had decided matters. If anything characterizes the victors of the Civil War it is that while the conflict lasted, instead of attempting experiments in new kinds of social structures as their enemies had done, they left that for later. If we consider Francoism in total, from the perspective of its earliest days, its end, and its duration, it is evident that a fundamental change did occur in Spanish society, but not in the way that those who exercised power had in mind. An observer able to compare the Spain of 1939 with the Spain of 1968 would have judged them to be two entirely different worlds. Yet, although there were evident changes, there were also undeniable examples of continuity, especially obvious in anything relating to the exercise of political power. There is, therefore, no better way of approaching the history of Francoism than by taking these factors as a starting-point.

## Franco: Biography and Political Practice

The traits of Franco's character, particularly his apparent impenetrability, may tempt historians to try to play amateur psychologist with a person who in actual fact was more straightforward than he appeared. When this happens, discussion remains superficial; yet a dictatorship which was by nature personal demands careful consideration of the one who held the monopoly of power.

Born in 1892 in El Ferrol into a family with a history of two centuries of service in the Spanish Navy, Franco's childhood was not a happy one, though this factor alone does not explain his life as a whole. His father lived apart from his mother and was not officially acknowledged until his death. This explains the boy's strong emotional attachment to his mother, which contributed to forging a cautious, withdrawn character but one that was, at the same time, susceptible to the wildest flights of ambition. An even stronger influence in the molding of his character must surely have been his early entry to the Military Academy at Toledo as the youngest cadet in his year. The sinking of the fleet denied him the possibility of joining the Navy: that is why he summed up 1898 in the three words "injustice, betrayal, desertion by Europe." At the Military Academy, his progress was not brilliant. In contrast, after a quick transfer to the Army in Africa, he gained a series of brilliant promotions and was mentioned in dispatches, always at the head of crack troops, first in the Regular Forces and then the Foreign Legion. On five occasions, he was rewarded for conduct on the battlefield. Although Franco's family had suffered no economic difficulties, it is possible that his marriage to Carmen Polo in 1923 was a step forward for him personally. In the 1920s he led an intense social life that, in his own words, allowed him to "make contact with men who were prepared." The general himself at 33 now felt "ready for great responsibilities."

He no doubt meant political responsibilities and it is important to remember in that respect that early on his opinion swung against what he considered dominant "myths." His *Diary of a Footsoldier* reveals the mistrust he felt towards liberal politics, in his view unable to achieve anything other than "years of stumbling steps and tentative truces." But it was the divergence in opinion on military policy in Morocco that brought about confrontation with Primo de Rivera, though it did not last for long. In the draft of his memoirs Franco acknowledges that he welcomed the Republic "enthusiastically." Disappointment followed swiftly, however, and he blamed all the ills of that regime on "ambitious failed politicians" and on Freemasonry. He soon adopted an attitude of "cold detachment" towards the regime, though not too obviously. From the end of the 1920s onwards he received anti-communist propaganda, and the revolution of October 1934, which he took an active part in putting down, was a turning-point in his life. His tardy commitment to the conspiracy against the Republic can be explained to an extent by his mixture of prudence and opportunism, but also by the fact that he had never been a "politicized" soldier to the same extent as many of his comrades-in-arms.

Over the course of the Civil War Franco finally became the figure of history that he would always remain. He based that figure on "a profoundly Catholic social conscience and on [a desire] to rid Spain forever of the causes of our decadence, our warring political parties, Freemasonry, and communism." He sincerely believed that he had "God's scandalous help" and that on his shoulders would rest in due course "total responsibility:

military, political and economic." He soon began to astound foreign ambassadors and close collaborators with his distinctly unorthodox opinions on all kinds of matters. With the war, too, there awoke in him secret desires brought together in *Race*, a text – later made into a film – that he wrote in 1940. The villain of the piece is a lawyer who has gone astray thanks to his membership of the Atheneum but is finally brought back onto the straight and narrow by his love for a young woman Falangist. In contrast, his brother – the hero – is a young officer; a third member of the family – a priest – is murdered during the Civil War. The story concludes with the victory parade in May 1939.

In light of what has been said so far, it is obvious that any study of the character of the dictator must go back in time to his professional life in the Army. Indeed, the first consideration to take into account is that Franco was first and foremost a soldier: "Without Africa," he declared, referring to his own personal experience there, "I can scarcely understand myself." From his personality, this was the only trait that really stood out, to such an extent that it is not possible to attribute to him, for example, the intellectual qualities shown by other officers. His intellectual horizons were for many years limited to attaining the post of high commissioner in Morocco. In certain senses that is what he did become, but in Spain.

It was from his experience in Morocco that he derived his strength of character, his impassivity, his hardness, and his sense of discipline. He did not hesitate in describing himself as a "sheep-like" officer – that is to say, scrupulous in obeying orders – even in front of young cadets. His austerity was closely linked to his experience in the Moroccan campaigns. "I do not object to luxury but I can do without it," he once told one of his closest associates. It would be over-generous to describe his residence at El Pardo as a palace when it could more properly be termed a barracks. His writings from Morocco bear witness not so much to cruelty as to a hardness which made him view death as commonplace. If it was in Soviet Russia that for the first time in the modern world a system was generated in which the state apparatus used modern methods of violence against any who opposed it, it was in Franco's Spain that such a system was first seen in western Europe.

His military career was the only reason why he became an influential national figure but he was by no means outstanding in his profession. His actual capabilities were those of an able tactician in guerrilla warfare against the indigenous peoples of Morocco, and they were also evident in his prudence, orderliness, and logistical skill in the management of his troops. These same strengths were the ones that he displayed during the Civil War, in which his allies always criticized his excessive slowness and prudence. It is often forgotten that Franco wrote a book entitled *The ABC of Defensive Warfare*; doubtless, in politics too he was a past master of defensive strategies. If life in the Army made him the figure he was, it also convinced him of the superiority of those who received an Army training. Franco always considered military training valuable in itself: he judged Eisenhower and De Gaulle favorably simply because they were generals. His concept of political power was close to his concept of military power and when talking about it he used terms such as "command and captaincy" and, beyond all doubt, tried to organize life in Spain as though it were a barracks. While exercising his political functions as Chief of State, Franco often gave important positions to soldiers. In the mid-1950s, half of the presidents of companies in the National Institute for Industry (*Instituto Nacional de Industria* or INI)[1] were soldiers.

His determination to revive in Spain the glories of the past translated in practice into far more prosaic attitudes as he confined himself to the "order, unity, and endurance" recommended by Luis Carrero Blanco. In the 1930s he reinforced this stance by adding to it another tragic yet firmly held conviction. He became convinced of the communist threat, to which, in his own mind, he added the dangers of a Masonic conspiracy dating back to the eighteenth century. From that time until his death Franco held the view that Freemasonry led inevitably to liberalism and that liberalism opened the way to the threat of communism. The unrelenting stubbornness with which a man who came to govern one of the world's leading industrial powers defended this nonsense appears excessive. His writings on the matter, signed with a pseudonym, show obsessive attention to detail, and his determination to pursue offenders was such that he managed to accumulate in the Salamanca Archives 80,000 files on supposed Freemasons in a country where there had never been more than 50,000.

Franco's experience of life in the 1930s also influenced him in another way. He had always been a Catholic but now his religious beliefs led him to view himself as a providential figure. The sincerity and spontaneity with which this conviction grew are astounding. He assured Don Juan de Borbón that he had won victory in the Civil War thanks to "divine favor repeatedly conferred." Catholicism and the Fatherland were in his mind one and the same thing to such an extent that, being responsible for the latter, he had no difficulty in pontificating on the former. The Spain of his day – at least up until the 1960s – was a country where bishops spoke out as though they were politicians, while the Chief of State at times seemed to perform the functions of a cardinal. His Catholicism was deeply sincere but it was not informed. He was not in any sense able to understand the changes brought about in the Catholic Church by the Second Vatican Council. It was only then that he felt disoriented.

Victory brought about a fundamental transformation in Franco's life. The terms he used when discussing taking on the duty of governing the Spanish nation precluded any suggestion that his attitude might in any way have been false or cynical. His own family were aware of the profound change that had taken place. If in the past he had been communicative and affectionate, now his position as *caudillo* made him "cold and distant" in his treatment of others. Franco's own convictions concerning his leadership would have been unimaginable were it not for the exalted role that others attributed to him. The consolidation of his position was largely managed by Ramón Serrano Suñer. In one book written in the 1940s Serrano Suñer suggested that the conditions of leadership which allowed the *caudillo* not to have to account for his actions to any official body set him on a par with the pope.

By that time Franco already had the unshakable conviction that no limits should be set on the scope or extent of his powers of command. Consequently, those on the right who wanted to limit his freedom of choice by institutional means, in accordance with the principles of their original plans of action in which he was seen as a temporary solution, he considered traitors. Those, on the other hand, who were flexible enough to explore other possibilities were found a post in the new regime. Nonetheless, their function within that regime depended entirely on what Franco wanted. During the Civil War he explained to anyone willing to listen the role he had planned for Falange and the traditionalists: the latter were to ensure that solid principles prevailed in the organization of postwar Spain, while the former was to become a vehicle for attracting the ordinary masses.

The role allocated to these two political forces reveals Franco's doctrinal limitations. It has been said that in 1939 his power was more absolute than that of any other dictator at the time, not only in terms of specific legislation but also because, as a politician, he did not consider himself bound by any ideology. His decisions were based on national militarism, national Catholicism, and national patriotism, and they drew strength from his obsessive hostility to Freemasonry. However, this was not so much a matter of doctrine as of deep-seated feelings. One minister, Mariano

Navarro Rubio, wrote that he was "short on doctrine but unshakable: his ideas were few, basic, clear, and productive." The first two adjectives no doubt correspond more closely to reality than the second two. At the height of the Civil War, an intelligent conservative such as Cambó did not know whether to be more astounded by how basic the ideas were – "like café conversations" – or by the "admiring tone" in which Franco described his periodic discoveries around the Mediterranean.

It is worth mentioning some of his ideas on different topics because they reveal his limitations. During the Franco years Spain experienced the radical transformation of her economy but not as a result of his economic ideas. What Franco naturally tended towards was a kind of "barracks autarchy." José Larraz, one of his Finance Ministers, used to say that never having managed to make the dictator pronounce the word "inflation" correctly – he always said "inflaction" – he had no hope of ever making him understand what the word actually meant. When the Plan for Economic Stabilization came into being in 1959 the man who had proposed it revealed in his memoirs Franco's "mistrust" of it, compounded by the fact that it was backed by international organizations. In actual fact, Francoism can be blamed for delaying a national economic development that could have occurred earlier. As Dionisio Ridruejo wrote, when the regime claimed credit for Spain's economic development, it was as if a harbor pilot sailing out to sea after a northwesterly gale had blown itself out were to claim that he himself had caused it to die down.

In the area of politics, too, Franco's notions were elementary, though he could concentrate his efforts jealously on holding on to power. During World War II he suggested to Don Juan de Borbón that he should follow the example of "revolutionary totalitarian monarchies" such as the Catholic monarchs had been, in his view. Years later, he sketched out for the same correspondent a curious theory of leadership by "prescribed acquisition." Nor did his theory of "organic democracy" in a previous era make any significant contribution to political science. These were mere words that he used to justify his position as *caudillo*.

It was not by chance that Franco's ideas on important matters were never anything but basic. His world was drably prosaic: his hobbies were fishing, hunting, and, towards the end of his life, watching films and television. He lacked any cultural interests, criticized intellectuals for their intolerable "pride," made spelling mistakes, and in meetings of the Council of Ministers – infuriating the Foreign Minister – he always referred to Eisenhower as "Aisenover." The best description sums him up in the word "mediocrity." The Duke of Alba wrote that "he possessed all the small virtues and none of the great ones," and General Kindelán said of him that he suffered from "mountain sickness" – that euphoria that swamps climbers when they reach heights beyond their physical capabilities. This also explains why loyalty was for him such a fundamental value. In the early days he very often used people from his close family circle, such as his brother or his brother-in-law, or those he had known during his childhood and youth in El Ferrol (Juan Antonio Suances or Camilo Alonso Vega, for example).

This notion of mediocrity may seem contradictory given the fact that Franco remained in power for a considerable length of time. One must remember, however, that his dictatorship was the product of a civil war whose cruel memory lasted a very long time. In contrast to this past, he himself presented an image of a shepherd who could bring all the diverse factions of the Spanish right together to graze in the same meadow and could avoid the divisive pluralism that had characterized the Republican years. Never was a phrase so accurate as when Francesc Cambó stated that "the one who stays in power is utterly determined to stay in power." José María de Areilza foresaw in 1945 that Franco would "always limit the scope of his politics to a short radius around his survival in the job." Such was the truth of this statement that the man who made it ended up working closely with the dictator, and he was not the only one.

This does not, however, explain how it was that Franco stayed in power for so long. Not being a professional politician himself and detesting those who were ("Do as I do; do not go into politics," he told one visitor), he nonetheless had the range of abilities without which he could not have played his part. A cynical Basque politician, José Félix Lequerica, gave up comparing him to great figures of the past and instead preferred to liken him to Gabino Bugallal, one of the best-known Galician *caciques*.[2] José Antonio Girón de Velasco, a leading Falangist, summed up Franco's virtues as "an ox-like tread, eagle-eyes, wolf's teeth, and playing the fool." Thanks to the last of these, Franco gave the impression of being harmless and manageable during the Civil War. "Wolf's teeth" refers to the hardness he displayed on more than one occasion and the "ox-like tread" to a sense of timing that his collaborators often found intensely irritating. Carrero Blanco, for whom this was particularly so, said to Laureano López Rodó: "We shall have to see just how hard he finds giving birth," alluding to his hesitancy over decisions on the question of the monarchy. And when Fraga suggested cosmetic changes such as no longer playing the

National Anthem at the end of radio broadcasting, Franco suggested that they did it in two stages.

His ox-like sense of timing would have been of little use to him had he not had "eagle-eyes." His perspicacity combined a clear perception of reality, a moderation that contrasted strongly with some of his supporters, and above all, a certain cool. "Even more than when he was on the attack," Navarro Rubio affirms, "the times when you saw him most sure of himself were when he had to ride out storms." Cautious cunning and discretion completed the panorama of his personality. "Anyone here who is not a fool is a crook," Franco told Areilza in a phrase devastating in its pessimism. It should come as no surprise that José María Pemán came to the conclusion that there was only one way to find out what his opinions were: to wait until they escaped from his grasp. Girón made no further zoomorphic comparisons but had he done so he would have had to mention the chameleon and its adaptability. The judgments that Franco pronounced on institutions within his regime seem so cynical that had they been expressed in public they would have been damned as subversive. He told López Rodó that he had never managed to understand what was meant by a "vertical trade union," unless the term was meant to depict an institution in which some people were higher up and others lower down. He told Antonio Garrigues quite shamelessly that the National Movement or *Movimiento* was a useful "claque" for stirring up the masses on public occasions.

These aspects of Franco's political character were translated into his daily activity in government; to describe that activity will help towards a definition of his dictatorship. He kept absolutely all political responsibility in his own hands and from the Civil War until his death he retained a degree of constitutive power that would, for example, have made his replacement by an heir quite feasible. So it is possible to say that in Spain what came into being was not a totalitarian system but a dictatorship in which power was vested in one single individual. At least from the legal point of view, Mussolini was constrained by fascist ideology and its institutions. Franco had significantly more political power.

However, this is not to say that he personally took charge of all the various ministries. The most important decisions and those relating to aspects of what he considered fenced-off areas of policy had to be submitted for his approval, but in practice he left a wide area of maneuver for ministers' initiative, just as he would have done as a commander-in-chief with his subordinate officers. His ministers' freedom of movement and "judicious" exercising of virtual omnipotence also drew strength from Franco's conception of his own function as one of arbitration. He had won a civil war thanks to the fact that he presided over a coalition of the Spanish right, and his dictatorship aimed to ensure that this situation continued. Having an arbiter in a regime that was not totalitarian meant that each sector could have a slice of power but no one could ever claim that any one sector of the right was entirely in opposition or entirely in the position of favorite. Franco's exercising of power as arbiter had climactic moments: replacing ministers. Once he had learned how to do it, he tried to make ministers last in office for 5 years. Changes were brought about through an intermediary and they allowed Franco to show his ability, almost like a homeopath, to combine together all the best ingredients.

According to Fraga, until 1962 "he never discussed politics in the Council of Ministers," which is true, though he talked even less about politics in the *Cortes*.[3] Franco kept all big political decisions to himself but from time to time the Council of Ministers became a kind of pocket parliament where fundamental issues or those that might in some way be seen as such were bitterly debated. True political enmity during the Franco years was to be found in the Council of Ministers where Franco's form of arbitration also meant turning a deaf ear to confrontation or doing away with anyone who caused conflict. In his opinion, forums of debate were dangerous institutions which might limit his power or slip into the bad habits of parliamentarianism. For that reason he always considered both organized pluralism and freedom of expression harmful, which explains why he took so long – from 1938 to 1966 – to draw up legislation governing the press, only then to modify its liberalizing content; or why his last political decision was to close the doors firmly on any possibility of providing an institutional framework for political pluralism.

It would be incorrect to state that Franco had "favorites" because that would suggest that he accepted the possibility of his own responsibilities being handed over to someone else, or that he saw no problem in sharing power. Serrano Suñer played a very significant role but never one that interfered with that of Franco who, on another front, needed him as a link to Falange as he had not yet completed his apprenticeship as dictator. Carrero Blanco's functions were more in the nature of support, as indeed became evident when his influence grew as Franco's health waned. Beyond this intimate circle were the most important members of the Army and emblematic figures in each and every sector of the Spanish right. The influence that these figures exerted could at times be great but it was never either decisive or constant.

The distance between Franco as dictator and those who collaborated with him was a product of a character that was neither particularly expressive nor effusive, and it explains the curious situation that occurred in the final phase of the regime. In the past this distance had served to enhance his role as arbiter but as his physical condition weakened he seemed barely able to play that role any more. Parkinson's disease brought out a trait that was the antithesis of his past behavior: weakness of character. His "eagle-eye" and "wolf's teeth" were apparently dulled unless one views his final repressive measures as their death throes; all that remained was the "ox-like tread." Franco had always been "a sphinx without a secret," but now, still indispensable and yet silent and inert, he was nothing more than a sphinx.

His ministers were perfectly aware of his physical decline. According to López Rodó, until 1965 meetings of the Council of Ministers began with a lengthy exposition by Franco and lasted all day, but after 1968 they only lasted the morning. It was also seen as quite an event, as Fraga recounts in his *Memoirs*, when in September the dictator interrupted a meeting to relieve himself. It was not by chance that from the following year on it became almost commonplace for confrontations between different factions to erupt at the nerve-center of the regime without intervention from the one whose mission it was to arbitrate and prevent this unforeseen conflict.

The last years of Franco's life were also characterized by his isolation. It was only to be expected that a person who had exercised power entirely alone should be condemned to end that way. Earlier on, his secretary had realized that the dictator was not so much talking to him as pronouncing "lengthy monologues." He seemed like a distant patriarch who had not entirely lost all his automatic responses and was still able to offer correction but now lacked information. Even so, he did retain a pale glimmer of what had been abilities in the past. In contrast, what turned the final years of his dictatorship into a burlesque farce were those close to him and his family. On the retina and in the memory of many Spaniards images persist from those years, and yet it would have been impossible for him to remain in power right up until his final days had he not played a very different role in the years up to that time.

It is not easy to compare Franco with other historical figures who have exercised power on their own. He has little in common with a professor of company law such as Salazar, or a former left-wing agitator like Mussolini. In one sense, on the other hand, he can be compared to Tito who, like him, rose to power after a civil war. Like him, too, the Yugoslav president, in the final stage of his rule, left his country with images of a distant patriarch with characteristics that were not entirely negative.

## Francoism: A Form of Dictatorship

The 1939 regime may often be referred to as a Francoist dictatorship but it did not owe its character solely to the man who personified it. It has clear similarities to other types of dictatorship in Europe and Latin America. What set it apart, however, was that while Franco was alive it stopped being one kind of dictatorship and became another, while keeping the same person at its head. All those characteristics that are attributed to Francoism as a form of dictatorship are present in other regimes at other times and in other places.

In Spain, rapid politicization under the Second Republic did not result in a strong Fascist Party; instead, what emerged as dominant on the right was Catholicism which, though essentially reactionary, nonetheless acted within the scope of the possible. Manuel Azaña was not wrong when he affirmed in the middle of the war that there might be fascists in Spain but there was no fascism, and were the opposition to win the war it would favor Congregations of the Sacred Heart of Jesus and military parades rather than imitating secular regimes with modernizing tendencies. Even if there was a Fascist Party, religious fervor and a proliferation of outmoded baroque ideals seemed to signal a return to Counter Reformation values.

In the midst of World War II, the point of comparison for the Franco dictatorship was never Germany; instead, the closest model was Italy and even more so the semi-, pseudo-, or para-fascist regimes that proliferated at the time. Franco's dictatorship was, without doubt, more like Vichy France or certain Eastern European countries than the Hitler regime. In Spain, for example, there was a struggle for power between the Army and the Fascist Party identical to that in Antonescu's Romania. As with Vichy France or Hungary, the Franco dictatorship, without ever going so far as to become totally fascist, went a long way down that path: indeed, far more so than those two countries, neither of which had only one single party. It made use of a populist façade and certain fascist political institutions but it cannot really be termed fascism as such.

Fascism provided a clear political framework of reference during World War II but after the war it ceased to feature as a viable alternative. After the 1940s the desire for totalitarianism in right-wing regimes, but not the regimes themselves, waned, though the regimes gained new strength during the 1960s and 1970s, albeit with different styles. Non-totalitarian regimes tolerated a certain degree of pluralism in their ranks. Rather than having a precisely formulated ideology, they were the product of a certain mentality and they too lacked a single party chanting a fascist liturgy. Into this category of dictatorship one could well put Francoism which, from a certain moment on, also used Spain's economic development as its main argument for remaining in power. Non-totalitarian dictatorships were a common phenomenon in Latin America, though with different variations: popular nationalism in Perón's Argentina, an anti-revolutionary military dictatorship in Pinochet's Chile, or regimes where the Army acted corporately (the praetorian model). Francoism had something in common with all these styles of regime. To sum it up, one might say that when studied as a whole it can be seen as far more than a mere conservative dictatorship such as that of Primo de Rivera, but also as far less than a fascist dictatorship. Certainly, it is not enough to point to possible similarities, which will be discussed again later; instead we must also emphasize those characteristics that remained constant throughout the regime's history.

One primary defining element has to do with the role of political ideology. An essentially authoritarian vision, national Catholicism, and a certain populist social agenda would together constitute keynotes of the regime, which remained hostile to the disruptive pluralism and freedom of opinion associated with a liberal society. Yet more than being just the result of a certain set of ideas, its character can more realistically be attributed to a particular mentality: that of those who won the Civil War. Francoism drew inspiration from a number of ideological sources (in the sense that they came from across the spectrum of the Spanish right), which were different in its infancy; however, it also allowed for modification of these ideas in response to changing circumstances.

The regime was, looked at another way and in contrast to certain Latin American or fascist dictatorships, personal not collective: hence its name "Francoism," for even if the man who personified it was a soldier, it was not dictatorship by the Army. Its personal nature did not preclude a desire for permanence which was never questioned, and this made it different from military regimes in Latin America and that of Primo de Rivera.

Nor did Franco try to do away entirely with powers other than those pertaining to the state. The regime did not even address seriously the task of establishing itself as an institution. Its founding legislation was a response to strategic reasoning and even looked ahead to projects in a distant future but it was never applied with even a minimum of sincerity.

One of the reasons why the regime was never institutionalized was that, having arisen out of a conservative coalition, its different component parts had different visions for the future. The Falangists were pro-Republican and the Carlists always rejected the notion of a single party, to cite just two examples. Therefore, potential conflict was a constant threat that Franco avoided periodically by direct intervention. This worked by splitting each of the groups within the conservative coalition into two sides: those who would collaborate and those who would not. The former reaped the benefits of a slice of power and so enhanced the legitimacy of the regime, while the latter remained on the margins of power.

Franco's style of government by arbitration was always informal in approach, for he never allowed strong political forces as such to be represented in the Council of Ministers. It was he who elected its members, though always with an eye to what would work best. He even assigned portfolios to each of the different groups, which might well be called "families": the Justice Ministry to the Carlists because it involved relations with the Vatican; portfolios relating to economic issues to the Alfonsine Monarchists because of their technical knowledge and contacts in economic circles; Labor and Agriculture to Falangists because of the social content, and Education and Foreign Affairs to the Catholics because for them the former was a burning issue and the latter might allow a more acceptable image to be projected to the outer world. The informal nature of the coalition meant that these groups never became institutionalized. The "families" of the dictatorship were above all a phenomenon in the early part of its history; with the passage of time, they were replaced by individuals.

It is typical of dictatorial regimes that they either mobilize ordinary citizens to support them or demobilize them as though passivity were a necessary response for survival. Fascist regimes always mobilize and the Franco regime did so right from the start; throughout all its life, when it thought it was in danger, its response was to mobilize support. Usually this took the form of a kind of "docile anarchy" which worked by cultivating an inarticulate, passive society. One person in the 1960s described the regime Spaniards were experiencing as neither Francoist nor anti-Francoist but just not interested in politics. The power of the regime was based not on a silent majority but quite simply on an absent one. Those years, as was the case with Italian fascism, could well be called "years of consensus," not in the sense that the regime was enthusiastically accepted but apathy meant that it was tolerated after earlier repression had utterly crushed the opposition.

Non-totalitarian dictatorships do not have this one single party. In the case of Francoism, there was one party initially intended to be the only actor on the political stage and the inspiration for the regime. However, this intention was frustrated. In due course, the party became bureaucratized and just another part of the state. The party had not conquered the state; what happened was quite the reverse. Yet the party always remained an important element at the heart of the Franco regime. Although its budget only ever reached at most 2 percent of the state budget, Falange did well out of this unification, and if it was not allowed a monopoly of power, it did receive a significant slice.

In general, in non-totalitarian dictatorial regimes there remain autonomous pockets outside the political sphere; the most influential are usually the Catholic Church and the Army. Obviously Catholicism played a hugely important role during the Franco years, so much so that it has been possible to look on it as the intellectual force behind the regime; however, this statement is only valid for the period up to 1962. The Church always had a sphere of autonomy that included control over a large part of education, a section of the press, and religious association. Yet Catholicism was, at the same time, just another family within the regime which took an important lead at certain key moments. It wanted to change the regime in 1945 but found itself forced to accept a portion of power without being able to introduce any changes.

Franco's dictatorship can much better be described as military than as Falangist. It is important to bear in mind that it was the Army that won the Civil War and that it had changed over the course of the conflict. Of the most high-ranking officers serving in 1936 only a quarter joined the uprising, but another factor was that during the conflict its ranks were swelled by provisional officers who would play a decisive role later on. The purge carried out at the heart of the military family was as harsh or harsher and even more arbitrary than in any other sector of the Administration in order to create a weapon capable of keeping in power those who had won it. At the end of the decade of the 1960s more than a third of all officers had been provisional lieutenants.

The regime that existed in Spain between 1939 and 1975 was that of a dictator – Franco – who happened to be a general. That brought opposition from sections of the Army, principally from those who considered him a kind of *primus inter pares*. From the 1950s onwards, changes in the Army made it unthinkable that opposition could arise within its ranks, but that did not mean that the regime could be termed military. Military officers played important roles at the heart of the governing class, especially in specific areas: public order was always under their jurisdiction. All vice-presidents and 40 of the 114 government ministers were from the Armed Services; eight of them held power for more than 10 years. They even held portfolios relating to economic affairs. Yet the regime was not praetorian because, for example, it did not endow officers with functions equivalent to those of university vice-chancellors, as happened in Pinochet's Chile. Military budgets gradually decreased and in 1975 Spain was one of the countries in Europe where the Army was least well subsidized.

Other aspects of the Francoist dictatorship are worth pointing out. The *Cortes* – which was supposedly equivalent to a legislative assembly – served merely as a sounding-board to give added weight to more important decisions taken by Franco himself; it also provided a forum in which the regime's political class could sound out different opinions. However, as López Rodó said, the unwritten rules of the constitutional game were that nobody argued with Franco and that it was the government that ran the country. The highest level that could be reached in Francoist politics was therefore that of minister. The qualities required to attain such a post were first and foremost loyalty to the person of Franco himself, also technical training, and finally membership of one of the regime families. Ministers always had considerable power because of an extensive "area of indifference" in which the dictator left those who collaborated with him a wide margin for freedom of movement.

In describing the dictatorship it is also necessary to take into account other factors such as, for example, the degree of political repression that existed. The sheer magnitude of the repression can only be understood if one views it in the light of the origin of Franco's dictatorship, which was during a civil war. It would be wrong, however, to focus analysis of the Franco regime solely on this initial repressive phase without considering the changes that occurred subsequently. Around 1965, for example, the numbers of those in prison came down to below 11,000 and the number of members of the security forces per thousand inhabitants was relatively low in comparison to the rest of Europe. Often repression took the form of detention for short periods with delayed court hearings, or it ended with light sentences already served before the trial took place. Although the level of repression rose in the final phase of the Franco years, it was never as severe as it had been in the 1940s or in the 1950s. Society had won new levels of tolerance.

In the economic sphere, freedom of initiative was only interfered with (and that was never done more than indirectly even if it was quite severely) during the first phase of the regime, because the state wanted to show favor to those who had been on the winning side. There was never freedom for trade unions, but from the 1950s onwards there were organizations that represented workers' interests within companies, and they were capable of reaching agreements with the owners on increases in productivity, so that in 1965 there was a relaxing of sanctions relating to strikes. Persecution of clandestine trade union organizations decreased in the 1960s but toughened up again in the final phase of the regime. Any other form of association was subject to strict controls, but there were marginal zones in which a certain degree of autonomy was allowed for chambers of commerce and – more especially – religious associations.

Legislation relating to the press, inspired by Mussolini's Italy, was in many respects harsher and more pedantic in the way it was applied. The preamble to the press law written during the Civil War (1938) railed against "freedom in the democratic style." As prescribed in the text of the law, newspaper editors were always government appointments. The purge among professional journalists was extremely severe: of 4,000 dossiers presented soliciting permission to work in the profession only 1,800 were accepted. Only in the 1950s did it become possible for newspapers to appoint editors of their own choice, and it was as late as 1966 that censorship prior to publication was abolished. Even so, the press always managed to maintain a certain pluralism, though it could only express opinions obliquely. The Catholic media controlled the same number of daily newspapers as there were official publications, and there were also a number in private ownership. The situation was similar for radio, but it was allowed only one single news and information program.

There are two contrary and equally inaccurate tendencies when attempts are made to define the role of the opposition in Franco's Spain. While it never entirely ceased to exist, probably after the war in Europe its chances of ever winning were slim right up until the moment of Franco's death. In its early years the regime used violent repressive measures against it, but it is also true that for much of the time it seemed willing to attract and even collaborate with its opponents. The opposition survived, however, because those who took over from those who were defeated in the Civil War were joined in the 1960s by a new opposition born as a consequence of Spain's newly developed society. As late as 1953 an important socialist leader died of maltreatment in prison, and in 1963 a communist leader purported to have committed crimes during the Civil War was executed. By the 1970s socialist leaders were known to the police who might occasionally arrest them, but they were not tortured, and when tried they were not sent to prison for long. There was always an opposition that was tolerated and not persecuted as long as it was not too active, and another that was illegal and the butt of extremely severe repression. In addition, the pluralism of the regime itself fostered the existence of a certain pseudo-opposition or opposition from within, of whom it could be said that the boundaries between it and the more moderate form of outside opposition became blurred during the final phase of Francoism.

This description allows us to gain a general impression of what the Franco dictatorship itself was always like; we can, therefore, try to compare it with other types of regime. The best comparison, because it allows us to consider similarities and differences, is with Italian fascism and with Salazar's Portugal. Relations between the three regimes were close but Franco – who on occasion could see Mussolini not only as someone worthy of admiration but also someone to be imitated – did not view Salazar as anything but a means of making contact indirectly with the democratic world. The origins of the three regimes were different. Only the Spanish regime had begun in civil war and had tried to rebuild a political system out of nothing; furthermore, it alone applied severe repression and always used a dialectic of victors and vanquished. Salazar was never totalitarian; his regime was conservative and based on Catholic corporativist ideas which used authoritarianism to reinforce republican institutions. Mussolini invented the word "totalitarian" but he himself never put it into practice (his totalitarianism was "imperfect" or "defective," at least in comparison with that of Hitler). Having risen to power by legal means he did not resort to violent repression, and when he institutionalized the regime, he left the way open to absolute totalitarianism, keeping it as a possible option.

A comparison of these two dictatorships with the Franco regime can be extended to examine many other areas too. The single-party model did not apply in Portugal, where Salazar sometimes allowed political opposition groups to exist legally during elections. He also allowed a certain degree of internal pluralism which brought monarchists face to face with those who were not, and confronted those with progressive views on the colonial problem with reactionaries. Italian fascism allowed for pluralism from different sources, but once in power the only diversity permitted was that of tone. In Portugal the Army, though guarantor of the system, did not play such a crucial role as to warrant the Salazar regime being called a military dictatorship. The Portuguese dictatorship, though personified by a man who had been a member of Catholic movements, was never clericalist, unlike what happened in Spain. In Italy, the more strongly totalitarian character of the dictatorship led to serious conflict between Mussolini and the Church, while the Army, though still maintaining a sphere of autonomy, was decapitated with the removal of those in command. In Portugal, there was the same selective repression as in Spain in the 1950s but it had little in common with the random ferocity of the Saló Republic at the end of the Mussolini era, which was comparable to the earliest Francoist repression. To sum up, in Italy autarchy was favored in the economic sphere, there was an actual cultural policy and even a form of Fascist art, and Italy also had imperialistic tendencies as part of its foreign policy. In Portugal, in contrast, economic policy was in the hands of the careful accountant that Salazar never ceased to be, and his imperialism remained purely defensive. In all these traits it is, of course, possible to see points of comparison with Francoism. If we were to attempt to consider together similarities and differences, we would have to say that the Franco dictatorship was a political regime which, on a hypothetical scale measuring the extent of fascist input, would have been placed in the 1940s between a higher score for Italy and a lower score for Portugal.

Francoism does not, therefore, have any distinguishing traits that make it a peculiar phenomenon. What does make it different is that it came into being as a result of a civil war and this meant that it had more chances of survival. Furthermore, its relative lack of any clear ideological basis allowed it to shift from one form of dictatorship to another, bordering on fascism in the 1940s and resembling more modernizing dictatorships in the 1960s. What is not at all common when a dictatorship disappears is for a peaceful transition to democracy to occur, though this did not depend on the regime itself but rather on changes within Spanish society and on the particular abilities of those in positions of leadership, both within the regime and in opposition.

## Victors and Vanquished: The Disasters
## of the Civil War and Repression

Any assessment of the disasters caused by the Spanish Civil War must begin with the number of those who died. To cite the figure of a million dead has become a cliché which could only be taken as correct if the number of those "not born" were taken into account. More realistically, the number who died as a direct consequence of the fighting would be just over 1 percent of the total population, which is similar to the percentage of deaths recorded in the civil war in Finland in 1918. In Spain's case demographic losses would not have exceeded the number of deaths caused by flu that year. The destruction was not materially comparable to that suffered in Europe during World War II. One need only compare the tens of thousands of deaths caused during the bombing of German cities with the 5,000 deaths suffered by Catalonia in the entire war. In this, as in so many other aspects, the Spanish Civil War was more like World War I than World War II. Figures show, however, that agricultural output went down by 20 percent and industrial production by 30 percent. More serious still than all this material destruction was the social fragmentation that was a direct result of repression.

In this respect it is true to say that the war of 1936 exceeded by a large margin what happened in other comparable situations: never before had any civil conflict in Spain ended with such persecution of the vanquished. The Carlist Wars of the nineteenth century, for example, had ended with "Embraces at Vergara" – symbols of reconciliation – but in this case that did not happen. Not only were the defeated put on trial, but in order to make such trials possible an entirely new form of judicial structure and new laws to address these exceptional circumstances were thought up. In addition to all that, economic sanctions were imposed and there was a general purge of the Administration.

The harshness of this repression becomes even more evident when the figures for executions in Spain are compared with those in postwar Europe in countries which experienced similar circumstances. In France and Italy, after 1945, repression was mild and did not last long because the democracy that triumphed was generous. In France only 800 collaborators were executed after being tried; in both countries the administrative purge was superficial and few remained in prison on these counts by the start of the 1950s. Julián Marías has written that in Spain the victors could have healed the country's Civil War wounds with only "a small dose of generosity," but there was no hint of any desire for reconciliation at all. Franco even went so far as to say that the debts of responsibility "could not be settled in a spirit of liberality." Some of his collaborators spoke of the need to "disinfect" the country. This was not a time to think of gaining a pardon but rather of serving a harsh sentence and choosing conversion.

A marked characteristic of the Franco regime was the appearance of a positive tangle of areas of special jurisdiction of which the most important was military jurisdiction. Unlike what happened in Italy or in Germany, repression was not implemented by the Party but by the Army (as had been the case in Vichy France) and in addition the notion of a political crime extended to cover unexpected areas. In 1939 it was decreed that military tribunals would have control over the monopoly on food products, in 1941 railway accidents came under its jurisdiction, and in 1943 it was also given the right to take action in the event of strikes. At the same time, there was a purge of the judiciary (14 percent of magistrates and 22 percent of public prosecutors received sanctions of some sort), areas of special jurisdiction within the service multiplied, and the sphere of action of normal tribunals was curtailed. Litigation and Administrative Jurisdiction were only partially restored in 1944 and had little effective power.

During the Civil War there were already signs of what was to come. In the summer of 1938 the death penalty was reintroduced into the Penal Code. At the start of February 1939 the so-called Law of Political Responsibilities (*Ley de Responsabilidades Políticas*) was made public; it was aimed at punishing "any who contributed substantially by action or omission to the formation of the subversive Red opposition, who kept it alive for more than 2 years, and who hindered the inevitable and providential victory of the National Movement." Responsibility was traced back to October 1934 and political or para-political associations that had been dissolved would subsequently lose all their possessions, which were handed over to the one single remaining Party. In January 1940 it was decreed that "no steps would be taken to apprehend any person without prior denunciation and a summons in writing," which seems to indicate that there had previously been a period of indiscriminate repression. The following March the Law for the Repression of Freemasonry and Communism (*Ley de Represión de la Masonería y del Comunismo*) was passed on the basis that it was these two groups who were responsible for "the loss of Spain's Colonial Empire, the cruel War of Independence, the civil wars that plagued the country throughout the nineteenth century, the disturbances that speeded up the fall of the constitutional monarchy and undermined the Dictatorship, as well as other numerous crimes against the state" during the period of the Republic. This legislation brought together a curious mixture of ideologies that would have been unacceptable to virtually all those it was designed to punish: it labeled as communist "Trotskyites, Anarchists and other such entities."

After outlining the measures themselves we can now move on to consider their results. Military tribunals played a major part in putting repressive measures into action from 1939 to 1942: indeed, up to April 1948 Spain remained under military jurisdiction. Compared to the repressive measures imposed by Hitler and Stalin, those enacted by Franco did not seek to do away with entire sections of the population (Jews or *Kulaks*) and therefore it seems inappropriate to use the term "genocide." Yet they were extremely harsh, making it plain that the intention was to crush any possible resistance arising within Spanish society. The length of the Civil War, the role of the Army in repression, the suffering experienced by the victors, and their determination to remain in power serve to explain what happened. The British Hispanist Gerald Brenan could write that Spain seemed to suffer from "Civil War neurosis," because it was willing to put up with any hardship if it meant avoiding such a disaster ever being repeated.

The data that we have on deaths in the postwar period is only partial. One might think that in a situation that had such an appearance of normality the number of executions might have been recorded in civil registers. That did not happen because the law in force at the time did not consider that any who lost their lives as the result of a penal sanction should be listed there. Calculations concerning the total number of executions vary considerably. Specialists today suggest some 50,000 but this figure is no more than a rough estimate which attempts to get close to the truth by looking at the cases that we do know about for certain (about 35,000).

Examination of such cases as these does, however, allow rather closer study of the form that the persecution of the vanquished actually took. In Catalonia – the region that has been most intensively studied – Francoist post-Civil War repression accounted for 3,385 executions. Catalonia was the only area which had seen a mass exodus of population across the border into France, which is why its leaders and even some lower-ranking members of the Popular Front were never located. Those affected were people who had never thought of themselves as targets for repression, such as political or union militants of no great significance especially in rural areas where there had been acute social tension, as it was easier to escape repression in Barcelona. In what is now the Community of Valencia where these circumstances did not pertain, the number of executions was higher: some 4,700. Another important piece of data refers to the number of cases dismissed in comparison to executions carried out. In Córdoba repression resulted in almost 1,600 deaths, but there were no fewer than 27,000 cases heard by 35 itinerant military tribunals (in Malaga there were 67 such courts). This disparity between the number of cases and the number of punishments reveals how diffuse the terror was. One might say that all those who had held any kind of position in Popular Front Spain were condemned for having supported the rebellion; punishment varied from the death penalty to 20 years in prison. Those who had held no position received lesser penalties being considered guilty of "helping the rebellion."

All such penal legislation was directed at a kind of crime of "inverted rebellion"; yet those accounted guilty of revolt were not in fact the ones who had rebelled. Marías has recounted how trials were conducted, and all kinds of sources testify in ways that bear his descriptions out. Procedural guarantees were virtually nil: the military tribunals used to deal with between 12 and 15 cases an hour or, for example, pass judgment on an entire group of 60 people accused on different counts. The brief time that elapsed between the courts martial and executions shows just how rapidly cases were expedited. Those defending the accused had to be soldiers but were not necessarily lawyers; a number of those called upon to do this job merely begged for clemency. Often the accused were not questioned, there were no witnesses, and there was no contact between the accused and their defense. Executions were carried out at night, the prisoners being called up for various "outings." The shooting took place against cemetery walls to save time. At Madrid's Eastern Cemetery (known now as the Almudena), 2,663 people were shot immediately following the war, of whom only 86 were women. The data pertaining to this site reveals that the executions were carried out mainly in the earliest months of the postwar period: almost a thousand were shot between May and December 1939.

There were instances where the fierce wave of retribution unleashed against the vanquished crossed frontiers, as was the case with Lluís Companys, President of the Catalan Generalitat. If his political career had been highly questionable, especially during the October insurrection of 1934, his presence in Barcelona nonetheless did much to prevent there being an even greater number of victims. Companys, in exile in France, was in Paris in June 1940, trying to track down a mentally ill son who had disappeared after the German invasion. The Spanish authorities managed to persuade the Germans to hand Companys and other Republican leaders over to them. Franco decided that he should be tried publicly in Barcelona. Some of the accusations against him came from grotesquely exaggerated police reports, but members of prominent Barcelona Falangist families testified in support of the case against him. After defending himself with dignity and poise Companys was executed, and even his bitterest political opponents, such as Cambó, pronounced that the court case had been an "immense error" experienced by all as a collective punishment.

There were also lesser punishments than the death penalty meted out, which showed the extent of the task of repression. Before the Civil War the number of prisoners in Spain was fewer than 10,000. In 1939 the number rose to 270,000, a figure which went down to 124,000 in 1942 and only fell dramatically by 1945 (43,000), and even more so by 1950 (30,000). From the summer of 1940 onwards pardons were granted as a result of the government's desire to free itself of the burden of its prison population; furthermore, the system of reducing sentences through work came into effect, though it soon degenerated into a means by which the state hired out cheap labor to construction companies. Prison, especially in the early postwar years, meant a lot more than the loss of liberty. The number who died owing to appallingly insanitary conditions or the lack of adequate nourishment in prisons was very high.

Another possible punishment took the form of economic sanctions. These bear witness to a genuine obsession with the existence of an "enemy within," and the arbitrariness of the sanctions was so extreme that not only specific individuals but entire families were accused. Legislation spoke of "erasing the errors of the past" but also of the need to display "a firm determination never to err again." On these terms it was possible to extend penalties to include politicians with reformist or even moderate tendencies, and add to the punishment of the loss of liberty that of economic sanctions. In each section of the population political authorities – which in matters of public order was the Civil Guard and in matters of religion the parish priest – issued reports on people's conduct that were powerfully influential.

There has not yet been sufficient study of the administrative purges that took place but certain data does give some idea of its magnitude. The principle on which it was based was the necessary replacement of all who held public posts of responsibility whether or not they had been punished according to the Penal Code in force at the time. Civil servants or even mere public employees were not allowed to be neutral: they had to be committed supporters of the regime.

We have already seen how the purging of the judicial system was carried out. The diplomatic service was, of course, hardly a revolutionary stronghold, yet despite this fact 26 percent of the profession received some form of punishment and 14 percent lost their job. Among university teachers, the purge affected 33 percent, and 44 percent in the case of Barcelona. In addition, the first time that competitive examinations for state posts were held, a fifth were reserved for soldiers fighting with the Blue Division (the level reached 80 percent for lower state employees). From the Civil War onwards, Franco took a special interest in the purging of the education system. It is possible that up to a third of all teachers received some kind of sanction but more significant still was the purge in the primary sector. Between 15,000 and 16,000 primary school teachers were punished, which was a quarter of the total number at work, and of those 6,000 were entirely banned from practicing their profession. As in other instances, often the geographical distribution of sanctions followed no perceptible reasoning but instead reflected the greater or lesser benevolence of the commission responsible for the purge. It was not just those employed by the State in the central Administration who were purged. In every town hall the existing municipal police were almost entirely replaced by newcomers. Among the workers employed on the Isabel II Canal which supplies Madrid with water, 57 percent received sanctions and 23 percent lost their jobs. Forty-two percent of workers on the trams in Barcelona were sacked. The impression one gains, then, is that the further down the ladder of public employment you went, the harsher the repression was.

All this suffering, taken as a whole, leads to the conclusion that when it is stated that the Franco regime was accepted passively the statement is only valid for the period immediately following World War II at the start of the 1950s. Also, we know about it from accounts of collective experience. It must be borne in mind too that quite apart from sanctions, there was also police surveillance. General José Ungría, who held major responsibility for surveillance, went so far as to say that under the new regime "denunciation by the police should be highly thought of, as a patriotic action." In Mallorca there was a military tribunal specially set up during World War II to try possible cases where there were disagreements. The entire population was divided into different categories identified with letters of the alphabet. Category B, for example, grouped together "former left-wing sympathizers who, after the *Movimiento*, joined the national militia." There was even a letter to refer to persons "of dubious morality, who are susceptible to financial inducements." With this mixture of repression and surveillance it is not surprising that the regime managed to ensconce itself so firmly in Spain.

## Exile and the Start of the Postwar Period in Spain

These repressive measures were aimed at the vanquished but some of the defeated escaped them by choosing to emigrate. In this sense too the end of the Civil War caused a rupture in the course of Spanish history. All previous internal conflicts had been followed by more or less emigration but always on a small scale and never lasting so long. On this occasion the exiles, in far greater numbers, retained strong emotional links with Spain but in certain instances lost all sense of what it was really like politically.

Emigration had begun before the Civil War ended. When Franco took the northern zone, some 200,000 people sought refuge in France in several waves and 35,000 remained there. There was a further huge wave of emigration when Catalonia fell, at which moment some 350,000 people crossed the frontier of whom 180,000 were combatants. A third occasion was at the final conclusion of the fighting: leaving via Alicante some 15,000 people abandoned their homeland and settled in North Africa. By March 1939, there were 450,000 Spaniards in exile of whom the immense majority (430,000) stayed in France while a small minority – principally or almost exclusively communists – ended up in Russia.

The circumstances in which Spanish emigrants found themselves in neighboring France were dreadful at this time. The majority were kept in concentration camps in the south where they lacked even the basic conditions for life. Some of them were treated as criminal offenders. France had not foreseen that such great numbers of refugees would flood across the frontier and soon decided that the economic burden of subsidizing these camps was excessive. By the end of 1939 only about 182,000 refugees remained, 140,000 living in France. Because more than 20,000 people returned to Spain during World War II, the final count of those in permanent exile, according to the most likely figures, would have been about 162,000 people – a high enough figure, but one proportionate to that of those who went into exile after the Russian Revolution of 1917. Yet if we take into account only the number of exiles in France at the end of World War II (about 100,000), the figure is higher than that of all cases of political emigration in the twentieth century added together.

These political exiles had to bear the weight of two added evils: the outbreak of World War II and internal strife. When Germany invaded Poland, the majority took up arms against the Germans. It is not surprising that the Germans considered them potentially dangerous and took action against them. Some of the leaders of the Popular Front were handed over to Franco; others did not suffer this fate, and some were deported to Germany, like Francisco Largo Caballero. About 13,000 Spaniards were taken from France to Germany where they ended up in concentration camps such as Mauthausen; only about 2,000 survived. In the resistance fighting against the German occupation in France there may have been 10,000 Spaniards or more. A large part of the south of France was liberated by Spanish combatants and among the first units to arrive in Paris were tanks bearing the names of battles fought during the Spanish Civil War.

Another misfortune for the exiles was disagreements among themselves – a continuation of the divisions that had existed between 1936 and 1939. In fact, rather than being a matter of ideological differences, this discord was linked to a clash between individual supporters and opponents of Juan Negrín and to the way that resources were shared out. From the time of the Civil War, Republican authorities answerable to Negrín had founded an Emigration Service for Spanish Republicans (*Servicio de Emigración de los Republicanos Españoles* or SERE). This organization was allowed to function in France until it was accused of conniving with communists and the French authorities closed down its offices in Paris. A rival organization soon emerged. In March 1939, the *Vita*, a ship belonging to SERE which was carrying what had been confiscated during the war in the zone controlled by the Popular Front, arrived in Mexico where it was seized by Indalecio Prieto with the approval of the Mexican authorities.

The socialist politician then set up a parallel organization to SERE, called the Junta for Aid to Spanish Republicans (*Junta de Auxilio a los Republicanos Españoles* or JARE). Past disagreements developed in exile into a bitter argument without either of the organizations ever giving a clear account of how their funds were being used. Meanwhile, there lurked an underlying question concerning the legitimacy of such Republican institutions which had been banned since the last phase of the Civil War. Only when an allied victory in World War II seemed possible did people begin to consider the possibility of rebuilding these institutions in Mexico.

The governments of the Basque Country and Catalonia were in equal crisis, to which was added a process of progressive radicalization.

The mention of Mexico says much about the Spaniards in exile. These splits in the middle classes on which Azaña blamed the outbreak of the Civil War highlighted the fact that large numbers of people (between 10,000 and 13,000) came from the classes that had led the country. The figures we have on this subject often vary but are nonetheless significant. Among the exiles there were possibly 2,500 professional members of the Armed Services, 500 doctors, 400 engineers, more than 1,000 lawyers and up to 12 percent of those who had held professorships in Spanish universities, including seven vice-chancellors. In Mexico a large number of Spanish intellectuals played a leading role in organizing important initiatives such as, for example, the founding of the College of Mexico or the Fondo de Cultura Económica publishing house. The contribution of Spaniards to Mexican life was so great that it could be called "a triumph" for this country. Integration into Mexican society was swift and in the 1940s half of the Spanish emigrants took Mexican nationality. In other parts of the world too, defeated Spaniards were warmly welcomed. In Cuba, the dictator Batista used Spanish immigration to give his regime a more liberal hue. Emigrants to Argentina were fewer and more predominantly intellectual, while Chile welcomed more proletarian elements.

Spanish emigration to Latin America as a consequence of the Civil War took on particular significance for world history. First and foremost, it was exile on a massive scale and of professional classes, something never seen before until that moment. In certain areas, such as the sciences or ideas, the emigrants represented a supremely important section of Spanish cultural life, which was therefore truncated in Spain. At the same time, emigration to Latin America was an intellectual experience: a discovery of the global nature of Spanish culture. So Juan Ramón Jiménez could write that he was "neither speechless nor exiled but reconciled." The mental world of the exiles was still on the other side of the Atlantic, and this explains their constant discourses on the nature of Spain. The poet León Felipe could write: "Franco, thine is the land, the house, the horse and the gun,/ mine is the ancient voice of the earth."[4]

Until now we have only referred to one of the Spains of the immediate postwar period. We must now return to the other side of the Atlantic where the victors, freed from all legal constraints, were preparing to write a new history of Spain from the very beginning and, at the same time, re-build its ancient imperial glory. They did so, of course, with the enthusiasm spawned by victory, "with an immense, constant, and perhaps absurd optimism" (the words are from Fernando Vizcaíno Casas), and in this case victory wore the dark blue shirt of the Falange.

Their enthusiasm was made up in equal parts of nationalism and Catholicism closely bound together with a strong determination to make an absolute break with the immediate past. Nationalism found a voice in stories such as the one that recounts how the dish known as "Russian Salad" was now called "National Salad," and hotels once called the "English Hotel" were now renamed "National Hotel." Stories such as these should not be thought of as trivial: a ministerial decree in May 1940 prohibited "the use of foreign generic words in the naming of establishments or services for recreation, commerce, industry, accommodation, the supplying of food, professional services, entertainment, and other such activities." An idealized past provided the ground plan for shaping the future, and of that past a peculiar vision was promoted from which the former liberal tradition and cultural pluralism of Spanish society had disappeared: hence the large posters put up in Barcelona bearing the words "Speak the Language of the Empire." At the same time the leaders of the New Spain were praised with almost religious devotion. Total identification with the person of Franco reached such an extreme that his image was used for commercial advertising, though this was banned in time. One film company claimed to be "the only one which never once produced an inch of celluloid for the Reds."

Another motto of the time ("From the Empire towards God") shows how close the relationship was between nationalism and Catholicism at this moment in the postwar years. What came to be called National Catholicism was not so much a theory as a way of looking at life. It was in no way false but rather deeply felt: the result of a reaction against the faith of the past which was seen as having been far too passive. This new faith was born as part of a fervent desire to reconquer society that was distinctly anti-modern and had no hesitation in conflating religion and politics. Its ideas were shared not only by the victors but even by some of the vanquished, for there were notable conversions and numerous late vocations that swelled the priesthood. What characterized National Catholicism was its "insatiability" – that is to say, its determination to gain total control and the idea that there was a direct and immediate link between Catholicism and politics or culture. The result was a deep-seated intolerance which led Ignacio Menéndez Reigada, the major propagandist of the Crusade ideal, to describe Protestants as "poisonous vermin."

It can come as no surprise, therefore, that one of the major preoccupations of Church authorities should have been to try to proscribe any dissident religious propaganda. The Spanish Church saw itself not as one possible version of Catholicism, or even the one that best suited Spain, but as absolutely the very best. In daily life National Catholicism was evident in what Agustín Foxá ironically called "national seminarism." What he meant was that there was a deeply felt but very elementary form of religion which was usually not just pretentious but also ignorant and which took the form of an extreme form of clericalism. Pemán used to say of Franco that he was the only world leader who, in his political discourses, did not just refer generally to the divine but made specific mention of particular elements of devotional practice associated with the Blessed Virgin Mary. In tune with the mentality of a society that had decided to take a step back in time, women were seen solely as destined for procreation. At the start of 1941, for example, a system of "financial loans for the wedded state" was set up which compelled those women who took advantage of them to give up any jobs they had, while official propaganda spoke of the need for "fertile families to send members of our race out into the world to build and uphold empires." Women were always portrayed as modest and traditional. In accordance with this image, Cardinal Plá y Deniel, the Archbishop Primate of Toledo, gave specific guidance on the length of women's sleeves and skirts and on their necklines. This reference to clothing will not be seen as coincidental if we take into account that in this sphere as well there was an attempt to turn the clock back. In explicit contrast to the image of proletarian women that Orwell had contemplated during his visit to revolutionary pre-Civil War Barcelona, Cambó was able to affirm that at the very moment that Franco's troops entered Madrid, "there were women wearing hats in Madrid, and that meant that once again there was civilization."

Along with all this enthusiasm on the part of the victors, there was a far more prosaic, even cruel reality. As Cambó had foreseen, the postwar period saw an accumulation of ills in the daily lives of ordinary Spaniards. One need only cast an eye over a few aspects of their daily diet and health conditions to see this. It appears that meat consumption went down to a third of its previous level and that in 1941 there were 50,000 deaths as a result of gastrointestinal infections. Five percent of university students were suffering from tuberculosis: an illness that accounted for about 26,000 deaths a year between 1940 and 1942.

Nothing shows the other side of the coin of the victors' enthusiasm better than the situation in which the press found itself. There were no general guidelines published or rules of censorship but the workings of the censors were so meticulous that newspapers were told to publish certain stories and not others, all "with due warmth." The novelist Miguel Delibes, who worked as a newspaper editor during those years, has written that "it is hard to imagine an inquisitorial machinery more "coercive, closed, and Machiavellian" than that put in place by the Franco Administration, which "left no loophole for personal initiative." Working on the subversion of freedom of expression at the lowest level, the censors, on minimal salaries and in precarious positions, rather than being enthusiastic supporters of the regime, were individuals forced to perform a lamentable task – or even to submit their own writings to scrutiny – because of their personal circumstances and in exchange for a pittance. One can imagine the inevitable mixture of humiliation descending into abjection that those who lived in such an atmosphere must have felt.

This was what Spain was like in the triumphal year 1939 in which the Civil War ended. It was this Spain that would have to face up to the years that followed and World War II, together with subsequent isolation that was a direct result of the peculiarities of the Franco regime. Whenever the time comes to pass judgment, it will always be important to bear in mind the contrast between the enthusiasm of the victors on the one hand and the actual reality of repression and exile on the other, and of the degree to which those in power tried to hide the reality that surrounded them.

## Bibliography

A good general discussion: Stanley PAYNE, *El régimen de Franco, 1936–1975*, Alianza Editorial, Madrid, 1987 (*The Franco regime 1936–1975*, Madison, WI: University of Wisconsin Press, 1987 and London: Phoenix Press, 2000). Aspects of the topic: Javier TUSELL, Susana SUEIRO, José María MARÍN, *El régimen de Franco (1936–1975). Política y relaciones exteriores*, UNED, Madrid, 1993, and "Franquismo," *Historia Social*, no. 30 (1998). Recent university publications about the period: Jesús A. MARTÍNEZ (coordinator), *Historia de España. Siglo XX*, Cátedra, Madrid, 1999, and volume XLI of the *Historia de España* by MENÉNDEZ PIDAL continued by JOVER, Espasa Calpe, Madrid, 1996, edited by Raymond CARR. A brief book: Juan Pablo FUSI, José Luis GARCÍA DELGADO, Santos JULIÁ, Edward MALEFAKIS, Stanley PAYNE, *Franquismo*, Temas de Hoy, Madrid, 2000.

There are many biographies of Franco, though they are of varying worth. The most extensive is Paul PRESTON, _Franco. A biography_, Harper Collins, London, 1993 (Spanish translation published by Grijalbo), which cannot be considered definitive. See also, Juan Pablo FUSI, _Franco. Autoritarismo y poder personal_, El País, Madrid, 1985; Stanley PAYNE, _Franco, el perfil de la Historia_, Espasa Calpe, Madrid, 1992, and Alberto REIG, _Franco, caudillo: mito y realidad_, Tecnos, Madrid, 1995. Franco's writings: _Apuntes personales del Generalísimo sobre la República y la guerra civil_, Fundación Francisco Franco, Madrid, 1977, and _Papeles sobre la guerra de Marruecos_, Fundación Francisco Franco, Madrid, 1986. The _Documentos inéditos para la Historia del Generalísimo Franco_, published in Madrid by the Fundación Nacional Francisco Franco, stop at the end of World War II. Studies on aspects of his personality, in J. A. FERRER BENIMELI, _El contubernio judeo-masónico comunista_, Istmo, Madrid, 1982; Román GUBERN, _Raza: el ensueño del general Franco_, Ediciones 99, Madrid, 1977; Herbert R. SOUTH-WORTH, _El lavado de cerebro de Francisco Franco_, Crítica, Barcelona, 2000 (_Conspiracy and the Spanish Civil War: the brainwashing of Francisco Franco_, New York: Routledge, 2001). The memoirs of those who lived closest to him during the long period of the dictatorship are most useful: Francisco FRANCO SALGADO ARAÚJO, _Mi vida junto a Franco_, Planeta, Barcelona, 1977, and _Mis conversaciones privadas con Franco_, Planeta, Barcelona, 1976. Highly debatable in terms of the interpretation it offers is Luis SUÁREZ FERNÁNDEZ's _Francisco Franco y su tiempo_, Fundación Francisco Franco, Madrid, 1984 and following.

Interpretations of Francoism as a political regime: Juan J. LINZ, "Opposition in and under an authoritarian regime: the case of Spain" in Robert DAHL, _Regimes and oppositions_, Yale University Press, New York, 1973; "An authoritarian Regime: Spain," in ALLARDT-LITTUNEN, _Cleavages, ideologies and party systems_, Helsinki, 1964; Amando DE MIGUEL, _Sociología del franquismo_, Euros, Barcelona, 1975; Ismael SAZ, _Fascismo y franquismo_, Universitat de València, Valencia, 2004, and Javier TUSELL, _La dictadura de Franco_, Alianza Editorial, Madrid, 1988. Monographs on political life throughout the Franco years in Richard GUNTHER, _Public policy in a no party state; Spanish planning in the twilight of the franquist era_, University of California Press, 1980; Guy HERMET, _Les catholiques dans l'Espagne franquiste_, PUF, Paris, 1980–1981; Javier TUSELL, Emilio GENTILE and Giuliana DI FEBO (eds.), _Fascismo y franquismo, cara a cara. Una perspectiva histórica_, Biblioteca Breve, Madrid, 2004.

Repression and purges during the Franco regime: Josep BENET, _La mort del president Companys_, Barcelona, 1962; J. CASANOVA, F. ESPINOSA, C. MIR and F. MORENO, _Vivir, matar, sobrevivir. La violencia en la dictadura de Franco_, Crítica, Barcelona, 2003; Santos JULIÁ, et al. (eds.), _Víctimas de la guerra civil_, Temas de Hoy, Madrid, 1999; Conxita MIR, et al., _Repressió econòmica i franquisme: l'actuació del Tribunal de Responsabilitats Polítiques a la provincia de Lleida_, Publicacions de l'Abadia de Montserrat, Barcelona, 1997; C. MOLINERO,

M. SALA and J. SOBREQUÉS, *Una inmensa prisión. Los campos de concentración y las prisiones durante la guerra civil y el franquismo*, Crítica, Barcelona, 2003; Francisco MORENTE, *La escuela y el Estado Nuevo. La depuración del magisterio nacional (1936–1943)*, Ámbito, Valladolid, 1977. On exile: José Luis ABELLÁN, *De la guerra civil al exilio republicano (1936–1977)*, Planeta, Madrid, 1982 and, especially, the anthology *El exilio español de 1939*, Taurus, Madrid, 1976, 5 vols., and Javier RUBIO, *La emigración de la guerra civil de 1936–1939*, San Martín, Madrid, 1977.

## Notes

1  A state holding company created by Franco in 1941 to promote economic viability and strengthen defence industries.
2  Gabino Bugallal Araujo (1861–1932), of a wealthy landowning family further enriched at the time of the 1830 selling off of Church lands, was the third generation to wield such power as local political bosses (*caciques*) that a movement – *bugallismo* – was named after them.
3  A one-chamber parliament to which the executive was not answerable, which served to rubber-stamp decisions.
4  "Franco, tuya es la hacienda, la casa, el caballo y la pistola, / mía es la voz antigua de la tierra."

# 1

# The Temptation of Fascism and the Will to Survive (1939–51)

If we view Francoism as a single period, we see that the year 1959 was crucial, not just economically as a result of the change that occurred at that moment, but also politically because that year saw a blurring of any identification with the fascist model and the dictatorship became more bureaucratic in style. It was no mere chance that the emphasis on politics in the period immediately following 1939 coincided with an economic situation that had become disastrous through mismanagement by those in power.

Dividing the Franco years into 5-year periods also makes sense. If 1959 is taken to be a pivotal year, the two decades preceding it can be seen as leading up to it while the following 15 years show the consequences of the change that occurred in that year. The first decade of the Franco regime was characterized by internal unity. During the early years of the dictatorship every effort was made to align the victorious Spain that had won the war with the powers that had been its allies during the conflict. That effort provides the key to the entire period and explains why Spain was later ostracized.

What happened in effect was that there was an attempt to rebuild Spain according to a model that was the complete antithesis of what had gone before. The attempt to establish fascism within the country was closely linked to an expansionist policy outside, in the same way as survival, thanks to cosmetic changes from 1945 onwards, focused Spain's foreign policy entirely on the need simply to survive. As for political opposition to the regime, during World War II and afterwards it kept going by remaining focused on how the Civil War had ended. One can even go so far as to say that Spanish culture of the period was deeply marked by the immediate impact of the recent conflict.

If it makes sense to view the period as a single chronological unit, it also makes just as much sense to divide it up. The World War II years were not only marked by Spain's foreign policy but were also the first moments in the new regime's political journey. Furthermore, it was the period in which Franco served his apprenticeship and learned his political skills. In the period that followed, one might say that this apprenticeship was completed, and what became central to life in Spain was its ability to resist outside pressure.

## A Failed Attempt to Make Spain Fascist

In the months following the Civil War Spain seemed to move towards an alignment with the Axis, more in terms of political institutions than foreign policy. Concerning the latter, the fact that Spain joined the anti-Komintern pact and left the League of Nations (*Sociedad de Naciones*) was proof of its ideological tendencies.

Visits by Spanish leaders to Germany and Italy confirm that this desire for alignment existed, especially the talks that took place in Rome in May 1939 between the fascist leaders and Serrano Suñer. This rising star in Franco's government enjoyed a close relationship with Ciano and even with Mussolini, and it was this that earned him a reputation as the representative of fascist politics in Spain. Nor was Serrano's reputation derived solely from the regime's international alignment; it came also from its internal politics. Mussolini, by advising Franco not to proclaim Spain a monarchy and by emphasizing the need to "talk to the people," was in effect suggesting that the regime become more fascist. Ciano's visit to Spain in July confirmed this sense of there being an alignment with Italy. Discussions in the Spanish Council of Ministers – Franco's cabinet – now revealed clear tension between those who were ready to follow the rising star, Serrano, and those who were not.

Although crisis had been brewing for some time, it finally erupted in August; by then Franco had already done away with the monarchist Pedro Sáinz Rodríguez. The change in government signaled victory for Serrano, who from that moment until 1942 was the key figure in Spanish politics. A cultured and intelligent lawyer, Serrano was superior to the rest of the regime's emerging political class, though he by no means lacked faults, being megalomaniac, ambitious, tending to foster a personality cult, intemperate, and secretive. As well as keeping his government portfolio, Serrano also managed to take on the presidency of the party's Political Junta; from then on he was addressed as "Minister President" by a press that he himself controlled. It is even perfectly possible that the young generals serving in various ministries for the Armed Services at that time (Juan Yagüe, Agustín Muñoz Grandes, and José Enrique Varela) were there not only because Franco trusted them more than those who had brought him to power but because from Serrano's point of view they were more susceptible to his own influence. There were in the new government personalities from the traditional Catholic right, but only as technical advisers or because they were close to Serrano (José Ibáñez Martín and José Larraz); the monarchist presence was much less evident – a clear sign that Franco saw it as potentially dangerous. The Carlist presence (Esteban Bilbao) was manageable.

The all-powerful Franco–Serrano duo was strengthened by a number of measures. Shortly before the governmental crisis, General Queipo de Llano was sent to Italy; in practice, he was exiled. At the same time, legislation was passed on the position of the Chief of State who, from then onwards, "on a permanent basis," would be able to exercise the functions of government without need of prior consultation with the cabinet. In fact, thanks to measures such as these, Franco acquired more absolute power than even Stalin – who had, at least in theory, to obey a Constitution – or Hitler, who was answerable to a parliament. The ratification of the party statutes, praised by Mussolini, took on characteristics that made them virtually identical to those of the fascists. Not only were the National Council and its Political Junta endowed with decisive political importance but also provision was made for controlling trade unions and armed militias. The economic plan approved in October 1939 was notable for its tendency towards autarchy.

If there was indeed a will to make Spain more fascist, one must ask why fascism never came anywhere near gaining control there. The reply to this question may be found in what actually happened in a situation in which internal politics were closely bound up with the international situation. In brief, it would only have been possible for the regime to become fascist if Franco's Spain had decided to join in World War II on the side of the Axis. In 1939 and 1940 any attempt to increase fascist influence would have been in its earliest stages and was unlikely to mature, and if the intention had been clear it nonetheless had fundamental weaknesses from the start.

The role of the army in the Spain that emerged victorious from the Civil War was of supreme importance and there was never the slightest doubt that it would have to be a major player were conflict to arise, in contrast to what happened in, say, Romania. One must bear in mind that in 1939, 80 percent of posts in the Administration were reserved for ex-combatants (and not, for example, for party militants) and that at least 25 percent of all political posts were given to men with an Army background. We have already noted that during the Civil War the military dominated the Administration in the rearguard and that in the wake of the conflict they took on the task of repression. Even in the Party's National Council, if 24 percent of its members were party veterans, about another 20 percent were from the Armed Services. As late as 1951, 27 percent of mayors and local councilors were Civil War ex-combatants. Any victory of the Party over the army could only have been possible if the Party had managed to establish for itself a more influential role in Spanish society.

The early years of the post-Civil War period illustrate clearly just how limited any growth in fascist influence actually was. The Party published figures which seemed to show its strength: in 1939 it had 650,000 members, and in 1945 1,000,000, in addition to 2,000 government employees and another 10,000 in the union organization, and it was no doubt monopolized by the most orthodox Falangists. The role of Carlism decreased: the position it occupied allowed it to retain some influence but it was marginalized and limited in the impact it might have. As regards the Party, the Carlist attitude can be summed up in what an ex-minister, the Conde de Rodezno, told Franco: it would not have been openly hostile but it certainly lacked solidarity. It was only in Navarre that Carlism had any real influence. Membership of the Party varied according to regions. In Catalonia it was tiny before the outbreak of the Civil War; it could only draw members from the anti-Catalanist right and a few local notables. In the Basque Country the Party managed to gain the support of traditionalists at a municipal level and of those linked to Falange in positions of power in the provinces. Over a large part of the Iberian Peninsula traditional elites were of the right. It is possible to discern a limited achievement of the aim of "nationalizing the masses" in the incorporation into the Party of former left-wing militants: A study of the Aljarafe district in the province of Seville shows that 15 percent of Party members came from left-wing militias and expressed radical opinions with uncompromising directness. This explains why it embarked on a mission of social action which went so far as to include speaking out strongly against monopolies. At the same time, the fact that it was a leading force in society meant that it could also play a policing role. Whatever the situation, its powers of coercion and its propaganda against its opponents had a far greater impact than any willingness to sign up to its ideas. Despite censorship, only sections of the press and the media could ever be considered tools of "fascist expansion" at the time. By around 1940 it was obvious that the result of the Party's attempt to influence society would remain ambiguous: in practice it fostered fear and passive acceptance rather than whole-hearted commitment.

Nor did the institutions that governed the Party work well. The National Council remained a divided body that in fact did very little, so much so that there is not much to be gained by discussing it further. More or less the same could be said of the Political Junta. The Institute of Political Studies (*Instituto de Estudios Políticos*), which was supposedly the intellectual breeding-ground of fascism, never matched up to its reputation. It might initially have been thought that in organizations aimed at young people there might have been a will to see fascism spread. However, the revolutionary Spanish Students' Union (*Sindicato Español Universitario* or SEU) finally lost its battle for life in 1941 with the disappearance in Russia of its principal radical leader, Enrique Sotomayor. Although the SEU had more than 50,000 members, there were always obvious gaps in its coverage of Spanish territory, the most obvious being in Catalonia and the Basque Country. In 1943, compulsory membership became the rule for all students. The Youth Front (*Frente de Juventudes*) created in December 1940 never had more than 13 percent of young people on its lists, and the percentage of women was even lower. Unlike what had been on offer in Germany, training was traditional, being run by soldiers and primary school teachers who had left their 20s far behind them, so without ever entirely losing its Falangist character, the Youth Front drifted towards educational and sporting activities. A parallel voluntary organization, Franco's Falange Youth Groups (*Falanges Juveniles de Franco*) – whose identification with the leader is itself significant – barely attracted 18 percent of young men and 8 percent of women. Last of all, the section of the Party aimed at women favored the domestic ideal of the model housewife that typified the traditional Spanish right. The *Sección Femenina* of Falange offered the mother as its role model rather than the young revolutionary. Its leader, Pilar Primo de Rivera, left no one in any doubt that "the real duty of women to their Fatherland is to bring up families on firm foundations of austerity and cheerfulness where all that is traditional can flourish." Nothing was so worthy of praise as a woman's "submissiveness" to men. Numbers of members never even reached a third of those in equivalent organizations in Italy; women barely took part in mass processions and could rarely be photographed doing gymnastics.

The Party quickly lost the political battle in two areas. In the summer of 1940 militias were set up but not much was achieved beyond laying down very elementary guidelines for mobilization. The military makes militias superfluous and in Franco's Spain the initial victory that had laid the foundations for the regime belonged unequivocally to the Army. Falangist union organizations did not play a major role in the national economy either. According to the Law on the Bases of Union Organization (*Ley de Bases de Organización Sindical*) of December 1940, although unions claimed to represent "the entire people organized as a working militia" the law did not include chambers of commerce or members of the professional classes. There is nothing of greater significance in the blocking of the revolutionary aims of the Falangist union organization than the fact that it was an army general, Andrés Saliquet, who denounced the man in charge of it, Merino, as a former Freemason. In Mussolini's Italy, the Party controlled and put blocks on union activity; in Spain, the force that exercised the greatest power – the Army – closed the door on Merino by denouncing him.

Mention of the Party takes us on into World War II. For Franco's Spain the invasion of Poland was not welcome news but it responded by aligning itself with its Civil War allies. For the first months of World War II Franco's Spain was closely aligned with fascist Italy but was in no state to think of taking part in the conflict, not even to the limited extent that the Duce considered his own country able to participate. In the event, in April 1940, when Mussolini decided to enter the war, he told Franco first, and when in May it became clear that France had been defeated, the Falangist press began to demand the return of Gibraltar. The spectacular defeat of France – Spain's traditional enemy in Morocco – immediately meant that Spain was tempted to join in the war in an attempt to gain some benefit in a radically new European order. Two days after Mussolini joined the war, Franco and Serrano modified Spain's position and put it on a footing of "non-belligerence," which in Italy's case had meant "pre-belligerence." The fact that over those same days Italian warplanes were allowed to overfly Spanish territory to bomb the British made participation seem more likely.

For Spain actually to take part in World War II it would have needed its economic situation to be better than it was and for there to be a greater

degree of internal cohesion. By December 1939 there was already discontent among the highest-ranking military officers directed at Franco
and strong reservations concerning Serrano who, in the eyes of many, had
too much power concentrated in his person, gave too much support to a
Falange that was too revolutionary, was dominant, megalomaniac, and
even seemed not to get on well with those who had helped to bring
him to power. In January 1940, General Muñoz Grandes was replaced as
Minister Secretary General of the *Movimiento* after only a few months in
the position. It is worth underlining the fact that a regime that prided
itself on following the model of fascist Italy should have appointed a
soldier as leader of the Party when it was in fact a soldier who would
replace Mussolini in 1943.

## The Temptation to Intervene and Internal Conflict (1940–2)

It has been written that a triumphant Germany immediately put pressure
on Spain to join in World War II and that this pressure was insistent and
lasting even if it never succeeded in breaking down Franco's resistance.
What actually happened, however, was that after Germany's victory in
France, the Spanish leadership identified totally with the Axis and this
situation lasted, with different nuances and some hesitations, until well
on into 1944. German pressure to induce Spain to intervene in the war,
though strong for several months, did not last very long. The initiative concerning Spain's possible entry into the conflict was taken not by Germany
but by the leaders of Franco's Spain. In mid June 1940, the *caudillo* sent
General Jorge Vigón to hold talks with Hitler and express Spain's willingness to become a participant in the conflict. On this occasion Spain for
the first time made substantial territorial demands. These consisted – and
remained so for some months – of the extension of its possessions in
the Sahara and Guinea and, above all, of the occupation of the whole of
Morocco and the part of Algeria that had been colonized by Spaniards.
There was not a single section of the Franco regime that was not in favor
of these imperialist ambitions. If for Falange Spain's imperial destiny
seemed likely to be fulfilled by this process, for Africanists who had fought
in North Africa long-cherished ambitions would be realized. The Falangists,
nonetheless, were the most ambitious (and least realistic) and at times
demanded Spanish expansion into the south of France and Portugal too.

There was never the slightest chance that the Franco regime's aims would ever be achieved because the position of Hitler's Germany on the issue was a far cry from what was widely desired in Madrid. The Führer was never a strong advocate of a historical justice that would allow Spain to fulfill its aspirations; for Hitler Spain was a not very important country that he expected to follow his lead of its own free will and be ready to furnish him with raw materials and strategic advantages in return for almost nothing. In Hitler's view, not even the Mediterranean was of any importance. Once France was defeated, he hesitated briefly over where Germany should next expand, finally deciding on eastern Europe with the result that Spain was no longer of any interest to him.

Having outlined the German position, we can now return to the events that were now unfolding. In July 1940, the Spanish Foreign Minister Juan Luis Beigbeder suggested occupying part of French Morocco on the pretext of controlling disturbances there. The operation never took place, probably because the French kept up a high level of military presence in the area and because Germany was never likely to authorize it. There was, however, an attempt to replicate this kind of spectacular decision in the style of Mussolini which, although it was somewhat of a caricature, did not, unlike the Italian model, end in a fiasco. At the very moment when German troops were entering Paris, Spanish troops occupied Tangiers, announcing the move as irreversible. The French representative was expelled from the city and a German consulate was set up there, whose actual aim was espionage. In practice it would be as late as 1944, when the war seemed to be turning decisively in favor of the Allies, that Spain would come round to considering the zone it controlled as international once more.

Shortly afterwards in 1940 Spain made concessions of considerable strategic advantage to the Germans: by July there was a German military mission in Spain preparing for an eventual retaking of Gibraltar, besides which, throughout 1940 and 1941, thanks to what was called Operation Moor, a total of 18 German submarines were re-provisioning in Spain. This allowed them to extend their radius of action considerably – so much so that they could reach as far as northern Brazil. The Germans also benefited from the information provided by the Spanish secret services, and even such people as Serrano handed over to Nazi diplomats dispatches from neutral ambassadors and anyone whose information might be interesting to them, such as, for example, the Duke of Alba, Spain's representative in London.

The German presence on the French–Spanish border signaled imminent danger for what was to become the United Kingdom's main base on the Old Continent: Portugal. The Portuguese might well have feared that Germany would attack through Spain with Spanish help and it was in these circumstances that negotiations took place, beginning at the end of June 1940 and ending a month later. The treaty was seen by the Spanish as a way of drawing Portugal away from the British cause and into its own camp. The British were not at all worried that their ally should sign up to such an agreement because it did not alter Britain's own policy towards Spain, outlined before Germany had ever become a threat. In Britain's view, a friendly Spain was desirable but a neutral Spain was essential. This was why it sent as its ambassador to Madrid an important Conservative, Sir Samuel Hoare. The ambassador, as eagerly as the Foreign Office, favored maintaining a stance that would incline Spain towards neutrality by exerting pressure on provisioning. The tactic used was typical of British Imperialism: to neutralize a dangerous area with the minimum of military effort and at only a limited economic cost. However, the policy went hand in hand with errors in execution and excessive fatuousness on the part of Hoare. On more than one occasion Churchill considered that invading part if not all of Spain's territory might prove to be a necessity given the possibility of Franco inclining towards the Axis and endangering the UK's strategic position.

Hoare tried to make his influence felt in military circles and used money to buy the support of monarchist generals. Yet his most effective policy consisted of a series of agreements from the final months of 1940 onwards that allowed Spain to be provided with enough oil and essential supplies to survive but not, on the other hand, to join in the war. However, despite all this, the possibility that Germany might invade Spain with the help of part if not all of those in power meant that plans were drawn up to block the way to Gibraltar and allow a takeover of the Canary Islands. A large amount of Britain's limited combat resources were kept on alert for many months in case of such an eventuality.

An important aspect of Britain's policy was the need to persuade the Americans to come into line with the British position. However, the United States tended to be even more anti-Francoist than Britain, perhaps as a result of the way that the two countries had chosen to distance themselves from each other after the Civil War. When an agreement with the United States to supply oil was finally reached at the start of 1942, only 60 percent of Spain's previous consumption of petroleum products was conceded.

If British policy was decided on and put into action swiftly in that crucial summer of 1940, remaining unchanged until the end of the war, German policy was formulated later and therefore was more subject to change. In fact, it was only in 1945 that Hitler realized that he should already have persuaded Spain to join in the conflict by the summer of 1940; that would have allowed him to take Gibraltar which in turn would have allowed him to gain a stranglehold on the UK's main communications route to its Empire. He had not done so because he believed that with his air force he could force Churchill to submit. In any case, Hitler did not want the French colonial empire to fall into British hands. All these factors meant that he could not satisfy Franco's excessive territorial demands, which were the essential condition for Spain's entry into the war.

Over the summer of 1940 and on into September the Spanish repeatedly presented their demands to Hitler but in the course of a visit in September Serrano, who was soon to take on the portfolio for Foreign Affairs, discovered to his great surprise that the rebuilding of Europe was not going to take the shape that Spain's notion of historical justice required but instead one that entirely suited Hitler's own personal interests. Not only were Serrano's requests barely granted a hearing but, moreover, he was faced with a German demand for one of the Canary Islands and another naval base in either Agadir or Mogador. He, as much as Franco, was strongly in favor of taking Spain into the war; as Franco wrote, "we shall benefit from being in the war but not by acting in haste." His idea was to gain substantial territorial advantages with the least possible intervention, but Hitler thought that Franco's Spain was a weak country lacking in resources which was asking too much and arrogantly attempting to mount an operation against Gibraltar for which it lacked the necessary means. This last factor was decisive: taking everything into account, the Führer himself explained to those working with him that by trying to reconcile the conflicting interests of Spain, Italy, and France, he was trying to bring off a "monumental deception."

This meant that Spanish desires never stood a chance of being met given Hitler's own agenda, while there was a distinct possibility that Franco might give way under the stubborn, calculated pressure exerted by the master of Europe. Nonetheless, accounts of their meeting at Hendaye in October 1940 have suggested that Franco managed to avoid committing himself while Hitler was in despair at his own failure to make him do so. What really happened was that Hitler, who had always despised the Spanish leaders, managed on that occasion to get them to sign a protocol that committed Spain to entering the conflict but on no precise date, which meant that the situation remained open. Franco himself had gone to the meeting with a memorandum in which he explained that he could not enter the war "just because he wanted to," reminding Germany that Italy had become a burden to its ally. The critical moment in Germany's pressurizing of Spain occurred in the last weeks of 1940. Hitler, whose main focus of concern was Central and Eastern Europe, had no strategy in mind for the Mediterranean except for a few brief weeks, and by January 1941 he considered the option of taking Gibraltar closed. In any case, his troops in the Balkans were having to cover for Italian defeats and when the invasion of Russia took place it became impossible to undertake sizeable operations at both extremes of Europe.

In February 1941, on one of only two journeys that Franco ever made outside Spain, accompanied by Serrano he met for talks with the Duce in Bordighera. He explained to the fascist leader that he not only wanted to enter the war but that he was afraid he might do so "too late." Mussolini, who must at that time have assumed that the war had already been won by Hitler, did not credit Spanish intervention with much importance: "How can a country which has not got bread to last the week go to war?" he asked one of his associates. It must be said that he himself had not won any great victories and Spain might become a competitor in the sharing of power around the Mediterranean. What happened after that was a repeat of what had gone before: Italy wanted Spain to join in the war but only when Italy said so and only when it best suited Italian interests.

From the start of 1941 on, Germany's military strategic planning on Spain was purely defensive: it anticipated only the creation of a protective front in the north which would move back gradually in the event of British troops taking the Iberian Peninsula. Spain no longer served Axis interests beyond its function as a defensive wall. That year Germany imported seven times as much military material from Spain and in 1943 Spain's trade with the Reich accounted for 25 percent of the country's total and was above the level of trade with Allied countries. This did not, however, mean that Spanish supplies were essential to the Reich except in certain strategic materials and at the end of the war. Germany gained significant trade concessions from Spain, yet at the same time instructions to the German ambassador in Madrid were to keep out of internal politics which, throughout 1941, were particularly uneasy.

A decisive factor in Spain's non-intervention in World War II was the lack of unity among the leaders of the regime which witnessed bitter confrontation between the military and Falange exacerbated by Serrano's determination to hold on to his own personal power. In June 1940 Franco had dismissed Yagüe, who had been accused of disloyalty, possibly by Serrano himself. More decisive still was the formation of a military party opposed to what Franco represented. Some generals favored intervention in the war but all of them were far more aware than the Falangists were of the dangers for Spain of insufficient preparedness. "With what?" asked one general when the possibility of Spain joining in the war was being discussed in his presence. The military feared that the exalted national sentiment stirred up by the Party might lead to an engagement in the conflict that would be suicidal; their high-ranking officers had advocated caution in any statements coming from those with political responsibility, and caution was not the style favored either by Falange or by Serrano. Yet there was also a question of the distribution of power. The military believed that they had won the Civil War and considered that it was they who had put Franco in the position he now enjoyed. In their view Falange was demagogic and ineffectual and Serrano was abusing the excessive power to which he clung.

In May 1941 a crisis-point was reached like no other in the entire history of Francoism. What made it different was how long it lasted and the fact that Franco, having tried to resolve it in one way, found himself forced to back down. At the start of May Falange, controlled by Serrano, declared itself no longer subject to censorship; at the same time, two members with the evocative surname Primo de Rivera – Pilar and Miguel – resigned from their posts in the organization. On May 5, it was announced that Galarza, who until then had been undersecretary to the Presidency, was moving over to be Minister of the Interior: a post that had in fact been vacant but in effect had been controlled by Serrano through the undersecretary since he himself had taken on the portfolio for Foreign Affairs. At the same time Carrero Blanco, who was destined to play such an important role later in internal politics, took over the post of Under-secretary to the Presidency.

However, Falange had the strength to retaliate. The Falangist news-paper *Arriba* launched a personal attack on the new Minister of the Interior and there followed a whole battery of resignations. Some, like Larraz, acted out of a conviction that the regime was handling the economy very badly, but those who resigned were above all leaders within Falange and Serrano himself was among them. He wrote to the Chief of State, address-ing him as "Dear General," and assured him in a menacing tone that "the case as far as we are concerned now offers no dignified solution." Franco was forced to make changes: on May 16, no fewer than four highly significant Falangists were appointed to ministerial posts: Arrese as Minister-Secretary of the *Movimiento*; Miguel Primo de Rivera as Agriculture Minister and Girón as Labor Minister; another Falangist, Joaquín Benjumea, became Finance Minister, taking over from Larraz. If we add to their number Serrano and Demetrio Carceller, we have to conclude that never before or subsequently did Falange play such a decisive role in government. Yet Franco managed to keep Galarza on as Minister of the Interior and Galarza, from that position of power, began to appoint provincial governors and leaders of the Party. At his side, Carrero started to make moves prejudicial to Falangist interests; what he saw as necessary was not a party in chaos confronting the military but rather a "select minority" with administrative skills. Finally, the star of the only person capable of leading Falange to a monopoly of power – Serrano Suñer – began its decline. From that moment on he controlled neither the Ministry of the Interior nor the press; he had also lost his monopoly in relations between Falange and Franco. In the future this role would be played by Arrese, who was more submissive and less intelligent but also less ambitious, and who would end up supplanting entirely the brother-in-law to the dictator.

It is significant that this crisis coincided almost exactly with the signing of an agreement between the Vatican and Spain which resolved the greatest problem that existed between the two powers: the appointment of bishops in Spain. The Spanish Church felt it had cause for grave concern in the final months of 1939. Its bishops feared at that stage that an attempt might be made to gag the Church. Pontifical documents were subjected to censorship, as actually happened when they spoke out against Nazi racism. The decisive issue was that of the appointment of bishops, as Franco's Spain wanted the right to nominate candidates. Disagreement was so profound that the appointment process ground to a halt and by the end of 1940 some 20 dioceses were vacant. Agreement was finally reached in the days following the governmental crisis, probably because Serrano felt he needed a diplomatic success. As a result, bishops were appointed according to a system whereby the Vatican was presented with a previously agreed list of candidates. Obviously, at the same time, the image of relations between Spain and the Vatican presented to the public was idyllic. The Saint Barbara festival was like a royal coronation and Franco was accompanied throughout those years and the period that followed by a relic of Saint Teresa's hand, captured from the enemy in Malaga in the Civil War.

In June 1941 the German offensive against Russia united the Francoist leadership for a time, all agreeing that, as Serrano put it, "Russia was guilty" of causing Spain's ills in the 1930s. Yet there was disagreement even on the subject of the Spanish Volunteer Division (*División Española de Voluntarios*) sent to Russia: not least concerning its name, since in Falangist circles it was called simply the Blue Division (*División Azul*). There also appear to have been differences of opinion on who should command it since some thought that it was a matter of political responsibility while others considered the operation strictly military. As happened on so many occasions, Franco opted for what seemed like a solution to suit both sides, which was to hand over command to a Falangist soldier, Muñoz Grandes. The Spanish Division numbered 18,000 men and saw action in the Leningrad sector. Muñoz Grandes met twice with Hitler in 1942 and expressed quite openly his own unequivocal support of the Axis. As time passed and Franco decided that Muñoz Grandes's position as commander of the Division had become problematic, he got rid of him by the simple device of making him a lieutenant general: a rank that meant he could no longer stay in Russia. German victories at the start of the conflict had made an early Soviet collapse seem likely. In July 1941 Franco had stated that the war "had been approached wrongly and that the Allies had lost it." Not even the entry of the United States into the war at the end of 1941 after the attack on Pearl Harbor induced the Spanish leadership to be more prudent in their pronouncements.

Over this time, confrontation between Falange and the Army was becoming more frequent. Spain's entire political life was taken up with a succession of confrontations between soldiers and Falangists that became increasingly violent. As Serrano's role had become less important, internal strife had built up such a store of acute tension that finally violence erupted. On August 16, 1942, a group of radical Falangists threw bombs at the close of a religious service in Begoña at which the Army Minister, the traditionalist Varela, had been present. The immediate result was a political crisis whose gravity can be measured by how long it lasted and how many people were dismissed from their posts. General Varela resigned, blaming Falange for what had happened. The crisis would have ended there had Franco, urged on by Carrero, not thought it necessary to compensate for Varela's resignation by distancing himself from Serrano. There was at this point no response from Falangists in support of Serrano to make Franco change his mind. On September 13, Varela was replaced by Carlos Asensio and Serrano Suñer by General Jordana, a former vice-president during the

Civil War. There was no indication that the crisis signaled a step towards a change in foreign policy; rather it appeared to be the result of internal factors. Foreign ambassadors judged quite correctly that what had happened showed that the only effective force within the Spanish regime was the Army; they were right, but only in part, because the ultimate winner was in fact Franco himself. No other political crisis would last as long as those that faced him in 1941 and 1942. The Falangists themselves, and more especially their Secretary General Arrese, submitted to the authority of the dictator despite the fact that a Falangist was executed. In the difficult times that lay ahead, Falangists and the *caudillo* would form a tight-knit group bound together by mutual interest.

During the period in which Serrano Suñer enjoyed political hegemony, attempts were made to endow relations with the Spanish-American world with special significance through cultural contacts. In defiance of democratic ideals Falange, working through diplomatic channels, launched a virulent campaign against the United States. The creation of the Council of the Hispanic World (*Consejo de la Hispanidad*) in November 1940, when the possibility of Spain joining in World War II had not been definitively dismissed, provided an administrative structure. The impact of this policy on Spanish interests was catastrophic: apart from the fact that there were no actual advantages gained, throughout the years following its implementation it was a heavy burden on the Franco regime.

## —— Stumbling Progress towards Neutrality (1942–5) ——

The change in direction in politics within Spain allowed the move towards neutrality that Jordana might have been working towards to benefit from the new turn the war was taking. The new Foreign Minister repeatedly assured the Axis that Spanish foreign policy was not going to change under any circumstances; nonetheless, at the first meeting of the government a resolution was approved that meant that the term "non-belligerence" disappeared.

The Allies had now gained the initiative in the war and were in action in a part of the world that directly affected Spain. Landings in North Africa were accompanied by British guarantees to Franco that the operation was not directed against him. After the British landings in December 1942 Jordana went to Portugal: a move indicative of the stance he wished to adopt from that moment on. The Salazar regime had remained neutral towards both sides in the conflict and could provide a useful means by which Franco's Spain could indicate a Spanish will to make overtures towards the Allies. Evidence of the ambiguity of the situation is seen in the fact that Carrero seemed still to think a German victory possible. Only after the Normandy landings did he suggest that Britain and Germany might broker a peace that would prevent the Russian advance.

Just as during the most fascist phase of the Franco regime's development relations with the Church had been plagued with difficulties, so now there were abundant signs of Spain's will to be on good terms with the Vatican. Franco went so far as to write a letter to the pope accusing the Americans of making concessions to Russia that would represent a serious threat to Catholicism. The pontiff replied in discreet terms that promised nothing. The Spanish position remained uncertain. The most clearly neutral position was that of Jordana and a section of Spain's diplomatic service which included, for example, the Duke of Alba.

One might well ask how the Spanish position was viewed by the warring parties. Germany had always taken a dual political approach where Spain was concerned and now this became especially relevant for a period of a few months. The very large German embassy staff (some 500 people of whom perhaps a third were spies) had been told repeatedly not to involve themselves in Spanish political affairs. On the other hand, the Nazi Party representative kept in close contact with radical Falangist groups. At the end of 1942 and start of 1943, the Germans also made contact with a number of high-ranking military officers, but what Hitler really wanted was for Spain, in the event of an Allied attack, to defend itself. In accordance with this stance, the Germans ended up agreeing to the Spanish proposal that Germany supply Spain with arms. The agreement they reached meant that half Spain's imports from Germany would be in the form of materials of war, principally artillery for coastal defense, while exports would take the form mainly of wolframite: a mineral of enormous strategic importance. As on other occasions, the position Italy adopted was substantially different from that of Germany. For Mussolini, the fact that the war was now centered around the Mediterranean was no longer a matter of choice based on Italy's own interests but rather of survival. He therefore suggested that Hitler attack the Allies through Spain.

Franco's policy in 1943 was still to foster a sense of being apart from the conflict while those who favored a more neutral political stance were having some successes without ever actually winning the debate. There was a significant move towards neutrality in April 1943 when, on the occasion of the commemoration of Columbus's landing in Barcelona on his return from America, Jordana spoke clearly of his desire for peace, no doubt largely as a result of his Catholic affiliation. It took time before Franco gradually began to adopt the language initially used by his Foreign Minister. Nonetheless, the Spanish position did shift millimeter by millimeter as the course of military operations changed. The fall of Tunis in May 1943 led Carrero to suggest that Germany should react quickly or try to make peace.

The collapse of Mussolini's regime was, however, to have an even greater impact since it had been a role model that Franco's Spain had imitated. It was information from Spanish military sources that convinced the Italians that the Allied landings would happen in Corsica or Greece rather than Sicily. When they happened in Sicily, Italy collapsed almost immediately, ruining any chance the fascist regime might have had of survival. Mussolini's removal from power had immediate repercussions in Spain, represented in Rome at the time by a Falangist of some importance: Raimundo Fernández Cuesta. Falange thought that something similar might happen in Spain. Once again this caused divisions at the heart of the regime's governing class. While Jordana tried to freeze Spanish diplomatic relations in Italy, Falange helped Mussolini's supporters in Spain. Of Europe's neutral countries, only Portugal and Switzerland maintained relations with the Saló Republic. Mussolini, some of whose closest collaborators ended up in Spain, was also on the point of fleeing there at the last moment. As is well known, he opted instead for Switzerland, was arrested on the way there, and summarily executed.

Yet Mussolini's fall had in effect happened much earlier, in July 1943 when, for the first time, he mobilized the members of Italy's political class who favored the restoration of the monarchy. This subsequently became an element of decisive importance in Spanish internal politics. The best evidence of the anxiety that Franco might well have felt when faced with this alternative is his affirmation, in front of an audience of Falangists, that "the liberal capitalist system," which he always linked to monarchist circles, "has gone for ever," at the same time announcing his firm decision that those who were not entirely loyal to him should "leave the ship."

To understand the monarchist position we must go back in time to the start of 1942. The previous year in Rome Alfonso XIII had died after acknowledging Don Juan as his heir and abdicating in his favor. The man who now took upon himself the future succession of the dynasty was someone who had identified himself with the extreme right and had not hesitated in trying to take up arms against the Republic in the middle of the Civil War. However, his cause soon came to represent something quite different because a certain sector of the political class was seeking a more viable political formula for Spain in view of a possible victory of the democratic powers. Already by March 1942 a monarchist committee had formed that was in contact with sections of the military that tended to express strong criticism of General Franco. Franco felt obliged to keep up some contact with Don Juan and in May wrote him a letter in which he lectured him on the characteristics required of any monarchy that might be restored in Spain; it must be "revolutionary", and by no means the "decadent" monarchy that in his view had ascended the throne in the eighteenth century.

In June, Pedro Sáinz Rodríguez and Eugenio Vegas Latapié had to go into hiding: the former into exile in Portugal and the latter in Switzerland. Don Juan de Borbón responded to Franco's letter at the end of 1942 by appointing as one of his advisers José María Gil Robles, a prominent leader of the most powerful right-wing faction during the Second Republic. As time passed, Don Juan's insistence that Franco accept the monarchist option became more pressing. In March 1943 the *Cortes* was set up. Franco had ensured that members of the nobility and the Armed Services sat alongside the Falangist leadership, thus indicating that he himself intended to stay in power. Don Juan then wrote to Franco outlining the "extremely grave risks" that would have to be faced if the monarchy were not restored, but the dictator merely pointed out that in actual fact those who supported the monarchy were an unreliable minority.

As has already been suggested, the moment when monarchist pressure on Franco became more insistent was in the summer of 1943. In June Franco might well have felt that his ranks were thinning when some 30 members of the *Cortes* approached him requesting the reinstitution of a traditional Catholic monarchy. The regime's reply was cautious. Carrero alerted the military to the existence of a Masonic plot to undermine the regime. In September 1943 Franco received via the Ministry for the Army a document signed by all lieutenant generals asking whether the time might not have come to make way for a new regime; in its original version the text was even more explicit since it suggested a return to monarchy and a dismantling of the totalitarian system. Not only those who had signed it but probably all Spain's high-ranking officers were in agreement with the proposed changes. Franco, on the other hand, was planning to stay in power and he had before him, in what had happened in Italy, the stark example of what not to do. He insisted that he had never received the document and refused to allow all the lieutenant generals to come and see him together, which might have resulted in a repetition of the last great Fascist Council meeting in which the Duce was done away with. What he did instead was receive the generals one by one and defuse in private conversations what might otherwise have become a dangerous force in opposition. In this way Franco freed himself from the possible threat of military opposition at the very moment when Allied pressure was becoming stronger.

Franco had no reason to hope that the Allies would treat him well after he had shown a decided inclination towards the Axis up to that time. The British, however, were too busy mopping up in Italy in 1943 to spend any time on Spain. At this point the position of British diplomatic representatives in Spain did undergo a marked change. The British ambassador, Hoare, soon realized that nothing was going to change Spanish politics; nonetheless, he did not recommended strong action against Franco. Jordana managed to have the Blue Division recalled; in total, over time, some 47,000 Spanish soldiers went to Russia, almost half of whom were wounded. What the British ambassador found hardest to take was the calm air of self-sufficiency that Franco displayed each time he received the diplomat and delivered one of his endless monologues. In circumstances such as these it is not surprising that Hoare's defense of a policy of non-aggression towards Spain lasted to the end of World War II.

For their part, the Americans had at this time another ambassador, the historian Peter Hayes, who was a Catholic and Roosevelt's personal representative but was not always in line with those in power in the State Department, who were more strongly anti-Francoist. Hayes tells in his memoirs how in Franco's office he came across photos of Hitler and Mussolini but soon reached the conclusion that the Spanish regime had little to do with fascism. Initially he tried to intervene in Spanish politics, for example asking Spain not to attack Russia, but in the postwar period he became an enthusiastic defender of the Franco regime. Nonetheless, neither Hoare nor Hayes can be held responsible for the Allies' harshest decision on Franco's Spain; that was taken by the US Department of State.

What happened can be explained by the position adopted by the Spanish up to that point and by Spain's slowness and insincerity in its move towards neutrality, but there was also a chance factor that led to the decision being taken. In November 1943 what came to be known as the "Laurel Affair" happened. Spain sent a telegram to the pro-Japanese government in the Philippines mentioning its "indestructible and proven relationship" with that country. The text did not, in fact, constitute recognition of the government but Washington was indignant about it.

The result was that in January 1944 all oil exports to Spain were suspended. The situation became extremely tense for the regime because at that time an Allied victory seemed highly likely after the Normandy landings. Finally, following very difficult negotiations, an agreement was reached in May by means of an exchange of notes between the Spanish Administration and the Allies. Franco's Spain confirmed the withdrawal of the Blue Division, promised to close the German consulate in Tangiers, and expressed willingness to resolve by arbitration the legal situation of Italian ships in Spanish harbors (which finally happened in line with American demands). It is probable that the question of greatest interest to the Allies concerning Spain was that of the Spanish export of wolframite to Germany. This mineral was of prime importance in the production of weapons of war (in warheads and armor-plating, for example) and Hitler had lost all other possible sources of supply apart from Spain. The agreement consisted of limiting supply to just a few tens of tons, the Allies buying up and using the rest. In this instance, as in so many others, Jordana's favorable attitude to neutrality met with disapproval from an Administration in which the Axis still had many supporters. No lesser figure than the Industry Minister, the Falangist Carceller, appears to have been one of them.

From that time on, Spain's foreign policy of neutrality was based on close identification with the pope and Catholicism, apart from one pronouncement on World War II that outlined three different theaters of war. As regards neutrality, efforts were made at the start of 1943 to draw together those neutral countries that shared Spain's religious position, but all attempts failed. As Franco himself explained, he was neutral as far as the war between Britain and Germany was concerned but he supported Germany in her war against the Soviet Union, as well as those countries that were fighting Japan. In fact these opinions were intended principally as camouflage to hide his former alignment with the Axis, but they also testify to the regime's interests and the mistakes it made. They show, for example, that Franco never took seriously the Allied demand for the unconditional surrender of the enemy, and they highlight his fear of a communist threat and his radical disagreement with those Americans who seemed to think that the communist regime might change.

At this point, however, a major about-turn had occurred in another aspect of Spain's foreign policy: in relation to Latin America. There was no more pro-Axis political propaganda and no Spanish interference in internal politics; indeed, Spain now accepted American influence in the area. At the same time ambassadors and organizations linked to Falange disappeared, though they had never been as important as the United States had thought. Spanish propaganda became purely cultural and had different objectives. The attempt to link Spain with a group of nations which had not been involved in the conflict underlined once and for all its own neutrality.

Its neutrality was evident in another area too. The Franco regime did not adopt a notably anti-Jewish stance; there was no racially based anti-Semitism, partly for the simple reason that numbers of members of this ethnic minority were small, though anti-Jewish discourses were at times used by leaders of the regime. Francoist anti-Semitism was a product of Catholic traditionalism and was compatible with both appreciation and the study of Spain's Sephardic heritage. There was, however, no policy of offering protection to Jews despite the fact that some were Sephardi and could therefore claim Spanish origins. There was a stage early on in which some 30,000 Jews passed through Spain but the regime had no policy aimed at saving them. Even towards the end of the war the regime did not offer them protection, although by then it was obvious that they were facing extermination. About 8,000 Jews were saved thanks to intervention by Spanish authorities, but these were instances in which Spanish diplomats took the initiative and acted on their own behalf, not on specific instructions from the government. In Greece and Hungary significant numbers of Jews were saved, and not only Sephardis; one Spanish ambassador, Ángel Sanz Briz, features in the Holocaust Museum in Jerusalem as one of those who defended the persecuted people.

All these factors are significant because they show that the Spanish authorities wanted to avoid any cause for confrontation with Nazi Germany but they also wanted to conform to conditions laid down by the Americans. At the same time, Franco's Spain tried hurriedly in the early stages of the war to give the impression that it was adhering strictly to a position of neutrality that had been far from clear up to that point. However, its true position was made evident to Allied ambassadors when Lequerica was made Foreign Minister. An intelligent man and skeptical to the point to cynicism, the new minister represented his country in its dealings with the Pétain regime and as a person he had always shown a clear preference for the Axis. As minister he never missed an opportunity to try to gloss over his pro-German past and to align himself almost to the point of adulation with the United States, which now seemed likely to be the undisputed winner in World War II.

When in the spring of 1944 Churchill stated in the House of Commons that he thought it was a mistake to insult Franco unnecessarily since he had done the Allies a favor by not entering the war, the regime thought this signaled a British attempt at rapprochement. That was not the case, however: Churchill responded in a tone that left no room for doubt on his strong disagreement with the political system in Spain. As for the United States, Lequerica directed all his diplomatic efforts at that country without any success. As time passed, Spain made concessions in relation to American warplanes and its neutrality turned into more positive support of those who were now quite clearly going to win the war. In April 1945 it broke off diplomatic relations with Japan; even so, the American president wrote to his ambassador that he did not want any involvement with Spanish politics, not believing that a regime that had been set up with the support of the fascist powers would be acceptable in the newly organized postwar world. Even those who were on the brink of defeat distanced themselves from Franco: after September 1944 the German ambassador was withdrawn from Madrid and when, months later, Hitler heard that Franco considered that he had not really been an ally of Germany, he spoke bluntly of Franco's "cheek."

What lay in wait for Franco was not just isolation from the outside world but also problems within Spain. As 1943 went by, several attempts were made to make him move ahead with the restoration of the monarchy on his own initiative. His refusal to do so had profoundly perplexed Don Juan's supporters who did not know whether or not to go for open confrontation with the regime. In the early months of 1944 a split did occur, mainly due to the attitude adopted by Franco himself. In January he wrote to Don Juan arguing at length that his own position was entirely legitimate, even claiming that it was providential. He also warned Don Juan that the exercise of power was "not a matter for bargaining." The dynastic heir retorted that Franco was overconfident about his regime and its likely duration. This so infuriated the *caudillo* that he wrote back stating that he would ask God to shed His light in Don Juan's mind and forgive him for the error of his ways. This exchange of letters, in which Franco always addressed Don Juan in a respectful tone rather like that of a schoolmaster with a not very intelligent child, left an open wound in the relationship between the two men that would never heal. Franco always considered the dynastic heir his closest rival, which explains the acerbic comments that he extended to encompass most of Don Juan's followers and advisers. At around the same time, several members of the monarchist cause were sanctioned. With the end of the war in sight, in March 1945 Don Juan, in the so-called Lausanne Manifesto, presented the monarchy that he personified as the means of bringing about a transition towards a regime with a constitution, respect for human rights, and certain regional freedoms. From that moment on, the monarchy remained on the horizon as a possible formula for political reconciliation and for a transition without trauma from dictatorship to something resembling political regimes elsewhere in postwar Europe. This option met with a total lack of any attempt at understanding on the part of those who had fought on both sides in the Civil War, whose memories of the conflict were still too acutely painful. Any gesture Don Juan might make could immediately be interpreted by either side (or both) as a betrayal, and the result was predictable. Even so, when World War II ended it not only seemed that the Franco regime was facing enormous difficulties but that its very survival was impossible.

We would do well at this point to draw up a final balance for the period 1939–45. As regards World War II it should be said from the start that it is difficult to offer a precise definition of the position taken by Franco's Spain, and not only because Franco himself did not want it clarified since Spain, having little actual power, could not change the final outcome of the war and so had to adapt to circumstances. If we were to try to define its position, we would have to start with Francoist Spain's links with the Axis. They explain why neutrality turned into non-belligerence when there was hope that some benefit could be gained with minimal involvement. After 1940 Spain again rejected the possibility of joining in the conflict to avoid coming up against the same demands. It is clear that the priority of the Spanish regime was clearly not so much victory for the Axis as its own survival.

Franco always maintained that his "capability and prudence" were what prevented Spain entering the war, but although he always thought carefully about what he considered to be national interests (which were synonymous in his mind with his own), he did not lack capability, though he was by no means prudent on every occasion. If he was often wrong about the direction the war was taking, at the same time he did not just give in to what others wanted and he always knew how to cover up unashamedly for past mistakes. But his politics were never the politics of neutrality. He gave help to the Axis that not only exceeded by far any help offered by truly neutral countries such as Switzerland, or those that adopted a stance favorable to Germany such as Sweden or Turkey, but was even greater than the help given by Finland which fought against the Soviet Union from the summer of 1941 on. A correct assessment of the Spanish position in relation to the war reveals that there were at least three occasions – in the summer of 1940, the following year, and in the autumn of 1942 – when Spain could have entered the war; that it did not do so was little short of a miracle.

The main reason why Spain did not join in was in all probability nothing to do with Franco or the regime's diplomacy. Conditions within the country at the time – it was poor and weak and its ruling class was in disarray – were a prime factor, but there were others too. Germany was only interested in Spanish involvement for a short time. Italy did not want a competitor when it came to the dividing of the spoils but it did want an ally at a time when its own strategies had not paid off. Britain, despite its naïveté at times on Spanish policy, is evidence of the value of intelligent diplomats capable of making the most of their resources in difficult circumstances. The United States could on occasion be thuggish, but never so much as to commit a gratuitous act of aggression against a Spain that it did not like.

It seems obvious that, unlike what had happened in 1914–18, Spain did not reap the benefits of true neutrality. Other countries had to stretch the definition of what was neutral (for example, allowing German troops to pass through them as Switzerland did), but none of them defined themselves as non-belligerent when what they were was pre-belligerent. The consequences would be felt later. When with constant ambiguity and repeated delays Spain gradually moved towards a firmer neutrality, no one could believe that this new stance was genuine. It is a curious paradox of the end of the World War II that the fate of Franco's Spain might well have been worse had Hitler won the war. He had never liked the Spanish leaders and, unlike those who did win, he had no qualms about interfering in the politics of other countries. And one can cite another paradox: the permanent hostility of Franco's Spain towards Soviet Russia throughout all these years proved more useful to him in the postwar period than friendship with Portugal, and at least as useful as his relations with the Vatican.

There is one more aspect to consider where it is important to examine the balance in relation to Spain's stance during World War II. We know that this was a very difficult time for Franco and not just because events in the rest of the world were putting pressure on him. In terms of Spanish politics too, these were the most complex years that he had to face, but they were also the years in which he served his final apprenticeship. What is surprising is not so much what he did in World War II as how capable he proved himself to be in the postwar period in Spain, despite the fact that this stage was only reached after a period of persistent crisis and bitter confrontation among those working alongside him, such as during the crisis of 1939–45. In this final year, he managed to combine his capacity for arbitration between the different tendencies within his regime with the ability to understand intuitively how foreign policy was going to change, or to stir up memories of the Civil War in a way that would permit him to survive after a very complex period of isolation.

## Cosmetic Change: Regime Politics between 1945 and 1951

In 1945 Franco's dictatorship was threatened at one and the same time by uncertainty inside the country on the direction it should take, by the possibility of internal opposition, and inevitably, by isolation from the outside world. All three factors were so closely linked that one cannot talk about one of them without also referring more or less directly to the others.

Franco discovered early on that it was important to give an appearance of institutional change and he found that the way to do this was by gaining approval for a number of constitutional measures that would in no way interfere with his own political power. This explains the 1942 Law of the *Cortes*: a procedure aimed at placing greater emphasis within the regime on the traditionalist element, as was obvious in the historic titles given to the assembly itself and to the parliamentary deputies or "*procuradores.*" It would come to be seen as typical of the Franco regime's hesitancy over institutionalization that this move was a direct result of advice from Mussolini to Serrano and Franco, and that in the end it would give satisfaction to a particular section of Falange. There was a similar occurrence in 1943 when a bill on fundamental legislation was drawn up but at the time did not see the light of day.

The defeat of the Axis made it obvious that what Lequerica had told Franco in 1945 had been wise: Arrese (and Falange with him) "should be removed from the limelight" – that is to say, as far as the outside world was concerned they should be as unobtrusive as possible. Franco, conscious of the wisdom of this advice, was not slow to act. From 1944 on there was evidence of him wanting to offer a more democratic image, for example when the first union elections were held in 1945 with a promise of municipal elections later on. After the summer of 1945 he understood what was happening on the international stage and responded effectively. As ever, his best weapon was his sense of timing which allowed him to prolong his stay in power while he made changes that were apparent rather than real. He actually told General Varela that he believed he was acting "with great tact but without haste," a phrase that says much about his political style as a whole. When Serrano Suñer proposed setting up a transitional cabinet to oversee the move towards a form of government acceptable to the rest of Europe, with some intellectuals included, Franco simply wrote "ha ha ha" alongside the proposal. His canniness – so like that of Sancho Panza – would stand him in very good stead.

He himself took the initiative in July 1945 when he brought forward new constitutional legislation and made changes in the government whose aim was crystal clear: to bring him into line with the political situation in Europe. Before doing so, however, he covered his own back with generals whose loyalty he knew he could count on at the time. Franco's most important decision from a tactical viewpoint was to adopt a Catholic stance in his politics. This was a clever move as one of the parties that was doing much to stabilize democracy in Europe at the time was the Christian Democrats. In Spain Franco did not go that far but he did call on support from Catholic associations that had remained in the background during the early days of the regime. There was one common element that united the official Catholic world and the Franco regime: their shared experience of a Civil War in which one in five parliamentary representatives of the Catholic Spanish Confederation of the Autonomous Right (*Confederación Española de Derechas Autónomas* or CEDA) had perished at the hands of the enemy. National Catholicism was not a doctrine practiced by only one section of the Spanish right but rather a common sentiment that united them all by linking together religion, nationalism, and the political regime. Nonetheless, the Catholic establishment did not exercise actual power until 1945, despite its clear support for the regime from the start. The Spanish Catholic Church expressed a clear desire for institutionalization and openness that went beyond a personal dictatorship.

Those Catholics prepared to collaborate who came to power in July 1945 had a program that coincided with the Church's overall wish that the dictatorship be institutionalized but should not be fascist. The person who best represented the will to collaborate was Alberto Martín Artajo, who moved from the position of President of Catholic Action to the Ministry of Foreign Affairs. In the summer of 1945 the regime's options seemed extremely limited, and, taking up a position in direct opposition to it, key figures in CEDA such as José María Gil Robles and Manuel Giménez Fernández condemned the degree of collaboration with the government that was beginning occur. It would not be fair to say that this was pure opportunism on their part, though it did become so in the end. Martín Artajo wanted – at least in theory – a return to monarchy, a declaration of political rights, and the necessary legislation to ensure that those rights were respected. In addition, according to his plans, citizens' views would be consulted. Furthermore, legislation governing the press would be modified and Falange would disappear, while the social services it had created would come under state control.

All in all it was a program that would allow for greater openness that was to an extent liberalizing but made no move towards democratization, offering only faint hope of some modest step towards closer relations with Europe. Franco never hid the fact that his own plans were altogether different. It was time once again to consider Spain as a kingdom, he affirmed, but Don Juan was no more than a "pretender" to the throne; it was up to Franco to decide who his successor should be. He was also quite blunt in the judgment he passed on the institution of monarchy. It could not, he said, be based on nothing more than the matter of who the offspring of "the last man to sleep with Queen Isabel (meaning Isabel II)" happened to be; rather they should wait and see whether or not "what emerged from the Queen's womb" was suitable, and the task of deciding that fell to him. He also made it quite clear to those who asked for some institutional structures to reflect political pluralism, that there would never be political parties. Of the press during the Civil War he stated that "I knew nothing of the matter and could not take charge of it during the war."

Political change did not result in the disappearance of Falangist ministers, who kept hold of the portfolios for Labor (Girón) and Justice (Fernández Cuesta). It did, however, signal the end of the office of General Secretary of the *Movimiento*. This was in fact an attempt to hide what was really going on in Spain from anyone outside as the organization itself remained in existence in the hands of a lower-ranking civil servant. This means that Girón was quite right when he said: "The men of Falange were going to do Spain a painful service by vanishing discreetly from the public stage." The raised-arm salute disappeared. Coinciding with the change of government, three important alterations became law. The Primary Education Law (*Ley de Enseñanza Primaria*) ensured that at this early level education was entirely Catholic. The Spaniards' Charter of Rights (*Fuero de los Españoles*) turned out to be a typical list of rights that were never made law. The passing of a Local Government Law (*Ley de Régimen Local*) implied that in local town halls a wider range of interests would be represented but this hope too was doomed to frustration. There was no change made on state control of the media which now came through the Ministry of Education. If censors had once been Falangists, now the job was done by members of the Catholic establishment.

In October 1945 the Referendum Law was approved, indicating a will to put before the people a major decision (that everyone suspected would be about the monarchy), though this did not mean that consultation would take place immediately. In that same month an amnesty was declared but a Law on Public Meetings, Associations, and Personal Guarantees (*Ley de Reunión, Asociación y Garantías Personales*) was immediately put on hold. There seems to have been a moment when a proposition was put forward to do away with the National Council, which was too strongly reminiscent of fascist organizations, but Franco was clearly reluctant to do without Falange. The proposal on the transformation of the *Cortes* never went further than effecting a slight variation in the rules governing it.

All in all, although there was much talk about "organic democracy," the reality on the ground in Spain was different from the Catholic corporativism of the 1930s. The regime was still a dictatorship which had changed its language but not the reality, which meant that all power was still concentrated in the person of Franco. Rather than being defined according to the principles of organic democracy, Francoism could be summed up in three words that appeared in one of the reports from Carrero to Franco written in those days as guidelines on how to resist pressure from outside Spain: "order, unity, and endurance" – with special emphasis on the last of the three. In the eyes of the man who now provided Franco with his greatest inspiration, what drove dissidents and democratic powers to try to change Spanish institutions was "sheer silliness" in the case of the first group, and a desire to rob Spain of its national independence in the case of the second.

Franco, who never harbored the slightest doubt about remaining in power but was not always able to keep up his appearance of confidence, clung on with grim determination. He turned against the monarchists and repeatedly voiced his anti-Masonic obsession. What seemed to him the greatest cause for concern was the possibility that the monarchy might manage to attract a large number of supporters from among those who had till then stood firm at his side. That was why, at the start of 1946, when Don Juan arrived in Estoril, he reacted decisively and violently. Statements on how "the regime must defend itself [against the defenders of the monarchy] and sink its teeth into their very soul" and "crush them like worms" show a level of excitement that was unusual in one so cold. This sense of anger is also evident in the anti-Masonic articles that he wrote in the press.

Yet Franco was always perfectly clear in his own mind as to what to do about the monarchist option. In the spring of 1947 he raised the matter in a Law of Succession on which a referendum was held in July and approval won by the inevitable overwhelming number of votes in favor. The law did not at any point address the issue of keeping the traditional dynastic line. It went no further than to make a general statement to the effect that Spain was a kingdom and to outline a very elementary mechanism for change in the event of the Chief of State passing away (a Regency Council (*Consejo de Regencia*) made up of high-ranking members of the political, military, and religious authorities). It was still Franco's prerogative to decide who would succeed to the throne but how this would happen was left vague. The only immediate practical consequence of the Law of Succession was that he was now able to bestow titles of nobility, which he did, giving dukedoms to the heirs of Primo de Rivera, Calvo Sotelo, and Mola, and other titles to the soldiers who had been in command under him during the Civil War. At the same time, over the course of 1948 and 1949, some of the monarchists who had fought with him in the war were sanctioned or dismissed from the Armed Services.

At the same time as the referendum, company juries (*jurados de empresa*) were set up as a complementary social strategy similar to the ballot in that they offered an appearance of democracy and were equally devoid of any real political effectiveness because of the delay in sorting out the regulations governing them. Rigid control of the press remained in place right up to that time; throughout the 1940s any criticism of the government of any sort was suppressed. The team responsible for the media, drawn from Catholic circles, was disbanded by political maneuvering before their program – modest though it was in scope – had had a chance to be implemented. In many areas – for example in relation to culture or to tolerance towards other religious groups – these Catholics had often been more closed-minded than even Falange.

At the end of this period Franco had every reason to feel extremely satisfied. In 1949 he was described by the major newspaper of the regime, *Arriba*, as "the man sent from God who always appears at the critical moment and defeats the enemy." That same year he visited Portugal and was awarded a doctorate at the University of Coimbra in the second and last journey outside Spain that he ever made in all his long time in power (and as on the previous occasion, he went once again to a dictatorship). In 1954 the *Cortes* would approve the renaming of his grandchildren to allow them to keep the surname of their grandfather the dictator. But there can have been no greater sign of his self-satisfaction than his governmental reshuffle. In 1951, with the storm effectively behind him, Franco gave himself the private satisfaction of not showing his true face. The Catholics retained their quota of places in the sharing-out of power and even increased it thanks to Ruiz Giménez being made Minister of Education, but Falange now made a comeback as the post of Secretary General of the *Movimiento* was resurrected and put once again in the hands of Fernández Cuesta. In addition, two men who had played key roles during World War II (and not exactly to the Allied advantage), General Muñoz Grandes and Arias Salgado in charge of the Blue Division and controlling the press respectively, were given a military portfolio and that of the Ministry of Tourism and Information. Carrero Blanco, Franco's principal adviser since World War II, who was critical of Falange's excessive power, was given a ministerial post.

Everything we have seen so far in this epigraph shows how measures implemented after 1945 brought minimal change, at least as regards Franco's personal power. However, if we compare the years immediately after the Civil War with the period after the end of World War II, there were evident changes in the mood of the country, and these become clear when we consider two questions: Catholicism and attitudes to particular cultures.

The desire to bring about a "neo-traditionalist reconquest" of Spanish society led on to the idea that the Catholic faith and the Spanish fatherland were consubstantial, to a messianic interpretation of past history, and to an authoritarian vision of a harmonious future for society. What made Falangists different from clericalists, and the years up to 1945 different from those that followed, was a difference in emphasis. Falangists accepted without question that the regime and the Party were both Catholic but they were not prepared to accept that the Catholic religion was autonomous and independent of politic control. They therefore pursued a political strategy aimed at achieving an "absolute monopoly" of power by preventing the formation of Catholic organizations. The more clericalist sector, on the other hand, saw Catholicism as a means of integration but at the same time claimed autonomy for itself.

Nonetheless, the fact that they agreed on certain fundamental principles means that it is almost impossible nowadays to understand the controversies that divided the two groups throughout the 1940s. The clericalists complained that the Civil War was not being viewed as a "Crusade": an essentially religious conflict. They also rejected the attempts that were being made to "nationalize" the intellectuals of the "98 Generation" or the liberals. The radical Falangists would have used the term "national revolution" to describe the regime. More than the traditionalists, they favored a secular culture with which they could identify and which they could imbue with Spanish nationalist sentiment.

What was most characteristic of the period after 1945 was not the disappearance of a National Catholic mentality so much as the greater degree of autonomy that was allowed to the Catholic Church in matters of social action. The regime accepted that the various movements within Acción Católica had their own areas of specialization. In 1947, following an example that had already been set the 1930s, a group of organizations emerged which were essentially apostolic in aim but could be seen as competing with organizations linked to the Party. Among these were the Workers' Catholic Action Guild (*Hermandades Obreras de Acción Católica*), Catholic Labor Youth (*Juventud Obrera Católica*), and Catholic Student Youth (*Juventud de Estudiantes Católicos*): HOAC, JOC, and JEC, respectively. As time passed, these would all come into serious conflict with the Party.

The example of Catalonia, which is by far the best known, shows very clearly the Franco regime's desire to implement a policy of homogenization that would lead to the disappearance of regional cultures, which would be replaced by the culture of Castile. The expression "cultural genocide" seems appropriate to describe what happened in those years. The Catalan language could only be spoken in the privacy of the home, while the renaming of streets seemed designed either to be offensive or as a gratuitous display of force. Not only was the use of Catalan prohibited in public life but an official propaganda campaign was mounted to promote the use of Castilian ("Speak the Language of the Empire," was the advice given by solemn posters all over Barcelona). A number of city monuments that might have been associated with Catalanism were removed and there was no more Catalan press, not even of a religious nature. From the summer of 1939 on, it was decided that as many obstacles as possible would be put in the way of publishing in Catalan. The only publications allowed were folkloric or religious pamphlets, the Bible, and classical Greek texts such as Plutarch – provided the introduction and notes were in Castilian.

In 1946 the situation changed slightly. There was a discernible "spring-time" in the world of publishing which allowed almost all Catalan poetry to be published, though the work of Joan Maragall, for example, could be published in Castilian but not in Catalan; the translation of recent authors into Catalan was forbidden. Preaching in Catalan was tolerated in rural areas but not until the 1950s in urban areas. Some grotesque cases occurred, such as that of writers such as Shakespeare having to be pub-lished in clandestine editions. Not surprisingly, the Catalans themselves wondered whether their culture would be able to survive. Even so, this period was in actual fact better than what could be termed the "blue era" when the Falange's influence was strongest.

## Opposition from Survivors: The Spanish Left from 1939 to 1951

In 1969 the former mayor of the little village of Mijas in the province of Malaga reappeared in public after an amnesty had been declared on crimes committed during the Civil War. He had spent 30 years of his life hiding in his home from 1934 to 1964, waiting for the chance to reappear. His experience, though remarkable, was only one of many similar stories that could be told by Spaniards on the side that lost the Civil War. In fact, until they could be reasonably certain of the outcome of World War II, no real attempt was made by the vanquished to regain power in Spain; once they did so, however, the international situation meant that the attempts of the opposition met with failure. It did, however, survive and enjoyed a moment of hope which was destined to die in the 1950s.

Probably the clearest example of dissent within a party was that of the socialists. The situation created during the Civil War continued or even intensified up to 1945, and only the hope of an Allied victory kept alive any desire to re-form the party. The one who did best out of this situation was Indalecio Prieto, who saw the ranks of his followers swelled by former supporters of Francisco Largo Caballero and Julián Besteiro, while Juan Negrín's influence waned noticeably. Negrín's influence had never been particularly strong in Spanish socialism, though he had been a powerful figure in the state apparatus of the Republic; now the frequent shifts in position of the Spanish Communist Party (*Partido Comunista Español* or PCE) weakened his position. Prieto began very early on to argue in favor of a plebiscite: an option he had favored at the end of the Civil War. His tactic never won unconditional support within the party but he did gain a majority.

Within Spain, the Spanish Socialist Workers' Party (*Partido Socialista Obrero Español* or PSOE) survived, though its position was very precarious. In Asturias guerrilla groups continued fighting until 1948, and from 1944 on a national executive existed inside the country. This executive, like the PSOE which had formed after emigration to France, adopted a strongly anti-communist stance. In France the principal organizer of the Socialist Party was Rodolfo Llopis, but Prieto, who combined greater prestige with tactical capabilities, provided the real thrust behind the PSOE in exile in France, and in 1946 the organization had 8,000 members. Taken as a whole, therefore, the Socialists were in a position to put forward a strategy based on external pressure on Spain and aimed at achieving a transition towards democracy. Even as they declared that they were Republicans, the Socialists were still open to change.

This attitude clashed with the opinion of those who wanted to restore the institutions of the Republic. The so-called Spanish Junta for Liberation (*Junta Española de Liberación*), founded in 1943, was the brainchild of Catalan Republicans with support from Socialists, though its most significant figure was Diego Martínez Barrio. The Junta came into being in opposition not only to the monarchist alternative but also to communist attempts to set up larger organizations. Inside Spain, what was known as the National Alliance of Democratic Forces (*Alianza Nacional de Fuerzas Democráticas* or ANFD), which came into being around the same time, insisted more strongly on the need for free elections in the present than on re-founding the institutions that had existed in 1931; closer to the monarchists, the ANFD also showed itself to be unequivocally anti-communist.

There had, then, emerged a possible source of confrontation between the ANFD and the Republicans in exile. It was as late as 1945 that the Republican *Cortes* was finally set up and functioning in Mexico. Martínez Barrio was elected President of the Republic and Negrín offered him his resignation. Not that this reunited the Republican camp. Prieto wanted Negrín as President of the Government and when a cabinet was formed under José Giral he refused to join it. It is therefore fair to say that the Republic was reborn with serious problems of disunity. At the start of November Giral completed his task of forming a government but Prieto, being more closely in touch with international relations at the time, was not slow to voice very different opinions from those of the official Republican government. Giral renounced violence but this was not enough to gain clear support from the western nations who, by asking in March 1946 for a transitional government to be set up, showed that they did not see the Republic as synonymous with democracy.

The Spanish Communist Party, whose political influence had increased over the course of the Civil War, found itself at the end of the conflict being accused by the rest of the Spanish left of harboring hegemonic ambitions. Confrontation was particularly bitter between the socialists and the communists and left the latter isolated. During the period that followed there was a first change in direction for the party when José Díaz committed suicide in 1942 and the leadership passed to Dolores Ibárruri: *La Pasionaria*. The bulk of the communist leadership was in South America and from there, via Portugal, they managed to reestablish some degree of organization within Spain. In 1941–2 Spanish communists suggested adopting a tactic of "National Union" against Franco, hoping thereby to group together very different factions, including some from the Spanish right, united by principles that were exclusively patriotic and anti-fascist. In reality, however, the communists attracted almost no support. They were, after all, as divided as any other group by internal disputes about the International and their diagnosis of what was going on in Spain. The defeat of an attempted guerrilla invasion via the Pyrenees allowed Santiago Carrillo to take over as communist leader in France. His position as leader there did not, however, mean a change in tactics, for the guerrilla war continued.

Compared with anarchism, Spanish communism had not been very strong in the 1930s but this situation changed in the first half of the 1940s. The reason was that the anarchists now faced the ultimate dilemma of whether or not to take part in politics. Now, with disputes intensifying within its ranks due to the split between anarchists inside Spain and those in exile, the possibility of moving towards syndicalism presented itself, or even of engaging in party politics alongside Republican groups or without them. But quite apart from these dilemmas, more than any other left-wing group the National Confederation of Labor (*Confederación Nacional del Trabajo* or CNT) received offers of support from members of the official Francoist union. As with the socialists and communists, by 1944 the anarchists had a clandestine organization that was active nation-wide, though it appears that they bore the brunt of Francoist repression.

The reason was that they tried to function as a union among the masses that could easily be infiltrated by the police. At the end of 1945 the new national executive of the CNT was imprisoned; of the first 14 such executives, 10 were dismantled by the police. In contrast to those who were in favor of joining the political process, the most extreme members who rejected any form of government advocated guerrilla war and acts of terrorism, though they were unlikely to achieve anything by these means. In the early post-Civil War years, the CNT lost 80 percent of its member-ship and by the start of the 1960s its leaders were longstanding militants who had fought in the Civil War, there being no one of a younger genera-tion to take their place.

As regards nationalist movements, one can detect in all of them, as a general trait, an initial tendency towards radicalization during the World War II years. It is significant that in 1944 the linking up of the nationalist groups from around Spain's periphery led to the re-forming of "Galeuzca," the group whose three syllables, taken from the names of the three historic regions, had united the most radical nationalist youth in the 1920s. However, after 1946 this group disappeared from the scene.

Up to the start of 1946 one might say that in fact the opposition in exile or of the left merely managed to survive. Then, with the defeat of the Axis, its members believed they could see light at the end of a very long tunnel. For Spaniards on the right, however, the Republic not only meant a return to the situation before the Civil War but also a reversal of the outcome of that war. From that time on, it seemed far more likely that it would be the monarchist option that would take Franco's place than the republican option.

Giral's government, from its moment of inception, had had problems that only increased in 1946 because it failed utterly to convince the demo-cratic nations that Franco might come to pose a serious threat to world peace. Objectively speaking, Giral was quite wrong in making this asser-tion and the United Nations' recommendation that the only action needed was to withdraw ambassadors from Spain might have been seen as a defeat by the socialists who were being increasingly spurred on by Indalecio Prieto to seek possible ways ahead. This explains why a government was formed with Llopis as president at the start of 1947. From the very beginning the main representative of Spanish socialism in France faced a difficult bal-ancing act. He belonged to a party which favored the democratic nations and therefore seemed able to offer some form of guarantee; yet it also had to try to unite all the opposition parties in exile and for that reason Llopis included a member of the Spanish Communist Party in his cabinet. In the summer of 1947 Prieto's position, which was always open to change, became the most powerful element in the PSOE, which meant that it was now impossible to hold the government together. The exclusively Republican government that then formed with Albornoz as president came to be seen as a kind of representative of Republican legitimacy and this enabled it to last a long time, though it was still incapable of providing any real alternative to the Franco regime.

From 1947 on, the PSOE in exile was still the most powerful party under Prieto's leadership. His attitude had proved to be the most clear-sighted on the left, but if his strategy was to succeed he had to find some way of working with the monarchists. His approaches to them over the course of 1948 proved fruitless, however. In 1948, at talks held in France they had failed to forge any solid hope of replacing Franco. Until 1951 the PSOE continued to argue at its conferences for the need to work with the monarchists but there was little it could do when faced with the democratic powers' increasing reluctance even to consider the problem of Spain. If for the socialist leaders outside Spain these were years of bitter disappointment, inside the country, after a brief period of hope, Spaniards experienced in their own flesh the full weight of repression. Between 1944 and 1947 there was some degree of organization inside Spain but it soon disappeared. At the end of the 1940s socialism was active only in areas where in the past it had been firmly rooted (Madrid, the Basque Country, and Asturias) and there it lacked coordination. By 1949 three national committees that had served one after another and some 1,300 militants were in Spanish jails.

As was the case in all communist parties in Western Europe at the time, the PCE obeyed directives from Moscow without question, to such an extent that Santiago Carrillo used the phrase "pole star" when talking of the Soviet Union, Jorge Semprún said that if the Soviet Union did not exist life would not be worth living, and Rafael Alberti described Stalin as "father, comrade, and master." As in other European communist parties, the Stalinist personality cult had its national equivalent: in Spain's case, Dolores Ibárruri. The particular stance of the PCE within the Spanish opposition was that it strongly supported the use of guerrilla warfare, though it by no means had a monopoly there. The fact that the PCE abandoned the option of guerrilla tactics in 1948 has been attributed to a decision by Stalin but it is more likely that circumstances outside Spain led to the change. Stalin only made a very general statement about the need to use armed combat in conjunction with legal processes. It is not true to say that this about-turn resulted in the PCE leading the strikes that happened in those years, which were in fact spontaneous.

At least as much as, or even more than, its support for guerrilla warfare, what characterized the PCE at the time was its isolation; it was so inward-looking as to adopt the defensive position typical of the Stalinist period which required constant purges driven by a fear of infiltration. In 1947 the PCE abandoned the Republican government at the same time as its marginalization was becoming obvious in other countries such as Belgium, France, and Italy. In 1948 it ceased to exist, as did the autonomous governments of Catalonia and the Basque Country. In 1950 it was declared illegal in France. Meanwhile, ideological purges were taking place which can be seen as clear evidence of heterodoxy in other countries. The party's self-destructiveness was evident in the fact that of the 17 PCE parliamentary deputies from the Republicans' last *Cortes*, four had died by this time but ten had left the party.

Although it drew its main support from the communists, the guerrilla war started up spontaneously in areas where there was a solid leftist tradition or where the geography was complex. With scant organization and few resources, the resistance fighters were simple "escapees" or people who had "taken to the hills," often after having broken out of prison. The communists used them to set up networks engaged in armed action which could count on limited supplies but never posed any serious threat to the regime. It was not, therefore, the most "serious" opposition group and it was not the reason why Spain did not enter World War II. Nor did it organize proper military action. As Carrero wrote to Franco in one of his reports, it was more a case of "banditry" aimed at creating an atmosphere of insecurity than an offensive reaction capable, for example, of cutting communications.

There was significant guerrilla activity between 1946 and 1948 but it decreased to a bare minimum after 1952, although there would still be occasional executions of resistance fighters in the mid 1950s. The most active group, which functioned on the eastern side of the country between Teruel, Cuenca, Castellón, and Valencia, depended on resources brought through from France. Unlike similar guerrilla warfare in other countries, the Spanish resistance did not have steady support from the local population, though they did have a network of some tens of thousands working with them or liaising; nor could they count on cross-border support and so they had to keep going by making small raids in isolated places.

Their action consisted mainly of assassinations, kidnappings, sabotage, or raids, and at most they occupied a small settlement for a short time. The guerrilla fighters did not work as large units but as small bands of men who remained hidden during the day and attacked at night. That is why it is impossible to give a detailed account of guerrilla operations. Some 2,200 guerrillas died in combat, while the Civil Guard, which was mainly in charge of fighting them, lost 250 men, and the losses to all the security forces combined can be put at about 300. Although there might have been as many as 7,000 guerrillas in total, there were never more than 2,000 to 2,500 in action at any one time in groups of no more than 300 people. On both sides the struggle was notable for its savagery: the guerrilla fighters executed real or supposed supporters of the regime, while the regime's counter-insurgency tactics included torture and application of the "law on attempts to escape." Carrero Blanco himself suggested using "a thrashing" as the most usual method for dealing with opposition terrorism.

It would be wrong to suggest that there was a fundamental difference between the guerrilla war and workers' protests in factories as if their strategies were incompatible: in fact, the first strikes in Franco's Spain occurred at the height of the guerrilla war. In May 1947 in the Basque Country the General Union of Workers (*Unión General de Trabajadores* or UGT) and the National Confederation of Labor (*Confederación Nacional del Trabajo* or CNT) joined in the strikes but so did the Basque Nationalist Union and the respective political groups which supported these movements. Asturias was the region that until the 1960s led in terms of workers' protests in Spain. From the start of the new regime a steady increase in the extraction of coal was recorded: in 1952 the numbers of miners employed topped 90,000, whereas in 1935 there had been only 44,000. After the Civil War there was also a marked militarization of working life which meant, for example, arrest for not turning up to work. Even though in the Spain of the time miners' salaries were above average, in practice until very late on they barely served to cover basic food needs. If all these factors are taken into account, along with the lack of modernization, the high accident rate in Spain is easily explained. Between 1941 and 1959 more than 1,500 miners died in Asturias and about 750 in León and Palencia as a result of accidents at work. Despite these statistics, in Asturias, the Basque Country, and Barcelona instances of protest were spontaneous, isolated, and unconnected, which can be explained by a general sense of defeat, fear, and repression.

In a context such as this, what happened in the Catalan capital at the start of the 1950s is of particular interest as it was something entirely new. The Barcelona Tram Strike of 1951 was not started by any clandestine organization; it happened as a result of a protest not about a political issue but about the price of public transport, which had been raised by 40 percent, far more than in Madrid. It meant that almost all trams stopped running for several days and had the added success of splitting those in power in the Catalan capital (Falange clashed with a governor whom they considered lukewarm). The wave of strikes spread from Barcelona to the Basque Country. There, in contrast, together with groups made up entirely of workers, members of Catholic organizations joined in too. All these factors, which go some way towards explaining the ministerial crisis that followed in April 1951, lead us on to consider a social protest that was to have a promising future, but only with the passage of time.

## The Monarchist Alternative

As we have already seen, the most active person on the Spanish left at this time, Prieto, knew only too well that replacing the Franco regime would depend on reaching an agreement with the monarchists. Although with some variations, the democratic forces also agreed on a transition towards democracy on the condition that the restoration of the monarchy would bring about reconciliation. We must therefore consider the monarchist alternative which now meant a clear break with the regime, however much the regime might try to bring about change by a peaceful process of transition. One could say that if ever there was a time when the Franco regime might have been replaced it was in 1946 and it would have been Don Juan who ruled as king in place of the dictator.

Over the course of 1945 Don Juan's and Franco's emissaries traveled to and fro between Switzerland and Spain but the chances of them reaching an agreement were scant because they differed on important issues. The dictator did not think for one moment that he should give up power; rather he clung to it with even greater determination. He had potent weapons to draw on: he could mobilize the younger elements in the Armed Services, and from the outset he thwarted any attempt to restore the monarchy by constantly suggesting new candidates. He used every argument possible to stay in power, including the need to hand out firm justice to those who had lost the war, but his most powerful weapon was his sense of timing and how slow he was to take action.

Don Juan's arrival in Portugal caused great commotion in Spain. An impressive committee of dignitaries, including 20 ex-ministers as well as aristocrats, members of the Armed Services, and Spain's five most important bankers, wrote Don Juan a letter which showed that support for Franco was less than one might have thought. However, most of the signatories were doing no more than putting their names to a formula that the international situation at the time seemed to demand, and they were unlikely to pursue it to its logical conclusion. This was how things stood when, a few days after Don Juan's arrival in Estoril, Franco broke off existing relations with him. It is obvious in what Carrero wrote to the dictator at the time that both men felt indignant about "the small smart salon set" whose common characteristics were "snobbery, frivolity, and stupidity."

At that time the monarchists had to play a "double game" which, as Gil Robles suggested, was so plagued by difficulties that in the end they simply could not win. It was, on the one hand, a matter of undermining the Spanish people's support for the regime by drawing into the monarchist camp sections of society that had been on Franco's side in the Civil War and, at the same time, reaching an agreement with the non-communist left. Although Don Juan de Borbón hesitated on more than one occasion and made many tactical mistakes, it was the monarchists' heterogeneity, their lack of unity, and their uncertainty as to the exact method they would use to remove Franco from power, as well as the state of post-Civil War Spain, that are the main factors that explain their failure. Certainly, if Franco was never deposed it was because it is very difficult, when a dictator has been brought to power by a civil war, to remove him without another civil war.

"Double politics" came into being in the early months of 1946. In February the so-called "Estoril Principles" ("*Bases de Estoril*") were signed with the result that a section of the Carlist movement joined Don Juan's cause, signing up to a program which mentioned "healthy representative institutions." At the same time contact was made with the moderate left inside Spain. It is probable, however, that the monarchists moved far too cautiously at this time, because in the months that followed Franco seized the initiative, never to lose it again. One must remember, too, that the socialists only adopted a more open stance later on.

Francoism benefited from a curious reaction that was evident in Spanish public opinion. The stance adopted by the democratic forces who condemned the regime was not widely understood and, as a result, the regime found it easy to stir up a mood of resistance like that when ancient Numantia defied the Romans. Carrero and Franco both realized this almost immediately and it was fundamental in shaping their decisions. It was in this atmosphere that Don Juan was contacted about the Law of Succession on which he had not yet had a chance to express an opinion. His conversation with Carrero, who was sent by Franco to report back on Don Juan's response, could not have been more significant. Don Juan complained that the text implied that the ruler was to be chosen; Franco's adviser retorted that in a civil war one could not bestride two trenches. "You will not succeed," replied Don Juan, warning of the difficulties they would face in terms of public opinion outside Spain. He was wrong about this. Declarations that he made shortly afterwards unfortunately clashed with monarchist public opinion in Spain. They made it seem as though it had been the monarchy that had won the Civil War and had restored civil liberties. Don Juan also stated that he was allowing contact between his followers and those who had fought on the opposite side during the Civil War: a fact that was confirmed when Gil Robles met Prieto in London in October 1947. The two leaders agreed on the reestablishment of civil liberties, on an amnesty, and on Spain's reintegration into Europe – that is to say, on the basic essentials. Both men were at the time open to possible change; they had had the support of the main political groups in the 1930s but there was no great difference between the final positions they now adopted. When news of this appeared in the Spanish press, accompanied by the usual propaganda, the conservative masses in the country adopted an attitude totally closed to any possibility of change. The unlikelihood of an immediate restoration of the monarchy at this point, the question of the education of Don Juan Carlos, the eldest royal child, and the divisions among the monarchists meant that from 1948 onwards Don Juan tried a series of different tactics. These included the meeting held on Franco's yacht the *Azor* off the Basque coast in August 1948. As with all other meetings between Franco and Don Juan, what was most important here was not its content so much as the fact that they met at all. "Whose gun is going to backfire on him?" Don Juan asked, referring to Franco and himself. "God will decide," he concluded. In the medium term the answer was undoubtedly Franco's but it changes totally if we consider the longer term. One must remember that Don Juan Carlos, merely by returning to Spain, could have been considered to have been confirmed as Franco's successor.

At the very same time as these talks were going on between Franco and Don Juan, monarchist and socialist representatives were meeting for discussions in San Juan de Luz, only a few kilometers away, and realizing that they agreed with each other on the outcome of the transition. Yet from the end of 1948 on, hopes of a return to monarchy gradually faded, while at the same time there was a slow shift among monarchists towards cooperation with the regime. Pressure from democratic forces had dwindled to nothing and there was puzzlement among the monarchist rank and file. By 1951 any possibility of agreement between monarchists and socialists had vanished totally.

At the end of 1951 Franco's new government had been named and a monarchist spokesman did not hesitate to label it the "most totalitarian" to date. In November 1948 Don Juan Carlos had been sent to Spain; at the same time Don Juan replaced the most anti-Francoist of the advisers who had been with him so far with others more closely in touch with government circles. The prince's education became a political issue once again when, after he had completed his Baccalaureate, the decision had to be made as to whether he should continue his studies in Spain or go abroad. Those working closely with Franco had their way, which meant that Franco himself could oversee the training of the one who would in time become King of Spain. Nonetheless, between father and son there was always a kind of "family pact" aimed at achieving an identical outcome, though that was not at all evident at the time, as became obvious after 1975: that is to say, 30 years after the Monarchist option first came to seem a real alternative.

## Franco in Isolation

The previous pages have allowed us to appreciate to just how great an extent outside pressures on Spain affected internal politics. The only reason for Spain's isolation was the continuance of a political regime that had not evolved to any degree since its beginnings in 1939. If Spain had done away with Franco and had evolved as Turkey had done, its collaboration with the Axis might have been forgotten. Something similar could have happened had it made a more radical about-turn as Brazil did, though Getulio Vargas did have to hand over power; or alternatively if Spain had opted in the past for a genuine neutrality like that of Salazar in Portugal, who also decided in 1945 to adopt a tentatively conciliatory political stance. However, nothing like this happened in Franco's Spain.

Despite triumphalist declarations by the regime's spokesmen, there were clear signs of diplomatic difficulties before the end of World War II. In the summer of 1945 an international conference was held in San

Francisco, out of which the United Nations Organization would emerge. The Mexican delegate proposed that nations whose regimes had been set up with the help of the fascist powers should not be granted membership. The "big four" meeting in Potsdam not long afterwards approved a resolution which stated that no request from Spain would be considered. Also, over the course of 1945 Spain's modest attempt at imperialist expansion ended pitifully: it was not allowed to take part in the international conference that was to decide on the future administration of Tangiers.

Within the regime Franco himself always had a major role in determining the direction that foreign policy would take, but this was even more the case at a time when he himself was having to play a hard game to stay in power. Franco showed no sign of personal greatness or statesman-like vision, but he did demonstrate that he was capable of astute analysis of the international situation when he judged that collaboration between the democratic countries and the Soviet Union could not last. If his foreign policy was successful it was because it was simple: he merely applied Carrero's maxim of "order, unity, and endurance" that governed his actions inside Spain to events on the world stage. Foreign policy consisted, then, of affirming repeatedly that Spain was a nation with an open and evolving constitution, capable of coming into line with the rest of Europe but with peculiarities that precluded political parties. The Civil War was seen as one episode in an ongoing struggle against communism and the regime was considered to have stayed neutral throughout World War II.

Many Spanish diplomats at the time knew full well that only the disappearance of the most notoriously dictatorial aspects of the regime would allow outside pressure on Spain to be eased. Lequerica – effectively Franco's representative in the United States – used a different type of argument based on material interests and on the political games played in American internal politics. In his view it was essential "to help businesses," which meant having the Republican Party in power: a group that was "not fanatically passionate but strong at administration and economics." That was the period of the reconstruction of a Europe that had been devastated by war, and Spain had resources that they might need.

It was above all in the early months of 1946 that Spanish diplomatic relations reached a particularly low point. Panama asked the United Nations member-countries to make their contacts with Spain conform to what had been decided at the San Francisco and Potsdam conferences.

France, still driven by memories of the Spanish Civil War, closed Spain's borders. One might have thought that the regime's days were numbered, which would explain both the monarchists' excitement and Franco's defensive attitude. However, the first references to the "iron curtain" date from this time. In March 1946, to avoid aligning themselves with the Soviet Union, the western Allies (France, Britain, and the United States) published a declaration which expressed both their desire for changes in Spain's political situation and that there should not be another civil war. In effect they were now giving the impression that they would have accepted a formula that allowed a modest pace of evolution. "The most we can hope for," wrote one British diplomat, "is modification of the present regime and the suppression of its most undesirable elements."

That position was taken much further by the United Nations. In April of that same year Poland, a country in which Soviet influence was now decisive, stated that the existence of a regime such Franco's posed a threat to world peace. However, in Ocaña where, according to the Polish delegate, atomic bombs were being made, all that was actually being produced was bricks. What the communist countries would have liked was for the United Nations to break all economic links with Franco's Spain. After a lengthy attempt to formulate a resolution, in December 1946 Spain was expelled from all international organizations and a recommendation was made that all diplomats in Madrid be called back to their own countries.

We already know that when these measures were made public in Spain the reaction was like that in ancient Numantia. They did of course give the clearest possible indication of just how isolated the Franco regime was at that time: in the United Nations voting there had only been six votes opposing the proposal, all from Latin American countries, against 34 votes in favor and 12 abstentions. Yet the UN measures made little impact in practical terms since Franco's Spain was already virtually isolated. Only three European ambassadors (including the British ambassador) and two Latin Americans were withdrawn from Madrid, while the Portuguese, the Swiss (interpreting their position as neutral), the Vatican nuncio, and the Irish representative, because he was from a country with a strong Catholic tradition, stayed on.

It was obvious what Franco had to do if he was to escape from the isolation imposed on him. He could hope that the Vatican and Catholic lobbies in all countries might join together to defend him. He also managed to persuade Portugal to act as intermediary between Spain and the democratic nations: between 1945 and 1957 Franco and Salazar met for talks five times. However, the regime actually broke out of its isolation first and foremost by exploiting divisions between the countries that had won World War II, attitudes to Spain in Latin American countries, and, to a lesser extent, in Arab countries too.

Although the main split between the countries that had won the war was between the Soviet Union and the others, there were some gray areas that need explaining in relation to the Spanish question. It suited the Soviet Union to have an area of ongoing instability in Southern Europe. In that sense the Soviets preferred Franco to a stable democratic monarchy. At the start of 1947 they made indirect contact with Franco to ensure that he would not align Spain with the western nations. It was the split between the Soviet Union and the democratic countries that was Franco's salvation – far more so than his own foreign policy. France saw that, as had happened in the Civil War, Spain's problematic state was becoming a cause for political debate within the country, but material considerations came to the fore: a trading agreement was signed in mid 1948. France would rather have kept its relations with Spain exclusively limited to trade, but Franco would agree only to full relations. The British position was the most coherent and consistent of any of the western nations: it involved trying to encourage the different elements of the Spanish opposition to engage in some form of cooperation presided over by the monarchy. The process leading up to this situation was also to be gradual: as Bevin said, it should be the result of a daily exercising of pressure and not of a total split. As early as March 1947 the British signed a trade agreement with Spain but, disappointed to find the opposition too divided, they finally came to the conclusion that there was no longer any point in applying more "pin-pricks" to Franco.

American policy was the most erratic of all the great powers. It was the United States that, in 1946, published the most hard-hitting document against Franco's claim to have been neutral while at the same time being reticent about a possible transition towards a monarchy. In the end, however, military interests won over all others. From 1947 onwards, all American strategic planning was based on the notion that if the Soviets launched an offensive against Europe, within 50 or 60 days they would reach the Pyrenees. Spain would be useful as a bastion of resistance and a base for a counter-offensive; in conditions such as these, Spain was as important on the southern flank of Europe as Britain was in the north. In October 1947, the State Department Office of Political Planning came to the conclusion that the Franco regime could not be removed except by force and recommended that pressure on it be eased.

At the same time, Lequerica's maneuvering in the American press and politics had a degree of success. From 1949 onwards the American House of Representatives began to approve aid to Spain – aid that was vetoed by President Truman. The first time aid was given definitive approval was as late as 1951. Apart from military reasoning, the Americans' change of heart owed much to the formation of an influential nucleus of Catholic senators and congressmen who were anti-communist, interested in exporting cotton, and who encouraged the arms industry or opposed Truman. The result of all these factors was a marked change in the American position: in 1945 public opinion had been largely hostile to Franco but in 1951 almost half of those polled were in favor of Spain joining NATO. Even so, one would have to say that what actually happened was that there was a shift from considering an alliance with Spain "extremely unpopular" to seeing it as "just not very popular."

Having explained the position of each of the western nations, it is also useful to look at the "substitution strategies" to which Franco resorted in order to alleviate his isolation. Foremost among them was his attitude towards the Latin American countries, and the tactic that the regime used to win support in that part of the world was its culture; as a result, funding increased substantially (by 40 percent). The Council of the Hispanic World (*Consejo de la Hispanidad*) was renamed the Institute of Hispanic Culture (*Instituto de Cultura Hispánica*). Spain's culture was presented in Latin America as offering a very particular, traditional, and Catholic alternative capable of challenging other, more materialistic options. In this way the Spanish regime could count on being favored by a section of Latin American opinion, even if at the same time it alienated more left-wing countries (such as Mexico, Chile, Costa Rica, and Colombia).

"We have hauled our body halfway out of the pit now and we shall never forget who it was who held out their hand to help us up when we were down in the depths," said Areilza in 1949, referring to Argentina in a speech which he made as Franco's representative. Indeed, Argentina's role in enabling Spain to emerge from isolation was so decisive that one could even suggest that "saving the dictatorship" depended on it. In the 1940s Argentina was the world's major exporter of wheat and beef but did not have a merchant fleet capable of transporting its products. In political terms Perón's government favored a populist "third way" with a "Latin identity" aimed at providing an alternative to American dominance in the new continent. At the time when Spain's isolation was at its worst the interests of the two countries coincided, which might give the impression – quite wrongly – that their politics also coincided. In fact Perón wanted to hold on to the support of the extreme right in his country while at the same time fostering a sense of national identity in opposition to American pressure; but his regime's popularism was markedly different from the National Catholic tone of Franco's Spain. Eva Perón had no hesitation in telling a Spanish minister that his country was overrun by those who "paraded around in cassocks sucking on communion wafers."

Cooperation between the two leaders, being a direct result of circumstances, was short-lived and caused trouble for Perón. For Franco, however, it proved decisive. At the very same moment when the UN was recommending the withdrawal of all ambassadors from Spain, Argentina was hastening to send its own to Madrid. In October 1946 a trade agreement was signed. In 1947 Eva Perón came to Spain on a visit that lasted 15 days and provided plenty of opportunities for displays of popularist demagogy. The following year saw the signing of what was known as the Franco-Perón Protocol aimed at fostering trade relations between the two countries. In this way Argentina made a crucial contribution to ensuring that Spain's supply lines did not collapse, although it received very little in return. In 1948 Spain imported almost 400,000 tons of wheat and 100,000 tons of maize – quantities which, in terms of price, were not a tenth of what Spain exported to Argentina. However, Cádiz did not become a free port facilitating the distribution of Argentine goods throughout Europe, investment in Spain did not increase, and Spain did not export industrial products to Argentina. In 1950 the balance of payments was already in Spain's favor and in 1954 rumors were rife of a possible breakdown in relations.

Spanish–Argentine relations – effectively an alliance between two pariahs – were characterized by misunderstandings. Argentina was a naturally rich country whose leaders were excessively overoptimistic about the future but it could not help Spain to gain any real benefits because the two economies were not complementary. There was also a divergence in foreign policy, for Perón had anticipated World War II and had adopted a neutral stance, while Franco wanted involvement in the western world. Each hoped to benefit from the other but it was Franco who gained real advantages. Meanwhile, the climate in the New World was changing. The clearest proof can be seen in the way the Latin American countries voted on the UN recommendation approved in December 1946. Whereas in 1946 some six countries had voted against the motion, in 1947, 1949, and

1950 respectively, the votes were eight, 12, and 16 against. The change in attitude towards Franco's Spain in Latin America can therefore be seen as widespread, early, and decisive, independently of Argentina.

Along with the support Spain received from Latin America, support from Arab countries must be taken into account. Even more so than with the former, Spain's policy in relation to the latter was the result of a process of substitution. It was a matter of managing through contact with the Arab nations to bring about some improvement in international relations as a whole. The Arabs did not have democratic institutions and usually abstained from voting in the UN; they also tended to reject any third-party interference in their own affairs, fearing communist intervention above all. This explains why Spanish diplomacy and propaganda had notable success. The problem facing Franco was that at any given moment the Arabs might demand independence for Morocco. Even so, in 1950 King Abd-Allah of Jordan visited Spain as the first Head of State to do so in this period. Then, in 1952, Martín Artajo traveled to various Arab countries with Franco's daughter and General Ben Mizzian, who was of Moroccan nationality but was an officer in the Spanish Army.

The successes achieved by Franco's Spain in its relations with Arab nations were due in part to the fact that they were more interested in the Palestine question than in Morocco. If Spain opposed the creation of the State of Israel and supported the Vatican proposal that the Holy Places should be under international control, the main reason for doing so was Israel's attitude. When independence was declared the news was not even announced to Spain: a country which the Israeli ambassador to the UN considered an "active sympathizer and ally" of the Nazis. In effect Israel gained the support of liberals and socialists. Not even firm reminders of the help afforded to escaping Jews during World War II, nor the degree of religious freedom allowed in Spain after 1945, impressed Israeli politicians one iota.

Having highlighted the support that Franco's Spain could call on, we can now describe how the country began to emerge from isolation. In 1947 Franco's Spain was expelled from the Universal Postal Union, the International Telecommunications Union, and the International Civil Aviation Organization. On the other hand, in the UN it received 16 votes in its favor in comparison to six the previous year. The western powers now decided that the withdrawal of ambassadors had, paradoxically, had the effect of increasing support for Franco and therefore that it was time to adopt a different stance. The "slow relaxing" of pressure on Francoist Spain recommended by planners in the State Department was helped by events on the international stage. In the summer of 1947, responding to Soviet pressure, Hungary had become a communist dictatorship and in February 1948 the same happened in Czechoslovakia. In the summer of 1948 the Soviets began the blockade of Berlin. By that time the chairman of the American Committee of the Armed Forces had visited Spain. In January 1950 the American Secretary of State did not agree to America approving a UN resolution allowing relations with Spain to be resumed. However, finally, in November 1950, the United Nations approved by 38 votes to 10, with 12 abstentions (which included France and Britain), a resolution which passed no judgment on the regime and gave approval for the resumption of diplomatic relations. In fact, by this time Spain already had representatives from 24 countries in Madrid. At the end of 1950 Spain took its first step towards membership of international organizations when it was admitted to the Food and Agriculture Organization (FAO).

At a glance it might seem that the attitude of the western nations had changed substantially, especially in the case of America. All the democracies thought from 1945 onwards that it would have been better had Franco handed over power but at no point were they prepared for military intervention, partly because it was not common practice and partly because Franco's Spain posed them no real threat. In response to what the Polish delegate had stated at the UN, a British diplomat said of Spain that "it is only a danger and a disgrace to itself." The western powers also discovered that the Spanish opposition was weak and divided and therefore Spain ended up being what might be termed "tolerantly ostracized." Truman stated that the withdrawal of ambassadors was "the wrong means to achieve the right ends," and Bevin, the British Foreign Secretary, described what had been his own attitude up to then as "neither effective nor intelligent behavior." This position did not imply any recognition of the benefits of the regime but only that it was immovable. The cold war increased tolerance towards the Franco regime but it was still ostracized and the clearest proof of that is that Spain was not allowed to benefit from the Marshall Plan or to join NATO.

## The "Dark Night": Autarchy and Rationing in the 1940s

As we already know, the level of destruction inflicted within Spain was nowhere near the level outside in Europe after World War II. In Spain a tenth of all cattle were lost during the Civil War but in Greece half perished in World War II; three-quarters of the Spanish merchant fleet survived while only a quarter of the French and Greek fleets were saved. In these two countries the drop in electricity production was 50 percent greater in France and 300 percent greater in Greece and the destruction of homes was twice and five times as bad, respectively. What made Spain different was how slowly reconstruction got under way – a fact that must to a great extent be blamed on the regime's economic policy which ensured that 1945 made no significant impact on the situation inside the country. Both before and after that date the political strategy favored autarchy and state intervention with a seasoning of revolutionary rhetoric which on several occasions conflicted with the measures put forward by Finance Ministers but satisfied the regime's Falangist members. During World War II Spain had an economic policy of strict rationing with no chance of cross-border trade against a background of stagnation. Once the war ended, the economic policy pursued previously could no longer be justified in any terms. Had Spain had more links with European foreign policy doubtless a profound transformation would have been possible, like that experienced by the rest of Europe from 1947 on. It has been estimated that without the Civil War Spain's economic growth could have increased by a third, and that with the Civil War – but with the Marshall Plan as well – growth could still have increased by a quarter.

What was most important in terms of foreign trade during the World War II years was Spain's relations with Italy and Germany. As time passed, involvement with these two countries became increasingly prejudicial to Spain at a time when the country was paying off a part of the debt incurred during the Civil War. Germany and Italy headed the list of countries buying Spanish products in 1941, and that did not alter until 1943. It was only in 1944 that a real change occurred in the theater of war that was clearly in the Allies' favor. It is true to say, therefore, that political factors made Spain dependent on the Axis, and that this dependency became particularly significant because Spanish trade had fallen to almost half its previous level as a result of the conflict. Estimates suggest that 12 percent of the value of its imports was transferred to Germany and 3 percent to Italy as a result of the debts incurred during the Civil War. Another aspect of the question relates to military expenditure by the Spanish state over this period, either to improve defenses or in preparation for joining in the world conflict. According to official figures, the budget for expenditure on such materials was always above 50 percent during the war and reached a maximum of 63 percent in 1943. This data all reveals the extent to which, if Spain had adopted a truly neutral position, it would have been of real benefit at the time. Improvements could have been made to industrial productivity by greater openness to trade with the Allies but in 1945 Spanish industrial productivity was 10 percent below what it had been in 1935 and the annual growth rate had not yet reached 1 percent.

The opportunity lost over these years can best be appreciated if one compares Spain with other neutral European nations. All of them improved more than Spain, which was the country with the lowest level of industrial expansion. Switzerland, Sweden, and Turkey faced difficulties that were, objectively speaking, much greater in terms of their geography and trade than any facing Spain, yet Spain made difficulties for itself by its bad relations with the Allies and by spurning foreign investment. On the one hand, public resources were used to build up industries that produced war materials, which swallowed up imports, energy, and money; on the other, no dams were built which could have eased the energy deficit and in effect the expansion of industries that could have exported their products was cut.

Autarchy and interventionism had been strong tendencies in the Spanish economy since the start of the century but now, being rooted in nationalist ideas, they became more pronounced than ever before. At the same time intervention proved to be extremely ineffectual. In Franco's startlingly simplistic opinion, "Spain is a privileged country which should be entirely self-sufficient"; as the peseta rose and fell in the only place where it was in free circulation (Tangiers), Franco imagined Jewish conspiracies at work. Self-sufficiency came to symbolize a revolt against the evils of degenerate economic liberalism. The hard-line nationalists of the time contended that prices of products and matters relating to productivity could be fixed by decree without any reference to the market; even the Labor Charter (*Fuero del Trabajo*) stated that "prices of major agricultural products will be subject to discipline and reevaluation." Any non-conformist behavior was viewed as a crime against the "Fatherland," with its corresponding guilty parties who had to be punished. Nor was the verb "punished" used purely theoretically, for we know only too well that in many militarized industries such as coal-mining, offenses led to arrests. The extreme simplicity of these ideas means that it is possible to say that Spain's political *caudillo* behaved like a quartermaster in matters relating to the economy.

A fundamental characteristic of economic interventionism at this time is that it was not at all original. At most what happened was that there was evidence of an effort to imitate the economic policies of fascist countries by setting up bodies to allow the state to act directly in Spain's economic affairs, such as the National Institute for Industry (*Instituto Nacional de Industria*) and the National Resettlement Institute (*Instituto Nacional de Colonización*). There are many examples of such imitation in Spanish legislation; so, for instance, the Spanish Foreign Currency Institute (*Instituto Español de Moneda Extranjera*) was renamed the Institute for Currencies and Exchange (*Instituto de Cambio y Divisas*), borrowing the title used in Italian law. Yet more probable still is the notion that all such changes owed more to the need to apply a coat of modern varnish to an old-fashioned "barrack-style autarchy" that could be traced back to Spanish military projects at the time of World War I. Another characteristic of Spain's economic policy was the extreme, almost militaristic zeal with which it was applied. Thirdly, state intervention created a "legal barrier to entry" which served principally to favor monopolistic practices and also, there-fore, behavior that would prove economically damaging, and one final characteristic of the Spanish economy at the time was the multiplicity of administrative organizations, which added to the general chaos and privileged those who supported the regime.

Never before had it been more obvious that autarchy made very little sense in Spain. Not only were there not enough rubber, cotton, fertilizers, and oil but not enough wheat either: a product in which Spain should have been self-sufficient a lot earlier. It is typical of a state that is so power-fully interventionist to have no real and effective plan for its own recon-struction. Dating back to the Civil War there was a National Service with responsibility for devastated areas which in due course (in 1940) became a Directorate General (*Dirección General*). There was also an Institute for Credit (*Instituto de Crédito*) whose function was exactly what its title sug-gests, and action was taken to ensure that specific places that had suffered particularly badly from the effects of war, such as Brunete and Belchite, were "adopted" according to a special scheme. However, these were isolated instances where action was actually taken and not a real overall plan.

Whatever area one considers it is clear that interventionism failed, being least relevant where it should have been most effective. The Ministry of Agriculture was still in Falange's hands but the program that it implemented was in fact a copy of the one that the traditional right had outlined under the Second Republic. Apart from returning land to those who had had it taken away from them during the Agrarian Reform, an attempt was made to increase productivity by various schemes aimed at repopulation that did not affect the question of land ownership. This led to the creation of the National Resettlement Institute (*Instituto Nacional de Colonización*) in October 1939. During the earliest period of the Franco regime the Institute concentrated almost exclusively on buying up land but did not really carry through its aims of repopulation. Estimates suggest that the yearly rate of resettlement for the period 1939–51 was only about 1,500 workers a year, which is a low figure when compared with attempts made by the Republic during its much briefer existence marked by failure. Only 23,000 families were settled on 10,000 hectares of land. In fact, the largest repopulation took place in the period immediately following (1956–60), when levels reached 2,000 per year thanks to the Badajoz Plan. Yet the efforts of the Institute affected only some 48,000 settlers and 6,000 agricultural workers up to 1975; of those, some 10,000 were resettled in Badajoz.

Despite this neglect of the countryside in the years following 1939, Spanish society did become more "rural": from a level of 45 percent of all workers being in agriculture the figure rose to 50 percent, breaking with a centuries-old trend. There is a very simple reason for this: the difficulty of getting hold of supplies meant that the population moved to where the foodstuffs were. Nonetheless, there are authors who point out that a higher percentage of big landowners cultivated their own land than had been the case under the Republic when most of these properties were farmed by tenant farmers. The deficiencies in agricultural productivity in the immediate postwar period have been blamed on what was termed the "persistent drought" but there was another reason as well. Although there were indeed some terrible years in terms of the lack of rain (1941 and especially 1945 when the wheat harvest was only 53 percent of the average harvest before the Civil War), a much more decisive factor was the lack of investment given that the state concentrated its efforts almost exclusively on autarchic industrialization.

No sector was as extensively regulated and no sector witnessed such total failure due to the regime's interventionism as that of commerce inside Spain. Immediately after the war a system of ration cards came into use: started as a "provisional" measure it was to remain in place for no fewer than 12 years. In fact rigid controls on agricultural productivity meant in effect that agricultural workers had to hand over a fixed quota of what they harvested for a ridiculous price. Shortages in supply in the first instance awakened a desire for yet more government intervention but, as well as not solving anything, this led to black marketeering known as "estraperlo." It would be hard to exaggerate the size of the black market; it has even been suggested that black market trading in wheat exceeded official trading and that in the case of olive oil figures were close. Interventionism was as ineffectual as the measure which "absolutely" forbade queuing. The black market became such a normal part of life that Ridruejo could conclude that "everybody has a finger in the pie."

In discussing problems of supply we have indirectly touched on Spain's industrial policy. The nationalistic obsession of its politicians at the time with Spain's greatness was more easily satisfied by huge factories than by more modest projects that were economically viable. Its grandiose industrial policy was the pride and joy of the regime, which tried by these means to achieve national greatness and prove the superiority of this political strategy over any other except increasing Spain's military capability. Measures concerning industry were implemented early on after being approved in 1939–40. However, the achievement the regime was most proud of was the founding of the National Institute for Industry which dates from 1941. Its founding statutes stated that its main aim would be to "foster the creation and revival of our industries, especially those whose principal purpose is to solve problems arising from the defense needs of this land or concerned with the development of our economic autarchy." This measure was to an extent an imitation of Italian legislation, though the politician responsible was not a fascist but Suances, a naval man and a personal friend of Franco's who had been Industry Minister in 1938–9 and in charge of devising these legal measures. In 1945 Suances once again took on a ministerial post with responsibility for Industry, a job that he managed to make compatible with being the President of the INI.

The fact that those principally responsible for Spain's economic policies were from the Armed Services is significant. It was been written of Suances that he "treated private capital as a schoolmaster treated pupils to whom he was giving lessons in patriotism"; he was "a paternalistic but severe schoolmaster" who threw himself into the task of making the most of Spain's "neglected resources" as though his sole aim was to create industries without any regard for cost. In a country where hunger was rife, clothing scarce, and shelter often lacking, Suances decided to invest huge sums of money to ensure that oil from the bitumous slate of Puertollano should still be available for the foreseeable future (it was in fact only obtainable in the 1950s and at uneconomical prices). Born in El Ferrol, Suances had spent a number of years working in naval shipbuilding and under the Republic he had had experience in a private company that had ended in failure, intensifying his suspicion of private initiatives. He equipped the INI with its own financial resources in the form of bonds (*obligaciones*) at savings banks (*cajas de ahorros*) guaranteed by the state. His main object-ive was the "vital nerve-centers of production" to such an extent that he effectively took on a "director's role" in the Spanish economy. Management was centralized and vertical. His efforts were mainly directed at produc-ing energy and they were profoundly unsuccessful on oil production, though there were better results on electricity thanks to the use of low quality coal in the thermo-electric industry (ENDESA and ENHER)[1] and to the fresh drive in the exploitation of available hydroelectric resources. A third aspect of the INI was that it functioned as a "hospital for sick companies" by means of an actual "socialización" of losses. Within 10 years the INI had also become the only company producing vehicles, it had a major share in fertilizers and aluminum, and it played a very import-ant role in oil-refining and artificial fibers. In other words, the public company had taken over from the private or foreign company in Spain.

As economic activities of dubious worth increased in number, the economic policy of the newly formed state did not pay enough attention to private industry which, against a background of interventionism at home and uncertainty in foreign trade, was forced to resort to extraordinary procedures. A mayor of Sabadell acknowledged in his memoirs that at that time two-thirds of the wool used in the Catalan textile mills did not come from official suppliers. Major businessmen were at times obliged to adopt the paternalistic tone that was imposed on them by the state but at the same time they also had virtually limitless powers within their companies as "bosses" answerable only to the state. Nor should one forget that there were serious deficiencies in Spain's energy supplies. In 1940 the country had consumed a million tons of oil but because of its pro-Axis stance it had restrictions imposed on its oil supplies by the Allies, so much so that it did not reach that level of consumption again until 1946. Once World War II was over, the difficulties that Spain was encountering in obtaining the currency to buy oil were starkly obvious and electricity supplies were found to be seriously inadequate. In years such as 1945 and 1949, elec-tricity supplies were on occasion some 30 percent below demand.

All of these factors contributed to the poor performance of Spain's index of industrial productivity in comparison with other countries. Available data reveals that the country's backwardness dated from this time. Growth was only 0.6 percent during the period 1935–50, while in the rest of Europe it was 2.7 percent. Only in 1950 did levels of industrial production once again equal the levels in 1930. Spain fell behind Italy and did not even begin to close the gap until 1963, and in 1975 the difference was as it had been in 1947. Between 1946 and 1950 Greece and Yugoslavia doubled their industrial production while Spain's rose by 1.1 percent. In 1950 the income per capita was 40 percent lower than in Italy, when in 1930 it had been only 10 percent lower. All of these factors must be taken into account when we encounter statements saying that the Franco regime was the driving force behind Spain's economic development.

A key factor in the economic policy of the time was public finance. Historians seem to agree on the effectiveness of the action taken by the Finance Minister Larraz who had been responsible for monetary reunification after the war. Other aspects of his time in office seem less positive. As regards taxation, the period was characterized by the shaky structure of direct personal taxation which was virtually nonexistent, and by widespread tax-avoidance, although there was marked success in indirect personal taxation and taxes levied on exceptional profits (*beneficios extraordinarios*). Even so, estimates on tax fraud suggest that only a third of what should have been collected actually reached the public coffers. Whereas taxes in Europe at that time were far higher, in Spain the tax problem prevented an interventionist state doing its job properly (in Britain tax was at 33 percent of the national income, in Italy 21 percent, and in Spain only 14 percent).

Also, maintaining the situation in banking virtually unchanged in effect created a *numerus clausus* preventing development, and this was reinforced by the Law on the Regulation of Banking (*Ley de Ordeanción Bancaria*) of 1946. Not surprisingly, in some operations banks obtained profits of 700 percent. In years that were not very good in economic terms, annual dividends of 12 or 13 percent on bank bonds were not uncommon. In addition, banks concentrated their growing power in industry. At the same time, banking legislation had a clearly inflationary effect. Debt became common throughout the system and it was automatically dealt with by the Bank of Spain (*Banco de España*). Yet this was not the only mechanism that drove inflation. Being unable to generate revenue by means of taxation, the state resorted to circulating debt. It is remarkable that as interventionist a state as Spain should have forgotten how vital it is to control debt. Circulation of debt by the state was as frequent as it was abundant: it can be shown that the national debt tripled over those 10 years. As for foreign investment, suffice it to say that Riotinto was viewed as an "economic Gibraltar" and everything that could be done to ensure that the mines ended up as capital in Spanish hands was done. Finally, in 1954, seven Spanish banks bought up two-thirds of the capital while the rest remained in British hands.

We once again find ourselves face to face with the state's interventionist policy as soon as we turn our attention to foreign trade, which was dominated by bilateralism, the awarding of licenses, and numerous exchange rates. The peseta kept the same exchange rate until 1948, which was entirely consistent with Franco's nationalist ideology since he viewed a strong currency as the best sign of economic power. After that there was a shift to a system of "multiple exchange rates" which came into force in an impenetrable jungle of highly elaborate regulations. Since foreign trade was also subject to a system of licensing, the demand to participate soon became overwhelming. In this as in so many other areas there were many instances of favoritism that were both irrational and corrupt. Certain surnames from the ruling classes, including many from a Falangist background, soon appeared on the list of those with large fortunes. It was only in mid 1950 that a free currency market was established – a date when, in any case, the chances of obtaining foreign finance were still small for political reasons. The problem was made worse by the fact that the Spanish state nationalized the greater part of all foreign capital in Spain (German companies set up during the Civil War, Barcelona Traction, Telefónica in 1945 . . . ).

As the moment comes to try to evaluate Spain's economic development at this time, it is worth calling to mind the opinion of the Hispanist Gerald Brenan: "The impression Spain gives at present is of a country for whom the road which leads to the basic conditions of what is human and tolerable is closed." This may seem an exaggeration and it contrasts strongly with what actually happened subsequently in Spain's economic development, but it does reflect the situation as it was at the time Brenan was writing. In 1945 the per capita income was close on a third of what it had been in 1935 and it only recovered completely in 1951; however, it was not until 1954 – that is to say, when the regime had been in existence for 18 years – that prewar macroeconomic levels were reached once again. In order to reveal the extent to which the 1940s were a time of sacrifice for Spaniards it has been possible to ascertain that the actual salaries of specialized workers fell by half. At the end of the decade Spain had fallen behind the most advanced countries in Latin America such as Argentina, Uruguay, and Venezuela. Instead of experiencing a process of reconstruction, political factors condemned Spaniards to a stagnation without parallel out of which there grew, as an inheritance for the future, a public sector whose value was questionable.

This examination of Spain's economic policy should conclude with reference to the government's social policy. Unlike what had happened in other countries with basically similar regimes, such as Peronism, Spain's social policy was not in the hands of unions but of the Labor Ministry. The Single Union Law (*Ley de Unidad Sindical*) and the Law on the Bases of Union Organization (*Ley de Bases de Organización Sindical*) of 1940 followed criteria that were clearly fascist. The union was conceived of as single, compulsory, and "ordered hierarchically under state direction," which meant that "since all democratic illusions have now been defeated, it brings together those who are choosing to take part and serve by their leadership." These unions were permeated by an ideology that used revolutionary language that in practice said very little. In this way negotiation was avoided, life inside companies was run like a barracks, and employers had exceptional disciplinary powers. Until late 1944 no election of representatives took place within companies and in October 1947 company juries were set up. However, at this point the owners managed to prevent their actual introduction into the workplace by suggesting that it was a "dangerous innovation" and in effect the measure only came into force after 1953 and then only in larger companies.

Since trade unionism had been emptied of all content, revolutionary rhetoric found an outlet in another sector of the Administration. The specific measures that were the outcome of these policies in the early years of the Franco regime meant expansion of the social welfare system inherited from the Republic and before. The next few years saw the first family allowance, the setting up of conciliation boards at work in 1938, old age pensions in 1939, a policy of Protection of the Family (1945), sickness benefit (1942), and the Law of Labor Contracts (*Ley de Contrato de Trabajo*) in 1944. There was also pay for public holidays and bonuses. Technical universities became the new starting-point for professional training. Of all these new provisions, the one that made the greatest impact on Spanish society was without doubt medical provision for children. Infant mortality fell by half in the period 1935–55 and deaths in childbirth to a quarter or even a fifth of previous levels. Other aspects of the regime's social policies were put into practice much more slowly or remained in the limbo of rhetorical declarations, such as those aimed at protection of the family. One must take into account the fact that salary rises were automatically made non-effective by inflation, and that however much social legislation intended to bring in new measures, levels of consumption clearly showed a downward trend once again.

## Culture: Penance and Survival

The situation of Spanish culture in 1936 has been described as a true "age of silver." The trauma of war meant that a section of Spain's creative writers and artists went into exile and also that a very particular interpretation was put on the country's past, as much by those who left Spain as by the ones who remained there. In neither case was there was a total break with the past, though some attempts were made to do just that.

The experience of exile made a powerful impact on many Spanish intellectuals. Prominent figures who went into exile included the musicians Manuel de Falla and Pablo Casals; philosophers such as José Gaos and Gabriel Ferrater; specialists in the social sciences such as Manuel García Pelayo and Francisco Ayala; men of letters such as José F. Montesinos and Guillermo de Torre; educationalists such as José Castillejo and Alberto Jiménez Fraud; playwrights such as Alejandro Casona and actresses such as Margarita Xirgu; the historians Rafael Altamira, Claudio Sánchez Albornoz, and Américo Castro; the novelists Max Aub, Arturo Barea, and Ramón Sender. Yet more important by far than drawing up a list of exiles is to determine the ways in which they might have been influenced by the extraordinary circumstances of their exile. Many saw their academic work disrupted and all of them experienced exile as an acutely painful mutilation. Yet as well as their pain we must consider other more fruitful consequences of exile. Many of them discovered the global nature of Spanish culture and felt that, rather than being driven from their own country, they had discovered another land, unlike numerous Central Europeans who had fled from Nazism.

This is why reflection on Spain and its past has been as insistent as it has been passionate. That has often been the case with all kinds of thinkers but is especially true of historians. In Américo Castro's opinion, Spain's past had been profoundly marked by its three religions – Christian, Muslim, and Jewish – and by a deep-rooted intolerance towards any dissenting minority. Nor, in his view, had this been totally negative since the anguish of the Jewish *conversos* had provided the inspiration for a large part of Spain's cultural creativity. In his famous debate with Claudio Sánchez Albornoz, what seems to have been most important was not the degree to which either of them might have been right or wrong but the fact that they were both so powerfully drawn to the study of Spain's past. Sánchez Albornoz, a positivist historian whose work had little in common with Spain's tradition of essay-writing, attacked Castro's thesis, rejecting what Castro claimed to have been the arabization of Spain and instead taking his own search for Spanishness further back in time as far as the Iberians. Essentially both historians felt strongly attracted by the notion of Spain's uniqueness and their results coincided. This type of preoccupation is also evident in novels written by exiles after the Civil War in which war itself also played a major role in the work of many writers. That is the case with Barea's *La forja de un rebelde* (*The forging of a rebel*), or Manuel Andújar's *Vísperas* (*The evening before*), and also with works by Aub, Sender, Ayala, and a great many others in which the theme of the Civil War mingles with memories of childhood, the problems of exile, and the difficulty of returning to Spain, or the threat of the dictatorship.

It has often been argued that given the caliber of those who left Spain, who were not only brilliant in terms of thought and narrative but also in disciplines such as poetry or the natural sciences, what was left behind in Spain was a barren desert with nothing but official art and official literature of more than dubious quality. However, to suggest that this was the case is to oversimplify and to ignore history. The exiling of intellectuals did not encompass even a fraction of Spain's cultural creativity; furthermore, it is far from certain that there ever was an official culture as such, quite apart from the fact that among the ranks of the victors too there was evidence of quite considerable brilliance.

Those who stayed in Spain had not all supported the winning side or even changed sides (though some had). As the Catalan journalist "Gaziel" wrote, clearly an effort was made by those in power to breathe life into "the relics of a past that has been obliterated in the rest of the world," and they had the "sickeningly submissive" approval of the Spanish bourgeoisie. Nonetheless, if Spain's liberal tradition could not survive as such, at least there still existed a "noble line of integrity." There were also those who, like Julián Marías, chose "to live with the scant liberty that exists at present but in all circumstances to be free." When writing, he adds, one had at times not to say everything that one was thinking but one could at least say some of it. It goes without saying that this was far from easy. We need only remember that many of the most important novels of the decade were censored. Cela's *La familia de Pascual Duarte* (*The family of Pascual Duarte*) was censored first of all and then he was thrown out of the Press Association (*Asociación de la Prensa*) on account of *La Colmena* (*The Beehive*). In the immediate postwar years Baroja's complete works were banned, more than 10 percent of all plays were subjected to censorship along with novels by well-known Falangists, while for years it was forbidden even to mention Spain's most successful playwright, Jacinto Benavente. Nonetheless, as Marías has said, "there was a considerable degree of personal and social freedom" because the regime was never entirely totalitarian and because it was not overly concerned with cultural issues. This explains, for example, how José Ortega y Gasset was able to return to Spain and try to reestablish a link with the liberal heritage of the past, as no lesser a person than Gregorio Marañón had done before him. In the aftermath of World War II, Spain's weighty legacy of tragic experience seemed to come through more clearly in Marañón's work because, in the biographies that he wrote, the theme of exile or the thirst for political power appeared more often than they did in the works of the more shy and reserved Ortega. It is highly likely that both men believed that Francoism might possibly move in a more liberal direction but in this respect they both soon had cause to give up hope. In Ortega's opinion, Madrid had reverted to being like any "unchanging small town in La Mancha," just as it always had been. As for Baroja and Azorín, they seemed to prefer someone who would "tame" revolutionary passions to the passions themselves.

There was little evidence in Franco's Spain of the real heirs to the liberal tradition, although 1947 did see an Institute for the Study of the Humanities (*Instituto de Humanidades*) founded, inspired by Ortega; it was also possible to begin publishing *Insula*, a literary review which put the literary world inside Spain in contact with those in exile. The problem is that this world was denied the opportunity to exercise any real influence and in consequence many prewar cultural institutions were left in a situation that was, to say the least, precarious. Marías wrote of the two great patriarchs of Spanish thought of the earlier period that "Unamuno was not seen in a very good light [but] it was not as bad as for Ortega [since] after all [the former] was dead and had been a less rigorous thinker." Nonetheless, in Franco's Spain as it was in its early stages, apart from those already mentioned and many others who were less important there was, for example, Ramón Menéndez Pidal who ended his literary career with a period of sparkling polemical syntheses. In other words, it was not the case that the literary masters gave in. However limited their chances of action were, liberal intellectuals with their slow silent labors made their contribution to Spain's transformation. The writer Carlos Barral could state that in the postwar years "the country set about doing penance [but] a transformation which years later seemed unimaginable happened at breakneck speed."

Rather than propounding only one kind of cultural orthodoxy the Franco regime had many kinds that overlapped to a greater or lesser extent and were neither clearly differentiated nor long-lasting. The mission to rebuild Spain's capacity for scientific research was entrusted to the National Scientific Research Council (*Consejo Superior de Investigaciones Científicas* or CSIC), part of whose directorship was of the traditionalist clericalist right and not at all in tune with Falange. In universities there was a sort of division of labor between the Party and Church groups when it came to formulating the 1943 Universities Act (*Ley Universitaria*). The result was a text which in essence did not in any way break with the university tradition of the nineteenth century: the lowest-level teaching posts were given to Catholic integrists. Continuity within Spain's universities was evident in their centralization and the continuation of the system of selection based on competitive examinations (*oposiciones*). Within 12 years three quarters of university chairs had new occupants. The only decisive change was the exponential rise in control in the sense that the vice-chancellor, who was appointed by the government, was seen as both a "head of the university and a government delegate." Power was shared between the most strongly clericalist sector and Falange in the sense that Falange controlled the Spanish University Students' Union (*Sindicato Español Universitario* or SEU) and the residential university colleges (*colegios mayores*) in order to maximize its impact on the young. As for academic staff, one would have to point out that the clericalists were the strongest element. Nor should one forget the drastic financial cuts that plagued the universities which, in the postwar period, had only 365 teaching staff in contrast to 553 under the Republic. Many of the students and academics who studied and taught there during those years have left in their memoirs a very negative testimony to their experiences. Carlos Castilla del Pino affirms that after the war in every academic subject there was someone whose aim was to start at the level that had previously been attained and to "to drag it down further than could ever have been imagined in the mid twentieth century." In many areas this may well have been the case but generalization can also distort the picture. In other areas political commitment was abandoned and essays and articles led on to serious academic study as a refuge from surrounding circumstances.

Falange and others associated with it took charge of what might be termed "high culture." The Party operated on two levels: one of lower quality production more directly controlled by more immediate political interests responsible for publications such as *El Español* or *La Estafeta Literaria*, and the other represented by the review *El Escorial*. The latter aimed to provide "propaganda in the grand style" but quality soon took precedence over the desire to persuade. It was hoped that in this way the roots of liberalism would be taken over and absorbed but it also ensured their survival. On another front, children's magazines published by Falange gave a first opportunity to write to authors who in time would become serious critics of the Franco regime. There is no doubt at all that there was more intelligence, sensitivity, and generosity of spirit in Falange circles than in other groups dominated by Church interests. Among such Falangists it was even possible at times to find an appreciation of new developments in the sciences that until then had never caught anyone's interest in Spain. The *Revista de Estudios Políticos* (Political Science Review), aimed in theory at setting out the regime's doctrinal position, in fact served to introduce sociology into Spain. Whatever the means might have been, by the middle of the 1950s there were no more than mere traces of fascism or any kind of cultural orthodoxy left.

In addition to this plurality of orthodox positions we should add to the general panorama of the moment a comment on the relative autonomy enjoyed within each of these areas and the drift among former hardliners towards greater apathy. There was of course an entire literature which chose to explore themes related to aspects of the whole experience of the Civil War but it belonged to the traditional right (Ricardo León, Concha Espina . . . ) and it did not last long. In the last analysis it is only of limited interest and does not of course invalidate their writing that Cela was a censor and Gonzalo Torrente Ballester wrote a book which spoke highly of the single party system, any more than Luis Rosales's or Luis Felipe Vivanco's fascination with epic or religious poetry should be paid undue attention. The most honest and obvious explanation for facts such as these will always be preferable to an attempt to claim that these writers were early dissidents when in fact such dissidence either did not exist or else came very much later. Another fact worth mentioning is that with one or two exceptions the novelists and intellectuals most closely associated with the regime in the area of ideology were more belligerent in their attitudes before it came to power than while it remained there. The case of Rafael Sánchez Mazas best typifies this as he soon devoted himself to an evocative style of writing, as is clear from *La vida nueva de Pedrito de Andía* (*The New Life of Pedrito de Andía*).

In exile as much as within the country, Spain's essential nature became not just a dominant theme but an obsession for essayists. This is evident in Menéndez Pidal's last works, especially *Los españoles en su historia* (*Spaniards through their history*) in which, like so many pro-Castilian historians of liberal background, he traces the origins of the nation back to a very distant past and condemns Spain's plurality as decadence. The fiercest argument of the period was the one that arose between different orthodox viewpoints at the end of the 1940s. The ensuing debate set Pedro Laín Entralgo, the most outstanding figure among the Falangist intellectuals, against the monarchist Catholic extremist position represented by the CSIC journal *Arbor*, founded in 1944, for which the author of *España sin problema* (*Spain without problems*), Rafael Calvo Serer, used to write. The Falangist position aimed to move closer to the intellectual attitudes of the liberal left in order to integrate them into its own way of thinking. Those opposing it, however, had since 1939 denied that there was anything essentially problematic about Spain because Menéndez Pidal "presented us with a Spain without problems." Laín's judgment was so very different that his starting-point was an alternative vision entirely unlike that of Menéndez Pidal and it was presented as being more liberal than the opposition's own view. All in all, this debate is evidence of the crucial importance of reflection on Spain's essential nature in the cultural world of the postwar period and throughout the Peninsula. It also allows us to trace the slow progress that was being made towards the recovery of liberal principles. For the Falangists it was the desire to draw in intellectuals in exile that in the long run led to them becoming more like them. The other faction was anti-totalitarian and monarchist and this last factor meant that it evolved too, at least in the case of Calvo Serer.

If we move on from these semi-political debates to the life of Spain's literary world we shall find a marked change in attitude from the Republican years. Prior to its politicization in the 1930s, the "1927 Generation" had been known for its experiments in form and its brilliant use of metaphor. The "1936 Generation" replaced these techniques with dense sentimental rhetoric and a preoccupation with human destiny. Germán Gullón sums it up more or less exactly: as a generation it would have been "moderate, tolerant, understanding, and an enemy of conventionally determined posturing and flag waving," reluctant to contribute to splitting Spain in two precisely because it had already witnessed that spectacle and had suffered in its own flesh because of it. As one can see, all this has very little to do with the mockery (*fumistería*) of official art (Josep Pla). For many of these writers both in exile and in Spain a supremely important influence was that of Ortega y Gasset.

Much of what has been said so far is even more relevant to any discussion of poetry at the time. Apart from its initial interest in religious or imperialistic poetry when it was founded, the journal *Garcilaso* represented a search for a lyricism that would be "neoclassical (in form), intimate, and nationalistic." Yet not even the supreme mentor of this group, José García Nieto, always adhered to these principles; perhaps more significant still was the return to a classical notion of discipline (the "scandal of rigid discipline"). In Rosales, as in Vivanco and Leopoldo María Panero, we find that political commitment and a commitment to this classical ideal were soon left far behind. At the same time, Damaso Alonso's 1944 work *Hijos de la ira* (*Sons of Wrath*) signaled the "rehumanizing of poetry" by presenting Madrid, in an agonizing way that has parallels with what was going on at this same time in *tremendista*[2] narratives (Cela), as "a city of more than a million corpses." The review *Espadaña* also marked a return to reality which contrasted with the process of "embalming" undertaken by those who had tried to link the world of poetry with the classical world. Even before the 1950s Gabriel Celaya had chosen to write politically committed poetry in opposition to the regime.

To an extent, in narrative too a backward step was taken towards classicism – to the tradition represented by Galdós and Baroja. The latter became the great master of the newly emerging generations, as Camilo José Cela – the most brilliant author of all those who had emerged in the 1940s – would recall. Cela's *La familia de Pascual Duarte* (*Pascual Duarte's family*, 1942) was the novel whose appalling version of reality, taken from the work of the painter José Gutiérrez Solana and the "Spanish Black Legend," brought the pain of the postwar period into a literature that seemed not to have experienced it until now. In fact *tremendismo* was born of this experience and became a dominant fashion. Less agonizing and more humbly imitative of Spain's "harsh, heartfelt, and painful day-to-day reality," as is stated in the prologue, was Cela's *La colmena* (*The Beehive*), written in 1946 but only allowed to be published in 1951 and then only abroad. Carmen Laforet's *Nada* (*Nothing*), published in 1945, explores beneath a prosaic story the general degeneration in collective morale in postwar Spain. At around this time the career of another writer began to make slow but sure upward progress: that of Miguel Delibes.

The theater, given its particular nature, would have had difficulty had it allowed discordant elements to have a voice. It has therefore been written that the 1940s were characterized by "humorous theater" that had "some novelty and was somewhat disconcerting and offered veiled social criticism of Spain's banal daily existence." The perennial bourgeois theater saw Benavente triumph in 1945 when he was once again allowed to put on a new play. Real novelty, though not immediately obvious, came in the form of plays in which humor and tenderness mingled, such as works by Miguel Mihura, author of *Ni pobre ni rico, sino todo lo contrario* (*Neither rich nor poor but quite the contrary*) of 1943 and *Tres sombreros de copa* (*Three bowler hats*), premiered in 1952. It was only in 1949 that *Historia de una escalera* (*Story of a staircase*) was first performed, introducing the short-lived but morally questioning theater of Antonio Buero Vallejo. For the time being, the vanguard was limited exclusively to writers in exile where in 1944 Rafael Alberti premiered *El adefesio* (*Looking a sight*).

There was never really one official orthodox position on architecture and the plastic arts either. Although the architecture of the time followed fascist models, in the postwar period there was virtually no possibility of rebuilding, and monuments commemorating the conflict used almost exclusively the form of the cross. There was practically no censorship in the plastic arts. In architecture – the art form most likely to have an immediate political impact – there is evidence of changing tastes and undefined intent in some of the greatest monuments of the time. This may well be the case with the Valle de los Caídos (Valley of the Fallen), begun in 1940 and very much the inspiration of Franco himself who even made some sketches for it. Initially there may have been an intention to imitate the architecture of Nazi Germany about which an exhibition was held in Madrid, and it was with these aesthetic notions in mind that designs were put forward for the Air Ministry building in Madrid. However, these plans went nowhere, partly due to the weakness of Spain's economy at the time and partly too because of changes within the regime. In this last respect, it is significant that the Air Ministry already mentioned was finally built according to architectural styles from Spain's own national heritage. Sánchez Mazas wrote that "El Escorial offers us the best lessons for the Falanges of the future" and indeed the Ministry owes much to the architectural principles of El Escorial. A style of monumental architecture that drew on national traditions is also to be found in other important examples of the architecture of the time, such as the Technical University (*Universidad Laboral*) in

Gijón designed by Luis Moya Blanco. National tradition was also evident in music, for example in the case of Joaquín Rodrigo's *Concierto de Aranjuez*. After 1951 it is clearly inappropriate to talk of official architecture in relation to the Franco regime.

As regards painting and sculpture, the most that one can say is that there was official art in areas such as illustration (Carlos Sáenz de Tejada) or murals (José Aguiar) but it did not last for long. Official tastes tended towards classicism and they were the dominant influence on sculpture (Enrique Pérez Comendador, Enric Monjo, José Clará . . . ) for obvious reasons. However, rather than a return to classicism, what in fact happened was that some aspects of the avant-garde of a previous period continued to exist but in a very limited market. One must also take into account the impact on new generations of outstanding figures from an early era of Spanish painting: as was the case with Daniel Vázquez Díaz in Madrid or Joaquín Sunyer and Pere Pruna in Barcelona. A further important factor to bear in mind was that painters such as Solana, who had until this time been demonized, became acceptable because they had so much in common with the literary phenomenon of the time known as *tremendismo*. Perhaps the strongest evidence of this link connecting the present with the past is to be found in the so-called *Academia Breve de Crítica de Arte* (Brief Academy of Art Criticism) and what was known as the "Vallecas School." The former, inspired by Eugenio D'Ors, existed from 1942 onwards and merits attention for its attentiveness to the most recent changes in painting and sculpture. D'Ors's efforts were devoted to raising the level of information on, and quality of, material on contemporary art in the capital. The Vallecas School did not represent a particular discipline or trend; rather, it was a group of young painters drawn to Benjamín Palencia: a figure who provided a link back to the vanguard of the 1930s. Many painters were interested in landscapes and still life, and in very uncertain circumstances they managed to keep up an admirable level of activity which only received public recognition in the 1960s. After 1948 the earliest attempts at abstract art began to appear, at first closely associated with surrealism and influenced by Klee and Miró, or with primitivism (the "Altamira School"). The first biennial Festival of Latin American Art, where the artistic merit of a young painter such as Palencia was acknowledged, marked the start of a new era. Conceived as a vehicle for political propaganda about Latin America, its importance lay in the fact that from that time on, the official Spanish art world came to accept the most varied artistic options.

Brief reference must be made to popular culture – to entertainment and leisure, for it is here that we can best observe the spirit of the age. In the history of Spanish cinema those were the years in which the popularity of the medium spread. The number of cinemas began to multiply and did not stop until the late 1960s. In 1952 the British historian Gerald Brenan stated that such a passion for the cinema was not to be found in any other country: an opinion confirmed by the fact that the number of establishments per thousand inhabitants equaled that of the United States. In those years too, an industrial style of production came into being. In 1941 the dubbing of films became standard: a nationalist measure initially, though it then became a lasting habit. In that same year, quotas were set for the showing of Spanish films and a system introduced which meant that anyone who produced Spanish films could also import foreign ones. Furthermore, the cinema was declared an industry of national interest and so received official funding.

During this period Spain produced an average of 37 films a year. In official circles the cinema was considered to have a vital function as a "formidable weapon for disseminating ideas," though this did not mean that pure entertainment was abandoned since the most popular genre at the time was comedy. However, films on historical themes (Juan Orduña) were thought to have greater significance. They were considered especially important in "shaping of the spirit of the nation" and common themes included heroic biographies, the formation of the Spanish state, and the colonial enterprise in America.

In song too, and in other forms of entertainment associated with it, there were notable changes in the 1940s. As well as a campaign to impose a certain morality in variety performances, the world of popular music saw a last revival of Spain's own style of operetta, the *zarzuela grande*, whose main exponents were Federico Moreno Torroba and Pablo Sorozábal. Its final crisis came as a result of a creative recession and a loss of prestige among the general public brought about by elitist criticism. In contrast, a genre that did flourish was a kind of folkloric spectacle introduced by Antonio Quintero, Rafael de León, and Manuel López-Quiroga which was almost entirely Andalusian. The success of this kind of production displaced for a time the music-hall songs of the past, the Argentinian tango, and Mexican ballads (*corridos*) which had given the musical entertainment of a previous era a cosmopolitan dimension.

Having made its appearance in the 1920s, radio became a social phenomenon in the 1930s. After the Francoist victory a new legal ruling came into force that was intended to last. Alongside the most widely broadcast private radio station *Unión Radio*, now rebaptized with the new name *Sociedad Española de Radiodifusión*, a state radio station came into being, *Radio Nacional*, and also one representing the Party. However, information – what was known as a *"parte"* or bulletin: a term with a military ring to it – was strictly the monopoly of *Radio Nacional* and at the same time a system of strict censorship was introduced. This did not, in fact, mean that radio broadcasting was in any way limited; in those years there were a million receivers: a figure three times the size of the figure at the start of the 1930s. Alongside political information, what is most remarkable about radio broadcasting in the postwar period is the sheer quantity of religious programming. Despite all difficulties, by the middle of the 1940s it was obvious that private radio had survived and indeed a new form of entertainment appeared: serials. The retransmission of popular music would have an immense impact both on the broadcasting companies (in commercial terms) and as a means of laying the foundations of a form of popular leisure entertainment.

## Bibliography

Political history: J. CAZORLA, *La consolidación del Nuevo Estado franquista*, Marcial Pons, Madrid, 2003; Giuliana di FEBO, *Ritos de guerra y de victoria en la España franquista*, Desclée de Brouwer, Bilbao, 2002; Álvaro FERRARI, *Franquismo y conflictos ideológicos, 1936–1956*, EUNSA, Pamplona, 1993; "El primer franquismo, 1936–1959," *Ayer*, no. 33 (1999), edited by Glicerio SÁNCHEZ RECIO; Javier TUSELL, *Franco y los católicos. La política interior española entre 1945 y 1957*, Alianza Editorial, Madrid, 1984.

On Falange: Miguel Ángel APARICIO, *El sindicalismo vertical y la formación del Estado franquista*, EUNIBAR, Barcelona, 1980; Ricardo CHUECA, *El fascismo en los comienzos del régimen de Franco. Un estudio sobre FET y de las JONS*, CIS, Madrid, 1983; Stanley PAYNE, *Franco y José Antonio. El extraño caso del fascismo español*, Barcelona, Planeta, 1997; Miguel A. RUIZ CARNICER, *El Sindicato Español Universitario (SEU), 1935–1965. La socialización política de la juventud universitaria en el franquismo*, Siglo XXI, Madrid, 1996; Joan María THOMAS, *Falange, guerra civil, franquisme. FET y de las JONS de Barcelona en els primers anys del règim franquista*, Publicacions de l'Abadia de Montserrat, Barcelona, 1992.

Political memoirs: José María AREILZA, *A lo largo del siglo, 1909–1991*, Planeta, Barcelona, 1992; Francesc CAMBÓ, *Meditacions. Dietari (1936–1946)*, Alpha, Barcelona, 1982; José M. GIL ROBLES, *La monarquía por la que yo luché*

(1941–1945), Taurus, Madrid, 1976; Alfredo KINDELÁN, *La verdad de mis relaciones con Franco*, Planeta, Barcelona, 1981; Pedro LAÍN ENTRALGO, *Descargo de conciencia (1930–1960)*, Barral, Barcelona, 1976; Dionisio RIDRUEJO, *Casi unas memorias*, Planeta, Barcelona, 1976; Ramón SERRANO SUÑER, *Entre el silencio y la propaganda, la historia como fue. Memorias*, Planeta, Barcelona, 1977, and *Entre Hendaya y Gibraltar*, Nauta, Barcelona, 1973; Eugenio VEGAS LATAPIE, *La frustración de la victoria. Memorias políticas, 1938–1942*, Actas, Madrid, 1995.

Spain's position on World War II: Charles B. BURDICK, *Germany's military strategy and Spain in World War II*, UP, Syracuse, 1968; Lorenzo DELGADO GÓMEZ ESCALONILLA, *Diplomacia franquista y política cultural hacia Iberoamérica (1939–1953)*, CSIC, Madrid, 1988; Donald D. DETWILER, *Hitler, Franco und Gibraltar. Die Frage des spanischen Eintritts in den Zweiten Weltkrieg*, Franz Steiner, Wiesbaden, 1962; Rafael GARCÍA PÉREZ, *Franquismo y Tercer Reich. Las relaciones económicas hispano-alemanas durante la segunda guerra mundial*, Centro de Estudios Constitucionales, Madrid, 1994; Massimiliano GUDERZO, *Madrid e l'arte della diplomazia. L'incognita spagnola nella seconda guerra mondiale*, Manent, Firenze, 1995; C. H. HALSTEAD, *Spain, the powers and the Second World War*, University of Virginia Ph. D., Virginia, 1962; Christian LEITZ, *Economic relations between Nazi Germany and Franco's Spain, 1936–1945*, Oxford University Press, Oxford, 1996; Antonio MARQUINA, *La diplomacia vaticana y la España de Franco, 1936–1945*, CSIC, Madrid, 1982; Rosa PARDO, *Con Franco hacia el Imperio. La política exterior española en América Latina, 1939–1945*, UNED, Madrid, 1994; Klaus Jorg RUHL, *Franco, Falange y el III Reich. España durante la II Guerra Mundial*, Akal, Madrid, 1986; Denis SMYTH, *Diplomacy and strategy of survival. British policy and Franco's Spain, 1940–1941*, Cambridge University Press, Cambridge, 1986; Javier TUSELL, *Franco, España y la segunda guerra mundial. Entre el Eje y la neutralidad*, Temas de Hoy, Madrid, 1995; Javier TUSELL and Genoveva GARCÍA QUEIPO DE LLANO, *Franco y Mussolini. La política española durante la segunda guerra mundial*, Planeta, Barcelona, 1985.

The period of isolation: María Dolores ALGORA, *Las relaciones hispano-árabes durante el régimen de Franco: la ruptura del aislamiento internacional*, Biblioteca Diplomática Española, Madrid, 1996; Paola BRUNDU, *Ostracismo e realpolitik. Gli alleati e la Spagna franchista negli anni del dopo guerra*, Università di Cagliari, 1984; Beatriz FIGALLO, *El protocolo Perón-Franco. Relaciones hispano-argentinas, 1942–1952*, Ediciones Corregidor, Buenos Aires, 1992; Juan Carlos JIMÉNEZ REDONDO, *Franco e Salazar. As relaçoes luso-espanholas durante a guerra fria*, Assirio e Alvim, Lisboa, 1996; A. J. LEONART, *España y la ONU*, CSIC, Madrid, 1978 ff.

The opposition during the early years of Francoism: Helmut HEINE, *La oposición política al franquismo de 1939 a 1952*, Crítica, Barcelona, 1983 and Javier TUSELL, *La oposición democrática al franquismo (1939–1962)*, Planeta, Barcelona, 1977. The Monarchists: Fernando de MEER, *Juan de Borbón, un hombre solo*

*(1941–1948)*, Junta de Castilla y León, 2001; José María TOQUERO, *Franco y don Juan. La oposición monárquica al franquismo* Plaza y Janés, Barcelona, 1989, and *Don Juan de Borbón, el rey padre*, Plaza y Janés-Cambio 16, Barcelona, 1992; A. VILLANUEVA MARTÍNEZ, *El carlismo navarro durante el primer franquismo, 1937–1951*, Actas, Madrid, 1998. Republicanism: José BORRÁS, *Políticas de los exiliados españoles, 1944–1950*, Ruedo Ibérico, Paris, 1976; José María DEL VALLE, *Las instituciones de la República en el exilio*, Ruedo Ibérico, Paris, 1976; David WINGEATE PIKE, *Vae victis! Los republicanos españoles refugiados en Francia, 1939–1944*, Ruedo Ibérico, Paris, 1969 (*The Spanish communists in exile 1939–1945*, Oxford: Clarendon, 1993).

On socialism: Luis ARIQUISTAIN, *Sobre la guerra civil y en la emigración*, Espasa Calpe, Madrid, 1983, edited and with a prologue by Javier Tusell; Julio AROSTEGUI, *Largo Caballero en el exilio. La última etapa de un líder obrero*, Fundación Largo Caballero, Madrid, 1990; *Congresos del PSOE en el exilio, 1944–1974*, Editorial Pablo Iglesias, Madrid, 1981; Richard GILLESPIE, *The Spanish Socialist Party. A history of factionalism*, Clarendon Press, Oxford, 1989; Santos JULIÁ, *Los socialistas en la política española, 1879–1982*, Taurus, Madrid, 1997; Abdón MATEOS, *Las izquierdas españolas desde la guerra civil hasta 1982. Organizaciones socialistas, culturas políticas y movimientos sociales*, Universidad Nacional de Educación a Distancia, Madrid, 1997; Amaro DEL ROSAL, *Historia de la UGT de España en la emigración*, Grijalbo, Barcelona, 1978; Juan A. SACALÚA, *La resistencia socialista en Asturias, 1937–1962*, Fundación Pablo Iglesias, Madrid, 1986; "El socialismo en España," *Anales de Historia de la Fundación Pablo Iglesias*, IV (1986); César TCHACH and Carmen REYES, *Clandestinidad y exilio. La reconstrucción del sindicato socialista, 1939–1953*, Fundación Pablo Iglesias, Madrid, 1986. On the Anarchists: Ángel HERRERÍN, *La CNT durante el franquismo. Clandestinidad y exilio (1939–1975)*, Siglo XXI, Madrid, 2004 and Eurico MARCO NADAL, *Todos contra Franco. La Alianza Nacional de Fuerzas Democráticas, 1944–1947*, Queimada, Madrid, 1982. On the Spanish Communist Party (PCE) and the guerrilla war: Fernando CLAUDÍN, *Santiago Carrillo. Crónica de un secretario general*, Planeta, Barcelona, 1983; Joan ESTRUCH, *El PCE en la clandestinidad, 1939–1956*, Siglo XXI, Madrid, 1982; Gregorio MORÁN, *Miseria y grandeza del Partido Comunista de España, 1939–1975*, Planeta, Barcelona, 1986; Secundino SERRANO, *Maquis. Historia de la guerrilla antifranquista*, Temas de Hoy, Madrid, 2001. On the opposition in the Basque Country: BELTZA, *El nacionalismo vasco en el exilio, 1937–1960*, Txertoa, San Sebastián, 1977 and Iñake BERNARDO, *Galíndez, la tumba abierta. Los vascos y los Estados Unidos*, Gobierno Vasco, Vitoria, 1993. On the opposition in Catalonia: Félix FANES, *La vaga de tramvies del 1951*, Laia, Barcelona, 1977; Miquel FERRER, *La Generalitat de Catalunya a l'exili*, Aymà, Barcelona, 1977; Carles PI SUNYER, *Memòries de l'exili. El Consell Nacional de Catalunya, 1940–1945*, Curial, Barcelona, 1978.

Living conditions and social protest: Carme MOLINERO and Pere YSÀS, *Patria, pan y justicia. Nivell de vida y condicions de treball a Catalunya, 1939–1951*, La Magrana, Barcelona, 1985; Carmen BENITO DEL POZO, *La clase obrera durante el franquismo. Empleo, condiciones de trabajo y conflicto (1940–1975)*, Siglo XXI, Madrid, 1993 and R. GARCÍA PIÑEIRO, *Los mineros asturianos bajo el franquismo (1937–1975)*, Fundación 1º de Mayo, Madrid, 1990.

Catalonia: Josep BENET, *L'intent franquista de genocidi cultural contra Catalunya*, Publicacions de l'Abadia de Montserrat, Barcelona, 1992; María Josepa GALLOFRÉ, *L'edició catalana i la censura franquista (1939–1951)*, Publicacions de l'Abadia de Montserrat, Barcelona, 1991; Borja de RIQUER, *L'últim Cambó (1936–1947). La dreta catalana davant la guerra civil i el franquisme*, Eumo, Vic, 1996; J. M. SOLÉ SABATÉ and J. M. VILLARROYA, *Cronologia de la repressió de la llengua i cultura catalanes (1936–1975)*, Curial, Barcelona, 1996.

Social and economic policy: Alfonso BALLESTEROS, *Juan Antonio Suances, 1891–1977. La política industrial de la posguerra*, Lid Editorial empresarial, León, 1993; Carlos BARCIELA, *La agricultura cerealista en la España contemporánea: el mercado triguero y el Servicio Nacional del Trigo*, UCM, Madrid, 1981; and *Autarquía y mercado negro: el fracaso económico del primer franquismo, 1939 – 1959*, Crítica, Barcelona, 2003; Jordi CATALÁN, *La economía española y la segunda guerra mundial*, Ariel, Barcelona, 1995; Antonio GÓMEZ MENDOZA, *El "Gibraltar económico": Franco y Riotinto, 1936–1954*, Civitas, Madrid, 1994; Pablo MARTÍN ACEÑA and Francisco COMÍN, *INI, cincuenta años de industrialización*, Espasa Calpe, Madrid, 1991; Carme MOLINERO and Pere YSÀS, *Els industrials catalans durant el franquisme*, Eumo, Vic, 1991; Pedro SCHWARTZ and Manuel Jesús GONZÁLEZ, *Una historia del Instituto Nacional de Industria, 1941–1975*, Tecnos, Madrid, 1978; Ángel VIÑAS *et al.*, *Política comercial exterior de España (1931–1975)*, Banco Exterior de España, Madrid, 1979.

Culture: José Luis ABELLÁN, *De la guerra civil al exilio republicano (1936–1977)*, Mezquita, Madrid, 1982, and *El exilio español de 1939*, Taurus, Madrid, 1978–79; Miguel DELIBES, *La censura de prensa en los años cuarenta*, Ámbito, Valladolid, 1985; Elías DÍAZ, *Pensamiento español, 1939–1975*, Tecnos, Madrid, 1992; Equipo RESEÑA, *La cultura española bajo el franquismo*, Mensajero, Bilbao, 1977; Jordi GRÀCIA and Miguel Ángel RUIZ CARNICER, *La España de Franco (1939–1975). Cultura y vida cotidiana*, Síntesis, Madrid, 2001; José Carlos MAINER, *Falange y literatura*, Labor, Barcelona, 1971; J. M. MARTÍNEZ CACHERO, *La novela española entre 1939 y el fin del siglo. Historia de una aventura*, Castalia, Madrid, 1997; Gregorio MORÁN, *El maestro en el erial. Ortega y Gasset y la cultura del franquismo*, Tusquets, Barcelona, 1998; Javier VARELA, *La novela de España. Los intelectuales y el problema español*, Taurus, Madrid, 1999. Plastic arts and architecture: *Arte para después de una guerra*, Comunidad de Madrid, 1993–4; José CORREDOR MATEOS, *Vida y obra de Benjamín Palencia*, Espasa,

Madrid, 1979; Ángel LLORENTE, *Arte e ideología en la España de la posguerra, 1939–1951*, Doctoral Thesis presented at the Complutense University (Madrid) (undated); Gabriel UREÑA, *Arquitectura y urbanística civil y militar en el período de la autarquía, 1936–1945*, Istmo, Madrid, 1979, and *Las vanguardias artísticas en la posguerra española, 1940–1959*, Istmo, Madrid, 1982. Cinema: Valeria CAMPORESI, *Para grandes y chicos. Un cine para los españoles*, Turfan, Madrid, 1993; Félix FANES, *Cifesa. La antorcha de los éxitos*, Institució Alfons el Magnànim, Valencia, 1981.

Memoirs by intellectuals: Carlos BARRAL, *Años de penitencia*, Alianza, Madrid, 1975; José Manuel CABALLERO BONALD, *Tiempo de guerras perdidas*, Anagrama, Barcelona, 1995; Carlos CASTILLA DEL PINO, *Pretérito imperfecto*, Tusquets, Barcelona, 1997; Camilo José CELA, *Memorias, entendimientos y voluntades*, Plaza y Janés-Cambio 16, Barcelona, 1993; Fernando FERNÁN GÓMEZ, *El tiempo amarillo. Memorias*, Debate, Madrid, 1990; Julián MARÍAS, *Una vida presente. Memorias*, Alianza Editorial, Madrid, 1988–9.

The role of Catholicism in these years: Alfonso BOTTI, *Cielo y dinero. El nacionalcatolicismo en España (1881–1975)*, Alianza, Madrid, 1992; Gregorio CÁMARA, *Nacional-catolicismo y escuela. La socialización política del franquismo (1936–1951)*, Hesperia, Jaén, 1984.

# Notes

1 The National Electric Company PLC (*Empresa Nacional de Electricidad, sociedad anónima*) and the Ribagorzana National Hydroelectric Company (*Empresa Nacional Hidroeléctrica del Ribagorzana*).
2 *Tremendismo* was a movement that depicted the harshness of life in graphic detail.

# The Years of Consensus: The High Point of the Regime (1951–65)

The middle years of the history of Francoism may be described as years of plenitude and the high point of the regime. When applied to those years but not to others there is truth in the paradox that while the regime was indeed a dictatorship it enjoyed a sufficient level of acceptance – even if it was only passive acceptance – for it to be able to say that there was a consensus in Spanish society that believed it should remain in power. There is no need to stress that repression and the dismantling of the opposition sufficed to explain this situation. By 1951 Franco's regime had in effect survived the worst period of its existence, which was the years immediately following World War II due to simultaneous pressure from within with guerrilla resistance and from outside coercion. But throughout the 1940s Spain remained a personal dictatorship whose doctrine was hard to define and was, in the European context, a marginalized country which seemed doomed to remain underdeveloped.

In 1951, in contrast, it began to win recognition of its international status, which never went as far as full acceptance as an equal but was radically different to its previous situation. The new Concordat with the Holy See contributed hardly at all to existing relations between the two powers but the mere fact that it had been signed came to signal a kind of recognition and acknowledgment. Spain's pact with the United States revealed in the world number one power an emphasis on strategic rather than ideological factors, which was distinctly to Franco's advantage. Even Moroccan independence, which one would have supposed would prove critical in the life of the regime, was achieved without trauma.

To a great extent these changing circumstances were due to international factors that had nothing whatever to do with the wishes of the Spanish. To a lesser extent the regime's high point was a result of the collapse of the opposition, which would not regain its potential for action until Franco's death. The 1950s was the worst period in opposition history in which, in the case of the monarchists, it was reduced to collaboration with the regime, and for the left, to fragmentation and looking back to the past. During the years we are about to analyze an opposition force did arise among the children of the Civil War victors in 1956. Also for the first time, in 1962, when the European powers met in Munich it did seem that reconciliation might be possible between opposition forces within Spain and those in exile. However, these events did not so much have an immediate impact on Spanish politics as forewarn of what lay ahead.

The Franco regime still lacked proper institutionalization but rather than being a sign of weakness, that proved to be clear evidence of its adaptability. Falange's return to the forefront of Spanish politics did not mean that the regime came together under its guiding principles, as indeed became obvious in 1956–7. The subsequent *Ley de Principios del Movimiento* (Law on the Principles of the *Movimiento*) was imprecise but did point the way ahead towards a kind of dictatorship unlike the Falangist model.

The high point of the regime was also appreciable in relation to initiatives in Spain's economic policy. Furthermore, when the regime took steps to change direction on the economy, this had the effect of increasing social support even if such support remained passive. The image that foreign visitors had of Spain in the early years of Francoism was of a country that had been condemned to irremediable poverty. Economic growth in the period after 1948 was inflationary and unbalanced and only allowed Spain to move from being an agricultural nation to one that was semi-industrialized. However, in the 1950s, a process of growth began that could even be described as strong in the first half of the 1960s. This process initiated a decisive change in the course of Spain's history: surely the most far-reaching change that occurred in our country during the Franco regime. At the time, the economic transformation seemed only to produce political conformism. Yet with all the provisos that might be made, one can nonetheless say that for Franco these years, as the years before World War II had been for Mussolini, were "the years of consensus."

## The End of International Isolation: The Concordat and Pacts with the United States

The international situation, with the intensification of the cold war, had an immense influence on the survival of the dictatorship. Two events that coincided will suffice to show this clearly: first, at the very same moment at which conflict began in Korea in 1950, Spain embarked on a fast-moving process of international rehabilitation that climaxed in 1953: a crucial date in the Korean War and for pacts between Spain and the United States. It is therefore obvious that for the leading western world power strategic factors far outweighed political considerations and this paved the way – albeit in very particular circumstances – for Spain to regain a role in international politics.

If the isolation of the Franco regime had been secured by a series of measures which excluded it from international organizations (or applied vetoes), its rehabilitation was achieved by reversing the process. In November 1950 the recommendations contained in the 1946 resolution were revoked. At the same time Franco's Spain began once again to join United Nations agencies whose technical, rather than political, character allowed discussion of a political nature to be avoided. At the end of 1950 Spain became a member of the Food and Agriculture Organization (FAO); then came membership of the International Civil Aviation Organization and in 1952 it joined UNESCO. Spain's entry into the United Nations took longer to achieve because it required prior agreement between the two major powers to admit a group of nations with conflicting ideological tendencies. In November 1955 Spain presented its candidature, which received immediate support from the United States. It was admitted, along with another 15 nations, in mid December after a speech in favor from no lesser person than the Soviet representative. At the same time, however, there were those among the western block nations who abstained from voting in favor of its inclusion.

It is possible to say, then, that at this point in time Franco's Spain had been fully accepted by the international community because acceptance had been ensured by an indirect procedure: the signing at almost the very same moment of the Concordat with the Holy See in August 1953 and the pact with the United States just a month later. Although these two diplomatic agreements were reached for different reasons, what they had in common was that their ratification would have been inconceivable only a few years earlier.

What is most surprising about the Concordat with the Vatican, given the advantages gained by the Church, is the fact that the idea actually came from the Spanish state. It was Ruiz-Giménez, who had been sent as Spain's ambassador to the Vatican in 1948, who announced his wish to take this step, which would in his opinion serve to consolidate the role of Catholicism in Spanish society and would at the same time, by strengthening the position of the Church in relation to Francoism, ensure that it gained a large share of autonomy. It goes without saying that a stance such as this cannot be understood except within the context of the Catholic mentality of the time, which had strong leanings towards extreme orthodoxy. Yet the Vatican did not share its vision and nor did a Madrid which favored royal over ecclesiastical power and considered Ruiz-Giménez not so much Spain's ambassador to the Vatican as the Vatican's ambassador to Spain.

After 1951, when the ex-ambassador took on the Education portfolio, negotiations were left in the hands of his successor, Fernando María de Castiella. All negotiation was now a matter for the state as supreme authority, as was typical of the regime. After a given moment, in a cold war atmosphere, Rome's reticence vanished. When the Concordat was signed everyone was complimentary about the text, especially in Catholic circles close to the government. One specialist in canon law went so far as to say that it "conformed more than any other" to Catholic doctrine; another went even further and stated that the Spanish Concordat "was a triumph far greater than that of any Concordat with any other nation over all time, so much so that it was a shame that it could not serve as a pattern for all others because not all nations could bear such a noble burden." For the future minister Gonzalo Fernández de la Mora the signing of the Concordat had "a purely political impact; it provided weighty and definitive backing for the legitimacy of the Spanish state both in its origins and in its exercising of government; it was a demonstration of exemplary concord between two sovereign states one of which, with its supreme moral authority, could ensure the international rehabilitation of the Spanish state."

Of course, a statement such as this would not have been publicly approved by the Vatican but the Church did quite unequivocally give the impression that it supported the Franco regime politically, and it received numerous favors in exchange. Spain's religious unity was reaffirmed, though non-Catholics had the right to practice their faith in private. The Church would receive an endowment from the state which would be officially approved and backed up with tax exemptions. The religious orders were granted a legal status that they had never enjoyed before in Spain's entire history. There was recognition of an ecclesiastical charter of rights together with acknowledgment of the Church's authority in matters of matrimonial law; in addition, a calendar of liturgical festivals was agreed which were then made part of the secular calendar, and religious associations were granted approval so long as their activities remained limited in scope.

What the Spanish state gained in return was relatively little. The existing system for the appointment of bishops remained unchanged. Also, all who held positions of political authority were obliged to pray during public religious events. All this, together with the various pontifical and liturgical honors bestowed on Franco, were in fact little more than mere formalities, but even so the Concordat was a diplomatic triumph for the state. Although its text had nothing substantially new to add, it did give the appearance of closer agreement than had been evident in the state's early relationship with the Holy See. Nonetheless, the Concordat was anachronistic, even for the Spain of the time, in the sense that it looked back to the past rather than forward to the future. Very soon problems began to surface concerning the exact interpretation of its contents, such as those relating to the appointment of auxiliary bishops, and this issue would later allow the Church to free itself from state intervention. In the last analysis, the Concordat did little more than contribute towards lessening Franco's Spain's isolation from the international community, though this situation had largely been resolved already by changing circumstances.

Virtually the same could be said of Spain's treaties with the United States. When in 1945 pressure on the regime began to be applied, the Foreign Minister, Martín Artajo, sent Spain's representatives abroad instructions recommending that they should "wait until the corpse of those defeated in 1939 had passed by." It took a long time for this to happen. In 1950 the United States had begun to offer economic aid to a Communist country, Yugoslavia, whereas Spain had to await developments in the Korean conflict – so much so that negotiations already under way between Spain and the USA halted until the battlefront was established – and also until the Truman Administration had been replaced by that of Eisenhower. Truman had always had a strong allergy to all that Francoism represented and he placed obstacles in the path of any aid to Spain voted by the American government to prevent it ever getting through. An Anabaptist, he was seriously concerned about religious freedom in Spain. Nonetheless, in the early months of 1951 a clear change had already taken place in the stance adopted by America. Indeed, it is significant that in the closing months of 1950 the United States set up bases in French Morocco and the Portuguese Azores. If Spanish negotiators were concerned about economic issues, military matters were the major concern for the Americans.

Negotiations began on the pretext of a visit to Spain in July 1951 by General Sherman. By then, after the ratification of American proposals on bases on Spanish soil, the Spanish position was already clear. Franco stated that his country did not want to join NATO – in actual fact he was well aware that this was not even possible – but that it was prepared to fight against the Soviet enemy on the European front. When discussion moved on to consider terms in greater detail, it became obvious that the discrepancy between the two countries was considerable: the United States wanted land to be ceded to them while the Spaniards preferred bases for joint use. In Spain's case representatives of the Armed Services appear to have played a greater role in the negotiations than diplomats. It was perfectly obvious anyway that the degree of recognition accorded to Franco's Spain proved in practice to be less than had been hoped for by those in positions of power in the regime. Carrero Blanco, for example, stated quite rightly that as regards America Spain "received entirely different treatment" from that accorded to other European countries. The truth is, however, that given the difficulties in the way of any closer agreement, Franco's representative recommended signing without delay that very year: 1952. It may well be that a delay would have been advantageous to Spanish interests but there was also a political advantage to be gained from a decision being taken quickly.

There is no clearer proof of the difference in treatment just mentioned than the details of the conditions laid down by both countries. What was signed concerned three agreements relating to defense and economic aid. "Agreement" is the term applied in American constitutional terminology to pacts signed by the executive powers that do not require ratification by the legislative assembly. In the legislative assembly, however great an interest the Pentagon took in the matter, it would have been beyond the bounds of possibility for any commitment ever to be agreed on with a regime that had maintained relations with the Axis powers. The pacts allowed for joint use of a series of bases over a period of 10 years and they would be renewable for a further 2 to 5 years. The bases would be built at Rota, Morón, Zaragoza, and Torrejón. The American garrisons on these bases were relatively small in number: some 6,700 men who, together with the civilian population, would reach a total of 15,000 (in 1958). An additional factor relating to these pacts was a commitment on the part of the Spaniards to stabilize the peseta and balance the budget, which meant a reciprocal obligation for the Americans to help Spain in material terms. On this issue there has not to date been sufficient emphasis placed on the significant role played by America in the transformation of Spanish economic policy.

The best description of the contents of the pacts that were signed may well be the one given by Franco himself when he stated that they were "military in origin with political consequences and definite implications for the economy." This is not the right moment to engage with this last aspect; suffice it to say at this stage that even though American aid to Spain was substantially less than that given to other countries, it was nonetheless of crucial importance. From a strategic point of view European defense acquired support and a weight that it had lacked previously, but advances in technology and strategy soon meant that a good number of Spanish bases became superfluous to requirements. In the medium term Rota was the most valuable acquisition for American and western defenses because it could provide logistical support for nuclear submarines. For its part, Franco's Spain won above all a diplomatic victory. That triumph meant that Spain won recognition for its contribution to the defense of the west, the start of an aid program, United States interest in political stability in Spain, and last of all the continuation – at least in theory – of overall military command on the bases.

Strictly speaking, the pacts also had clear disadvantages due to the glaring lack of equality in the treatment Spain received. The terms relating to the use of the bases by the Americans were very imprecise, as were the conditions that the Americans must fulfill. Spain did not get any explicit guarantee concerning her own defense, had no control over operations mounted from within Spanish territory, and, in addition, it was dependent as regards the actual functioning of economic aid on the allocation of funds voted by the United States Congress. Spain suffered the disadvantage of being a potential object of reprisals for the simple reason that the bases were within its territory, and in exchange it did not gain any of the advantages that might have accrued had it been viewed as an equal by its allies. All in all, nothing altered the substantial differences between the two countries in terms of their political structures. In the United States the alliance with Franco's Spain moved from being hugely unpopular to being merely not very popular.

With this as a starting-point, one can well imagine that the next few years saw an upsurge of countless causes for friction between the two nations. They related in the first instance to questions of compensation by the Americans. The Spanish authorities do not seem to have been aware initially of the dangers of a nuclear threat for centers of population near the bases, though these soon became evident. When in 1962 the renewal of the treaties was negotiated, Spain did not gain any advantage other than a vague allusion to the fact that there would be consultation in the event of any threat from outside. Differences in treatment were also evident in the matter of resources allocated to Spain by the United States. The Spanish Army relied on material from America, though this served only to prevent it falling even further behind in technical terms; also Spain did receive economic aid but this was incomparably less than what it would have received under the Marshall Plan. Figures show that it achieved little in comparison with other European countries. Between 1946 and 1960, Spain received 456 million dollars in military aid, which was a tenth of what France got, a quarter of what went to Italy and Turkey, and half of what was sent to Luxemburg. Over the same period economic aid was around 1,013 million dollars – a figure lower than that received by Holland or Turkey and only a fifth of aid to France, a seventh of that given to Britain, and a quarter of what Germany managed to obtain. Under conditions such as these it is not at all surprising that relations with the United States were constantly plagued by misunderstandings, for all their calm appearance. In 1959 the President of the United States, General Eisenhower, with whom Franco seemed to have some affinity, visited Spain. However, the affinity proved insufficient to ensure that Spain was treated as an equal. In the course of the next renewal of the pacts in 1963 Spain managed to obtain one aircraft-carrier but did not see any sign of the status of relations between the two countries being raised to that of a proper treaty.

## ——  Spain and Europe: Colonization of Morocco Ends  ——

As far as the Americans were concerned, Franco's Spain was a far-off land whose development was not a subject on which for the most part the general public was kept informed since its only importance for the United States was strategic. In contrast, this was never the case in the democratic countries of Europe where the memory of the Spanish Civil War continued to be an important consideration in internal politics. Economic interests, realism in terms of recognition that Spain's opposition was unlikely to achieve much, and the realization that a blockade was a bad method to use to achieve a good result are all factors that go some way towards explaining why relations between Franco's Spain and other European countries were maintained. However, that is not to say that Franco's Spain was accepted as one of those countries. It was always seen as a chronic invalid whose eventual recovery might just happen in the distant future. In complete contrast to this vision from outside Spain, the regime considered itself stable and well satisfied, and it would continue to be so at least until 1964: the year in which Spain celebrated 25 years of peace. Many people saw Franco as the supreme guarantor that there would be no more conflict.

Relations with other countries depended to a great extent on the make-up of their governments. Two clear examples of how huge a gulf could divide even two conservative governments are France and Germany, whose two leaders, De Gaulle and Adenauer, were in favor of Spain joining the Common Market at the start of the 1960s. Nevertheless, the Spanish ambassador in the French capital, José María Areilza, encountered serious difficulties in official Spanish circles concerned that he should not offer help in any obvious way to anyone trying to destabilize the Fifth Republic. As for the Federal Republic of Germany, Spain established relations with it in the spring of 1951 but a year went by before Adenauer sent an ambassador to Madrid. In early 1960 Germany tried to reach an agreement with Spain on military facilities but it was enough for the international press to get wind of it for the possibility to vanish.

What was far more significant than these factors was what happened to Spain when moves were made to form a Common Market. At the start of the 1950s, when the Americans asked Franco what he thought about European unity, he replied that he detected socialist leanings in everyone who was working towards that unity. In March 1957, before the signing of the Treaty of Rome which brought the Common Market into being, there were ten European regional organizations and Spain belonged to only three of them. A country such as Austria, which at that time had a singularly curious neutral status, was a member of five and even Turkey was in seven. The paradox is that at this time Spain was already sending 61 percent of its exports to Europe.

At a time when the creation of more economic open spaces in Europe could be glimpsed on the horizon, the regime's reaction was hesitant and it finally opted for a long period of waiting. At the heart of the regime there were those who were not ready to accept the obvious fact that Spain needed some form of integration in, and association with, Europe. In Falangist circles, for example, a kind of "Ibero-market" was favored, though in fact it was not viable because the Spanish and Latin-American economies did not in any way complement each other. What weighed more heavily still was the fact that the leaders of the regime had strong political reservations about a united Europe. Carrero Blanco, for example, was of the opinion that economic cooperation would inevitably lead to political submission; he foresaw a world controlled by international companies and this vision, colored by conspiracy theory, always raised the specter of imminent danger for Spanish interests. Franco shared this view but, being more pragmatic, judged that "it would punish Spaniards of this generation and the next" if Spain had no contact at all with the Common Market.

However, the driving force behind relations with the Common Market was principally a new generation of politicians, characterized by their professional experience in economic and diplomatic affairs, who had no political program other than a shared realism. And so, along paths that at times coincided and were certainly tortuous, chosen by the Ministries for Foreign Affairs and Trade, a way ahead for a decision to be reached was opened up in about 1957. After 1960 Spain had diplomatic representation in the Common Market. For its part, Alberto Ullastres's trade policy, presented by the Trade Ministry, aimed initially to open up the way ahead by means of bilateral pacts. The pressures of the actual circumstances at the time made themselves felt. After 1955 Spanish diplomats began to realize that the Organization for European Economic Cooperation (OEEC) was "the only means of gaining entry into" Europe. In the second half of 1958 Spain became a member both of this organization, then known as the OECD (Organization for Economic Cooperation and Development), and of the International Monetary Fund, and this had important consequences for the formulation of a new economic policy. The decision to seek entry to the Common Market itself was finally taken in 1962.

At that same time Franco's Spain had begun to face new problems in the context of international relations, such as the question of decolonization. In this respect it had always shown quite clearly that it was out of touch with the spirit of the age, which explains why its achievements so far had been distinctly unsatisfactory, as is evident in the case of Morocco.

As we have already shown, Franco's Spain, even during its worst period of isolation, had kept up contact with Arab countries and continued to do so after 1951, as is evident from a visit that Martín Artajo made to some of those countries in 1952. In recognition of the part played by Moroccan troops in his Army during the Civil War, Franco made vague promises to the effect that the Moroccans would receive "the finest roses from the rose-garden of peace." After World War II the education system set up in Spanish Morocco used Arabic primarily, whereas the French zone prioritized the use of French. In contrast to what was happening to the south of

Morocco and in Spain itself, within the Spanish protectorate there was freedom of the press and for political parties. Franco was always able to use the fact that Spain had high-ranking officers such as General Mohammed Mizzian, who had been born in Morocco, as an argument in support of his policy, but as he did not entirely trust Mizzian he put him in charge of the Captaincy General in Galicia in the far north of Spain.

Initially, demands for independence in these circumstances did not come from within the Spanish protectorate but from French Morocco. From 1947 onwards the French authorities had had serious trouble with the Sultan Mohammed V who had not forgotten the promises of independence made by the Americans in 1943. In 1952 and 1953 violent incidents caused hundreds of deaths. The Palestinian question was no longer in the forefront of international relations and instead the problem of Moroccan independence became the most urgent issue still to be resolved. Restlessness increased in the Arab world as a whole, as is evident in the proclamation of the Republic of Egypt and in the struggle for independence in Algeria.

The moment of crisis in Spanish politics came when on the one hand the demands of the nationalists intensified, and at the same time it became obvious that Spain was out of tune with the other colonial power: France. Morocco had continued to be an economic burden for Spain to bear but it had not yet posed any problems in terms of public order or uprisings. In 1952 the Spanish protectorate gave a degree of autonomy to the indigenous population which seemed to conflict with policy in the French protectorate. The indigenous authorities in the Spanish zone played with various options and finally chose nationalism. The gravest problems emerged after 1953, at which time the policy of the Spanish government was rash and came to a bad end. In that year, the French expelled the Sultan Mohammed V and replaced him with a colorless character who supported them. The Spanish reaction was of indignation. The Spaniard in charge at the time was General Rafael García Valiño, whose policy was always firm but daring. On hearing that the Sultan had been dethroned, the Spanish general declared: "They have entirely ignored our presence in this area . . . it seems unlikely that in the future there will be a climate of confidence to facilitate collaboration." Spain continued to recognize the authority of the Caliph appointed by Mohammed V in the Spanish protectorate and also backed the setting up of Moroccan nationalist propaganda organizations in its territory. This policy was, it appears, a joint decision by Franco and García Valiño; nonetheless, there were also significant differences between them. García Valiño, for example, did not hesitate in adopting a permissive stance on the selling of arms to the nationalists. Franco considered sacking him but finally decided against it.

The failure of Spanish policy was already apparent by the time the French suddenly changed their approach. Though France was in fact much more deeply concerned about Algeria than Morocco, in 1955 it accepted a transitional formula – "interdependence" – and, at the end of that year, allowed Mohammed V to return to his country. In March 1956 France finally accepted Moroccan independence and Spain was obliged to do the same the following month. If for its neighbor this had not meant very much, for Spain it undoubtedly meant a lot more because of the constant Moroccan demands concerning land that Spain considered Spanish. On the very same day that the Spanish Head of state accepted Moroccan independence he also contacted the Americans to say that the new situation represented a grave danger because he saw the spread of communist ideology as inevitable.

However, the Moroccan question was not resolved by the declaration of independence. The new nation, like so many others, adopted a nationalistic political stance right from the outset. Eight of its ministers belonged to the Istiqlal party, one of whose ideologues, Allal al-Fasi, backed the idea of a larger Morocco that would encompass the entire Sahara. In addition, in the south of the country a so-called National Liberation Army was active which in actual fact consisted of independent factions in part armed with weapons kindly provided by the Spanish authorities of the Protectorate. In November 1957 there were armed clashes in Ifni and the northern Sahara (only a month before, at the UN, Morocco had demanded control of the Tarfaya area) and many small Spanish positions had fallen to these armed groups. It may indeed have been an exaggeration to say that what happened was a "little Annual",[1] for casualties were no more than two or three hundred dead. With French help the Spanish managed to stabilize the situation in the Sahara, though they were less successful in Ifni. In February 1958 it became possible to initiate talks with the Moroccans in the Portuguese city of Cintra, as a result of which, at the end of the year, the Tarfaya area was handed over to Morocco.

Despite this development Morocco continued to press its demands for repossession of Ifni, the Sahara, and the two Spanish sovereign enclaves of Ceuta and Melilla. Only as late as 1968 would Ifni be handed over, by which time it was of little interest anyway. Decolonization of Morocco only came about because pressure was brought to bear on Spain, and even then the result was never satisfactory for either party, which meant that collaboration with Spain was not at all good in the years that followed. The mistakes made by the French were worse at first, but France's material wealth made later collaboration between the metropolis and its former colony possible. From that point on, Franco, and even more so Carrero Blanco, was reluctant to make the move towards decolonization, which was put off for as long as possible. In 1960 there was still a substantial Spanish garrison in Moroccan territory, whereas the French had already entirely abandoned the country; the Spanish would only do so finally in 1961. Franco could do nothing whatever to prevent his allies, the Americans, providing arms for Morocco, which eventually meant a dangerous strategic situation for Spain.

In contrast to what went on in Africa, in Latin America the Franco regime's foreign policy was more original and better adapted to circumstances. The stance adopted on the Cuban revolution was not conservative and did not fall in line with United States policy. Spain's presence was palpable in Cuban society through its religious institutions. When Cuban Catholics joined the opposition, the Spanish Ambassador Juan Pablo Lojendio afforded protection to many of who were persecuted in the last days of the Bautista regime. When the new regime in turn began to take repressive action – notably against Catholics – there was a major clash between no lesser personage than Castro and Lojendio in January 1960. Although the ambassador was forced to leave Cuba, diplomatic relations were not broken off and Spain did not take part in the economic blockade instigated by the Americans. The Spanish stance shows, therefore, that the Franco regime was capable of a certain ideological ambiguity in international affairs. If decolonization of its own territories must have been seen by many in high places as a tragedy, the Falangists, unlike the United Kingdom and France, rejoiced to see a nationalist leader triumph rather than a democrat such as Nasser.

## The Regime and the Opposition up to 1956

Having reached this point we should once again consider the evolution of Spain's internal politics, which did not undergo any major changes in the period under discussion: a telling fact in itself. The opposition showed no signs of being ready for action until the middle of the 1950s and circumstances outside Spain did not provide any pressure for change as they had done in 1945. One might even say that the crisis in 1956 was only partial and due to one simple incident, though it is certainly the case that it would have profound repercussions on the emergence of a new Spanish opposition. There would be no crisis that was more than a "changing of the guard" until 1957.

Mention has already been made of the ministerial reshuffle of 1951 which saw the greatest changes ever made in the history of the regime. Although as ever they were the result of Franco's arbitration in balancing up conflicting tendencies within his government, they did mean – to an extent at least – that Falange returned to the political stage. In fact, not only was the organization represented in the cabinet by Girón, Fernández Cuesta, and Muñoz Grandes, but the post of General Secretary of the *Movimiento* was officially reestablished – a job which, in effect, Fernández Cuesta had done since 1948, controlling Falange while at the same time combining this mission with the Justice portfolio. Furthermore, this is not the only evidence we have of Falange's evolution from 1951 on; it also held its one and only Congress in October 1953, showing an entire lack of reticence about making its presence felt in public. Falange's increasing influence was also obvious in the weakening of the other regime "families." In 1954 Falange used all its power and influence to prevent several front-line candidates winning the municipal elections held that year, while the role of political figures who were members of Catholic organizations (Martín Artajo and Ruiz-Giménez) was basically limited to carrying out the ministerial duties incumbent upon them. In theory the Party had 2 million members but only some tens of thousands of these were politically active: perhaps fewer than those belonging to Catholic organizations. Falange controlled a bare 1 percent of the budget, while the Home Office controlled 10 percent. In other words, what was most significant at this point was the single Party's visibility rather than its actual power.

One figure who remained in the shadows only to emerge later as a powerful influence was Carrero Blanco, who became a minister for the first time in 1951. In reality Carrero wanted to take advantage of these governmental changes not to bring Falange back into power but rather the exact opposite: that is to say, to pension it off. "The Girón phase," he wrote, "is now over," but the Labor Minister would remain in place until 1957. If Carrero was listened to on the matter of removing Fernández Cuesta from the Justice Ministry, he was ignored on the suppression of the post of general secretary of the *Movimiento*. It is significant that Carrero Blanco approved of the Home Office taking over the regime's political institutions, but of far greater interest than all that he advised against is what he proposed, which would only be implemented 6 years later. He was concerned about Spain's economic policy and his stance on it was very different from that of the majority of the government up to that point. "What really matters is that it should be effective," he pointed out, adding "What would be ideal would be for private enterprise to do whatever is necessary." This, as one would expect, brought him into confrontation with Suances who, in Carrero's view, deserved "severe criticism" for his pushy attitude and failure to accomplish tasks committed to his charge. It may well be that Carrero's intervention was responsible for Suances quitting the Ministry for Industry, but he did not leave the INI; Carrero may also have been behind the appointment of certain ministers to posts in economic affairs. Whether or not this is the case, it was not until 1957 that the aims of this trend were fulfilled. What is obvious is that the mind of the sub-secretary to the presidency, though eager for effective action, was very different from the classic mentality of the market economy: he thought that he could solve the problem of monopolies by sending offenders to work camps.

One or two other aspects of Carrero's position should be mentioned at this point. Nervous because of the opposition that had reared its head once again in 1951 in mass actions such as the Barcelona Tram Strike, Carrero proposed a general, Alonso Vega, to take on a Home Office post of responsibility for public order. Another general, Jorge Vigón, could take on foreign policy. Finally, one question which for the moment did not bother Carrero concerned the institutional mechanisms of the regime: "The regime has now totally and finally taken shape," he affirmed. It is also worth noting that Franco was a stronger supporter than Carrero of Falange which, now tamed, was proving useful in serving his aims.

We should now consider the running of the 1951 government, though economic factors will be discussed later. It was Joaquín Ruiz-Giménez who, as a minister, caused most political controversy, not so much because of what he said as because of the reaction of groups opposed to his ideas. Ruiz-Giménez was at the time the most important young member of the regime's Catholic family and it was this that led him to make up his ministerial team with figures who, at least in part, were of Falange. The combination of the cultural "liberalism" of this group – in the sense of its desire to prove its openness to intellectuals on the left – with the Ministry of Education's usual financial problems and also with the reactionary nature of the most strongly clericalist sectors in power made Ruiz-Giménez's

Administration controversial and brought it to an abrupt end. The only surprise here is that its demise came about through confrontation with the most hard-line sector of Falange and not with the most strongly clericalist elements in cultural affairs.

Difficulties arose early on for Ruiz-Giménez, initially linked to the approval of the Law on Secondary Education which provoked strong protest from those in the clericalist camp who were of the opinion that it would "cut the throat" of secondary education in religious schools. The law was passed in February 1953 but only after facing a hard battle. Even so, this was nothing compared to the problems that faced any attempt to open Spain up culturally. As has already been suggested, Ruiz-Giménez had relied on figures in university circles who favored such a policy: Pedro Laín Entralgo, Antonio Tovar, and Torcuato Fernández Miranda, the vice-chancellors of the Universities of Madrid, Salamanca, and Oviedo, and indeed on the Director General for Universities, Joaquín Pérez Villanueva. The policies adopted on universities were of no great import but in practice they signaled the advent of a kind of cultural openness that was extremely influential. The three vice-chancellors mentioned above and the Falange youth press, inspired in great part by Dionisio Ridruejo, tried to revive the Spanish liberal intellectual tradition of the turn of the century (more specifically that of Unamuno and Ortega, its emblematic leading figures). From an intellectual point of view this revival of an important aspect of Spain's pre-Civil War cultural life was an important – perhaps even irreversible – move, but it would be wrong to suggest in any way that these groups wanted to break with the regime; rather, they were a particular part of it characterized by their secular nature and the attraction of the objective quality of their cultural tradition. They nonetheless had some formidable enemies in the most strongly clericalist circles which followed in the footsteps of Ramiro de Maeztu and *Acción Española*.

Controversy had first arisen on cultural issues when Laín Entralgo and Calvo Serer published two books at the end of the 1940s and start of the 1950s. The most traditional right-wing groups, associated with Opus Dei by their opponents, had a firm foothold in the Ministry of Tourism and Information and the Atheneum in the person of Florentino Pérez Embid, and also in the National Scientific Research Council (CSIC). The most combative representative of this tendency was Rafael Calvo Serer. The group's approach was very different from that of the supposedly "liberal" Falange: they loathed liberal culture and considered their opponents' stance both collaborationist and revolutionary at the same time. However, as this extreme traditional right-wing group was also Monarchist, paradoxically it favored a formula that might open the way to replacing the Franco regime.

Friction between these two factions was glaringly obvious in 1951, 1952, and 1953 but it came to an abrupt halt in the closing months of 1953, probably because Franco himself intervened. Calvo Serer published an article in a French periodical in which he denounced the Falangists as "revolutionary opportunists" and condemned "compliant Christian-Democrats" such as Ruiz-Giménez. For this he was sent into temporary exile. In the Falange Congress already mentioned, a "third force" that Calvo Serer had identified with his own stance was openly ridiculed.

Yet the failure of one of the two parties in the dispute did not mean victory for the other; rather, both ended up suffering the same fate. After the end of 1953, any worthwhile intellectual debate in various cultural publications on both sides was silenced. Moreover, a biting attack on Unamuno by the Bishop of Las Palmas resulted in the cancellation of an act of homage that was being organized in Unamuno's honor. Despite the fact that Franco was given a doctorate *honoris causa* by the University of Salamanca – a title that he received with visible emotion – his attitude towards the worlds of culture and intellectualism remained cautious and reticent. That attitude effectively blocked most of Ruiz-Giménez's attempts to incorporate into the teaching body any who had a Republican past.

The upsurge of a certain amount of student agitation in 1954 on the issue of the British presence in Gibraltar, the existence of cultural clubs under the aegis of the Spanish University Students' Union (SEU), and the show of solidarity with Ortega y Gasset on the occasion of his death in October 1955 were three catalysts which produced a situation that would become positively explosive in the early months of 1956. Yet we should note that the burning questions about the structure of the regime which had dogged public life from 1945 to 1951 were no longer seen as relevant, perhaps because Franco considered them resolved or because he did not even wish to address them having achieved his main aim: that is, to remain in power. During the last months of 1955 there seemed to be no reason to anticipate any trouble but events in fact led to a double confrontation: on the one hand at the heart of the regime and on the other among a section of university students at the same time.

By this point the republican option had ceased to be viable and any opportunity the monarchist cause might ever have had no longer existed. There were monarchists who had liberal inclinations but were not exactly democratic, such as those who, in the municipal elections in Madrid in 1954, voted against the official *Movimiento* candidate. However, on the whole, the tendency to go along with the regime was strong at the time. When the moment came to decide where Don Juan Carlos was to study, the decision was made by Franco himself who at the same time had no hesitation in stating that he might well consider the possibility of the succession passing down the line of Don Juan's older brother, Don Jaime. During the conversation that took place between Franco and Don Juan at Las Fincas at the end of 1954 the two men seemed to share the same views. However, the monarchist collaboration with the regime only reached its peak in 1955 when in certain declarations attributed to Don Juan the heir to the royal line appeared in public praising Fernández Cuesta and speaking of the need to come together in a "tight bunch" in order to protect existing political institutions. It was only from this moment on that collaborationist support that had in effect meant total support for the person of Franco himself was withdrawn.

If this was the situation among those who had in the past nourished the strongest hopes on the matter of replacing the Franco regime, how much worse was the situation of those in opposition who had seen the great opportunities of the period from 1945 to 1947 vanish without trace. This was the case for the Socialist party, whose membership outside Spain dwindled substantially over the 1950s: the number of sections represented at conferences organized by the General Workers' Union (*Unión General de Trabajadores* or UGT) in exile totaled 469 in 1951 and only 186 in 1959. At the same time, uncertainty on strategy grew. The failure of the monarchists' policy of collaboration with the regime led to an "isolation cure" from 1952 on, but the party was aware that it needed to work together with other options, which meant that the years that followed saw a constant weaving and unpicking of attempts to do so.

The main leader of the PSOE in exile after the start of the 1950s was Rodolfo Llopis, who came from the left of the party but would end up becoming, in the eyes of the new generations inside Spain, the very epitome of conformity. A fairer judgment from a historical point of view would point out that it was Llopis who also managed outside Spain to sustain a structure capable of bridging the gap between the party's historic tradition and these same new generations. Indeed, he did so by effecting considerable transformations in the party's basic approach, though more in practice than in theory. This is perfectly evident and can even be seen in those leading lights of the party who, throughout the 1930s, had adopted a more radical stance. Such was the case, for example, for Araquistain, whose ideological trajectory shifted from a deeply felt anti-communist position to one favoring a reversion to democracy that allowed for a certain openness on the matter of the regime.

As for the Spanish Communist Party, one has to consider, along with the defeat of the guerrilla resistance to the regime and the impossibility of linking up with other opposition groups during those years, the continuing Stalinist purges and the apathy displayed by Vicente Uribe between 1952 and 1954. The target for expulsions was a central committee made up of 65 members of whom 27 had already been expelled from Spain by this time. Then at last the party's Fifth Congress held in Prague in November 1954 saw a leadership reshuffle and support given to those sectors who had come through from the Socialist youth movements (Santiago Carrillo, Fernando Claudín, and Ignacio Gallego).

At the same time, even if there was a reshuffle of the Communist Party leadership, the same cannot be said of its understanding of what was happening in Spain. During the party conference the suggestion was made that an Anti-Francoist National Front (*Frente Nacional Antifran-quista*) should be formed, whose aim would be to create a provisional revolutionary government which would follow a program intended to bring about the disappearance of the "last remains of feudalism" in the country. As a result the communists failed to anticipate the process of economic development that would shortly be under way in Spain. In their minds – in their imaginations – the memory of Spain's republican phase and the conviction that a regime such as that of Franco could suddenly collapse remained strong. Reality would soon show that Spanish society could evolve without that affecting the political system in the least in the short term.

It seems obvious in the light of this overview of the opposition between 1951 and 1954 that this was the period when its chances of success were fewest. Nonetheless, in February 1956 it was clear that this did not mean that the opposition was going to vanish; rather, it was in fact seen to have enough potential to manage to reshape itself, even if this was a result of the stance taken by a section of society and not by what the leadership wanted. What happened that month should not be exaggerated to such an extent as to suggest that there was ever any real threat to the regime. It was not only the new student opposition that played a part in events; what occurred was also due in large part to developments within the regime itself.

Up until this moment the attitude of specifically student groups had not played a significant role in political opposition to the regime. The events of February 1956, however, involved students from the social classes that supported the regime, though several interpretations of what happened were possible. First, there were dissident Falangists who acted with the support of the SEU in some institutions, such as the University Employment Service (*Servicio Universitario del Trabajo*), and of some periodicals. The official students' union, which still had considerable influence at the time, organized demonstrations to protest against the British presence in Gibraltar but then it could not control them. Disaffected monarchist students also joined in and there was undoubtedly an upsurge of religious fervor that would have a significant political impact, which was seen in those who gathered around the priest Father José María Llanos,[2] who were initially Falangists and then later Communists. There was in fact communist agitation during the protest due to infiltration by a handful of militants but it was only minor.

In 1955 the press in exile realized that there was ferment in Spanish university circles but only in the closing months of that year did any direct clashes between students and the regime take place. The first incidents occurred on the occasion of the death of Ortega y Gasset whose liberal tradition some students wished to continue. Activities of a literary nature (such as plans for a conference of young writers) served to bring together students and some Francoist leaders such as Dionisio Ridruejo who now adopted a more dissident stance. The leaders of the student protests (Javier Pradera and Enrique Múgica) were communists who turned what was initially disaffected cultural ferment into a more clearly political protest, pushing for a Student Congress entirely separate from the official students' union.

At the start of February 1956 a collection of signatures in support of setting up the Congress caused the first incidents involving Falangist students, who retaliated by attacking the Law Faculty at Madrid's Complutense University. The fiercest confrontation resulted in a serious bullet wound for one young Falangist, inflicted by a member of his own side wielding a gun. This event resulted in the immediate arrest of Ridruejo and the dissident students. For a few days political tensions were so high in Spain's capital that several senior academic authority figures had to go into hiding to avoid being targeted in Falangist reprisals. Most important of all, however, was the fact that actions carried out by the opposition had an immediate impact on Spain's internal politics. This was the first occasion on which anything like this had happened since the earlier disturbances in Begoña[3] had been caused by militants from within the regime. Unlike what had happened on that occasion, it seems that Franco did not hesitate for one moment.

In the circumstances the dictator followed his usual strategy of arbitration. Ruiz-Giménez represented an openness that had caused conflict; he had also not proved capable – because he lacked the means – of tackling the deficiencies in public sector education or bringing private and religious schools to heel. Falange's main spokesman (and at the same time its controller) was Fernández Cuesta. Both men were dismissed immediately. Such was not the case with Blas Pérez who was in charge of public order which was under threat at the time. The marginalization of both contenders, as had been the case in 1942 with Varela and Serrano, proved in the short term to be to Falange's advantage since it meant that Arrese was once more given a ministerial post. From that time on, there would be no more cultural openness within the regime, or at least only in areas that were specifically designated (cinematography) or uncontroversial (painting), unless it occurred outside the framework of the regime or indeed in opposition to it. If in the past Francoism had enjoyed the support of intellectuals, most of that was now lost, though attitudes remained passive rather than openly confrontational. In political terms, it would perhaps be wrong to exaggerate the effect of these events on life within the regime. If Ridruejo chose the path of opposition, the same cannot be said for Ruiz-Giménez whose ideas would only take a similar turn much later on as a result of the impact of Vatican II. In fact the significance of the events of February 1956 was only relative. The political life of the regime continued on its way, unaffected by attempts to achieve a greater degree of cultural openness.

It was nonetheless at this moment perhaps that a definitive image of Franco emerged that is worth discussing at this point because it remained so until the time of his death. It was no longer the image of the man who had won the Civil War, nor even of the one who, according to regime propaganda, had kept Spain out of World War II; it now was also the image of the man whose vigilance could ensure that discord would never return to Spain, even at the heart of the regime. Official propaganda instructions relating to the cinema news documentaries or NODO (*Noticiario y Documentales*) stipulated that "all news items about the *caudillo* or in which he takes a leading part should appear at the end of the newsreel and if possible provide a final apotheosis." Franco, even more than a leader, seemed to have become a kind of paternalistic guardian protecting Spain from the inclemencies of that national evil: discord.

The repercussions of the events of February 1956 had a far greater impact on the opposition, particularly in the long term. In the weeks that followed, demonstrations and arrests continued; the defense lawyers acting on behalf of the detainees were often prominent members of the opposition such as Gil Robles. Yet very soon student protest died down and it is probably true to say that until well on into the 1960s the universities generally conformed. However, those who did not swelled the ranks of an opposition that would in time become influential in university circles. Not long afterwards, when Franco was talking with Don Juan about Don Juan's son's education inside Spain, he mentioned the presence at university of those he called "rowdy and troublesome." In fact, in student circles political groups were forming that would play an important political role later on. First and foremost there was the Socialist Association (*Agrupación Socialista* or ASU) which was never very large and did not last long (it disappeared in 1962), but what was important about it was that it was the means by which figures who were destined to play significant roles with greater strategic flexibility were allowed to make their appearance on the political stage. So it was that the young members of the ASU were in favor of approaches being made to Don Juan and to the Spanish Communist party at the same time: attitudes that were sheer heresy in terms of traditional socialism and even more so if they were combined. The same was true of the other opposition groups that emerged at this point.

## A New Political Opposition

In the interests of cohesion it would be better to continue with our discussion of the opposition before moving on to consider the evolution of the regime. It is important to remember that the political groups who will be mentioned here were tiny – so much so that it is almost flattery to call them parties at all. Yet they did represent something new that would bear fruit in due season. Those involved with opposition groups have contrasted the figure of Indalecio Prieto, "his face drowned in sadness," with the "ethical men" of the new opposition who acted on principle but also felt a "fascination with danger faced knowingly." The role played by the opposition in Spanish life would doubtless be greater in the period after 1965 but its starting-point was now.

The newest development in the period after 1956 was the appearance of an opposition inside Spain which had little to do either with prewar opposition groups or with groups in exile. They can be viewed as the seed-bed for what would in the final years of the Franco regime be termed the "moderate opposition." Strictly speaking, it was not because this opposition looked kindly on the dictatorship but because it did not aim to use violence and it did not demand the return of the long-gone legitimate prewar government. It was more a matter of groups with largely centrist tendencies against whom on the whole the fiercest repressive measures were never used; rather, they were viewed as having a paralegal status based on the understanding that they would in no way harm the regime. The forerunners of this kind of opposition can be found in the circles that gathered around Don Juan. After all, since the monarchy was supposed to draw all elements together, its aim continued to be to maintain the "dual role" it had had in 1945, which meant drawing people from the right and left together to share in a common purpose.

Don Juan did not repeat the statements that in 1951 and 1955 had led to him being identified with Francoism, but by maintaining a collaborationist stance he finally managed at the end of 1957 to draw into his camp a section of the Carlist cause. This closer association with the right did not prevent him keeping contact with the left-wing opposition or having occasional disagreements with Franco. In March 1960 Franco and Don Juan met and talked for the third time, once again focusing on the matter of Don Juan Carlos's education. In fact the lack of any real understanding between the two men is evident in Franco's repeated attempts to discredit Don Juan's advisers, whom he branded as Masons, and also to impose what were in effect guardians to watch out for his own interests.

Ambivalence on the form the monarchy might take was especially obvious at the start of the 1960s. So, for example, the wedding of Don Juan Carlos to Princess Sofia in Athens (1962) was organized without the regime playing any part at all in the proceedings. In 1961 the most notable representative of the monarchist cause in Spain was José María Pemán in the position of President of the Cabinet (*Consejo privado*). José María Pemán, an intellectual without any political pretensions who came from the extreme right but had liberal tendencies, was at that time Spain's most renowned man of letters. Favoring the institutionalization of the regime and a monarchy that would work with it, he realized that the monarchy would have to be accepted by the anti-Francoist opposition as well. Perhaps acting on his advice, Don Juan tried to build bridges between the monarchy and liberal intellectuals and he had some success: in 1958 he even visited Juan Ramón Jiménez, that most outstanding of Spain's cultural figures in exile.

Most of the groups that made up the new opposition that emerged after 1956 gravitated towards the monarchist opposition. The most surprising case was the group inspired by Dionisio Ridruejo, named Democratic Action (*Acción Democrática*). In fact Ridruejo had been gradually distancing himself from the regime, after an orthodox start, because he believed that it was not Falangist enough. However, after the events at the universities he increasingly favored democracy as an alternative to Francoism. Blessed with a gift for words and a brilliant intellectual who was warm, effusive, and charming, he could in time have played a key role in drawing the opposition together. His political affiliation never went beyond a left-wing liberalism. What was most significant about Ridruejo's position was that it represented in effect a turnaround of Copernican proportions for a man who had once been one of the main leaders of Falange. His position had also changed on the monarchy, which at one time he had considered a reactionary symbol.

If Ridruejo was a newcomer to the monarchist camp whose presence there seemed almost accidental, other political groups that emerged at this time were more clearly monarchist as a result of their past. This was the case with the groups with Christian democrat tendencies who drew their inspiration from José María Gil Robles and Manuel Giménez Fernández. The former had been one of Don Juan's principal advisers but had distanced himself somewhat in the first half of the 1950s when Don Juan's collaborationism had become more marked. Further left still there was the group led by Manuel Giménez Fernández who spoke out openly against Catholic collaboration with the regime and took up a stance even further to the left in all his public statements. He therefore expressed support for agrarian reform and proposed a federal structure for Spain. This group would have liked closer contact with the left in exile and that indeed came about; it also tried to define itself as provisional (*accidentalista*).

Unlike the Christian democrats, the monarchist factions that came together to form the Spanish Union (*Unión Española*) in 1957 were unambiguous in their stance on the monarchy. As was the case with Ridruejo, they too epitomized the conversion to democratic ideals of a sector of society that had come from the extreme right at the time of the Second Republic. Now, however, the ideologues of *Unión Española* reproached the regime for justifying its existence on the basis of a civil war rather than trying to heal the wounds caused by that war. A strong defender of democratic principles, like all the groups mentioned so far, *Unión Española* had its own particular strategy which included an interest in the Armed Services, participation in some of the regime's electoral processes (like the 1954 elections), and the adoption of an economic policy based on strictly liberal principles. In fact, in one of its documents circulated internally *Unión Española* declared itself to be a "moral" link rather than a political party. This is most significant not only in relation to this particular group but also to the other groups that came into existence at that time. We are in actual fact talking about groups with very small numbers which were really more like social discussion groups or friendly "brotherhoods" and whose capacity for action was extremely limited.

As a result of the events in the universities in 1956 and of these groups, which may be described as representing a "moderate" opposition, others appeared which would come to play a decisive role on the left in Spanish politics either immediately, as in the case of the Popular Liberation Front (*Frente de Liberación Popular* or FLP), or as time passed, like the group led by Tierno Galván.

What made the Popular Liberation Front different was probably that it was ahead of what would, as time passed, come to be the life experience of an entire generation of university students. At first its motivation was in part religious; in that sense, too, it was a forerunner of what was to come later in circles involved in secular apostolate after Vatican II. Also typical of the Popular Liberation Front was the type of revolutionary ideals which meant that at times its leaders were quick to criticize the Spanish Communist Party which it saw as competition, or it would even go so far in the Basque Country as to collaborate with ETA. The FLP was also the first concrete evidence of the impact in Spain of a revolutionary tendency linked to the Third World, notably Tito's Yugoslavia, the Algeria of the *Front de Libération Nationale* (FLN), and Castro's Cuba. It was so sensitive on the issue of Spain's plurality that it took on different names in the Basque Country and Catalonia: the Basque Socialist Party (*Euzkadiko Sozialisten Batasuna* or ESBA) and the Catalan Workers' Front (*Frent Obrer Català* or FOC) respectively. Its attitude remained ambiguous on the use of violence but, like the University Socialist Association (*Agrupacion Socialista Universitaria* or ASU), it never actually used it. It was typical of a certain historical moment but it gradually lost all its members to other groups that were usually more moderate after the start of the 1960s and particularly after

1968. Its leaders could well be described as "radical aesthetes," though they then became leaders of other groups in opposition to the regime.

Although in time it joined up with the PSOE, the group that originated in Salamanca and gathered around Tierno Galván with notable successes in university circles cannot be said to have identified with the left at the start. This was typically a consequence of the character of the person who led it. Reserved, courteous, academic, and introspective, Tierno invented for himself a left-wing republican past and an image like that of a sober, incorruptible Old Castilian, especially after the end of the 1960s when he shifted towards a socialism that was theoretically very radical. His initial doctrinal position could be described as monarchist. For Tierno, monarchy could pave the way to a liberty that, according to his view at the time which was strongly influenced by Anglo-Saxon neo-positivist philosophy, was the "effective" solution *par excellence*.

From the end of the 1950s on, the PSOE endured the worst phase of its opposition to Francoism. This was in part due to the fact that it lost some of its support among the working classes: during the strikes in Asturias in 1957 and 1958 socialists had played an important role but this was decidedly less so in 1962. The tactic of the UGT, which consisted of not taking part in union elections, was to blame. After the student protests of 1956 the ASU clashed with its leadership outside Spain, despite the fact that these leaders allowed them a certain latitude in their affiliation to the party. In 1959 the UGT party conference had to be suspended, while in the 1960s the PSOE conference had to move from close to the French border much further up into France. For a time it was not possible to publish the party newspaper and later they had to resort to the trick of using a French title. Meanwhile, inside Spain the first splits with the party leadership had occurred. They were the inevitable result of the logical disparity of viewpoint between the realism of those inside Spain and the idealism of those in exile, though there were also differences of approach. The militant socialists inside Spain were more inclined to agree to work with the monarchists, but also with the communists; most important of all, they demanded greater freedom of action. In support of their case they argued that they alone were the target for repression by those in power, and that repression was harsh right up to the end of the 1950s. As late as 1959 a final attempt was made to net socialists' leaders without any political activity having taken place to justify it. Political repression on the part of the regime diminished after that and there was a substantial reduction in prison sentences, which barely lasted 1 year for mere militancy.

The section of the party that diverged most strongly from the leadership outside Spain was the *Agrupación Socialista Universitaria*. Some of these young people showed monarchist tendencies but were above all inclined to criticize what they called "the blinkered anti-communism" of the leaders outside while in fact joining the PCE in some of their protest activities. Indeed, the ASU went even further and declared its support for a "revolutionary socialism," and in 1961 one of its members, Luis Gómez Llorente, had a confrontation with the now very elderly Indalecio Prieto. In fact, the groups of professional lawyers who led the party in Madrid and the Socialist Movement of Catalonia (*Moviment Socialista de Catalunya* or MSC) had similar disagreements with Rodolfo Llopis.

One aspect of the new opposition within Spain that deserves attention, given the importance it acquired in the 1960s, is its contacts with the opposition in exile. The huge decline of the opposition between 1951 and 1956 was accompanied by the severing of contacts between the opposition inside Spain and that in exile, but it was not by chance that these contacts were renewed in 1956. In 1957 Tierno Galván presented a document to the opposition in which he put forward three "hypotheses" on ways of replacing the regime in which it was clear what his own opinion – also widely held among the opposition in Spain – was: namely that a monarchy was the most realistic and viable solution. They would have to wait until 1959 for a formula to be decided upon that could unite the opposition and even then it would not see the light of day until 1961. This formula gave rise to what was called the "Union of Democratic Forces" ("*Unión de Fuerzas Democráticas*") and at its core were the Christian Democrat Left (*Izquierda Demócrata Cristiana*) and the PSOE in exile. Both proved that it was possible to devise a process whereby those in opposition inside and outside Spain could work together, which would bear fruit at the pro-Europe meeting in Munich in 1962.

A common feature of all the groups formed inside Spain in and around 1956 was in fact their pro-European bias. The regime had applied for Spain to join Europe as though it had at last realized that in the short term there was no other possibility for the Spanish economy than this. However, the European option also had at this moment a precise aim: the aim was that by Spain aligning itself with democratic processes the PCE, which was not at the time in favor of Spain's entry into the European Common Market, would be excluded.

Inside Spain pro-European feeling started in political Catholic circles but soon spread widely throughout a range of different political tendencies.

In exile the occasional monarchist, the Basque nationalists, and above all Salvador de Madariaga had done much to promote European unity. Madariaga and those closely linked to him must be credited with taking the initiative in calling for a pro-European joint conference. It was finally decided that the conference would be held on the theme of "Europe and Spain" at the same time as a second conference organized by the European Movement in Munich at the start of June 1982. By the time the conference took place Spain had suffered a wave of strikes – perhaps the most significant in terms of size and distribution since the end of the Civil War. Most opposition groups inside Spain had expressed their solidarity with the strikers while others outside encouraged or defended the protest.

On the date mentioned, in the Bavarian city over a hundred Spaniards gathered, two-thirds of whom were from inside Spain. All opposition groups were represented, both those in exile and those inside the Peninsula, and at last agreement on replacing the Franco regime was reached among all of them. Questions relating to the regime were sidestepped and instead discussion focused on what points they all had in common, which were based on a common acceptance of human rights, of representative institutions, of the identities of the different regions, and the possibility of setting up political parties and trade unions. At the final conference session the two figures who best represented the two worlds spoke and jointly emphasized their close alignment. Madariaga reminded those present that Europe was not just a commercial entity and therefore Europeans could not accept a dictatorial regime in their midst. For his part, Gil Robles reiterated that it was not the desire of the European Movement to teach Spain any lessons. The fact that these two sectors came together in this way was definitive proof that by 1962 reconciliation had been achieved between those who had been on opposite sides during the Civil War. In fact the Munich Conference was the moment at which the transition to democracy became a possibility.

Franco's reply was, nonetheless, immediate and must be understood in the context both of his ability to exploit outside interference in the life of his regime and of his habitual fear lest moderate sectors in politics were to rob him of the support of the middle classes which had until then been firmly behind him. All these factors meant that his reaction was excessive: he suspended the Charter of Spaniards' Rights (*Fuero de los Españoles*) and the press mounted a bitter campaign against any who had attended the conference which was immediately labeled a "conspiracy." Once back in Madrid, the participants had to choose between being confined to the

Canary Islands or emigration. In total nine people were confined to the Canaries, all of whom would later play important roles in Spanish politics during the transition, especially as members of the Union of the Democratic Center (*Unión de Centro Democrático* or UCD). At the same time demonstrations were organized throughout Spain in which, as in 1946, those who supported the regime were encouraged to stand firm like the people of ancient Numantia.

The Munich "conspiracy" was an important event in Spanish history for several reasons. For the first time ever, the opposition inside Spain seemed to exceed in numbers and relevance the opposition in exile. However, more important by far was the fact that on the occasion of that meeting the wound left by the Civil War began at last to heal. As for the possibility of the opposition being able to show the Franco regime a united front, Munich was a significant step forward, though unity among the entire opposition was still a long way off. The communists, who were more manifestly reticent on the subject of the European institutions, did not officially take part in the conference; the FLP was present but again not officially. The meeting in the Bavarian city was evidence that in the course of time, which was slowly but surely pushing Spain towards Europe, the winds of history were blowing in favor of the opposition. It was, however, also evidence of the fragility of that same opposition.

In the memoirs of an official journalist at the time, Emilio Romero, one can find a disparaging comment regarding the pro-European lobby who attended the Munich conference which suggests that "Franco could eat them up with potatoes." Indeed he could, because he had instruments of repression at his disposal and he knew only too well how to use them. But the scant threat posed by the opposition was due not only to the possible use of repressive measures but also to simple misunderstandings. Immediately after Munich a crisis situation arose between the Christian democrats and the monarchists. A note from Don Juan de Borbón stating that he had not been represented at Munich was taken by Gil Robles as a denial of his own personal authority, and at the same time a split occurred between those who thought Don Juan's declaration positive and those who did not.

The repercussions of Munich for the regime were no less significant. The problem of the incompatibility of the dictatorship with Europe would continue until the death of the dictator. However, at the same time and in the short term, Franco's regime had managed to steer clear of any greater dangers. All in all he reacted to Munich exactly as he had reacted in 1946 and, as on that occasion, his success was undeniable, which would prove to be much more troublesome in the years that followed. It should also be borne in mind that if there were signs of renewal within the opposition, it is also true that some sectors that in the past had been more dynamic dwindled and faded away. In the mid 1960s the last traces of violent anarchist action were eliminated and at the same time a section of anarchist syndicalism was induced by Solis to collaborate with the regime. It was sufficient to offer a five-point agreement that was never actually put into effect. "Five-pointism" ("*Cincopuntismo*") was the name given to this tendency which brought about the demise of part of the Spanish left.

##  For or against Falange: Political Life under  the Regime between 1956 and 1965

The years immediately following 1956 witnessed the first serious attempt to provide the regime with an institutional framework: a process that Franco had been reluctant to undertake. The process that would actually achieve the desired result would only reach completion later, after the formation of the cabinet in 1965, but the general direction that change was to take was made clear, even if only with typical caution, in those early years. It was then that for a few months it became conceivable that the regime might take on once again the blue tinge associated with Falange that had colored its politics at the start of World War II. Once that possibility was eliminated, the process of institutionalization moved ahead slowly along a different path, starting with a first very simple step – a generic Law on the Principles of the *Movimiento* (*Ley de Principios del Movimiento*) – while the drafting of real constitutional change did not even begin until Franco had been in power for 25 years and had had a first reminder of death: his hunting accident at the end of 1961.

Given that it seemed as though the choices facing Franco were either to favor Falange or to do away with it, we should briefly recall the role that he had allotted to it within his regime. Falange was on the one hand merely a tool but on the other it was indispensable. Statements by Falangists to the effect that Franco was not one of their own abound: this explains the loathing that the most radical Falangists felt for Carrero Blanco. We have already quoted one of the Chief of state's statements about Falange's supporting role, which have a somewhat cynical ring to them. Two statements that he made in the presence of the doctors who looked after him throughout all his illnesses flesh out this image and both show the General's displeasure when confronted by a party such as Falange. He told Vicente Gil, who was a Falangist, that the members of his party were "*unos chulos*" – thugs – revealing on that occasion a nervous irritability that was not at all usual among the postures he habitually adopted. He told Dr Ramón Soriano more calmly that Falange was like a kind of OAS (the *Organisation de l'Armée Secrète* – the terrorist group that supported the French presence in Algeria) which "I soon taught how to behave properly."

This was the situation by 1956, but it is true nonetheless that faced with the other political groups that supported him, Franco had to be able to count on the support of the Falangists. He had used them against the military chiefs during World War II and he had kept Fernández Cuesta in power after 1945, charged with the unpleasant task of disciplining Falange. When he resolved the tensions between the cultural openness of Ruiz-Giménez and Fernández Cuesta by following Solomon's example, it occurred to him to turn to Arrese for help because he thought that José Luis Arrese might be more useful to him in controlling this sector. The Falangists believed that Franco thought the new secretary-general of the *Movimiento* a highly gifted intellectual but it is far more likely that the dictator knew Arrese's limitations and used him for his own ends.

Unlike another Falangist, Jesús Rubio, who succeeded Ruiz-Giménez, Arrese tried to win a more active political role for his faction of the "reactionary coalition" and indeed, had he been successful, he would have done so almost on his own and irreversibly. In 1945 he had commented on what he called in the Charter of Spaniards' Rights "the sly introduction of vague, threatening rights." Nor was he wrong in this, for the text gave that impression even if it was never in any way put into action. Now Rubio tried to set the regime on a firm institutional footing, taking advantage of the political situation as it appeared to be. For his part Franco remained clearly skeptical about the possibility of providing a clear structure for a form of power such as his, which was all the stronger when less well defined. Arrese, with his statements and initiatives, applied indirect pressure aimed at institutionalization on Franco whose own intentions were very different.

In March 1956 Arrese stated before a Falangist audience that the political structure of the state was not fixed since there was as yet no law to regulate either the government or the *Movimiento*. For an instant it appeared that his intention of launching these two initiatives was going to succeed and even herald a clear Falangist majority in the cabinet. However, after the summer, in October, he began to meet with unexpected difficulties and, from having virtually been the man Franco trusted most, he came to be seen as a danger to the unity of the regime.

At that point Franco handed him 15 comments on the initiatives he had in progress, which the Falangist realized were like so many death sentences. He had managed to surround himself with a solid team whose main mentor was Emilio Lamo de Espinosa. Lamo de Espinosa believed that if the regime was to be institutionalized the question of the monarchy ought to be left to one side and that what was needed instead was a National Council as the most appropriate organ of government. What was particular about the *Movimiento* was the degree of absolute independence it would enjoy in relation to Franco's eventual successor. It would be led by a secretary-general elected by the Council who would have very wide powers equivalent, in Arrese's own words, to those of "a political commissar on active service." The law aimed at regulating the government was intended to set out new areas of responsibility. The National Council was to take on the responsibilities of a kind of tribunal on constitutional guarantees, the government could be dismissed by the Council, and the secretary-general of the *Movimiento* had the power to veto specific initiatives from ministerial departments. Had all these measures been approved, the result would quite obviously have been out and out hegemony for a Falange that would have been the one and probably the only beneficiary of this unification.

It was not surprising, therefore, that there was a storm of protest against what Arrese was trying to achieve. The military had no interest at all in the implementation of the initiatives and were spurred on to oppose them by the monarchists. From the monarchist camp the president of the *Cortes*, Esteban Bilbao, considered the proposals "a straightjacket" and refused to attend the National Council. His future successor, the Carlist Antonio Iturmendi, described the *Movimiento* as a "rigid, state-bound organism incapable of popular warmth." Another minister affirmed that if the proposals were to be allowed through, the Spanish regime would be identified with "those political systems most lacking in the most basic liberties." However, perhaps the most ironic interpretation was the one that stated that the changes that would occur might make Spain into something like Russia "but with priests." The Church also opposed the proposals in a document signed by the three serving cardinals. In addition, some 15 bishops subjected the man primarily responsible for drawing up the proposals to a grueling interrogation. The Catholic family put forward a counter-proposal which suggested reinforcing representative institutions, the creation of a Council of the Realm (*Consejo del Reino*) with greater powers, and a reduction of Falange's powers to the point where they would cease to exist. Faced with all these proposals, the only reaction of which Arrese was capable was limited and defensive.

At the end of 1956 there was such turmoil at the heart of the regime that at a meeting of the Council of Ministers the Count of Vallellano left the room after a confrontation with Franco and then returned later. In January 1957 Carrero Blanco, who had outlined on paper his negative response to the proposals, advised Franco to dismiss Arrese despite the fact that the latter was a "good, loyal, and excellent person." He also suggested the possibility of putting a soldier in the post of Secretary-General of the *Movimiento*. Carrero's judgment was definitive in ensuring that Arrese's proposals went no further for, by this time, as one Falangist said, Franco effectively spoke "through Carrero's brain." In a private note the General wrote that "everyone wants laws to be made which will define and guarantee these functions [sic] but not for such a situation to be reached in a way that pleases everyone." This was what led him to request that the proposals be withdrawn and any institutional change be put on hold until some distant future date.

Arrese never really stood a chance of carrying through to completion his plans to provide the regime with an institutional structure; he soon made public the possibility that he would choose "a quiet return to the warmth of a loving home." He even went further than this: he agreed to being relieved of his post if instead he was given the Housing portfolio (he was an architect), so it is not possible to suggest that his experience was the starting-point for Falangist dissidence. There was, however, little that he could do in his new ministerial post owing to a lack of funding. Meanwhile, the purists in Falange had decided that from that moment on, the state was actually in crisis and that the doctrinal line that it was taking was insincere and a corruption of the ideals of the founder, José Antonio Primo de Rivera. In his memoirs the Falangist Girón states that the proposals he outlined were nothing but "a castle of fireworks which burned out in a few months." Those who came to play a prominent role later on were considered heirs of this "third force" at the start of the 1950s and it is confidently said of them that "they invented nothing: it was a kind of enlightened despotism with no wig and no snuff."

The government reshuffle of 1957 was one of the changes of personnel that Franco did not want to happen, which would suddenly explode on him without warning. This does not mean in any way that it was of no significance: quite the opposite. In the first place it created an opportunity for a large number of the leaders of the official Spain to be replaced, and out of 18 ministers 12 changed. One of the key issues in these changes was the relegation of Martín Artajo, who had drawn attention to himself by his opposition to Arrese. It is typical of the complicated game of balance and counterbalance that Franco played that Falange suffered the worst defeat of all, yet Arrese remained a minister while the most significant member of the Catholic family disappeared (Castiella could only be considered loosely attached). The disappearance of Girón, together with Arrese's relegation, reduced Falange to little more than a sigh. José Solís represented for Falange purists a turnaround of Copernican proportions and, above all, a way of watering down the "revolution waiting to happen." So charming that he was forgiven for his constant maneuvering, slippery in the extreme, crafty as a mouse, and lacking both training and reading, Solís was living proof that it was impossible for Falange ever to gain overall control of power in Spain.

The most significant characteristic of the crisis was that Carrero Blanco's opinion carried the day and in his wake a whole new political class appeared on the scene. His role was so decisive that in the majority of cases he subjected candidates for ministerial posts to rigorous examination before they ever got to speak to Franco. It was also his program that was put into action subsequently. He had always thought that what would be far better than a single party like Falange would be a limited number of well-trained Catholic administrators. The question of efficiency in the functioning of the state bureaucracy and economic matters had worried him for some time. As for the appointment to government posts of Mariano Navarro Rubio and Alberto Ullastres as Ministers of the Treasury and Commerce, all that is certain is that the appearance of the latter owed much to the former, though it seems that they did not share a precise political aim. Stabilization, which Franco accepted was inevitable, was made essential by circumstances. What these ministers represented at the time was a different kind of political leader not associated with any of the regime families. This was, in any case, a world that had little in common with Falange. Navarro Rubio, for example, although he had spent a large part of his career in the Trade Union Organization (*Organización Sindical*), ended up in confrontation with Fernández Cuesta and in his memoirs he calls a certain type of Falangist "gun-slingers." Like Ullastres he was a member of Opus Dei, but one must also acknowledge more generally in other men who appeared on the public stage at this time a certain common identity or similarity of approach: a high level of training, a predominance of specialization in a specific discipline, and an absence of strictly political criteria. All of these characteristics were what Carrero was looking for.

It is essential above all to consider the position of those who lost out during the crisis. The measures of a political nature that were approved during the mandate of the 1957 government did not really have any serious impact on Falange and nor did they erode its power, but despite this they were received with angry suspicion. Although none of the party's most important hierarchies made any difficulties over the turn the regime took from 1945 on, there were tensions in those years. Falange faced a serious disadvantage owing to the lack of high-level leaders and to internal divisions. Arrese, for example, had to contend with opposition from Fernández Cuesta, and even Girón criticized him for stating that Falange had never exercised power. At the end of the 1950s the Falangists felt sufficiently vulnerable from an ideological point of view to set up a number of José Antonio Doctrinal Study Groups (*Círculos Doctrinales José Antonio*) which came to form a kind of parallel structure to the organizations of the *Movimiento*.

Although the old structure of the single party allowed this sector of Falange to continue to exercise an important influence in Spanish political life, it was beginning to creak. By the middle of the 1960s half of those signed up with Falange had been members in the 1940s and the average age of its members was over 50. The organizations which were enjoying the greatest success at the time were perhaps the youth organizations but in fact their success depended in large part on their ability to provide social services and only 2 percent of members of these organizations went on to join the *Movimiento*. The main consequence of Solís's administration as head of the unions and then of the party was the "depoliticization" of these organizations brought about by turning the bureaucratic apparatus into a machine to ensure conformity. It was, at the same time, a machine of power which drew a large clientele and in itself provided a justification for those whose role was to lead it. There were occasional glimmers of protest but any effects were definitely negligible and easy to suppress. In 1950 a report on the *Movimiento* concluded that "in all sectors politics is no longer a factor under discussion." Yet the books in Spanish schools that were supposed to be disseminating the official doctrine of the regime throughout society were doing so less and less by the end of the 1950s, while support for this kind of political education was even less among teachers (barely 10 percent in large cities). Obviously there was no evidence of open opposition (in the referendum of 1946, only in the Basque provinces of Vizcaya and Guipúzcoa was the opposition the strongest voice).

Once Arrese's proposals had been defeated, the focus of political initiative shifted to those around Carrero Blanco where Laureano López Rodó was beginning to be a prominent figure. The son of a manufacturer who had suffered in the dramatic social instability of the 1920s and himself a university professor of company law (*derecho administrativo*), López Rodó states in one of his books that he was a Falangist in his youth only because there was nothing else he could be. He rose through the ranks thanks to Carrero, who was the means by which López Rodó ensured that his political proposals reached Franco. As he says in his *Memoirs*, when Franco asked for a text relating to some legal measure it was López Rodó who provided the "withies to weave the basket." He stated in the 1960s that two fundamental objectives should be "economic development" and the establishment of "a legally constituted social state." In these same memoirs he transcribes a few paragraphs from his diaries according to which he thought that his actions should lead to "a degree of evolution in politics." When faced with Arrese's attempt to promote fascism, the new forces emerging within the regime came to represent a tendency towards a dictatorship that would be bureaucratic and administrative with a strong element of clericalism.

In this sense the Law on the Judicial Structure of the State Administration (*Ley de Régimen Jurídico de la Administración del Estado*) of June 1957 was highly significant because from a political point of view it could have been a reaction to the law on government dreamed up by Arrese. The Falangists were angered by it because it did not address political issues and because it made no mention of the *Movimiento Nacional*. A few of the more intelligent among them came to realize that a measure such as this "profoundly altered the very foundations of the regime," which had been a state controlled by one party and was now becoming dependent on an Administration. While discussing these measures mention must be made of the approval one year later of the Law on Administrative Procedures (*Ley de Procedimiento Administrativo*) which allowed private individuals to challenge government decisions in the courts, with the result that the government itself became subject to fixed rules that were now laid down by the law. From then on, the functioning of the machinery of the state became much more even and organized: minutes were taken at meetings of the Council of Ministers by the secretary, Carrero himself, and also at meetings of the various commissions set up by the government to deal with different areas of administration, principal among which was the Commission on Economic Affairs.

More political by far was the Law on the Principles of the *Movimiento Nacional* (*Ley de Principios del Movimiento Nacional*) promulgated by Franco himself before a *Cortes* summoned to act merely as a "sounding-board." Once definitive judgment had been passed pronouncing Arrese's proposals not viable, the three areas they addressed were passed on, not to the National Council, but to the Office of the Chief of state for consideration. Only one of them was judged viable, because it always had been so: the Law on the Principles of the *Movimiento Nacional*. Begun in the summer of 1957, what characterized the drafting of the text was the number of people involved in it and, at the same time, the gradual reduction of the text itself. All the different regime families took part in its composition and the number of principles enumerated – which had originally started at 40 – was cut to 12. In fact the text became so generic that it was acceptable to all but also aroused suspicion among the Falange purists, more for what it did not say than for what it did contain. The law did not at any stage refer to the *Movimiento* as an organization; nor did it pronounce a clear ban on pluralism in relation to associations or unions. At the same time, the appointment of a military judge to deal specifically with terrorist activities, the Law on Public Order (*Ley de Orden Público*) of the summer of 1959, and the legislation on military rebellion of 1960 provided those in power with the necessary tools to ensure that they need not be afraid of an opposition which was in any case was still in a desperate state at that time.

Other important bills were drafted but with little hope of their becoming law in the short term. The drift in favor of the monarchy seemed to be becoming more pronounced despite the fact that it was still imprecise, and this meant that in 1959 young Falangists repeated their protests – which were still fairly harmless – against Franco and Carrero. It is important to remember that at the end of the 1950s a return to monarchy – which irritated part of Falange – was no longer as remote a possibility as it had been in the past. In 1959 Don Juan Carlos completed his civilian studies and in 1961 began his military training. Given the legal situation at the time, if Falange could not express its republican leanings openly it did at least do all it could to make the choice of Franco's successor as complicated as possible. The maintenance of a certain ambiguity in the debate on the monarchy, at least on the actual person involved, and the alternative of a choice between the *Movimiento* and a single party, were issues that continued to cause division within the regime itself. There continued to be indecision on the matter of institutionalization but by 1959 it was generally thought to be inevitable that there would be a return to monarchy at some point.

The government formed in 1957 spanned the 5-year period that Franco considered an appropriate length of time for a cabinet to last, but before we discuss the cabinet that took its place we should consider one fact that is important if we are to explain one of the resolutions made the moment it was replaced. In December 1961 Franco had a hunting accident when his gun exploded because it was of an insufficient caliber. His wound was slow to heal and this served as a reminder that such an accident could happen at any moment. The reaction of Franco himself is worth noting because it was so typical of the man. It was two soldiers, Alonso Vega and Arias Navarro – both responsible for public order, who drafted the press release informing the nation of what had happened and it was another soldier, Muñoz Grandes, who, the following year, was made vice-president of the Council of Ministers. So the question of the succession was raised and it became clear that Franco's own thinking tended towards preference being given to the Army.

As usual, the change of government happened in July and apart from the appointment of Muñoz Grandes as vice-president – a job that was compatible with that of Chief of Staff of the Armed Services – other important moves were also made. Arrese disappeared once and for all from the government but more significant still was the appearance of Manuel Fraga Iribarne to replace Gabriel Arias Salgado, who had been badly hit by the events in Munich that have already been discussed. The new Minister for Information was able – even if it took a long time to draft it – to bring out a Press Law to replace the legislation dating from 1938. In the cabinet there was soon evidence of a shifting of positions which must be taken into account if we are to understand the rest of the history of Francoism. Muñoz Grandes was unable to play an important part politically in what followed because of bad health, among other reasons, but he normally sided with ministers with Falangist tendencies such as Pedro Nieto Antúñez, who was in charge of the Navy, Solís, Castiella, and Fraga. As typified by Fraga, this tendency could be defined as "open" (*aperturista*) in contrast to the position adopted by Carrero Blanco whose mind was closed to all processes of change. These categorizations, apart from being of dubious value, depended on the matters under discussion and indeed ministers did not always side with the same cabinet colleagues. What should be underlined is that there existed a struggle between differing tendencies which was not characteristic of the entire Franco period and most especially had up to this time been subject to Franco's arbitration as he saw fit, and now his health had begun to fail. The tendency that Carrero Blanco represented was described by his adversaries as technocratic and linked to Opus Dei. There is no doubt at all that within that tendency there was a constant shifting of alignments, there were clashes between its members, and in matters such as economic policy there was a tentative effort at liberalization but those in positions of leadership preferred coordinated action and a common will. In his memoirs Fraga ascribes to López Rodó the nature of an "octopus," as if the latter were trying to control the whole state apparatus with Carrero's help. His judgment is not without foundation. In fact, López Rodó himself states in his memoirs that 13 ministers came from the commissions who drew up the first development plan and another 13 from the second and third plans.

As 1962 approached, although the regime still had 13 years to run, the problem of the succession was already being openly discussed and at the same time as the question of the institutionalization of the regime: a particular preoccupation of Carrero Blanco. After his hunting accident, although Franco would still present a healthy appearance until well on into the mid 1960s, he did suffer from Parkinson's disease and if it allowed him to live a normal life nonetheless, as time passed it weakened his capacity to make decisions, which had never been the case before. As a result, some of his ministers insisted that there was urgent need to give the regime firm institutional foundations of some kind. Franco's usual tendency to avoid this happening caused stormy scenes on more than one occasion during plenary sessions of the Council of Ministers. On one such occasion, speaking to a persistent Fraga, Franco replied by asking if Fraga thought that he was a "circus clown" unable to grasp the need to prepare for the future. There were of course plans to draw up a constitution but in Franco's mind the time did not seem ripe for any such schemes to win approval. From outside Spain pressure was brought to bear on the ruling classes of the regime so that there might at least be an appearance of liberalization. At the start of 1962 an international commission of jurists wrote an extensive report which pronounced clearly on the human rights abuses taking place in our country. However, the regime remained content with its institutions (or lack of them) and ample proof of this was given when in 1964 it celebrated 25 years in power, which it described as "years of peace."

Yet all these factors together did not add up to any sense of urgency about the institutionalization of the regime because of the preeminence of the issue of the monarchy. In 1963, as we know, Don Juan Carlos settled permanently in Madrid in the Zarzuela Palace after a brief period in which relations with Franco had been somewhat tense. His father had wanted him to return to Spain with the title of Prince of Asturias, thereby acknow-ledged as heir to the throne. The *caudillo* finally reminded him indirectly that the Zarzuela Palace was vacant and could be occupied by someone else. This game of ambiguity on the matter of the succession continued through the years that followed. The following January Franco received Don Hugo, the eldest son of Don Javier and heir to the Carlist line. That same year, Franco himself had to reply before the Council of Ministers to Solís, who stated that the question of the monarchy did not seem all that clearly defined, and he retorted "that is the only thing that is clearly defined." As late as 1965 Carrero, who was the driving force behind this policy on institutionalization, expressed the view that it was now not possible to get Franco to decide on both naming a successor and the insti-tutionalization of the regime at the same time.

Meanwhile the regime was facing problems arising from the changes that had taken place in Spanish society since the start of the 1960s. The most important of these concerned social change brought about by Spain's economic development. Those sections of the population that had initially put their trust in autarchy were already sensing defeat in 1963 when Suances, the inspiration behind the autarchic work of the INI, left office. Franco, who had accepted the Stabilization Plan with some reservations, made statements from time to time that were reminiscent of his perennial desire to intervene in economic affairs ("I am becoming a communist," he said on one occasion), yet at the same time he benefited from the general air of success that surrounded the running of the economy.

There is another factor to be borne in mind which had an impact on developments within the Catholic Church. As early as the start of the 1960s there were already signs of a drift away from the Church on the part of many former members, which was a source of concern for Franco and the leaders of the regime. The publication of the encyclical *Mater et Magistra* caused problems, but more problematic by far were the Second Vatican Council and the election of Pope Paul VI, which was for Spain's Head of state like "a cold shower" as he said quite openly to those closest to him. The results of these changes within the Catholic Church were significant in three ways. First, they led in 1964 to discussion of issues such as the statute relating to non-Catholics. Second, they gave rise to complaints from bishops about certain aspects of the regime. One of the strongest of these related to the official unions which had been the subject of a heated correspondence between the Cardinal Primate of Spain and Solís in 1960. Third, they provided fresh arguments in support of protest on the subject of the social effects of Spain's economic development. "I am not afraid of the workers but of the priests who stir them up," Franco stated in 1965. A few years earlier (1962) he had still seemed convinced that in the case of these anti-regime Catholics "the perfection of the Church cancels them out and the Church corrects the error of their ways."

By 1965 it had become clear that the government had to change: a notion to which Franco, as ever, turned a blind eye. When Carrero tried to make him address the issue Franco attempted to put off any change and his adviser protested: "that is what Your Excellency said to me last summer." Franco's physical decline had already begun by then, which made it harder for him to practice his usual strategy of arbitration and also made him reticent when decisions had to be taken. Although these signs would become increasingly obvious, it was only after 1965 that one of his ministers, Manuel Fraga, could think, as he says in his memoirs, that this historic figure was fading away just at the very time when he was needed most.

Nonetheless, at that point, however clear it was that Franco had begun to decline physically, a process of economic development had begun which not a few of his supporters identified at the time with his regime. We know to what an extent it was false to make this identification because the very nature of the regime had made any sustained economic development impossible since 1945. Yet all in all and despite the fact that the regime played a far smaller role in Spain's economic growth than the role it attributed to itself, there is no doubt that it was the single most important factor in the history of Spain over this period.

## The Easing of Autarchy and the Change in Economic Policy

At the start of the 1950s, for the first time in the history of the Franco regime there was a significant rise in national earnings: in 1954 ration books disappeared. Until then Spain had been the exception in the context of a postwar Europe of economic "miracles": it had remained one of the countries on the old continent with the lowest energy consumption per inhabitant and its per capita income was on a level with Costa Rica. After the start of the 1950s there was significant economic growth, especially in industry. The average rate of growth in industrial production was at about 8 percent during the 1950s and in some years, such as 1952, it reached the extraordinary level of 15 percent. The Spanish economy moved once more from being agrarian to being largely semi-industrial and agriculture accounted for no more than 25 percent of the gross domestic product. Spain's economic development was therefore notable and exceeded that of any previous period, including during the Primo de Rivera dictatorship. Growth was nonetheless uneven, unbalanced, and unhealthy. In the last instance this type of growth would in time end up requiring the adoption of a more orthodox policy after 1957, and one that was more unequivocally liberalizing in 1959, with all the leeway and flaws that will be examined in due course. It is important to emphasize, therefore, that change was slow and had its foundations in the restraints imposed under the previous autarchy, and it was brought about far more by letting things happen than by defining a new economic policy.

There is one prime factor that does much to explain the change that came about in the years we are discussing. That was the acceptance on the part of the democratic countries and – more especially – the United States, that Franco's Spain was a necessary evil. This fact had immediate repercussions on the Spanish economy in the sense that it allowed it to be supplied with some of the currency it needed. As we know, in 1951 and 1952 the United States Congress agreed loans to the Franco regime that the American Administration did not want to make. After 1952 economic help began to filter through, but it was only at the time of the pacts between Spain and America that they came fully into effect. In the period between 1951 and 1963 economic help reached 1,183 million dollars – a figure which, though small in comparison with that given to other countries, played a vital role in making growth possible in a stagnant nation. Of this total sum, only 414 million were donations (35 percent), while the building of bases on Spanish soil accounted for some 230 million and the rest took the form of loans.

The impact of this help on the Spanish economy has been described graphically in the words "it fell on Spain like water on parched ground." The effect it had was both to stabilize and to allow expansion. Despite the fact that the aid given was less that that received by a communist country – Yugoslavia – it meant not only allowing imports to grow but also stimulating growth within Spain. Had it not been for this aid Spain's program of a new economic policy could not even have been contemplated in 1959.

A second important factor that should be discussed relates to the program initiated by the government. On the one hand there seemed to be no doubt that the program drawn up in 1951 was far more competent in technical terms and seemed far more capable than its predecessors of dealing with the conditions imposed on Spain by membership of a western world economy. In addition, from time to time there were critical moments (for example in 1951 or in 1956) which forced changes to be made. However, historians disagree over the extent to which the economic policy pursued by the cabinet in 1951 amounted to a direct precedent for the 1959 Stabilization Plan. One writer has pointed out that "large-scale expansion began but it tended to produce an imbalance because it did not in any essential way diverge from the intellectual framework of the previous policy." Another has indicated, for his part, that "adopting a liberal perspective . . . had enough force behind it to have some influence but implementing it later was less decisive and – needless to say – less energetic." What resulted was a decrease in the previous use of discretionary powers and of irrational moves but official declarations which tended to accept, for example, international commercial exchange, the market economy, and private initiative clashed with the Administration itself, which did not follow the program that had been outlined.

What happened from 1951 onwards shows just how much potential for development the Spanish economy had and the difficulties that government policy created. In the period 1951–4, growth – sizeable growth – allowed income levels to reach prewar levels once again and prices stabilized; between 1955 and 1957 the increase remained rapid but became inflationary. Industry not agriculture was the motor for this economic development. The average rate of increase in industrial production was 8 percent. In contrast, the part played by agriculture, though there were some positive changes, decreased in relation to the overall national income. The Agriculture Minister appointed in 1951, Rafael Cavestany – a pragmatist and former businessman – took steps to ensure that over the decade the use of fertilizers doubled and numbers of tractors quadrupled. The hectares under irrigation grew by a third.

Spain's industrial policy hardly changed at all but the splitting up of the former Ministry of Industry and Commerce seems to show a desire to break with the interventionism of the former, though not in the case of the latter. The INI under its president Suances was still being financed by the state and over the period 1946–59 it embarked on three large-scale industrial projects that still seemed autarchic in style even though autarchy was no longer the official policy: REPESA (petrol refining), ENSIDESA (steel), and SEAT (cars). Criteria such as industrial quality and productivity did not seem to play the decisive role that they should play. As if this were not enough, there were other areas in which state action should have been much more decisive if it was to bring about real industrial development, but that did not happen. Restrictions on electricity consumption continued on into 1954 but state intervention in the three areas mentioned did have a positive effect. While the autarchic aim to produce petrol from raw materials within Spain had meant 7 years without producing a single barrel, petrol refining now tripled in 1951–2. In steel production the INI took over from a private company that had proved incapable of embarking on the adventure that lay ahead and by 1967 production levels beat those of Spain's entire steel production in 1929. SEAT, founded in 1950 thanks to the importation of cheap Italian technology, produced more than 10 million cars in 1956.

There is perhaps no area where the heterodoxy of the government's performance on the economy is more obvious than in its monetary policy. The growth in money supply remained disproportionate over the entire period. The Treasury continually defaulted on payment of debt and forced the banks to absorb it, though it did allow them to transfer it. The consequences of this situation were predictable. Between 1953 and 1957 the official price index rose by 50 percent, though the real figures would have been higher. The reaction from the economic authorities was arbitrary and impotent and consisted of nothing more than a whole raft of controls and restrictions to no effect. The government's wage policy had in the past been very strict but now it had found it necessary to adapt to new circumstances. The sharp wage rises under Girón as Labor Minister, for example in 1956 (when pay rose by about 40 or even 60 percent), had no effect other than to contribute to spiraling inflation. Nor did the state show itself to be either active or efficient in the matter of fiscal policy.

At the same time there were important changes made to the situation so far in areas such as internal and foreign trade. As regards the former, the previous period was seen as "abnormal" and therefore required radical change. April 1952 saw free trade, price-setting, and the circulation of the majority of products approved, though measures did no more than establish a system described as "semi-normality." For example, preferential tariffs still existed for rail transport and "supervised" prices on designated products. As for Spain's policy on foreign trade, there was at first a sense that there would be rapid and substantial changes made. The new Ministry of Commerce under Manuel Arburúa aimed its policy at increasing exports and improving the exchange rate. In 1951, for the first time but not the last, Spain's gold reserves fell so low that only the chance occurrence of a good harvest would save the situation. Under Arburúa between 1951 and 1952 the number of import licenses tripled. However, once again an economic policy that began decisively ended up bogged down in ineffectual delay tactics (*gradualismo*). The minister took a liberalizing approach to foreign trade: in theory at least foreign trade was accepted as the usual means of solving problems arising from weaknesses in internal supply. However, unlike what happened in Italy at that time Spanish exports remained weak because they consisted largely of agricultural products for "aperitifs and desserts."

In fact the rise in imports was due entirely to American aid. Although the types of exchange rate were reduced from the original 34 to no more than 5, the entire system became a cumbersome device: the rate of exchange with the dollar went from 11 to 127 pesetas per dollar. What those in charge of Spain's economic policy at the time did not manage to do was to improve exports of industrial goods. The fragility of Spain's trade situation became abundantly clear when in 1956 a severe frost hit citrus production, coinciding with a poor olive harvest. Spain's capacity to buy from outside was more than 70 percent dependent on agricultural products and raw materials.

From an economic point of view, then, it is obvious that the 1951 government found itself caught up in a series of contradictions arising from confrontation between different sectors within it, of which the most important were on the one hand the economics ministers and on the other the sectors who favored of the old political autarchy, who were usually Falangist sympathizers. This was not so for all of them, for they ranged from members of the INI and the Industry Ministry to those in the Agriculture Ministry, and they also included some from the Labor Ministry. The position in which the Spanish economy found itself had become unsustainable. The new government of 1957 provided the "ideological *substratum*" for a change in economic policy. It did so under pressure from circumstances and in the absence of any other possible option.

It is worth asking whether or not Franco was aware of the change that he himself made possible with this ministerial reshuffle. In all probability the answer is no because even though the new government team's arrival in power coincided with the end of Arrese's Falangist-inspired projects, Franco showed little or no enthusiasm for any stabilization plans. He still did not understand why the dollar bought more in the United States than it did in Spain, and only when under pressure from the mere possibility that a bad orange harvest might result in bankruptcy for Spain did he finally accept what his economics ministers were proposing. When it was suggested that the exchange rate should be set at 58 pesetas per dollar he finally agreed to 60 pesetas "because it is a nice round figure." Quite clearly his mind was still unable to grasp the principles of capitalist economic thought. When the Industry Minister Joaquín Planell defended state intervention via the INI Franco was delighted with the minister's speech ("give him both ears and the tail," he commented in a plenary session of the Council of Ministers). Although two of the new ministers belonged to Opus Dei (Mariano Navarro Rubio and Alberto Ullastres, in addition to the highly influential post held by López Rodó), this team should not be seen as having a coherent program as many of its members held widely divergent views on a number of major issues. The Stabilization Plan was the work of Navarro Rubio while Ullastres had wanted a slower transition towards liberalization and the aims of López Rodó and later López Bravo were very different from the initial aims of the 1959 Stabilization Plan.

"It all happened as though the monetary authorities had had a fairly precise process for achieving stabilization ready in their heads," wrote one of the most outstanding economic historians of this period. Nonetheless, what mainly operated was, as Fuentes Quintana wrote, "a survival instinct" – that is to say, circumstances proved stronger than Franco's wishes. He, on the other hand, had such absolute control in the political sphere that he was not too worried about changes in the economic sphere. The memoirs of Navarro Rubio, who was principally responsible for economic change, confirm that. One has the sensation that the period 1957–8 was a time of preparation for the much more decisive measures that would be taken in 1959. It is important to underline the fact that these measures coincided with others of a different sort such as the Administrative Procedures Law (*Ley de Procedimiento Administrativo*) of 1958 and before it the State Administration Law (*Ley de Administración del Estado*) of 1957 which paved the way for the move from a dictatorship with fascist leanings to one that was more bureaucratic in nature.

This is obvious if one examines measures implemented in the period between 1957 and 1959. Fiscal reforms in December 1957 increased revenue by a seventh by rough but effective means such as "global evaluation" and a system of standing agreements (*convenios*); in addition, a new tax on the sale of companies (*tráfico de empresas*) came into existence. Also, for the first time the usual resources of the monetary policy were actually applied. An attempt was made to reduce the extent to which public organizations could issue debt and it was made harder to transfer it by rediscounting. The Treasury thereby played a clearly anti-inflationist role. Together with the Foreign Ministry it was also responsible for Spain joining the Organization for European Economic Cooperation (OEEC) in 1958, and the International Monetary Fund and the International Bank for Reconstruction and Development. When representatives of these various institutions appeared in Spain, stabilization gained powerful support.

Following these early measures, Navarro Rubio read out a document in which he set out his program before the Council of Ministers at the start of the summer of 1958. Essentially the text stressed that Spain was not different from other countries and that therefore the rules that would ensure a sound economy in other countries would do the same in our own. At the end of the year Navarro made a speech identical in tone before the *Cortes*. Franco wanted to be on good terms with the envoys from the International Monetary Fund and, without going so far as to admit to the flaws in the Spanish economy, he seemed ready to allow a general overhaul. It was only in June 1959 that the plan was accepted in its entirety by the Council of Ministers.

There is a further complementary aspect of the political strategy adopted by those who favored stabilization which allows some explanation of the success of the plan. In January 1959 a questionnaire on economic matters was sent to various institutions. On reading their answers it was deduced that there seemed to be a general consensus in favor of the liberalization of foreign trade, monetary stability, a leveling of the balance of payments, and even the integration of Spain into wider economic spheres. The truth is, however, that the INI was hesitant about an economic program of this type, as indeed, only a few months earlier, the secretary-general of the *Movimiento* also had been when putting forward a proposal for a kind of Iberian Benelux agreement instead of integration into Europe. However, the difficulties in implementing such a program did not come from these groups only but also from others such as the Industry Ministry; even the Labor Ministry only took action following these events once it had decided that what lay ahead was inevitable. From the very moment that the Stabilization Plan was approved, disagreement between Navarro Rubio and Ullastres became so obvious that the former describes it in his memoirs as "extremely dramatic in character."

Over the period in which preparation for what came to be called the Stabilization Plan was moving ahead, a slow rate of growth was sustained in agricultural production while industrial growth increased much more rapidly. All in all, the growth in revenue stood at 4 to 6 percent per annum and the per capita income at 3 to 5.6 percent, but where the situation changed completely was in foreign trade, showing the extent to which the policies of the time had been inadequate. Towards the end of 1958 a report by the OEEC described the situation as "precarious" and proposed not only a devaluation of the peseta but also "the abolition once and for all" of all interventionist devices. By the very end of 1958 the situation of Spain's gold reserves was clearly disastrous since there was an enormous deficit which in 1959 reached over 76 million dollars.

What is remarkable is not that those in power in Spanish politics changed the focus of its economic policy drastically but that they took so long doing it. The situation was desperate: there loomed over Spain the threat that vital imports such as oil would be suspended. The following winter, with a likely decrease in exports and increase in imports, could bankrupt the country at a time when, in addition, its level of imports was higher than it had been in the past. On the other hand, there was an obvious solution to Spain's economic problems. The program that all the specialists from the international organizations that Spain had just joined were recommending to its leaders meant a return to financial orthodoxy, the liberalization of trade, and the elimination of restrictive practices. Any other solution would not only mean a return to the past but would also be to lapse back into a situation that was sheer madness.

It was in these circumstances that, under pressure from Navarro Rubio, Franco finally gave in and – only for the time being and with notable bad grace – gave up on what had until now been his own ideas on economic matters: "Do whatever you like," he told his Treasury Minister. This decision gave rise to a government memorandum dated the end of June 1959 and addressed to the IMF and the OEEC. In a tone that was both down to earth and laconic, this text defined the turn that Spanish economic policy was now going to take. "The Spanish government," it said, "believes that the moment has come to bring our economic policy in line with that of the nations of the western world and to free it from controls which, being a legacy of the past, are no longer appropriate to our present situation." This presupposed that private initiative would be respected and interventionism would be cut. In addition, the memorandum made the following statement: "The government will continue with its present policy of authorizing wage increases only in cases where they are justified by a parallel increase in productivity." Although it was never made public, the document contained entire paragraphs of reports written by foreign experts.

This memorandum was followed halfway through July by the publication of a decree law described as a "Stabilization Plan" – an inappropriate title because it stressed its monetary aspects when its scope was very much wider than this suggested. In fact, "the most notable of the measures put forward . . . was its very extensive package of regulations and its high standard of internal coherence" which set it apart from measures put forward not only in the past but also in the future under Francoism. The regime had "changed its shirt and even its body in terms of its economic policy yet it remained essentially the same."

The decree contained a great variety of initiatives. First and foremost it limited annual public spending to 80,000 million pesetas and promised to keep it under control in subsequent budgets. Secondly, it also capped growth in bank credits, setting the figure at 163,000 million, a reform in banking was announced, and the immediate pledging of debt was done away with. Similarly, steps were taken to ensure better coordination of state policies on investment. Fourthly, a new trade policy was introduced by the state: only 20 percent of foreign trade would be trade by the state and the exchange rate was unified after a large devaluation of the peseta in relation to the dollar which would now be worth 62 pesetas. The Plan also made a modification of tariffs possible and this immediately meant the liberalization of the majority of foreign trade. Finally, another important aspect of the Stabilization Plan was that it called on foreign financial assistance, principally from the international organizations that Spain had recently joined. Nonetheless, directly or indirectly most of the finance for the new Plan came from American sources.

What was most important of all, however, was not so much what this decree contained as the extent to which it allowed a glimpse of what the future held in store. The impact of the Stabilization Plan immediately had a positive effect on the balance of payments. In no more than the space of a year, from the end of 1958 to the end of 1959, the Spanish Foreign Currency Institute (*Instituto Español de Moneda Extranjera* or IEME) balance moved from 58 million dollars in the red to 52 million in credit. A year after the Plan came into action, currency reserves topped 400 million dollars. On the other hand, as could well have been predicted, this meant a recession in the short term because of the reduction in consumer demand and the collapse of investment. Industrial production suffered a severe stoppage in growth but agricultural growth continued to increase. By 1960 Spain saw a significant improvement in these areas and by 1961 it was fair to say that the crisis was past. This situation coincided with the beginnings of foreign tourism and of emigration as two new factors which made an impact on the Spanish economy.

It was in this climate that the inevitable offensive against the policy of stabilization began. The meetings of the Council of Ministers became, in Navarro's words, "sorrowful Fridays" because all the ministers were fighting against the limits imposed on the resources available to them. The *Movimiento* and the unions led the resistance for obvious reasons, arguing against the lack of social content in the measures. From 1960 onwards, expansionist economic measures began to be implemented with reference principally to public investment. In April 1962 the banking system underwent a reform with the nationalization of the official bank and the creation of three types of private banks: commercial, industrial, and mixed, all subject to different legal requirements. The savings banks (*cajas de ahorros*) were no longer dependent on the Labor Ministry and now came under the umbrella of the Treasury. In 1960 the liberalization of foreign investment in Spain had begun but a legal frame of reference was only finalized in April 1963. In July 1964 a generalized tax reform was approved. One might say that this represented a decisive move towards laying down a legal framework for economic life in Spain.

Yet other initiatives by reformers on economic policy never got anywhere near seeing the light of day. Restrictions on public spending happened in certain sectors such as the Spanish Railways (*Red Nacional de Ferrocarriles Españoles* or RENFE) but not in the INI or in housing. Even before stabilization, attempts had been made to coordinate public sector spending by an office created for that very purpose. However, the "investment plans" ("*ordenaciones de inversión*") of 1959 and 1960 were only for 1 year. Navarro Rubio's own success helps to explain why from a certain moment on, the main protagonist of stabilization should come up against political difficulties. He did not manage to release the IEME from Commerce Ministry control and when he was spoken of as a possible candidate for a position of economic vice-president the bid was a failure and he was never appointed. Nonetheless, the way ahead, leading to fresh discussion of Spain's economic problems, remained open. A delegation from the International Bank for Reconstruction and Development (World Bank) visited Spain in the summer of 1961 and then published a report which was distributed widely – 20,000 copies were sold – which could be considered the first serious text offering a global perspective to discuss the subject of Spain in depth since the Civil War. This document stated that "Spain had the human and physical resources to achieve and sustain a high level of economic development" but that if it was to do so it would have to pay adequate attention to the matter of costs.

In February 1962 a new body – the Commission for the Development Plan (*Comisaría del Plan de Desarrollo*) answerable to the Presidency – was set up and came to be seen as so vital that it was soon given ministerial rank. With collaboration from international institutions, the first Development Plan was published in December 1963. Formulating it had been the work of a series of commissions and reports in which 400 people took part, of whom 250 were businessmen. In practice the role of these groups was purely advisory. According to López Rodó, who name was linked to the process of drafting the development plans, these were intended to be "an effective means of reducing uncertainty and making a real commitment to solidarity." Like all the plans that would follow, the first Development Plan, based on of the notion of "indicative planning," whose main European theoretician was Monnet, aimed to commit the public sector to a series of projects while the private sector was only given suggestions for possible action.

A consequence of the drafting of the first of the Development Plans was the opening up of a public debate on Spain's economic problems. Proof of this is found in the passion with which pronouncements were made on the report by the World Bank earlier on in 1962. In general there was protest from Falangist groups and those who favored planning based on interventionism but this was neither widespread nor a frontal attack. There was also reticence on the part of those on the left who were critical of the first plan's neo-liberal economic perspective. However, before the drafting of the first Development Plan had even been completed rapid economic growth had already begun.

Indeed, between 1961 and 1964 the growth in industrial production oscillated between 11 and 13 percent per year – a figure that would not be repeated until 1969. This showed that the Stabilization Plan, not the Development Plans, was the factor that set in motion the transformation of the Spanish economy. The measures taken in 1959 had an effect like that described by Adam Smith when mercantilist initiatives disappeared.

All in all, the reasons why economic development happened from this moment on can be traced back to possibilities that had existed in the 1950s, the initial implementation of the measures put in place in 1959, and the income of a country situated at the western extreme of a flourishing industrial civilization.

These reasons reveal, on the other hand, the limitations of both the development that took place at the start of the 1960s and the people who took part in the process. The Stabilization Plan was the starter-motor that set in motion Spain's industrial development but its center of gravity was its liberalization and this remained within certain modest limits. At a moment when the dominant figure on the Spanish political stage was Carrero Blanco it could not be otherwise, because his mind was not receptive to the opening up of the Spanish economy to international competition. When stabilization had shown proof of being successful Carrero wrote in a report that the world was dominated by three international powers: communism, socialism, and freemasonry, the last of which "will help us because they need us, but even as they help us they will be trying to control us." His attitude to the world outside Spain was quite clearly suspicious in the extreme. His caution combined with his nationalism to cause him to write in another report: "The ideal would be not to have to import anything other than what we need for production."

Liberalization ended in about 1967 and López Rodó and López Bravo "understood the market economy to be like another form of discretionary decision-making centered on stimulating private initiative and offering direct help to employers." It is possible that this was because of fears that liberalization might find a way to enter into politics, but it is even more probable that in a regime such as the Spanish regime at the time the natural tendency was to encourage a kind of development in which the state, through prizes and agreements with interest groups, might carry on playing the same decisive role as ever. Those who replaced Navarro Rubio – one historian has commented – watered down the wine from 1959 onwards.

Yet they also brought to completion a renewal of the leadership team central to the regime's economic policy. Between 1951 and 1963 Suances, who until then had been Franco's main adviser on industrial policy, saw his influence decline dramatically. Carrero had accused him – and not without some cause – of trying to direct Spain's entire economy from his office. At that time it was said that the president of the INI manipulated as though it were one economic unit what was at that time the astronomic sum of 1,000 million pesetas, which was nicknamed the "*suancio*" after

Suances himself. In 1953 Suances resigned for the fifth time and a few years later he broke off in practice all personal relations with the Industry Minister. From 1958 on links were cut between the INI and the budget and it had to finance itself through the savings banks. In 1963, when Suances felt nothing less than persecuted and his blunt pronouncements were beginning to cause serious problems in relation to Spain's economic policy, he ended up resigning once and for all. In the last stages of his time there the INI made a commitment on the construction of power stations.

It is important to note in conclusion that Spain's change in economic policy was accompanied by a parallel loosening up of social policy. As we have seen, in the stage of autarchy the Labor Ministry had played the major role in determining social policy. After that time, on the other hand, a much more decisive role was played by the Trade Union Organization (*Organización Sindical*).

This change illustrates very well the developments that had taken place at the heart of the regime. In 1953 rules were drawn up governing the company juries formed 6 years earlier. In 1957 – that is to say, halfway through the 2 years that led up to the Stabilization Plan – the first elections were held to choose trades union delegates (*enlaces*) and in 1958 the Law on Collective Standing Agreements (*Ley de Convenios Colectivos*) was passed and had an important impact on Spanish life. From that time on, within businesses, the renewal of a *convenio* would be an element that would further politicize the social struggle, but it had now become possible to avoid wage claims, leading inevitably to conflict and the disruption of public order. It was a matter, quite definitely, of an initiative aimed at making the labor market more flexible by making it more like the market economy outside Spain.

In 1965 Spain's economic development was still too recent a phenomenon to allow political conclusions to be drawn that might threaten the stability of the Franco regime. However, it is essential at this point to turn our attention back to the political opposition because it was to make a significant contribution later as a mediator between the politics of the regime and a society that had modernized thanks to the country's economic transformation.

## —— From Political Opposition to Social Opposition ——

If 1962 represents a certain turning-point in the political history of Francoism, the same can be said of the history of Spain's political opposition.

In effect, after Munich a new phase opened up which would be characterized by the emergence of a form of protest that was social rather than strictly political. This new reality showed clearly how limited political opposition had been in the past, apparently unable to achieve anything more than symbolic gestures. Social protest could give the impression that it was directed against specific aspects of daily life in Spain rather than against the regime. Yet social opposition provided a justification for political opposition. It was not directed by it but it gave hope to the political opposition; it broke down the walls separating small opposition coteries and made the last years of the life of the regime a time of constant uncertainty.

Spain's "social opposition" reached its peak in the second half of the 1960s but there had been a previous phase which helps to explain what it was like. Halfway through the decade it was not possible to state categorically that it actually existed. One should point out that from the very outset it had had three driving forces which took over one from another. It began with opposition from a section of organized Catholicism, then it took the form of student rebellion, and in its third manifestation it was led by protest from workers.

Organized Catholicism distanced itself from the Franco regime before Vatican II. During the first phase of Francoism, various organizations committed to the workers' apostolate channeled much of their protest against bad working conditions and played an important role in the strikes of 1951 and 1956. In 1956 the main leaders of Workers' Brotherhoods of Catholic Action (*Hermandades Obreras de Acción Católica* or HOAC) were dismissed from their jobs. There had by this time been a move in all areas of Catholic Action in Spain away from a kind of pastoral work which one might describe as based on "authority" to one requiring "consent." There were also other sources of conflict between the state and the Church. In 1956, for example, the editor of the periodical of the Episcopate that was not subject to censorship, *Ecclesia*, was dismissed on issues to do with the freedom of the press. In the 1960s there had already been initiatives from trade unions spurred on by members of Catholic Action and, in 1963, the ZYX publishing house was founded to provide a link between Spanish Catholicism and social action.

What is important is that by the middle of the 1960s there had been a decisive change in the thinking of the leaders of the apostolic organizations. The majority of the leaders of Catholic Action had nothing whatever to do with revolutionary attitudes, to such an extent that, as the future Cardinal Vicente Enrique Tarancón would say, even to suggest that they had was not only a grave mistake but one that might prove damaging to the Catholic Church itself. Whatever the situation, apostolic movements were the first means by which political opposition became social opposition among Spain's young people.

Viewed in this light, Jorge Semprún's statement in 1965 to the effect that the two organizations with any future in the Spanish opposition were the Communist Party and the Christian democrats makes sense. One might add that Catholicism performed a crucial function in that it disseminated democratic principles through its communications media. An example of this would be the periodical *Cuadernos para el Diálogo* founded in October 1963 which, from Catholic origins, in time brought together the entire opposition. *Cuadernos* was not only a fundamental means by which the ideological guidelines of democratic thought were disseminated but was also evidence of the shift of a section of Spanish Catholics towards the opposition. Its founder, Joaquín Ruiz-Giménez, did not break his links with the regime until the moment in 1964 when a new law on associations was discussed in the *Cortes*. With the passage of time Ruiz-Giménez took over leadership of the most left-wing section of the Christian democrats after the disappearance of the man who had led it until then, Giménez Fernández (1968). However, by that time the moment of opportunity had passed for that particular political group. If it had been useful in spreading democratic ideas, it ran out of energy doing so. Many members of the socialist leadership in 1975 had been Christian democrats 10 years earlier.

We would have to locate the forerunners of student protest in the events of 1956, but also in the transformations that took place at the start of the 1960s in the official students' union. This had lost its fascist character and had adapted to circumstances, allowing free elections to the student year-group councils (*consejos de curso*) and to autonomous faculty committees (*cámaras*), though the top hierarchy were still appointed from above. At first the apathy predominant among students allowed them to be controlled from above but soon these timid beginnings gave way to a strongly contentious mobilization by university students while the more moderate proposals put forward by the union leadership proved a failure.

In any case, even as late as the middle of the 1960s anti-Francoist students at Spanish universities were in a minority, though they had no adversary to fight other than the general level of depoliticization. The initiative in the protests against the regime had been taken originally by the University of Barcelona where a Committee for Inter-University

Coordination (*Comité de Coordinación Universitaria*) was set up. It would subsequently move in 1961–2 to Madrid where it would be led by groups that claimed to have no party agenda, such as the Spanish Democratic University Federation (*Federación Universitaria Democrática Española* or FUDE) and the Union of Student Democrats (*Unión de Estudiantes Demócratas* or UED), the former on the left and the latter largely Christian democrat though it also included other tendencies. The protest against those in positions of leadership in the SEU spread so fast that by 1964 the majority of university regions did not in fact recognize the official union.

The academic year in which student protest became most intense was 1964–5 and the climax came with a student demonstration in February 1965 in which several university teachers took part (José Luis López Aranguren, Agustín García Calvo, Santiago Montero, and Enrique Tierno Galván). From that moment on, both the protest itself and government reactions to it took on a different tone. By 1965, in terms of action, clandestine unions had been replaced by student assemblies, which were more effective as a means of calling immediately for demonstrations, but they also took the place of the representative democracy of the faculty *cámaras*. The difficulty was that this opened up a way that led to a form of radicalization that did not take into account Spain's actual political situation. A stable students' union became an impossibility because state repression set about dismantling it. In March 1966 the initiative was taken once again in Barcelona when 500 people gathered at the Capuchin Monastery in the Sarrià district of the city (in what came to be known as the *caputxinada*) founded the Barcelona University Students' Union (*Sindicato de Estudiantes de la Universidad de Barcelona* or SDEUB). The regime's reaction, far from attempting to revive the fascist SEU, was to set up Student Professional Associations (*Asociaciones Profesionales de Estudiantes*) which proved to be no more stable. In April 1965, after the vice secretary-general of the *Movimiento*, Fernando Herrero Tejedor, had met with students, a decree was approved which allowed the bureaucratic and administrative functions of the SEU to be separated off from its representative function.

By the second half of the 1960s the regime seemed to have accepted that the situation in the Spanish universities was impossible without finding any solution, and to have decided to live with it. The universities had by this time become a kind of world apart where political principles alien to those that governed the Franco regime were circulated and a degree of tolerance was exercised in relation to political dissidence. If at the beginning of the 1960s dissident students were in a minority, from the second half of the decade on they became a clear majority. One might even add that among the younger academics, to be a Francoist was not just exceptional but truly eccentric. This situation was evidence of the weakness of the regime but also, in some sense, of its strength because it survived, despite these oddities, within the body politic without any difficulty at all.

The working classes also won a certain limited degree of autonomy just as the university students had done. There had always been union opposition to the regime but earlier, halfway through the 1950s, it had largely been dismantled. What brought about the change in the situation was the strategy adopted by the clandestine unions which had until then been reluctant to take part in official union life.

The situation began to change after the start of the 1960s, which makes it necessary to consider first of all the role played by the official unions up to this point. They had never had the means to deal with possible demands from workers who had traditionally enjoyed a higher level of union autonomy. At the start of the 1940s, for example, the leaders of the union movement acknowledged the "manifest hostility" of the workers. As time passed, however, conflict between individual workers and companies was channeled through union organizations or work tribunals (*Magistraturas de trabajo*).

The regime tried by means of legislation to avoid the situation becoming too damaging to its own interests. The Work Contract Law (*Ley de Contratos de Trabajo*) of 1958, which was not enacted until 1961, set out a new framework for labor relations according to which from time to time the signing of a *convenio* created conflict within companies over workers' demands. In addition to this, in 1965 strikes on purely economic issues were legalized under the heading of "collective conflict at work." Meanwhile, the creation of a National Board of Employers (*Consejo Nacional de Empresarios*) broke with the structure of the vertical union and separated the workers from the employers. In turn, all of these changes owed much to the circumstances of conflict experienced in earlier times. It is possible that the strikes in Asturias in 1962 triggered much of the union activity in the final phase of the regime and even on in our own time, because it was not a matter of spontaneous conflict (as had been the case with the Barcelona Tram Strike of 1951); nor was it the result of agitation by those who had lost the Civil War, as in the 1947 strike in Bilbao; rather, it happened as a consequence of a specific conflict and ended with a demand for the freedom to strike and the creation of trade unions – two areas which enjoyed support from intellectuals. It is from 1962 that an important

and irreversible change in Spanish history can be dated: namely, the transformation of strikes into a daily reality in labor relations.

One factor which explained this consolidation of social protest and
the birth of a new kind of union movement was the appearance on the
scene of groups of workers from Catholic organizations. The Workers'
Union Front (*Frente Sindical de los Trabajadores*) was a product of the
HOAC. The Workers' Trade Union (*Unión Sindical Obrera*) too, founded
in 1961, had similar roots even though it declared itself non-confessional.
It described itself as socialist but was not linked to any party in particular. Last of all, the Workers' Union Alliance (*Alianza Sindical de los
Obreros*) was founded in 1964 on the foundations of what had been called
the Workers' Vanguard (*Vanguardias Obreras*): an apostolic organization
of Jesuit inspiration.

All these organizations with Catholic roots, like the Spanish Communist
Party, took advantage of the legal status enjoyed by the unions. However,
it was the PCE that got the best results from this tactic thanks to the
founding of the Union Confederation of Workers' Commissions (*Confederación Sindical de Comisiones Obreras* or CC.OO*). It seems that in a
region such as Asturias the initiative for this move came entirely from the
Communists, while in other places such as Madrid Catholics and even
disaffected Falangists played a significant role. In general the *Comisiones
Obreras* spread during the cycle of conflict that began in 1962, though
its organization was not really consolidated until the second half of the
1960s. From 1964–5 onwards, *Comisiones Obreras* began to organize
action on a provincial level and by 1966, when union elections were held
throughout Spain, this clandestine union was very successful. It no longer
depended for support on a proletariat that remembered the republican
years but could now draw on a much younger membership. In 1967
*Comisiones* held its first congress where the powerful influence of the Spanish
Communists was seen to dominate proceedings, leaving other groups
clearly in the minority. What really mattered was that by this means the
Communist Party had begun to break out of its former isolation. In this
sense the profile of those elected in the union elections mentioned earlier
was typical: more than half were under 30 and therefore had experienced
the economic growth of the last few years. For people such as these,
*Comisiones*, as a loosely organized unitarian assembly able to accept part
of the legal situation of the time while also pushing for concrete changes,
was an ideal formula. This was the Spanish Communist Party's second
achievement. Yet even earlier, from the second half of the 1950s on, it had

managed to attract a good number of figures from intellectual circles and most important of all it had won a degree of respectability among all the groups who opposed the regime.

This reference to *Comisiones Obreras* and to the political groups with which it had contact serves as an introduction to a discussion of changes that took place within the Spanish Communist Party. It would not be right to think that these changes were the result of careful thought from within the Party – at least, not at the start. The PCE did not in any way alter its traditional stance and that is why the revolt against the Soviets in Hungary was condemned out of hand; however, after the summer of 1956 at least there were more insistent calls for reconciliation to end warfare between Spaniards.

The policy of national reconciliation became the main Communist Party slogan at the time when the leadership was taken over by a younger generation of those who, in the Civil War, had joined from the United Socialist Youth (*Juventudes Socialistas Unificadas*): Santiago Carrillo and Fernando Claudín to name but two. In contrast, by 1959 Dolores Ibárruri had already been relegated to a position that was little more than decorative. The new team embarked on much more explicit action inside Spain. Already by this time Jorge Semprún, using the pseudonym "Federico Sánchez," had played an important part in the student protest of 1956. However, it would be wrong to exaggerate the success of the propaganda in favor of "reconciliation" or the calls for a "day of peaceful protest" such as the one attempted at the time. Also, the immediate result of the party's increased activity was even harsher repression. The execution of Julián Grimau in April 1963 for supposed crimes committed during the Civil War is evidence that the regime would not be slow to recall how it was that it had come to power whenever it wanted to justify repressive action.

The failure of the "national days of protest" was so glaringly obvious that in no time at all there was intense debate inside the party on how to interpret the situation in which Spain now found itself. Carrillo played the role of the willful political pragmatist and relied on the prestige of Dolores Ibárruri who described the dissidents as "feather-brained intellectuals." Claudín and Semprún, who were right when they recognized "the changes in Spanish society, now far removed from feudalism," ended up criticizing Stalinism and the lack of democracy inside the party from which, after a long debate which dragged on from 1962 to 1964, they were both expelled. This separation in actual fact was not seriously problematic for the PCE. In practice Carrillo began, though slowly, to adopt many of the views formerly held by his adversaries. The purely utilitarian argument that Carrillo developed in his various writings of memoirs consists of affirmations that if Claudín's theory was accepted it would mean a significant decrease in militancy.

##        Culture in the Francoist Middle Period:        
###        The End of the Penitential Years

Developments in Spanish culture in the middle of the Franco period provide interesting parallels with what was going on in the economic sphere and in political opposition groups. These developments came about thanks to Spain's opening up to the outside world and the unequivocal desire to modernize. Economic and political changes are understandable if we take into account the fact that it was the cultural media who contributed to them to a quite remarkable extent.

This is not to suggest that the cultural media had no contact whatever with official circles. It seems quite clear that if in terms of politics there was a definite break made with the past, there were in contrast elements of continuity that were much in evidence linking cultural life before 1939 with that after it. Meditation on the essential nature of Spain, the presence of José Ortega y Gasset and the inheritance from the Generation of '98 in much of current Spanish thinking, the militancy of writers in politics and their confidence in the state as the instrument of collective salvation are all evidence of a continuous line of thinking which linked the pre-Civil War intellectual world with that after the war. It is quite another matter, however, that their ways of resolving issues were radically different. Nonetheless, one cannot dispute the fact that a large number of front-line intellectuals in Spain at this time were active members of organizations that formed part of the regime. Many of the best writers (Jesús Fernández Santos, Rafael Sánchez Ferlosio, Ignacio Aldecoa . . . ) had been members of Falange. Their reasons for not conforming as writers were ethical and literary rather than strictly political. It is true that their Falangist origins left their mark on the attitudes of such writers who later became dissidents. Hence Juan Francisco Marsal has quite rightly spoken about the "objective Francoism" of writers who had abandoned their earlier attitudes favorable to the regime and had adopted others that were more in line with opposition thinking because, even as they did so, they nonetheless retained a "unitarian" and totalizing concept that had little in common with a liberal position.

If in the 1950s and early 1960s there emerged a political class that is still present in Spanish public life even today, the same can be said of the intellectual world. It was this that led Spain down the road to identification with the thought and concepts of life of the western world. What Carlos Barral termed evolution "in a gently easing direction" on the part of the regime helped to develop these possibilities further. In this respect a parallel can be drawn with Spain's economic development. What happened in Spanish culture at this time can be summed up by saying that there was a significant catching up on time lost since the Civil War. In the economy too there was a return to the macroeconomics of the prewar period and the foundations were laid for what would later be growth in the 1960s.

The first intellectual opening up to the outside world during the Franco regime was made possible by the presence of Joaquín Ruiz-Giménez in the Ministry of Education. What is of most interest to us here is not that there was now a far more open attitude, nor that it aroused strong opposition, but rather the fact that this political phenomenon coincided with others of an intellectual nature. The evolution of many of the most significant thinkers in the Spain of that time and later is characterized specifically by the building of bridges between them and Spaniards in exile and Spain's liberal tradition. Nonetheless, the paths they took were different. Aranguren, starting from a Catholic critique, shifted over this period from a position of concern to one of ethical disquiet and resistance to the power of the regime which necessarily became political. In the case of Tierno Galván, his thinking moved from the linguistic abstraction of the neo-tacit approach to a functionalism that was directly critical of the ideological monopoly imposed by the present political system. The work of Julián Marías, for its part, was characterized at this time by a dual emphasis: the need to maintain links with Spain's liberal tradition whose most iconic representative was Ortega, and the affirmation that the Spain of that time had not lost all of its vital intellectual tradition which indeed was at work within those precise ideological coordinates. It was on this particular point that he held a most interesting debate with the American Hispanist Robert G. Mead.

Nonetheless, the debate that best represents this cultural moment was the one that raged around the figure of Ortega y Gasset himself. Accused of religious heterodoxy, Ortega was in the line of fire of those whose attitude was staunchly National Catholic because his thinking was more systematic than that of Unamuno and therefore seemed to them to be far more dangerous. The main participants in the debate were Julián Marías, who insists that he took part reluctantly out of a certain sense of duty, and the Dominican Santiago Ramírez, whose basic position was one of intolerance. It is significant that a large number of intellectuals whose views had coincided with those of the regime or who shared its ideals (ranging from Aranguren to Laín Entralgo and Maravall) also took part in the discussion expressing their sense of indebtedness to Ortega y Gasset.

This fact proves that the philosopher's presence in Spain was a factor that led the Spanish intellectual universe of the time in a more liberal direction. Some of the great intellectual minds (apart from José Antonio Maravall, another example would be Luis Díez del Corral) were able to grow from the original seed of Ortega's thought. So we can see quite unequivocally that a gradual recovery of liberal ideals was under way among those who had started off from very different positions. At the end of the 1950s liberals from a Falange background took part in intellectual events organized by the Congress for the Freedom of Culture (*Congreso por la Libertad de la Cultura*) whose ideology was pro-western and funding American. Outside Spain this institution published some "Notebooks" which for the first time featured signatures of intellectuals both in exile and inside Spain. No doubt an offshoot of the debate on Ortega, Marías denounced the fact that there were those who were prepared to use the Congress against the regime but who then immediately afterwards decided that it should be done away with along with liberalism itself. In fact, it was at this time that members of the new generation broke with liberalism (and also with Catholicism which was seen as suffocating and oppressive). Marías in fact presented as "converging aims" the directions now taken by the Spanish Communist Party and the regime on the subject of Ortega-style liberalism.

The crucial moment in the split between these intellectuals and their past took place around the events of 1956. For some of those who took part in these events, what happened was "a crisis very like a crisis of faith." Ridruejo himself went so far as to say that "we were on the other side." Yet, as has been indicated, appearances changed but the underlying totalitarian thought often did nothing more than move from extreme right to extreme left. To understand how these changes came about, there is no better method than to ask to what extent the official world of the regime had at its disposal resources and centers of activity capable of attracting a more creative youth. It was the cultural activities organized by the SEU – the Spanish University Theater (*Teatro Español Universitario*) or film-clubs – that fueled the transformations that were taking place at the time.

The *Servicio Universitario del Trabajo*, conceived in an atmosphere of close harmony between Falange and Catholicism, gave birth to a pro-communist Catholicism. In a different way the cultural periodicals that appeared in these years were evidence of a plurality of attitudes all essentially derived from positions of political dissidence. So in *Laye* and in *Alcalá* – two intellectual publications associated with Falange of which the first was more secular and the second more Catholic – one can detect a drift in the radicalism of some of its writers towards a vague kindof Marxism. In *El Ciervo* a self-critical Christianity, in its acceptance of the ideas of the French philosopher Emmanuel Mounier, made possible a certain attitude that represented a compromise with communism; we have already noted the relationship between this publication and the FLP. In *Praxis*, published in Córdoba, it is again possible to see the link between religion and revolution. The periodical *Índice* was associated with some of the major figures of the regime but its enthusiasm for Third World revolutions and for the reintegration of exiles is clearly evident. Perhaps the most respectable approach of all the periodicals of the time was that of *Ínsula*, of which Enrique Lafuente Ferrari commented that it was evidence of "a will to protect the continuity of true Spanish intellectualism," and *Papeles de San Armadans*, whose patron, Camilo José Cela, stated in a letter to someone in exile that he wanted it to serve "to unite Spaniards by means of their intelligence."

There are several other interesting aspects of the development of Spanish thought at the start of the 1960s. It is from this time, for example, that we can date the beginnings of the recovery of the cultures of Spain's periphery: about 50 titles were already being published in Catalan. In fact, "the recovery of Catalan literature was only one piece in a far more complex mosaic" (Jordi Gràcia). Poetry festivals between 1952 and 1954 gave the sense that a brotherly relationship was possible between Castilian and Catalan, closely tied in with opposition culture. It was also in this period that the first signs of a genuinely Spanish form of Marxism appeared, suitably disguised to pass through the customs control of the censors. Censorship, as far as books were concerned, had by now become much more flexible. One man who worked as a censor told the Peruvian writer Mario Vargas Llosa, who was living in Barcelona at the time, that in one of his books the word "whale" had had to be replaced with "cetacean" when referring to a soldier.

It is proof of the obvious pluralism of the Spanish cultural scene that alongside the traditionalist *Atlántida* there appeared the *Revista de*

*Occidente*. However, perhaps the periodical that is most representative of this moment was *Cuadernos para el Diálogo*, whose inspiration was clearly Christian democrat at the start. It allowed the branch of Catholicism that favored renewal (whose main forerunner was Manuel Giménez Fernández) to play an important intellectual role in the propagation of the democratic ideal of peaceful coexistence. Similarly, the emergence of the social sciences at a later stage was to have an increasing impact by exercising a distinctly critical function in relation to traditional views of Spain at the time. This was so, for example, with history which now followed the principles of the French school as a result of the work of a historian of no lesser prestige than Jaume Vicens Vives whose concepts broke with the imperialistic notions that had once characterized traditional Spanish historiography. Finally, there remains one last intellectual debate that is of interest, which considered whether or not Spanish culture was European in nature. In fact, in opposition to Fernández Santos, the position defended by Juan Goytisolo, which argued that it was not, presented a key political issue which drew strength from the revolutionary potential that existed in the so-called Third World.

There was, then, a political element in all the major aspects of developments in Spanish thought at the time which was also to be found in literary fiction. Around 1950 a change occurred in Spanish narrative that tended to depict day-to-day reality. It bore witness to the world around it and was very explicit in novels such as Cela's *La colmena* (1951), Luis Romero's *La noria* (1951) and *Proceso personal* by José Suárez Carreño (1955). This realist trend can be seen as the most outstanding single trait in that entire period of Spanish literature, not only in narrative but also in social poetry and even in quite a large part of Spanish theater.

As regards the novel, the aesthetic influences on which this realist approach was based were Italian neo-realism, French objectivism, the so-called American "generation of the damned," and, above all, Sartre's theory of political engagement. The Spanish mentor chosen by the new generation of writers was Antonio Machado, who was celebrated in many acts of homage in his honor. From a political point of view their so-called "operation realism" received strong support from the PCE and its emissary inside Spain at that time, Jorge Semprún, but in actual fact the links between exponents of the new aesthetic style and the party were frequent but only short-lived. If indeed the populist social style of writing continued to flow from the pens of some authors during the second half of the 1960s (Francisco Candel, for example), it fairly much died out after that.

One must remember, after all, that there were many different ways of adopting this new approach: one need only point to the difference between the more cosmopolitan literature that came from Barcelona and what was produced in Madrid.

All in all, the realist approach and political engagement produced many diverse approaches to writing. In the majority of young writers of the time one can detect a clear disillusionment with politics, the deprivation suffered by a generation that had been a silent victim of the Civil War, and a resolutely accusatory stance towards society, at least in moral terms. The protagonists of these narratives were always anti-heroes with no sense of any transcendental mission. The most typical novel of this period without doubt was Rafael Sánchez Ferlosio's *El Jarama* (1956), a story about a group of Madrid young people's mundane excursion to the Jarama river during which the total absence of any meaningful events reveals the stunted nature of their existence, which is barely affected at all by the death of one of their number. There is in contrast a much clearer social critique as a backdrop to García Hortelano's novels *Nuevas amistades* (*New friendships*, 1959) and *Tormenta de verano* (*Summer Storm*, 1961), which are about Spain's middle classes at the time, and this tendency is even more marked in the writings of the Goytisolo brothers. In *Juego de manos* (*The Young Assassins*, 1954) Juan Goytisolo depicted political inconsistencies in a group of angry young people before moving on to report on the conditions of poverty in daily life in Almeria in *La Chanca* (*The Salthouse*, 1962) and *Campos de Níjar* (*The fields around Níjar*, 1950), while Luis Goytisolo described life in the urban slums around big cities in *Las afueras* (*The Outskirts*, 1958).

These examples of the social novel of the period achieved extraordinarily wide distribution figures as a literary fashion. In less notable works this type of narrative later became the object of acerbic criticism which Carlos Barral tried to disarm by reminding critics that the "thinness and coarseness" of such social literature was merely a response to the forms against which it was reacting which were themselves "so poor and so obstinately and introvertedly Spanish and Hispanicizing." Nonetheless, it is essential to stress once again that there were many different forms of realist writing at this time. The greatest success in terms of conventional writing in the period, José María Gironella's Civil War trilogy of 1953–66 which began with *Los cipreses creen en Dios* (*Cypresses believe in God*), was imbued with this same critical tone. On the other hand, a novelist who produced reasonable work that became increasingly interesting, Miguel Delibes, focused on issues where a clear social critique, combined with a profoundly humanist approach, played a major role in his writing, as was the case in *Mi idolatrado hijo Sisi* (*My idolized son Sisi*, 1953). Ignacio Aldecoa's short stories and the exploration of the inner world of Fernández Santos in *Los bravos* (*The Bold*, 1954) illustrate aspects of Spanish narrative which connected with the literary fashion of the moment.

Historicity, realism, political commitment, testimony and social critique were also characteristics of the poetry of the 1950s and first half of the 1960s. It is, in any case, worth emphasizing that the new poets' consciousness of generational differences were provided with a means of promotion by the writings and anthologies of José María Castellet, who considered the replacement of Juan Ramón Jiménez by Antonio Machado as these writers' main source of inspiration a phenomenon of prime importance. Gabriel Celaya, Blas de Otero, and José Hierro, who began work before the 1950s, perhaps afford the best example of this kind of poetic approach. From Celaya came a characteristic condemnation of arguments in defense of the notion of art for art's sake ("I curse poetry that is conceived as a luxury. I curse the poetry of those who will not take sides and get their hands dirty") and a defense of lyricism viewed as a tool: a "weapon loaded with the future." *Pido la paz y la palabra* (*I demand peace and the word*, 1955) may well be the most moving work by Blas de Otero: an act of solidarity with mankind, peaceful coexistence, and the fatherland. Years later the poet said that his work expressed his identification with Marx: "I copy him a bit and make it sound better." In Hierro's *Quinta del 42* (*The year-group of 1942*) a similar attitude exists ("I confess that I loath ivory towers," the poet would say), yet if his work contains what he terms "reports" linked to this notion of social poetry, there are also "hallucinations" which lay bare the poet's personal life experiences. The younger poets rebelled against the lack of realism of the 1940s. "More than setting themselves against them they simply turned their backs on their elders": a kind of attitude that can be seen as representative of the time. Skepticism or even pessimism permeates the work of José Ángel Valente, and of Jaime Gil de Biedma which presents as an ideal "to live like a ruined noble amid the ruins of my intelligence." The two major themes of the poetry produced in Barcelona in those years relate either to remembering the Civil War: ("I was awoken out of the purest childhood by gunfire / by men in Spain who were giving themselves up to death": Goytisolo)[4] or to the destruction left behind in the wake of the war ("You go out into the street / and you kiss a girl or buy a book / or walk around happily and they strike you down": Gil de Biedma).[5] Their personal identification with a line of political dissidence is also quite explicit in some of these writers such as Claudio Rodríguez, who took part in the subversive activities in Madrid University in February 1956.

In the best theater – not escapist theater – political commitment also gave rise to substantial debate in this period. It set Alfonso Sastre against Antonio Buero Vallejo, the former advocating "impossibilism" and the latter "possibilism" in terms of politically committed theater. Sastre, who had originally been associated with the Falangist media, had argued for a "theater of agitation" which was to have an "inflammatory" impact on Spanish life. Given the circumstances, his dramatic works such as *En la red* (*In the net*, 1959) suffer from a distinct lack of depth, but above all they were so badly maltreated by the censors that they could not even be performed. Buero Vallejo's theater, based on moral reflexion but not pamphleteering, dealt with human nature and its misfortunes based in history but with clear allusions to immediate present reality. It was, without doubt, *Historia de una escalera* (*Story of a staircase*, 1949) that was the start of a whole realist school whose interiors had nothing whatever in common with the bourgeois interiors of conventional theater. There was, however, a second and much younger generation of realists represented by Carlos Muñiz, Lauro Olmo – notably *La camisa* (*The shirt*, 1962), José Martín Recuerda, and Ricardo Rodríguez Buded who presented, with numerous references to the present, the spectacle of the poverty and spiritual prostration of a Spain on which they would never cease to show their profound disagreement.

The theater in its conventional or its comic guise had no limits imposed on what it could present as realist theater did. Pemán moved on from historical drama to a traditionally *costumbrista*-style comedy of manners. However, the greatest theatrical success of this entire period was Joaquín Calvo Sotelo's *La muralla* (*The wall*, 1954), which dealt with a moral conflict that could easily connect with the Catholic mentality of the moment. It was characteristic of the circumstances in which the theater was functioning at the time that a considerable part of the renewal of the drama scene had to be achieved through humor. Fantasy, the improbable, and sentiment provide the dramatic foundation for the work of Enrique Jardiel Poncela and Miguel Mihura. The tardy appearance of Mihura's *Tres sombreros de copa* (*Three top hats*) in 1952, some 20 years after its first draft, shows how difficult it was to bring about change in Spanish dramatic life. Mihura had to adapt to circumstances but he then put on a great many new plays in the 1950s. Jardiel Poncela, who described humor as a "disinfectant," never came to be viewed as bringing any profound renewal to the theater which sees him rather as following the formulae of the theater of the absurd. A formula that did little towards renewal but was better adapted to the tastes of the Spanish theater-going public of the period as well as being endowed with undeniable wit and wisdom was that of Alfonso Paso, an extremely prolific writer who, for some 20 years, was the main playwright to be staged in Spanish theaters. As for the extremely personal "panic theater" of Fernando Arrabal, which had much in common with surrealist theater, it was in reality a dramatic phenomenon from beyond our own frontiers and was hardly performed at all in Spain before 1975.

As we come to the end of these paragraphs dedicated to literary creativity it would be wise to offer a brief summary of the consequences of these writers' political commitment. It has been said that "with Franco acids that would destroy the flotation line of their future did not run out but were shared around" (Jordi Gràcia). This quotation may well be right, but in the short term what actually happened was that their initial urgent sense of commitment was replaced by more demanding standards in formal aspects of literary production. In that respect it is significant that the Biblioteca Breve Prize was set up in 1958, whose significance in terms of literary history is that it set out to achieve just that. It is possible to glimpse similar moves being made in other areas: for example, in the 1960s Taurus published editions that made the major works of western thought available throughout Spain. The legacy of those years, far more than any supposed political transformation, lies in the setting up of structures to allow the diffusion of culture that proved to be enduring.

It is perhaps in regard to painting that we can best appreciate the cultural changes that ran parallel to changes in literature during the middle years of Francoism. In both cases there was a certain recovery of historical memory and, at the same time, an eagerness to open Spain up to the world outside. It is also possible to detect in these two areas elements critical of the reality surrounding the artists in Spain. It is also important to bear in mind that this period, in the cinema as well as the plastic arts, had seen commercial networks set up for the first time, individual reputations made, and indeed a reaching out to the outside world that would prove vital for Spain in the future.

In painting, surrealism was beyond any doubt the spark that set the aesthetic creativity of Spain's artistic avant-garde alight but it was just that:

a spark. Apart from those for whom this avant-garde movement was a continuation of their previous development (José Caballero), it was also the case that some members of *El Paso* followed surrealist principles at first (Antonio Saura). In either case, in the surrealism that preceded abstract art it was possible to detect the influence of Central European surrealism (especially of Paul Klee) but also of Miró who had returned to Spain in 1942. Klee represented a crossroads where the abstract and the figurative, the concrete and the transcendent all met, together with a magical aura which explains his success. However, as a group, only the so-called *Dau al Set*, which included Antoni Tàpies, Joan Josep Tharrats, Modest Cuixart, Joan Ponç . . . , can rightly be termed surrealist. In the rest of the Peninsula we have to go back to the end of the 1940s to find any signs of an artistic avant-garde at work, and what did exist never really developed. The so-called Altamira School (1948) was a friendly gathering of very diverse personalities among whom there were writers and critics too.

Moving on to the 1950s, there were for the first time indications that avant-garde art was being accepted and even promoted with official backing. This was evident in a series of biennials of Spanish American Art in the third of which, held in Barcelona (1955), Tàpies presented his first densely textured mixed medium pictures, and before that at the art course put on at the Santander Summer University in 1953. By this time it had become almost normal to find in Spain exhibitions of recent work by American, Italian, or French artists. It was only after the second half of the 1950s that informalism came to dominate the art scene. The years 1956 and 1957 saw the blossoming of initiatives such as the "First Exhibition of Non-Figurative Art" or the exhibiting of an "art other." All in all, the most decisive step was the coming together of groups such as *Parpalló* (1956), *Equipo 57*, and *El Paso* (1957). *El Paso* was one of the most important and although it did not survive long and its doctrinal baggage was no more than an expression of a desire to stir up stagnant waters, it did bring together some of the best abstract painters of the moment (others such as Lucio Muñoz stayed on the sidelines) who shared many of the same concerns. *El Paso* brought together Manuel Millares, Antonio Saura, Manuel Rivera, Luis Feito, Juana Francés, Rafael Canogar, and others, who shared an aesthetic which, if on the one hand linked them to the American avant-garde, on the other was full of specifically Spanish references. The basic nature of the materials they used, their critical approach to Spanishness, and their recourse to a certain type of dramatic abstract style are what have been considered essential characteristics of *El Paso* whose members over time either continued in their initial tragic vein (Saura) or evolved towards more lyrical forms of expression (Rivera). In the case of *El Paso* enthusiasm for informalism was evidence of a desire to break with the general panorama of Spanish art at the time but it was also sufficiently cosmopolitan to be successful beyond our frontiers. Official policy backed these signs of modernity. In the final years of the 1950s and the early 1960s Spain's new abstract art enjoyed important successes in Venice, Paris, and the United States. This was also true of the first figures to emerge in Spanish avant-garde sculpture. It was Ángel Ferrant's mobiles that re-awoke the interest in the avant-garde that had existed before the Civil War but Basque sculpture (Eduardo Chillida, Jorge de Oteiza) – monumental and rounded in style – was the product of a very different sensibility.

At the end of the 1950s and start of the 1960s there had also appeared in both sculpture and painting an abstract geometrical style (Eusebio Sempere, José María Labra, Andreu Alfaro, Pablo Palazuelos) which showed that the paths that led towards pictoric modernity in Spain were not limited to the abstract expressionism that gathered around the *El Paso* group. Some of these creative artists (above all Sempere but also Francisco Farreras) can be seen to have shared a form of lyrical abstract art whose origins may lie in France rather than America. There were other painters too who have become associated with Cuenca, although that particular town in La Mancha was a meeting-place for the most diverse options in the most advanced plastic arts (Gerardo Rueda, Gustavo Torner, Fernando Zóbel) whose dominant characteristic is a style devoid of extravagance, anguish, or the violence of *tremendismo*, combined with a subtle poetic language. If for abstract expressionism a picture had to be like a violation, for this lyrical abstract art the work became a careful decanting that owed nothing to improvisation. For its part, from the starting-point of geometric abstraction *Equipo 57* found its artistic voice in an attitude of criticism and rupture which preferred collective to individual work and then took the path towards design. Of course not all art was abstract in Spanish painting over these years. In the middle of the 1950s there also appeared in the general panorama of Spanish art representatives of a realism imbued with a particular forcefulness (Antonio López and the brothers Julio and Francisco López Hernández) which came to be one of those examples of originality that can be detected from time to time in the history of painting.

Although it is difficult to set architecture alongside other cultural movements, one can appreciate an identical sense of a cosmopolitan modernizing urge in some of the examples of architectural design from the 1950s onwards. Miguel Fisac, who achieved in the CSIC buildings in Madrid what may be considered the very finest example of classicism, is also the man who introduced new materials such as bare concrete, or kinds of lighting such as lateral lighting through stained-glass windows (the church in Alcobendas, 1955). Another important feature was the work of José Luis Fernández del Amo, collaborating with the *Instituto de Colonización* (Institute for Repopulation) to promote the building of mass housing in accordance with the canons of Spanish architectural style. From the 1950s onwards, organicist architecture exemplified by the work of José Antonio Coderch began to appear, while Spanish architects such as José Antonio Corrales and Ramón Vázquez Molezún enjoyed a significant degree of international success.

———————— **Daily Life and Leisure Activities** ————————

We already know about the spread of the cinema in post-Civil War Spain since it is without doubt the art form that aroused the greatest interest among ordinary people. In 1951 the Ministry of Information and Tourism was created and it featured for the first time ever a department responsible for cinema. State protectionism continued to play a crucial role in Spanish cinema. A process for funding it was negotiated according to which the essential criteria were those to do with costing and with quality as judged by a commission set up for that purpose. Between 1951 and 1962 the number of films produced in Spain rose from 40 to about 80. Suevia Films took over from Cifesa as the most successful company in Spanish film-making. At the start of the 1960s the American producer Samuel Bronston settled in Spain and it was here that some of the greatest films of the period were made.

Cinema production had its ups and downs as a result of the appearance of a new generation of producers with a distinctly critical approach. We should nonetheless bear in mind that the quality of the work of this more critical section of the film world was no guarantee of success. The films that had the longest runs in the period were Juan de Orduña's *El último cuplé* (*The last song*, 1957) and Luis César Amadori's *La violetera* (*The violet-seller*, 1958). Luis García Berlanga's *Bienvenido míster Marshall* (*Welcome, Mr Marshall*, 1952) only appeared in eighteenth place. Comedy was undoubtedly successful in a more gentle form such as José Luis Sáenz de Heredia's *Historias de la radio* (*Stories from the radio*, 1955), or the most critical of Fernando Fernán Gómez's films. However, public preference showed the extent to which the folkloric musical remained the genre most resistant to change and also the most influential. At this time too, the rural melodrama and historical film disappeared from the scene: indeed, the granting of the label "of national interest" to *Surcos* (*Furrows*, 1951) by the radical Falangist José Antonio Nieves Conde, and not to Juan de Orduña's *Alba de América* (*American Dawn*, 1951) whose script was said to have been written by Franco, was in effect the swan song of this genre. Other kinds of cinema characteristic of this period were "films with children" which usually included singing and were often edifying and religious. Suffice it to say that of the ten Spanish films with the highest viewing figures, three were religious.

In contrast to what might be called National Catholic cinema such as *Marcelino pan y vino* (*Marcelino bread and wine*, 1954), neo-realism, of which good examples to cite might be *Plácido* (1961) and *El verdugo* (*The Executioner*, 1963) by Luis Berlanga or *Muerte de un ciclista* (*Death of a cyclist*, 1955) and *Calle Mayor* (*Main Street*, 1956) by Juan Antonio Bardem, presented a critical realist view of Spanish life. From the middle of the 1950s on, there was a phase of self-criticism aimed at Spanish film-making by the directors themselves. Bardem, in a phrase that would become famous, described it as "politically ineffectual, of minimal intellectual worth, aesthetically void, and extremely shaky as an industry." These were also the times in which cinema clubs flourished, many of them made possible by the SEU and discussions on the problems facing Spanish cinema that took place in Salamanca. Thanks to the presence of José María García Escudero in the post of greatest responsibility in the Ministry of Information and Tourism during the Fraga years, there was in the early 1960s a certain flowering of what came to be called new Spanish cinema which was much more closely tied to the reality of daily life. It was accompanied by the production of one of Luis Buñuel's most remarkable films, *Viridiana* (1961), which posed serious problems for the censors.

In the 1950s, sport, and most especially football, was confirmed as being one of the major pastimes for Spaniards. Physical education was introduced into the school curriculum as early as the 1940s. The popularity of football is demonstrated by the fact that the daily newspaper *Marca*, which is principally but not exclusively dedicated to the sport, was selling 350,000 copies and became the best-selling of all Spain's newspapers. Sports organization after the Civil War was the responsibility of the General Secretariat of the *Movimiento* (*Secretaría General el Movimiento*) and it was only after the 1960s that the National Sports Delegation (*Delegación Nacional de Deportes*) could act to a certain degree independently of political power. The first national delegate for Sports was General José Moscardó who had been decorated for his defense of the Alcázar of Toledo, while the second, José Antonio Elola, was a well-known Falangist politician.

The social implications of football are of particular interest to us. Of the 73 leagues or cups that there were, 60 were won by the biggest clubs, each of which had a very clearly defined profile. The Madrid team, under its president Santiago Bernabeu, a civil servant working at the Treasury who enjoyed a healthy economic lifestyle, had a number of cabinet ministers as members of the club during the middle years of the Franco period. Barcelona always enjoyed the best economic situation because it had so many members but its sporting results were often poor: between 1961 and 1984 it won only one league. It usually had a certain Catalan dissident tone. In 1968 it had its first non-Francoist president, Narcís de Carreras, who had in the past served as secretary to Francesc Cambó. In 1973 Agustí Montal's bid to become chairman of the club was successful and he was elected after stating during the campaign that "we are who we say we are: Barcelona is more than a club." *Atlético de Bilbao*, which had dominated Spanish football in the first decade of the century, did so again in the 1940s despite the fact that, of the Basque players who had remained permanently on tour outside Spain throughout the Civil War, all but one decided to stay in exile. Its links with the Air Force team *Atlético de Aviación* allowed *Atlético de Madrid*, which joined up with it, to take on all the players who had been in that particular branch of the Armed Services.

Political intervention by the state affected even the football clubs themselves: all teams had to include at least two Falangists, a ruling that did not disappear until 1967. Nationalism not only meant that naming clubs in English had to cease but that foreigners themselves had to disappear during the 1960s. The language of sports journalism had to be Castilianized by order of the censors and it sometimes acquired a certain epic tone. Football club chairmen had initially been appointed by the national delegates themselves. Then, in the 1940s a new system was introduced which meant that only a few select people attended club meetings, though by the 1950s there were once again democratic elections.

A large number of Hungarian players appeared in Spanish football during the 1950s. The first was Ladislao Kubala whose career started with the decade and who gave Barcelona an unaccustomed series of wins.

Spanish football became international, although it was far from easy to do so after the Civil War. Ferenc Puskas did the same for Madrid, but the foreign player *par excellence* in that team was Alfredo di Stefano whose arrival in Spain was controversial because of the rivalry between Madrid and Barcelona, which it did much to sharpen.

In World Championships the results gained by Spanish teams were not brilliant. Spain only just managed to qualify for the final rounds in 1961 and 1966. In 1960 it refused to compete against Russia and in 1964 it did and it won the European Championship in the presence of Franco, the event being celebrated as though it were a military triumph. However, the most important role in relation to the public projection of Spanish football outside its own frontiers was without doubt played by Real Madrid. When in 1955 it won the Latin Cup in Paris the players were awarded the Imperial Order of the Yoke and Arrows (the emblem of the Catholic Monarchs and Falange). Its greatest successes were winning the European Cup for 5 years, as a consequence of which the Foreign Minister made Di Stefano and one of the club's directors, Raimundo Saporta, Commanders of the Order of Isabel the Catholic. On another occasion it was stated entirely seriously that the influence of football in Spanish society would be a cause of alienation but that opinion could not be justified: at most one might say that the impact of football was more a result than a cause of political passivity in Spain.

"The radio came into its full glory in the 1950s," wrote Manuel Vázquez Montalbán. It is proof of the popularity and attractiveness of radio that there were even rented sets with a slot for coins for those with little money. A decisive factor was a new form of programming with spaces for comedy, serials, and "magazines" with very varied content ranging from competitions to music broadcasts. *Lo que nunca muere* (*What will never die*), a series by Guillermo Sautier Casaseca, the most successful scriptwriter of this genre, was about a family split by the Civil War which finally sees toleration and understanding triumph among its members. In short, serials on the radio became rather like the reediting of the serials that had appeared in newspapers in an earlier period.

In the area of popular culture too we should mention music which underwent a transformation after the start of the 1960s. Before that time the typically Spanish form of operetta known as *zarzuela* – by now "a distortion, stinking of formalin, of an old style of authentic rural sentimentality" – had virtually disappeared. In an earlier period a recovery of the short musical pieces known as *tonadillas* and other forms associated with the one-act comedies known as *género chico* and of a more international melodic trend had all converged, with uncertain results. From the middle of the 1950s both Italian and American records began to be found in Spain.

Pop culture reached the Peninsula much later and in a rather peculiar way. It triumphed due largely to requests by listeners to the radio, but at first there was strong nationalist resistance. "What is so lamentable," wrote one enemy of the new music, "is that Spanish writers are themselves contributing to the increasing popularity of a style whose spread we should be preventing rather than imitating." Even so, in only a short space of time pop culture had given birth to an entire industry. In *ABC* in February 1964 there was a statement to the effect that "today any song, if it becomes popular, can make the writer a millionaire."

Pop reached Spain stripped of "much of its explosive charge." Caution about the subversive side of the new music can also be seen as regards the cinema: *Rebel without a cause*, the film by Nicholas Ray starring James Dean which came to symbolize a generation that had broken with its parents, was first shown in Spain 8 years after it was first premiered. The true pioneers of pop were Manuel de la Calva and Ramón Arcusa – The Dynamic Duo (*El Dúo Dinámico*) – from 1957 on. They were the "friendly, responsible, familiar face of rock and roll," which was destined to become the background music at the parties of the younger generations of the middle classes (these were the years of the definitive triumph of Elvis Presley). The two Spanish singers worked for an aircraft company and had to turn professional quickly; they managed on the one hand to adapt songs by other writers and also to write their own. *Quince años tiene mi amor* (*My love is 15 years old*, 1960) was their first original success. After the second half of the 1960s they were overtaken by other groups but much later, at the end of the 1980s, they made a comeback due to nostalgia shared with others of their generation.

However, at the end of the 1950s and beginning of the 1960s the general public still preferred the music of the *copla*, the *bolero*, and the *ranchera*. The transition from the *copla* to pop music of Anglo-Saxon origins was made by Latin American groups who played the more moderate forms of rock and sang in Spanish. This was so with *Los Cinco Latinos* from Argentina, and *Los Llopis*, who were a Cuban band with a contract in Spain to sing tropical-style songs, but who also translated and performed rock. More immediately the Mexicans Enrique Guzmán and Teen Tops introduced versions of rock songs in Spanish into the Peninsula.

Apart from the radio, a decisive role in the diffusion of the new style of music was played by festivals organized for young people and schools. The lead in these was taken by "tall, good-looking students with a good presence," people "with a minimum of money, contacts and technical knowledge." It was above all a phenomenon among university students. From November 1962 on, the morning shows at the *Circo Price* in Madrid offered a mass experience featuring music for the young, but this was finally stopped on governmental authority without ever having given rise to any serious conflict. As in Italy, music festivals played a significant part in promoting popular music. The festival in Benidorm known as the Spanish Song Festival (*Festival Español de la Canción*) was the main event aimed at promoting the city's beaches. It is interesting to note that it was started in collaboration with The Broadcasting Network of the *Movimiento* (*Red de Emisoras del Movimiento*) in 1959 and it launched Raphael in 1962. But there were many more festivals, each with its own particular character. Some served to promote the singers who later came together as exponents of the Catalan "nova cançó."

Halfway through the 1960s there were two important new features on the Spanish pop scene: the attempt to develop an original style and an impact at last being made outside Spain. *Los Brincos* aimed explicitly to become "a typically Spanish beat group": *Flamenco* was its first attempt at a kind of music that had its roots in popular songs of another era. *Los Brincos* were immensely successful and earned five times more per performance than any other group, even selling more records than the Beatles at times. In the second half of the 1960s other groups appeared who often did not themselves record but had musicians do so in the studio. This was what happened with *Los Bravos*. Their *Black is Black*, sung in English, was second in the hit parade in Britain in 1966 and sold two and a half million copies worldwide. In the world of popular music, which is a very important part of daily life for Spaniards, a very important change had occurred. It was, however, merely a consequence of what had happened in the rest of Spanish society.

## Bibliography

There is no specific bibliography on this period but there are many memoirs: S. ÁLVAREZ, *La larga marcha de una lucha sin cuartel*, Ed. Nos, A Coruña, 1994; Alfonso ARMADA, *Al servicio de la Corona*, Planeta, Barcelona, 1982;

"CÁNDIDO," *Memorias prohibidas*, Ediciones B, Barcelona, 1995; Fabià ESTAPÉ, *De tots colors*. *Memòries*, Edicions 62, Barcelona, 2000; José María GARCÍA ESCUDERO, *La primera apertura*. *Diario de un director general*, Planeta, Barcelona, 1978, and *Mis siete vidas*. *De las brigadas anarquistas a juez del 23-F*, Planeta, Barcelona, 1995; Antonio GARRIGUES Y DÍAZ CAÑABATE, *Diálogos conmigo mismo*, Planeta, Barcelona, 1978; Laureano LÓPEZ RODÓ, *La larga marcha hacia la Monarquía*, Noguer, Barcelona, 1977, and *Memorias*, Plaza y Janés-Cambio 16, Barcelona, 1990–2; Raúl MORODO, *Atando cabos*. *Memorias de un conspirador moderado*, Taurus, Madrid, 2001; Mariano NAVARRO RUBIO, *Mis memorias*, Plaza y Janés-Cambio 16, Barcelona, 1991; Dionisio RIDRUEJO, *Escrito en España*, Losada, Buenos Aires, 1962; Emilio ROMERO, *Tragicomedia de España*. *Unas memorias sin contemplaciones*, Planeta, Barcelona, 1985; Federico SILVA MUÑOZ, *Memorias políticas*, Planeta, Barcelona, 1993.

Partial aspects of politics: Juan José del ÁGUILA, *EL TOP. La represión de la libertad*, Planeta, Barcelona, 2001; José Ignacio CRUZ, *El yunque azul. Frente de Juventudes y sistema de educación*. *Razones de un fracaso*, Alianza, Madrid, 2001; Luis Fernando CRESPO, *Las reformas de la administración española (1957–1967)*, Centro de Estudios Políticos y Constitucionales, Madrid, 2000; Francisco SEVILLANO, *Ecos de papel. La opinión de los españoles en la época de Franco*, Biblioteca Nueva, Madrid, 2000.

The Opposition: Donato BARBA, *La democracia cristiana durante el franquismo*, Encuentro, Madrid, 2001; Sergio VILAR, *Protagonistas de la España democrática. La oposición a la dictadura. 1939–1959*, Éditions Sociales, Paris, 1969. Social protest: José BABIANO, *Emigrantes, cronómetro y huelgas. Un estudio sobre el trabajo y los trabajadores durante el franquismo*, Siglo XXI-Fundación 1º de Mayo, Madrid, 1995; Carmen MOLINERO y Pere YSÀS, *Patria, pan y justicia. Nivell de vida i condicions de treball a Catalunya. 1939–1951*, La Magrana, Barcelona, 1985, and *Productores disciplinados y minorías subversivas. Clase obrera y conflictividad en la España franquista*, Siglo XXI, Madrid, 1998. On Ridruejo one can consult his *Dionisio Ridruejo: de la Falange a la oposición*, Taurus, Madrid, 1976. On the Socialist Party: Abdón MATEOS, *El PSOE contra Franco. Continuidad y renovación del socialismo español, 1953–1974*, Fundación Pablo Iglesias, Madrid, 1993; Raúl MORODO, *Tierno Galván y otros precursores políticos*, El País, Madrid, 1987; Enrique TIERNO GALVÁN, *Cabos sueltos*, Bruguera, Barcelona, 1981; César ALONSO DE LOS RÍOS, *La verdad sobre Tierno Galván*, Anaya and Mario Muchnik, Madrid, 1997. About the PCE: Fernando CLAUDÍN, *Documentos de una divergencia comunista*, Iniciativas Editoriales, Barcelona, 1978; David RUIZ, *Historia de las Comisiones Obreras (1958–1988)*, Siglo XXI, Madrid, 1993. On the student revolt of 1956: *Jaraneros y alborotadores. Documentos sobre los sucesos estudiantiles . . .* , Universidad Complutense, Madrid, 1982. On the "Munich conspiracy": Joaquín SATRÚSTEGUI *et al.*, *Cuando la transición se hizo posible. El "contubernio" de Múnich*, Tecnos, Madrid, 1993. On the Anarchists: Ángel

HERRERÍN, *La CNT durante el franquismo*, Siglo XXI, Madrid, 2004. On Catalonia: Josep M. COLOMER, *Els estudiants de Barcelona sota el franquisme*, Curial, Barcelona, 1978, and *Espanyolisme i catalanisme. La idea de nació en el pensament polític català (1939–1979)*, L'Avenç, Barcelona, 1984; Hank JOHNSTON, *Tales of nationalism*, Rutgers University Press, Piscataway, NJ, 1991; *El President Tarradellas en els seus textos, 1954–1988*, Empúries, Barcelona, 1992. Others: José Antonio GARCÍA ALCALÁ, *Historia del FLP. De Julio Cerón a la Liga Comunista Revolucionaria*, Centro de Estudios Políticos y Constitucionales, Madrid, 2001.

On foreign policy, for Spain's relations with the United States, apart from the texts already mentioned, see: María Jesús CAVA MESA, *Los diplomáticos de Franco. J. F. de Lequerica. Temple y tenacidad (1890–1966)*, Universidad de Deusto, Bilbao, 1989; Ángel VIÑAS, *En las garras del águila. Los pactos con los Estados Unidos de Francisco Franco y Felipe González (1945–1995)*, Crítica, Barcelona, 2003, and Arthur P. WHITAKER, *Spain and the defense of the West. Ally and liability*, Harper, New York, 1961. On Moroccan independence: Víctor MORALES LEZCANO, *El final del protectorado hispano-francés en Marruecos. El desafío magrebí (1945–1962)*, Instituto Egipcio de Estudios Islámicos, Madrid, 1998, and María Concepción YBARRA, *España y la descolonización del Magreb. Rivalidad hispano-francesa en Marruecos (1951–1956)*, UNED, Madrid, 1998. On relations with Portugal: Juan Carlos JIMÉNEZ REDONDO, *El ocaso de la amistad entre las dictaduras ibéricas, 1955–1968*, UNED, Mérida, 1996. On European politics and other international organizations: María Teresa LAPORTE, *La política europea del régimen de Franco, 1957–1962*, EUNSA, Pamplona, 1992. On relations with Cuba: Manuel de PAZ SÁNCHEZ. *La diplomacia española ante la revolución cubana (1957–1960)*, Centro de la Cultura Popular Canaria, Santa Cruz de Tenerife, 1997.

On economic policy before and after the Stabilization Plan: Charles W. ANDERSON, *The political economy of Modern Spain. Policy making in an authoritarian system*, University of Wisconsin Press, Madison, WI, 1970; Manuel Jesús GONZÁLEZ, *La economía política del franquismo (1940–1970). Dirigismo, mercado y planificación*, Tecnos, Madrid, 1979.

On culture in the second third of the Franco period, memoirs: Carlos BARRAL, *Años de penitencia*, Alianza, Madrid, 1975, and *Los años sin excusa*, Seix Barral, Barcelona, 1978; J. M. CASTELLET, *Los escenarios de la memoria*, Anagrama, Barcelona, 1988; Jaime GIL DE BIEDMA, *Diario del artista seriamente enfermo*, Lumen, Barcelona, 1974; Juan GOYTISOLO, *En los reinos de Taifas*, Seix Barral, Barcelona, 1986; Manuel MILLARES, *Memorias de la infancia y juventud*, IVAM, Valencia, 1998; Antonio MARTÍNEZ SARRIÓN, *Infancia y corrupciones*, Alfaguara, Madrid, 1993, and *Una juventud*, Alfaguara, Madrid, 1997; Antoni TÀPIES, *Memoria personal. Fragmento para una autobiografía*, Crítica, Barcelona, 1979.

General: Jordi GRÀCIA, *Estado y cultura. El despertar de una conciencia crítica bajo el franquismo (1940–1962)*, Presses Universitaires du Mirail, Toulouse, 1996; Shirley MANGINI, *Rojos y rebeldes. La cultura de la disidencia durante el*

*franquismo*, Anthropos, Barcelona, 1987; Juan F. MARSAM, *Pensar bajo el franquismo. Intelectuales y política en la generación de los años cincuenta*, Península, Barcelona, 1979.
    Literary aspects: Laureano BONET, *La revista "Laye." Estudio y antología*, Península, Barcelona, 1988, and *El jardín quebrado. La escuela de Barcelona y la cultura del medio siglo*, Península, Barcelona, 1994; José Luis CANO, *Poesía española contemporánea. Las generaciones de la posguerra*, Guadarrama, Madrid, 1974; Víctor DE LA CONCHA, *La poesía española de la posguerra. Teoría e historia de sus movimientos*, Prensa Española, Madrid, 1973; *España, vanguardia artística y realidad social: 1936–1976*, Gustavo Gili, Barcelona, 1979; Román GUBERN, *La censura: función política y ordenamiento jurídico bajo el franquismo (1936–1975)*, Península, Barcelona, 1981; Alfonso LÓPEZ QUINTAS, *Filosofía española contemporánea*, BAC, Madrid, 1970; Fernando MÉNDEZ LEITE, *Historia del cine español*, Rialp, Madrid, 1965; Thomas MERMALL, *La retórica del humanismo. La cultura española después de Ortega*, Taurus, Madrid, 1978; Santos SANZ VILLANUEVA, *Historia de la literatura española. Literatura actual*, Ariel, Barcelona, 1984.
    Intellectuals: Josep M. MUÑOZ I LLORET, *Jaume Vicens i Vives. Una biografía intel.lectual*, Edicions 62, Barcelona, 1997; Enric PUJOL, *Ferran Soldevila. Els fonaments de la historiografia catalana*, Affers, Barcelona-Catarroja, 1995; Javier TUSELL y Gonzalo ÁLVAREZ CHILLIDA, *Pemán. Un trayecto intelectual desde la extrema derecha a la democracia*, Planeta, Barcelona, 1998; Javier VARELA, *La novela de España. Los intelectuales y el problema español*, Taurus, Madrid, 1999.
    Aspects of the plastic arts: "Artistas españoles de París en Praga, 1946," exhibition held in 1993–1994 in the Sala de Exposiciones Casa Monte de Madrid; Lourdes CIRLOT, *El grupo* Dau al Set, Cátedra, Madrid, 1986; "Exposición Antológica de la Escuela de Madrid," exhibition held at Caja Madrid, Madrid, May–July 1990; "Equipo 57," exhibition at the Centro de Arte Reina Sofía, Madrid, 1993; "El grupo de Cuenca," exhibition held in the Casa de Alhajas de Caja Madrid, 1997; Víctor NIETO, *Lucio Muñoz*, Lerner y Lerner, Madrid, 1990; *Pintura española de vanguardia (1950–1990)*, Fundación Argentaria-Visor, Madrid, 1998; "Grupo Pórtico, 1947–1952," exhibition organized by the Gobierno de Aragón and the Ministerio de Cultura in 1993–1994; "Del surrealismo al informalismo. Arte de los años cincuenta en Madrid," exhibition organized by the Comunidad de Madrid in 1991; "Tomás Seral y Casas. Un galerista de la posguerra" exhibition organized at the Centro Cultural Conde Duque, Madrid, 1993; Laurent TOUSSAINT, El Paso *y el arte abstracto en España*, Cátedra, Madrid, 1983; Gabriel UREÑA, *Las vanguardias artísticas en la posguerra española, 1940–1960*, Istmo, Madrid, 1982.
    History of the Church: Jesús IRIBARREN, *Papeles y memorias. Medio siglo de relaciones Estado-Iglesia en España, 1936–1986*, BAC, Madrid, 1992; Antonio MURCIA, *Obreros y obispos en el franquismo*, Ediciones HOAC, Madrid, 1995.

Leisure activities: Jesús GARCÍA JIMÉNEZ, *Radiotelevisión y política cultural en el franquismo*, CSIC, Madrid, 1980; C. F. HEREDERO, *Las huellas del tiempo. Cine español 1951–1961*, Generalitat Valenciana–Ministerio de Cultura, 1993; Jesús ORDOVÁS, *Historia de la música "pop" española*, Alianza, Madrid, 1987; Duncan SHAW, *Fútbol y franquismo*, Alianza, Madrid, 1987 (*The political instrumentalization of professional football in Francoist Spain*. PhD Thesis, 1988. British Library); Manuel VÁZQUEZ MONTALBÁN, *Crónica sentimental de España*, Espasa Calpe, Madrid, 1986.

## Notes

1 In the Defeat at Annual in 1921 some 15,000 Spanish troops and civilians lost their lives.
2 A Jesuit, after the war Llanos embarked on a work of apostolate among Falangist youth, became chaplain to the Youth Front (*Frente de Juventudes*) in 1946, and subsequently assistant director of the Catholic student *Congregación Universitaria de Madrid*, maintaining a high public profile.
3 On August 16, 1942, at the shrine of Our Lady of Begoña in Bilbao, anti-Francoist Falangists mounted a protest. A bomb exploded and a Falangist, Juan Domínguez, was sentenced to death as a result.
4 "Fui despertado a tiros de la infancia más pura / por hombres que en España se daban a la muerte."
5 "Uno sale a la calle / y besa a una muchacha o compra un libro/ se pasea feliz y le fulminan."

# 3

# Economic Development, *Apertura*, and the Late Franco Years (1966–75)

The traits that characterize the last decade of the Franco regime are closely linked to the person of Franco himself. At other times, either he was in full possession of his physical faculties or the life of his regime was focused elsewhere on areas that did not require his intervention. He was not required to play an active role, for example in economic matters. Now, in contrast, in the second half of the 1960s, political uncertainty inside Spain became the most burning issue in the life of the regime.

Economic growth, which continued throughout these years, had by now begun to make Spanish society less authoritarian. It therefore became at this time not merely a propaganda weapon used by the regime but also a source of conflict. There was also worsening conflict brought on by the transformation of society, which was substantial from the mid 1960s onwards, leading not only to social democratization but also to the adoption of different cultural attitudes. For example, those years saw an effective alignment of Spain's cultural and intellectual worlds against the regime which was to a great extent aware of what was going on.

However, the capacity for reaction of those in positions of political leadership in the regime had diminished considerably. This was particularly so in the case of Franco himself, who could sense that concepts deeply rooted in his way of thinking were being eroded, while at the same time there was a gradual weakening of his former ability to arbitrate between different elements within the right-wing coalition over which he presided. The overwhelming impression given by the Franco of the last 10 years of the dictatorship is one of a governor who was becoming increasingly disconcerted by a reality that he no longer found easy to understand and direct.

Scholars who study the last decade of Francoism cannot but sense the pathos of a regime that was dying after turning its back on society. Franco was no longer the victorious *caudillo* who had won the Civil War but an

old man who was still capable of resorting to the harshest forms of repression from time to time but now found himself at an inconceivable
distance from the Spanish people. Before the crisis of October 1969 he said
to Manuel Fraga: "I've been here for so many years, inside the walls of this
place [The Palace of El Pardo], that I don't know anybody any more."
More pathetic still is a reading of the private notes that he wrote about the
Church distancing itself from the regime: "What do the people who were
involved with Vatican II know about Spain?" he asked himself in 1968. As
time passed he was more and more perplexed and pained by what was
going on, which he described as nothing less than "a stab in the back" and,
"faced with a historic responsibility," he considered consulting the pope.
He presided, stony-faced and silent, at several cabinet meetings at which
more and more of the members were technocrats rather than politicians
and important discussions were turning into increasingly bitter arguments.
His opinions became so defensive that they were often difficult to interpret. Those who consulted him usually found him hesitant, his character
weakened by the weight of years and a prey to uncertainty. Sometimes he
was simply not there: on the two occasions that he received Henry
Kissinger he fell asleep. He had always been "a sphinx without a secret" in
the sense that his character and personality were far more straightforward
than the lengthy theories put forward in an attempt to interpret them.
Now he was just "a sphinx" and no more, and the clues he gave were even
fewer. It was Franco's physical decline that made the institutionalization
of the regime essential, but it remained impracticable, in the first instance
because it was a personal dictatorship, and also because an institutional
framework threatened to bring increasing internal conflict. Rodolfo
Martín Villa points out in his memoirs that Spanish society played no part
in official politics, and that official politics had no moral legitimacy for
imposing rulings on society. The regime was confronting an ever more
active opposition, but the opposition was as yet unable to pose any real
immediate threat. The most positive aspect of a situation such as the one
described, which corresponds most closely to the years after 1973, is that
it can be seen as a preamble – and perhaps a necessary one – that allowed
what followed to take the form of a peaceful transition.

Events proved that the regime was unable to evolve, but before 1969 this
was not so obvious to the majority of Spaniards. In that year Francoism
still enjoyed some of the consensus support that had lingered on from
the 1950s. Nonetheless, over the 1960s much of that disappeared. The
regime's successes held the seeds of its own destruction.

###### ——— Economic Development in the 1960s and 1970s ———

Economic growth in Spain was on a par with that in Italy, France, and Germany even though it happened somewhat later: it was very strong at the start – indeed, almost explosively so – but it became more uneven subsequently. It was the result of a better use of resources and increased productivity as a consequence of using new technology, cheap energy – electricity consumption in Spain tripled between 1960 and 1975 – and a workforce that had been underemployed until now. Its origins can also be seen in a "boundless eagerness for an improved economic performance" evident in the working class political leadership.

If we are to grasp the true extent of the profound transformation which occurred in Spanish society over a decade we have to consider the question of revenue. It was the source of the three great driving forces behind Spain's development. These three driving forces were tourism, foreign investment, and the emigration of the workforce, mainly to Europe.

First of all we must look at the important part played by tourism which, in a very short time, became the nation's primary industry. The so-called "tourism revolution" was seen as being so fundamental that at the time of greatest growth in this area there were some who concluded that Spain could now import without limit or anxiety of any kind. From 1966 to 1970 the number of tourists grew from a little over 17 million to 24 million, whereas in 1961 the number had only been a little above 7 million. Somewhat more than half of the tourists came from Europe's first Common Market. In 1966 there were almost 9 million French and almost 2 million Germans, while the number of British topped 2.5 million. Tourism proved crucial for the Spanish balance of payments because it allowed Spain to do away with its trade deficit. In the initial stage of its industrial development, tourism played a decisive role as the revenue it brought in tripled in the period 1960–6 alone. Tourism was – and still is – primarily a summer phenomenon, middle class and concentrated in already developed areas, and it helped not so much to industrialize but to "dilute" Spanish society. There is no doubt whatever that, in part at least, the transformation of the cultural habits and way of life of Spaniards at the time was a direct result of contact with the outside world.

Government policy played a decisive role in the matter of foreign investment. In the period 1956–8 foreign investment represented only some 3 million dollars. After 1959, investments of under 50 percent of capital were liberalized but over 50 percent they needed government approval. It has been estimated that between 1959 and 1974 Spain received investments of foreign capital amounting to about 6,000 million dollars. The sources of this capital were largely North American (40 percent), Swiss (20 percent), German (11 percent), French (6 percent), and British (5 percent). Investment was aimed mostly at the chemical industry (perhaps 25 percent) but also at commerce and foodstuffs. What attracted European capital was the existence of a cheap labor force and an expanding market. Spanish industrialization would have been inconceivable without this support, which accounted for perhaps 20 percent of investment in industry.

In third place, another driving force behind the Spanish economy, which also was a result of low income, was the export of Spain's workers to Europe. Unlike what happened in other countries such as Portugal, the Spanish state not only did not discourage emigration but even followed a consistent policy of channeling it. Franco himself stated in private that he could not prevent Spaniards seeking a better life outside Spain. The annual number of emigrants in the 1960s, with the exception of 1967–8, was over 100,000 and in some years, such as 1964, it touched on 200,000. Between 1960 and 1973 a million workers left Spain, of whom 93 percent were heading for Europe. It has been estimated that in some years money sent home by Spanish emigrant workers brought the country double the revenue that it earned exporting citrus fruits. From a strictly economic point of view emigration had positive effects as it brought with it capitalization and a better professional training, and it even caused a significant wage rise in rural areas.

Only after having touched on these three fundamental driving forces is it possible to turn our attention to the reality that they engendered. The growth experienced by Spain was largely dependent on industry, but at the same time there were profound changes affecting agriculture that should be mentioned here. What happened in this period could well be described as a crisis for traditional agriculture.

In order to explain this process we must look back to the measures on agriculture introduced in the 1950s. First of all it is essential to remember that those were the years when repopulation programs were implemented (it was the time of the Badajoz and Jaen Plans). At the start of the 1960s one could say that the Spanish state was financing very slow transformation of the physical environment, while in contrast it showed no concern whatever about agricultural productivity. That impression is confirmed by the fact that its agrarian policy was obviously having a minimal effect.

The first Law on Land Consolidation (*Ley de Concentración Parcelaria*) was provisionally approved in 1952 and passed in July 1955; in February 1953 the National Service for Land Consolidation (*Servicio Nacional de Concentración Parcelaria*) was set up to implement these measures. Its objective was to fight against the existing system of smallholdings (*minifundios*); even as late as the 1960s, half of the farms in Galicia were smaller than 20 hectares in size. Between 1953 and 1968 – that is to say, a space of time that corresponds roughly to a half generation – only a little over 5 million hectares were brought together to form larger farms. Calculations showed that at this average speed it would take 30 years to effect the transformation that Spanish agriculture needed. The first measure aimed at farms that could obviously be improved dates from December 1953, but the revision of this kind of measure (in 1971 another law was passed) itself shows that the existing laws were not very effective. At the end of the 1960s, in terms of agriculture, Spain was still reminiscent of some Third World countries: agricultural production was 17 percent of the national total.

However, if government measures did not bring about any great changes, it is possible to say that demographic factors contributed towards Spain's transformation. As regards the countryside, the single factor that made the greatest impact was the fact that the government backed emigration. The loss to the agricultural environment of a million working people who went abroad, and of perhaps four times that number who went to live in towns of more than 100,000 inhabitants, had an immediate effect on salaries. Estimates suggest that whereas in the period 1950–70 prices rose from an index of 651 to 1,465, rural salaries went up from 424 to 5,030. We have to bear in mind that this salary rise affected landless laborers (*jornaleros*) as well as small property-owners. As a result, the smallest and least profitable properties from an economic point of view tended to disappear. In the 1950s this meant those of fewer than 6 hectares, and in the 1960s those smaller than 50 hectares; between 1962 and 1972 something in the order of half a million farms disappeared.

It was, therefore, this single factor that drove forward the modernization of Spanish agriculture. Large farms (*latifundios*) remained a reality but they were no longer presented as an irrational form of agricultural organization. On the contrary, the lack of a labor force had introduced a modernizing and profit-making mentality that had in fact already been typical of Spanish agriculture before this time. In the 1970s the role of agriculture in the overall Spanish economy was diminishing, even in terms

of exports, but it was only in 1973 that Spanish agriculture began to respond to the real demands of the internal market. Towards the end of the
Franco period, although Spain was still below the level of the majority
of European countries in terms of its use of agricultural machinery and
fertilizers, it had managed to increase its production of maize per hectare,
while barley and wheat production had increased by 60 percent. Over
the same period the production of meat per inhabitant quadrupled and
that of eggs doubled. For the first time in Spanish history, by the 1970s
an entire generation had had no direct experience of that habitual
phenomenon of the past: hunger.

Notwithstanding all of this, Spain's economic growth in the 1960s and
1970s was primarily industrial. Throughout the 1960s indicative planning
was presented in official propaganda as the cause of Spain's development.
In reality the role planning played was far smaller than was suggested
at the time. In accordance with this reading of the situation, the role of
economic policy was crucial during the period of stabilization. At that time
those in charge of Spain's economic life were being advised by an efficient
team of economists among whom, for example, were Joan Sardá and
Enrique Fuentes Quintana. The measures adopted in 1959 were accepted
because they were inevitable, and also because they were successful in the
short term, but by 1962 a report by the World Bank awoke much stronger
resistance from within the political system.

On some imprecise date around 1964–5 the liberalization program had
reached crisis-point. One of the experts, Fuentes Quintana, could write
that Spanish development was in fact a result of stabilization and that the
plans had put a brake on it. Far from being a magical form of salvation,
the plans were simply an imperfect form of prediction based on European
models imported into Spain. They were not really the work of economists,
and with them and the reintroduction of state interventionism the
economy was once more subject to interference.

To view as relative the impact of the various Development Plans on
Spanish economic growth is, then, a notion based on sound arguments.
For many the plans were nothing more than "simple projections or estimates, which were more or less fallible about events that would have come
about anyway." Perhaps the best proof of this is the anecdote that tells how
the adjective "social" was added to the title of the first plan in response to
complaints by Falangists, but not a single comma was changed in the text.
What is striking about these government estimates is the number of
factors that were simply not taken into account. They did not, for example,

foresee the expansion of tourism, nor imagine that there would be such migratory movements as there were, which, by the time of the first plan, were already four times larger than had been anticipated. What is more, paradoxically, planning was to become more compulsory for the private sector than the public sector because the latter was unable to control costs. As if that were not enough, the absence of any real planning became more acute over time. The last development plan was the least well implemented and in several sections there was a deviation of more than 50 percent from what had originally been predicted. Many of the basic economic targets were not taken into account or were allowed to go down paths that had never been anticipated by those who had drawn up the plan. Prices, for example, which should have risen by 12 percent according to the second plan, in fact rose by 20 percent. It is possible that the only fundamental achievement of the Development Plans was to show Spaniards the importance of having an economic policy and of the economy in general.

An examination of government interventionism in Spain's industrial policy makes it clear that the liberalizing ideas of 1959 were far from having been implemented by 1964. Issues such as the MATESA scandal (*Maquinaria Textil del Norte de España Sociedad Anónima*: North of Spain Textile Machinery Ltd) reveal that in an economy such as Spain's economy was at the time, what was essential for good business was not technological innovation or entrepreneurial imaginativeness but to be "well connected" in official circles. The case of this particular firm also shows that it was virtually essential to break out of the constraints of the tight interventionist straitjacket.

The constraints that existed – the legacy of an earlier period – took a long time to dismantle: it was as late as 1967 before the government prerequisites authorizing the setting up of an industry disappeared. By now there were no businesses of national interest but there were, on the other hand, many designated of "preferential interest." This was just one of the many main ways – perhaps as many as nine of them – of favoring certain businesses. In this respect it is worth mentioning, above all, what was called "concerted action," which meant that by means of low interest rates and tax exemptions it was possible to finance up to 60 percent of a factory in exchange for reaching certain production targets. Another common form of state intervention in the industrial sector was in the creation of development areas. In this way it could be said that the industrial policy adopted, rather than being geared to a market economy, favored private enterprise. The World Bank had said that the state should not enter any economic field that private enterprise had plans to enter, but now everyone was dependent on the benevolence of the state. It can come as no surprise that the man principally responsible for Spain's industrial policy, Gregorio López Bravo, was described as a genuine entrepreneur in national industry rather than as the one who created the best framework for that industry.

Nor was there a clear policy relating to the INI. In 1959 it was forced to seek finance through the savings banks or *Cajas de Ahorro* – a measure that enraged those in charge of it – but until 1963 it was presided over by Juan Antonio Suances. By the 1960s Suances's relations with Franco were bad and although when he resigned he was thanked for "extraordinary services rendered" and given the title of marquis, he never forgave being dismissed from his position as Franco's principal adviser on economic matters. From 1968 on, the INI was directly dependent on the Ministry for Industry. In López Bravo's view, the INI should have had a subsidiary function in relation to private enterprise and should have gone into areas where private enterprise did not operate, and, at the same time, act as a hospital for companies in difficulties. Given these criteria, it is not surprising that the INI should have continued to take on new commitments and, above all, that companies experiencing difficulties with solvency would come to land on its shoulders. After the state had spent enormous sums of money trying to restructure the steel industry by concerted action, it had to accept the creation of ENSIDESA (*Empresa Nacional Siderúrgica Sociedad Anónima*: National Steel Company Ltd), an INI company which was in competition with another privately owned company in which the state holding company itself had interests. Only after 1970 did the INI begin to be guided by criteria which took profitability into account while still keeping up its levels of activity even in new fields (such as shipbuilding and gas).

Even facing limitations such as these, the growth in Spain's industrial production was spectacular. The rise in industrial productivity was truly impressive: 160 percent between 1963 and 1972; between 1960 and 1973 Spain multiplied its productivity by three and a half. In a short space of time the most thriving industries were chemicals, paper, and metal-mechanical industries such as car production. Not only did production increase but productivity as well, doubling in the period 1961–70 and growing at an annual rate twice that of Germany and more than twice that of Britain. We can explain this extraordinary industrial development principally in terms of the existence of an internal market capable of providing huge demand. In the period 1960–72 capital goods increased at an annual rate of 20 percent, while exports of manufactured goods over a similar period grew by 14 percent.

The very speed at which Spanish industry grew also had its disadvantages since it meant that industry was located in limited areas of Spain. Halfway through the 1970s, 49 percent of Spanish industry was in Madrid, the Basque Country, and Catalonia and, with the exception of steel production, Catalonia had a clear lead in all other branches of industry. At around that time Julián Marías wrote that Spain was not underdeveloped but "badly developed," a statement that seems correct if attention is focused principally on the destruction of the natural landscape and the kind of urban development that took place in those years.

In terms of foreign trade as well, many positive changes occurred over the years following the Stabilization Plan. If we consider nothing other than exports, it is possible to say that in the period 1960–75 they grew by a factor of ten; the annual growth rate was especially strong between 1967 and 1973. It is also significant that what Spain was exporting changed considerably. Agricultural products decreased to a third of their original level in the period 1961–75, while exports of intermediate, capital, and consumer goods increased. All in all, although at the end of the Franco regime tourism and the remittances sent back home by emigrant workers played an essential part in achieving a balance of payments, Spain had broken with its traditional image as an exporter of citrus fruits. For example, it also exported ships (in 1971 it was the fourth largest producer in the world) and machine tools.

Even so, experts have described Spain's opening up to trade as "limited and contradictory." In 1963 free trade already accounted for 63 percent of the total and by 1967 that rose to 75 percent, yet by 1974 it had only reached 80 percent. Customs tariffs protected the Spanish market, but there were other procedures too which had similar effects. Tax concessions on exports increased by so much that if, in 1961, 3 percent of the export market benefited from them, by 1975 that figure had risen to 13 percent. Although Spanish foreign trade grew, it did not attain the level of development that it could have reached. It represented only 9 percent of GDP when in the majority of Common Market countries it was at least double that. A third of Spain's trade was within the Community but it was only in the summer of 1970 that a treaty was signed, and then it was not a treaty of membership, since that was impossible until the political conditions required were achieved, but at least it was one of association.

Taken as a whole, Spain's economic growth after 1959 was spectacular. In the 1960s and 1970s it featured as one of the five countries in the world with the best economic results. In 1966–71 the annual growth rate was only 5.5 percent, but if we take a longer period, such as 1960–75, it was a little higher than 7 percent, which was the highest figure in Europe and one of the highest in the world after Japan and Iran. By the 1970s Spain was already the tenth or eleventh most industrialized country in the world. A true and genuine revolution had taken place which was much more far-reaching and irreversible than the revolution during the Civil War. The paradox is that, as we have seen, this revolution had not been foreseen by those in positions of power in politics; nor, most importantly of all, had change come about in the way that they had planned.

Change had in large part been spontaneous. It generated new problems and raised many questions. The spontaneity of Spain's development meant that in the future its foundations would have to be laid once again. Industry continued to be overprotected to combat competition from outside, while internally it was subject to government intervention. The problem was not that public sector industry was too large (within the Common Market figures were virtually double those in Spain) but that state intervention determined what would happen to 4 out of every 10 pesetas worth of credit. Agriculture faced problems with modernization and competitiveness. The Spanish state was impotent because it lacked the necessary tax mechanisms. At the end of the Franco period it was draining off little more than 13 percent of the GNP, whereas in Japan that figure was 15 percent and in France 22 percent. Only between 1958 and 1965 was there a tax surplus. In addition, the system was extremely behind the times, with income tax representing a very small sum whereas, in the Netherlands, it was already at 50 percent. A direct consequence of this was that Spanish infrastructures left much to be desired. The Spanish state had, in effect, at one and the same time, an interventionist lion's head and a mouse's tax and budgetary tail. The glossy image of its economic development has to be set alongside the actual "aluminosis" that weakened a large number of the beams that had been used in its construction.

Finally, we must take into account the fact that Spain's development had been affected from time to time by problems with prices. Since the Civil War the peseta had been devalued eight times, and in the period 1963–70 the price index rose from 100 to 151. The average annual price rise during Spain's period of greatest development was at 7 percent, while in the rest of Europe it was usually under half a percent. The government should have imposed deflationary measures in 1964, but in 1967 it adopted new policies which did completely the opposite. Even more serious for the country's political leaders was the fact that they had engendered a society in which the regime itself now made no sense at all.

## The Modernization of Spanish Society

At the same time as Spain's economy was growing, a profound transformation was also taking place in society that would inevitably have political implications. If the Spain of the 1950s had quite a lot in common with Latin American countries – indeed, it was actually trailing behind them according to many indices of economic and social development – by the final phase of the Franco regime it had in many senses become a European country.

Between the census of 1960 and the one carried out in 1970, the number of Spaniards had increased from 30 million to over 33 million. Indeed, the first area in which the modernization of Spanish society became manifestly obvious was in relation to demographic change. The change in the mortality rate occurred in the 1950s, at which time Spanish figures were similar to those in other European countries such as France and Italy. In contrast, the birth rate went down later than elsewhere; it was only in the final phase of the Franco period that it went down from 21 to 18 per 1,000. The factors that caused this were late marriages and birth control, which only became widespread to the point of reaching the same level as other countries in Europe after the transition. The overall growth in population was very strong at this point, oscillating between 12 and 10 per 1,000. The aging of the population characteristic of European societies was, in the Spanish case, a late phenomenon.

Significant changes came about, too, as a result of internal migrations. In the 1960s, 4 million Spaniards changed their place of residence. The biggest migratory phenomenon was of landless laborers moving to urban centers where there was more chance of them finding work and a different way of life. What happened as a result was that the Spanish population became urbanized. The number of Spaniards living in towns of more that 20,000 inhabitants rose from 40 to 54 percent, though in European countries such as Germany the figure was already in the order of 80 percent. In 1970, the year in which the last census of the Franco era was taken, only 33 percent of the population lived in towns of fewer than

10,000 inhabitants. This means that a huge process of urbanization had taken place.

There was also significant redistribution of the population, which tended to move towards the periphery rather than towards the center of the Peninsula and become part of new urban centers of growth. At the start of the last century, the demographic weight of the center was still superior to that of the periphery, but this situation had changed by 1970 when the center accounted for 44 percent and the periphery 56 percent of the total population. The centers which received internal migrations were the central province of Madrid, the coast – particularly the Basque Country and Catalonia – and the valleys leading through to France and the valley of the Ebro. Then, during the 1970s, emigration continued towards Madrid and the east coast, but not so much into Catalonia and the Basque Country. There had appeared once again in Spanish history a factor that had been a strong characteristic of our past: a duality that was not only demographic but also social and cultural. Alongside the Spain of modern development, huddled together in the poorer districts of its industrial areas, there lived another depopulated Spain – a kind of internal Lusitania condemned to desertification and underdevelopment.

The changes that took place in Spanish society were occupational as well as demographic and migratory, and in this respect we should underline the fact that the speed at which they happened was meteoric. In the space of just one generation the transformation that occurred exceeded anything of the kind over the entire previous century. In the period between the censuses of 1960 and 1970, the rural population decreased from 42 to 25 percent of the total – a change similar to levels over the previous 60 years. With Franco's death now close, Spain's working population took on a modern appearance, and although the role of agriculture was still far greater than in other countries (22 percent), the service sector now employed 40 percent of the working population, while 38 percent were employed in industry. The working population grew from 34 to 38 percent and added to it there was a female workforce which rose to 24 percent: an already sizeable figure, though one that fell far short of levels in the rest of Europe. Spaniards now clearly saw a job and a desire to improve one's personal and family life as priorities, as is evident from the fact that ten-hour days were not uncommon and one in five workers in Madrid had more than one job at the start of the 1970s. The generation that took an active part in Spain's development was, above all else, a hardworking generation.

Spain saw much more growth than redistribution of its population, yet the data relating to per capita income and consumption show that the majority of the population benefited from these economic changes. It could not be otherwise when in the period 1964–72 industrial wages rose by 287 percent, while the cost of living rose by only 70 percent. The average Spanish income in 1960 was around 300 dollars, in 1964 it was 500 dollars, and in 1973 it reached 2,000 dollars, a figure achieved by Japan only 4 years earlier. Given these spectacular statistics, it is worth comparing them with those of other nations: in 1967, for example, the per capita income in Spain was 50 percent higher than in Portugal but only two-thirds of the level in Italy.

It is doubtless in relation to consumption that we can best appreciate the change experienced by Spanish society as a result of economic growth. Consumption began to take off between 1962 and 1966, but it only became generalized in the second half of the 1960s and the beginning of the 1970s. In the first phase, for example, the number of cars per inhabitant doubled, the number of telephones increased by 50 percent, and the number of kilos of meat consumed per head of the population rose by a little less than 50 percent. The figures were almost more startling in the period 1966–74, which saw a spectacular rise in the production of certain goods. Spain moved from producing 250,000 cars per year to 700,000, from 570,000 television sets to 730,000, from around 300,000 fridges to more than a million, and from around 400,000 washing-machines to more than double that number. By the time of Franco's death, certain household goods were to be found everywhere. If in 1968 the percentage of households with fridge, television, and washing-machine was at around 40 percent, by 1975 it was close on 80 percent for some of those goods, while at least 60 percent of households had all of them. The rise in the standard of living also was evident in the reduction of the percentage of the family budget spent on food, which had been 55 percent at the start of the period and went down to 38 percent.

If we examine the stratification of Spanish society we can see who the people were who benefited most and who was marginalized by this process of development. A phenomenon which was crucially important was the emergence of what were termed "new middle classes" consisting of office workers, sales people, and technicians with different trainings. These new middle classes were the main protagonists of Spain's development and increase in consumption, but they were also the sector that was mainly involved in *pluriempleo*: holding several jobs at a time.

Now, if these new layers of society were evidence of the very real social transformation that Spain had undergone by this time, social inequality nonetheless remained a feature of daily life and represented a marked difference between Spain and the majority of other European countries. At the end of the Franco period, around 1.2 percent of the Spanish population owned 22 percent of the nation's wealth, while another 52 percent held another 21 percent. The economic development of the 1960s was, on the whole, a widespread phenomenon but even so it did not reach sizeable pockets of the population. By the 1970s, 80 percent of households still lacked running water in Orense, and 23 percent of heads of households in Huelva were illiterate. To this "old poverty" should be added the new poverty of immigrants into cities, who lacked any kind of training (one sociologist labeled them "pre-workers") and lived in miserable conditions in slums around the edges of conurbations, marginalized by a thriving consumerist society.

This was one sign of the "bad development" that was characteristic of the Spanish society of the time, but it was not the only one. The state was clearly incapable of responding to social demands. It was as late as 1970 before it spent more on education than on the Army (at the height of World War II, in 1943, the military budget had been set at 54 percent of the total). Even so, the deficiencies in Spanish education were still obvious, with a large part of the population of school age not attending classes, poor pre-school provision, and in contrast, universities which had seen the number of students rise (and of teachers too, whose numbers increased by 66 percent). Something similar could be said about housing, where demand grew 50 percent more than had been anticipated in the First Development Plan.

As one would expect, economic development did not only produce a quantitative change in social terms; there were also qualitative changes in the characters of the different social groups, two of which in particular deserve some brief comment. The Armed Services had adopted a progressively more professional approach after 1963. Although a high percentage of senior posts remained in the hands of the 10,000 men still serving who had been given temporary rank as *alféreces provisionales* during the Civil War, as time passed the mentality of younger recruits changed. A survey conducted in 1975 among the members of the eighth year to graduate as officers from the Military Academy at Zaragoza revealed that only 48 percent did not have other jobs as well. Moreover, by this time more than 10 percent had a university degree and up to

46 percent some lower qualification. More than half thought that the religious component of military ceremonies in barracks was inappropriate. Among an officer body whose form of Catholicism tended to confuse politics with religion but ended up being viewed merely as an imposition, the first tentative signs of nonconformity – such as the *Forja* group – began to appear in the 1950s. In Spain, unlike Portugal, the Armed Services did not distance themselves from the dictatorship, but by the 1970s a wide gap now separated the high command from the younger officers. Along with the Democratic Military Union (*Unión Militar Democrática*), which will be discussed later, we should mention the four cadets expelled from the Zaragoza Military Academy in 1973 for reading dissident publications such as *Cuadernos para el Diálogo* and *Triunfo*, for having university friends, or for having renounced their Catholic faith.

There were also qualitative changes taking place that affected women. The immediate postwar period had meant a considerable step backward in terms of the social and professional role of women in Spain. This was due to a particular conception of woman which linked her to reproduction and to family life. "We love the sweet, passive woman who waits for us, glimpsed behind a curtain, occupied with her work and her prayers," said one text in a women's magazine of the time. Characteristics such as these continued to be assigned to women in a very special way in the Spanish case because of the view that "where woman is at her most womanly is here, in Spain." Women had to "get engaged" or they would end up "dressing saints." If a man did not marry it was because he did not want to, whereas for a woman it was because she was not able to do so. The only other variant on this domestic vision for women was, in exceptional cases, the empty-headed product of modernity which, in the 1940s, was called the "*niña topolino*" after the fashionable wedge-heeled shoes that such girls wore. Legislation on family subsidies penalized women who worked, while in other instances a misconceived desire to protect women was a factor that did much towards keeping them out of the workplace. The women's section of Falange (*Sección Femenina*) devoted itself principally to training girls in domestic skills. The separation of the sexes in schools fueled a kind of mystique about masculinity and about the sinfulness of contact between the two sexes.

From the middle of the 1950s on, and even more clearly a decade later, changes did begin to occur. In 1958 a reform of the Civil Code (*Código Civil*) went part of the way towards declaring the roles of men and women equal in marriage. After the middle of the 1940s, a new generation of women wrote autobiographical novels (Carmen Laforet, Carmen Martín Gaite, Mercè Rodoreda . . . ) which were evidence of a renewed commitment to literature on the part of women graduates. In the 1960s, María Campo Alange wrote two books about the situation of women in the society of the time, and from the middle of the 1960s on, the philosopher and essayist José Luis López Aranguren could comment that, in contrast to the virtual absence of any mention of sexuality in previous years, there was now, more than anything else, a lack of inhibitions. This was a consequence of the fact that there was now also a move towards sexual equality in the workplace. In 1950 women represented only 15 percent of the working population, whereas by the end of the Franco period the figure had reached 28 percent, though the percentage in domestic service was still very high. Some figures from these years show that there were, at one and the same time, progress and limitations. Less than a tenth of directorships were in female hands, and in 1969 only 20 percent of those receiving public sector salaries were women. By the 1960s, among university graduates it was thought of as normal for women to work, yet in the year that Franco died, 80 percent of the population as a whole thought that woman's place was in the home.

## The Change in Spanish Catholicism

The data offered so far are only part of the evidence that we have of a change of mentality in Spain. A process of evolution in the Catholic Church, principally as a result of the impact on our country of the Second Vatican Council, provides yet more evidence of change at the same time as being itself a driving force for change. Given the Church's enormous power in the society of the 1950s it is unlikely that any other social institution could have played a comparable role.

If we are to appreciate the sheer magnitude of the change that took place we must inevitably look back to an earlier period. Well on into the 1950s a large part of the Church hierarchy and its members shared at a deep level the fact that they identified Spain with the Franco regime and with Catholicism. The Bishop of Lérida, Aurelio del Pino, stated that "what raises Franco to levels that few have attained in the whole of human history is his marvelous work in the Christian transfiguration of individuals." Spanish specialists in social Catholicism affirmed that "the whole of Christendom is one gigantic vertical union," and in December 1957 it was even suggested that Franco should be made a cardinal, setting him on a par with the emperors Constantine and Charlemagne.

Yet, at about this same time, attitudes such as these came to be seen as somewhat extravagant because of changes occurring within the Spanish Catholic Church itself. Characterized by its close links to the state, by an "insatiability" that wanted Spanish Catholicism to be purer than any other form, and demanding a higher level of orthodoxy from it and everything to do with it, intolerant and out of touch with current trends of thought beyond our frontiers, National Catholicism was also autocratic. Those in the hierarchy who expressed reservations about the regime in the 1950s were doing so from an extreme integrist position.

Yet National Catholicism also had at its heart a genuine spontaneity and sincerity, and for that very reason it could not ignore the reality of religious life in Spain. Characteristic of this religious life was the intense level of mobilization by groups devoted to the work of apostolate; however, to have a deep religious sentiment free from any ties to politics or religious culture is quite another matter. As far back as the 1940s Catholic groups such as the workers' movement *Hermandades Obreras de Acción Católica* or the youth organization *Juventud Obrera Católica* clashed on more than a few occasions with representatives of the official state unions. In different ways, the quest for purity and religious commitment clashed with the way of life in the huge seminaries built in those years which housed some more than dubious theology reduced in practice to a formalist morality.

The self-critical approach that surfaced in the Spanish Catholic Church towards the end of the 1950s was sometimes centered on social issues, but it was largely limited to intellectual strongholds, lay or otherwise. Even some members of the hierarchy, like the future Cardinal Enrique Tarancón, addressed in their teaching the disparity between the appearance of a thriving Catholicism and the reality of social doctrines that were hardly ever put into practice. What is certain is that the movement that was self-critical was also didactic in tone. In the so-called *Conversaciones Católicas* held in San Sebastián and the Gredos Mountains, in which some of the best-known Spanish intellectuals of the time took part, from Julián Marías to José Luis López Aranguren and including Pedro Laín Entralgo, this self-critical tendency anticipated – albeit hesitantly – the impact that Vatican II would make on Spain. Marías, who defended what we might describe as "liberal Catholicism," wrote that if this type of encounter had only continued, the Spanish Church could have been spared much of its subsequent crisis. However, perhaps Aranguren was more influential in Catholic circles, in time moving from identification with the intellectual world of the regime to a position further to the left. His book *Catolicismo y protestantismo como formas de existencia* (*Catholicism and Protestantism as different ways of life*: 1952) took the first step in that process of evolution.

While the Catholicism of that generation of intellectuals had been personal, the generations that followed experienced a stifling form of religion, particularly in the education system but also imposed on society as a whole, and this explains their subsequent anti-clericalism. It was possible to see in this self-critical intellectual world an expression of a new mentality which had little in common with at least one of the most important functions that Catholicism had had in relation to the regime so far. During the Franco period, Catholicism had performed a para-political function – providing the regime with leaders from one of the regime families typified by its particular kind of pluralism – or else it had increasingly acted as an unofficial court of appeal: a voice for social protest. Catholicism had also provided an intellectual underpinning for the political system and its new revisionist thinking came into conflict with the old ways.

Alongside this change in thinking in intellectual circles it is important to note that as time passed there also emerged a growing dissident attitude among those committed to social Catholicism, or else in associations characterized by a strong cultural identity of their own. At the start of the 1960s Franco himself considered writing a letter to the pope to complain that the "revolutionary urgency" of Spain's movements of apostolate was intolerable and that certain Basque bishops lacked the qualities necessary to run their dioceses. After 1959 Catholic Action in Spain had adopted a form of organization based on specialization and on a commitment to specific circumstances, and over time this inevitably led to conflict with the political system. That was quite evidently the case in relation to the official state trade union, which members of the hierarchy considered "a mere shell emptied of all content." The situation worsened when in 1962 militant members of the HOAC and JOC joined in the strikes in Asturias, as a consequence of which the presidents of both organizations received huge fines, while the JOC's representative, who would later become a bishop, was stripped of his ecclesiastical licenses.

Also at the start of the 1960s, there was evidence of dissidence in Basque and Catalan Catholic circles. As early as 1960, during protests over Franco's presence in Barcelona, among the leaders of the disturbances was

Jordi Pujol, who came from these Catholic circles and was condemned to 7 years in prison. That same year more than 300 Basque priests wrote a letter of protest voicing their disagreement with the regime; 4 years later some 400 Catalan priests did the same. In 1963 the Abbot of Montserrat declared that although the regime might called itself Catholic it was not so. Stances such as these, though initially only representative of a minority, soon become commonplace. The fact that they happened on a daily basis did not, however, represent a serious threat to the regime. As late as 1964, when the regime celebrated 25 years in office, it was possible to publish in their entirety and with no evidence of any resistance the official declarations by the Church hierarchy reaffirming their close links with the regime. It was in that same year that more than a million people gathered in Madrid to recite the rosary – a ceremony inspired by an American priest but one that reveals our weakness for baroque ceremonial.

However, it was without doubt Vatican II that contributed most towards changing Spanish Catholicism, so much so that we can say that it played a much more decisive role in Spain than in other parts of the world. The position from which the majority of the Spanish Catholic Church approached the proceedings was clearly very different from the overall spirit that inspired the Council. As late as 1961, not only was the Spanish Church hierarchy intent on condemning communism as "intrinsically perverse," but its members, as result of their own experience and their antecedents, were totally hostile to notions of religious freedom and pluralism and the very concept of the Church and a Catholic state being independent of one another. When Cardinal Montini spoke out in favor of the latter, the Spanish Foreign Minister tried to persuade the four Spanish cardinals present to speak out against the notion. Later, Montini was chosen as pope – a decision that Franco received "like a jug of cold water."

In circumstances such as these, the part played by the Spanish Church in the sessions of the Second Vatican Council could not be described as brilliant; it provided barely 5 percent of the Council Fathers, and that 5 percent inevitably aligned itself with those resisting progress. One Spanish bishop was denied the right to speak after he had stated that religious freedom was "inadmissible." Another question that was much debated, as one would expect, concerned the appointment of bishops. In many matters Vatican II did nothing other than ratify practices that had been in existence for years, but that were for Spanish Catholics a revelation that Spain's representatives at the Council accepted sincerely though they were also somewhat perplexed. The vision of the rights of the individual that permeated the texts approved by the Council in relation to political institutions was in stark contrast to what was actually going on in Spain.

One direct, immediate, and unavoidable consequence of Vatican II was the approval of a Law on Religious Freedom in 1967. Until this date the situation for Protestants in Spain had been lamentable: they had had problems with the civil authorities on account of their versions of the Bible, their religious ceremonies which could not be conducted in public, and even their buildings on which no notices were allowed to appear. The original bill drawn up by Castiella as Minister for Foreign Affairs was received by Carrero Blanco with strong reservations and was cut by the Ministry of Justice, only to suffer further cuts when it came before the *Cortes*. From now on, civil marriage would be permissible for non-Catholics, who also would not be obliged to take part in religious ceremonies either during military service or in state education. Even so, even Catholic organizations considered the law inadequate.

Much more decisive than this, however, was the change that took place in Spanish Catholicism. The Second Vatican Council began by having an undoubted impact on the Church hierarchy. One must remember that in 1966, a year after it ended, 83 percent of Spanish bishops had been appointed according to the right of presentation that had been set out in the 1953 Concordat. In addition, two-thirds were over 60 years of age, a quarter were over 75, and only three were under 45. Almost half had been bishops for over 20 years and the vast majority had been ordained before the Civil War and came from rural areas. During the period 1965–71 no fewer than 42 new bishops were appointed – that is to say, more than half the total number. Moreover, in the last stages of the Franco period, given the discrepancies that existed between civil and ecclesiastical authorities, it became customary to appoint auxiliary bishops because it did not require state intervention.

This change brought about in the hierarchy by replacing older members with younger men did much towards changing the content of its teaching. After 1966 the Episcopal Conference functioned like an electoral college in place of the former Conference of Metropolitans. Nonetheless, even at this time the document that was approved on "The Church and temporal power" still showed a determination to maintain a relationship with the state identical to the one already in existence.

The situation changed from the end of the 1960s onwards. A very important part in this process was played by Rome itself in the first instance, and more especially by Pope Paul VI. Spanish Catholicism must have given him frequent cause for concern because of its continuing resistance to renewal despite high numbers of religious vocations and the confessional state. It seems that no important decisions on Spain were taken without the pope's consent, but a decisive role in the process of change was played by Vicente Enrique y Tarancón, then a cardinal. Having become a bishop at the early age of 38, Tarancón can be viewed within the episcopate as self-critical, though the content of his pastoral letters in the 1940s and 1950s made no reference at all to any aspects of the political regime but rather dealt with practical problems such as rationing. He never used the term "dictatorship" when referring to the Franco regime, and he always spoke of Franco as the "*caudillo.*" He was not, then, in contrast to the image that existed in the mind of the extreme right wing, a "political" bishop or a schemer. Nor was he typified by having moved from one extreme to the other but rather by a desire to hold together the two tendencies that divided the Spanish Catholic Church. He had a deep pastoral concern, a gift for communication and leadership, and a good dose of common sense. As secretary of the Conference of Metropolitans he was seen as representative of the Spanish hierarchy for a good number of years.

It was only in the 1970s that he emerged at the forefront of the Episcopal Conference. Tarancón's rapid succession as Bishop of the Diocese of Madrid when this fell vacant was evidence of the direction in which the Holy See was leaning. Until the situation had been consolidated with Tarancón at the head of the Episcopal Conference, there were numerous incidents involving the civil authorities. The Minister of the Interior, General Alonso Vega, commented in 1970 that "the Catholic Faith is no longer our best weapon against our family demons."

The victory of the tendency that Tarancón represented also meant victory for a renewed Catholic Church. A survey carried out among thousands of priests showed that only a fifth approved of existing relations between the Church and the state and that a higher percentage had ideas that were not far off a kind of socialism. In September 1971 the so-called Joint Assembly of Bishops and Priests met. One of the proposals that the majority of the assembly voted for but could not approve because it required a qualified majority referred to the Civil War and asked for forgiveness because the Church had not in the past been a means of reconciliation. In January 1973 an episcopal document on "The Church and the Political Community" declared the faith incompatible with a system "that does not seek equality, liberty, and participation." Later, in November 1974, the Episcopal Conference stated that it felt "obliged to support deep changes in our institutions in order to guarantee . . . the fundamental rights of all citizens."

As Cardinal Tarancón would later state, this change came about due to reasons that were clearly and strictly to do with the Church and religion even if later they would be interpreted according to other criteria. In fact the Spanish bishops acted as "pontiffs" in the strictest etymological sense of the word – that is to say, as builders of bridges between Spaniards. It is hard, therefore, to overstate the importance of the role of the Spanish Church in this respect. It contributed "more than any other social institution towards the recovery of the real Spain"; if another institution existed that could be compared with it, it would without doubt be the press. In a traditionalist authoritarian society, the Church was a dynamic driving force that was critical and committed to renewal, and that helped to spread the principles of pluralism, participation, and democratization. The democratic Spain that emerged after the transition was to a large extent the heir to the forward-looking Catholicism of the 1960s and 1970s. This was no doubt because the transition happened in the Church before it happened in politics and indeed it made the political transition easier than it would otherwise have been.

Nonetheless, this change in thinking and the move towards peaceful coexistence on the part of the Spanish Catholics was not achieved without difficulty. There occurred within the Catholic Church a severe split that would have lasting consequences. If the majority of Spanish Catholics followed the example of their bishops, there were also those who opted for a reactionary stance. Publications with a strong right-wing bias proliferated and some bishops continued to occupy political posts such as that of Member of the *Cortes* or Counselor of the Realm. The crisis affected life in religious orders as solid and disciplined as the Jesuits, who were on the point of splitting into two provinces. There is no doubt at all that at a certain moment members of Opus Dei, an organization characterized by its traditional attitudes in matters of religion, tried from Rome to minimize the importance of the decisions of the Joint Assembly.

Vatican II did so much towards bringing about a change in thinking that it is no surprise that it produced a sense of religious disorientation that took the form of a loss of vocations and of clear targets for action. The incidences of secularization were at their worst at the end of the 1960s, but the decrease in vocations carried on into the 1970s: if in 1963 there were about 8,000 seminarists, by 1974 there were only 2,500. If, for a large part of the Spanish Church, this crisis meant a more real and sincere faith free of any compromise with worldly criteria, for another section it meant that the Christian message was trivialized and the religious element of life reduced almost entirely to a commitment to a politics of protest. The crisis that arose at the heart of the Spanish Catholic Church as a result of Vatican II also brought other painful traumas with it. One such trauma was the crisis in movements of apostolate between 1966 and 1968 which Cardinal Tarancón would subsequently believe was seriously badly diagnosed by the Church hierarchy. These factors all lead one to think that in fact the idea that the movements of apostolate were all committedly Marxist organizations – a view defended by Bishop José Guerra Campos, their representative – lacked any justification.

Spain's movements of apostolate had acquired a significant degree of autonomy by the end of the 1950s and this was confirmed at the time of Vatican II, but they also came into conflict with the Church hierarchy which had not yet undergone renewal. In June 1966 a meeting of all the leaders of the various Catholic movements was held at the Valle de los Caídos and its decisions were not approved by the hierarchy. In June 1968 a huge number of people in high positions in Catholic Action resigned, and in the last years of the 1960s the organization lost at least half of its membership. Despite this loss, those who stayed on as members (perhaps more than 300,000 of them) totaled more than all the opposition groups put together, and probably all those signed up as more than a mere formality in the files of the single Party – facts which go to prove just how much social weight Catholicism still had in the Spain of the time. The greatest problem perhaps lay in their lack of direction and of a sense of having their own identity that continued well on into the 1970s.

Something that was not the case at the start – the supposed move towards Marxism on the part of the movements of apostolate – ended up becoming true, at least in part, because of the bitterness of confrontation, the attitude of the regime and of a section of the Church hierarchy, and the tendency towards Marxism that was a result of a lack of experience of democracy. Catholic movements with progressive tendencies that came into being in the 1960s had an intellectual middle-class component which, on the one hand, meant that they adopted radical positions on certain issues (an early preoccupation with the Third World and the search for a third way as an alternative to capitalism and communism). On the other hand, however, they did not remain fixed because they had built into them an element of systematic heterodoxy which meant the rejection of any totalitarian option in the mid term. That is what happened, for example, in the case of the Popular Liberation Front (*Frente de Liberación Popular*), disbanded at the end of the 1960s, or of the periodical *El Ciervo*. The radicalization of the world of left-wing Catholicism produced the most surprising results in the 1970s. In a region with as strong a Catholic tradition as Navarre, extreme left-wing political movements far more extreme than orthodox communism saw their ranks swelled by former Catholic militants who had been members of movements of apostolate. In this way a hyper-traditionalist region became the most strongly Maoist area in Europe.

The regime reacted in a typical way when faced by this new battlefront. The entire leadership of the Franco regime not only kept faith with its National Catholic position but became even more resolutely committed to it as the discrepancy between its own view and that of the Church became increasingly obvious. Nothing shows this determination more clearly than the conversation between Carrero Blanco and Tarancón recounted by the latter. Faced with growing conflict, the Admiral promised to give the Church "whatever it wanted" but only on the condition that it became "our main support." Then, in the *Cortes*, he valued the benefits that the Church had received as a reward for its collaboration with the regime at 300,000 million pesetas. This statement was crude, but it also revealed Carrero's anxiety and was clear proof of the profound crisis in relations between these two power blocks.

The situation had changed by the start of the 1970s, with a Church "entirely distanced" from the regime, in whose ranks protests became more frequent as the days went by. It was normal to find in the press news that meetings of a religious nature had been suspended, priests had been arrested, and searches of church buildings had been carried out by the police. In total some 150 priests suffered some kind of sanction and many of them spent time in a prison specially set up for them in Zamora. The regime's own internal reports calculated that 45 percent of the Church hierarchy and 10 percent of priests held dissident views. A situation of conflict between Church and state had become a reality on an almost daily basis.

The Spanish Church effectively embraced change before the political transformation brought about by the transition actual took place, and in this sense it was ahead of the rest of society. This fact should be acknowledged now that time has passed. Nowadays it almost has been forgotten and what remains are anti-clerical and reactionary attitudes and a considerable degree of confusion within the Church itself about its direction and leadership.

---------------------------------- *Apertura* (1965–9) ----------------------------------

From 1965 on, the regime's domestic policy was dominated by one word – *apertura* – whose meaning requires some explanation. *Apertura* never meant substantial transformation but did suggest a desire to loosen the severe controls that had been in place in earlier times. It did not mean anything beyond change within the regime, and it certainly did not mean a change of regime. An essential factor that goes some way towards explaining it is rooted in the optimism born of Spain's economic growth at the time, and of the absence of any real opposition (it was precisely because there was no danger of the country being destabilized that the experiment could be attempted at all). This situation was actually able to influence Franco himself on matters such as the Press Law (*Ley de Prensa*), but logically it had an even more far-reaching impact on younger politicians. They were better administrators than their predecessors had been and they viewed themselves as having moved on from the old world of the single Party. They were conscious of the need to provide the regime with the support of an institution rather than depend on the life of one man. Hence their sense of urgency about providing a legal framework for what had for years lacked any decisive formulation. Had it not been for the ministerial changes that took place the Press Law, for example, would have remained forever dormant. These younger politicians were conscious in the mid term of the fragility of a regime that would drag them down with it were it to fall. In López Rodó's diary there is a note from the start of 1968 which expresses the view that the regime was "an anachronism and an obstacle" standing in the way of Spanish society.

*Apertura* did not mean the same as the institutionalization of the regime, though the two were related. Carrero, for example, could not be said to support *apertura* because he had always argued in favor of institutionalization. For younger ministers institutionalization meant proceeding in a manner that was far from being fascist but was equally far from being democratic. Institutionalization and *apertura* were decidedly not the work of any one sector of the regime; rather they involved a whole generation of political leaders. Nor was the freezing of the process the responsibility of any one sector but rather a result of the sense of danger that affected them all. Because what was at issue was all the major political preoccupations of the time, positions intersected and took on different meanings according to the particular questions under discussion. Fraga can be said to have been in favor of *apertura* as regards the *Movimiento*, and of government approval of the Press Law, but not on how this law was applied. The ambiguity of the term *apertura* can best be appreciated in the way that it affected issues such as trade unions. It could be thought *aperturista* to limit the power of unions that were not democratic and also to make them more representative. Yet no one would have suggested for one moment that unions should be made completely democratic.

*Apertura* has usually been linked to the technocrats of the 1962 government that was reshuffled in 1965. In fact there had always been members of the Francoist camp who had reached high positions because of their technical training but now, in the last phase of the regime, there were increasing numbers of technocrats, while the old regime "families" were fading from the political scene, or alternatively becoming too rigidly defined to make a career in politics possible; or they became rather like closed coteries. Before all else, the technocrats were the coterie that formed around Carrero Blanco, whose influence was on the increase and whose opponents linked this group to Opus Dei. In fact those who belonged to Opus Dei took up many different political stances, but many of its members, whether or not they were associated with López Rodó, played a crucial role in Franco's governments in the years under discussion.

It is worth mentioning here the two most significant figures who joined the government in 1965. Laureano López Rodó joined it after having been technical general secretary to the Presidency in 1956 and under-secretary for the Development Plan from 1962 onwards. A member of Opus Dei, in his case it is possible to speak of his close identification with Carrero Blanco which gave him considerable influence. His rather gray, orderly, focused personality did not win him popularity, but the Commission for the Plan (*Comisaría del Plan*), of which he was the director, allowed him to gather together a substantial coterie of followers. The "technocracy" that he represented was like the groups during the reign of Fernando VII who came to represent a certain moderate tendency that was rejected equally by the extreme right-wing "Ultras" and the Liberals. The other very important minister in the 1965 government was Federico Silva Muñoz, in charge of Public Works, who became typically representative of the transformation taking place in the regime's "Catholic family." He could also be said to follow the same political line and he too had a coterie, though in his case it was a more modest one.

In September 1967 Carrero Blanco was made vice-president of the Government in place of Muñoz Grandes. Muñoz Grandes had come to represent the Falange element in the Armed Services that one might call "*moviment-ista*" which, since 1962, had taken up a different stance on the question of the institutionalization of the regime. The dismissal of Muñoz Grandes, who was still Chief of Staff of the Armed Services, was probably due to disagreements with Franco ("We are tired of arguing," he told Fraga) on the question of the monarchy towards which Muñoz Grandes, as a Falangist, was hostile. Carrero's influence was derived from the fact that he was the person whom Franco trusted most, while he himself always declared that he was entirely committed to his political master. Not a very ambitious man and one who shunned publicity, Carrero was not as flexible as Franco but had earned the dictator's appreciation because he identified absolutely with him despite the fact that his religious integrism was stronger than Franco's and he shared no common ground with Falange or its sympathizers. From the 1940s on, he always played the role of the dictator's *éminence grise*, though Franco did not always follow his advice. As if to make up for this strong preference, Franco gave Fraga the job of cabinet secretary, not López Rodó as Carrero would have liked.

It was the 1965 government that brought about the institutionalization and opening up of the regime in a short space of time, but then it ended up back-tracking immediately. Foremost among the legal rulings and initiatives that were approved was one – the Press Law – which was import-ant because it would change the cultural parameters of Spanish society. Other measures affected the political class within the regime, such as the Organic Law (*Ley Orgánica*), the Law on the *Movimiento* (*Ley sobre el Movimiento*), and the Union Reform Law (*Ley de Reforma Sindical*), while the election of a successor to Franco would prove of decisive importance for the future of Spain.

It would be hard to overstate the importance of the 1966 Press Law. Until this time the regime had taken an extremely hard line, having begun its life in a time of war; one need only remember that Arias Salgado had described it as having a "guided press." With characteristic tenacity, Fraga announced the immediate approval of the new law in 1962, but the process that lay behind the composition of the text had been extremely complex. Franco told Pemán on numerous occasions that he would not mind governing with a free press; nonetheless, there is no doubt at all that notes he wrote betrayed a profound mistrust of the freedom of the press. His attitude was born of a certain prejudice that led him to view as crim-inal not only anything that appeared to attack the basic principles of the *Movimiento* (which were vague enough as it was) but also the unhealthy dissemination of immoral material. Furthermore, he insisted on the clear responsibility of the heads of the public media for whatever might appear in those media, and on the possibility that censorship prior to publication might be reestablished by a simple governmental decision. Yet even if we admit that he did not believe in the freedom of the press, he nonetheless ended up accepting it.

The Press Law put forward by Fraga as "a means of keeping Spain clean, not staining her and even less destroying her," contained a great many strict provisos to prevent any threat to the regime. The state reserved the right to inspect newspapers before they went into print and even to prevent publication; it could confiscate copies of any banned material and it could also impose sanctions via administrative channels. As if that were not enough, the limits imposed on freedom of speech were nonspecific, speaking of "respect for truth and morality" and respect due to "institutions and persons when making critical comments on political and administrative action." In other words, the law was extremely ambiguous: only in this way could it be passed.

All in all though, the effect was positive overall. The writer and newspaper editor Miguel Delibes could say that if "in the past they used to make you write what you felt and now they are content with forbidding you to feel anything, so we have gained something." In the first instance there was an immediate increase in press publications: there were 129 new publications, of which 8 were daily newspapers and 3 were published in Madrid. In the second instance – and this is more important still – the press could break with what had until this time been its usual way of behaving; according to Josep Pla, this had meant padding the news out with events that had not actually taken place and cutting reports on what had actually happened. Yet, thirdly and most importantly of all, the press could now takes steps to publicize the principles and norms that were the basis of democracy, and even to make democracy itself both known and acceptable to ordinary Spaniards. None of this was achieved without difficulties, and in some cases these were considerable.

The first difficulties arose with the immediate introduction of restrictive measures only a few months after the law was passed; these included modification of the Penal Code and an abusive Official Secrets Act (*Ley de Secretos Oficiales*). This legislation also allowed severe sanctions to be imposed. By the end of 1966 there were already 22 cases open which ended in fines, and this figure grew to 72 and then 91 in the following 2 years; in general they affected small publications that were religious in nature. In

September 1968, the Madrid daily paper *El Alcázar* had both its editors and its status changed by the simple procedure of the government altering its status in the relevant register. This newspaper had increased its circulation from 25,000 to 140,000 copies between 1963 and 1968, but under the new far right-wing company that took it over these figures would plummet to 13,000 copies in circulation in 1975. These sanctions were a result both of the law itself and of the harshness with which it was applied by those responsible for it, but also of pressure from the rest of Spain's governmental class and from Franco himself. López Rodó stated that with the Press Law the government was "always in the dock." The man in charge of the Interior Ministry, Alonso Vega, was even more explicit, saying "I shit on the law." Fraga's idea of the freedom of the press was frankly limited, but all these pressures led him to conclude that "better than losing the Press Law would be to apply it with all its consequences," by which he meant sanctions. Among his opponents – which was how he viewed members of Opus Dei – he saw a desire on the one hand to boycott the law because it was too liberal, but on the other to cause the downfall of the regime from outside (in the daily newspaper *Madrid*). As well as applying all the appropriate sanctions, he did not neglect any propaganda opportunities. "Since much is being published that is openly hostile to the regime on the subject of the Civil War," Franco had written to him, "we should abandon the politics of abstention and offer our support to works which merit it and for which we can provide documentation." From then on a service within the Ministry of Information and Tourism was set up to attend to this task.

The remote antecedents of the Organic Law can be traced back to bills put forward by Arrese. The Organic Law bill was drawn up in what would be its final form in the summer of 1966, it was submitted to a referendum at the end of that year, and became law in January 1967. Responsibility for its contents should basically go to Carrero and his closest collaborators, though many pens had been involved in writing it. There was, nonetheless, no lack of tensions between different sectors of the regime when the moment came to determine what it should contain: at the very last minute Carrero managed to do away with the requirement that the general secretary of the *Movimiento* should be chosen by the National Council from a list of three candidates. The most strongly Falangist sectors would have liked the Council to perform the same functions as a constitutional court. Fraga stated in his memoirs that this was an opportunity for bringing about changes in the regime that had been lost. Nonetheless, it was clear from the start that the Organic Law had only limited aims and that it could not contribute towards making the Spanish regime in any way similar to a democratic regime.

The foremost scholar on the Organic Law defined it as an attempt to convert a constituent dictatorship into a limited monarchy, counterbalanced by institutions that curtailed the role of the Chief of State. The National Council continued to exist as a left-over of *movimentista* ideology reserved for those who had had a long history in the regime or could claim to act as a kind of supreme guardian of the essence of Spain. What was truly new was that there was now a sector of the *Cortes* that was entirely made up of what were called "family" members (*procuradores familiares*), who were chosen by a kind of direct election that was subject to all kinds of provisos but did nonetheless mean that public opinion had been taken into account. There were only 108 *procuradores familiares* (compared with 150 union members), and they also accounted for numbers of votes that varied widely given that there were two votes per province, and therefore Soria had far more votes than Barcelona. The absence of political associations also created a new kind of selection procedure in that only those with an enormous personal fortune could take part in the electoral processes.

All in all, the elections which produced this new composition of the *Cortes* were lively and resulted, for example, in the defeat of two civil governors, while in some places independent candidates managed to get elected. The first stage of the legislature that began its existence in 1967 was dominated by the actions of the *procuradores familiares*. Yet in August 1968, the Interior Ministry prevented those members meeting, and from that moment on their action tended to weaken and lose any ability to effect change.

In reality the Organic Law did not determine the shape of the political system; what were needed were additional measures whose discussion made for increasingly embittered relations between the different regime families. The Law on the National *Movimiento* passed at the start of 1969 did not in fact reduce its function to that of a vague, generic communion of Spaniards; it did, however, reinforce its bureaucratic aspect. Cabinet discussion on the Law was hard and relentless. Silva Muñoz recounts in his memoirs that amendments as innocuous as replacing the term Provincial "chief" with "president" were vetoed. Linked to this project was another aimed at restructuring political associations so as to make them answerable to the National Council. It was approved in the summer of

1969 but immediately hit crisis due to Franco's customary reluctance to formalize the pluralism that was nonetheless growing inside his regime. The bill was never presented before the *Cortes*.

The Organic Law pushed through a revision of official trade unionism which had to adapt to the new constitutional framework. In 1967 there was extensive consultation on particulars, and at its Congress held in Tarragona in May 1968 the Union Organization itself put forward a proposal which began by demanding autonomy, only to end by expressing a wish that the minister responsible for it be chosen by the Union Organization itself. As could be expected, the final outcome was that the official unions had a minister imposed on them. For the moment, however, the main difficulties confronting the union came from the Church, which was not slow to state in a document from the summer of 1968 that Spanish legislation on the freedom of trade unions had little to do with pontifical teachings.

## The Succession. Matesa and Internal Splits in the Regime

The decision on institutionalization that was most pregnant with consequences for the future, and was also the last on which the ruling elite of the regime managed to reach an agreement, was on the naming of Don Juan Carlos as Franco's successor. It proved a painfully slow process until a final decision was reached, but once agreed on, everything moved ahead very fast. In his memoirs López Rodó calls it "operation salmon," because Carrero and he had to act with the patience demanded of salmon fishermen.

In 1963 Don Juan Carlos had moved into the Zarzuela Palace after his wedding, though not without some hesitation on the part of himself, his father, and Franco. Without ever giving up completely on collaborating with the regime Don Juan had manage to keep Franco out of the decision-making on his son's marriage and would also have preferred some clear acknowledgment of his son before Don Juan Carlos took up residence permanently in Spain. Franco, for his part, had seriously considered other alternatives to the succession – a regency renewable every ten years or Don Alfonso de Borbón; he demanded "absolute identification" with his aims and "commitment" on the part of whoever was to succeed him. As late as 1964 he wrote in a private note that "the worst that could happen would be for the nation to fall into the hands of a liberal prince who would act as a bridge towards Communism."

As time passed, the presence in Spain of Don Juan Carlos and his wife, and their apparent identification with the regime, seemed clear indications that Franco was inclining towards this option. Don Juan Carlos tried to condition his response to his circumstances by avoiding too close contact with those who gathered around his father, while maintaining the underlying closeness that had always linked father and son. At the same time, he met once a month with Franco, who felt for him the affection that he might have felt for the son he never had. Don Juan did not think that Franco would ever name his successor in his lifetime. Don Juan Carlos, being closer than his father to the day-to-day reality of political life in Spain, always thought that he would. From 1966 onwards, José María Areilza took change of the monarchist cause and gave it a new dynamism in the form of a more liberal content. In any case, Franco had by now completely rejected the possibility of choosing the son of Alfonso XIII. If Areilza was wrong about the candidate to the throne, he was not wrong about the kind of monarchy that Spain would have in the future.

Franco's decision on the succession seems to have been reached in the early months of 1968. By that time Don Juan Carlos had turned 30 and any statements he made emphasized the need to respect Spain's present legal structures. At the end of 1968 Don Carlos Hugo, eldest son of Don Javier de Borbón-Parma who, like Don Alfonso, had shown no hesitation in supporting Franco during the referendum on the Organic Law, was made to leave Spain. If Solís, the minister in charge of the unions, could not at this juncture openly declare that he was a republican, he could at least do his very best to make the issue of the monarchy as complicated as possible. Finally a decision was reached: "He has just given birth," Carrero told López Rodó, referring to Franco, and Don Juan Carlos wrote to his family in Estoril: "The seed has sprouted." Both expressions show that the decision was both personal and sudden. The title Prince of Spain bestowed on Franco's successor was suggested by López Rodó to avoid direct confrontation with Don Juan, but it proved useful for the monarchy because it left free the traditional title of Prince of Asturias, usually given to the heir to the throne.

Don Juan declared that he remained "like a mere spectator" in relation to a decision in which he had played no part, and that at the same time he represented a liberal alternative to the kind of monarchy that it seemed probable his son was going to represent. Declarations by Don Juan Carlos at the time of his accession were clearly aimed at satisfying a Francoist audience, since he stated that the historic legitimacy of his position dated from July 18, 1936. Only 19 members of the *Cortes* voted against the appointment and nine abstained. Years later, the present monarch would say that he had spent years "playing the fool in this country." Yet his line of thinking was clear, and it was unmistakably linked to what his father represented. The choice of successor was the result of Franco's will and of passive acceptance on the part of the man designated, yet without a doubt there was also a section of the regime, identified with Carrero, that played a key role in pushing the decision through. Nonetheless, to a greater extent than any other decision taken in this period, the decision on the succession was shared by all other sectors that went to make up the regime.

Yet that same year also saw the end of consensus and even Franco was unable to heal the disagreements that arose. The months that followed were anything but peaceful. Silva Muñoz, who stayed neutral in the face of the ensuing confrontations, describes in his memoirs his "lonely agony" in the Council of Ministers when confronted with the "rage" and "frenzy" of the opposing sides. It is not easy to determine exactly what characterized the two schools of thought that clashed in the cabinet. Carrero Blanco's position on foreign policy was clearly pro-American; also, in his view, the decolonization of Morocco had to lead to the area being made into provinces of Spain's overseas territories. All of these factors set him in radical opposition to Castiella. His attitude was hardly compatible with the margins of tolerance recently allowed by the regime and his attitude on religion was firmly integrist. He criticized Solís to Franco for proposing "a trade unionism independent of the authority of the state," and he also criticized Fraga for his policy of openness in relation to the press, for his supposed moral laxness, and for the wave of anti-clericalism, arguing against undermining the Church.

The opposite viewpoint took as its starting-point on foreign policy an altogether less compliant attitude towards America, and also wanted to use the decolonization issue to have Gibraltar returned to Spain. It was also closer to Falange or the *Movimiento*, and it placed more importance on social concerns than on the Development Plans. There was a tendency in its ranks to favor the regency option, at least on Solís's part, and it aimed to reform the political system on the basis of its own presuppositions, accusing its opponents of being opposed to progress. Among the most active members of this second group were Castiella, Solís, Fraga, and Admiral Nieto Antúnez. In view of Carrero's influence with Franco, it looked unlikely that this group would ever succeed. The year 1968 was a very tense one which Fraga describes in his memoirs as the "decisive pulse-beat." The issue only turned into a head-on struggle in the summer of 1969 with the so-called "Matesa Affair."

Matesa was a company that produced machinery for the textile industry which had been very successful thanks to official credit provisions. Legislation on official credit was very probably less than perfect, and the management of the company was somewhat megalomaniac, but it was up to date with interest payments which were safeguarded anyway by insurance. Over a period of time the company could only be accused of irregularities associated with tax evasion, and of not paying back currency obtained from exports to the Spanish Institute for Foreign Currency (*Instituto Español de Moneda Extranjera*). Apart from this, Matesa often sold its products to subsidiaries set up abroad in order to have access to foreign markets. The whole affair offers a very clear insight into the nature of an economy that depended on favors bestowed through official channels.

What is of interest to us is not the specific case of this one company so much as the question of how it became the factor that brought existing political tensions to a head. July 1969 saw both the case and its politicization turn into a major issue. Fraga tells in his memoirs how, in the Council of Ministers, there were two tendencies confronting each other: the one with which he was associated that was ready to introduce light and shorthand typists, and the other which wanted to "throw earth over the whole issue." In fact, the Minister for Information allowed the press unique freedom in this particular instance, such as it was not allowed in relation to any other matters. The *Movimiento* press, too, immediately launched accusations at the sector furthest removed from its own positions. "This is the end; it's either Fraga or me," said Carrero. Both sides were spurred on by an urgent need to eliminate their opponent. Faced with Franco's inability to arbitrate in any real sense at all, an open squabble began which seemed much like a settling of scores. In October there was a government crisis and the leading figures on the side which had opposed Carrero – Fraga, Solís, and Castiella – and the technocrats all left power.

The government formed in October 1969 was described as "homogeneous" and was accused of being little more than "an offshoot of the Commission for the Development Plan," which was not exactly true. Silva Muñoz stayed on until April 1970, and several institutions often acted in ways that were not in line with government policy. The National Council, as well as the *Cortes*, set up commissions of enquiry to look into the

Matesa affair, and the Supreme Court went so far as to prosecute the president of the Bank of Spain and the ex-Treasury Minister Navarro Rubio. Many who would be ministers after 1973, when Carrero Blanco had disappeared, played an important role in the Supreme Court, the *Cortes*, or the National Council when the time came to try to establish real or supposed responsibility in the case. This split at the very heart of the ruling elite was, then, the lasting legacy of 1969 to the rest of the history of the Franco period.

------------------ **Worker Protest. Terrorism** ------------------

Meanwhile, the impact of the opposition was growing, though this is not to say that it posed any real threat to the regime. What is more important from the historical point of view is that the regime was able to stand firm under opposition pressure but could not eliminate it, even when it resorted to using its most drastic methods. The most important role played by the opposition was to keep the regime in a permanent state of tension, to deny its legitimacy, and to ensure that it stood no chance of surviving after the eventual disappearance of the dictator. The fact that there was opposition at all forced the regime's political classes to offer an option of reform, while, at the same time, public opinion was drawn to the opposition even if people did not join its ranks in great numbers. Furthermore, there now seemed to be signs of a linking up of political, social, and professional protest movements that had not been seen before.

As regards social protest, it is striking that from the second half of the 1970s on, the relevance of student movements decreased while protest among workers became increasingly vigorous. The process of *apertura* begun in 1961 had in practice led to the disappearance of the SEU and to a change in legislation on education (1970). It was obvious, however, that a democratic union of students was not viable due both to repression and to internal dissentions. From that time on there were many groups preaching spontaneity, direct action, or extreme activism. During the three states of emergency that were declared between 1968 and 1970, disturbances in universities played a role equal to that of the labor movement: in 1969, for example, out of a total of 739 arrests, 315 were of students. Among those who suffered reprisals were teachers who did not yet have fixed teaching posts. In the university sector, Francoism had disappeared from among students and was almost seen as eccentric in teachers, but this did not put the regime in any real danger either. One could say much the same thing about intellectual circles. Between 1962 and 1969 up to 30 written protests against government policy were received by the Ministry for Information but they made no serious impact despite the increasing number of signatories.

If the student protest movement had engaged in active dissent before the labor movement, in the final phase of the Franco period it was the workers who had more impact. From the middle of the 1960s to the time of Franco's death, the number of strikes increased fast. If in 1966 there were about a hundred, in 1968 the number had tripled to 309. For the time being protests were focused on areas that had a tradition of working-class dissent: Asturias being particularly relevant, then Barcelona, the Basque Country and, to a lesser extent, Madrid. Conflict was especially intense in those sectors of production that were characterized by a greater class awareness: mining and metallurgy. Marcelino Camacho, the main leader of the communist *Comisiones Obreras*, was a metalworker. The pressure of these strikes did not diminish in the final Franco years, and now is the best moment to discuss it because, although to do so means moving ahead of the events themselves, it allows us to observe them as they develop. In 1971 almost 7 million working days were lost through strikes; in 1973 the figure was around 9 million, in 1974 and 1975 they were around 14 million, and the figure rose even higher in 1976. These facts were not solely the result of political factors; economic circumstances also played a decisive role. Yet if we compare these data with those in other European countries, we shall discover the true nature of the labor situation in Spain. In the mid 1970s France, with more inhabitants than Spain, did not go above 3 million work days lost through strikes. Spain was losing five times more. It was the very system that was supposed to regulate conflict that was itself in crisis in Spain.

It is worth taking time to analyze the available data on social protest. In the first place, the pace would seem to have been that of a society that was just waking up and stretching, and that after a period of trial and error then began to take rather timid action before finally freeing itself from any bonds of a legal system that it no longer respected. In the 1970s there was a genuine generational split in the leadership of the unions so that the continuing presence of Camacho, for example, who was about 50 years old, stood out as an exception. This youth phenomenon was often accompanied by more extreme virulence and radicalization, yet it did not therefore mean that social protest had become revolutionary in nature.

There were always specific demands being made, mainly on pay. An examination of the geography of these protest movements is also interesting in that it shows that over time protest spread throughout the whole of Spain. In the 1960s Asturias and the Basque Country had headed union protest; then the main focus seemed to move to Barcelona, but social conflict also broke out in other places such as Madrid, Pamplona, Vitoria, El Ferrol, Vigo, Seville, Valencia, and Valladolid. The groups leading the protest movements also changed. Initially they had been miners and metalworkers but protest soon spread to the textile industry, building, chemical production, transport, and even banking. One very significant factor in the final phase of Francoism was the number of strikes that took place for reasons of "solidarity," which was high.

As protest increased, so did repression. Nevertheless, one would be wrong to think that the regime reacted as it would have done in the 1940s. Harshness was often accompanied by brutality but at this time it lacked conviction because the seeds of discontent had now spread too widely and society itself was demanding a more tolerant form of behavior. During this final phase of the regime, opposition no longer took the form of small groups, as figures show. In 1974, 25,000 workers were suspended from work without pay; not all of them were political dissidents but by now the figure was very high. That same year the courts issued 1,400 indictments on political charges affecting 6,000 individuals; not all of them were union members, but it is fair to suppose that the majority were. From 1971 onwards there were per year about 1,000 convictions in civil courts and about 200 in military courts. In addition, in 1969 and 1974 there were 17 deaths as a result of confrontations between the forces of law and order and workers demonstrating. The number was so high because of the size of the demonstrations, but there was also another factor which leads us back once again to the issue of the regime's inability to keep the peace. The forces of law and order were not trained to deal with peaceful demonstrations, and by now not even reactionary leaders such as Carrero seemed prepared to allow the level of repression that these forces envisaged.

Another important piece of data that sheds light on social protest in this period concerns the position adopted by the official vertical trade union. Its leaders had no intention other than to continue to exercise a degree of influence but, because of circumstances, the way in which they did so contributed towards making the actions of illegal unions easier. As time went by, the Union Organization could only harbor modest hopes that the majority of those elected would be independent candidates, and things being as they were, these hopes were often not realized; when elections were held in Baix Llobregat, in only three out of 50 large companies was the *Comisiones Obreras* candidate not voted in. The official union needed to be acknowledged inside and outside Spain. In order to achieve that, it tried to win from the International Labor Organization some degree of recognition of the essentially single nature of Spain's union movement – an issue on which, curiously, it agreed with the Communists. Also, legislation was applied more moderately in comparison to its initial harshness. Strikes were still illegal, but after 1970 strikers could not be sacked, thought they could have their contract suspended. After 1975 striking ceased to be a public order offense at all, although conditions were set with which it was difficult to comply.

In the final decade of Francoism the most important clandestine trade union was *Comisiones Obreras*. Although within its ranks there were sectors that were not communist (and they also played a fundamental role in some of the provinces), the PCE was the major component of the organization. This became clear when, in May 1972, the union leaders were arrested at a monastery in Pozuelo. The punishments meted out were as severe as 20 years in prison for those reoffending. The most important figure in *Comisiones* at this time was Marcelino Camacho, a Communist condemned to 12 years in prison after the Civil War who had lived in the part of North Africa colonized by the French and had returned to Spain in 1957. The second most important union, though it was far less significant than *Comisiones*, used in the provinces to be the *Unión Sindical Obrera* (USO), whose numbers were only exceeded in some regions in the final years of the Franco period by the UGT. This highlights a fact that has often been forgotten: that militants from a Catholic background played a vital role in the reconstruction of Spanish trade unionism.

Although, as Camacho states in his memoirs, he never met a single entrepreneur in prison in the Franco years, workers' protests did in fact do much to bring about changes in attitude among employers. The position adopted by Catalan employers in the final stage of the regime proves that their doubts were growing about an economic policy that they considered far too interventionist. Younger, more dynamic employers were by now in favor of democratic unions with which, in fact, they were now already having dealings. A month before Franco's death, the National Labor Organization (*Fomento del Trabajo Nacional*) proposed "a kind of contract by means of which the more favored classes . . . would resign some of their privileges and give ground on some of the positions they held," while "the working classes would in turn consider the capitalist model as a valid playing-field." This was an indication of what was to happen later, during the transition.

During this period, as well as this kind of protest, a number of other social collectives who had so far not taken any action at all began to make their voices heard. We have already noted the crucial role of the press in disseminating democratic ideals. While Fraga was still minister, there were the highest number of indictments that led to convictions and penalties in line with the legislation in force at the time: 125 in 1967 and 228 in 1968. Yet this should not be taken to mean that the pressure exerted by his successors weakened; rather, indirect methods were applied that were often far more effective. The daily newspaper *Madrid*, after suffering its first confiscation in 1967, two more in 1968 and a 4-month suspension, was finally closed down in 1971, so completely that the building where it had been housed was blown up. This newspaper's experience is significant because it signaled the definitive shift of the brain behind it – that of Calvo Serer – from an extreme right-wing monarchic position to one of democratic pro-European liberalism. His newspaper offices were the training-ground for the bulk of journalists who approached the transition with attitudes very different to their submissiveness in previous periods. The most spectacular success of the press was the periodical *Cambio 16*, which achieved distribution figures of 300,000 copies. As for the attitude of professional journalists, the same comment might well apply: that as a profession, and with very few exceptions, they took up a position in opposition to the regime.

By the end of the 1960s, the protest movement had spread to Spain's law colleges. In 1970, at a Law Congress held in León, a speech given by the Justice Minister was greeted by a large number of delegates walking out of the hall. Yet in this profession dissident attitudes towards the regime were not so widespread. Only younger lawyers and certain sections of older members saw themselves as guardians of human rights. Elections to the College of Lawyers (*Colegio de Abogados*) in Madrid turned into semi-political electoral confrontations in which the opposition always looked set to win but never quite did. In the graduate law schools (*Colegios de Licenciados*) mobilization came later, though it too was beginning in the mid 1960s. In 1974 a candidate put forward by the PSOE and the PCE was elected to the College in Madrid.

From the second half of the 1960s on, together with these forms of social protest which were spreading, another phenomenon appeared that was strongly represented in the ranks of the opposition but had little to do with what we have discussed so far. The appearance of terrorism – impossible to eliminate and evidence of the ferocity of repression in the Franco years – had such an important impact on the life of the regime that at times it almost seemed as though it was shaping that life. The decision by ETA (*Euskadi ta Askatasuna*) to use terrorism dates from 1967; it never stood the slightest chance of achieving its objectives by these means, but it did have a decisive influence on Spanish politics. In this respect we need only recall the manifestations of solidarity in opposition to the trials of ETA members – *etarras* – at a time when people had not yet appreciated the fact that terrorism would be the most tragic legacy that Francoism would leave behind it. One must remember that ETA was the most significant terrorist movement in Europe, with the exception of the IRA in Ireland, and it has caused four times as many deaths. Unlike what happened in other countries such as, for example, Italy or Germany, terrorism enjoyed popular support from ordinary people in Basque society, which explains how it has lasted so long.

Basque nationalism has a whole historical tradition of independent radicalism which can be viewed as a forerunner of ETA. There was also, in the 1920s and 1930s, a link between the nationalist struggle and anti-colonialism in some theoretical writings. However, the birth of ETA cannot be understood apart from the profound disillusionment experienced by Basque nationalists in the mid 1950s, in a period when even left-wing ministers in France, such as François Mitterand, were closing down centers linked to the production of nationalist propaganda.

Around 1952, at the heart of the Basque student organization, the Basque Revolutionary Party (*Euskal Iraulzarako Alderdia* or EIA), a group appeared calling itself *Ekin* which, as its name (the equivalent of "*Hacer*": "Do") suggests, showed a distinct lack of confidence in the traditional Basque opposition. It was this group that provided ETA with a large number of its early leaders: Julen Madariaga, José Luis Álvarez Emparanza, Benito del Valle . . . In 1956 the *Ekin* group managed to attract a section of the youth movement of the Basque Nationalist Party (*Partido Nacional Vasco* or PNV). In July 1959 ETA was born, its name meaning "Euskadi and Freedom." It defined itself as a revolutionary movement for Basque national liberation, but the term "revolutionary" did not imply that it was Marxist or that it would use violence. As has often been the case throughout history, at the start the membership of ETA, which would in time become a terrorist organization, consisted of students, not proletarian members.

The internal history of ETA, after these beginnings, has been punctuated by a series of ideological debates. What is paradoxical is that these debates always ended up by producing splits that did not in fact weaken the movement, and it continued to enjoy popular support that was not at all affected by such evidence of dissension. The subject of the debates can be summed up quite simply. First, an issue that has always been there at the heart of ETA has been the tension between its commitment to nationalism and its role as a labor movement, and this has resulted in part of the organization taking the form of small political groups. Also, another source of internal contradictions at the heart of the organization has been the role allocated to activism. In general there has been a predominance of tendencies advocating activism. So, in its early years, the text that was read most widely by its members was Federico Krutwig's *Vasconia*, which likened the Basque situation to that of Third World countries fighting for their independence from colonial powers.

ETA's early years were the period of its ideological radicalization and its transformation into a revolutionary organization. During that time it was influenced by anti-colonial theory, and it became a violent critic of traditional nationalism. It adopted Marxist terminology and propounded the theory of the spiraling nature of violence, according to which repression had to be countered with equal force to provoke it yet further. It was between 1966 and 1968 that ETA finally became a terrorist movement. That was due in part to the victory at its heart of a group that advocated a guerrilla-style struggle supposedly similar to the guerrilla war going on in Vietnam. Another section of ETA, more committed to action as a labor movement, was thrown out of the so-called Fifth Assembly held at the end of 1966 and start of 1967.

The repression that resulted from the state of emergency that was declared in 1967, and the victory of the supporters within ETA of a guerrilla-style armed struggle, together led the organization to embark on a program of violence in 1968 that would in fact prove irreversible. In June, the *etarra* Echevarrieta died in a confrontation with the Civil Guard, who also lost one man, and in August a police inspector was murdered. The regime's reaction was harsh in the extreme; the Basque Country was put under an almost permanent state of emergency. In 1969, ETA was on the brink of collapse, and this would happen again on subsequent occasions. However, the Franco regime was by now too far removed from its Civil War victory to get away with using the level of violence that it had deployed at that time in the past. Indeed, as theorists of terrorism had foreseen, indiscriminate harsh repression only attracted more militants to ETA.

All in all, the early months of 1970 were a time of severe crisis for the movement. The trial in Burgos of a group of ETA militants brought expressions of solidarity both from the opposition in general and from the whole of the Basque Country. The conduct of the trial under military law, and the absence of guarantees on correct procedure, mobilized widespread protest, while ETA's kidnapping of the German consul in San Sebastián, Eugen Beihl, had important international repercussions. The regime was prudent enough to spare the men convicted the death penalty.

Nonetheless, there continued to be splits in ETA despite repression. The men tried in Burgos belonged to a tendency that appeared to have done well at the start but was later criticized for its lack of nationalist feeling. It came to be known as ETA-VI, but a result of its commitment to the labor movement was that it went on to become a Trotskyite organization. The other tendency, ETA-V, which was refused admission to the Sixth Assembly, grew fast and managed to persuade members of the middle and working classes in certain regions (the whole central and southern areas of Guipúzcoa) to join it. Its principal leader was Eustaquio Mendizábal, *Txiquía*, and his most significant actions were the kidnappings of the industrialists Lorenzo Zabala and Felipe Huarte in 1971 and 1973; all of these actions were attempts to copy Black September or the *Tupamarus*. The attack on Admiral Carrero Blanco was initially conceived as a kidnapping to bring about the liberation of 150 ETA-V prisoners in jail at the time.

## ———  Late Francoism: Carrero Blanco as President  ———

If there is any one factor that can explain the crisis Spain experienced in 1969 it is the personal decline of Franco who, 2 years earlier, had reached the age of 75. Had he remained in full possession of his political faculties he would not have failed to carry on arbitrating in the way that had been the main function of his leadership over the forces that had won the Civil War. Foreign dignitaries who visited him in his latter years, such as General Vernon A. Walters, deputy chief of the CIA, have described him as an old man who barely muttered more than a few words in an interview, and those bore no relation whatever to the matters under discussion.

Yet Franco's physical decline is not the only factor to be taken into account when considering the historical period that can be referred to as *"tardofranquismo"*: "the late Franco period." Other decisive characteristics of that period were the lack of a clear sense of direction, problems with law and order, fragmentation within the governing class, a proliferation of conflicting positions within the leadership, and obvious paralysis when the moment came to confront problems. In this final phase, Francoism gave the distinct impression that the political regime was in decline.

The government of October 1969, with its vice-president Carrero Blanco, was described as colorless by all its opponents and this view has not altered in later histories of Spain. López Rodó questions the appropriateness of the description in his memoirs: after all, several ministers were from a Falange background. However, what is beyond all doubt is that the pairing of Carrero and López Rodó had acquired overwhelming political influence, although in the medium term they would suffer for it. Four of the 11 new ministers had been members of the Commission for the Development Plan, but this does not mean that they dominated the entire Francoist political system. A program set out by Carrero Blanco in January 1971 had raised the issue of political associations and established good relations with the *Cortes* as though to satisfy the *Movimiento*, but in actual fact what Carrero did was a response to the turbulent nature of a part of the regime's ruling class. López Rodó states that the government found itself caught up in a process of "attack and demolish" ("acoso y derribo"). As one of the losers following the crisis, Fraga described what happened as a "huge national disaster" and became Carrero's fiercest opponent. In April 1970 Silva resigned. In 1971 an old and influential member of the government, Admiral Nieto Antúñez, begged Franco not to rely solely on his own powerful charisma but also on the "moral strength" of a team.

Even greater problems were posed by other situations that came about within the existing institutions. The Matesa Affair was used by one faction in the *Cortes* as a weapon against the government, but the government dealt with the issue by decreeing an amnesty in October 1971 in which 3,000 prisoners were set free, including political leaders who had not yet stood trial. Franco had assured Navarro Rubio that the issue would "come to nothing," but his solution meant that these men were left with suspicion hanging over them. A solution as botched as this was only conceivable once Franco had begun his final decline.

Much the same could be said of the new questions on the succession which reared their heads shortly after Don Juan Carlos was given the title Prince of Spain. In December 1971 the engagement was announced between Don Alfonso de Borbón and Franco's grand-daughter, María del Carmen. The wedding took place in March 1972, and what was notable about it was the error in the bridegroom's marriage strategy. It was by now too late for Franco to change his successor, but a whole series of tensions arose as a result of the marriage. Don Alfonso had requested the title of Prince of Borbón but had to content himself with being called the Duke of Cádiz, though he insisted that he should be considered second in line to the throne. It was the Prince of Spain himself who came up with the formula that was finally adopted officially, as proof of his desire for "collaboration and union," and with the added promise that the Dukes of Cadiz would in due course be accorded the title reserved for the children of monarchs: *Infantes* of Spain. A situation such as this would have been unthinkable until Franco's declining years when, as indeed happened at this point, he was for the first time ever manipulated by members of his own family. Even Carrero had to put up with the Chief of State's wife reproaching him because, in her view, there were "incompetents and traitors" in the government. In López Rodó's memoirs the chapter that deals with 1972 is entitled "The Year of the Wedding," which proves just how far family matters had become bound up with public life.

In a similar way, the turbulent nature of events relating to the *Movimiento* can best be understood when viewed in the light of Franco's advanced age. The 1969 government had a bitter enemy in a clericalist extreme right represented by Blas Piñar, and in 1972 there also reappeared on the political scene a notable representative of the most fascist element within the regime, José Antonio Girón de Velasco. When Silva Muñoz was replaced by Fernández de la Mora, who had come up with the theory of a "State of Public Works" and had legitimized his position by devoting himself to this cause, his departure effectively meant the disappearance from the political scene of the regime's Catholic family. The theory of a "State of Public Works," on the other hand, was nothing other than an extension and rationalization of certain proposals that had first been made by the monarchist extreme right under the Republic. The number of law cases resulting in punishment decreased, but the press, now the responsibility of Alfredo Sánchez Bella, was subject to even greater pressure by indirect means such as telephone calls. Other aspects of government behavior were not so much reactionary as fairly much in line with the particular character of the regime. The Trade Union Law (*Ley Sindical*) of 1971 meant that the minister for Trade Union Relations was not elected by the official Trade Union Organization, but a minister chosen by the president of the government was imposed instead. This being so, the decision could be viewed as retrograde by union representatives in the *Cortes* because it was in effect what had always happened under the regime. An attempt to draft a Law on Local Administration (*Ley de Administración Local*) was soon abandoned. The key political issue was still the problematic question of political association. Fraga had pronounced in favor of it. Fernández Miranda, the new general secretary of the *Movimiento*, knew that as long as Franco lasted genuine association would be impossible, while Don Juan Carlos, who had been taught by Fernández Miranda, had advised him in this particular matter to "glide and not land": that is to say, to avoid proposing legislation that would not bring real results. There was no genuine struggle between *aperturistas* and reactionaries; both groups were on the defensive and used arguments to fence with their opponents. Neither was in favor of democracy but equally, neither was completely resistant to change.

The atmosphere was worsening for the regime. Bad relations with the Church gave rise to bitter reproaches from members of the government who could remember the economic aid given to the Church by the state. As Ridruejo wrote at the time, the opposition was for the regime like a kind of guerrilla war which may have been wearying but also drove it to take action. It seemed impossible to curb opposition activity, even by resorting to the harshest of measures. In September 1968 Carrero had set up a service answerable to the Presidency aimed at combating subversion; it was made up of military personnel and was under the command of Colonel José Ignacio San Martín. Neither the service's impact nor the information it provided seems to have been particularly effective. When Franco was questioned by Carrero about it continuing, he answered "neither yes nor no," and what words he did utter were puzzling. In all dictatorial regimes, in their final phase, there comes a "paralysis in decision-making," and that occurred in Spain before the death of Carrero Blanco. The phrase we have just quoted is an excellent example of it.

Franco himself must have been conscious of his own inability to exercise power directly, and the proof of this came when in June 1973 he made Carrero president of the government. The political transition that would follow Franco's death now seemed close at hand – hence Carrero's attempt to form a government characterized by its pluralistic composition (it included future ministers with whom he had no personal connection whatever), and hence too López Rodó's desire to take on a political post as Minister for Foreign Affairs. The vice-presidency fell to Fernández Miranda as proof of Carrero's growing confidence in him. The 1973 government was, beyond doubt, a government of transition towards a monarchy, but also of continuing Francoism in a version in which the Falangist element appeared weaker.

The short duration of Carrero's term in office in the Presidency confirms the impression of the non-viability of a regime in which, if the Chief of State was in his 80s, the head of government had himself turned 79. "The years are passing; I'm tired and my head feels as though it's splitting," Carrero confided to López Rodó. If he had any guiding principle for government it was his sheer stubborn resistance. In the last weeks of his life it seems that Carrero was thinking about launching an "institutional offensive." He considered *apertura* "a load of nonsense," and he imagined he saw universal Masonic conspiracies at work on all sides. The last political document that came through his hands begged the state to "train men not pansies" [*sic*], and he repudiated the "long-haired twitchers" whose music provided entertainment for the young.

These were the circumstances in which "Operation Ogre" was carried out in which, towards the end of 1973, ETA murdered the president of the Spanish government. It was the organization's first action outside the Basque Country and nobody had really seriously believed that they could actually achieve such a feat, although the police authorities had been convinced for a long time that they might attempt a kidnapping. The rashness of the action by the Madrid commando, and the scant surveillance in place at the time, led some people to wonder if there was strange conniving going on in certain sectors of the regime. However, there is no objective evidence to support this theory: it is the result of an inevitable tendency in human beings to find the most extravagant explanations to account for any events that are out of the ordinary.

There is no doubt at all that had Carrero not died he would have been a major factor to consider in the political panorama after Franco's death – a man whom the King would have had to take into account during the transition process. Carrero's immediate successors did not carry enough weight in the regime to take on that role. The sense that the country was drifting without any clear aim became even more pronounced than before.

──────  **Late Francoism: Arias Navarro's Government**  ──────

Almost the only element of continuity between the governments of Carrero and Carlos Arias Navarro was the irremediable decline in Franco's physical health. Growing daily more senile, an expressionless Franco who articulated his words badly and shuffled along without moving his arms, or who said nothing at all and ended up crying, was pathetic. Fraga has spoken in his memoirs of one of his last interviews with Franco, which he left with the impression that the dictator "was listening but not hearing." López Rodó stated that Franco listened to him "without moving a muscle in his face." Franco's state explains to some extent at least why the brief parenthesis of crisis first became "frenzied" and then degenerated into a witch-hunt, or so those who experienced it felt at the time.

Arias Navarro's appointment was clear evidence of the growing strength of his political family or close circle within the regime. The final decision in favor of Arias might also have been influenced by Alejandro Rodríguez de Valcárcel, president of the *Cortes*. It certainly seems that Fraga was right when he stated that Franco's "will was written for him" in this respect. Fernández Miranda, who as vice-president had harbored hopes of taking on the job, was rejected. Don Juan Carlos was not consulted when the new cabinet was being set up. If the previous presidency had taken it upon itself to promote the monarchy – even though the monarchy that actually came into existence would in time become very different from what it had originally anticipated – the presidency did not now appear to have any links worth mentioning with the man who took the place of Carrero Blanco.

As a political figure, Carlos Arias Navarro remains somewhat of a mystery. He was a man of no great importance within the regime and seemed unlikely to have either a team or a plan for government to put forward at what was in fact the most difficult moment in the entire life of the Franco regime. It soon became clear that the impression he gave of hidden energy in fact concealed hesitancy, and that if he was at all able to convince himself that political reform was essential, he retained those ideas only for a very short time because his inclination was to keep the system just as it was. It seems that even Franco himself, shortly after proposing Arias, had doubts about the wisdom of his choice. Though he had been made a minister thanks to Franco's intervention, Carrero thought Arias lacking in "judgment."

There was in Carrero's government a basic core of men with major responsibilities – Carrero as president, García Hernández at the Home

Office, Cabanillas as Minister for Information – and a minimum of continuity with the past in those in charge of the economy (Antonio Barrera de Irimo) and in social affairs (Licinio de la Fuente). Ministers were often disloyal to each other and there was a lack of a common purpose: one minister stated that during Carrero's time there had been doubts about his ability to do the job of president, but compared with Arias, if likened to orchestral conductors, "he was just like Von Karajan." Considering the ministers as a whole, one can see a clear tendency to react which contrasted with the period when Carrero took all the decisions in Spanish politics. Reshuffles of those in lesser government posts were numerous (about 150 in more important positions) and the aim seems to have been to create an impression that a break had been made with the past. Franco explained to one minister who was on his way out of government that he had approved the changes because "every bullfighter must negotiate with the team he has to work with."

The so-called "spirit of February 12" was a result of these particular circumstances. Against all predictions based on his past experience as Director General of Security, Arias Navarro made an opening speech on February 12, 1974 in which he stated his intention of effecting political reform within the system's existing guidelines. The actual content of his program was frankly limited: it consisted of a reform of the Trade Union Law and the approval of a Local Government Law, of another law on Associations and on a system to deal with issues of incompatibility. At the time, however, these measures were enough to create an impression of a new way opening up to allow political change to take place.

Yet the spirit of February met a quick death in March when the Archbishop of Bilbao, Antonio Añoveros, put his signature to a document that caused such an uproar that the prelate was on the point of being expelled from Spain. His pastoral letter referred to the "specific identity of the Basque people" and their right to preserve their "spiritual heritage." Although it did not contain anything directly subversive, Archbishop Tarancón recommended that it should not be read out in public. When it was, there followed a few days of mutual exasperation. Tarancón had, ready to hand, the document of excommunication that would be pronounced on anyone who tried to expel Añoveros from his diocese. In his memoirs Fraga calls what happened a "false step" on the part of the government. Three ministers were on the point of resigning and the situation was saved only by intervention from moderate sectors within the government and by the primate, who dealt directly with Franco. Añoveros left his diocese but out of personal choice and only for a time, despite the fact that this had been the most serious incident ever to occur between the Church and the regime. Franco, in one of his moments of political prudence, played a part in avoiding further progress down the path towards confrontation that the president of the government seemed inclined to follow.

Meanwhile, circumstances quickly became more difficult for the new government. By this time the impact of the first crisis resulting from the rise in oil prices was being felt and also, between the spring and the summer of 1974, two European dictatorships that shared certain characteristics with Francoism suffered crises, in Greece and Portugal. The end of the Salazar regime in Portugal meant much to Franco, who had once said that if one of their regimes perished, the other would have to "carry the dead."

The main factor that led to organized dissidence in the Armed Services in Spain was the example set by the revolution in Portugal. It was evident in only one organization in the summer of 1974, in the Democratic Military Union (*Unión Militar Democrático*). Its members were from fairly non-conformist Catholic backgrounds and they took up positions close to those of the PCE and PSOE. Their proposals, which were moderate, did not go so far as taking any significant action. When the organization came to light it did not have specific enough strategies. All that was clear was its willingness to take part in any coup against the state, and its aims were retrograde.

In July 1976, a military commander and ten captains were arrested, tried in 1976 and sentenced to between 2 and 8 years in prison. In the summer of 1974, too, General Díez Alegría, whom some saw as a liberal general who could have played a part in the transition to democracy but who chose to abide by the strictest discipline, was dismissed from his post as Chief of Staff of the Armed Forces. The excessive politicization of the Army during the dictatorship had vaccinated it against any attempts to turn against Franco.

What happened in Portugal had an impact on Spanish politics, as much by awakening hopes in the opposition as by further irritating the more reactionary sectors of the regime. As had been the case for Carrero, Arias Navarro found himself under pressure from the political bunker. In June 1974, finally bringing to an end the "spirit of February 12", Arias openly identified the Spanish people with the National *Movimiento*. By the time of Franco's death, only two of the proposals that Arias had put forward had been approved and both were clearly unimportant and inadequate. In January 1975, after a partial crisis in which Arias distanced himself from the more forward-thinking element in the government, he managed to extract from Franco approval for a Statute on Associations (*Estatuto de Asociaciones*), which stipulated that membership had to be over 25,000 and must cover 15 provinces, and of course such conditions did nothing to encourage people to join associations. The question of associations had been an old warhorse for a long time, and they depended for their legal constitution on the National Council, which ensured that they would not attract anyone who was already a member of the *Movimiento*.

Meanwhile, uncertainty created by a political reform that was not actually being implemented, though it was being announced and then denied, was intensified by further uncertainty surrounding Franco's state of health. In July 1974 a first illness forced him to hand over power temporarily to Don Juan Carlos, and just 1 day before that happened, the first opposition organization, the Democratic Junta (*Junta Democrática*), had come into being. The Prince of Spain, from the moment he had been given that title, had tried to keep a certain distance between himself and the regime while also contacting moderate opposition groups. He managed to create at least a certain sense of expectancy about his person, which would have been unimaginable back in 1969. The appearance in those years of books and articles about the future of the regime and the Prince's role seem to confirm this new interest in him.

When Franco took up the reins of power once more, the Prince heard about it only as it was actually taking place, though he had asked to be kept informed of what was happening. One can well imagine that for the Prince this must have been a humiliating experience. An undercover "family pact" continued to function as his father made statements which supported the image of the monarchy as an institution that had relevance for all Spaniards. In the summer of 1975, Don Juan declared that he had never in his entire life submitted to "that limitless, irresistible power exercised by Franco" that had come into being as a response to a particular set of circumstances. After making this declaration he was forbidden ever to take up residence in Spanish territory.

Differences of opinion within the government now began to increase exponentially. The government itself became the epitome of incoherence and gave an impression of being permanently unable to implement any common decision. After the death of his president, Carrero Blanco, Franco was a sick man who had lost "the last thread that tied me to this world," and who had no idea at all of what the "spirit of February 12" even was, though Arias had talked to him about it. When the most reactionary elements in the regime suggested to him that his successor might have strayed outside the orbit of the system, he was upset and replied that "there are promises that cannot be broken." Yet as soon as he took power again in September 1974, he immediately began an offensive against the more *aperturista* elements in the government. In October 1974 Pío Cabanillas was dismissed, but the economic vice-president, Barrero de Irimo, and with him the occupants of several lesser posts, expressed their solidarity with Cabanillas and were also removed from office. Later on, for the reasons already mentioned, another of the vice-presidents, Licinio de la Fuente, was replaced by Fernando Suárez, while Fernando Herrero Tejedor replaced José Utrera Molina, who was unable to control the rebellious elements within Falange. Then, to cap all these problems, Herrero Tejedor was killed in a traffic accident.

Arias Navarro's government was, by October 1975, the very incarnation of disorientation. When in September 1975 five terrorists were executed as a drastic measure intended to put a stop to any further opposition demonstrations, there was general protest against the regime throughout the rest of Europe. The regime responded by resorting to a procedure that it had used twice in the past. As it had done in 1970 and 1971, it organized a mass rally in the Plaza de Oriente in Madrid to allow its adherents to show their support. This display of strength was again rather pathetic because Franco's tremulous voice was once more heard accusing liberals, Freemasons, and communists of causing all Spain's present ills. Meanwhile, for the first time in almost 30 years the situation worsened for Spain in relation to foreign affairs. Both issues – the opposition and foreign policy – must be discussed before we turn our attention to the last weeks of Franco's life.

## Opposition Activity: The Road to Unity

The backdrop against which the politics of the regime were played out in this period was one of increasing social protest. It did not have an exclusively socialist or revolutionary agenda and nor was it capable on its own of bringing about regime change, but it did show the extent to which society had become independent of the state. One cannot even say that it was the work of opposition organizations.

By this time terrorist brutality had alienated the support that a section of the opposition had expressed for ETA up to the start of the 1970s. After the murder of Carrero, the Spanish Communist Party totally rejected ETA, and condemnation was even stronger when, in September 1974, a bomb was set off in the Cafetería Orlando in Madrid. This attack was made possible by help from communists who were subsequently rejected by their party. At the same time, there was a tendency in the PCE – and in the opposition in general – to blame terrorist acts on extreme right-wing movements.

Repression, combined with the support for ETA of a significant percentage of Basques, goes a long way towards explaining the final split in radical nationalism that occurred before Franco's demise. There was one faction that tended to combine violent action with non-terrorist acts; it was referred to as political-militant ETA and was drawn towards political activism. Nonetheless, the dominant tendency at the heart of the movement was fully committed to outright terrorist action and was called militant ETA. From the start of the 1970s on, terrorist attacks were not limited to the Basque Country but spread throughout all Spain's territory.

At the end of the Franco period terrorist violence increased and reached a level at which, unfortunately, it was destined to remain well on into the start of the transition. Between October 1974 and October 1975 ETA murdered 22 members of the security forces and 14 civilians, but most significant of all was the fact that in the days following the execution in September 1975, 200,000 people joined the strike organized in the Basque Country to express solidarity with the terrorist organization. That fact reveals the extent of public support and the gulf that existed between the Basque Country and the Franco regime. After 1973 ETA was not alone in resorting to terrorism, which spread to pro-China groups such as the reconstructed PCE and the Spanish Marxist–Leninist Organization (*Organización Marxista Leninista de España* or OMLE). The former set up the Armed Revolutionary Groups of October 1 (*Grupos Revolucionarios Armados Primero de Octubre* or GRAPO), specifically in response to the executions; these groups were particularly brutal in their actions but lacked any public support. Their militants were from humble backgrounds and came from industrial areas which were experiencing crisis (naval ship-building, for example), and they had to steal weapons from the police and did not even have their own means of producing pamphlets. Nonetheless, in the final moments of Francoism the GRAPO provoked repressive action from the regime that exposed its very worst aspects. The anti-terrorist decree that was to apply to them (and to ETA) in retrospect was aimed at holding responsible not only those who defended terrorism but also anyone who tried to "play down" its effects. The long-forgotten anarchist movement experienced a certain resurgence. There were groups committed to violent action, and in 1974 a militant from this tendency (Salvador Puig Antich) was executed.

Yet even this proliferation of terrorist activity could not hide the fact that there was another kind of opposition which might have had a much lower profile in the public media at the time but would later play a very much more decisive role. The moderate opposition of the PSOE and PCE chose their leaders and outlined their positions at this crucial moment when Spaniards sensed that the final demise of the regime was close at hand.

At this point the moderate opposition seemed not to be at the forefront of what was going on, but we must bear in mind that its role was not immediate and direct confrontation but rather to offer an alternative for the future. As time passed there was a gradual blurring of the boundaries between the opposition and the regime. There was now a "buffer-zone" in Spanish politics with a clear, unequivocal desire for democratization, although there were differences of opinion on the strategies to be adopted, and also disparities in terms of their origins.

Much of the moderate opposition had in the past identified with Don Juan de Borbón who, in this final phase of Francoism, stressed the differences between his own position and that of the regime, and so attracted the support of those who saw in him a liberal alternative to his son's kind of monarchy. In the last years of the regime Areilza put himself forward as representative of a civilized, democratic, and constitutional right wing, which explains why he was the target of angry reactions in official circles, especially from Carrero. For his part, Calvo Serer, with a past as the mentor of a certain version of an extreme right-wing monarchist tendency, and with an already democratic perspective on events, provided the inspiration behind the daily newspaper *Madrid*.

Two other groups that had in the past been part of this moderate opposition were the Christian Democrats and the followers of Dionisio Ridruejo. It was as late as 1973, when there was little time left before Franco died, that the Christian Democrat Team of the Spanish state (*Equipo de la Democracia Cristiana del Estado Español* or EDCEE) was founded. It was made up of Spanish Christian Democrat groups, the Democratic Union of Catalonia (*Unió Democràtica de Catalunya* or UDC), and the Basque Nationalist Party (PNV). Though there were exceptions, a semi-tolerant policy on the part of the government allowed Spanish Christian

Democrats to hold meetings with a certain amount of publicity through-out 1975. Certainly, the aim of the progressive liberal Catholic lobby was to promote the democratic ideal, and many of its members joined other, more left-wing groups. From 1973 on, when the Chilean govern-ment of the socialist president Salvador Allende was overthrown – initially to applause from the Christian Democrats – a group who supported Ruiz-Giménez shifted their position and joined the ranks of the PSOE. That same year saw the founding of the association Christians for Socialism (*Cristianos por el Socialismo*). For his part, having been forced into exile after the Munich Conference, Dionisio Ridruejo now returned to Spain where his valiant, caustic declarations led to prosecutions in 1972. His early death prevented his group playing a decisive role in Spain's transition to democracy.

In both the Basque Country and in Catalonia the opposition had followed its own particular path, but this now became the case even more than ever before. In the mid 1960s, the Basque Nationalist Party no longer had the religious affiliation that had been characteristic of it until that point. In Catalonia, the decline of Francoism coincided with a political formula that was to achieve even greater success after the transition. This option was linked to the person of Jordi Pujol who began his public life in Catholic organizations, like a large part of the political class that emerged in Spain during the transition. In May 1960 he led a protest movement against Franco on the occasion of a visit by the latter to Catalonia; as a result he was tortured and received a prison sentence of which he served two and a half years. After his release, his life became focused on the rebuilding of Catalan culture and a sense of national identity. The Democratic Convergence Party of Catalonia (*Convergència Democràtica de Catalunya* or CDC) came into being towards the end of 1974 and drew together elements from different backgrounds including the left, as was the case with Miquel Roca Junyent. Apart from mention-ing the political parties at the time, it is important that we stress the significance of certain changes taking place in Catalan nationalist thought in the final phase of the Franco period. Nationalism, critical Marxism, and progressive Catholicism came together to form the basis of a common understanding that allowed the creation of a single, unified consciousness.

For the time being, regionalist and nationalist movements were of only limited significance in the rest of Spain. Nevertheless, one group in Andalusia, that was nationalist in character with its roots in the distant past, was actually older than the CDC in Catalonia. The origins of Andalusian political nationalism must be traced back to the 1966 elections, when Alejandro Rojas Marcos became a councilor for Seville representing the city's big families. His actions and those of his followers led to the creation in 1972 of the Socialist Alliance of Andalusia (*Alianza Socialista de Andalucía* or ASA), which is where the pro-Andalusian movements of today originated.

Perhaps most characteristic of this period in the history of the opposition in Franco's Spain was the appearance of intermediate political groupings which acted within the legal framework but were committed to bringing about change. In mid 1973, a group formed called *Tácito*, which had as a platform for reaching the public the articles it published in *Ya*, and which advocated a shift towards nonconformity on the part of the regime's Catholic family. *Tácito* brought together committed members of the opposition who, with the Franco regime still in place, nonetheless continued to hold to a reformist position. Articles signed by *Tácito* had important repercussions and on some occasions meant prosecution for their authors.

More unexpected still were developments taking place in the thinking of Carlists and Falangists. In the late Franco period these two political blocks not only refused to accept Franco's arbitration any longer but even took up positions on the fringes of the regime, splitting into one sector composed largely of young members, which joined the opposition, and another that was more conventional and remained faithful to the regime. One might therefore talk of a degree of genuine heterodoxy among these most orthodox of groups. Only an utterly anachronistic viewpoint that tries to interpret past events from a present perspective could underestimate the importance of this kind of dissidence at the time.

Once the Carlists had given up all hope of Don Javier's son Carlos Hugo becoming heir to the throne, they moved towards a position which might seem unlikely but was not in fact so. In practice, Carlism had survived in a dormant state, keeping its organization functioning in some places – principally Navarra – but without confronting the *Movimiento*. If at times in the past it had allowed itself to be guided by leading figures from the *Movimiento*, its younger members now chose to associate themselves with the pretender himself. What resulted was a profound transformation of traditional Carlism, which became what Carlos Hugo himself described as socialist, self-regulating, and federal. At a deep level, there was a certain logic in the identification of socialism with Carlism since traditional Carlism had always had a popular tendency.

The change in Carlism became more obvious in the way that the annual gathering of the movement in Montejurra was organized and then gradually modified its position over time. Having been the site of a popular religious pilgrimage until 1966, Montejurra gradually became increasingly politicized. By 1972 the Carlists were arguing in favor of a socialist monarchy, and by 1974 the traditional Montejurra gathering claimed to be self-governing. Later on, Carlist propaganda began to contain what might be termed a "cry of the people." From 1968 on, there were even Carlist groups who had no hesitation in carrying out terrorist attacks and raids. Obviously not everyone followed the Carlist Pretender and his youth groups down this particular road. Attendance at the Montejurra gatherings, which had brought together 70,000 people at the end of the 1960s, barely reached five or six thousand in the 1970s.

Activities such as these brought Carlism to the brink of suicide by the time of the transition, and the Falangist youth movements went the same way. There was always space for a degree of dissidence within Falangism, but until the end of the 1960s it could hardly be said to have been of any significance at all. As with Carlism, the situation changed for young Falangists towards the end of the 1960s. A so-called Student Union Front (*Frente de Estudiantes Sindicalistas* or FES), inspired by the trade union movement, was active in universities after 1963 and enjoyed considerable support. After the early years of the 1960s there were also the José Antonio Doctrinal Circles (*Círculos Doctrinales José Antonio*) that were linked to the *Movimiento* but increasingly critical of it. They tried in 1970 to organize a meeting in Alicante with the intention of coming up with some means of promoting Falange that was independent of the regime. The fact that these discontented sectors of Falange existed meant that, after 1970, the celebration of the anniversary of the founding of the party had to take place in a meeting of the National Council.

It was not merely by chance that Carlism tried to develop along more socialist lines since, at this very moment, the Carlist movement, which had until now consisted of no more than a handful of exiles and a few young people inside Spain, suddenly became a rallying-point for a wide range of political tendencies. If it was to make the most of this situation, it needed first of all to replace the traditional leaders of the party with others better suited to the real Spain of the 1960s. In the second half of the decade, the party leader was an octogenarian who had been in that position for almost 30 years. Rodolfo Llopis was characterized by a strong mistrust of spontaneity within Spain and a determination to safeguard the essential nature of the party, and this effectively stood in the way of any chance of moving ahead.

Inside Spain socialism had followed a path that had little in common with Rodolfo Llopis's strategy. In 1967 the Catalan Socialist Movement (*Moviment Socialista de Catalunya* or MSC) held its party conference and its leading figures showed a clear commitment to autonomy as opposed to direction from outside. The following year the Interior Socialist Party (*Partido Socialista del Interior* or PSI) was founded, though this was nothing other than a new name for the followers of Tierno Galván, who in 1965 had been a PSOE militant, though he was expelled from the organization shortly afterwards. The PSI was almost exclusively a party of university teachers led by that overwhelming personality Enrique Tierno Galván. As for the PSOE in exile, there were two new significant developments which were more in tune than before with changes occurring within Spain at the time: anti-communist feeling disappeared and a certain libertarian atmosphere made itself felt. The mission of renewing the PSOE fell to three groups of young leaders from within the organization who came from different geographical regions and different militant tendencies and who were, in some cases, fresh on the scene: Enrique Múgica and Nicolás Redondo were the main driving force behind Basque socialism, Pablo Castellanos represented the party in Madrid, and Alfonso Guerra and Felipe González were leaders of the organization in Seville.

The leaders who breathed new life into Spanish socialism moved ahead slowly and had to contend with hard-fought controversy before a final solution was reached. It was only in 1967 that the socialist leadership could count on sizeable representation inside Spain (7 people); 2 years later, at meetings of the leadership outside Spain, Felipe González made his first public appearance. In 1970, for the first time, Llopis allowed a certain sharing of responsibilities: he would take on representing the party abroad while inside Spain those on the ground would be in charge. In 1971 the UGT came under the direction of a mixed committee of members on both sides of the frontier, though most were from inside Spain. However, the decisive moment came in 1973 when, after a series of earlier skirmishes, all members inside Spain who were committed to renewal had their way with Llopis. In fact, this was due more to the Basque and Madrid leaders than to those from Seville, but the latter would in time become more important because they had Felipe González among them, and his leadership potential was already visible for all to see.

Nonetheless, the reformers' victory was not complete until the start of 1974. The Socialist International's confidence in the young party leaders ensured that the reformist tendency did finally win through, but they continued to face problems inside the party. In 1973, for example, Guerra and González resigned from their posts; it was they who were taking a radical stance, which meant that they were putting obstacles in the path of Christian Democrats joining the party leadership.

The final triumph of the reformist tendency, and the consolidation of their previous success, occurred in October 1974, on the occasion of a Congress in Suresnes, near Paris. Just how limited the strength of Spanish socialism was barely a year before Franco's death is obvious from some simple statistics: the PSOE had 2,500 militants inside Spain (a fifth of them in Guipúzcoa) and 1,000 outside. The leaders who were elected signaled a final victory for Felipe González (*Isidoro*), but he only won it by publishing a statement of political intent and thanks to Nicolás Redondo's voluntary withdrawal from the leadership race. The decisions taken at the Congress were characterized by the markedly radical tone with which they rejected capitalism and the so-called "military blocks," which included the Western Block. Nonetheless, socialism had won for itself a promising position that boded well for future elections. In the first instance, it had in its favor a symbolic continuity with Spain's left-wing past, as well as representing effectively a youthful radicalism that did not in fact last long but was evidence of a pragmatic attitude. In addition, it was cross-class: a high proportion of its leaders had been to university. Suresnes was, then the culmination of a process and meant both a generational and an ideological renewal.

After this moment the PSOE could move ahead and become a kind of magnet for very different sectors who had adopted the label "socialist." By the time of Franco's death, it was still a party with severe deficiencies. It lacked organization, but as early as 1974, González had moved to Madrid and begun to work on remedying that, and it was at this point that a good number of its future leaders joined the party. It lacked a strong union movement, but it was never short of support from outside Spain, and although in Madrid and Seville it was predominantly a party of students and young professionals rather than workers, it did finally manage to build up the UGT, with the help of militants from the USO.

At the start of the 1970s, however, the PCE was the party of the left that seemed most likely to gain the strongest position. At this point it had a larger membership and better organization than the PSOE, and under its leader Santiago Carrillo it was becoming independent of the Soviet Union while, at the same time, avoiding isolation in Spain's opposition. The PCE may indeed have accepted the Soviet invasion of Hungary in 1956, but it was sharply critical of the invasion of Czechoslovakia in 1968. Its leaders even went so far as to state that what they wanted for Spain was a political situation like the "Prague spring." The Communist Party of the Soviet Union (*Partido Comunista de la Unión Soviética* or PCUS) reacted swiftly and angrily, and this no doubt fueled the dissident movement towards the end of 1969 led by two former Soviet ex-functionaries. More relevant by far, though, was the reaction of Enrique Líster – a significant historical figure in the Spanish Communist Party who also enjoyed direct support from the USSR. The PCUS criticized the Spanish leadership on several occasions, but Carrillo continued to maintain close relations with considerable sections of the international Communist movement that favored autonomy over Soviet control, such as the parties in Romania, Korea, and even in China.

He also adopted a stance aimed at attracting wider sectors of the Spanish population. Furthermore, Spain's particular situation favored an emphasis on democratic principles and consequently the PCE strategy could be summed up in the proposal of a "pact for freedom." In 1973 its "manifesto-program" suggested a "new democracy" for Spain but was vague on its exact content. The PCE even came round to accepting Spain's membership of the Common Market, which initially it had rejected. On the other hand, what did not appear to have changed at all was the way that the party was run, still following the principles of a rigid "democratic centralization." Carrillo held the reins of power; a third of the central committee was over 70. Nonetheless, the memory of the past and the enthusiasm felt in the present both did much to blur differences between those demanding freedom on the one hand and membership of the Communist Party on the other. In the eyes of many Spaniards the opposition was in practice identified with communism.

At the same time, however, other political groups split with the Communist Party because they considered it either reformist or too moderate. In the mid 1960s there emerged among Communists who had emigrated from Spain a self-styled Marxist–Leninist PCE with pro-China tendencies. It in turn gave birth to the Anti-Fascist Patriotic Revolutionary Front (*Frente Revolucionario Antifascista y Patriótico* or FRAP), which committed acts of terrorism in the 1970s and was not the only extreme left-wing group to come out of the PCE. From the

PSUC came the International Communist Party (*Partido Comunista Internacional* or PCI), which then became the Spanish Labor Party (*Partido del Trabajo de España* or PTE), along with some Trotskyite cells which joined together to form the Communist Revolutionary League (*Liga Comunista Revolucionaria* or LCR). There was one extreme left-wing organization that did not come from this source but was an offshoot of the more working-class side of ETA, and another called the Workers' Revolutionary Organization (*Organización Revolucionaria de los Trabajadores* or ORT), whose members came from Catholic workers' organizations of apostolate.

After outlining the groups that made up the political opposition to the regime, it is important to emphasize their disunity, which persisted right up to the time of Franco's death. Rather than focusing on removing the dictator, what the opposition tried to do in the last years of Francoism was to use collective action to obtain the guarantees that would make a transition to democracy possible.

At any given moment agreements were made that allowed collaboration between different opposition groups. There were, for example, collective demonstrations about the way that the referendum on the Organic Law was conducted in 1967. In 1970, the visit of the German Foreign Minister provided an opportunity for Tierno Galván, Ruiz-Giménez, Areilza, and Satrústegui to be interviewed, who also contacted the American Secretary of State shortly afterwards. There was even an example of far wider collaboration that did not rely on help from outside in Catalonia, where the Catalan Assembly (*Asamblea de Cataluña*) was set up at the end of 1972. In October 1973 its leading members were all arrested.

In the rest of Spain no one single representative organization was formed before Franco's death. In the summer of 1974, the Democratic Junta (*Junta Democrática*), spurred on by the PCE, was formed in Paris and attracted supporters of Don Juan de Borbón. There were also other groups that joined it such as, for example, Tierno Galván's *Partido Socialista Popular* (Popular Socialist Party or PSP) or, for a time at least, the Carlist Party. In fact it was obvious that to join this party merely meant taking up a position with a view to the immediate future, and we can therefore say that what was most important about it was not what it achieved at the time. Just as the *Junta Democrática* was backed by the PCE, so too the PSOE, working with Christian Democrats, formed the Platform for Democratic Convergence (*Plataforma de Convergencia Democrática* or PCD), and it was far more pluralistic.

---------------------------- **Spain and the Western World** ----------------------------

If we are to understand the final phase of Francoism, it is essential that we take into account the situation outside Spain at the time. This had an impact on the final weeks of the life of the regime when war broke out in Morocco, though this final conflict involving Spain in fact affected the whole Sahara. First we must look back to the mid 1960s. Fernando María Castiella had become Foreign Minister in 1957, and the fact that his term of office ended in 1969 meant that he was the longest-serving member of government working on foreign policy in the entire Franco period. A Spanish nationalist, Castiella had felt drawn to Falange in his youth but had also been a member of the regime's Catholic family. Although his commitment to the regime was beyond all doubt, his realism and competence pushed him in the direction of being more ready to adapt to circumstances. His attitude on foreign policy was often revisionist, especially in relation to the United States. Concerning other aspects of foreign policy, Castiella introduced a particular focus on the struggle for decolonization in Third World countries. The problem with this policy was that Spain was now increasingly obviously part of the western world: of Castiella's official visits abroad (of which there were over 70), only one was to Latin America and only 10 percent to Arab countries.

A brilliant man but also often superficial and intemperate, Gregorio López Bravo, who was Foreign Minister from 1969 to 1973, gave Spain's foreign policy a more clearly western orientation. During his time in office, the Ministry for Foreign Affairs took on responsibility for foreign trade and opened up markets in Eastern Europe. His successors, Laureano López Rodó and Pedro Cortina Mauri, did not last long enough to leave their own mark on foreign policy. López Rodó, however, did at least show clearly that he intended to continue along the same lines as his predecessor, though somewhat more discreetly. Cortina, rather than devising his own foreign policy, was, one might say, like many other politicians in the final stages of the Franco period, governed by circumstances.

If each of Spain's Foreign Ministers made their own particular mark on the country's foreign policy, it nonetheless developed within a fixed framework. According to the way it had been defined after 1953, it was basically determined by relations with the United States. In dealings with the Americans in a relationship between two very unequal partners – and military aid to Spain was very much less than that given to Yugoslavia

– Castiella's approach as a diplomat was often somewhat irritable, while Franco's attitude was consistent with his usual mixture of caution and stubbornness, and therefore much more compliant. On the matter of relations with the United States, Franco used to say that if "one can't do anything but marry, it's better to marry the richest girl in the village"; and of course, America did not intervene in Spanish internal politics. Franco's personal papers reveal that he was very much aware of the nuclear threat to Madrid posed by the closeness of the airbase at Torrejón. Carrero's position was the same: he approved of the USA's anti-communist stance, but thought Americans "infantile," and he was also aware that it was only the Pentagon that looked kindly on Franco's Spain.

The Americans gave Spain some unpleasant surprises such as, for example, their refusal to let American weapons be used in north Africa, and the American warplane carrying an atomic bomb that crashed into the sea off Palomares (Almería) in 1966. At times Spain made concessions without gaining anything in exchange; Muñoz Grandes allowed Rota to be used as a base for submarines armed with nuclear weapons without imposing any conditions. From the end of 1967 on, the possibility of a renegotiation of the treaty gave voice to increasing Spanish dissatisfaction, especially from Castiella. He warned that Spanish collaboration should not be taken for granted and at the same time lodged a complaint about the American fleet visiting Gibraltar, and he demanded more American aid. Negotiations became very tense between the summers of 1968 and 1969. What is certain is that there was a deep lack of understanding which would be difficult to overcome; the Americans complained about what they considered unreasonable demands at a time when they were facing other more pressing problems such as Vietnam, while the Spaniards considered that they were not getting enough diplomatic support from the United States. It was proving impossible for the American leaders to obtain the Legislative Assembly's approval on signing a treaty with Spain. Although Castiella modified his position and became slightly more flexible, his original rigidity – he had gone so far as to suggest that the Americans, as well as the Soviets, should move out of the Mediterranean – made relations with Carrero much worse. López Bravo then made a new agreement in the summer of 1970. At last Franco's own theory had triumphed, according to which "if we don't negotiate, what else are we going to do?"

The new pact replaced what had in 1953 been termed "military bases for joint use" with "facilities available at Spanish bases," and it placed more emphasis on technical and cultural aspects and economic cooperation;

however, the balance of the two sides remained unequal. In the case of minor conflicts, of which there were many taking place around the world, the Americans could use bases in Spanish territory for support or supply without taking Spanish attitudes into consideration. Essentially, from 1953 until the end of the regime, the situation remained unchanged because of the inequality of the conditions outlined in the pacts. The more conservative among the American leaders on foreign policy, including Kissinger, wanted Spain to be allowed to join NATO, but opposition from a sizeable number of members vetoed this possibility of increased Spanish integration into the Western Block.

If Spain's relations with America suffered because of imbalances such as these in areas of mutual interest, the situation was even worse as regards other European countries. In 1961 Franco still thought that proposals to unite Europe were "unrealistic," which allows doubts to arise about the perspicacity that he was sometimes considered to have shown in this area. Yet, despite this attitude, that very same year the decision was taken to request some kind of membership of the Common Market, showing that the realism of diplomats and economic experts could also make an impact at a high level in Spanish politics. In February 1962, Franco's Spain requested an "association that could in time lead to full membership of the Common Market." One should note that the terminology suggested no more than a secondary form of entry into the organization. What was of most interest was negotiation on trade. The request made no allusion whatever to Spain adopting the political principles on which the Common Market was based.

Spain's petition made scant impact in pro-European circles at home. In the rest of Europe, the Franco regime gained the support of a few nations who, while not considering its government on a par with their own, were not worried about closer contact (Germany and France); however, the Benelux countries and those further north were more reticent. Political resistance was strong in certain instances such as, for example, the European Parliament and the Council of Europe. On Spain's part, reports were written stating that "there was not a single party as such" – words taken from a report by Fraga which are further evidence of the increasing flexibility of the new generation of leaders. However, the regime's reaction on those who had taken part in the Munich Conference ruined the effect of any such compromise.

Given these circumstances, it is not surprising that negotiations did not get under way for another 5 years. The Spanish petition on entry into the Common Market consolidated and – one might even say – made irreversible the economic reforms of the late 1950s, but it was only in the summer of 1970 that an agreement was actually reached, and that was after lengthy discussions. The content was limited in scope, not going beyond preferential agreement which allowed Spain to be termed a "Mediterranean country." What was important, however, was that the results were very positive for Spanish trade. Exports to Common Market countries rose by 30 percent. López Bravo summed up the impact of the agreement very well when he referred to the "practically irreversible nature" of Spain's closer relations with the European Community. This did not, however, mean closer identification in political terms. Indeed, Franco's Spain continued to be viewed by Europe with profound reservations in political terms, and with the hope that change would come about as soon as possible.

Fears of isolation loomed again at the time of the executions in September 1975, seeming to hark back to Spain's situation at the end of World War II. Now, in addition, the Franco regime could not rely on Catholic support. Relations between Franco's Spain and the Vatican were bad in the period known as *tardofranquismo*, especially during López Bravo's time in office, so much so that the Spanish Foreign minister had a tense, even hostile interview with the pope. Franco used to be cautious in matters that might cause conflict with the Church ("priest-meat is hard to digest," he told Alonso Vega), but he was confused and angry at the Church's distancing of itself from his regime. In the last private text that he wrote on the subject, he went so far as to say that the position that Rome was adopting was like "a stab in the back" for him.

From the end of the 1960s on, there had been discussion on the need for a new Concordat between the Church and the Spanish state. In 1965 the Vatican had asked those countries with the privilege of nominating bishops to renounce it and the pope insisted that Franco should do so in 1968. The Chief of State took the line that this could only happen with due reference to overall relations between the two powers. In 1971 a draft Concordat was drawn up in which the state chose the impossible option of complete renegotiation as a means of blocking the attempt to do away with its role in the appointment of bishops.

The draft Concordat was very soon out of date, and the bishops as much as the press and Rome itself made clear their preference for partial agreements. In October, on the issue of Church–state relations, the Foreign Minister López Bravo told Archbiship Tarancón that the state would go no further because "the cup was now so full that one more drop would make it overflow." In January 1973 he visited the pope, and the tone of their discussion was so sharp that Paul VI later told Tarancón that on no fewer than three occasions he had signaled for the minister to leave the room. When López Rodó took over from López Bravo he tried to restart negotiations. At the end of 1973, Agostino Casaroli, in charge of Vatican diplomacy, went to Spain. However, his efforts came too late and were impracticable: the conviction that it was the Vatican's intention to avoid consultation with the Spanish hierarchy was the project's death-knell. By 1974 Rome was already aware that it should not move too fast to establish a new relationship with the Franco regime.

If López Bravo failed in his attempt to improve relations with the Vatican, his name was linked with the establishment of a new kind of relations with Eastern Europe. There had been covert contact between the Franco regime and the Soviet Union since the 1940s. Kruschev's letter to Franco in 1961 on problems in the Mediterranean signaled tacit recognition of the regime on the part of the USSR. From 1966 on, the Eastern Block countries were willing to maintain relations with Spain, and by the end of the decade the process of setting up trade agreements was unstoppable. In Castiella's time agreements were made with Romania (1967), then with Poland (1969), Bulgaria and Czechoslovakia (1970). In 1970 López Bravo stopped off in Moscow to make direct contact with the Soviet authorities, and trade relations were followed by full diplomatic relations: the first Spanish embassy in an Eastern Block country was set up in the German Democratic Republic.

Probably the aspect of Spanish foreign policy that took up most of the government's time was the question of decolonization. As presented by Castiella, it had two facets which, according to his way of thinking, were complementary. Spain was to benefit from decolonization by regaining control of Gibraltar, but it would also acquire certain obligations because of its position as an administrative power in the colonies. This last point was agreed on after some hesitation. On this basis Spain tried to gain support from Third World countries for its plan to repossess Gibraltar. In fact, the two problems it was addressing were entirely separate issues.

The United Kingdom had taken advantage of Spain's weakness in the post-Civil War period to extend its territory in Gibraltar by occupying a strip of the isthmus between the Rock and the mainland and building an airport there. The first diplomatic contacts between the two countries on the subject of Gibraltar took place at the start of the 1960s. The distance between their positions led Spain to decide to take the matter to the United Nations, where Castiella's strategy became clear when two countries such as Cambodia and Bulgaria (that is to say, one neutral and one communist) were the ones to open the debate in 1963. In 1964 the UN suggested that negotiation should start at once, but the positions of the two participants were too far apart. Spain insisted that when it had ceded Gibraltar in the first place it had been on the understanding that it would regain control rather than Gibraltar be handed over to another nation. At the same time, it affirmed its willingness to grant a special statute to the inhabitants. In 1966 Spain closed the frontier with Gibraltar, cutting off all contact by land, and in 1969 it did the same by sea, also making repeated protests on violations of Spanish air-space. For their part, the British demanded from the start that the will of the people be taken into account, and in September 1967 a plebiscite was held which voted in favor of maintaining existing relations with Britain.

Tensions rose still further when, in 1969, Castiella went so far as to suggest a cordon of tethered balloons to stop the British airport being used, while Franco was proposing the creation of a new province of Gibraltar. Neither suggestion came to anything because Franco's usual caution won the day and he told his Foreign Minister that "the only Spaniard who did not have the right to feel passionately" about the problem was Castiella himself. However, López Bravo was no more successful when he used a more conciliatory and friendly approach. In 1973, Franco's Spain was once again trying to dream up harsher measures to put an end to the Gibraltar situation, such as building a large airport close by. The conflict had no chance of a solution being found given the terms in which it was framed.

## ———— Late Decolonization: Guinea and the Sahara ————

Meanwhile, Spain's decolonization of Morocco was actually going ahead, surrounded by tensions because Carrero's position on the matter was that it should not be taking place at all, while Castiella's was completely different as he had to back the move in order to win back Gibraltar, which explains why Spain's policy changed in a very short period of time. In 1958–9 the Sahara and Guinea were both declared Spanish provinces, but by the start of the 1970s it was already obvious that in the case of Guinea the situation was not sustainable. Castiella's solution was to decolonize, and he was strongly supported by members of Spain's diplomatic corps because his solution was realistic. In the Presidency, however, many civil servants agreed with Carrero Blanco, seeing decolonization as personal torture (it was like "having strips of skin torn off," commented one diplomat).

One important aspect of Spanish decolonization to note is that it was approached very differently from the way that the Salazar regime in Portugal had gone about it, although the two regimes had many significant traits in common. In the case of Portugal, its colonies meant more to it from many points of view, but in addition Salazar exercised political power there directly. His regime had become more rigid in its final years, acting very much in the way that Carrero favored acting, and it had made the colonies provinces of Portugal, investing public funds and setting about implementing egalitarian legislation. The attempt was bound to fail and it caused a cooling in Spanish–Portuguese relations. The last occasion on which Franco and Salazar met was in 1963. Portugal not only refused to inform the United Nations on what was going on in its colonized territories but also refused to support Spain's demands for the return of Gibraltar. This meant the breakup of a solidarity between the two dictatorships that had begun during the Spanish Civil War.

Guinea, in terms of its viability as a nation, faced particular problems, first because of the distance that separated the island of Fernando Poo from its territory on the African continent (300 kilometers), and also because of the ethnic diversity of the inhabitants of the two areas. The island had been colonized first, and had even a developed Creole elite. Spanish colonization of the African mainland had started late (it was only in 1935 that Spaniards had moved inland) and it was characterized by a Church presence and a concept of a relationship with the indigenous peoples that was like that of a guardian. Spain gained undoubted economic benefits from its exploitation of Guinea. At the start of the 1960s this Spanish possession had a relatively high income for the African continent as well as one of the highest levels of export. A good sign of its prosperity is the number of Nigerian laborers who worked there: some 60,000 at the time of independence.

It was as late as the 1960s, a long time after other powers had begun decolonization, that the possibility of Guinea's independence came under discussion. In 1964 it was granted a degree of autonomy, and both municipal and regional elections were held resulting in a proliferation of parties which formed along tribal rather than ideological lines. At the end of 1968, after a visit by a member of the UN, a referendum took place which favored independence.

Independence did not, however, bring either freedom or prosperity to the former colony. The worst problem was that its leader, Francisco Macías, became a bloody dictator capable of murdering his own ministers,

with the result that a considerable proportion of the population emigrated. The sheer barbarity of his government was later concealed under
the banner of "scientific socialism," as happened in so many other African
countries, with the creation of a single party "of workers" and an anti-
colonialist demagogy that blamed the Spaniards for every imaginable ill.
In 1972 there was severe tension between the metropolitan power and
the ex-colony, and in 1975 relations effectively broke down.

The question of the Sahara seemed, at least in theory, to be less problematic than that of Guinea. The desert was home to some 70,000 nomads
whose lifestyle had barely changed in centuries, and this population
had a certain distinct cultural identity in that its language, "Hassania,"
shares only 75 percent of its characteristics with Arabic. These people had
always lived according to forms of social and political organization that
predated the state, but they had maintained some sort of relations with
the Moroccan and Mauritanian authorities. Until 1934 Spain occupied
only three sites on the coast; it was during the Civil War that the whole
territory was brought under its control and the town of El Aaiún (Laâyoune)
was founded. In principle, then, the Sahara seemed controlable, but this
proved not to be the case because of an accumulation of different factors
which ranged from international conflict in North Africa to uncertainty
on the subject among Spain's political leaders.

The situation did not alter in the Sahara until huge deposits of phosphates were discovered which, in economic terms, meant that mining
began there in 1969. Transportation of the mineral first happened in 1972
after the opening up of an open-cast mine and the construction of an
immensely long conveyor-belt which took it right to the coast. In 1975,
the year in which Spain decided to withdraw from the area, the price of
phosphates rose steeply worldwide. One of the neighboring countries,
Morocco, was already a major producer of these minerals, which are
essential for making fertilizers. By the end of the 1960s, the nomadic
herds of the Saharaui people had lost any importance they had ever had;
only about 8,000 people still kept them. As usually happens in such
circumstances, the first nationalists made their appearance, either in the
country's administration or among indigenous troops.

For quite a long time the Sahara was far from being a major preoccupation for Spain's foreign policy. Franco never managed to achieve sincere
collaboration or effective friendship with Hassan II. The king of Morocco
had managed to gain control of Ifni in 1969, but by the following year
he was telling Franco's son-in-law that next he would be demanding the

Sahara. At around the same time as its withdrawal from Guinea, Spain gave the impression that it was prepared to make a move in the same direction in the Sahara by holding a referendum. In fact, a resolution on a referendum had already been approved by the UN and Spain had voted in favor. In the mid 1960s there had been an ongoing struggle between Morocco and Mauritania over the Spanish Sahara. When the interested parties managed to reach an agreement in about 1968, Algeria – a political regime with a revolutionary element – also became involved. Meanwhile, as though this were not enough, disagreements arose over fishing rights and the activities of armed groups. The situation was worsening. One gains the impression that Carrero tried to hold to a position of resistance at all costs in hopes of achieving a spurious independence. Arias's policy was much more uncertain because he was finding the situation inside Spain far more taxing than in Africa. Whatever the truth of the matter, caught between its inability to make a move and its uncertainty over what to do, in practice Spanish policy meant trying to "play for time only to run out of it in the end."

The modest attempts in the Sahara at supposed self-government – the creation of an assembly or *Yemáa* – came so late and were so flawed that they proved counterproductive in dealings with the United Nations. Furthermore, the party set up with Spanish help was soon overwhelmed by genuine nationalist sentiment. From 1970 on, the nationalists took part in a series of significant incidents. After initial repression in response to demonstrations that already had resulted in deaths, there was armed action in 1973. The Polisario Front (*Frente Popular de Liberación de Saguía y Río de Oro*) – the name adopted by this nationalist faction – soon won support in the whole of Algeria which allowed camps for exiles and fighters to be set up within its frontiers.

That situation was a powerful factor in bringing the Spanish authorities to the point of deciding to go ahead with holding a referendum on self-determination; however, just a few months before it was due to take place, Morocco appealed before the International Court of Justice in The Hague. The question put before the Tribunal was whether the Sahara could be considered to have been dependent on any other state authority before the arrival of the Spaniards. While discussions were being held at a high level in the Tribunal, a certain rapprochement took place between Spain and the Polisario Front; fighting ceased and prisoners were exchanged.

However, the Spanish Administration's ability to act was seriously hampered by Franco's final illness. In October 1975, the Tribunal in The

Hague pronounced in Spain's favor on holding the referendum, but Morocco reacted immediately by acting as though its own standpoint had been confirmed. Hassan II announced the so-called "Green March," which was intended to be a kind of peaceful pilgrimage to the Sahara involving thousands of unarmed civilians. Franco's sense of duty – but also his stubborn determination to remain in power – meant that he actually presided at a meeting of the Council of Ministers at this dramatic juncture, and it was there that his final illness began.

Hassan II, for his part, was both lucky and clever. When Don Juan de Borbón reproached him for having taken advantage of Spain's critical situation as Franco lay dying, the king of Morocco retorted: "Tell me what other moment would be better to address the Saharaui problem." The decision to hold the "Green March" circumvented any criticism from within Morocco and won support from a good number of African and Third World countries. As for Algeria, its actions at the United Nations were utterly incoherent. The Soviet block did not take any decisive stand, while the Western Block countries sided with Morocco.

Spain's action after the start of Franco's final illness was an example of the weakness and paralysis typical of dictatorial regimes at certain crucial moments. At the UN it managed to comply with the policy to which it had signed up, while also negotiating with Hassan II. With Franco at death's door, the regime could not handle any more problems. In November, as a result of the Madrid Treaty (*Tratado de Madrid*), Spain entered into a pact with Morocco and Mauritania on forming a joint administration. This was always a fiction and the Moroccans soon set about occupying Saharaui territory, which in practice simply gave in to them. Spain, with Moroccan assent, sold two-thirds of the company handling the phosphates and received in exchange false assurances that its fishing rights would be guaranteed. In this way the regime freed itself from one problem but failed to prevent conflict continuing in North Africa because the Polisario Front, armed by Algeria, stopped the Moroccan takeover of the Sahara happening peacefully. A quarter of a century later the UN decisions on the right of the Sahara to self-determination have still not been put into action.

────────────  **A Politically Committed Culture?**  ────────────

Spanish culture was full of paradoxes during the final phase of Francoism. There was not always open hostility on the part of the cultural media towards the regime but nor was there unquestioning conformity. Like Spanish society, Spanish culture developed in its own way alongside the regime, with periodic bouts of conflict between them. This is not only true of high culture but also of popular forms – after all, this was the time of protest songs and the so-called *gauche divine*: a rebellion against intolerable official solemnity and moral hypocrisy. While in terms of ideas and the social sciences there existed assumptions that were alien to the official political standpoint, literature often chose a path that led to an experimentalism that had nothing to do with any political position. Art did offer some examples of political commitment, but it also resorted to irony or parody. In the theater and in the cinema there was a very significant level of open hostility in specific cases (25 percent of films could be termed dissident). In Spanish culture as a whole there was an obvious gulf between Spain's official politics and its real politics, both being autonomous and for the most part not interfering with each other. However, after 1969 points of conflict did multiply.

Evolution in the worlds of ideas and the social sciences tended to take the form of identification and rediscovery. The interpretations of Spain's past that were put forward often likened its experience to what had gone on in other countries in similar circumstances. The term "rediscovery" also indicates a trait that was typical of this period, though in fact it was a phenomenon that dated from an earlier time, but that now began to move faster. At the end of the 1960s, for example, the liberal Krausist tradition, which had at times been viewed as rather an unfortunate aspect of Spain's past, became the object of serious research. The first work on Spain's left-wing tradition also dates from that time, as does the appearance of Spain's very few contributions to Marxist thought (Manuel Sacristán, Tierno Galván . . . ). Also highly representative of the period was the interest that social scientists took in Spain's experiences in the Republican years which indicated – albeit with a degree of uncertainty – both the desire for and imminence of a democratic state of peaceful coexistence. At the same time, however, in terms of ideas, there was a return to individualism and neo-Nietzschian theories, both of which were far removed from the political commitment of other periods, even if those involved took up a dissident stance towards the regime. It is from this final period of Francoism that we have inherited a certain breadth in Spanish cultural life in terms of material aspects such as, for example, cultural networks, a reading public, and a small amount of structuring.

While these developments were taking place in the academic world and the world of high culture, a number of publications were helping to spread and popularize dissident values. Among them it is worth mentioning two periodicals, *Triunfo* and *Cuadernos para el Diálogo*, neither of which lasted beyond the transition. *Triunfo* was, in origin, a film weekly which, in 1968, broadened out and disseminated left-wing ideas, though usually with no reference at all to the situation in Spain. In 1971 an edition on the subject of marriage earned it a 4-month suspension, but in 1975, when it dared go so far as to mention the revolution in Portugal, the suspension lasted until after Franco's death. *Cuadernos para el Diálogo* started out in 1963 as a monthly publication with Catholic origins and a post-Vatican II spirit. From 1969 on, it could be viewed as a publication representing the opposition as a whole, and in 1973 it adopted a left-wing tone when events in Chile brought its editorial team to a point of crisis. More closely related to political concerns in Spain, *Cuadernos para el Diálogo* helped to create an important link between culture and politics, and in so doing fomented solidarity among different sectors who opposed the regime.

The change that occurred in the mid 1960s was perhaps more obvious in literature than in any other cultural sphere. New writers were by now openly critical of what they called the "cabbage generation" that was prosaic, stark, and provincial; the new generation would be "the sandalwood generation": cosmopolitan, reveling in artifice, and experimental. At the same time the critics (José María Castellet) and publishers (Carlos Barral) who had encouraged the former now became advocates of the latter. Anecdotes apart, it seems clear that the end of social realism came about as a result of sheer tiredness. Social realist narrators and poets felt that neither their political commitment, nor the popularist literature through which they had tried to reach out to a public that they had never really had, had managed to bring down the regime; instead, the quality of their work had gone down.

As regards narrative, the change that took place in the mid 1960s had been anticipated in earlier works. The appearance of Luis Martín-Santos's *Tiempo de silencio* (*Time of silence*, 1962) marked the start of the change. At the same time, the publication of Mario Vargas Llosa's first novel, *La ciudad y los perros* (*The Time of the Hero*) in the same year sparked off a trend in experimentalist writing. For at least a decade the best novels from Latin America exerted a very positive influence on Spanish narrative. Three novels that all appeared in 1966 exemplify the changes that took place in narrative writing. In *Últimas tardes con Teresa* (*Last afternoons with Teresa*) Juan Marsé re-creates the sense of political disillusionment and, at the same time, offers a story that is sharply critical of certain sectors of the opposition. Miguel Delibes's *Cinco horas con Mario* (*Five hours with Mario*) is a fine example of the stylistic concerns of the time, and it describes the tragedy of a mind alert to the destructiveness of an atmosphere of provincial conservatism. As for Juan Goytisolo, one of the writers who best characterizes social narrative, in *Señas de identidad* (*Signs of identity*) he began a kind of spiritual autobiography which also aims to offer a form of critical meditation on Spain itself.

The year 1969 could equally be considered immensely important in Spanish literature. It was then that the publishing house Planeta awarded two of its major prizes to writers in exile – Ramón Sender and Mercè Rodoreda – and at the same time Spain itself witnessed an explosion of experimentalism: Delibes's *Parábola del naufragio* (*Parable of a Shipwreck*), Camilo José Cela's *San Camilo 1936*... (alluding to the day the Civil War started: the saint's day, July 18). People also began talking about the novelist who would be a crucial influence on new generations of writers: Juan Benet. Novelists who had begun writing in the 1940s now opted for experimentalism, which could be said to have become established as a style around 1973. Cela and Delibes chose the baroque, with its complicated syntax. Gonzalo Torrente Ballester, who had chosen a structure and thematic content typical of the nineteenth century in *Los gozos y las sombras* (*Joys and shadows*, 1957–62), in *La saga-fuga de J. B.* (*The saga-flight of JB*, 1972), immersed himself in culturalism and the fantastic.

As had been the case in the 1950s, it was an anthology by Castellet – *Nueve novísimos poetas* (*Nine very new poets*, 1970) – that offered an account of the newest trends to appear in Spanish poetry. Also in this same area of literature, one poetic mentor – Antonio Machado – was replaced by another – Luis Cernuda. Spain's new poets, like its novelists, showed clear cosmopolitan leanings that led them to choose their models from Latin America, or alternatively from more heterodox writers associated with surrealism such as Carlos Edmundo de Ory. The new poetry was characterized by its freedom of form, its close links to contemporary communications media, its exoticism, artifice, and fascination with experimentalism. *Arde el mar* (*The Sea is Burning*, 1966) by Pere Gimferrer exemplifies these new tendencies.

The same fascination with experimentalism is evident, of course, in the theater. The works of Antonio Buero Vallejo from this period, such as *El tragaluz* (*The skylight*, 1967), take place in a far more complex theatrical space and show this fascination, which is also to be found in the dramatists who best represent the period: Euloxio R. Ruibal, Ángel García Pintado, José María Rodríguez Méndez ... Reference to themes linked to politics in these works was, it must be said, indirect and allegorical rather than testimonial and precise, but all of these factors taken together meant that Lázaro Carreter could quite rightly label this kind of production "underground" theater. At the same time as these works, there was also a kind of performance or *función* (the word used very often at this time) which was rather like a collage of elements akin to the absurd *esperpento* theater of Ramón del Valle-Inclán. Adolfo Marsillach, at the time a fellow-traveler of the PCE, who in 1968 staged Peter Weiss's *Marat-Sade*, put on a performance of Molière's *Tartuffe* barely a month after the crisis of October 1969, which gave him the opportunity to be sharply sarcastic about the ministers who were members of Opus Dei. If Spain's poets rediscovered Luis Cernuda at this point, in much the same way dramatists rediscovered Valle-Inclán as a means of exploring political concerns. One of the dramatists mentioned would later recall that the Galician Valle-Inclán was able to "make a caricature out of a grand gesture, not to lament but to destroy." Indeed, in an attempt to find a term to describe this kind of theater, the dramatist Francisco Nieva invented a new word, "*reópera*." In terms of more conventional theater, this period saw the decline in popularity with theater-goers of Alfonso Paso, his place being taken by Antonio Gala, whose humor and command of language made him one of the most successful writers of the time. One of the most surprising strikes organized in the year that Franco died was the actors' strike in which popular personalities with no particular political affiliation took part.

It is virtually impossible to present a complete overview of the wide diversity of tendencies in Spanish painting in the last phase of Francoism. From the end of the 1960s on, there was a degree of politicization in the world of the plastic arts, but it did not necessarily lead to any change in aesthetic styles. There was also evidence of a certain move backward towards figurative representation as abstract expressionism began to lose pace. The hint of a return to realism was linked to political commitment. Juan Genovés and Rafael Canogar offer a clear example of a figurative style which aligned itself with the values of the avant-garde and was at the same time politically committed, and there were others as well who had recourse to irony or parody, for example, as was the case with Eduardo Arroyo and the *Equipo Crónica*. Through narrative images that used the visual language of the poster or popular cartoon-like *aleluya*, these artists offered a bitterly corrosive image of Francoism and of its particular inter-pretation of Spain's past. The abstract expressionists themselves exagger-ated their sense of anguish (Manuel Rivera in his *Retablo por las víctimas de la violencia*). At the same time, however, some of the youngest painters drawn to *Nueva Generación* expressed their rejection of the traditional concept of Spanishness (*casticismo*) and of the blackness of *El Paso*, while at the same time they dissociated themselves from politics, declaring that they were "apolitical and devoid of respect." Among these new painters, perhaps Luis Gordillo and Darío Villalba were the most influential. The ironic tone that Gordillo adopted when talking about painting as a task, and his rejection of any values relating to the materials he used or the style of his work, pointed the way ahead for subsequent generations.

Diversity was an even stronger characteristic in Spanish film-making at this time. There was, for example, a certain "*apertura*" while José María García Escudero was director general after 1962. "It's not that nothing has happened in politics in ten years, it's that nothing has happened at all," he stated in his memoirs. After that time, written norms came into effect governing censorship (the percentage of films that were censored went down from 10 to 7 percent), while film production was promoted through the establishment of an automatic subsidy of 15 percent of takings.

García Escudero's policies brought positive results. A "new Spanish cinema" emerged which tended to choose themes from daily experience and often explored the contrast between provincial and city life, such as Jorge Fons's *La busca* (*The search*, 1966), made a few timid references to polit-ical dissidence and frustration among Spain's youth like Basilio Martín Patino's *Nueve cartas a Berta* (*Nine letters to Berta*, 1965), or depicted the tension of hidden violence about to break out, as in the case of Carlos Saura's *La caza* (*The hunt*, 1965). These quality films did not, however, have much international success or even reach a wide audience inside Spain. The official protection that the cinema enjoyed mostly benefited poor quality comedies: *La ciudad no es para mí* by Paco Martínez Soria (*The city's not for me*, 1965) was the biggest box-office success of the decade. The general public was even less receptive towards the so-called "Barcelona school" characterized by cultural allusions, experimentalism, and the hermeticism that is well illustrated by the title of one of their works: *Dante no es únicamente severo* (*Dante is not only severe*, 1967).

The 1970s began most inauspiciously for the Spanish film industry. Faced with comedies whose vulgarity took the form of "sexual voyeurism" – *No desearás al vecino del quinto* (*You won't fancy the neighbor on the fifth floor*, 1970) had the highest box-office takings until 1987 – Spanish cinema of the 1970s offered plentiful evidence of dissidence. There are perhaps three films that best illustrate this particular stance: Patino's *Canciones para después de una guerra* (*Songs for after a war*, 1971), which shows the difficulties inherent in depicting the immediate past; Víctor Erice's *El espiritu de la colmena* (*The spirit of the beehive*, 1973), which has a backdrop of armed resistance to the regime, and Carlos Saura's *La prima Angélica* (*Cousin Angélica*, 1973), which borders on more or less explicit anti-Francoism. Carlos Saura's oblique and intellectualized style perhaps gives the best idea of the realities of film-making in these closing moments of the Franco period. What is remarkable is that cinema such as this was profitable from an economic point of view; Saura's film cost 12 million pesetas and brought in 80 million, and Elías Querejeta became one of the most powerful producers in the industry. Those who did not have such pretensions also achieved considerable successes by means of a "third way" which was sufficiently accessible for the general public and dealt with themes that at another time would have been considered unacceptable, such as Roberto Bodegas's *Españolas en París* (*Spanish Women in París*, 1969).

In 1969 the French writer Max Aub visited Spain, and his deep sense of disappointment is captured clearly in *La gallina ciega* (*Blindman's Buff*). Yet his vision was too firmly rooted in the past and lacked a firm foundation. Hesitantly and not without difficulty a new culture was growing up independently of the state, and it had a critical edge and provided a space in which voices that had previously formed part of Spain's ancient heritage could once again be heard.

———————— **Spain at the Time of Franco's Death** ————————

The last year of Franco's life afforded a pathetic image, reminiscent of Valle-Inclán's definition of *esperpento*, due to the dictator's blind determination to remain in power, to the atmosphere conjured up by his close family circle, and to the grotesque nature of some of the political conspiracies that were being dreamed up in the wings. In July 1974 Franco suffered a thrombophlebitis which meant that the last year of his life was almost entirely taken up with learning to speak and walk again. It was his earnest desire to accomplish the mission that he believed had been entrusted to him which, at the time of the Green March, meant that he took up the reins of power once again, under pressure to do so from those in government and from his own family. His activities on a typical working day, on which he received dozens of people, and his sedentary pastimes such as watching television, exacerbated his illness to an extent, but not as much as the susceptibility to pressure that was a product of his age and Parkinson's disease, and of the impact on him of the recent events in the Sahara. Keeping in contact with Hassan II by means of personal messengers, which shows how little confidence he had in Arias Navarro, he himself took all the major decisions on the crisis which had essentially been resolved by the time he died. On October 15, 1975 he suffered a first heart-attack, which was followed by two more on October 19 and 20, due in part to his determination to live a normal life when he was no longer in a state to do so. From October 23 on, his condition became critical and problems with circulation caused peritonitis, for which he underwent an operation on November 3. The slow process of dying that began at this point cannot but inspire pity. The historian should bear in mind that its very duration had the effect of allowing Spanish society to grow accustomed to the idea that he would soon no longer be there, and this did much to prevent greater commotion and to allow caution to rule the day.

Franco's death also signaled the death of his regime. Conscious of his duty, prudent and able though he was, the most positive judgment that can be pronounced on Franco means remembering what he was not. His regime habitually violated the freedom and rights of the individual, showed exceptional cruelty over many years, and having come into being as a result of a Civil War, was remarkable for the length of time it stayed in power. It was not, however, a totalitarian system in the way that other dictatorships at the time were. Its advocates have attributed to Francoism Spain's economic development of the 1960s, and the 1975 monarchy, but the former was a product of circumstances rather than of any action on his part, while the monarchy was restored to power with very different results from those he originally intended. Neither event would have been possible had Francoism been a totalitarian regime. Just as within Spanish society a desire for freedom had begun to grow like grass in the cracks between the paving-stones of a patio, so too, in relation to the question of the succession, hopes grew that Spaniards would soon recover their freedom. Don Juan Carlos who, as Franco lay dying, had to intervene to prevent Arias Navarro resigning, was under attack from the left and was ignored by the center, while the right wanted to manipulate him; yet he himself was destined to play a crucial role in the transition that was about to occur.

The weeks in which he exercised power for the second time as interim Chief of State were his first chance at an apprenticeship. He had resisted taking power, and he only did so once he knew that Franco would not recover. Apart from facing problems such as those already mentioned, he had to take the initiative on several important matters: for example, to prevent his father taking up a confrontational anti-regime stance, to gain the trust of the military, to persuade the United States to help Spain solve the problem of the Sahara, and to keep the communist opposition waiting expectantly to see how events were going to turn out.

Nothing could in fact have been further from the truth than to assume that this transition would be easy. At the time of General Franco's death certain factors led Spaniards to suspect that problems were going to multiply in the near future and that some of them were going to be extremely challenging. For the first time the process of Spain's development seemed to falter. After 1973 the economies of the western world, which had been experiencing self-sustaining growth after post-World War II reconstruction, now faced acute crisis. The most immediate trigger was the rise in oil prices which went up by 500 percent in 1 year. There were, however, other contributory factors, such as weaknesses in the international monetary system and the tendency throughout the west to increase public spending. A consequence of the crisis was that the Keynesian strategy that had until now been the founding principle on which economic policy stood was now brought into question.

Spain's experience differed in many respects from that of other western economies, and not only because of its lack of any energy sources of its own. Our country had not enjoyed such a long period of economic growth. The weakness of the dictatorial regime had raised expectations of a better standard of living, and as if that were not enough, there were a series of factors that did not apply to other countries and contributed to making Spain's situation worse. While in the European countries that were members of the OECD oil represented 55 percent of energy consumption, in Spain the figure was 66 percent; furthermore, almost all of this oil was imported, while in the rest of Europe that figure was only 70 percent of the total. Finally, emigration changed direction. Whereas in the period 1961–73 there had been a leakage of population out of Spain, in 1973–5 the number of those returning was about 140,000 and, as one would expect, the immigrants made problems in the internal labor market worse.

The impact of the oil crisis was felt later in Spain than elsewhere in Europe but, on the other hand, it was to prove even more severe and long-lasting.

As late as 1974 growth was still at 5.7 percent, but by 1975 it had gone down to a mere 1.1 percent. This meant that at the same time inflation rose at a much faster rate than in the countries of the OECD. In the last three years of the Franco regime it rose by 11, 15 and then 17 percent, which was the equivalent of four, two and six points above the average rate in other countries. Problems that had not existed until then suddenly appeared in an acute form. During the best period of economic development between 1964 and 1974, the average unemployment figure had not been above between 1 and 2.4 percent of the working population, but in 1975 it came close to 5 percent. The major causes were stagnation in industrial development and rigidity in labor relations. The economic perspectives for 1975 were therefore anything but optimistic. For these reasons two experts could describe the first year of the transition as "the worst year for the Spanish economy since 1960," and not only economic but social factors too contributed to making the overall picture more problematic still. The lack of freedom for trade unions meant that protest suddenly arose on purely political issues and was often irresponsible; in 1975 the rise in productivity was the lowest since 1965, but the real rise in salaries was four times higher.

Nonetheless, can the state in which the regime found itself in 1975 be described as terminal and therefore beyond hope of survival? The answer to this question may be positive or negative according to the perspective from which one considers it.

From the point of view of the regime's governing class, there was a general belief, especially among the younger members, that Franco's death would bring about sweeping changes in Spain. As Rodolfo Martín Villa has recounted in his memoirs, young leaders were conscious of a loss of prestige in the eyes of a society in which Francoism had been firmly rooted in time past. Because of this loss of prestige, the regime had finally taken a decision not to take control of large areas of the nation's life, and Spanish society had chosen to go its own way with a supreme disregard for political institutions.

What was widely referred to as "sociological Francoism" in the final years of the regime was increasingly less clearly Francoist, less representative of society as a whole, and therefore open to other possibilities. As one would expect, there were leaders within the regime who were indignant about a situation that they would have liked to challenge if only they had known how. The younger ones, however, accepted it and looked for a way out of the present political system, even if only hesitantly and questioningly.

If we look at the crisis in the regime from the point of view not of those involved in politics but of Spanish society as a whole, we find a paradoxical scenario. It is, or course, true to say, as Martín Villa does, that there were not "pressing concerns" over the transition towards freedom and democracy. Society's attitude was much more passive, though that did not mean that it did not want a democratic regime in power. It seems beyond any shadow of doubt that in the last phase of Francoism, thanks to a greater degree of toleration on the part of those in government on matters such as the press, and also to a greater sense of equality among Spaniards as a whole, democratic principles had begun to filter through to a society that had in the past been more authoritarian than the regime itself. An official survey conducted in 1966 posed questions on attitudes to democratic and authoritarian ideas. While 54 percent of those consulted did not know how to answer, or chose not to do so, only 35 percent said that it was better if decisions were taken by "those elected by the people" rather than the alternative, which was that "a man of outstanding qualities should take decisions on our behalf." In 1974 the percentage had already risen to 60 percent; the number of those who preferred one man had gone down to 8 percent, and there are numerous surveys which have come up with similar results. The number of those "very interested in politics" doubled in the last years of the regime. At the time of Franco's death a survey revealed that 72 percent of Spaniards wanted the King to grant freedom of expression, and 70 percent wanted universal suffrage. Religious freedom and freedom for trade unions were considered by a large majority to be essential, and as regards the founding of political parties – the most controversial issue for the more orthodox members of the regime – a decisive change in opinion had taken place in a very short time. In 1971 only 12 percent believed that the existence of political parties would be "beneficial," but by 1973 the figure was 37 percent, which was more than the opposite opinion, and in the spring of 1975 the figure reached 56 percent. Running parallel to these statistics, in 1968 some 55 percent of Spaniards considered Spain's political situation good, but by 1975 that figure had gone down to 8 percent.

With all its contradictions, that was the overall picture of Spain at the time of Franco's death. That a transition was possible without trauma was due in part to this starting position, but also to the political skills of those who took the lead at a moment as difficult as the one we have just described.

# Bibliography

Political aspects: Francisco Javier CAPISTEGUI, *El naufragio de las ortodoxias. El carlismo, 1962–1977*, Eunsa, Pamplona, 1997; Jorge DE ESTEBAN *et al.*, *Desarrollo político y Constitución española*, Ariel, Barcelona, 1973; Rodrigo FERNÁNDEZ CARVAJAL, *La Constitución española*, Editora Nacional, Madrid, 1969; Luis HERRERO, *El ocaso de un régimen. Del asesinato de Carrero a la muerte de Franco*, Temas de Hoy, Madrid, 1995; Santiago MÍNGUEZ, *La preparación de la transición a la democracia en España*, Universidad de Zaragoza, Zaragoza, 1990; Jesús PALACIOS, *Los papeles secretos de Franco*, Temas de Hoy, Madrid, 1996; Pedro J. RAMÍREZ, *El año que murió Franco*, Argos Vergara, Barcelona, 1985; Álvaro SOTO, *¿Atado y bien atado? Institucionalización y crisis del franquismo*, Biblioteca Nueva, Madrid, 2004; Javier TUSELL, *Carrero. La eminencia gris del régimen de Franco*, Temas de Hoy, Madrid, 1993; *Juan Carlos I. La restauración de la monarquía*, Temas de Hoy, Madrid, 1995, and in collaboration with Genoveva G. QUEIPO DE LLANO, *Tiempo de incertidumbre. Carlos Arias Navarro entre el franquismo y la transición, 1973–1976*, Crítica, Barcelona, 2003.

The press: Carlos BARRERA, *El diario "Madrid," realidad y símbolo de una época*, Ediciones Universidad de Navarra, Pamplona, 1995.

Memoirs by political figures: Jose María AREILZA, *Crónica de libertad, 1965–1975*, Planeta, Barcelona, 1985; Vicente ENRIQUE Y TARANCÓN, *Confesiones*, PPC, Madrid, 1996; Gonzalo FERNÁNDEZ DE LA MORA, *Río arriba. Memorias*, Planeta, Barcelona, 1995; Manuel FRAGA IRIBARNE, *Memoria breve de una vida pública*, Planeta, Barcelona, 1980; José Antonio GIRÓN DE VELASCO, *Si la memoria no me falla*, Planeta, Barcelona, 1994; Laureano LÓPEZ RODÓ, *Testimonio de una política de Estado*, Planeta, Barcelona, 1987; Mariano NAVARRO RUBIO, *El caso Matesa (Datos para la historia)*, Dossat, Madrid, 1978, and "El caso Matesa explicado por completo," *ABC*, March 25 and 28 and April 4, 1988; José Ignacio SAN MARTÍN, *Servicio especial. A las órdenes de Carrero Blanco*, Planeta, Barcelona, 1983; Jordi SOLÉ TURA, *Una història optimista. Memòries*, Edicions 62, Barcelona, 1999; José UTRERA MOLINA, *Sin cambios de bandera*, Planeta, Barcelona, 1989; Juan VILA REYES, *El atropello Matesa*, Plaza y Janés-Cambio 16, Barcelona, 1992.

Anti-Francoist opposition: Sebastian BALFOUR, *La dictadura, los trabajadores y la ciudad. El movimiento obrero en el área metropolitana de Barcelona (1939–1988)*, Edicions Alfons el Magnànim, Valencia, 1994 (*Dictatorship, workers and the city: labour in Greater Barcelona since 1939*, Oxford, OUP, 1989); Francesc ESCRIBANO, *Cuenta atrás. La historia de Salvador Puig Antich*, Península, Barcelona, 2001; José María MARAVALL, *Dictadura y disentimiento político. Obreros y estudiantes bajo el franquismo*, Alfaguara, Madrid, 1978; Pere YSÀS, *Disidencia y subversión. La lucha del régimen franquista por su supervivencia, 1960–1975*, Crítica,

Barcelona, 2004. On the Monarchist groups: José María GIL ROBLES, *Un final de jornada, 1975–1977*, Tordesillas, Madrid, 1977. The role of Catholic organizations: Javier DOMÍNGUEZ, *Organizaciones obreras cristianas en la oposición al franquismo (1951–1976)*, Ediciones Mensajero, Bilbao, 1985; Pedro IBARRA GÜELL, *El movimiento obrero en Vizcaya, 1967–1977. Ideología, organización y conflictividad*, Universidad del País Vasco, Bilbao, 1987. On the Socialist Party: Carlos and José MARTÍNEZ COBO, *La segunda renovación*, Plaza y Janés, Barcelona, 1991; Miguel PEYDRÓ CARO, *Las escisiones del PSOE*, Plaza y Janés, Barcelona, 1980. On the Communists: Marco CALAMAI, *Storia del movimento operaio spagnolo dal 1960 al 1975*, Da Donato, Bari, 1975. On trade unions: Abdón MATEOS, *La denuncia del sindicato vertical. Las relaciones entre España y la OIT*, Consejo Económico y Social, Madrid, 1997. On the UMD: *La UMD y la causa 250/75*, Ministerio del Ejército, Estado Mayor Central, Madrid, 1976. On ETA and terrorism: Ángel AMIGO, *Pertur. ETA. 1971–1976*, Hordago, San Sebastián, 1978; Julián AGUIRRE, *Operación Ogro. Cómo y por qué ejecutamos a Carrero Blanco*, San Sebastián, 1978; Robert P. CLARKE, *The Basque insurgents. ETA. 1952–1980*, The University of Wisconsin Press, Madison, WI, 1984; Gurutz JÁUREGUI, *Ideología y estrategia política de ETA. Análisis de su evolución entre 1959 y 1968*, Siglo XXI, Madrid, 1981, and John SULLIVAN, *El nacionalismo vasco radical, 1959–1986*, Alianza Editorial, Madrid, 1986 (*ETA and Basque Nationalism: the fight for Euskadi 1890–1986*, London: Routledge, 1988).

Foreign policy: Javier TUSELL, Juan AVILÉS, Rosa PARDO, Marina CASANOVA, Abdón MATEOS, Isidro SEPÚLVEDA, and Álvaro SOTO, *La política internacional de España en el siglo XX*, Biblioteca Nueva-UNED, 1997. Also: Vicente CÁRCEL ORTÍ, *Pablo VI y España*, BAC, Madrid, 1997; María Jesús CAVA MESA, *Los diplomáticos de Franco. J. F. de Lequerica. Temple y tenacidad (1890–1976)*, Universidad de Deusto, Bilbao, 1989; José Ramón DIEGO AGUIRRE, *Guerra en el Sáhara*, Istmo, Madrid, 1991; Jaime PINIES, *La descolonización del Sáhara. Un tema sin concluir*, Espasa Calpe, Madrid, 1990, and *Episodios de un diplomático*, Editorial Dos Soles, Burgos, 2000; Tomás BARBULLO, *La historia prohibida del Sáhara español*, Destino, Barcelona, 2002.

The final stage of the Spanish economy during the Franco period: J. D. DONGES, *La industrialización en España. Políticas, logros, perspectivas*, Oikos-Tau, Barcelona, 1976; Arturo LÓPEZ-MUÑOZ and José Luis GARCÍA DELGADO, *Crecimiento y crisis del capitalismo español*, Edicusa, Madrid, 1968; Jesús PRADOS ARRARTE, *El Plan de desarrollo de España (1964–1967). Exposición y crítica*, Tecnos, Madrid, 1965; Jacinto ROS HOMBRAVELLA, *Política económica española. 1959–1973*, Blume, Barcelona, 1979, and Ramón TAMAMES, *España ante el segundo plan de desarrollo*, Nova Terra, Barcelona, 1968.

Changes in Spanish society and mentality: Mariano AGUILAR OLIVENCIA, *El Ejército español durante el franquismo*, Akal, Madrid, 1999; Alfonso G. BARBAN-CHO, *Las migraciones interiores españolas*, Instituto de Desarrollo Económico,

Madrid, 1967; Julio BUSQUETS BRAGULAT, *El militar de carrera en España. Estudio de sociología militar*, Ariel, Barcelona, 1967; Fundación FOESSA, *Informe sociológico sobre la situación social de España*, Euramérica, Madrid, 1966 and 1970; Rafael LÓPEZ PINTOR, *Los españoles de los años sesenta: una versión sociológica*, Tecnos, Madrid, 1975; Carmen MARTÍN GAITE, *Usos amorosos de la posguerra española*, Anagrama, Barcelona, 1987; Jesús M. DE MIGUEL, *El ritmo de la vida social. Análisis sociológico de la población en España*, Tecnos, Madrid, 1973; Eduardo SEVILLA GUZMÁN, *La evolución del campesinado en España*, Península, Barcelona, 1979; José Félix TEZANOS, *Estructura de clases en la España actual*, Edicusa, Madrid, 1975, and José Juan TOHARIA, *El juez español. Un análisis sociológico*, Tecnos, Madrid, 1975.

The Church: Feliciano BLÁZQUEZ, *La traición de los clérigos en la España de Franco*, Trotta, Madrid, 1991; Audrey BRASSLOFF, *Religion and Politics in Spain. The Spanish Church in transition. 1962–1996*, Macmillan, London, 1998; José CASTAÑO, *La JOC en España (1946–1970)*, Sígueme, Salamanca, 1978; Juan GONZÁLEZ ANLEO, *Catolicismo nacional: nostalgia y crisis*, Ediciones Paulinas, Madrid, 1975; Juan GONZÁLEZ CASANOVAS, *La revista* El Ciervo. *Historia y teoría de cuarenta años*, Península, Barcelona, 1992; Juan María LABOA (ed.), *El posconcilio en España*, Ediciones Encuentro, Madrid, 1988; José Luis MARTÍN DESCALZO, *Tarancón, el cardenal del cambio*, Planeta, Barcelona, 1982; Sylvie ROUXEL, *Espagne. La transformation des relations Église – État du Concile Vatican II à l'arrivée au pouvoir du PSOE*, Presse Universitaire de Rennes, Rennes, 2004; Joaquín RUIZ-GIMÉNEZ, *El camino hacia la democracia. Escritos en Cuadernos para el diálogo (1963–1976)*, Centro de Estudios Constitucionales, Madrid, 1985; Ángel TELLO, *Ideología y política. La Iglesia Católica española (1936–1959)*, Pórtico, Zaragoza, 1984.

Culture: Eduardo HARO TECGLEN, *El niño repúblicano, Hijo del siglo, El refugio*, Alfaguara-El País-Aguilar, Madrid, 1996–9; Adolfo MARSILLACH, *Tan lejos, tan cerca. Mi vida*, Tusquets, Barcelona, 1998; *Triunfo en su época*, Conference at the Casa de Velázquez in October 1992, École des Hautes Études-Casa de Velázquez, Ediciones Pléyades, Madrid, 1995; *Pintura española de vanguardia (1950–1990)*, Fundación Argentaria-Visor, Madrid, 1998.

# 4

# The Transition to Democracy (1975–82)

Over the course of the twentieth century Spain's role on the world stage has been limited. During the crisis years of the 1930s it was the only example of a country where democracy was destroyed by civil war, and as such it awoke passions all over the globe. Then, in the 1970s, it played a decisive role in a third wave of democratization that began in the Mediterranean, spread to Latin America, and finally reached Eastern Europe.

Spain's transition happened at a time when it seemed unlikely that democracy would spread further elsewhere, though subsequent events showed that it was in fact possible. Democracy was achieved very quickly in Spain, and that served as an example for other areas of the world. Also – and this was even more important – the cost to society was not high, which meant that the democratic regime was consolidated in a very short space of time even though its starting position was not promising. Although the break with the past was not as sharp as the opposition had expected, there clearly was a break, but it came about by means of reform. The transition happened with no uncertainty about the particular road it should take (as proved to be the case in Gorbachev's Russia), and no "pockets of authoritarianism" were allowed to survive, as happened in Pinochet's Chile. Furthermore, those in politics did not try to perpetuate their own power but rather seemed to adapt well to the new institutional scenario, as happened in some countries in the Balkans. Spain's diversity might seem comparable to that of Yugoslavia, but there was no internal armed conflict; on the contrary, at the same time as the transition to democracy there was a move from a model of a centralized state to one that was far more decentralized. To sum up these changes: if the model of a collapse of democracy could lead to a Weimar Republic in Germany, the reverse process was seen in the Spanish model of a transition which exemplified the building of a democracy.

This process cannot be understood without taking into account what had gone before. Spain, whose rate of development in the 1950s had been below that of some Latin American countries, by 1975, in contrast, was among the 12 most developed countries in the world. If Poland's income in the 1950s was 50 percent higher than Spain's, by 1975 Spain's was four times larger than Poland's. The change was highly significant, bearing out what Aristotle had written about democracy being all the more possible the more egalitarian society was. Yet there were also cultural changes taking place. By 1973, three out of every four Spaniards were in favor of freedom of the press and of religion (allowed, if only to a limited extent, by the Franco regime), but the majority were also in favor of freedom for trade unions. When Franco died, the majority began to think that freedom to form political parties was essential. In such circumstances the government became aware that its legitimacy was now being questioned and Spain's transition to democracy cannot be understood without also considering the opening up, or "*apertura*," that occurred after 1966, despite all its limitations, or without taking into account the splits that became evident among the ruling elite after 1969 and even more so after 1973. Arias Navarro's period in office makes sense if we view it as having overseen the final and irreversible decline of the Franco regime. If it did not allow the will of the nation to be expressed, it did at least show clearly what Spain did not want.

The building of a national consensus on the subject of a democratic system was to a great extent the result of the weight of history bearing down on the nation and the will to rid Spain of it. Very few of those who played leading roles in the transition had experienced the Civil War for themselves, but its memory nonetheless weighed heavy on them – far more so than the threat of a Soviet invasion in Poland, or in Hungary the memory of 1956. There was no amnesia in Spain as some have stated, but rather a desire to forget – to "make oneself forget" – in order to avoid a repeat of the conflict, and this explains the will to grant a general amnesty. The process was the work of individuals, and should be understood as essentially imaginative and inventive; equally obviously, there were difficulties to be faced until the very end of the regime. There was no alternative but to dream up solutions, for the simple reason that there simply did not exist any historical or political foundations on which to build. It is not true that any of the main protagonists had a detailed plan in mind as well as good intentions.

As was usually the case in the Mediterranean and in Latin America, the major role in Spain's transition to democracy basically fell to elements in the political center, and more precisely to the government of Adolfo Suárez who, in effect, directed the operation, set the timetable, and took the main initiatives. It is quite clear that the way he went about effecting change was entirely unexpected from a man of his background; he learned lessons from Spanish society itself, and also in part from the opposition. In general terms, Rodolfo Martín Villa has attributed the major responsibility for the transition to the younger, more reformist members of the previous regime, and to the oldest members of the opposition. The vital and essential role that the socialist opposition would play after a given moment was that of constituting an alternative to the government, thus providing the spare wheel that the political system needed.

What was particular in Spain's case was not so much that elements of the center played a major part in the transition, or that the role of the left was to neutralize other more revolutionary options, but that these two events happened at the same time. This was not the case, for example, in either Portugal or Greece. However, at the same time, the reformists would not have accomplished their mission had there not been pressure on them from ordinary Spaniards. Until 1973, and even at the time of Franco's death in 1975, the process would not have come about in this particular way; nor would it have been possible in the first half of 1976. Then the situation did change, but how it happened cannot be understood unless the mobilization of the population is taken into account; in general the transition in Spain was peaceful, though there were 460 deaths during the period 1975–80. Even so, the majority of mass gatherings were peaceful; in the decade that followed the death of Franco, 36 demonstrations of more than 100,000 people took place in Madrid, despite which the opposition was never in a position to replace or overthrow the government merely by calling on all its supporters to act. This combination of factors means that it does not make sense to ask whether reform won the day or rupture. Rather, it was a matter of a break with the past being made possible by processes of reform, or alternatively, such far-reaching reform that what had been reformed effectively disappeared. Spain was, in this sense, an exception in the overall context of the "third wave" of democratization, and it also clearly set an example.

## The Monarchy: King Juan Carlos I

One characteristic feature of the Spanish transition is the role played by the institution of the monarchy. It did not legitimize Spain's new democracy – rather the opposite – but at a moment when the legitimacy of Spain's political institutions hung in the balance, monarchy was the kind of regime that Franco wanted, with Don Juan Carlos as his undisputed heir, and that disarmed any possible suggestion that this option represented a break with regime policy. On the other hand, however, Don Juan Carlos was also the representative of a legitimate dynasty and, moreover, his person was linked to his father's activity in – or at least his degree of collaboration with – the liberal opposition to the dictatorship. Had the monarchy been entirely identified with the ruling regime, as it had been in Portugal, it probably would not have been able to play any role at all, any more than that would have been possible if it had adopted an entirely oppositionist stance. In this way one can say that Don Juan Carlos represented what might be called a legitimate democratic option in waiting, but one that nonetheless still had an overlap with past institutions that strengthened its claim to legitimacy.

While the Franco regime had lasted, Don Juan Carlos's political status had been variable and unstable. His relations with Franco were always cordial but they were not easy and complex moments had to be got through, especially after he had been named as Franco's successor. It was at this point that "I saw my husband suffer most," as the future queen would later testify. He started with a sense of mission, but he could not count either on those who wanted to keep the old system or on others who wanted to break with it completely. The monarch knew perfectly well what the principles of reconciliation were that would provide the foundations for *convivencia* – peaceful coexistence – within the Iberian Peninsula. He had discussed them with leaders of democratic countries and had raised expectations in political, social, and intellectual circles that favored change. That his stance coincided with the greater openness to change in the Church is clear from two public addresses by Cardinal Tarancón. To a great extent, what Don Juan Carlos did cannot be understood without considering the "reign in the shadows" of his father, with whom he always shared a deep understanding although their perspectives were very different. His father had the viewpoint of the emigrant. "I realized that the key to success was the Army; I had to join the Army in order to be able to count on its support," said Don Juan Carlos in contrast. Many people thought that he was a bland, insubstantial representative of an autocratic regime firmly anchored in the past. His discretion was seen as ignorance, his discipline as docility, and his silence as a lack of imagination or absence of ideas. Yet when his moment came he showed that although he might not know how, he certainly did know what he intended to do. At that moment he showed balance and caution, self-control and cool judgment – though not coolness in his dealings with people – directness and clarity, no great intellectual capability but a real concern that the monarchy should not lose contact with the world of culture as had happened with his grandfather Alfonso XIII.

It was obvious from the start that he was to play a major role in the transition. He was asked to facilitate the break with the past, or *ruptura*, by ruling as an absolute monarch while he enabled Spain to move towards democracy; however, rather than ruling, what he actually did was to point the way ahead. He was described as the "motor for change," and a historical work that focuses on him was aptly titled *The Driver of Change* (*El piloto del cambio*). In fact, it was his job to cut the Gordian knot of the Spanish political situation at the end of 1975 by making two key appointments – of Fernández Miranda as President of the *Cortes*, and of Suárez as President of the Government – and in addition to act as a shield to prevent the military breaking in on the political process. That was the extent of his active involvement, which means that he could quite fairly be described as a constitutional monarch before there was a Constitution. He did not even play a part in drawing up the Constitution, and on the day when he approved the draft text he declared that he himself was now "legalized." To the extent that it is possible to simplify this account by establishing an order of precedence among the individuals who took leading roles in the transition, one might well say that Don Juan Carlos headed the list, though one can in no way say that he did anything to make that happen. For reasons already cited, Adolfo Suárez would be in second place, and Santiago Carrillo would come third. This does not mean that the king did not make mistakes, especially in the first months of his reign. His conduct clearly had a positive effect in general terms but he, like all the other actors on the political stage at the time, had to serve his apprenticeship.

Apart from the matter of these main characters, the process of transition can be compared to a kind of greyhound race from which various participants withdrew when their moment passed. The first to retire was

Carlos Arias Navarro, whom Franco had left as president of the government at the time of his death.

## The Death-throes of the Past

Although the aim in Spain was reconciliation, the way to achieve it was not immediately clear. Don Juan Carlos seems originally to have thought of a technocrat for the post of President of the Government, but he was more interested initially in appointing Torcuato Fernández Miranda as President of the *Cortes* and the Council of the Realm. Able, with extensive legal and political knowledge and experience inside the regime, in the early 1970s Fernández Miranda had managed to stall discussion on political association within the regime by resorting to his "relentless ability to make people dizzy with words." He did so both because he knew that Franco did not want the issue resolved and because the future king was not interested in political associations unless they were genuine. Despite his past, Fernández Miranda was very much aware that it was essential for the monarchy at that time to "sweep out the bunker and include the left"; he had also persuaded the king that this could all be done by legal means. Nevertheless, there is a danger of exaggerating the part he played in the transition, which may have been decisive but was only instrumental. Fernández Miranda seems to have ensured that the transition script was his own even if the king directed the play and Suárez was the main actor; nonetheless, the most decisive roles in the production were those of the last two characters. In fact, Fernández Miranda was not even informed of some of the most fundamental decisions (for example, concerning contact with the PCE or relations with the military).

The appointment of Fernández Miranda, which gave him an immediate leadership role in the *Cortes* and the Council of the Realm, could not have come about without the support of the president of the government. Arias wanted to avoid his job being interfered with by the king after the coronation, basing his decision on the idea that he had been appointed by Franco for a period of 5 years and therefore he supposed that he would remain in power. He had no great regard for the king, any more than the king did for him, always considering the president "as stubborn as a mule." It was not just a matter of personal differences. Arias's moment of opportunity in history had long since passed. He wanted to reform the regime, but he was still plagued by doubts on his own loyalties and his actual ignorance as to how to effect change. He could not even bring himself to consider the possibility of talking with more moderate elements within the opposition, and he saw Spanish society as a passive object upon which he could act, as though it would accept without question any decision he might make on its behalf. The reform proposed by the government over which he presided was in fact devised by Fraga, and it seems as if Arias was not even very much in favor of it. His political experience had been limited to the security forces; and being ignorant of all else, he often mistrusted his own ministers. His opinions were not infrequently those of an extreme traditionalist who had become anti-clericalist as a result of the Church's distancing of itself from the regime. There may never have been another president of the government who was so strongly criticized in his own ministers' memoirs as Arias Navarro was, and as if that were not enough, the cabinet that he formed was not his own but was imposed on him either by circumstances or by the king.

Fraga enhanced the standing of his own Home Office portfolio (*Ministro de Gobernación*) by taking on the job of vice-president as well. This appeared to give him a rank higher than that of a minister, and also prime responsibility for bringing about the transformation of Spain's political institutions; however, he had to joust with serious problems of law and order at the time and this, as we shall see, did not make it easy to implement political measures. In addition, the way that Fraga set about the task of reform was quite wrong: his main idea was to enact a series of reforms of the institutional system which he intended to impose from on high. He did on occasion realize that he must negotiate with the opposition, but his treatment of them was high-handed. Alongside Fraga, two pro-reformists, José María Areilza and Antonio Garrigues in the Foreign Office and Ministry of Justice respectively, could have played a significant role but did not often do so because, being isolated as politicians, they did not have any support from within the system or from the ranks of the moderate opposition. Areilza soon realized that he was "a foreigner trying to sell local merchandise that had been tampered with," but seeing things in a more positive light, he in fact made no small contribution to change merely by the content of his statements. The rest of the government at the time was barely relevant and even less united. "There is here no agreement, no common aim, no coherence, no unity," a despairing Areilza would write in his diaries.

Arias made a few vague verbal concessions (a legislative assembly consisting of two houses whose character remained imprecise, a reform of rulings on political associations and the right to demonstrate . . . ), but they were not enough in the face of quite unprecedented social mobilization that could not be channeled by existing structures. At the start of 1976, there was within the space of just 1 month a series of strikes that were larger and more radical than anything in the entire preceding year. It was, as Areilza said, like a gale blowing up just off the coast. There were even moments when the government lost control of a town the size of Sabadell. The channels afforded by the official trade union, which had served until now to resolve labor conflict, were no longer up to the task. Worse still, what began as public order incidents degenerated into pitched battles due to the fact that the security forces were unprepared to face Spain's new conditions of freedom and toleration.

Fortunately, the wave of strikes in January 1976 in the industrial belt surrounding Madrid did not cause any deaths, but in the following months there were two violent incidents that did cause bloodshed. In March there was a serious outbreak of social conflict in Vitoria which resulted in five deaths as a result of an absolute power vacuum and inability to channel the protest by means of negotiation. As for the events in Montejurra in May, they represented confrontation between the two factions of extreme traditionalists and pseudo-socialists into which the Carlist movement had now split.

Faced with this patently obvious political failure and subsequent deterioration in circumstances, the political reform that had been announced actually moved ahead slowly and tentatively. A mixed commission composed of members of the government and the National Council undertook to effect reform, and it soon became clear that their greatest priority was to decide what elements from the past were to be retained in institutional and personal terms. Their starting-point was always continuity, without consulting anyone on the issue, and this was unacceptable to the opposition; it also began to be clear that there were serious differences within the various organizations at the heart of the regime. A new ruling on political associations was passed by the *Cortes*, and this meant that for the first time Adolfo Suárez, the general secretary of the *Movimiento*, could make his presence felt as a political figure with a role to play. He did so realistically and without excessive rhetoric: it was a matter of "making normal in politics what was already considered normal in the street." But if 338 members voted in favor, the number of those who abstained or were absent, or who opposed the proposals, was only some hundred votes fewer. In June the reform of the Penal Code – relating to the prohibition of political groups of a totalitarian nature – ran aground so badly that it endangered support for the government in the *Cortes*. In the minds of those opposed to change, what was essentially at stake was the possible legalization of the Spanish Communist Party.

The events described here reveal a situation which could perhaps suggest that there was a political vacuum, begging the question as to whether it could have been filled by the opposition, and if the opposition would in fact be up to the task of forming a social force or political alternative. The answer to this question is without doubt no, and to explain why that is the case requires discussion of the political opposition during the period under discussion.

However widespread social protest was in Spain, at no time was the opposition able to forge links with important sectors of the armed forces. In this sense, the situation was very different from that in Portugal. One might even say that the *Unión Militar Democrática*, whose members were involved with left-wing politics, emphasized the professional commitment of Spain's military personnel and persuaded them to keep off the political stage. We need only remember that the membership was never above 140 officers, and then not all at the same time. This group, which also was more moderate than Portugal's revolutionary soldiers, always took up a defensive position; their moment of greatest activity was before Franco died. Furthermore, any real danger of military intervention came more from high-ranking officers rather than from sheer numbers of men. In March, coinciding with disturbances in Vitoria and the trial of the members of the UMD, there was an attempt on the part of the military to exert pressure on the king through General Fernando de Santiago, but the king himself put a stop to it.

The opposition, on the other hand, though it gained no support from the armed forces, did benefit from the increasing loosening of controls and the evident deterioration of the regime, now condemned to disappear in the eyes of the general public, though it was not at all clear how, when, or why it was going to be replaced. From January 1976 on, clandestine groups began to hold public demonstrations. The Christian Democrats organized talks at the start of the year and a conference in April, and that same month the UGT was also able to organize a conference and it was actually allowed to take place. To this extent the opposition was also an important motor for change. However, it would be an exaggeration to make it seem like the only active element in the events of the time: the same cry that served as a slogan in all demonstrations ("Juan Carlos, listen") is evidence of the opposition's inability to bring about changes in the political system on its own.

It was as late as March 1976 when a single opposition organization finally came together, containing such widely diverse elements that the task of negotiating with the government was not at all easy; nonetheless, its members began to play with this possibility, conscious of their weakness (but also that Spanish society supported them). As an alternative term to that used to denote government proposals identified with "*reforma*," the term that had been used in opposition ranks to express the desire for fundamental modification of the political institutions at present in power was "*ruptura*": a break with the past. This break was, however, only temporary and some saw it as a kind of enjoyment of an inheritance gained without any effort that would reverse the outcome of the Civil War. Among the vast majority of opposition members, including left-wing groups, there was a desire to avoid any kind of trauma while moving from a dictatorial regime to a democratic one. As a result, very soon – indeed, from March 1976 on – the term that began to be used was a "concerted break" ("*ruptura pactada*"), an apparently self-contradictory phrase, but one that would in fact become a reality.

From all that has been discussed so far we can deduce that by the summer of 1976 *ruptura* was impossible and a *ruptura pactada* seemed even less likely. Even the reform that was constantly being discussed on all sides was unlikely to happen in the foreseeable future, both in terms of its content and of the means of implementing it. Yet the more positive image of the king and the decreasing likelihood of the older reformists coming up with solutions now altered the situation. In preceding months the king's popularity had increased, in part due to official visits to difficult regions (Asturias and Catalonia). Furthermore, his presence in the United States in May and June gave him an added international dimension and also provided the opportunity for him to confirm what his own guiding aim for Spain was: full and complete democracy. On his return from the States, the king was quite clearly in a position to achieve what it had been impossible for him to attempt 6 months earlier. He had learned a lot in difficult circumstances, he benefited greatly from the positive efforts of certain ministers, and he personified the as yet ill-defined but nonetheless deeply felt desire of Spaniards to bring about change in a peaceful way.

Relations between the monarch and the president, which had always been bad, had by now worsened considerably. The king had not thought of the president as anything but a temporary expedient. According to the official version of what happened, Arias's departure from the presidency was at his own request, put before the Council of the Realm and approved by the king, but what happened was in fact exactly the opposite. The king summoned the president after an audience with diplomats in the *Palacio de Oriente* at one in the afternoon; there, dressed in military uniform, he asked the president to resign from his post. Although at the time Arias did not react, the necessary steps had already been taken – the Council of the Realm was to meet that afternoon – to prevent any attempt to block the move.

So ended Arias Navarro's period in power, which had served a useful purpose in Spain's process of transition to democracy. From a historical point of view, what was most relevant about this period was that, without doubt, it ended all possibility that Francoism could survive in any form, and it contributed decisively towards making a sweeping reform seem inevitable, including in the eyes of the majority of the ruling classes of the previous regime. Even more important was the change that took place at the heart of Spanish society. It was during these months that it became glaringly obvious that there was a need for a reform that was not purely cosmetic. Had the Arias–Fraga reform been implemented, it would have led to an incomplete form of democracy which, in the mid term, would have meant much more political and social conflict. Fraga is not right, then, when he states that the reform that he put forward would have had "more solid" foundations; on the contrary, with his reform the outcome would have been far worse.

In the matter of the replacement of Carlos Arias Navarro as president, conditions were now right for the monarch to exert some influence in the Council of the Realm and put forward his own candidate. This was, in the words of the one who would be his candidate's successor, "a new man but not completely so, young but not overly young, a Falangist but not excessively so, a Monarchist but not exclusively so." Along with Adolfo Suárez, younger members of the regime's political class also came to power. The new reformist generation did not have the personal enemies that the grand old patriarchs of the politics of the dictatorship had gathered over their time in power; it had sufficient experience and influence at the heart of the Francoist state and, at the same time, it could connect more easily with the widespread changes that had taken place in Spanish society over the previous years. It was also the king's generation, and alongside him it would play a leading and outstanding role in Spain's transition to democracy. At the time, however, this was not understood either by the media or by public opinion.

## Adolfo Suárez: The Road from Liberalization to Democracy

The new president did not actually appear to have had a very brilliant political career so far – indeed, it had even seemed that it might be in some danger after 1973 with Arias's rise to power. His most important post had been as director of the Spanish radio and television network RTVE (*Radiotelevisión Española*), but in the first government of the new monarchy he had played a secondary role. His victory in an election to fill a place on the National Council over Franco's son-in-law, the Marquis of Villaverde, and the success he had achieved presenting the new law on political associations were clear evidence of his ability to exercise leadership over the regime's political class. During the crucial months of the transition he was very popular, but in just a quarter of a century since then historical judgment of him has fluctuated widely. Vilified after 1980, his value in the eyes of public opinion was minimal 2 years later, was variable throughout the 1980s, and only rose definitively in 1995, 20 years after Franco's death.

Adolfo Suárez was born in 1932, in Cebreros in the province of Avila. A deeply religious man, his first public activity was linked to Catholic lay associations. His entry into government service after the necessary competitive public exams came late, and he did not belong to any of the major groups within the Administration. Bold and likeable, his political career can to an extent be explained by the support he received throughout from Herrero Tejedor, who was a minister for a few months in 1975. When facing adversity he proved able to survive and ambitious. He professed a humility that was heartfelt, but it was also a product of his weaknesses and, in the words of Calvo Sotelo, it would give him an obvious complex about being no more than an "average student." That in itself made him able to deal with political realities without trying to force them to conform to his own predetermined notions. "I am an ordinary man and I have many gaps in my knowledge," he told the philosopher Julián Marías the first day they met, and he described himself as "an ordinary straightforward man" in the *Cortes* on one occasion. His gaps in knowledge were generally a matter of his cultural education and – and this would prove rather more relevant – of a lack of insight into what were likely to be the implications of Spain's new life as a democracy. His famous phrase from one of his first public speeches ("making normal in politics what was already considered normal in the street") may seem bold, but it was a basic assumption for any liberal. His apparent modesty proved successful. His greatest accomplishment in government was a succession of performances in which he grew and shrank like Louis Carroll's Alice. He began by almost begging the opposition's pardon, and then went on to achieve what it could not have done better than he did. He was helped by an astute political sense that was a result of his ability to seize the moment, of his cool and his sense of timing. Despite having been a member of the political ruling class under the dictatorship, if anything characterized Suárez it was his lack of stiffness when exercising power and his genuine desire to serve the common good. His past did not in any way prevent him having perfectly clear ideas about the final results of his political actions, and it also made him cultivate personally the virtues that provided the basis for peaceful coexistence at the same time as Spanish society was doing so. His identification with the king was absolute for a good many months. On the one hand he had something that the opposition lacked, and that was a grasp of the notion of the state (its strengths and weaknesses). At the same time, he took advantage not only of the opposition's impotence but also its deep-seated desire to reach agreements and avoid social disruption during the transition. Santiago Carrillo, general secretary of the PCE, came away from their first secret conversation convinced that Suárez was no different in essence from any other democratic politician that he knew in Europe.

The composition of Suárez's government caused as much surprise as the name of the man who was to lead it as its president. The vice-president Alfonso Ossorio was a key figure who brought with him the support of the younger elements of the Catholic "family" of the Franco regime which included, for example, Landelino Lavilla, the Minister for Justice. In general the government had two defining characteristics which were also characteristics of Suárez himself: they were young and they were new. Only one of its members, Admiral Pita da Veiga, had served as a minister under Franco, and the average age of cabinet members was 44. The greatest novelty, however, was the language they used. Suárez declared that he was a "legitimate agent engaged in a process of setting out a political arena which would be open to all." He would play this role until he ensured, as his "final goal," that governments of the future would be "the result of the free choice of the majority of Spaniards." "Let us try to achieve this together," he concluded.

This unhurried and realistic approach, with democracy on the horizon, brought about a significant change in the political atmosphere in Spain in a short space of time, between July and September 1976. The amnesty that was approved was incomplete, but it did cover all crimes that did not involve the use of violence. There was no real negotiation with the opposition, which asked for a cabinet with a "wide democratic consensus," but there was dialogue and even concessions were made. There were still difficulties with the armed forces. The military vice-president General Fernando de Santiago's reservations about the way the political situation was going led to his resignation in September; he was replaced by Manuel Gutiérrez Mellado, one of the very few high-ranking military officers who was unambiguously in favor of the developments taking place in politics.

The way ahead that had by now been chosen – following the course set out by Fernández Miranda but implemented by Landelino Lavilla – consisted basically of moving "from law to law." In order to do this, in the summer of 1976 moves were made to draw up a law to allow *for* political reform, not as a result *of* political reform in the sense that the final decision and definitive content of the changes to be effected would rest in the hands of the citizens of Spain. In essence, too, it differed from the Arias–Fraga plan in that it was not a law from *within* the regime but *about* the regime. It was merely a matter of approving a text which would enable Spain to end up with a democracy, but without creating too closed and rigid a framework dependent on observing legislation put in place by the previous regime, and without determining the shape of the institutions of the future. The flexibility of the final text was such that one might call it a law of transaction that would allow the transition to take place. What was fundamental to the Political Reform Law (*Ley de Reforma Política*) was that elections were called and a minimal institutional framework came into being to permit them to take place.

This framework was, nonetheless, already democratic in character since, as stated, "the fundamental rights of the individual are inviolable and binding on all organs of the state." There would be two houses in Parliament, the Congress of Deputies and the Senate, with 204 and 350 members respectively, who would be elected by universal suffrage, with the exception of a small number of senators (40) who would be royal appointments. The mission of these two houses would be to draw up a new Constitution. The Senate would be elected according to a law of electoral majority, while a law of proportional representation would apply to elections to the Congress of Deputies. In law, the right to hold a referendum was reserved for the king in cases where it was necessary. This measure hung like a kind of sword of Damocles over the heads of any who might resist the process of reform.

Predictably, problems arose between the military and the regime's ruling class. Suárez explained the projected reform to the high-ranking officers in general terms at the start of September, and later this brought a complaint that he had made no reference to the possible legalization of the Communist Party. However, from an institutional point of view, the fate of the reform was in the hands of the *Cortes*. The report produced by the National Council of the *Movimiento*, which had been given the task of drawing up a report that would offer guidelines but would not be binding, was ignored by the government. The only group that actually had a functioning organization in the *Cortes* was the group that supported Fraga and numbered almost 200 members; in order to counteract it, an agreement had to be reached on the electoral law to introduce a restriction on a simple majority. The traditionally docile behavior towards the government of those who had served under Francoism, together with Fernández Miranda's skillful touch, the hopes of being reelected of a great many existing members, the use of people who combined an illustrious surname with the ability to match up to the task in hand, were all factors that helped to ensure that the law was in fact approved. The number of members who voted in favor was 435 in comparison with only 59 against, seven of whom were generals. The voting ended with a spectacle that was both moving and impressive as the government and members of the *Cortes* applauded one other. In fact, and despite appearances, the continuity of the previous institution had now ended and those who had been part of it had gone – for the most part at least. The proof that this was so is that although 35 UCD parliamentarians had been members of the *Cortes* of 1976, some of those who had voted to approve the Political Reform Law had not been members of the constituent *Cortes* of 1977.

As stipulated in the Political Reform Law itself, its text had to be ratified in a national referendum. This took place in December under curious conditions. A large part of the opposition, which anticipated a high level of abstention, wanted a yes vote; as for the government, it used public resources to bring in a positive result. Nonetheless, the referendum gave the Spanish people more freedom to express their opinions than at any other time since the Civil War, and the majority of the population felt that they had done so without the vote being manipulated. In this sense one might add that it was a chance to express its views for a society that was not yet democratic but was well on the way to genuine liberalization. There was only 2.6 percent of the vote against the motion and 3 percent left blank out of a total of 77 percent of the population that took part in the referendum. This meant that there was significant social support for the process of democratization that was already under way but was as yet incomplete.

## —  Facing Difficulties: Terrorism and the Military Coup  —

To speak of the apparent ease with which the transition came about is to focus exclusively on the final result, although this could not be taken for granted even at the end of 1976. There were at least two occasions on which the move towards reform was in serious danger: in January 1977, when the double pressure of terrorism from diverse sources might have brought the country to the brink of conflict again, and in Holy Week in May, when the Communist Party was legalized, and at the same time what had in the past been a single party was dismantled and its powers and people were transferred to the new Administration. It was also, without doubt, Adolfo Suárez's finest hour. He clearly demonstrated at that time his capacity for work, though his timetable was often anarchic, and also his ability to absorb the hostility of his political enemies and, above all, his intelligence in reading the moment. This explains the speed with which the transition process moved ahead, so that only 6 months after the referendum circumstances were favorable enough to allow free elections aimed at producing a constituent assembly. Viewed from a comparative historical perspective, what happened during this period of the Suárez government shows the extent to which a government that had emerged from within the previous dictatorial regime managed to achieve its constituent aims better than a provisional government that had come from the ranks of the democratic opposition could ever have done.

To succeed politically meant setting aside the possibility of action on other matters such as the economy. Despite the crisis there, a conscious effort was made to avoid setting up a coherent program that might increase social pressure on the government. During the summer of 1976 little more was achieved than the implementation of a very few partial measures, and that year ended up being the worst for the Spanish economy since 1970. The rise in the GNP did not reach 2 percent, unemployment figure rose to 6 percent – an almost inconceivable figure in the past – and inflation was running at about 20 percent. At the same time, the state saw itself plunging further into debt and the balance of payments went into deficit. None of these problems would be addressed until after the elections.

We have already talked about the serious public order incidents that were a consequence of the economic crisis during the first months of the monarchy. Subsequently the worst public order problems occurred around the time that the Political Reform Law was being approved. They were the result of action by terrorist groups that had seen their number of militants grow thanks to the clumsy, over-bearing action of the police, and they had above all won social support, which may not have been widespread but was enough to make a political impact.

During the period 1976–80 ETA, which was backed by a substantial section of Basque society, was responsible for about 70 percent of the terrorist acts committed, and after this date, practically speaking, it had a tragic monopoly on actions of this type. In these early stages the number killed by terrorism stayed relatively stable, with figures under 30 dead (26 in 1975, 21 in 1976, and 28 in 1977), but then the numbers rose sharply to reach a total of 85 in 1978, 118 in 1979, and 124 in 1980. After this peak in 1980, the minister Juan José Rosón's policy of reinsertion at the same time as offenders were being pursued saw a drastic drop in numbers of victims with 38 dead in 1981 and 44 in 1982. Therefore the peak of ETA terrorism can be seen to have coincided with the drawing up of the Constitution and the attempted military coup shortly afterwards.

Yet although ETA had become more lethal and was now contributing far more towards provoking a reaction from the Army, in an earlier period extremist organizations with scant social support had already been able by their actions to make a significant political impact. The GRAPO were a group from within the PCE – the Spanish Marxist–Leninist Communist Party with pro-China leanings which was notable for its members' markedly proletarian background, its extreme sectarianism which induced them to live in almost family-style groups, by how few members there were (about 200), and by the scarcity of its resources which meant that they had to obtain weapons from the security forces. On some occasions their almost total lack of means even prevented them printing pamphlets justifying the murders they committed. Their members came in their entirety from areas where there had been acute social conflict during the closing stages of Francoism (Cádiz, Vigo, the Basque Country . . . ). The mindless violence that they practiced was the product of extremely simplistic theorizing, but their greatest impact on public opinion was achieved by two of their kidnappings: of Antonio Oriol, President of the Council of State, in December 1976 when the Political Reform Law had not yet been approved, and of General Villaescusa, President of the Military Supreme Council of Justice, only days later. For weeks, at an extremely delicate moment in political terms, public attention was focused on this one question until the security forces freed the hostages in mid February 1977.

Meanwhile, on January 24 there had been an attack by an extreme right-wing group on the offices of a firm of labor lawyers who worked for the PCE which caused seven deaths. This event had enormous political repercussions because it drew widespread expressions of solidarity and, above all, showed that the PCE was able to control its masses and act so responsibly that any attempt by the military to intervene and justify their actions on the basis of public order would have lacked any appearance of legitimacy.

This fact provides a clear illustration of the PCE's particular circumstances, whose problems were only finally resolved when it was legalized on April 9, 1977. In fact the PCE had enjoyed a degree of toleration since December 1976. Its main leader, Santiago Carrillo, had returned secretly from exile in February 1976. He doubtless tried to force through some further recognition of the PCE by the simple expedient of being less and less careful about being seen around the capital, and in so doing he brought into question the legitimacy of any election that might be held without the participation of the Communist Party. His arrest in the final days of December 1976 can not only be explained by his own desire to make his presence felt in public life but also by the Suárez government's need to prove its authority and the efficiency of the police. For a moment the government considered the possibility of expelling Carrillo from Spain but the Minister for Justice, Lavilla, drew attention to the fact that it was simply not possible to do so under the pre-Constitution legislation in force at the time. Suárez was perfectly aware that the Communist leader had engineered his own arrest and that this posed a problem that he must solve. Carrillo, who was subjected to bad treatment in police custody (such as being stripped naked), realized that those holding him had no idea what to do with him, as he himself said. However, in the police stations where he was held there hung portraits not of the king but of Franco.

It is probable, as has already been suggested, that all those members of the government who played a part in the transition thought initially that it was not going to be possible to legalize the Communist Party before the elections because the Army would oppose it. This is a case which shows just how complicated a process the transition was, with the positions of the government and the opposition intertwining in different configurations; both changed over time. The PCE, with scant support from the other parties of the opposition, insisted that it must be legalized and the government (in effect, Suárez) finally agreed at exactly the right moment. Yet this result would not have been possible had public opinion not altered on this issue which had in the past been such a bone of contention. After Franco's death the percentage of those in favor of the legalization of the PCE was very low. Opinion polls in March 1977 revealed that 40 percent of the population was in favor of legalization and 25 percent against, but the following month the figures were already 55 and 12 percent respectively.

There were, in addition, personal factors that influenced the political process. In February contact was made for the very first time between the president and the general secretary of the Communist Party, and out of this meeting grew an understanding between the two politicians that would last the entire duration of the transition. Although it would be incorrect to suggest that the meeting produced a pact, it was understood that Suárez would bring about the legalization of the PCE if the PCE accepted the Spanish flag and the crown (despite the fact that Carrillo would have preferred the order to be reversed). What was achieved in effect was to an extent one of the many moments of consensus that paved the way ahead for Spain's transition to democracy. In accordance with current legislation, the means by which the legalization of the Communist Party was to be effected was left in the hands of the judicial authorities, though deadlines were set for issues to be resolved. While these authorities were coming to a decision, toleration was increasing and in March a Euro-Communist summit was held in Madrid.

At last, on April 9 – an Easter Saturday on which the potential for reaction of politicians and the press was less than at other times – the Spanish Communist Party was legalized. The judicial authorities communicated the decision to the political authorities. It was the most risky step in the entire transition because it could have provoked an immediate right-wing backlash. There was also evidence of a remarkable lack of preparation for the possible event of a reaction on the part of the military. Gutiérrez Mellado was in the Canary Islands, the Army Minister was ill, and therefore the Chief of Staff who presided over the Army's supreme consultative body found himself in an extremely unfortunate situation. There was acute tension at this point among the highest-ranking officers in the Armed Services, who went so far as to express their firm opposition to the measure although they accepted it because of their "discipline and patriotism." Fortunately the most retrogressive section of the Army lacked both a leader and a clear political will at that time, though the Navy Minister did resign, which could be seen as the second military crisis of the transition after that involving General Fernando de Santiago.

Over the course of that month of April and almost simultaneously, the government carried on with its headlong dismantling of the existing political regime. A few hours after legalizing the PCE it had decided to abolish the *Movimiento* whose minister then became secretary to the government. This decision meant the disappearance of the symbols of the *Movimiento*, though in reality it had already lost its political content and its ability to mobilize support; nonetheless, it remained entirely incompatible with Spain's democratic future. The official trade union and old single-party bureaucracy was integrated into the Administration as it had wished and as the opposition agreed it should be. In this way the process of liberalization ended and the door to democracy was opened wide.

------------------------------ **Parties and Elections** ------------------------------

From April onwards public opinion was focused on the forthcoming election campaign which would precede the general election. In mid March an electoral law had been approved, and it is worth underlining that all sides accepted it. The main opposition leaders met with Suárez but there was certainly no pact – only an exchange of views; nonetheless, what is also certain is that the content of the law was no different in essence from what the opposition would have wanted anyway.

The emergence of a system that allowed political parties to exist proved more problematic. The number of initials identifying these parties spiraled to infinity and the different groups were "as hard to identify as microbes in a droplet of water" (Marías). There were no historical precedents to follow because so many years had passed since elections had last been held – even more than the 12 years in Germany in 1945 (or the 19 in Italy). Nonetheless, the underlying attitude of Spanish society as a whole was at the same time perfectly clear. As the polls suggested, only 4 percent of Spaniards claimed to be very interested in politics while those who were hardly or not at all concerned topped 70 percent. One public figure had, however, managed to win a high level of support among the population: the king, of whom 77 percent said that he had a crucially important role to play. Forty-two percent of Spaniards said that they were of the center – a figure which, added to that of the right, totaled 52 percent – while the left could claim about 44 percent support which, together with the extreme left, could almost reach a total of 48 percent.

In short, everything seemed to suggest that in the future Spanish political life would group around two political formulae, both of which would be centrist and moderate. There were, however, a few surprises in store concerning these initial predictions. On the one hand, although in general Spaniards tended to position themselves in the center of politics, at the time the right seemed stronger than in any other European country. Meanwhile, on the other hand, pre-election polls revealed the existence of a popular mass vote that might be attracted by democratic socialism, though the form of socialism that was prevalent in Spain at the time appeared – for the moment at least – to be more radical than among Social Democrats in the rest of Europe. Finally, offering obvious points of comparison with Italy at the time, there were those who predicted that Spain would see the rise of a significant Christian Democrat tendency, and perhaps even a strong yet moderate Communist Party. All of these expectations proved wrong, not because they were based on wrong assumptions but for the simple reason that their common point of departure was altered by the way that the parties presented themselves to the electorate.

Paradoxically, if one considers what the final results would be, the right formed a political party which it called the Popular Alliance (*Alianza Popular* or AP), whose destiny was to stay linked to the man who had at the start been its principal motivating force, Manuel Fraga. Another detail about this party was that it formed early on (September to October 1976), and that this was greatly to its disadvantage because it immediately aroused fear and hostility in all other areas of politics. In fact, rather than winning over all those who had previously supported Francoism, it attracted only older members; the majority of what had been Francoism's sociological base would go to swell the ranks of the party in government. Over the course of the electoral campaign, Fraga's temperament inevitably led him into situations of confrontation and that meant that the group supporting him came under ever-increasing attack.

The almost infinite numbers of groups that clustered more or less in the center and that were in existence by the end of 1976 began at this time to consider the possibility of working together on wider political issues. The first to do so was the Popular Alliance whose party conference in February 1977 was on about the same scale as that held by the PSOE just a short time before. Although this was an initiative outside government, it was already obvious by the spring of that year that any candidate from the center had to be able to count on the presence of Adolfo Suárez in order to attract an electorate that now identified with Suárez. An electoral alternative known by the initials UCD – *Unión de Centro Democrático* or Union of the Democratic Center – only stumbled onto the political stage very late with not a few conflicts still to be resolved. It was to be a kind of archipelago of a party made up of young reformists from the regime together with most of the non-socialist and independent opposition. Strictly speaking it could not really be described as a residue left by the previous regime: the percentage of UCD parliamentary *diputados* who had been *procuradores* in Franco's government was only 17.5 percent, while 13 of the 16 Popular Alliance members had been ministers under the previous regime. There remained a scattering of political groups with centrist leanings who did not join the coalition presided over by Suárez, the reason being a certain overconfidence that the names chosen by these groups – especially the title "Christian Democracy" – would be enough on their own to draw voters.

The Spanish Workers' Socialist Party (*Partido Socialista Obrero Español* or PSOE) held its 27th conference in December 1976 in conditions that amounted to toleration rather than actual freedom, despite which it then began its spectacular rise in popularity. In reality it had not played a fundamental part in the protest movements of the 1960s (by 1974 it still had barely 2,500 members, a thousand of them in Vizcaya and Guipúzcoa). Nonetheless, after Franco's death socialism was sufficiently closely identified with freedom and the desire for social change to prove attractive to a large part of Spanish society. Reading the texts approved at the congress leads one to deduce that the PSOE of the time sought to define itself as radical. Nonetheless, it is equally clear that these declarations did not go beyond mere words. Felipe González has said of himself that he was always a moderate, and this is probably true, though at that time his party did not appear moderate to the same extent.

Unlike the PSOE, the Spanish Communist Party had not altered its political leadership during its years in exile and could still boast such emblematic figures as Dolores Ibárruri, *La Pasionaria*. With the dictatorship now well in the past, the attraction of a communism that had always been viewed as the arch-enemy of the regime had faded. Carrillo, for his part, showed a clear desire to avoid any danger of becoming inward-looking, and this led him during the election campaign to launch attacks on the AP but, in contrast, not against the UCD. This may have lost him votes which went instead to groups on the extreme left.

This description of the political scene would not be complete without some reference to nationalist movements within Spain. In Catalonia, Catalanism of the center was represented by Jordi Pujol and his Democratic Pact for Catalonia (*Pacte Democràtic per Catalunya* or PDC) which included people of widely differing tendencies and self-definition such as liberals and social democrats, many of whom came from a Catholic background, the only element linking them being their Catalanist sentiment. We should add to this primary Catalan nationalist force that of the Christian Democrats of the Democratic Union (*Unió Democràtica* or UD), whose origins can be traced back to the time of Spain's Second Republic and which stood for election on its own merits. In the Basque Country the nationalist party had kept small nuclei of members and some organizational framework functioning throughout the Franco years, and this made it remarkably long-lasting in historical terms.

It is obvious that the final weeks of the election campaign must have had a considerable impact on the election results. There is no doubt at all that the PSOE displayed the greatest dynamism, and along with its technical and organizational capabilities this meant that expectations continued to grow, almost tripling the initial prediction of 10 percent of the vote suggested by opinion polls. Although, for example, civil governors had a major say in choosing UCD candidates, one can say with confidence that the results were nonetheless fairly representative of Spanish society at the time.

As for the election results themselves, voting numbers were high: some 78 percent; abstention on previous occasions may well have been the main reason for this comparatively high figure. The Union of the Democratic Center won approximately 34 percent of the votes cast and 165 members of parliament, which would make it the largest minority in the government. The PSOE won 29 percent of the vote and a total of 118 deputies, which made it quite clearly the country's second largest political party. Coming in far behind these two political frontrunners, the Spanish Communist Party won 20 seats and the Popular Alliance 16. Tierno Galván's Popular Socialist Party (*Partido Socialist Popular* or PSP) managed to gain only a tiny minority of 6 seats, and the Christian Democrats gained no representation except in Catalonia, beyond a handful of senators, and that was thanks to an alliance with forces on the left. In contrast, nationalist parties won over 20 seats in the Spanish Congress of Deputies (8 going to the Basque Nationalist PNV and 13 to Catalans due to various coalitions). Thanks to the peculiarities of the electoral system, which was by straight majority voting in elections to the Senate, the distance between the UCD and the PSOE was larger in the upper chamber: 106 seats as opposed to 35, despite which the party in government was far from having an absolute majority.

Any attempt to interpret these election results must take into account Spain's historical electoral tradition. In part the geographical distribution of votes was the same as it had been in the 1930s and, as then, the party system revealed a pluralistic picture and a polarization not just between right and left but also according to cultural identity. In Catalonia and the Basque Country the picture was even more diverse for this very reason, but now there was one difference in comparison with the 1930s: the earlier centrifugal tendency had given way to a centripetal force after 1977. This would become obvious in the following months, but for the time being the will of the Spanish people had the power to affect the decisions of what was a minority government of one color and therefore fragile as it faced up to conflicting opinions from competing political forces.

## The Long Road towards a Constitution

As has already been said, the Political Reform Law had put off the drawing up of what was to be a foundational political text until after the elections had taken place. This process now unfolded under conditions that were peculiar but did nonetheless respect the essential agreement reached previously between all the political parties. There was, for example, no legal text in force that could determine the government's responsibility before parliament, and therefore this had to be improvised as a pre-liminary step towards achieving a Constitution whose content was to some extent predetermined by Spain's prior acceptance in April 1977 of international agreements on human rights. The electoral law put in place for the elections of June 1977 had also anticipated the contents of the Constitution. However, it was the amnesty that had first been suggested in a debate in mid July, and had actually been decreed in mid October, that put forward the essentials of what would in time be the Spanish Constitution. Weeks before the elections, the government had freed all prisoners who had not been directly implicated in causing deaths, and had even gone so far as to make pacts with people close to ETA. On the date mentioned, the process of reconciliation took another step forward. With only the Popular Alliance abstaining, a general amnesty was decreed which included not only those who had committed acts of violence against the Franco regime but also those who had used violence in defense of the regime. It was one of the most generous amnesties of the entire third wave of democratization, its generosity no doubt being made easier because the worst of Francoist repression was by now well in the past. A slight drawback was that Spain's historical memory of the past did not last long.

The most urgent task facing Suárez at that time was to form a government. The Union of the Democratic Center was purely an electoral coalition, and the allocation of portfolios gave it the appearance of a mosaic containing a plurality of political families very similar to what had existed under Franco's dictatorship. Nonetheless, as had been the case then, so now too there were men who enjoyed Suárez's closer confidence, or technocrats whose capability was generally acknowledged, who occupied the most important posts. Gutiérrez Mellado controlled – or tried to control – the military. Fernando Abril Martorell acted as second-in-command on political issues, and Enrique Fuentes Quintana directed economic policy. After December 1977, the different groups that had existed in the center folded, though not without some attempt to resist dissolution. The life of the party was rather languid after its initial moments. Álvarez Miranda was elected President of the Congress of Deputies, and Antonio Fontán President of the Senate: both of the center after having started off in opposition.

The second Suárez government had to deal with numerous difficulties at the same time as embarking on drawing up the Constitution. There was now no alternative but to confront the economic crisis. Indeed, in the summer of 1977 the rate of inflation had reached almost Latin American levels (in the order of 50 percent per annum), unemployment had reached 6 percent, which had been unheard of in the past, and Spain went badly into debt. The country had to get to grips with the previous lack of any economic policy and at the same time create a framework that would allow it to face up to the challenge of writing a new Constitution that would ensure sufficient latitude and social peace to avoid a dangerous spiraling of demands in response to political change. The Moncloa Pacts came to represent in socio-economic terms an attitude parallel to that of the political consensus achieved in the electoral law and the amnesty. In effect it was a matter of reaching a political agreement for which Suárez and Carrillo were primarily responsible, though they were not the main actors, having discussed the matter in earlier meetings. The pacts did not arouse a great deal of enthusiasm among socialists, who said that they would accept them "critically," while the Popular Alliance was more reticent, and employers' organizations even more so. The guidelines on economic matters agreed in the pacts were the work of Fuentes Quintana, who had been insisting on the need to make adjustments since the previous summer. They stated that political parties, employers' organizations and unions, and the social forces of the left were committed to a policy of austerity on salaries in exchange for a series of countermeasures that were to tackle issues ranging from the start of fiscal reform, including the setting up of new taxes such as inheritance tax, to the provision of a large number of school places, the extension of loans to Social Security, and the regulation of Spaniards' new freedoms. To a certain extent one can also say that it was at this time that Spaniards began to learn the basic principles of the social market economy that was to feature in their Constitution.

While the Constitution was under discussion there were several episodes of civil disturbances which aroused fears of tensions turning the clock back. By this time it had become clear that ETA was going to be an even greater problem for the infant democracy than it had been for the dying dictatorship. In the 11 months running up to June 1977 – a year in which, as readers will remember, there were three successive amnesties – ETA murdered several more members of the security forces.

Obviously there was also a general move towards normality. At the start of 1978 union elections were held and produced a victory for *Comisiones Obreras* (CCOO), the union that had been most firmly rooted in Spain since the 1960s, which had by now opted for association with the PCE and other political groups to its left. This tendency did not, however, mean that the average industrial worker had communist leanings, as there were members of *Comisiones* who voted PSOE. For their part, the UGT had not gained as much ground, given that it had begun to make progress quite a lot later; it was only when it added to its ranks the leaders of the *Unión Sindical Obrera* that it could match the strength of CCOO. The left also demanded immediate municipal elections: a request which was not heeded because the UCD government realized that to hold elections at the very same time as the debate on the Constitution, because of the language that would be used during the election campaign, would endanger the survival of a consensus.

As one would expect, the greatest political challenge was to determine the basic text of the Constitution. This has been the case throughout the entire third wave of democratization. Portugal, which due to the lack of any peripheral nationalist groups had fewer problems to solve than Spain, after serious difficulties keeping the peace within its frontiers, ended up modifying its original Constitution not long after it was first drawn up. The situation has been similar in countries of the former Soviet Union such as Poland, which were without a Constitution for many years. In Spain, after 18 months on the drawing-board, in a text that comprised more than 160 articles, general agreement was finally reached.

There could have been a government initiative at this point, but in the end it did not happen and this had a positive effect. However, the Constitution had to be lengthy because the left insisted on an extensive enumeration of rights and intentions which was, to a large degree, logical given circumstances in Spain at the end of the dictatorship. For this reason Miquel Roca could well say that if in Sweden, where freedom to hold meetings had always existed, there was no need to mention it in the Constitution, it was in contrast essential to do so in Spain. Political groups of all complexions took part in writing the Constitution, though the two largest parties in the *Cortes* took the lead. The Catalanists also played a major role in the process, principally as mediators representing other options and by putting forward their own precise demands on territorial organization within the Spanish state, not on their own behalf alone but more generally. In contrast, the Basque nationalists only demanded sovereignty, which proved unacceptable to all other groups but did force some quite significant amendments to be made. The amendment agreed on with the Popular Socialist Party forms the preamble to the entire document.

The draft constitution was written by a commission of seven people: three of the center, one socialist, one communist, one Catalan nationalist, and a representative of the right. The process was not without complications: in November 1977 its contents were made public by being leaked via a newspaper, and in March 1978, shortly before the text was completed, the socialists withdrew from the commission. Later, the right-wing members were on the point of doing the same, but on neither occasion was the fundamental consensus of the group under any real threat. In the final stages, more thorny questions began to be resolved without any publicity, by Fernando Abril and Alfonso Guerra, who had risen to be second-in-command in the UCD and PSOE respectively. Abril had begun to stand out from his colleagues immediately after the elections. This was the time of what came to be known as the "re-consensus" – a dreadful term which highlighted the fragility of the pacts agreed upon up to that time and the need to work very hard indeed to maintain overall agreement. The only party that was not in on this agreement was the PNV, but it did make it clear that it would act within the constitutional framework and it recalled that in the past, though it had not voted on the 1931 Republican Constitution, it had fought alongside those who took up arms in its defense in 1936.

In October 1978 the Constitution was approved in a joint session of both houses, as had been set out in the Political Reform Law. It was then put to a referendum in December, again as the law demanded. In no other transition in the "third wave" of democratizations was such complete agreement achieved between all the participating political groups in the first instance, and then with the participation of ordinary citizens to ratify the decision. When the matter was put to the vote in the referendum of December 1978, polling figures were low – only about 69 percent – which meant that only about 70 percent of electors used the vote to ratify the contents of the Constitution. In fact, it was only in the Basque Country that there was an actual shortfall that challenged the legitimacy of the document. One has to bear in mind how repetitive such consultation of the Spanish population had become, and there was also a certain degree of "disenchantment" felt by many citizens concerning the democracy that had just been achieved.

The final text of the Constitution was the result of an extremely laborious process that had had to deal with significant contradictions and no doubt had had a negative impact on the clarity and even the grammatical accuracy of the final document. Nonetheless, thanks to all these factors the Constitution, for the first time in Spain's entire history, was the product of a genuine consensus, and the constitutional arch spanned a far wider range of views than had originally been hoped for at the start. Only groups on the far right and far left objected to the Constitution, but the fact that both Fraga and Carrillo voted in favor denied them any possible support from wider sections of the population.

The main characteristics of the text of the Constitution can be understood according to these premises. The great advantage of the way it was formulated was that it was the result of a consensus, but it was nevertheless often based on "apocryphal compromises": that is to say, a layering of statements that tried to satisfy a range of contradictory requirements at one and the same time. There was evidence in it of the influence of Spain's constitutional history – primarily the texts from 1812 and 1931 – but it was in fact not very original in its essential elements. In deciding on its exact content, efforts had been made to avoid repeating the experience of the 1930s by using procedures such as the constructive vote of censure.

The 1978 Constitution had 11 sections and 169 articles. What first catches the reader's attention on perusing it is that in order to produce it agreement had to be reached on several bitterly disputed issues. The enumeration of human rights and liberties is lengthy, but on the matter of education all parties were in agreement. That the state was declared to be non-denominational did not cause problems either, and the same might be said on the question of the monarchy despite the fact that the PSOE maintained its original republican stance. Concerning institutions, the Spanish political system can be described as a very diluted form of bicameral government in the sense that, although the two chambers exist, the Congress of Deputies has far more power than the Senate. One determining trait that is essentially Spanish is that it provides for what are described as "organic laws" which require a virtually absolute majority if they are to be approved rather than just one vote over a half of those present. For this reason the Catalan leader Miquel Roca has been able to write that the Constitution was not merely the result *of* consensus voting but was intended to provide *for* future consensus on certain issues.

Nonetheless, it remains the case that on one very important issue agreement was basic and incomplete. Section VIII of the Constitution, which deals with the territorial organization of the state, tried to offer a framework in which it was possible to encompass, at one and the same time, the claims of Basque nationalists concerning their historic rights, the demands from Catalan nationalists if not for sovereignty then at least for a situation similar to that of the Generalitat in the 1930s, and also the diffuse regional sentiments that stirred throughout Spain with the advent of democracy. The way that Catalonia, the Basque Country, and Galicia were satisfied was by the use of the term "nationality" when referring to them, though there was then no precise clarification of their exact nature as "nations without a state." This meant that guidelines were laid down fairly imprecisely, which had the advantage of not closing off any options and leaving open for a future time the possibility of further changes, but only on the basis of a consensus. From the administrative point of view this means several levels of responsibility in competition with each other and various ways of achieving autonomy, the fastest being that open to those regions that had in the past had a Statute of Autonomy.

Consensus on this one issue was, then, left for later. This is why, in a book on the Constitution written to celebrate its twentieth anniversary by some of those who had worked on it, the authors disagreed on this question. The lines of confrontation did not coincide strictly with party lines but rather according to attitudes towards the notion of a pluralistic cultural identity in Spain.

## —— An Unresolved Issue: Nationalism and Terrorism ——

The fact that a text that was imprecise and technically incorrect was generally accepted can be explained in essence by Spain's particular character. If indeed its degree of cultural plurality is greater than in any other Western European country, and comparable to that in central Europe and the Balkans, it is nonetheless a far cry from the situation in part of the former USSR. There, for example, in the seven largest cities in Lithuania the majority of the population is Russian – and speaks that language – while in Central Asia there are also religious differences to take into account. The Spanish case is different too from that of Canada (two nations) and Belgium (two nations and four language regions), or of Scotland (which emerged late as a nation). The situation in Spain can be summed up in very few words by saying that although for all Spaniards Spain is a state, and it is also true that for most of them state and nation are one and the same, for sizeable minorities in the Peninsula Spain was a state but not a nation. Moreover, feelings were not the same across different communities, but were different in some aspects and in others mixed, and not always in the same degree everywhere. This was the result of a genuine historical "counter-experience" which contrasted with what had happened in other countries (Pierre Vilar). If in Germany and Italy the last few decades of the century saw national unity achieved, Spain's experience was radically different. In addition, linked to its plurality though different from it, there is the incidence of terrorism with a possible impact on Spain's general political life. Even Ulster, which had suffered a form of terrorism that was far more brutal than was the case in the Basque County (almost 1,400 dead between 1969 and 1975), has been able to maintain a greater degree of democracy without any attempt to turn the clock back by violent means, as was always a threat in Spain.

Setting up a state on the basis of principles of decentralization or federalism was not felt to be a major priority in the initial phase of political change except in the Basque Country and Catalonia (and somewhat less so in Galicia). One gains the impression that if, after a given moment, a continuous succession of demands of this kind were made, it was due to the fact that decisions had initially been taken by a political ruling class that had then passed the decision-making on to the population at large, where the demands did not immediately get beyond the larval stage. As time passed, Basque and Catalan demands acted as a trigger for regional sentiment all over Spain, though it took very different forms in different places. That is not to say that the sentiments that gave rise to demands for a pluralistic society were in any sense false. On the contrary, what had happened in the 1930s shows that the spread of such attitudes was to be expected and was even inevitable.

We should in the first instance consider Catalonia and the Basque Country, for the blossoming of regionalist sentiment in other regions and nationalities belongs to a later period, after the elections in 1979 when it at last became relevant in political terms. In the case of these two nationalities Francoism, although it had enjoyed solid political and social support, had been a minority viewpoint, and during the dictatorship autonomous governments had existed in exile. First of all, however, it is important to underline the fact that the two cases were different. The Basque Country embarked on its democratic journey without a sufficient consensus; so, for example, only about one in four inhabitants of Guipúzcoa agreed with the text of the Constitution. A degree more support for the existing political system was only reached as late as October 1979, on the occasion of the referendum on the Basque Statute. Counting up all those who agreed with the Constitution, the Statute, or only one of the two documents, a figure of 50 percent of the Basque population was now reached. Even so, at the end of the 1970s between 13 and 16 percent of Basques considered ETA terrorists patriots, and between 29 and 35 percent believed that they were idealists.

In Catalonia there was a greater degree of social consensus and agreement with the general direction that the transition was taking. After the elections, 62 of the 63 parliamentarians elected asked for a return to the 1932 Statute of Autonomy, and it became obvious that a demand that was being made by so many in such a peaceful manner must be satisfied. Josep Tarradellas, President of the Generalitat in exile, and Suárez, after an initial disagreement, were both able to act swiftly, decisively, and competently. Only a few days after the elections they met together in Madrid and, despite an inauspicious start, the meeting ended well. Once more in place, the Generalitat had powers that were more symbolic than real, but Tarradellas's return to Barcelona at the start of October meant that a decisive step was taken towards finding a practical way forward for a

Catalonia whose behavior in the elections had actually differed considerably from that of the rest of Spain. This was the only instance of rupture in the transition process in Spain, as the institution that was now in place had come into being under republican legislation before the Civil War. Although Catalan nationalists still demanded sovereignty, the Catalan Statute and the referendum on its implementation in October 1979 won the support of all political groups. There was, nonetheless, an undoubted duality in the Catalan electorate which often voted differently in local, Catalan, and general elections.

Circumstances were not the same in the Basque Country as in Catalonia. Even before the 1977 elections the PNV had shown a willingness to compromise that distanced it from ETA's position; however, its attitude to the constitutional process, and the attitude of a section of the Basque population towards terrorism, remained one of disapproval or condescension. On the day on which the amnesty was approved, three people were murdered by the terrorist organization. It was only in December 1977 that agreement was finally reached on setting up a provisional governing body. Even then, this was only possible because resolving the problem of Navarra was put off until a future date and Navarra remained for the time being separate from the autonomous Basque community. In the early months of 1979 difficult negotiations took place on the matter of the content of the Basque Statute. When at last it was approved and put to the vote in a referendum, 90 percent of those who took part voted in favor, which was about 60 percent of the population as a whole. This was at last a sufficient degree of consensus to satisfy Basque society and the government in Madrid, though conflict did continue. In January 1980, the Basque nationalist members withdrew from the Spanish Parliament in protest against the way that the transfer of powers was being handled. Furthermore, given the political fragmentation in the region, the autonomous institutions could only function if Herri Batasuna, the political wing of ETA, did not take part, leaving the PNV with an artificial majority.

The question of Basque autonomy cannot be discussed without reference to ETA terrorism which made normalizing democracy in Spain infinitely more complicated than it would otherwise have been. Reference has already been made to the number of victims it caused and to the times when it was most active. It is quite easy to sum up the evolution of ETA and the groups associated with it in terms of general tendencies. After political freedom was established in Spain a debate arose on the relative merits of politics complementing violence, or alternatively, as the only way ahead. This meant that ETA activists trod a path that would lead to legal political action sooner or later. In general the older members opted for political solutions, but there were always younger groups willing to swell the ranks of a violent form of activism that ended up winning most support.

Towards the end of the Franco years ETA appeared to be split into two factions: militant ETA (ETAm) was the old militant wing of the organization; it consisted of only a very few militants and it professed a form of radicalism that was more nationalistic than revolutionary. Political-militant ETA (ETApm) had originally been able to count on the support of the majority of the movement, and had at one time considered the possibility of other forms of action besides terrorism. Being more strongly Marxist and revolutionary, it managed through its political organization, the Basque Left (*Euzkadiko Ezkerra* or EE), to gain 10 percent of the vote in Guipúzcoa and the election of two members of parliament and one senator. After 1979, however, its attempt to make its voice heard resulted in violence as criminal as that of ETAm, which proved incomprehensible even to radical Basque nationalists. After the summer of 1979 the distance separating EE and ETApm grew. The policy of repression and reinsertion implemented by the Interior Minister Rosón, with the support of EE, meant that ETA's organization effectively crumbled at the start of the 1980s, which meant that the number of deaths from terrorism was considerably reduced. ETApm finally announced that it was folding in September 1982. As for ETAm, initially reduced to a very few militants, it set up a leadership structure at the end of the 1970s which remained in place until 1992 and proved capable of forming a commando group every 2 weeks, which shows just how firmly rooted it was in certain sections of Basque society. Although in the spring of 1978 it also formed its own parallel political organization, the Union of the Basque People (*Herri Batasuna* or HB), for ETAm terrorism was really a substitute, not a complement, for mass action.

Despite these factors and the rise in the number of terrorist attacks in the months after the approval of the Constitution, it was already clear by the summer of 1979 that not only was the PNV supported by the majority of Basque nationalists (gaining twice the vote won by HB) but that it was prepared to begin to speak out against ETA terrorism and act within the framework of the Constitution.

───────     ## The Triumph and Fall of Adolfo Suárez     ───────

In dealing at this stage with the approval of the Catalan and Basque Statutes we have moved ahead beyond the point in time that we had actually reached in our narrative. Now we must return to it and remember that these events were preceded by another general election victory for Adolfo Suárez.

In October 1978 the UCD held its first party conference and saw the increasing success of the younger element of the party which was more closely linked than it had been in 1977 to moderate sectors of the opposition to Francoism. In fact, the party conference was a first step towards preparing for the elections that, once the Constitution was approved, were to be held in March 1979. There had been serious doubts in government circles on the wisdom of calling elections, but the decision had been taken to do so because in any case one confrontation via the ballot-box was unavoidable, in municipal elections. The atmosphere in which the elections – whose results could not be predicted – took place was not without a certain dramatic tension. The result would be determined primarily by the high level of voters who were still undecided (some 40 percent), while a third of those of the center decided how they would vote at the very last minute on the basis of the final television programs in which Suárez himself took part.

Suárez presented center politics as the fundamental enemy of the socialists with whom no further pacts would now be made. The right, calling itself the Democratic Coalition (*Coalición Democrática*), was in fact none other than the Popular Alliance, which had now distanced itself from much of its past collaboration with Francoism and had come up instead with some ideas of its own. There were few changes in the PSOE. Approximately two-thirds of the socialist members of the 1977 government stood as candidates once again, though on this occasion some of the historic leaders who had been in exile tended to disappear while members of the PSP put themselves forward for relevant posts. As for the communists, their candidates came from *Comisiones Obreras*, which was by now Spain's major trade union.

The election results in March brought few changes. Of course, the party system allowed for numerous groups among which differences were slight but significant. The UCD lost a little under 1 percent of its vote but gained three seats because of the nature of electoral law. These facts give the lie to the statement from socialist circles that it was a transient party without any real possibility of surviving for any length of time. For its part, the PSOE went from having 118 members of parliament to 121 but, if we take into account that it had already taken over the PSP, its results meant an effective loss of seats and of votes (somewhat more than 3 percent). The deep disappointment that was felt among socialists finally led to disagreement. The PCE increased its share of the vote by a bare 1 percent and therefore continued to exist without a firm base within the nation. Almost half of its votes and 15 of the 23 seats that it gained were in Catalonia and Andalusia. As for the Democratic Coalition, it lost something over 2 percent of those who had voted for it in the past and this was enough to ensure that its number of seats went down from 16 to 9, which was comparable with the Popular Alliance result in 1977.

These results were confirmation that Spaniards had accepted both the means and the results of the transition to democracy. In opinion polls at the time Adolfo Suárez was awarded 7 out of 10, which was quite unheard of for a European politician at the time. The municipal elections that followed modified the situation somewhat. The UCD emerged as winner once again if we consider the number of councilors elected (more than 29,000 in comparison to 12,000 socialists). Yet these figures are deceptive if taken in isolation, because the PSOE gained a significant slice of political power thanks to agreements it signed at the start of April with the communists, who now had 3,600 councilors, which meant that they controlled a large percentage of Spanish cities.

Over the following year and a half, however, Suárez's decline in popularity as a politician and as Spain's prime minister accelerated as he appeared perplexed on matters of government and unable to resolve disputes within the party he led, which indeed owed its existence in large part to him. In the debate on the occasion of the investiture he appeared to resist parliamentary intervention and only managed to win the support of pro-Andalusian and other regionalist groups. From May 1979 to May 1980, out of 2,046 votes in parliament, Suárez was present for only 1,555.

Once the investiture had taken place, a new political phase opened up in Spain, in theory marked by the disappearance of a general consensus once the Constitution had been approved. An attempt was made to counteract the fragmentation of the party in power by the way the government was made up. In this government and the one that followed it, Fernando Abril, who was a close friend of the prime minister, played a major role as Suárez had delegated important political functions to him. Shy, hardworking, demanding, well intentioned, and always deeply conscious of his responsibility before the state, Abril was, nonetheless, a bad parliamentarian who was disorganized when the time came to act, even though he was an able negotiator; nor did he have the training to deal with the economic matters committed to his charge, which was also irritating for the other UCD leaders precisely because he was so powerful. A government reshuffle in May 1980, which followed on in the same direction as the previous changes, only aggravated the situation. Abril was at his most influential between the summers of 1977 and 1980, and in the end he ruined his relationship with Suárez. If Suárez erred by omission and indolence, his deputy, who was a good but interminable negotiator, erred in the opposite direction, interfering in matters that were outside the scope of his own job.

The real problem was that the government appeared impotent and uncertain when facing the problems that repeatedly confronted it. In June 1978 ten regions – the equivalent of three-quarters of Spain's entire population – already had what amounted to pre-autonomous governing bodies. The entire political class at the time, including the socialists, believed deep down that it was necessary to alter the procedure by which autonomy was to be attained in order to prevent Spain's other regions catching up with the "historic nationalities" in terms of the political powers accorded to them. Yet in February 1980, when the question arose of Andalusia achieving autonomy on a fast track, the combination of very clumsy presentation of the issue on the part of the UCD, and a certain demogogy from the opposition, resulted in an outright rejection by the majority of Andalusians of any delay in bringing in the Statute.

The situation became even more complex with the reappearance of internal conflict within the UCD at a time when it was extremely weak in parliament. A crucial moment was reached when the PSOE presented a vote of censure in May 1980. It could not succeed, but according to opinion polls after the parliamentary session only 26 percent of Spaniards approved of Suárez's response. This gave Felipe González a chance to make a good showing as a serious alternative in government.

These poor prospects accentuated the crisis facing the party in government. At the start of July 1980 the UCD leaders accused the prime minister of adopting an excessively personal style of leadership in the party and the government, and of not asking or accepting advice. Suárez agreed to yet more changes in the government when everyone returned after the summer recess, and he also got rid of Abril who had offered his resignation about five times. Even so, after October 1980 the most right-wing sections of the party began to mobilize. A few weeks later a group that was openly "critical" appeared at the heart of the UCD which had managed to persuade Lavilla, the President of the Congress of Deputies, to lead it in mid January 1981. It pushed for clearer ideological definition and more political confrontation, but this helped to create a general climate of irresponsibility and stagnation in the government and the opposition. Fraga tells in his memoirs of an interview with the king in which he spoke to him of "crisis facing the state, crisis in society, and the need for a change of direction." There were others expressing themselves in much the same terms in almost all parties (Ramón Tamames in the PCE, Alfonso Ossorio in the AP, Enrique Múgica in the PSOE . . . ). Meanwhile, in the newspaper *El Alcázar*, whose circulation increased from 15,000 to 70,000 copies, there were rumors of possible military intervention.

On January 29, 1981 the situation took a surprising turn: that day, quite unexpectedly for the immense majority of Spaniards and most of his own ministers, Adolfo Suárez tendered his resignation. "I do not believe that there was only one cause, or that it remained hidden," wrote his successor. He had not given up his job for any one particular reason, "but rather because of his state of mind." He was at that time the longest-serving president of a European government and he knew that he could not hold on in that position until 1983 when elections were next due. He realized his own limitations and that over time the popularity he had once enjoyed had dwindled. Doubtless he showed great moral strength in admitting it; he was not directly pressurized and he did not retire in the face of imminent danger.

───────     **The Army and the Transition: February 23**     ───────

One of the enigmas of Spain's transition to democracy is the role that the Army played in the whole process. In Turkey, Italy, Portugal, and Greece the military played an important part in the move to democracy, either initially, overseeing the process and then stepping in to correct it (Turkey, 1945), or as a decisive factor in the removal of the dictator, only without playing any leading role immediately afterwards (Italy, 1945), or as the trigger for ending the dictatorship in a society that at first did nothing and then became more radical and moved towards the left (Portugal, 1974), or else as a decisive factor in the previous dictatorship which ended up divided, thus opening the way to democracy (Greece, 1974). In Spain the military did not appear to play an important part at all in the transition, which was curious if one takes into account the fact that Spain's starting-point was a military dictatorship. There was no split into different tendencies and nor was there any evidence of any strong desire to play an active role in politics.

In seeking an explanation for what happened, the fact that Don Juan Carlos was Franco's successor, duly appointed by him quite unequivocally, and that he was also the supreme head of the armed forces is obviously of prime importance. Looked at another way, Francoism was a dictatorship with a soldier at its head rather than a regime run by the Army as a body. Furthermore, in order to preempt any possible opposition, the Army as an institution had been increasingly discouraged from attempting to intervene in Spanish political life, while at the same time remaining in general in a world apart from normal society, with the exception of its youngest officers. Because of the lack of modern technology and on poor salaries, the majority of the officer corps was obliged to take up a number of different jobs (*pluriempleo*) when stationed in big cities.

The transfer of allegiance from Franco to the king avoided any threat of military intervention, or else channeled it into a tense dialogue with the civil authorities. The Spanish Constitution itself contained calculated ambiguities on the exact responsibilities of the monarch, one article attributing to him "supreme command" of the Army, while another made the government responsible for the defense of the realm. This meant that those who favored a coup never gained a majority because of the question of loyalty to the monarch.

The stance that most high-ranking military officers adopted is another matter altogether. In 1976, 68 of Spain's 95 brigadier-generals had fought in the Civil War; the way the Armed Services were organized at the time meant in addition that men would only retire at 70. The four lieutenant-generals in the *Cortes* voted against the Political Reform Law. All officers with this rank and that of divisional commander could be placed on the extreme right wing of politics, and it was also the case that all those awaiting promotion to the rank of brigadier-general were colonels who shared the same ideas. Among the younger officers there was a very different mentality to be found: the majority of captains and lieutenants had far more contact with ordinary society and had had no experience whatever of the Civil War. One should in any case underline the fact that the Democratic Military Union – which, as a movement, opposed the regime – only ever had 140 officer members, three-quarters of whom were stationed in Barcelona or Madrid. Nonetheless, for the king and the transition itself there was always the danger that young officers might in time be drawn into becoming involved in some form of revolutionary left. The king had only 2 or 3 years during which he had at one and the same time to keep older and younger officers loyal to him. The process of reforming the Armed Services had in effect made little progress. In 1979 the only civilian in the ministry was the minister himself and that remained so throughout the 2 years that followed.

Looking back over this period it appears that military intervention could only ever have been effective had it happened at the very start of the transition, at the time of the Political Reform Law, or else at extraordinary moments such as when the Communist Party was legalized, but at the highest levels of command there was no one to take the lead and no plan beyond the notion of resistance to change. Military leaders often talked of the possibility of armed intervention, but what happened in actual fact was that there were several moments of tension between different levels of authority and civilian politicians or the king, but these were clashes that ended with the generals submitting to discipline. When Fernando de Santiago left power there was constant psychological sparring between military and civilian authorities. De Santiago, like many other public figures, always gave the impression that he believed that the transition should not go beyond "tolerable limits" and that the Army had a sphere of autonomous action. However, Spain's civilian politicians did not agree. In practice the military high command only had any impact on one aspect of the transition: when they vetoed the amnesty in the case of soldiers who had belonged to the Democratic Military Union.

A key figure in the transition was Manuel Gutiérrez Mellado who, as vice-president with responsibility for matters of Defense, was the principal person in change of determining policy on military affairs – a job that would later be shared by Agustín Rodríguez Sahagún. Gutiérrez Mellado could be described as the soldier with the soundest judgment in the Spanish Army at the time that he was collaborating most closely with Adolfo Suárez. His political activity was based on the need to keep politics out of Army barracks, and this made him the person most subject to the worst tension throughout the entire transition. During his term as vice-president he undertook the modernization of the armed forces. One might question whether this was accompanied by an adequate policy on service appointments, though obviously it is not possible now to determine whether a more decisive policy might not have provoked an adverse reaction among commanding officers at the time. According to Abril, Spain's generals were as resistant to change and as immovable as the statues in the Plaza de Oriente, and Gutiérrez Mellado did not enforce discipline when cases occurred where he should have done so.

Worst of all, however, was the leniency with which open opposition to the transition was treated. The man who was the inspiration behind the Cafetería Galaxia conspiracy of November 1978, Colonel Antonio Tejero, was sentenced to only 7 months in prison, which was a trivial sentence even if his aim – to attack the Moncloa Palace – was utterly hair-brained. A special case was that of General Armada who, having been very close to the king, appeared totally loyal to the monarch, although he did not hide his conservative inclinations and would have been appalled by the legalization of the PCE. Despite Suárez's reservations as he handed in his resignation, Armada had just taken up the second most senior post in the Army's high command.

On the night of February 23 to 24, during the second vote on the investiture of Suárez's successor, Colonel Tejero, together with 400 civil guards, boldly invaded the Spanish Parliament and held the members hostage. He had gained access to the building "in the king's name," but most of the guards had no idea at all why they had come to the Parliament building. If the coup was to succeed they had to gain control of Madrid and the military uprising also had to spread right to the coast. The strongest doubts were felt by the military authorities in Seville, Zaragoza, and Valladolid, but we can gain a measure of the seriousness of the events from the fact that at the start only a very few captaincies-general were in total agreement with the legal position set out in the Constitution. In Valencia General Jaime Milans del Bosch failed to complete the success of the conspiracy in Madrid, in part because some of his divisions remained loyal to the government and others were unsure what to do, and this proved decisive. Nonetheless, for some hours the situation hung in the balance.

The coup's entire strategy was based on creating a state of emergency that would induce the military authorities to intervene with backing from the king. Therefore the king played a decisive role when he contacted not only generals but also colonels to persuade them not to support the uprising. General Armada's presence in the Zarzuela Palace was unauthorized, and it was the king himself who suggested an immediate meeting between the Chiefs of Staff of the Armed Forces and one of his closest collaborators who managed to ensure that the units that had taken over the

Spanish radio and television headquarters left the building so that the royal message could be broadcast.

Acting entirely without authorization from the king, General Armada went to the Parliament building to negotiate an interim situation – military government but with the consent of the parties – which would validate Army intervention in Spanish politics. It was already quite clear that there was a discrepancy between Tejero, who wanted a return to a purely military government and rejected political parties, and Armada, who considered it essential to gain parliamentary support for a government that he himself would lead.

The beginning of the end of the coup came when Don Juan Carlos declared on television that the crown "cannot tolerate any kind of action or attitude from those who would try to use force to disrupt the democratic process that the Constitution – for which the Spanish people voted – determined by a referendum would take place." The king had before him two prime examples of the way he should act: his grandfather Alfonso XIII and his brother-in-law Constantine had paid with their crowns for their ambiguous response to military coups or their collaboration. The stance that Don Juan Carlos adopted may incidentally have revealed his true intentions for the left, but his action was in fact a continuation of the role he had played since the very start of democratization, as a shield protecting the transition process.

Apart from the king's intervention, it was flaws in the conspiracy itself that caused it to fail. First there were internal divisions: Tejero was against democracy and monarchy, Milans against democracy but not monarchy, and Armada wanted to manipulate both but avoid confrontation with either. There is also no doubt that it failed because Spaniards all knew immediately that it was happening and could actually listen to it being broadcast.

As regards the impact of the coup on Spain's political development, it would prove to be less significant than was first thought in 1981: rather than a democracy that needed to be carefully watched there was a watchful democracy. If the officers who opposed change but did not take part were not punished, nor were they given key posts. It may be that these officers never became ardent democrats, but they had nonetheless a sense of discipline and loyalty to the monarchy. In contrast, a lack of cohesion and a lack of unity rather than any swing to the right were what caused havoc in the UCD. In fact, the attempted coup's strongest impact on Spanish politics was that it made any subsequent attempt by the military to turn the clock back totally unthinkable. Along with this surprising result, one might also cite another, which was no less important but was less expected. The coup alerted all sides – politicians and civilians – to the dangers of irresponsible attitudes.

## Calvo Sotelo's Government and the Crisis in Center Politics

It was Suárez himself who suggested as his successor Leopoldo Calvo Sotelo, who did not at the time belong to any particular tendency within the UCD. Calvo Sotelo's close collaboration with Suárez does not mean that their background or personalities were in any way similar. Intelligent, cultured, capable, and a sharp-tongued parliamentarian, Calvo Sotelo gave the impression that he was more right-wing than Suárez but also more solid. At the time he took office as prime minister, some commentators went so far as to compare him to a kind of Adenauer destined to set Spain on the rails towards normalized democracy. What is certain is that Calvo Sotelo, in his first months in the post, managed to raise the levels of acceptability of his government considerably, reaching as high as 40 percent in contrast to Suárez's final phase, when support was a low as 26 percent. However, Calvo Sotelo could not prevent the latest rise in petrol prices hitting the Spanish economy; nor could he hold the UCD together. His main weakness was his lack of tenacity and even ambition. In October 1981 Fraga was higher in the opinion polls than the prime minister, though the UCD still had more potential votes than the AP.

After the attempted coup it became possible to consider either forming a coalition or carrying on alone without making pacts in either direction. Calvo Sotelo chose to do the latter in hopes – vain hopes, as it turned out – of keeping the UCD together. This decision did not prevent him appointing Fraga's brother-in-law, Carlos Robles Piquer, as director of RTVE. However, the so-called "natural majority" of the right that could supposedly hold its ground proved to be neither natural nor a majority and this ensured that the right-wing option would not come to power. The Organic Law on the Harmonization of the Autonomy Process (*Ley Orgánica de Armonización del Proceso Autonómico* or LOAPA) aimed at harmonizing legislation on the move towards regional autonomy was approved with the support of the two majority parties.

Despite the fact that, during his term of office, Calvo Sotelo was the object of fiercely polemical debate, no one could doubt his merit in the matter of judging those on trial for the events of February 23. A Defense of Democracy Law (*Ley de Defensa de la Democracia*) provided a legal framework that ensured that any further attempted coup would be quashed, and even went so far as to allow for the temporary suspension of any section of the media that expressed support for it. The prime minister discovered that the senior Army officers involved had no actual notion of an overall political plan and instead were protesting in very general terms about the autonomous regions, terrorism, the lack of law and order, and even pornography. The promotions that he proposed and implemented in the Army were mainly automatic and did not discriminate in favor of right-wing ideology. In the months following the coup, various incidents occurred that brought the military and civil authorities into confrontation. When the sentences of the court became known, public opinion and student opposition were on the side of the prime minister – and of Suárez – in the sense that they judged the punishment insufficient. The case then went to the Supreme Court which increased the sentences considerably.

Together with Spain's entry into NATO, of which more will be said later, these were the areas in which Calvo Sotelo managed to formulate a program. In many other areas he failed to do so, either because of the size of the task he faced or – above all – because of divisions within the party that supported him. The economic crisis, for example, had now become acute due to the second oil price rise worldwide in 1979. In Spain the situation was more serious because it was hitting a country that had not yet resolved its first crisis, whose dependency on foreign energy sources was enormous and whose institutions were too rigid to make an appropriate response. Calvo Sotelo's government found itself at this point facing an immensely difficult situation which worsened because of its weakness in parliament, which meant that it managed to bring about only a limited lowering of prices and a very partial slowing down of the rate of unemployment.

On issues such as the divorce law, private television channels, and the autonomy of Spain's universities, divisions within the UCD turned debates into battlefields and prevented any matters being resolved by parliament. Calvo Sotelo's government began to go downhill at the same time as the UCD was breaking up. The final result was that a political party that had played a supremely important part in Spain's transition to democracy ended its life in the parliamentary elections in 1982. It was a case that was unique in European political history. That year, after a past that had drawn applause from all sides, it managed to get only 7 percent of the vote and 11 seats. Between 1992 and 1994, the Italian socialists' share of the vote went down from 13 to 2 percent and that of the Christian democrats from 29 to 11 percent, but only after much longer periods of crisis.

These events might seem to suggest that the sole reason for the UCD's existence was the transition, and that once this had been achieved the party was bound to fold. Yet this idea conflicts with what happened in other transitions to democracy. In Spain it was difficult to get a consensus, and this meant that while the Constitution was being drawn up, the party in power had to avoid the kind of confrontation that Adenauer had faced in Germany, which allowed it to consolidate its party policy. Most important of all, the Spanish center-party leaders failed to find a means of reaching agreement among themselves. There were ideological differences, though none of them was impossible to overcome; more serious by far were the personal differences which later became more sharply focused on matters of relatively little importance such as divorce, for example. In Italy, on the other hand, the Christian democrats who oversaw the transition in 1945 did not suffer from such splits within the party until later, in the 1960s. It was the UCD's internal crisis that caused its decline in the polls, not the reverse, despite the fact that surveys after the 1979 elections showed that three out of every four UCD voters could be considered firm supporters of the party.

Leaders from the center party scattered in all directions. While Suárez showed a disturbing propensity to return to politics, the "moderate platform" pulled the right together and Francisco Fernández Ordóñez, the most outstanding representative of the social democrats, expressed a desire to "reestablish his own identity" which would lead to him leaving the party in November.

After the summer of 1981, a truce was declared among a UCD leadership faced with the prospect of imminent elections in Galicia in October. In these elections the Popular Alliance vote rose by 17 percentage points, while the UCD went down by 9; compared with the right's 26 seats, the center could only muster 24 (the PSOE won 17). This was the first time that the AP had defeated the UCD in an important region. The right was beginning to win over the urban middle classes who had until now voted largely for the UCD. In the elections in Andalusia in May 1982, the Popular Alliance won 350,000 votes more than in the previous elections, quadrupling its strength, while the UCD lost half a million votes. The election campaign was accompanied by very belligerent action against the government on the part of the employers' organizations.

Calvo Sotelo now wanted to try a collegiate leadership alongside Suárez and Landelino Lavilla, president of the Congress of Deputies, but he did not succeed. Lavilla's subsequent attempt to lead the party would only make sense if he managed to form some kind of "showcase government," and this would require some reshuffling. However, Calvo Sotelo was by now overwhelmed by a succession of defeats and he dissolved the *Cortes* and called elections for October. So the UCD did not have its votes snatched from it by a political adversary. Although Fraga's energetic oratory managed to attract a section of the middle-class vote and some younger political leaders, he was, as we shall see, a long way off winning all the political space previously occupied by the UCD. The UCD had never been a political party with a base in society; it also erred on the side of being opportunistic, lacking clear definition and also lacking direction. The worst aspect of this party was, however, what one of its members – Emilio Attard – has described as "ferocious cannibalism" among its leaders.

## Foreign Policy

Before turning our attention to the 1982 elections, we should consider certain factors that would influence the results and that we have so far only touched on circumstantially when they really require consideration as a whole.

Without doubt the transition to democracy meant that internal politics took priority over foreign affairs. In general terms foreign policy developed according to a consensus, except on the matter of Spain's entry into NATO, despite the fact that the models the socialists favored were Sweden and Austria: that is to say, a third route. The communists, unlike their colleagues in Greece, for example, had been pro-European since 1972, as were reformist elements within the regime.

Did any factors outside Spain have an impact on the transition to democracy? If we compare the cases of Spain and Portugal, there is no doubt whatever that in the latter intervention by the western powers played a far greater role, especially when the Carnation Revolution began to move towards less democratic solutions. There was only vague general pressure on Spain, and this can be demonstrated quite easily by comparing the presence or absence of representatives from other countries at the ceremonies that marked Franco's death and Juan Carlos I's coronation. Nevertheless, given that Spain itself took the lead in its transitional process, the democratic countries did not feel obliged to offer continuing help or even a minimum of cooperation. The United States, which initially had not understood the need to legalize the Communist Party, then later, at the time of the attempted coup on February 23, published an unfortunate communiqué in which it seemed to be turning its back on Spain's political evolution. The agreement between Spain and America in 1976 had been the start of a more mature, evenly balanced relationship between the two countries, which resulted in a reduction in the number of service personnel stationed in Zaragoza and a Spanish refusal to store American nuclear weapons. France was the country that put the most obstacles in the way of Spain's entry into the Common Market and it also did nothing to help in the fight against terrorism. As for transnational political organizations, they did perform an important function, but it was one that did not act decisively on the configuration of the system of political parties in Spain. Finally, we must refer to the way in which events in Portugal affected Spain. Each country influenced the other and the results were positive. Portugal, which took the lead, exposed the fragility of the dictatorships in the Iberian Peninsula. Then, over the course of 1975 – the most revolutionary phase of the Portuguese transition – what was happening there might well have struck fear into the hearts of Spanish Conservatives, but by the time the transition began in Spain the situation had settled down in Portugal. Last but not least, the political solution that was finally chosen in the neighboring country was actually similar to the UCD in Spain.

It is important to mention briefly the foreign policy that Spain's governments pursued over this period. During Arias's time in office, an initiative was brought forward to take a step towards improving relations with the Catholic Church by giving up the right to nominate bishops. In fact this measure was implemented by Areilza and his under-secretary Oreja and at first some of the king's advisers opposed it. After January 1976, full diplomatic relations with the rest of Europe were renewed, but real change came later; Spain's withdrawal from the Sahara in a shorter time than that anticipated in Franco's day shows how extremely weak its political circumstances were, and this inevitably affected foreign policy.

Marcelino Oreja, as Minister for Foreign Affairs, was himself the key person in the first stage of the transition, even more so than Suárez. In July 1976 agreements were signed which meant that, at the moment when the state renounced its right to nominate bishops, the Vatican gave up its ecclesiastical privileges in Spain. The role of mediator was entrusted to the king, whose prestige therefore increased. The ratification of agreements on human rights underwritten by international organizations anticipated what would later be set out in the Constitution. The state applied for membership of certain bodies such as the European Economic Community and the Council of Europe, access to which had been impossible during the Franco years. In October 1977 it asked to join the Parliamentary Assembly of the Council of Europe. In only 4 months, at the start of 1977, while Areilza was still Foreign Minister, Spain established full diplomatic relations with the countries of Eastern Europe with whom it already had trading contacts from an earlier stage.

The legacy left by the Sahara question put Spain in a precarious position, but Oreja made it quite clear that the Saharaui people must be consulted. Spanish foreign policy zigzagged between the different countries of North Africa, to such an extent that at the end of 1977 it broke off relations with Algeria and in 1980 seemed instead to align itself more with Morocco. At the end of 1977 it seemed conceivable that the existence of an artificially generated independence movement in the Canaries might serve as a pretext for possible decolonization of the islands to feature on the agenda of the Organization for African Unity. In January 1979 – that is to say, only a few days after the Constitution was ratified – four concordats were signed which governed all areas of relations between Church and state. On this matter, and on the regulation of the religious question in the Constitution, there was consensus on the part of all political factions.

Approval of the Constitution brought with it a change in Spain's foreign policy. Until that moment all political parties had agreed on a negative stance, while priority had undoubtedly been given to internal affairs. Now parties all had their own priorities and disagreements arose. Entry into the European Common Market, which was for the majority of Spaniards an obvious part of Spain's democratic transformation, was one factor that united them, but was also, at the same time, impossible. In June 1980 the French president, Giscard D'Estaing, voiced his outright opposition to Spain's entry into the Community. On the other hand, it seemed that for once Spain's relations with another major European power, the United Kingdom, were set to improve considerably. In April 1980, for the first time, the British agreed to hold talks on all questions relating to Gibraltar and therefore also to the matter of the sovereignty of the Rock.

The partial modification of Spain's foreign policy after 1978 was due to a change not only in priorities but also in more fundamental questions. The main responsibility for this turn of events probably belonged to Suárez.

The split between him and Oreja in part explains the latter's dismissal. In any event, the prime minister's attitude was based on a mixture of remembering the politically ambiguous stance of an earlier period, the desire to avoid terrorism in Spain and, above all, a wish to play every trump card he had in order to arrive at a clear definition of Spain's future role on the world stage. The Spanish prime minister's position may have "relied overmuch on having a nose for politics" but in the event it went no further than making gestures aimed at asserting his own independence.

Calvo's Sotelo's rise to power also meant a slight change in direction for Spain's foreign policy, and this became evident as soon as José Pedro Pérez Llorca was made Minister for Foreign Affairs. The UCD was trying to achieve clearer definition and this could happen if its foreign policy were brought into line with that of the rest of the western world. In fact Spain had been a part of the Western Block since its treaties with the United States in 1953, but it had been something of a poor relation with no authority, only able exert indirect pressure and without an effective role to play. It may well be that a consideration of some weight in the decision to join NATO was a desire for the Spanish Army to be involved in a wider European context, but this meant confrontation with the PSOE. What the UCD did was to put the PSOE in the position in which the German social democrats found themselves when they agreed to membership of NATO after a Christian Democrat government had decided that the Federal Republic would become a member.

Calvo Sotelo's solution was clearly viable and a move in the right direction. Spain was invited to join NATO by all the organization's existing members, including Greece which had a socialist government. In Parliament he won the support of sectors other than the UCD (189 votes – that is to say the center, the right, and the Basque and Catalan nationalists – against 146 votes). "It was," commented Pérez Llorca, "the last time that the government had such a clear majority and the unanimous support of its own parliamentary party."

The PSOE's attitude of dogged opposition was nonetheless expressed in terms so firm that they caused a decisive change in public opinion. If in 1975 some 57 percent of Spaniards were in favor of entry into NATO and only 24 percent were against, the percentages had altered dramatically by 1981 to 17 and 56 percent respectively. This swing, which would prove very inconvenient when the PSOE opted to stay in NATO, produced significant electoral dividends in the short term. The catch-phrase that the PSOE used to attract tens of thousands of followers at this moment ("No to entry") seemed to hold out a promise, if only an ambiguous one, of leaving the organization.

There was, on the other hand, clear continuity on two matters in Spanish policy over the entire political spectrum from the governments of the center through to the socialists: Latin America and Israel. Concerning the former, the Spanish Constitution gave the crown a vital role that it had taken on a few months after Franco's death. Don Juan Carlos very quickly showed his eagerness to contribute to the existence of a Latin American Community of Nations. In March 1977 relations were resumed with Mexico which had received a significant percentage of Spanish exiles in 1939. As for Israel, the killing of Palestinians in Sabra and Shatila in the summer of 1982 prevented relations being resumed, which was another sign of Spain's close identification with the other European countries.

## Economic Policy and Social Change

"It fell to me to govern Spain at the worst moment in the entire economic crisis," wrote Calvo Sotelo in his memoirs, and Miguel Boyer, a future socialist minister, has agreed. Calvo Sotelo's statement applies and is valid for the whole political transition, which we should also examine through this particular lens even if only in general terms.

In 1973 the Spanish economy still seemed buoyant but appearances were belied by reality. In that year economic growth stood at 8 percent, unemployment was barely above 1 percent and inflation was at 11 percent. However, although the public sector was smaller, that did not prevent the state intervening in all areas because the process of liberalization had ground to a halt. The business sector was not very innovative, and since 1964 only a million jobs had been created. A youthful population and women's access to the work market were about to cause a sharp rise in unemployment. The state was handicapped by its lack of revenue from taxation. The trebling of the price of crude oil at the start of the 1970s reduced its purchasing power abroad by a fifth, or a loss of three points in terms of GDP. The decisions that were taken after the oil price rise went contrary to decisions taken by other OECD countries. Instead of transferring the rise in energy prices onto costs, an attempt was made to avoid any impact on the Spanish economy by generating a widespread public response. This is why the timing of Spain's economic crisis was different from that in other countries. In Spain, in practice, the effects of the first rise in petrol prices had not dissipated before the second crisis hit the country in 1979. It was only resolved finally in 1985–6, 3 years after the rest of the west began its recovery.

As had been the case in 1931, these events gave the impression that democracy had arrived in Spain at the worst possible moment. Indeed, in the period 1976–82 the average yearly growth rate was a mere 1.4 percent, far below that not only of the 1960s but also of the years after 1985. In 1977 – the decisive year of the transition – the state was in effect bankrupt and inflation reached 30 percent in the month following the elections (having reached 42 percent in some earlier years).

The policies that were pursued with more or less success by governments of the center continued to be implemented by successive socialist governments; indeed, there were no "substantial differences in terms of their concerns, their focus, or the priorities they set" between the two tendencies, which is understandable if we consider that the measures were implemented by members of a uniform class of leading civil servants who were at first social democrats and then more strongly liberal, all of whom believed that the state had the major responsibility in the economic field.

There were few advances made while the center was in power. After a devaluation of 20 percent, and thanks to a restrictive monetary policy towards the end of 1978 as a result of the Moncloa Pacts, inflation had been brought down to 16.5 percent (that is, down by a third of the previous difference between Spain and the rest of Europe) and the balance of payments was at last showing a positive figure of 1,500 million dollars. However it was simply no longer possible to continue with the economic policy devised after 1979 despite the fact that it had been intended to serve for a further year, besides which the most recent rise in the price of crude cost two more points of the GDP. What became characteristic of this situation was the tendency to put off necessary decisions. Re-conversion did not begin until 1981 because before that date there was nothing more on offer than state aid and a timid plan for Spain's shipyards. At the same time, there was explosive social conflict fanned by the belligerent attitude of the UGT: there were more strikes in 1979 than in the 2 preceding years. The one exception was the banking sector. Between 1975 and the start of the 1980s, almost half of Spain's financial organizations suffered badly during the crisis and many collapsed or changed hands. To solve this problem an institution had to be set up to mediate between the state and private banks: the Fund to Guarantee Deposits (*Fondo de Garantía de Depósitos*). By 1982 a billion pesetas had been spent in this way. In the mean time, between 1978 and 1984 more than 20 percent of employment in industry had been destroyed: a figure higher than that in Italy or France but below the figure in Britain. There was negative economic growth in 1980 and 1981, while inflation remained fixed at around 14 to 15 percent and the balance of payments deficit that had accumulated in the period 1980–2 rose to 14,270 million dollars.

Although the process was only in its early stages, during the transition itself there was discernible social change which worked towards greater equality. The main factor behind such changes was increased funding for social affairs, which was a volatile sector between 1977 and 1981. This tendency in Spanish life at the time, which would become irreversible over the 1980s, can best be appreciated by considering the state's involvement with the GDP, which rose by 50 percent while in the rest of the Common Market it remained more or less stationary. It was not for nothing that Spain, during the period of the transition, was one of the countries in the world where fiscal pressures increased fastest.

Another important factor to be borne in mind was the presence of trade unions in the world of work. One might say that in general they tailored their demands to circumstances, partly due to their links with the political parties. So, for example, *Comisiones Obreras*, along with the PCE, always judged that Spain had barely had time to consolidate as a democracy and therefore demands had to be reasonable. The UGT was at times more pushy in accordance with the Socialists' policy of harassing the government.

Very soon, however, Spanish trade unions began to coordinate their action. The Moncloa Pacts brought about a decrease in salaries in real terms, with a commitment to increased public spending and a leveling of pay for different types of workers. Spanish trade unionism had soon moved light years away from the northern European model, keeping going with very low percentages of members. This did not mean that workers did not vote in union elections. They did, and as time went by there was also a growing if imperfect dual unionism, evident in the fact that if the two main groups between them barely gained 55 percent of posts in the first election, by the 1980s, in contrast, they won 80 percent. As we know, *Comisiones* won a clear victory over the UGT in the first elections (34 percent as against 21 percent), but in 1982 it was the UGT that won. Political circumstances at the time can be seen as explaining this change, but it is important to bear in mind too that the third trade union – the USO – split, and most of its leadership went to swell the ranks of the socialist union. The great paradox was that the emergence of trade union power coincided with the moment at which a new phenomenon came to the fore: unemployment.

There were other changes taking place in the midst of a kind of "anomia," as though the old norms of conduct had ceased to apply without any new ones replacing them. At the start of the 1980s, for example, only a third of Spaniards were practicing Catholics, though the influence of Catholicism in Spanish society remained far greater than these figures would seem to suggest.

By 1982 it was already evident that the role of women was increasing. The first women's associations had appeared around the 1960s, but it was only in the 1970s that they began to have any social impact. In 1974 the first family-planning clinic opened its doors though it was still illegal, and that same year, the Mayor of Madrid declared that women who wanted to work should not get married. The situation began to change more rapidly after 1975, the year in which the wife's obligation to obey her husband disappeared, although the legal equality of husband and wife in marriage did not become effective until 1981. Meanwhile, women were beginning to win acceptance for their changing role in society. Between 1974 and 1982 the number of women with technical qualifications working in state civil administration rose from 19 to 34 percent. In 1980 the percentage of women with university qualifications was 11 percent for the age bracket 40–9, while among those between 20 and 29 the percentage was as high as 50 percent. In the Francoist *Cortes* there had barely been 1.4 percent of women but by 1979 this figure had risen to 6 percent; in union elections the figure of women elected was 11 percent. Women had begun to move forward in a way that would now be unstoppable.

## October 1982: The End of the Transition

As regards Spanish socialism, the transformation it underwent over the course of its two party conferences in 1979 proved decisive as it moved from a very radical position – at least in theory – to a more reformist stance that was able to connect more effectively with the majority of Spanish society.

The first conference was held in May 1979. The left wing argued at that time that the position the party had adopted was too compliant, with the added disadvantage that this had not resulted in major electoral gains. In contrast, those closest to González who had declared his opposition to Marxism, believed that the program should quite simply be aiming to "modernize" Spanish society from a position of power. When the first socialist conference took place there was an explosion of tensions that proved impossible to control. It was the result of an ideological overload, and of a kind of frustration in the face of a process of adaptation to reality by a political group that had come from opposing a regime that had only disappeared just 2 years earlier. A debate such as this had little or nothing to do with the interests and preoccupations of the socialist voters and even less so with voters in general. González refused to continue as the party's general secretary and thus created a vacuum and provoked an ideological debate that did not go very far but did resolve some issues.

At the September conference only about 400 delegates took part in comparison to the 1,000 or so in May. Those who voiced criticism were soundly defeated, obtaining only 7 percent of the votes. Alfonso Guerra, at the head of the Andalusian delegation, voted on behalf of 30 percent of those attending the conference. Whatever the circumstances, the ideological problem seemed to disappear. The political resolution of differences began with the program that had been approved by the party in 1979; it then stated clearly that the PSOE was a democratic party that represented the masses and favored federalism. On a matter of political theory, it now stated that Marxism was a "theoretical and critical tool, not a dogma," to be used for analysis and for transforming reality. In fact, the tone used remained radical, and capitalism and "social-democratization" were rejected, though it was clear that appearance and reality were now further apart than ever.

Along with all these issues, there had been a change in the make-up of the party and this had set an enormous distance between the new PSOE and that of the 1930s. At the start of the 1980s only one in six members were non-specialized workers and only one in three had not had more than basic schooling. Spain's new socialist party now had members in the middle and professional classes. It was a very young party with 63 percent of active members under 35, while 45 percent had joined after 1977. Four in every ten of them claimed to hold religious beliefs. The 1981 conference was entirely peaceful and there were no serious disagreements; the resolutions taken retained a radical ideological component which would end up contrasting strongly with the politics of Felipe González's later governments. Before the economic crisis, the PSOE had tried to stimulate demand by increasing the deficit to kick-start reactivation and to widen the distribution of labor. On foreign policy, too, the PSOE held to a position that was further to the left than was usual elsewhere in Europe (though it was more common in French and Greek socialism). According to the conference resolution, Spain could make an important contribution towards diffusing tensions between the two world power-blocks if it delayed its entry into NATO, and it should work towards building a stable relationship with the group of non-aligned countries.

More important than the PSOE's program was its strategy. In the resolutions just mentioned the Socialist Party defined the UCD as a party that had shifted from Suárez's lukewarm vote-winning reformism to an attitude that inclined more towards conservatism and capitalism: the position represented by Calvo Sotelo. The new UCD would be incapable of "dismantling the network of the civil conspiracy" against democracy. Doubtless the party in government did much to damage its own position.

The PSOE was also helped by a process similar to the one facing the PCE. October 1977 saw the publication of Jorge Semprún's *Autobiografía de Federico Sánchez* (*Federico Sánchez's Autobiography*) in which the author launched a fierce attack on Santiago Carrillo's past history and fired a first salvo in the demythification of communism. Carrillo managed to put forward a proposal and remove Leninism from among the inspirational elements of his party, but he never gave up his belief that the dictatorship of the proletariat was necessary in Russia. His "revolutionary Marxism" continued to advocate a high level of "democratic centralism," and a personalized style of party leadership.

After the 1979 elections all the tensions that had plagued the PCE suddenly came to a head and exploded. The party gained some 220,000 additional votes and topped 10 percent of the electoral total, but it nonetheless saw its position as a party with little influence in parliament accentuated. Carrillo then tried to increase party unity by launching an offensive against the Catalan communists who had seen their share of the vote remain fixed, and whom he considered far too strongly nationalist and pro-Russia. By intervening he not only failed to restore discipline within the party but also aggravated existing dissentions. In the Basque Country a large part of the PCE ended up joining nationalist left-wing groups as a reaction against these events. As a last-ditch attempt, Carrillo faced up to the professional sectors of the party and that was, perhaps, when his worst problems began.

The general elections in October 1982 can be seen as the final moments of Spain's transition to democracy. Although in terms of institutionalization the transition had ended in December 1978, it should nonetheless be seen as having continued right up to the elections because stable democracy was not confirmed until the socialist victory of 1982, which is evident in the fact that the figure of 9 percent of Spaniards with an anti-constitutional stance before February 1981 went down to 5 percent by the time of the 1982 elections. What happened in 1982 was an obvious electoral earthquake of enduring impact, which was seen as a deep incision forever severing the present from the past. In October 1982, 10,000,000 Spaniards changed the way they voted: the equivalent of 40 percent of the electorate as a whole and half of those who actually voted.

This change in electoral choices had a long history. From April to June 1982 the PSOE share of the vote went from 24 to 30 percent, while the UCD went down from 13 to 10 percent. October 1982 was probably when pre-electoral campaigning had the least impact on the results of the polls. The socialist motto "For change" was not so much an electoral manifesto as the expression of a general will to change the way that politics was practiced. The spectacle of splits within parties had been too transparently obvious for the UCD or PCE to set the situation to rights now. Many left-wing voters saw the PSOE as the only real possibility of change in government and 3,200,000 members of the electorate moved from doing nothing to voting.

The PSOE won more than 10 million votes, of which some 4.5 million came from previous abstentions or other political parties. In total, 48 percent of voters chose the PSOE, which therefore had 202 deputies in comparison to the AP–PDP coalition (Christian democrats from the UCD), whose vote was around half that of the socialists. The latter had managed to win massive support from young people who were now voting for the first time, and also from the urban middle classes who were especially responsive to the information put out daily by the media. The socialists swallowed up half the previously communist vote and 30 percent of the center, and were a clear winner in all professional and occupational sectors except among employers. In addition, 35 percent of practicing and 55 percent of non-practicing Catholics also voted socialist. It was clear that the PSOE had moved from being the party in power on the left to being the party in power over the entire political spectrum. It was as though a pluralist party system had become like that in Sweden at the time, choosing one party with a great many more votes than its nearest rival, and therefore capable of offering a long period of stability in government with only a few minor changes.

The AP–PDP coalition gained vastly more votes than Fraga had done in 1979. If earlier on only 6 percent of the vote had been won, now in contrast the figure was almost 5.5 million or 26 percent. It was more a right-wing vote than a vote of the center, and it therefore had the disadvantage that if any attempt was made to satisfy this particular electorate, any party doing so would distance itself from where the majority of Spanish society situated itself politically. For its part, the UCD suffered a total collapse. After having had 35 percent of the vote it went down to something less than 7 percent. Its members scattered in both directions: 30 percent of those who had voted UCD in 1979 now voted PSOE, while 40 percent opted for the AP–PDP. This was not, however, the worst blow; rather it was that the voters who remained were marginal and only deferred to whoever was in power. The typical UCD voter in these elections was a country housewife. Hopes for the future looked brighter for the PCE, but they won only 4 percent of the vote in 1982 whereas in 1979 the figure had been 10 percent. As a result, Spanish communism scored lowest on the electoral scale over the whole western Mediterranean. The imperturbable loyalty of the nationalist electorate in Catalonia and the Basque Country was confirmed in these and subsequent elections.

In fact the changes were far less sweeping than they seemed, as only 13 percent of voters changed their allegiance on the self-positioning political scale. Be that as it may, the PSOE took power at that moment under the best possible auspices. González managed to gain a popularity rating of 7.5 out of 10, which was not only higher than any other European leader including Suárez when he was at his most popular, but for the first and only time topped the rating of the king at that moment. In other words, a new political journey was beginning in the most favorable conditions imaginable.

To conclude this chapter it seems that we must draw up a balance of Spain's transition to democracy in terms of its positive and negative points. Compared with the rest of the "third wave" of democratization, the Spanish case comes out as clearly positive. Many Latin American countries still had "pockets of authoritarianism." The fragility of their democracy was evident in the emergence of all-powerful leaders or popular power-blocks or, most of all, in the fact that a large section of their populations did not believe in democracy as the only possible political system. As for the dozens of ex-communist countries, apart from the grave problems they faced concerning territorial boundaries, in the 1990s only about five or six at most were clearly on the road to democracy. If we take the case of Greece and Portugal as points of comparison, the difficulties facing Spain in her transition to democracy were greater, and yet the different kinds of traumas experienced were fewer. The consensus in Spain was exemplary, as was the will to offer an amnesty to the former enemy, pardoning all crimes committed before June 1977. In this sense the Spanish transition can only really be compared to the transition in Poland.

It would, however, be a mistake to consider that what happened in Spain was unrepeatable and a model case. There are also negative elements to be weighed up. Many of the decisions that won a consensus vote were the result of agreements reached at the very last moment. "It's going to get through!" a journalist heard someone exclaim from the back row at a constitutional commission when the prime minister requested an amendment on educational matters. The mobilization of the population as a whole was limited and even went down, and the measures in place to avoid a repetition of the events in the 1930s created a kind of excessively tutelary attitude towards Spanish citizens, who seemed straitjacketed by formulae that did much to distance the political system from the popular dynamism that it needed. A quarter of a century after the Constitution was approved, the life of Spain's democracy would be threatened more by the cancer of skepticism than the coronary of a military coup, and yet this attitude was also proof that Spain is not so very different from other democratic countries.

## Bibliography

The transition to democracy in a wider context: Juan José LINZ in collaboration with Alfred STEPAN, *Problems of democratic transition and consolidation. Southern Europe, South America and postcommunist Europe*, The Johns Hopkins University Press, Baltimore and London, 1996; José María MARAVALL, *Los resultados de la democracia. Un estudio del sur y del este de Europa*, Alianza Editorial, Madrid, 1995; Guillermo O'DONNELL, Philippe SCHMITTER, and Laurence WHITE-HEAD, *Transitions from authoritarian rule*, 4 vols. The Johns Hopkins University Press, Baltimore and London, 1986.

Immediate forerunners and general works: Raymond CARR and Juan Pablo FUSI, *España, de la dictadura a la democracia*, Planeta, Barcelona, 1979 (*Spain, dictatorship to democracy*, London: Allen & Unwin, 1979); Ramón COTARELO, *Transición política y consolidación democrática (1975–1986)*, CIS, Madrid, 1992; Rafael LÓPEZ PINTOR, *La opinión pública española: del franquismo a la democracia*, CIS, Madrid, 1982; José María MARÍN, in *Historia política, 1939–2000*, vol. XVIII, Istmo, Madrid, 2001; Álvaro SOTO, *La transición a la democracia en España, 1975–1982*, Alianza Editorial, Madrid, 1996; *Veinticinco años de reinado de S.M. Don Juan Carlos I*, Espasa Calpe-Real Academia de la Historia,

Madrid, 2002; Charles POWELL, *España en democracia, 1975–2000*, Plaza y Janés, Barcelona, 2001.

Essays: Josep M. COLOMER, *El arte de la manipulación política*, Anagrama, Barcelona, 1990; Julián MARÍAS, *La España real*, Espasa Calpe, Madrid, 1976, *La devolución de España*, Espasa Calpe, Madrid, 1977 and *España en nuestras manos*, Espasa Calpe, Madrid, 1978.

Journalistic accounts: Joaquín BARDAVIO, *Sábado Santo Rojo*, Ediciones Uve, Madrid, 1980; Josep MELIÀ, *Así cayó Adolfo Suárez*, Planeta, Barcelona, 1981; Santos JULIÀ, Javier PRADERA, and Joaquín PRIETO (coordinators), *Memoria de la transición*, Taurus, Madrid, 1996; José ONETO, *Los últimos días de un presidente. De la dimisión al golpe de Estado*, Planeta, Barcelona, 1981, and *La noche de Tejero*, Planeta, Barcelona, 1981; Victoria PREGO, *Así se hizo la transición*, Plaza y Janés, Barcelona, 1995.

On King Juan Carlos: Charles T. POWELL, *El piloto del cambio. El rey, la monarquía y la transición a la democracia*, Planeta, Barcelona, 1991, and *Juan Carlos. Un rey para la democracia*, Ariel-Planeta, Barcelona, 1995 (*Juan Carlos of Spain, self-made monarch*, Houndmills (Hampshire), Macmillan, 1996); Carlos SECO SERRANO, *Juan Carlos I*, Anaya, Madrid, 1989; Javier TUSELL, *Juan Carlos I. La restauración de la monarquía*, Temas de Hoy, Madrid, 1995; José Luis VILLA-LONGA, *El rey*, Plaza y Janés, Barcelona, 1993.

Memoirs: José María de AREILZA, *Cuadernos de la transición*, Planeta, Barcelona, 1983, and *Diario de un ministro de la monarquía*, Planeta, Barcelona, 1977; Leopoldo CALVO SOTELO, *Memoria viva de la transición*, Plaza y Janés, Barcelona, 1990; Santiago CARRILLO, *Memorias*, Planeta, Barcelona, 1993; Manuel FRAGA IRIBARNE, *En busca del tiempo servido*, Planeta, Barcelona, 1987; Miguel HERRERO, *Memorias de estío*, Temas de Hoy, Madrid, 1993; Carlos GARAICOE-CHEA, *Euskadi: la transición inacabada. Memorias políticas*, Planeta, Barcelona, 2002; Laureano LÓPEZ RODÓ, *Claves de la transición. Memorias*, Plaza y Janés-Cambio 16, Barcelona, 1993; Rodolfo MARTÍN VILLA, *Al servicio del Estado*, Planeta, Barcelona, 1984; Alfonso OSSORIO, *Trayectoria de un ministro de la Corona*, Planeta, Barcelona, 1980; Salvador SÁNCHEZ TERÁN, *De Franco a la Generalitat*, Planeta, Barcelona, 1988; Josep TARRADELLAS, *Ja soc aquí. Recuerdo de un retorno*, Planeta, Barcelona, 1990.

Biographies: Carlos ABELLA, *Adolfo Suárez*, Espasa Calpe, Madrid, 1997; Alfonso FERNÁNDEZ MIRANDA, *Lo que el rey me ha pedido. Torcuato Fernández Miranda y la reforma política*, Plaza y Janés, Barcelona, 1995; Antonio LAMELAS, *La transición en Abril. Biografía de Fernando Abril*, Ariel, Barcelona, 2004.

Monographs: Paloma AGUILAR, *Memoria y olvido de la guerra civil*, Alianza Editorial, Madrid, 1996; Felipe AGÜERO, *Militares, civiles y democracia. La España posfranquista en perspectiva comparada*, Alianza Editorial, Madrid, 1995; Javier FERNÁNDEZ LÓPEZ, *El rey y otros militares*, Trotta, Madrid, 1998, and *Dieciséis horas y media. El enigma del 23-F*, Taurus, Madrid, 2000.

Writing the Constitution: G. CISNEROS, M. FRAGA, M. HERRERO DE MIÑÓN, G. PECES BARBA, J. P. PÉREZ LLORCA, M. ROCA JUNYENT, and J. SOLÉ TURA, *Veinte años después. La Constitución cara al siglo XXI*, Taurus, Madrid, 1998; Soledad GALLEGO-DÍAZ and Bonifacio de la CUADRA, *Crónica secreta de la Constitución*, Tecnos, Madrid, 1989; Gregorio PECES BARBA, *La elaboración de la Constitución de 1978*, Centro de Estudios Constitucionales, Madrid, 1988.

Political groups: Juan José LINZ and José Ramón MONTERO, *Crisis y cambio. Electores y partidos en la España de los años ochenta*, Centro de Estudios Constitucionales, Madrid, 1986; Jonathan HOPKIN, *Party formation and democratic transition in Spain. The creation and collapse of the Union of the Democratic Center*, Macmillan, London, 1999; Carlos HUNNEUS, *La Unión de Centro Democrático y la transición a la democracia en España*, CIS-Siglo XXI, Madrid, 1985; José María MARAVALL, *La política de la transición, 1975–1980*, Taurus, Madrid, 1981. Trade unions: Robert M. FISHMAN, *Organización obrera y retorno de la democracia en España*, CIS, Madrid, 1996.

The question of autonomy: Juan José LINZ, *Conflicto en Euskadi*, Espasa Calpe, Madrid, 1986; Francisco J. LLERA, *Posfranquismo y fuerzas políticas en Euskadi. Sociología electoral del País Vasco*, Universidad del País Vasco, Bilbao, 1985; Gregorio MORÁN, *Los españoles que dejaron de serlo*, Planeta, Barcelona, 1982; John SULLIVAN, *El nacionalismo vasco radical, 1969–1986*, Alianza Editorial, Madrid, 1988 (*ETA and Basque Nationalism: the fight for Euskadi 1890–1986*, London, Routledge, 1988).

Foreign policy: Richard GILLESPIE, Fernando RODRIGO, and Jonathan STORY, *Las relaciones exteriores de la España democrática* Alianza Editorial, Madrid, 1995 (*Democratic Spain: reshaping external relations in a changing world*, London, Routledge, 1995); Charles T. POWELL, "Un 'hombre-puente' en la política exterior española: el caso de Marcelino Oreja," *Historia Contemporánea*, no. 15 (1996); Josep SÁNCHEZ CERVELLÓ, *La revolución portuguesa y su influencia en la transición española (1961–1976)*, Nerea, Madrid, 1995.

On the economy: José Luis GARCÍA DELGADO (ed.), *Economía española de la transición y la democracia*, CIS, Madrid, 1990; Joan TRULLEN, *Fundamentos económicos de la transición política. La política económica de los acuerdos de la Moncloa*, Ministerio de Trabajo, Madrid, 1993.

# 5

# Consolidating Democracy: The Socialist Government (1982–96)

Spain's most recent history – the consequences of which are still being felt in the political arena today – has been marked by a desire to synthesize, and by an attempt to leave behind anything that is no longer relevant after a time, and which therefore may be considered of purely topical interest. One of Borges's characters, Ireneo, known as the Rememberer because he remembered everything and was unable to forget, in the end was unable to grasp the overall sense of all he knew. This should be the aim of the historian, despite the doubtful nature of the sources he has at his disposal when he studies his own period.

By 1982 Spanish democracy had consolidated in terms of its general outline. The socialist victory had strengthened it and had brought the transition to a close in areas that had remained for a time open to discussion, such as foreign policy and the armed forces. The new executive allowed governmental action to move its center of gravity away from the strictly and essentially political into other areas such as economic updating, the organization of a Spanish state with autonomous regions, and the defining and implementing of a true Welfare State.

It is without doubt the socialist government that should be identified most closely with the normalization of democracy, which is the usual final phase for any transitional process in any country. The content of its legislation did not mean a complete overturning of the past; instead it kept some continuity, for example in economic matters. It has therefore been possible to describe this stage as a kind of "decade of moderation" (Ernest Lluch), though there is no doubt that for a large section of the Spanish population – the left – this was felt to be the real start of democracy in Spain, and there was also a kind of resurgence of the enthusiasm that had last been experienced in April 1931, at the proclamation of the Second

Republic. When Felipe González chose his ministers and determined his party's foreign policy, he bore in mind at every moment what had happened in Spain in the 1930s when the left had first tried to bring about sweeping reforms.

## Felipe González and the Two Souls of Spanish Socialism

In one of the books on political propaganda published in 1982, Felipe González was described as a mixture of "didacticism [ ... ], common sense, a lack of formality, and a certain dose of illusion tempered with pragmatism." "A feeling of approachability" did much to ensure that he had an excellent public image over a long period of time. Even during elections, when he was under attack from his opponents, he managed nevertheless to keep his popularity ratings high. What is unusual about him is that he did so across the entire ideological spectrum. The extreme left, for example, gave him a rating that was not far short of excellent (6.4 out of 10).

As a personality on the political stage, Felipe González dominated Spanish public life for almost 15 years and played a leading role both before and after this time. He came to the party leadership when he was only 32 years old, and he was 40 when he became prime minister. He was born in Seville in 1942, into a very hardworking middle-class family which was quite well-off but lived simply and had strong links with the agricultural community. A mediocre student, his early background was in progressive Catholic circles rather than the traditional left. Once he had finished his degree, he worked for a time as a labor lawyer: a job that he combined with activities in opposition politics. His personal style of leadership tended to attract followers naturally from early on, which also explains how it was that his popularity lasted so long. His achievement was largely due to his accessibility and his capacity for analysis of the current political situation. He was not influenced during the final phase of Francoism by the political persecution to which he was subjected – which was relatively light in comparison with what many suffered – but he was affected, in contrast, by the loneliness he experienced when he first moved from Seville to Madrid.

He was soon seen in political circles as the representative of a new political generation – the very antithesis of Franco and Francoist politics. Eduardo

Haro wrote that Felipe González was the first face of anti-Francoism, and that is a good description: he represented, as nobody else did, the youthful impulse for change in Spain, which was often accompanied by oversimplification and ingenuousness but was also sincere and enthusiastic. Unlike the rest of this younger generation, however, it is almost impossible to detect in González any sign of an initial radicalism that would with time become more temperate. "I must confess that I always was a moderate," he stated in 2002, on the twentieth anniversary of his rise to power. The model he favored was always northern European social democracy and not any kind of "nonexistent socialism," somewhere between communism and labor politics, towards which not a few of his followers had leanings. He maintained close ties of friendship with Willy Brandt, but perhaps he can be seen to have had the closest affinity of all with Olof Palme; he once said that Palme could produce "the most simple analysis thanks to the most complex knowledge." He never, for example, doubted for one moment that he should keep to the most orthodox economic policies in order then to be able to share out the social benefits, and in general he was able to keep control among his ministers on this matter.

Felipe González managed to become one of the longest-lasting political leaders in Europe, ahead of the British prime minister Margaret Thatcher and second only to Helmuth Kohl in Germany. An excellent public speaker, as much in Parliament as in election campaigns or when facing the media, González always had a complementary and most enviable gift for simplifying his message. Together with his idealism and pragmatism, he also knew how to enable the majority of people to share his interpretation of matters under discussion, and this enabled him, even at moments of crisis for his government, to maintain a high level of support for him as leader, well above that enjoyed by his party. His leadership was never seriously questioned until the electoral defeat of 1996, but as he himself declared, it had become a "leadership living beyond its capabilities" which, with the passage of time, became part of the PSOE's problem rather than its solution. Even so, he was not only the party's best candidate throughout all those years but he also had the ability to rise above internal disputes, both when they were trivial and when they were directed against him personally, and the prudence not to stir up trouble unnecessarily.

He was able to do this because he was exceptionally well endowed with the skills needed for political life in a democracy. Those around him were always impressed by his ability to anticipate and analyze: "Listening to Felipe thinking aloud was an inestimable privilege," wrote one minister. Suárez lacked all these qualities, and this explains why he was unable to hold a political party together. Not only that, but as can be shown with many examples, González often imposed his own direction on a party that was not itself tending to go that way. The truth is that he could seem quite detached as regards the party – at times excessively so – at moments when the party tended to be weighed down by radical ideology and in need of a more pragmatic approach.

González brought a breath of fresh air to Spanish politics, almost as though the country was now in the hands of a nonprofessional. Nonetheless, although they remained imperceptible at first, he had some of the most dubious propensities of which politics, in the worst sense of the word, is capable. He was not generally a leader who courted unnecessary confrontation, though this was not because of any personal insecurity or lack of confidence in his own strengths. It meant that he was able to affirm, towards the end of his time in office, that he had exercised power "without resentment." At the same time, he seems to have been unaware that he could not risk failing to keeping a vigilant eye on all aspects of action taken by his own party – not forgetting a certain inevitable "leakage" via cracks in the basic structures of financial affairs. Nor did respect for the delicate balance between Spain's democratic institutions weigh heavily enough with him; rather, he tended to count exclusively on his election victories to justify passing legislation that could have worked better with a degree of consensus. Above all, he could sometimes give the impression, by word and deed, that seeing how well supported he was by an impressive harvest of votes, he felt entitled to choose – or let others choose – measures that were quick-acting in the short term but entirely reprehensible from a moral standpoint in order to reach his objective. The scale of his political power, and his move from an overly strong ideological emphasis to pragmatism, also help to explain his tendency to take shortcuts that seemed effective but later produced dangerous results that were also more than debatable from an ethical point of view.

It remains the case that under Felipe González Spanish democracy had its first leader who could handle the ordinary everyday business of democratic politics under normal conditions. Although he was far less intellectually able than Manuel Azaña in the 1930s, while González was in power he was much more successful at performing the tasks of setting the calendar, the priorities, and the content for implementing reform. It is true that circumstances were, logically, very different from the 1930s. Looking back, González was far kinder than he had been in opposition towards governments of the center and towards the man who had led them. González stated that he had always respected Adolfo Suárez, in the same way as he had been aware of the constraints that Suárez faced in the political climate that existed between 1976 and 1981. In many more respects than are usually stated, there was in Spain's socialist governments a marked degree of continuity with what had gone before.

Shortly after leaving power, in a speech given before a university audience, González summed up the achievements of his Administration in five points and one sentence. The sentence spoke of the lack of any feeling of resentment that we have already mentioned, and it has to be said that previously, in his opposition years, he had often insisted on this point, even when it was not necessary to do so. The problem during his term in office was not one of resentment – which may indeed have been more of a factor for the opposition – so much as overconfidence. The five points that the ex-prime minister cited in summing up his achievement in office were: the modernization and liberalization of the Spanish economy; improvements in the quality of life due to greater social cohesion; the improvement in physical conditions; the drawing up of the Constitution, as much in terms of the reform of the Armed Services as of the setting up of a Spanish state composed of autonomous regions; and finally the breaking down of barriers, inherited from the past, that had cut Spain off from the rest of the world. In none of these areas is it possible to say that the actions of the socialist government were entirely original or flawless, but the points that the ex-prime minister listed were in general terms an apt choice. Not even the most severe of his critics can deny that, even if there is room for disagreement on the methods used and the degrees of change. We shall return to these issues as we draw up our final balance of the period.

With the passing of time it has become clear to any analyst that there were in Spain two versions of socialism existing alongside each other at one and the same time, which seemed complementary at first but in due course proved to be mutually contradictory. It is surprising to note how bitter the exchanges between them were on occasion, and yet how stable the relationship remained despite all their difficulties.

The opposite pole of socialism to González's was led by Alfonso Guerra. Between González and Guerra there ran a strong current not so much of friendship as of genuine affection that had grown up in the early days of their political and party struggles; even in the worst moments of the conflict that was to come, they remained loyal to each other (perhaps Guerra more than González). Guerra simplifies what happened by contrasting his own meticulously systematic way of proceeding with González's brilliant capacity for improvisation. However, setting aside for a moment the fact that this statement is incorrect even if it does reflect the two men's different abilities, what is most important is that in their tastes and relationships, Guerra and González could never be described as close to each other. When they were in power there was from the start a deep gulf separating them. The leadership always fell to González because of his analytical and debating skills. During the 1980s Guerra was given a major role to play, but it was never entirely clearly defined, as became obvious even when he was vice-president from 1982 onwards. Even then he was never in a position to take major decisions, though he was able to veto a few quite important ones and make his mark on a number of more minor issues.

Having reached this point we must now sketch a brief biography of Alfonso Guerra. A controversial personality who used direct language and a seemingly radical tone, he was born in Seville in 1942 into a humble background (his father kept pigs). He studied industrial engineering and philosophy and then worked in teaching, the theater, and as a bookseller, before moving into politics as a profession. At the moment when the PSOE came to power, he was extremely popular – almost as much so as González – but Guerra's popularity would prove the more ephemeral of the two. In the 1970s he was known for his extreme position exemplified by his article entitled "The foci of praxis" ("Los enfoques de la praxis"). For all his appearance of being a sharp-tongued demagogue, Guerra was gifted with political skills that were far from negligible, among which one could mention his organizational capabilities within the party, his early apprenticeship in electoral techniques, and his capacity for negotiation aimed at obtaining a consensus: a virtue that contrasted strongly with his somewhat harsh image. He achieved consensus on the basis of dramatic stagings of confrontation that inevitably ended in agreement.

The foundations on which his political position was based were weakened by a form of left-wing populist politics that tried to find a third way that was dependent neither on the United States nor on the USSR, and that was critical of NATO, for example, or else prone to extreme oversimplification in economic and social matters. This "left-wing opportunism," as Semprún calls it in his memoirs, had no real success in luring the government towards more radical attitudes. In fact "*guerrismo*," as it came to be called after Guerra himself, had no real political program and was more a matter of making grand gestures with "social" implications in a tone that purported to be radical. Nevertheless, in cabinet meetings, with the backing of like-minded colleagues, he waged an "ongoing guerrilla war" against social democrat or liberal socialist ministers. Like Suárez, Guerra was a more perishable product of the political system than he had at first seemed to be. He was more fragile and ingenuous than his image as an apparently hard man seemed to suggest.

Even more important, though, was the fact that what he had to offer without a political program was not viable. For him politics was essentially the exercise of power by means of a party viewed as a kind of extended family or clan, whose members should be governed by the strictest discipline. This was what made "*guerrismo*" attractive to many leaders within the party. It offered sufficient security in the face of possible attack to allow them to pursue their professional career. On the other hand, it created problems for those who had been chosen to run the autonomous communities. Manuel Chaves and José Bono have both recounted how they felt that, in Andalusia and Castilla-La Mancha respectively, they were being manipulated by the media and let down by a deputy prime minister who thought himself omnipotent. Guerra's power within the government was never decisive though it was significant, and at times it was limited to areas that were either fairly unpredictable (relations with Algeria), or were of no great importance. On the other hand, he was a major figure in the party until the 1990s.

In 1982 Guerra displayed a "certain reluctance" to take his place on the party executive and even seems to have suggested that the prime minister's office should be reorganized in such a way as to ensure, beyond any doubt, that he and his supporters would be in a position of power. Uncertainty over the matter lasted a month. González realized what was going on, though he never admitted as much, and he acted skillfully. If Guerra were not on the party executive, it would suggest that there were in effect two opposing poles of power. The prime minister must therefore have decided that it was altogether better to have Guerra in the Moncloa Palace, though Guerra soon discovered that his role there was limited: he did not even manage to ensure that he was in charge of all official publications.

In fact, within the party, once González had been accepted as leader there were no opposing poles of power other than that led by Guerra. The movement of those who favored "renewal" came much later – some

10 years after the socialists came to power – and in González's opinion some of their leaders and some elements of their political program were either dull or inane from an ideological and a pragmatic point of view. In reality, the character of the party was determined by the personality and political weight of González himself, by his moderation and his desire to take Spain down the road towards a northern European style of social democracy.

Yet we should also mention the kind of personal support that he required. A fair number of his ministers, encouraged by González himself, had already made a move towards social democracy. Others, such as Miguel Boyer, who had opposed Francoism but was now well settled in social and economic circles, could be described as liberal socialists. Boyer, who had joined the University Socialist Association (*Agrupación Socialista Universitaria* or ASU) very early on, had spent 6 months in prison in 1962, and this meant that he bore an early stamp of opposition membership that marked him out as different. Though a physicist by training, he always worked as an economist, most notably in the Bank of Spain where many of Fernández Ordóñez's supporters had also been trained. On receiving the Treasury portfolio, Boyer became the main force behind the government's economic policy. González found in him the economic orthodoxy favored by Northern European socialists. The relationship between the two men was forged early on and was strong: what proved decisive in Miguel Boyer's political life was having got to know Felipe González in 1969 in a Madrid which González had found hostile. However, the Finance Minister and Alfonso Guerra, who would in due course become deputy prime minister, would always see things from opposing viewpoints.

## The Socialists' First Term in Office.
## Reform of the Armed Services, an
## Economic Update and Foreign Policy

To help him in the task of governing Spain, González had a leadership team that remained constant throughout the 1980s with the sole but extremely important exception of Boyer. In the 1990s the situation changed, but the fact that certain ministers remained proves that the prime minister had quite clear in his own mind the sort of successor he wanted to replace him.

Be that as it may, when González formed his government he took into account both technocrats and nonaligned independents as well as members of his own party with different tendencies. He himself chose successive party executives, but he always bore the actual nature of the party in mind as he did so. Boyer was a key player in the first executive, but so was Guerra, whose reluctance to be a member – whether purely strategic or out of genuine conviction – we have already mentioned. Once he did accept, he was given only a limited role in managing the rest of the team, but he did retain clear control over the party organization. On the other hand, the main portfolios concerned with the economy always went to specialists who had for a long time been associated with Boyer's liberal socialist circles, or with the social democracy of the UCD. González also made use of the organizational structures of the party and the UGT: it was they who took charge of the administration of the state's social funding, and this brought them within Guerra's sphere of influence.

Three people would play key roles in Spain's socialist governments, in different but always important areas of responsibility: Serra, Solana, and Solchaga. Narcís Serra, who had been Mayor of Barcelona from 1979 on, was made Minister for Defense and successor to Guerra as deputy prime minister in 1991. Javier Solana, a professor of physics, had three portfolios in 13 years, having been one of the small nucleus of Madrid socialists who had made González feel welcome on his arrival in the capital at the end of the 1960s. Carlos Solchaga, after being Minister for Industry in 1982, was responsible for economic policy from 1985 to 1993 and then took on for a short time the leadership of the Socialist Party in Parliament.

González had first offered Serra a ministerial post before the elections were held, and he then repeated his offer at the time of the attempted military coup during the pre-election campaigning. Serra had had experience of municipal management, had organized the annual celebration to honor the armed forces in Barcelona, and was a calm man who had until then taken charge of relations between the PSOE and the Army. Javier Solana, a university teacher who had studied in England, demonstrated his versatility by taking on a series of portfolios and by his skills in communicating with the information media. He was also an important enough figure in the Socialist Party to be put second on the electoral list for Madrid, and enough of a friend to González to accept the situation when, in 1993, the prime minister put an independent candidate ahead of him. Carlos Solchaga, a technocrat with a background in the economic circles we have already mentioned, was indubitably the strongest opponent of the left-wing populism represented by Guerra, and of the position adopted by UGT trade unionists. During the first socialist government, which lasted until 1985, disagreements were already surfacing between him and the unions. Nicolás Redondo quickly showed his lack of training and flexibility in negotiation; he was also fiercely jealous of other possible candidates competing for leadership positions within the union.

The new executive had to confront three crucial problems: the final consolidation of democracy in the face of possible attempted military coups, the updating of the economy, and bringing Spain firmly within the orbit of the alliance of western democratic nations.

When the idea of a "soft" takeover of power failed, the soldiers who favored the option of a coup began in 1982 to plan action that would use violence from the outset, including the assassination of targets in top positions of power. However, the Center for Defense Information (*Centro Superior de Información de la Defensa* or CESID) was now on the alert and was able to thwart an attempted coup planned for election day in October 1982. It was indirectly linked to both Milans del Bosch and Tejero. The conspirators, who had long lists of possible collaborators, were sentenced to 12 years in prison and were expelled from the Army in 1984. There were further attempted military coups, the most important of which was planned to coincide with the Day of the Armed Forces in La Coruña in the summer of 1985. On that occasion an attempt was made to blow up the stand where leading figures would be watching the event. However, when the coup was prevented there was insufficient evidence to take the suspects to court.

From then on, attitudes to the relationship between civil and military power changed, and this led at last to a decisive and total reform of the Army. Action was fast and unequivocal whenever there was any hint of a challenge to discipline. Shortly after the government was formed, the Supreme Council for Military Justice (*Consejo Supremo de Justicia Militar*) tried to free those serving sentences for the attempted coup of February 23. González himself threatened to dissolve the Council if it took such a decision. After that, no kind of declaration on political matters by Army officers was even countenanced, and any declarations that were made meant that, whatever their status, the officers were immediately removed from their posts. It was suggested to Serra that the members of the Democratic Military Union who had been forced to leave the Army should be allowed to rejoin; initially he replied that this was "not at all important," but in 1986 he finally gave way, and this showed that it was in his mind to do so but the timing had been set with an eye to circumstances. The UCD could obviously never have taken such action because it lacked the necessary political strength.

The new Minister for Defense found himself in a peculiar situation that was far from ideal in terms of the relationship that existed between civil and military power. The Joint Chiefs of Staff (*Junta de Jefes de Estado Mayor* or JUJEM), whose task it was to decide on such matters, had let months pass by without sharing out the new investment provided for materials because of disagreement over the weapons themselves; it was not the minister who had to decide on the particulars but the military themselves. At the same time, the different provincial and local commanders were sending "reports on the opinions" of their units to the ministry in an attempt to push the authorities in one political direction or another. There was, then, a certain degree of military autonomy beyond the reach of civil power which was unjustifiable and could potentially reach a point where it posed a serious danger.

Military reform came about by means of a large number of measures that do not need detailed examination. What really mattered was that they established once and for all the primacy of civil power over military power. In 1985, the bringing into line of salaries in Army administration (a brigadier-general would now earn the same as a deputy director general) did much to bring the two sides closer together. For a time under socialist governments military spending increased but then, after 1985, changes in the international situation made it unnecessary: in practice the budget in Spain remained at 1.6 percent of the GDP, while in NATO countries the figure was 2.7 percent. At the start of the 1990s, the Spanish Army had 180,000 members, half of whom were professional soldiers. A growing problem that needed to be faced was the impact of pacifism on the young: in 1993 the number of conscientious objectors reached 70,000 a year. They were made to do social work, and as this was not very demanding, many young people chose it in preference to military service. As a result, recruitment figures were lower than predicted.

The socialist government also brought in important changes in terms of citizens' rights and judicial organization. So it was that a law on abortion was passed in November 1983, which legislated on timings and limited the possibility of aborting to the existence of danger for the pregnant woman. Modifications were also brought in on matters such as the laws on criminal justice, asylum, conditions for detainees, the Penal Code, and *habeas corpus*. Some of these measures have been blamed for the freeing of too many prisoners and the impact on crime figures. The Organic Law on the Judiciary (*Ley Orgánica del Poder Judicial*) introduced a new system for electing the members of the General Council of the Judiciary (*Consejo General del Poder Judicial*): they had previously been elected in part by judges' associations but they would now be chosen entirely by Parliament. A measure such as this no doubt meant that the judges' supreme governing body took on party allegiances, and this process was to become even more pronounced as time passed.

When the socialists came to power Spain's economy was in a disastrous state. The impact of the second energy crisis compounded the unresolved problems of the first, and the political situation was such that the government did not respond with coherent and lasting solutions. Meanwhile, investment was diminishing, unemployment was over 15 percent, the deficit topped 5 percent of GDP, foreign trade showed a seriously negative balance, and growth remained below 1 percent. The economy and Spain's energy policy still had to be updated, and as if that were not enough, future perspectives were also overshadowed by the fact that the PSOE had come to power with an electoral program that was far from orthodox in economic terms. The promise that it would create 800,000 new jobs by direct investment and by employment provided by the Administration could not have any outcome other than that already experienced in other countries: devaluation of the currency and inflation. That had already happened in Mitterand's France, which had also carried out a program of nationalization. Other aspects proved more positive: revenue from taxes grew at a rate of 6.4 percent per annum in real terms, so that by 1990 the government managed to double the original figure. The reform introduced by Fernández Ordóñez had been the main reason for this positive result.

The first phase of the socialist economic policy piloted by Boyer consisted in practical terms of a classic operation of updating that was vital at the time. The main priority was to reduce inflation, and it went down from 14 to 8 percent between 1982 and 1985. This adjustment was achieved at some cost to employment, and meant that the figure of those out of work, instead of going down, rose to 22 percent. The re-conversion program affected a third of the country's industry and cost a billion and a half pesetas. The worst affected sectors were textiles and steel. Re-conversion now became a cause of personal crisis not only for left-wing populists but also for social democrats as those in ministerial posts found that they had come to power with ideas that were now proving to be very different from their colleagues' ideas. The theory behind Spain's economic policy itself was always orthodox. Unlike what had happened in France, not only was there no nationalization of industries but there was no policy of slimming industry down. SEAT, the Spanish state's major car manufacturer, was sold to the German company Volkswagen without the government making any attempt to keep it in Spanish hands. At the time, Guerra saw the first Spanish government as a coalition between the socialists and Boyer. In one sense he was not wrong, because however strong Guerra's own influence was in politics, in economic matters González gave all the credit to Boyer. Yet Guerra's opinion seems to assume that at a given moment González was able, or could choose, to do something different from what he did do, and that is most unlikely.

The only decision that deviated from economic orthodoxy was a result of circumstances. Rumasa, a holding company with multiple interests in the industrial sector, had found itself in a critical financial situation for some time and had caused serious concern in the banking world. Its sudden expropriation, after lengthy discussions with the government, was viewed as inevitable: the only means of avoiding worse evils. Nonetheless, this operation was seen as dubious in constitutional terms because the takeover had actually happened by decree and had then been validated by law after the event. Furthermore, the Constitutional Court had reached its decision solely on the basis of its president's vote, and he was undoubtedly under political pressure and also stated that such an operation was only legal in this one specific instance.

The first stage of the socialists' time in power also saw some measures for social reform being passed, though they became more far-reaching once the economic crisis was over. The working week was set at 40 hours, with the option of reducing it to 35 hours; the holiday period was extended to up to 30 days a year, and retirement conditions were modified. Pension funds were also set up along with provision for social tourism. Above all, these were the years in which a major effort was made to improve conditions in education. For example, the school-leaving age was raised from 11 to 14 and the number of education grants was multiplied by eight. Measures were also introduced in relation to the structure of the curriculum. The Organic Law on Education (*Ley Orgánica de la Educación* or LODE) set out the criteria governing the running of private schools. The fears it aroused, especially in Church circles, proved unfounded in the medium term. The LODE stipulated that teachers in private education would be paid directly, but by means of subsidies it managed to stabilize most of the private sector. After that time relations between the government and the Church were cold and distant but not openly confrontational. There were, for example, no problems on the matter of financing the Church, but the tax on income did not change in the way that the Church wanted it to.

In the first phase of the socialist Administration, which coincided with its first term in office, Spain became once and for all a full member of the western world and defined its strategic interests and major priorities accordingly. The UCD had been the first party to choose this road, but it was not the reason why the journey did not end as had originally been foreseen. The PSOE on the one hand adjusted its policy because of NATO, and on the other finally took Spain into the Common Market under the very best circumstances.

It should be noted that while Felipe González's position was not so very different from that of the majority of his party, he was more able than most to foresee how events were going to develop. Very soon, and going against his Foreign Minister Fernando Morán, he expressed his support for the deployment of new missiles in Germany. At the end of 1984 he spoke out at the PSOE party conference and managed to gain a fair majority (394 votes to 266 after his speech on the subject) in favor of the decision that had been taken, which meant that the content and organization of the referendum on NATO would remain in government hands – that is to say his own. González was no doubt disappointed when Morán was appointed shortly afterwards, because he could never really connect with him. He probably remained anchored in a position that was intended to be equidistant from both of the superpowers of the time, or else he tried to gain special benefits because of the position that Spain adopted. Whatever the case, the lack of communication between the two men was absolute. According to Morán, on the NATO question that was so crucial to the way Spain defined its foreign policy, "there was never once a time when the President and I had clear, detailed discussion to clarify our positions." González finally opted in 1986 for a line that clearly favored the western and Atlanticist interests represented by Fernández Ordóñez.

Nonetheless, the road that led to this decision was tortuous, problematic, and long. It was only in the last months of 1984 that the government finally reached agreement on wanting to join the European Community and become a member of NATO. In October González listed ten points on Spain's defense needs which in practice linked these two organizations together. They certainly were related but not directly and not at that very moment. There had been no pressing demand by NATO for Spain to join the alliance in the first instance, but were it to leave now it would set a very bad precedent. Even Guerra acknowledged that.

Meanwhile, negotiations with Brussels on Spain's entry into the European Community went ahead. The treaty was signed in June 1985 and came into effect at the start of the following year. Spain became at that moment "a fragment of a superpower" and this meant that its economy and its foreign policy now took a different and very clear direction. In 1985 the percentage of Spanish exports destined for Europe was 55 percent, but by 1987 the figure had reached 63 percent, and in 1992 it topped 71 percent. After joining the EEC in the second half of the 1980s, Spain received some 80,000 million dollars of foreign investment, which helps to explain the economic prosperity of the period. In political terms, our country was given two seats in the European Commission and 60 euro-deputies out of a total of over 500. Very early on, Spain aligned itself clearly with the countries most in favor of integration, following the climate of opinion within the Peninsula, as much on the left as on the right, both before and after it joined. The Spanish government contributed to European integration by proposing that "membership funds" be made available to help out the least developed nations among which, more especially, Spain itself featured.

On March 12, 1986, the promised referendum on NATO membership took place, which González considered one of the worst mistakes of his time in office. As he explained later, the question that the majority of Spaniards would have wanted to hear on the lips of their government was "if they would agree to Spain staying in NATO if they had voted against it." There was, therefore, a basic supposition that Spain would not become part of the organization's military structure, the installation of atomic weapons on Spanish soil would be prohibited, and, last but not least, the American military presence would gradually be reduced.

All parties were disconcerted at the result of the referendum, for if the PSOE went back on its previous position, the right abstained from voting, having valid reasons for doing so given the content of the questions posed. There was no sense in joining a military organization without prior serious discussion of the appropriateness of such a step and remaining outside its military structures. González's big mistake was to commit himself to a referendum without accepting that both he and his party would have to make changes. Nonetheless, it would have been worse still to do what the Greek socialists did, which was to promise a referendum and then not hold it. Clearly González himself had caused the problem, but he was then honest enough not to go back on his word; he would doubtless have resigned had his proposal not been accepted.

It was not known until the very last moment what the results of the referendum would be. Twenty-eight percent of voters reached a decision only the day before, and another 21 percent did so during the campaign. Sixty percent voted, and of that figure only 52 percent were in favor, while 40 percent voted against and 6.5 percent put in blank voting-slips. Two-thirds of all voters voted against their normal position: one in three on the right did not go along with their leaders' proposals and a fifth voted in favor. Thirty-eight percent of socialist voters voted no, but only a very small minority "changed sides" in the general election that followed.

In these three aspects of the socialist government's actions – military reform, updating the economy, and integrating Spain into the western alliance – there was continuity with previous policies and the results were quite positive. Remaining firm on implementing policies became easier because of the massive support obtained via the ballot-box. On the other hand, the results were not so much the consequences of a carefully laid plan or the unfolding of a predetermined program as of having a stable government, a day-to-day learning process, and decisiveness on the part of the new socialist leadership. Government action taken with the backing of an absolute majority of Spaniards made possible what had until that moment seemed inconceivable in three such crucial areas.

## ——— A Means of Consolidating Democracy. The GAL ———

In October 1982 Spanish society as a whole yearned for stable government and had a very negative opinion of the UCD whose internal disputes seemed to prevent such government ever being achieved. In its hands, democracy seemed threatened by bad management and a lack of any clear sense of direction. A reaction against this situation gave the PSOE an absolute majority in the elections in October 1982, and the result was a peculiar political system which had some very positive aspects and others that were decidedly ambivalent.

The legitimacy of the democratic system itself seemed by now to be firmly consolidated, given that 70 percent of the population was stating that the best political system was this and no other. The number of disaffected had gone down to 5 percent or less. However, there was at the same time a persistent attitude of "noninvolvement" in public life in a large majority of ordinary citizens. A maximum of only 30 percent of Spaniards were quite or very interested in what went on in the public sphere. This attitude to politics has been described as "cynical democracy" in that if, on the one hand, the average Spaniard is in no doubt at all that his political system is the best, his basic assumptions about politicians are very negative, and this gives the impression that he is not interested in viewing democracy as an enterprise in which he has a part to play through his own efforts. To a certain extent the PSOE's absolute majority served to lull the nation's desire to participate actively in politics; at any rate, it did not awaken it. Nor did the opposition do so, being simply not viable for the whole of the 1980s.

In addition, however, quite apart from attitudes within society, there were dangers in the way that Spain's institutions were functioning, and responsibility for this must, objectively speaking, be placed principally on those in government. Suddenly Spain had a political system in which, in actual practice, one party alone held power until 1993. This was in every way a surprise that could hardly have been foreseen given the characteristics of Spanish society and of the electoral law. The result, even in the short term, was that people expected little from democracy in Spain because the country lacked the vital elements of proper controls, civic ethics, and participation in the political process.

This situation meant that institutions that should have been totally autonomous in fact acted with a clear pro-government bias for no other reason than that the government had an absolute majority in Parliament. That was the case with the Constitutional Court, as we have been able to observe in the Rumasa case. For its part, the Department of the Attorney General of the State (*Fiscalía General del Estado*) quite obviously became a mere appendage of the Administration, to such a point that in the end a person was appointed to the post of Attorney General who did not even have the necessary legal qualifications for the job. Yet he was only dismissed when the Supreme Court was on the point of declaring the procedure illegal. The General Council of the Judiciary also behaved differently, in accordance with the new way that its members were elected. In other words, Parliament ceased to be a means of controlling the government executive because it had become virtually impossible to set up parliamentary committees of enquiry. Two further pieces of information complete the picture and reveal the extent to which Spain's socialist governments felt that they had a free hand to act as they chose. The worst cases of fraud in the funding of political parties happened immediately after legislation had been altered to increase the sums of money the parties were to receive. Secondly, the public media were used consciously and repeatedly to back the party interests of those in power.

Despite all these issues, up until 1991 the fact that Felipe González was a figure who enjoyed almost universal esteem contributed towards stabilizing Spain's democracy. After 1991 the problems of corruption that had arisen because of the hegemony of this one particular party did much to tarnish his image, but they also brought the political problem firmly into the foreground amid Spaniards' major concerns. Between 30 and 40 percent of the population thought it the most serious of all their worries, and this meant that it soon became imperative to improve the atmosphere in politics. It was this that would result in the defeat of the PSOE in 1996.

We have not yet mentioned what must be considered the worst violation of the ethics of democracy. The anti-terrorist policies of the socialist governments had been considered one of their worst failures, though this conclusion was reached principally and almost exclusively after consideration of the trouble caused in the medium term by the Anti-terrorist Liberation Groups (*Grupos Antiterroristas de Liberación* or GAL).

Of course the GAL did not on their own take up all the time that successive socialist governments spent on the terrorist problem. If an overall assessment of the government's performance must be seen as negative, the reasons for this are in fact more far-reaching. In order to understand the situation we need to look back to the moment when the socialists came to power. The "dirty war" against ETA that had begun during the Franco regime and had continued throughout the transition in the form of action that, beyond any shadow of doubt, already involved sections of the police, ended while Calvo Sotelo was in government. Earlier on, in the triangle between San Sebastián, Rentería, and Andoain, ten people with close ETA connections had been assassinated between 1979 and 1981.

In 1982, however much socialist leaders felt bemused by ETA attacks and interpreted declarations of support for the organization from third parties as mere "rhetoric and empty words," it is certain, objectively speaking, that the worst period of ETA terrorism was by now in the past. During the first socialist term in office, the number of those killed was about 40 a year: a figure that was a third of the number killed in the worst year of terrorist activity. Therefore, terrorist pressure cannot be taken as an excuse for what happened. The explanation for the mistakes made by the socialists in this affair is to be found in the atmosphere generated around the notion of "change," in the government's lack of experience and beginners' mistakes, and in a series of unfortunate appointments in the ministry of Home Affairs.

The fear that the chronic instability that Spain had suffered in the 1930s would be repeated, and the socialist leadership's euphoria at their resounding electoral victory, led them to think very soon about the possibility of rapid action and decisive shortcuts to deal once and for all with ETA. The Interior Minister, José Barrionuevo, himself admits in his memoirs that in 1983 that he authorized a raid over the French frontier and the kidnapping of an Army pharmacist – Martín Barrios – who was later murdered. On the other hand, the anti-terrorist law voted on in the Congress of Deputies in December 1984 met with opposition on all sides, including from the Constitutional Court. One might say that the policy of the Home Office at this early stage, quite apart from the GAL question, consisted of trying to appear severe while in fact being inefficient when it came to devising effective legislation. The same could later be said of the Interior Minister José Luis Corcuera on the question of law and order. Drastic oversimplification, combined with methods of dubious legality, seems to have been the best recipe that the next two Home Office Ministers could devise to solve serious issues.

In contrast, the socialists' most positive and decisive achievement was the change brought about in France's attitude, and this made it increasingly easy after 1984 to have terrorist suspects expelled from France initially, and then finally allowed them to be extradited to Spain. It is a paradox worth noting that one element that fanned the flames of the dirty war was the fact that France still had doubts about Spanish democracy. In any event, from 1986 onwards the extradition procedure became fairly rapid. On the other hand, French courts would not for the time being put any member of ETA on trial. At the same time, the police scored a number of successes in dismantling terrorist commando groups. The most brilliant operation was the finding and taking over of a logistical center in Sokoa in the south of France, which proved beyond doubt that the ETA leadership was living in that country.

Until that point, the "dirty war" had seemed to involve little more than small groups that appeared and disappeared and did not seem in any way to be directly linked to the government. Those known to have killed had been individuals from the extreme right, often foreign nationals, and in a few instances it seemed that the inspiration behind their actions came from individuals not in any way associated with the Administration. Another possibility is that the police themselves used these methods without their superiors being in any way responsible (though it certainly appears that they did nothing to investigate any cases that came up).

The GAL were active from October 1983 to 1987 and killed over 30 victims. They often acted on incorrect information, even in instances where they killed. There can be no doubt at all that they were the inspiration of members of the police and of the government in the Basque Country, and that Madrid initially chose not to be troubled by questions of responsibility. From the point of view of the fight against terrorism, and setting aside any moral judgment, the GAL did not have a significant impact. In 1986 ETA killed 40 people – eight more than in 1983. One might even conclude that they were counterproductive. The most barbarous acts of terrorism happened in 1987, immediately after the GAL's key operations. That year ETA terrorism once again hit a target of 52 deaths a year. Nor was there any sign that this had any impact at all in the French authorities' attitude towards ETA.

The worst effect of the GAL was that among the most extreme young Basque nationalists they prolonged the sense that their struggle was basically the same as it had been under Francoism. The funerals in honor of the dead, attended by huge crowds, powerfully reinforced that impression. There will always be some doubt about the ultimate responsibility for what happened. There is, however, no doubt at all about the failure to investigate the events, even at the highest levels of government. It is less certain that the main body of ministers knew what was going on. Given the personality of the Interior Minister (Barrionuevo) and of his Secretary of State (Vera), it seems unlikely that they could on their own initiative have taken a decision such as that which led to the creation of the GAL unless they could at least count on understanding from those above them. Whatever the truth of the matter, the most direct backing for the dirty war came from the governing authorities and the socialist leaders in the Basque Country itself.

It soon became obvious in that same decade – the 1980s – that at lower levels in the police, quite apart from unacceptably immoral acts, there had been some remarkable blunders. Not only had attempts been made to kill or kidnap people who had nothing whatever to do with ETA, but public funds had been used for private entertainment, so blatantly that the lifestyle of the corrupt betrayed them in a most ostentatious way. In 1988 the Police Chief José Amedo and his colleague Michel Domínguez were arrested and the following year they stood trial, charged with being GAL members paid for with reserved funding. At the time they did not reveal the names of those who had inspired them and funded their activities.

Worse still, the most perverse aspect of the GAL case was that at that very moment, at the end of the 1980s, there was a palpably obstructionist attitude towards the Justice Department on the part of members of the Administration, and more especially of the Interior Minister himself. It would have been logical to attempt then what would be attempted later – that is, what one of the colleagues working with the Minister of Justice and the Interior, Juan Alberto Belloch, has described as "a reasonable settling of accounts with the past." Yet just the opposite happened and then it was too late to set matters to rights.

## Elections and Public Opinion in the Second Half of the 1980s

In 1986, once it became clear that González and Morán were incompatible, the prime minister would have liked a short government crisis that would require a very few changes to his cabinet. What happened instead exposed the tensions that existed within the socialist camp, the prime minister's own doubts, and the difficult interplay between the foremost personalities in government. Boyer hoped at the time to become the "major player" in the crisis and he demanded one of the posts of deputy prime minister which would allow him to bring to heel ministries that were overspending. However, Guerra refused point blank to share the post of deputy prime minister with anyone. It must have seemed to him that he had sacrificed enough when he had accepted a post with far more limited powers than he had wanted. The final result was that Boyer left the government, but there were no further political consequences. González put Carlos Solchaga in charge of directing the economy, and at the same time he got rid of ministers who now seemed to have little to offer. What also happened was that the center of gravity of his interim policy shifted from industrial re-conversion to social welfare. That would probably have happened in any case, though with Boyer the change would doubtless have been slower and more difficult.

Throughout the 1980s, public opinion – between 30 and 40 percent of all citizens – remained strongly in favor of the socialist government. However, González's popularity was even greater, ranging from 46 to 70 percent of the electorate. This stable support meant stability for the government too, and for the time being serious internal disagreements over the party program were not in evidence.

Election results confirmed the data from surveys. In the 1986 general election there was clearly continuity, but paradoxically this did not give the impression that the party political system was firmly consolidated. Polling figures were down by about 9 percentage points – 50 percent lower than in the previous elections (which were municipal). The PSOE lost somewhat more than a million votes but had 184 deputies, keeping 79 seats more than the right (105 compared with their previous 107). Apart from an increase in apathy – basically due to dissatisfaction with present policies – it was clear that blame for the failure to consolidate the party system lay fairly and squarely with the right, and with the center where there was an immense vacuum. Adolfo Suárez's Democratic and Social Center Party (*Centro Democrático y Social* or CDS) went from having two seats to 19, but this was a somewhat spurious success because they still had many fewer votes than the total gained by the UCD and CDS combined in the decisive elections in 1982. On the other hand, the Catalanist Miquel Roca's Democratic Reformist Party (*Partido Reformista Democrático* or PRD) barely won 1 percent of the vote, topping 2 percent in only seven districts. Since the party was well financed, these results spelt downright failure and took away from the Catalan nationalists any desire they might have had to be involved with the rest of Spain through a party based on such ideas. In practice it had never been a real alternative, and without doing any irremediable damage to Fraga's party – which had never been viable anyway – it did it no favors either.

Against all the forecasts, in the 1989 elections the Socialist party once again won an absolute majority, though only by one seat this time. Votes continued to seep away from the PSOE which, on this occasion, lost some 800,000 and went down from 8,900,000 to 8,100,000, although these figures were still sufficient to ensure it had 176 seats. The Popular Party did not lose votes as it had done in the previous elections, but it won only about 40,000 new votes and only one more seat in the Congress of Deputies. Now, too, any immediate possibility of the center coming up with a formula that could seriously threaten the stronger party disappeared completely. Suárez's CDS was once again left with less than 8 percent of the vote (1,600,000 and only 14 deputies) and was overtaken by the communists who, with only four seats and 800,000 votes in 1982, had barely grown in 1986, despite having three more seats, but on this occasion won 1,800,000 votes and 17 seats. This was a result of a proportion of left-wing voters who turned their backs on the ruling socialists. What was less obvious but in fact more dangerous in the medium term was that the majority of those aged between 25 and 40, and the urban middle classes, had begun to turn their backs on the PSOE and on González himself.

Nonetheless, what stands out most immediately from the results of the 1989 elections is the impotence of the opposition, and more especially the section of it that had seemed to offer the best chance of taking over power, which was the far right wing. The Popular Alliance had believed in 1982 that a two-party system had been set up which would mean that sooner or later it would inevitably come to power, but this assumption was manifestly wrong. Whenever the Popular Alliance stood as the obvious alternative to the PSOE, it proved unable to seize the reins of government, and so Spain's situation with one all-powerful party continued. Even the habit of holding once a year a solemn debate on the "state of the nation," given the curious circumstances in which it took place, gave clear advantages to the party in power and only illusory advantages to the so-called leader of the opposition, who was not even seen as such by his parliamentary colleagues. Fraga, who deserves recognition for having organized the right and integrated it into Spain's democratic structures, was clearly rejected personally by a majority of up to 60 percent of the electorate.

Circumstances first made the leader of the AP an apparent victim of his allies in the mid 1980s, and then finally made him the outright winner of the leadership struggle on the right, so that he in fact became his own successor. Fraga himself was mainly to blame for the weakness of his coalition. The opposition politics of the Popular Coalition (*Coalición Popular*) were overdramatic and it appealed far too often to the Constitutional Court against government measures as though they all represented violations of constitutional agreements. Yet what in fact characterized the socialists' policies at the time was that they often made continuity their priority and therefore were not at all radical. This meant that Fraga was opposing something that no longer existed because the socialists were no longer as extreme as they had been in the past. González became the butt of personal attacks from Fraga when in fact he was a force for moderation; nor was he using moderation as a subterfuge. It is important to bear in mind that it was at the end of the 1980s that the GAL and corruption both erupted onto the political scene. Quite apart from that, mistrust among members of Fraga's coalition was so great that it became necessary to decide on percentages (65.7 percent for the AP and 21 percent for the PDP) of possible posts in every single constituency and in the elections themselves. Fraga also provided a counterbalance to the Christian democrats of the PDP by inventing some virtually nonexistent liberals.

Apart from proving that Fraga's option was simply not viable with or without allies, if the "alternative to the alternative" (PRD) brought about its own rapid downfall, there was a third case to consider where there was a long slow death due causes that were easy to foresee. In the case of Suárez's CDS, it was hesitation about making pacts with other forces in politics (the PSOE or AP) that brought it to crisis-point at the start of the 1990s. On the left, too, no other force capable of taking votes away from the socialists had appeared by 1986. The lack of unity among the communists not only did not diminish but actually increased with the founding in 1983 of a Communist Party for the Peoples of Spain (*Partido Comunista de los Pueblos de España*) led by Ignacio Gallego, and also of a Table for Communist Unity (*Mesa por la Unidad de los Comunistas*) inspired, and indeed dominated, by Santiago Carrillo. Contrary to what its name suggested, the latter in fact took the fragmentation of Spanish Communism to ultimate extremes. The Socialist party faced no real danger until the 1990s, and then it was more a result of the passage of time and the government's own mistakes than of any initiatives on the part of the opposition.

Splits in the opposition became a frequent spectacle in Spanish politics. In July 1986 poor election results led the Christian democrats (PDP) to break their alliance with the AP and adopt a stance that was not in itself unreasonable, but they acted with such haste that their move seemed hard to understand, with the sole result that they ruined the political chances of one valuable political figure, Óscar Alzaga. Paradoxically, as time passed it became clearer that in fact, as the Christian democrats had declared, the Popular Coalition option was nothing whatever like a true political alternative. When Alzaga lost his position as leader, his successor, Javier Rupérez, continued to stumble along uncertainly until inevitably he merged with the right. In fact, by 1987 the Christian democrats had lost all credibility as a political force.

Despite all of these factors, it remained clear that Fraga still did not re-present a viable political alternative. His own colleagues and voters had shown him that this was the case in the preceding months. After the 1986 elections, at the heart of the AP leadership there was a storm of conspir-acies. There were even splits, among them the departure of the party's general secretary, Jorge Verstrynge. The autonomous communities that had previously been the most solid bastion of the right now saw how the government was being taken over by the left. In Galicia, before splitting off and after elections, the PSOE had a chance to govern for the first (and only) time in the region, but what finished Fraga off was the Basque elections in November 1986, in which the Popular Coalition won only two seats – as did the CDS. From having been seen as a veteran of politics betrayed by his closest and most treacherous colleagues, Franco's ex-minister had become an epitome of political impossibilities. He had to resign, but many months would pass before stable leadership would be achieved on the right, and during that time some of its best leaders – such as Herrero Tejedor – would find themselves marginalized.

Herrero came closest to succeeding Fraga, and there is no doubt whatever that he had the personality and the ability to make the takeover effective and positive for the right. However, at the AP party conference in February 1987, it was clear from the start that there was nothing Herrero could do. He had fewer than half the votes of his opponent, the Andalusian Antonio Hernández Mancha. Nor did he get any help from Fraga or the older members of the party. What weighed heavily in Hernández Mancha's favor was a freshness that people longed for after 3 years of Fraga's chairmanship. Nor was his election without good cause. He was, after all, young, he was much applauded at meetings, and he was the leader of the regional organization with the greatest number of members: Andalusia.

However, Hernández Mancha quickly proved to be an utter failure. Entirely without direction in strategic and tactical matters, his proposals were often extravagant. When he called for a vote of censure against González, the result returned was completely the opposite of what had happened when González had done the same to Suárez. In 1988 a new conspiracy brought Fraga back to lead the party. It was only a temporary measure, but it also offered an opportunity to increase support for the right at the time. The Christian democrats who had led a passive existence throughout 1988 now decided to join the AP group in Parliament in January 1989 in the person of Marcelino Oreja.

On the left, it also took until the end of 1988 for the new leadership to take shape and a line of opposition to be devised that would be capable of offering at least an alternative to the ruling socialist party. In February 1988, Julio Anguita, who for quite some time had been Mayor of Córdoba – the only provincial capital where the PCE headed the polls – took on the leadership of the United Left (*Izquierda Unida* or IU). This party aimed to be a broad front with the communists at its center but which would also include in its ranks those dissatisfied with socialism, ecologists, and pacifists. Anguita expressed his firm opposition to any lasting pacts with the PSOE, while for the PSOE, those were months when it was beginning to need such pacts urgently.

## The Second Term in Office: Social Policies and Union Protests. Spain and the World

Guerra and his supporters hoped that during the socialists' second term in office the supposed coalition between Boyer and socialism would break up, though as we know – as González had decided – the government's economic policy did not change. Carlos Solchaga tried to steer it in the direction in which it had traveled up to 1986. As a politician he was sincere, tough, and flexible, and he held to a clear line and often clashed with ministries with big expenditure and presidents of the autonomous communities. He also confronted the unions – even the UGT. In 1990 he tried to reach an agreement with the unions but was unsuccessful. In 1991 he would have preferred to be made deputy prime minister in charge of the economy in order to be able to combat was described by Javier Pradera as "rebellion by the public spending commando," or alternatively to be given a different portfolio such as Foreign Affairs. He did not have his way. Although González backed him, he was not entirely satisfied with Solchaga's way of addressing difficulties, which he thought too confrontational without actually getting the desired results.

However, the economic situation had improved by the middle of the 1980s. After 1985 and especially in 1987 – rather later than in other European countries – the cycle changed direction and the Spanish economy began to grow at a yearly rate of 4.5 to 5 percent, which was very high – indeed, one or two points higher than the average for the other countries of Europe, and fairly comparable with the levels attained in the years of the "economic miracle" of the 1960s. During this period 1,800,000 jobs were created, which was a response – even if only a partial one – to previous demands for more work, especially from young people and from women. Economic prosperity also allowed extensive public spending on infrastructure which increased at a rate of 0.5 percent per year and in 1991 reached a figure of five points of the GDP.

Given this feeling of prosperity, it is not surprising that during this period foreign investment multiplied by five. The sizeable flow of foreign capital into Spain was attracted there by high interest rates. This capital, which was allowed to purchase 25 percent of Spanish businesses, went more towards buying existing firms than starting up new ones. Investors' interest centered on certain sectors, notable foodstuffs and cars.

One final aspect of Spain's prosperity was due to a widespread program of privatization of public sector businesses. Not only did the socialist government not nationalize but, like other governments with the same ideological background, it sold a significant proportion of publicly owned companies into the hands of private enterprise. This accounted for the sale of 15 percent of Telefónica, 20 percent of ENDESA, 50 percent of Argentaria, 80 percent of Repsol, and 91 percent of ENAGAS. These sales prevented the formation of a new, autonomous economic power. Nor does it appear that the government would have held back from total privatization given the right circumstances (the Stock Exchange, for example).

Economic prosperity at last made possible a very substantial increase in social spending which allowed the setting up of a Welfare State that had not really existed until that time. Progress was made simultaneously in areas such as pensions, health, and in education as already mentioned. In a few instances, such as research and scientific development, the increases were spectacular. The number of scholarships went up from 162,000 to 750,000; the number of university students rose from 700,000 to 1,200,000. Furthermore, between 1989 and 1992 funds available to cover unemployment almost doubled at a time when the economic cycle was only just beginning to change. Even so, halfway through the 1990s the Welfare State in Spain was still a long way behind the level usual in the rest of Europe: the proportion of beds per thousand inhabitants available in Social Security hospitals was only half that of Germany or France.

When considering Spain's economic policy, it was also necessary to add to this increase in social spending the setting up of the autonomous regions that multiplied the state's debt by six, and also the extra expenditure destined for the events celebrated in 1992: the Universal Exhibition in Seville and the Olympic Games in Barcelona. The consequences of these events were horrendous in terms of cost to the general public. In 1993 the state deficit stood at higher than 6 percent in terms of GDP. Nonetheless, the economic situation had changed and had moved in a very positive direction. Inflation began to stabilize around 6 percent: a figure rare until then in the Spanish economy and one that suggested a break with its normal patterns of behavior. The price control achieved at this point has proved irreversible in relative historical terms, but it remains at the same distance as ever from the European average. The income per capita in 1994 was 36 percent higher than it had been in 1974 and 9 percent higher than in 1985.

The worst aspect of the Spanish situation was the level of unemployment. The number of workers with jobs went up from around 11 million to 12.5 million at the start of the 1990s, but when the economic situation worsened, unemployment rose again to reach a previously unknown level of no less than 24 percent: a figure far out of line with the other European economies.

But let us return to the mid 1980s to find the explanation for social confrontation in Spain at this time. Economic recovery acted as a stimulus to union demands, while the fact that the PSOE remained in power with an absolute majority and no effective political opposition led the government to think that it had little to fear from the unions. At the end of 1988 a relatively minor issue – the government's attempt to introduce a Youth Employment Scheme (*Plan de Empleo Juvenil*) – resulted in an explosive general strike in December. What one first notices about this strike is that it caught the government completely unawares. González has described it as "a huge act of stupidity" and in one sense he was right. By not negotiating to achieve a satisfactory solution for both sides at the opportune moment, the government ended up giving way on matters where it should not have had to do so. One of the ministers who later became general secretary of the PSOE, Joaquín Almunia, has written in his memoirs: "We did not know beforehand what was coming and nor did we learn all the lessons we could have learned." The "dragon" of public spending, as Boyer had once called it, took to the air in a way that had not been foreseen.

González, one of whose enduring characteristics was always to "have one foot in the stirrup," even thought that it might be possible after the 1989 elections for someone else to stand for the post of prime minister. He suggested as much to the man he had in mind – Narcís Serra – of whom he had an excellent opinion because of the work Serra had done in Defense. It is very likely that Serra would have accepted but, as we shall see, circumstances did not allow it. In any case, the election results meant that there was no great haste.

Along with factors such as these, Spain's position had altered on the international stage. As anticipated, major changes were made in the bilateral agreements with the United States. There was a desire to "reshape" the US military presence on Spanish soil, and this amounted to a substantial reduction in personnel. It was in part a consequence of left-wing anti-American feeling; the renewal of the pacts in 1983 had been noticeably chilly. According to González the Americans were "used to doing whatever they liked" as regards Spain, and their presence had to be limited in accordance with the ten-point plan agreed by the *Cortes*. When in April 1986 the United States bombed Libya, they had to do so without overflying Spanish territory because permission to do so was withheld. As on other occasions, serious argument on matters of defense, or on Spain's responsibilities in the western world, was avoided. During negotiations, according to Serra who played a major role on Spain's behalf, there were "dramatic moments" to be lived through with a succession of American negotiators, especially with the last of them, Reginald Bartholomew. Yet, all in all, the question was not of ultimate importance. Between 1986 and 1988 the government negotiated the withdrawal of some American Air Force units and finally achieved its aim: 72 warplanes with a nuclear capability left the airbase at Torrejón. In December 1988 a treaty was signed in which, besides addressing the transportation of "nuclear weapons" within Spanish territory, there was a commitment "not to ask." Spain had, in any case, managed to achieve what it had set out to do at almost the very same moment at which the Berlin Wall was brought down and a new world view opened up. For this reason its own decision made less of an impact in the context of the West's defense policy.

As soon as Fernández Ordóñez – who had been a key figure during the transition to democracy – replaced Fernando Morán, he managed to implement a policy that was totally in line with that of the West and also took advantage of the possibilities opened up by Spain's unique position in the western alliance. Javier Solana took on the post of Minister for Foreign Affairs after June 1992 when illness forced Fernández Ordóñez to resign. That Spain was completely in tune with the rest of Europe was once again evident – especially so – when Irak invaded Kuwait at the start of 1991. A comfortable majority of Spaniards supported their government in the action it took, thanks in large part to Fernández Ordóñez's educational skills. Spain allowed 35 percent of American flights, though the position taken did not prevent Madrid being chosen to host the start of the peace negotiations between the Israelis and the Palestinians in October 1991.

After that time, what came to be a decisive facet of Spain's involvement in international affairs was its support of control and peace-making operations. Having become the ninth largest contributor to the UN in economic terms, from 1988 on it sent officers and troops or security forces to some of the parts of the world caught up in the worst conflicts, such as Namibia, Angola, Haiti, Nicaragua, El Salvador, Somalia, and the former Yugoslavia. It played a very important role in the foreign intervention in

Yugoslavia, even to the point of taking a limited part in the bombardment of Serb positions in 1995.

Finally, it is worth referring to two regions of the world with which Spain has always had rather curious if close relations for reasons either of cultural tradition or of geographical proximity: Latin America and the Magreb.

In Latin America, the example set by Spain's transition to democracy was seen as both as a model to imitate and a means of exerting influence in other areas. Spain was influential in the advance of democratization in Central America and the Southern Cone. In Nicaragua the socialist government was initially dead set against the United States putting any pressure on the Sandinista rebels, but it distanced itself from the rebels when it saw that they had little interest in the path to democracy and seemed to be moving instead towards adopting a revolutionary position. Part of the negotiations between the government and the opposition took place in the Spanish embassy (1989) and, at a moment of greater stability later on, Spanish troops formed a large contingent of the force sent by the UN. As for El Salvador, González himself was present at the signing of an agreement between the government and guerrilla forces (1992). The peace negotiations in Guatemala took place in Madrid from 1987 onwards. In that same area of the Caribbean, Spanish policy in the socialist years was significantly different from that of the United States. In 1986 González traveled to Cuba in accordance with the particular policy that Spain was pursuing on that country, and in the 1990s he tried to influence the Cuban dictator and bring about a degree of liberalization, but to no other effect than that a few prisoners were freed. In the case of Panama, Spain showed that it was prepared to help towards a peaceful solution by offering asylum to General Noriega when the Americans threatened to invade the country. As for the Southern Cone, Spain's role was also important there at the time of the first contact between the opposition and Pinochet's dictatorial government. In 1990, when the process of change was complete, the king, as well as González, visited Chile, where the political classes had kept the Spanish transition very much in mind during their own march towards freedom.

In wider terms, the Ibero-American Community began to take shape in practical terms in the 1990s, viewing cooperation as its main tool and giving the word a very particular sense. In effect, after 1991, summits were held which were attended by Chiefs of State and presidents of Latin American countries at which the king of Spain played a very important role. These summits were initially held once a year (then every other year) and the main problem they faced was drawing up a program. However, 1985 saw the creation of the Secretariat of State for International Cooperation, which then became an Agency, and after 1986 annual plans for cooperation were put into effect each year. The Spanish Parliament played quite a significant part in the development of this policy and in 1987 approved a series of general directives on aid. By 1993 the level of aid topped 300,000 million pesetas, of which 44 percent went to Latin America.

Another area in which it was obvious that Spanish foreign policy would have an important role to play, again throughout the entire time that the UCD and PSOE were in power, was in the Mediterranean. The finalizing of substantial agreements defining Spain's policy in that area happened in 1986 when full diplomatic relations with Israel were restored.

As for the Magreb, which would soon have a total of some 100 million inhabitants, Spain never had anything remotely like the influence that France had, but from the 1980s on it became an area of special interest, conflict having diminished greatly since Spain's entry into the European Union. Only 7 percent of Spanish exports were going to the Magreb, but Spain now gets from the area all its imports of super-phosphates (Morocco) and natural gas (Algeria). As early as 1983 Felipe González traveled to Morocco, so initiating in practice early contact with the Magreb each time that there is a change of government in a country with which relations had always been a source of conflict, though it is more easily resolved now that Spain is a member of the European Community.

## Policy on the Autonomous Communities: A New Vertebrate Structure for the Spanish State

During the time that Spain was ruled by socialist governments a decisive and irreversible political change took place when Article VIII of the Constitution was put into effect. In fact, up to 1981, only five statutes of autonomy had been approved, but in the period 1982–3 another 12 came into being. It then took until well on into the 1990s for Ceuta and Melilla to have their statues approved and made operative. Nonetheless, the essential work of transforming a state that had been hugely centralized into one that was very decentralized had been done in the 1980s.

What helped greatly was that in August 1983 the controversial Organic Law on the Harmonization of the Autonomy Process (LOAPA), approved while the UCD was in power but with PSOE collaboration, was declared by the Constitutional Court to be invalid in terms of a large part of its content. This High Court endowed itself with the powers to achieve what politicians had not been allowed to attempt, but at least this procedure meant that there was a principle of orderliness in the process of setting up Spain's autonomous regions. In this way too there was an independent body capable of resisting the centralizing tradition of the Spanish Administration. As time passed, though faster than could ever have been predicted, a process of such massive decentralization was implemented that it could even be said to have surpassed any such process in other countries that describe their structures as federal. In this sense one can actually say that Spain did not effect one transition but two: the first from dictatorship to democracy, and the second from an extremely centralized state to one that was notably decentralized.

This change was brought about in successive and fairly unpredictable phases. In actual fact it did not follow any predetermined plan, nor was any plan agreed between the different political groupings. It even took some time for a particular sense of identity to develop in certain regions. There were some autonomous communities which started out from a position in which they lacked any real, deep feeling of identity, which they then created in response to demands aimed at ending a situation of underdevelopment. On this particular subject, the testimonies of Juan Carlos Rodríguez Ibarra and José Bono, presidents of Extremadura and Castilla-La Mancha respectively, coincide and are useful. In both these instances there was no sense of particular regional identity and no demand for political autonomy, but the change proved to be the best thing that could happen to areas that had been neglected in terms of their level of development or public funding. Their state of underdevelopment was such that demands were made for public infrastructures (or, for example, for the closing of nuclear power-stations) and that in itself created a regional consciousness.

There were many different ways of viewing policies on autonomy among the members of the socialist leadership. In the first half of the 1980s, responsibility for policies on autonomy went to Alfonso Guerra who, quite apart from his known preference for centralization, was forever interfering in the affairs of the party's regional organizations. Conflict with Catalan nationalists was severe, and when it was resolved the result was damaging to the PSOE. In the period when Almunia took over ministerial responsibility from Guerra after the first government reshuffle, he showed a greater desire to reach agreements with the nationalists, and more especially with the Basques.

Despite these differences in the processes involved in setting up a Spanish state with autonomous regions, the general architecture of state institutions progressed as the two major parties worked together on approving general measures. The first of these meant the creation of the so-called Interregional Compensation Fund (*Fondo de Compensación Interterritorial* or FCI) in 1984. More decisive still was the Organic Law on the Funding of Autonomous Communities (*Ley Orgánica de Financiación de las Comunidades Autónomas* or LOFCA).

Throughout this whole process, and apart from conflicts arising from different viewpoints within the party in government, there were permanent problems emerging on specific matters. One example was the conflict over the relative powers of the autonomous institutions in the different regions and nationalities in relation to the Constitutional Court, principally in the case of Catalonia and Euskadi (it was these two communities that appealed on almost half of the proposed laws). It was at the height of these conflicts that the first socialist government met its end in 1985, at a time when there had been 130 appeals made, followed by about 100 in the following years, though by 1989 the figure was down to 60, and in 1993 was only 15. It is, however, clear that the level of conflict in Spain was far higher than in a federal state such as Germany.

Once Spain had set her foot on the road to a vertebrate style of articulation as a state with autonomous regions, the autonomies with fewer powers demanded equality with those with more. Under pressure from the regional governments, the two major parties decided in time that they saw no major disadvantage in forging agreements that would raise the ceiling of the powers invested in the autonomous communities to levels equal in all cases. The latest of these agreements (framed in the Organic Law on the Transfer of Powers or *Ley Orgánica de Tranferencia* of December 1992) was aimed at raising the level of the powers invested in all autonomous communities to such an extent that the regions would take major responsibility for matters such as Health and Education. Furthermore, in March 1994 the statutes of the autonomies that did not yet have powers in these areas were amended.

In this way and in a very short time Spain became one of the most decentralized countries in the world. While 90 percent of the public budget was handled by the central government (and the rest by municipalities (*ayuntamientos*) and provincial councils (*diputaciones*)), by the start of the 1990s this figure had gone down to less than 2 percent of the total. By 1992 the autonomous communities were handling 25 percent of public spending. However, one cannot say that at the end of the socialists' time in office the process of setting up a new way of organizing Spain as a state with autonomous regions was complete.

It was a clear instance of the classic problem of the race between the hare and the tortoise: the hare runs faster but the tortoise always catches up in the end, and there is no doubt whatever that a certain level of devolution of power was reached by some regions which stimulated and attracted the other autonomous communities. Yet the race restarted automatically over and over again because however much was gained, more demands were then made by the "historic nationalities." Spurred on by the appearance of galaxies of new nations in Eastern Europe after the crisis in communism in 1989–91, these historic nationalities also claimed the "right to self-determination." A demand for "sovereignty" that would prove difficult to address and that provoked hostile responses became the preferred alternative for the most strongly nationalistic parties. These reactive tendencies proved beneficial to the Popular Party and it encouraged them in return.

Meanwhile, in general terms, each autonomous community took shape politically according to one of four models. There are predominantly left-wing communities such as Andalusia, Castilla-La Mancha, and Extremadura – Andalusia having periods of nationalistic feeling that have not been very influential except in Seville – and to them, up to 1995, we should add Asturias, Murcia, and Valencia. As regards the predominantly right-wing communities – the Balearic Islands, Cantabria, and Castilla-León – they all remained loyal to their political affiliation with one exception for a time, and that was in Castilla-León. There was one very special case in this last community, and that was Galicia, where the moderate conservatism of Galician nationalism meant that most nationalists were subsumed into the right-wing party during the entire period in which the socialists were in power. The third group was made up of communities where there were regionalist or nationalist movements which acted like a hinge and so became a crucial element in stabilizing government by opting on most occasions for the center-right. These regions were the Canary Islands, Aragon, Navarre, and La Rioja.

It is worth mentioning especially the two historic nationalities that had the strongest sense of their own identity and were able, through their deputies in the Congress, to make a greater political impact within the Spanish government.

In Catalonia the main nationalist group, Convergence and Union (*Convergència i Unió* or CiU), came to power in the autonomous community in 1980, and after the elections that year exercised it for most of the time without having to collaborate with other groups. Jordi Pujol, an outstanding political figure and an enduring force in Spanish public life for over a quarter of a century, managed as Tarradellas had done before him to become identified in people's minds with the community he led. A distinctive feature of Catalanism was the fact that, unlike the leaders of the rest of the Spanish right and center-right, its leading figures had all emerged from anti-Francoist or dissident groups. Pujol had been arrested and ill-treated and had spent months in prison during the 1960s. CiU Catalanists not only took part in drawing up the Constitution but also in the Moncloa Pacts. As Pujol himself has recounted, he also managed to avoid involvement in the removal of Suárez, as many leaders of the UCD would have liked to do. Roca, who was the deputy-leader of the party and favored the reformist tendency was, in 1992–3, keen to be part of the last socialist cabinets, but Pujol, warned off by what had happened in 1986, held out against it. The failure of this two-headed politics led in effect to Roca's resignation. Nonetheless, Catalanists provided the socialist government with useful support from 1989 to 1993 and were an indispensable ally in the period 1993–6.

The peculiar circumstances of Catalanism in Spanish politics after 1993 meant that it provided a hinge for whatever national government might emerge at a time when there was no absolute majority in Parliament. González's bringing forward of the elections in 1996 was preceded by a letter from Pujol in September 1995 in which, for a range of reasons among which was the fact that the GAL affair had come to the attention of the Supreme Court, Pujol told the prime minister that he could not support him.

In general there has not been real conflict in Catalan society over the superimposing of one cultural identity on another, nor even over the implementation of so-called "linguistic immersion" which presupposes that on the first rungs of the educational ladder all teaching will take place in Catalan. As a result of the bringing down of the Berlin Wall and the flowering of new nationalities, the entire Catalan Parliament, with the exception of the right, approved a declaration demanding the right to self-determination. This was the first case in which a vote was taken on such a decision and typically there were no immediate consequences.

The force that was shaping Basque politics was, in contrast, an extreme form of fragmentation and polarization in addition to the presence of terrorism in the region. As though the region's existing problems were not enough, the removal from power after 1984 of the first president or *lehendakari*, Carlos Garaicoechea, was a result of the dissolution of the PNV organization in Navarre with which he was associated, and of the respective powers invested in the regional councils, as laid down in the Historic Territories Law (*Ley de Territorios Históricos*). When a new party, Eusko Alkartasuna (EA), made its appearance in September 1986, it was defined as social democrat and in favor of self-determination, but in fact it was not so very different from the PNV, except in terms of differences in distribution (greater numbers in Guipúzcoa in the case of EA). Another instance of fragmentation in Basque politics was that of the political groupings which came from positions close to ETA but evolved in a way that turned not only against terrorism but also against nationalism itself.

This meant that after 1986 the political system in the Basque Country had seven parties: four that were nationalist (PNV, EA, EE or Euskadiko Ezkerra, and HB), two state parties (PSOE and AP and later PP) and a seventh provincialist party: Alavese Unity (*Unidad Alavesa* or UA). Despite this degree of fragmentation, or perhaps precisely because of it, political pacts between these contending forces were a constant factor in Basque politics. The PNV always had the Presidency of the Executive despite the fact that at the start of the 1980s it failed to win more votes than the PSOE. Furthermore – and this was supremely ironic – it even ended up governing along with the political group that had split off from it: Eusko Alkartasuna. However, the most significant aspect of this pragmatic pacting from a political and historical point of view was that there was a succession of governments in the autonomous community that were based on "transversal" agreements between the socialists and Basque nationalists. In this way a kind of politics that took the form of "permanent pacts" came into being at all the most crucial levels of government, not just in Vitoria but also in Madrid.

This experience of transversal government contributed to, and was at the same time helped by, changing attitudes towards terrorism in Basque society. At the end of the 1980s only just over one in five Basques considered ETA members patriots. There was now potential for a front against terrorism among the region's democratic political forces. After ETA's most brutal attacks, such as the bombing of the Hipercor hypermarket in

Barcelona in 1987, the democratic parties managed to agree on taking joint action in protest against terrorism thanks to the Madrid and Ajuria Enea agreements in November 1987 and January 1988 respectively. The new *lehendakari*, José Antonio Ardanza, repeatedly emphasized the differences between the PNV and ETA, not only in terms of means but also of ends.

However, after the start of the 1990s several factors came together to threaten the survival of transversal government. In the first instance, as had already happened in the Catalan Parliament, in February 1990 the Basque Parliament voted in favor of a resolution on self-determination. At the same time, a decline in the socialist vote presented its leaders with the constant temptation to break with the central Spanish party as this seemed to be the only way of keeping its own electorate. Basque nationalism in this period tended to seek electoral support from among even the most hard-line nationalists.

What characterized ETA's evolution on the terrorist question was, throughout the 1980s and at the start of the 1990s, its very slow return to the political process. When the socialists came to power, the number of dead as a result of terrorism was, as we have said, around 40 people a year; at the same time, it was only after 1986 that the vote in favor of Herri Batasuna went down.

In the final years of the 1980s and at the start of the 1990s, with exceptions such as 1991, the numbers of deaths went down to around 20 a year, and by the end of the socialist time in government the number of deaths as a result of terrorist activity was around ten per year. If in 1986 Operation Sokoa had provided a large amount of information on the terrorist organization, Operation Bidart subsequently succeeded in dismantling a large part of ETA's support network. While the socialists were in power there was a discernible aging of the *etarras* in prison and a growing number of members from Guipúzcoa, the province where hard-line nationalism was most widespread and most deeply rooted. Finally, we must bear in mind that the use of methods such as the GAL up to 1986 did not mean that there was no government contact with the terrorist organization. After having held talks with ETA in Algiers in 1986 which failed, contact continued to be maintained until 1988 in other localities – Bordeaux, for example – without any success. The last socialist Interior Minister, Juan Alberto Belloch, kept contact with the terrorist organization. Like so many others, he was convinced that he would gain results in the end, but he too was disappointed.

———————— **The Loss of an Absolute Majority** ————————

During the period between 1986 and 1992, the level of the intention to vote PSOE remained very high – at between 24 and 33 percent – while on the right the figures fluctuated a great deal, and only towards the final phase of the government did they reach anywhere near the lowest percentage scored by the socialists. The moment when a fundamental change began to take place in public opinion was in 1991, the year in which the PSOE began quite definitely to lose the hegemony it had enjoyed until then among urban voters. By 1991, 56 percent of those questioned in surveys thought that they were already paying too much tax for the public services that were being provided in exchange. That was proof both of a change in direction of public opinion and of mistrust of the party in government.

At the same time, there was a marked decrease in the rate at which laws were being passed in the 1990s, and at times attention was switched to areas in which legislation provoked unnecessary conflict. The clearest such case was the minister José Corcuera's Law on Public Safety (*Ley de Seguridad Ciudadana*), which was from the very start considered unconstitutional by a large percentage of the public. In the end, the Constitutional Court would declare a large part of the law contrary to the fundamental law of 1978, and this would bring about the resignation of the minister, who had promised to go if the Court pronounced in this way.

Be that as it may, what was even worse for the socialist government was the advent of a spate of political scandals. These began in the months that immediately preceded the 1989 elections and they worsened as time went by. Although it is unfair to blame all socialists for what was in fact the responsibility of a very few, at the same time there is no doubt whatever that their excessively pragmatic approach, their conviction that the eventual result would be the best possible and therefore that any shortcut was permissible, the length of time they had stayed in power which led to them forgetting their responsibilities, and, last but not least, a tendency to react badly as soon as any adverse criticism was made, were all vices that were widespread in the party in government. As we shall have the opportunity to see in due course, a large part of the scandals dated back to the socialists' first term of office and can only be understood in the light of their euphoria at their triumph in effecting a change in government. As we know, in 1991 the PSOE began to lose the urban vote, and this meant that the following year, when the Olympic Games were going to be held in Spain, as well as the celebrations for the quincentenary of the discovery of America, far from being the moment of greatest glory for González's government, was a time of crisis in the eyes of the general public. Worse still, it became obvious to any independent observer that at the heart of the ruling party there were two souls that could not work together easily, to whom we have already referred: Felipe González and Alfonso Guerra.

The first matter to attract public attention concerned the behavior in Seville of Juan Guerra, Alfonso Guerra's brother. His case was reminiscent of the kind of anecdotes that were told about the abuses of power by political bosses known as *caciquismo* at the time of the Restoration of the Monarchy in 1876. Acting as a kind of secretary to his brother, Juan Guerra had used an office in the Government Delegation in Seville for his own personal business. It was understood that he had created for himself a means of bestowing personal favors. He had, furthermore, been involved in all kinds of minor business dealings that were more or less dubious. Although the whole affair was not on a very large scale, the deputy prime minister reacted in a most unfortunate way in denying all guilt and trying to shift the blame, when it was quite clear where responsibility actually lay. This matter brought Alfonso Guerra into head-on confrontation with Felipe González, but despite several skirmishes, he did not finally leave the government until 1991; before that, and in the years afterwards up to 1996, he waged all-out guerrilla war against the sections of the party that were closest to González.

To everyone who was watching the PSOE in the 1980s, the González–Guerra duo seemed more or less indestructible. That is how the press and the opposition saw it too. However, the crisis that arose between them showed that in fact the situation was very different. The relationship between these two major protagonists in Spanish public life was never very close from a personal point of view, and it also became obvious that their opinions differed greatly on how to govern and on the way they saw the party itself. Rather than being a close relationship based on shared experience outside work, the relationship between González and Guerra seems to have been strictly political. They complemented each other only at the time they came to power, but very soon the gulf separating them became obvious. González finally reached the point where he considered Guerra's position "abusive" because of the latter's demands for support, and more importantly still, the prime minister finally realized that his deputy was "part of the problem rather than the solution." The thirty-second PSOE party conference (1990) might have given the impression that the situation was becoming more stable because in fact 80 percent of the most important figures within the party could be described as Guerra supporters who had signed up to "*guerrismo*." This would have meant that the party remained in Guerra's hands while González took charge of governing the country. In January 1991 the deputy prime minister, who had offered to resign earlier on, was dismissed from his post.

If this separation of functions had ever come about, circumstances would soon have made it impossible for the agreement to work. In the spring of 1991 information began to appear in the press about FILESA – a network of companies whose aim was to increase socialist party funding. A paradox occurred, in that in 1987 a generous law on party funding allowed the PSOE to increase the sums it received from around 3,600 million pesetas per year to 6,700 million. However, the political parties – and not just the socialists – always showed a kind of insatiable thirst when it came to public funding, which they tried to increase by any means at their disposal.

During its short life, FILESA charged diverse companies around 1,000 million pesetas for work that was never actually done and, at the same time, it paid the Socialist Party's bills for election campaigns and also the renting of property for party use. As if this were not enough, the company did not pay taxes when these should have been in the region of almost 300 million pesetas. All of this inevitably leads one to think that the companies that had paid the bills had done so in exchange for some sort of compensation from the party that was then in government. Faced with this indisputable reality, the PSOE immediately split. Guerra's faction tried to deny what was obvious to everyone and resorted to the tactic of accusing its opponents. It was claimed that González should also have been held responsible – if only because he did nothing – but the latter was aware that a situation such as this was unacceptable.

There were other controversial questions tangled up in the FILESA affair. From the end of the 1980s on, Felipe González had made clear his desire not to stand again as a candidate for the party leadership. Guerra's supporters, without showing any opposition to González, built their hopes on this state of affairs and tried constantly to take a hand in the matter of the succession. Above all, they vetoed any possibility of Narcís Serra ever benefiting from González's departure. The ex-deputy prime minister's followers believed that they had good arguments against all of his rivals in the party. When at the start of 1992 it was discovered that a finance company called Ibercorp was guilty of irregularities that seemed to have benefited individuals linked to some of the most influential areas of government economic policy, there was even rejoicing in the Guerra camp.

However, González, who was prone to changes of heart on the matter of his dedication to politics, seems to have reacted vehemently and decisively when faced with the possibility of the party ending up in the hands of the man who was now his rival. In October 1992, after much doubting, he announced that he would agree to stand again as a candidate for the party leadership, but he then immediately set out his conditions and demanded independence for the government in relation to the party, which he had always assumed to be the case anyway. Meanwhile, the situation at the time proved favorable for the emergence of a new tendency within the party. It would be an exaggeration to say that those who advocated "renewal" ever came to have any group structure. They would have liked the PSOE to be less inward-looking, but they never reached the point of setting out a program or offering an alternative way ahead as such. In fact they were waiting for González to lead them, but never saw it happen because he was already doing so without any difficulty in that he already exercised direct control over the party organization as a whole. In April 1993, the secretary of the party organization, José María Benegas (who as such was also number three in the party hierarchy), resigned from his post complaining about the attitude of several nameless ministers and "renewers of nothing." This event meant that elections were called even though the government had not lost its original support in Parliament. This also meant that there was another paradox in that a candidate who did not want to stand (González) was forced by circumstances to lead a party with which he found it hard to communicate, and bring forward elections when nobody wanted them.

To complicate the parliamentary situation still further, as well as the lack of unity in the PSOE there was the matter of continuing political scandals. In 1991 José Amedo had been sentenced to more than a century in prison, but he remained silent (it came to light later that he had done so in exchange for remuneration) on the identities of those ultimately responsible for the GAL. All these circumstances taken together meant as a consequence that the 1989–93 term of office was somewhat sterile in terms of what it achieved and became very complex as a result of the need to maintain a vital degree of stability. Although, as the results of the 1989 elections had suggested, the PSOE had a virtually absolute majority, in the final period of its time in power it felt a need to be able to count on help from nationalist and/or centrist groups (PNV, CiU, and CDS) who were given the totally inappropriate name "constitutional block," as though the PP was not constitutional. In the medium term, the result of this collaboration was none other than the disappearance of the few chances that the CDS had ever had, and an image of the nationalist groups that made them seem willing to sell themselves to the highest bidder. That is how the right tried to present them through the media, at the same time as it attributed to González an ability to seduce such political groups that was as infinite as it was perverse.

Meanwhile, the change in attitude in public opinion as regards the PSOE had become more marked. At the start of the 1990s, some 89 percent of Spaniards were convinced that there was much or a fair amount of corruption in Spain, and 76 percent described the PSOE as a "divided" party. Around 1991, sociological changes had begun to show clearly in the political make-up of town-halls and the parliaments of the autonomous communities. In 1983, the PSOE had held power in 50 of the 70 largest municipalities, of which 45 remained in its hands in 1987. By 1991, however, it had only 37. In 1983, the PSOE had governed 12 of the autonomous communities while the PP only governed three, but in 1991 the PSOE held only ten and the PP now held five.

The elections held in 1993 were preceded by results that had been gathered in earlier surveys which suggested that a socialist defeat was almost a certainty. Divisions within the socialist camp were obvious even while the election campaign was being organized. Still today the socialist leaders continue to argue over who was responsible for leading the campaign, and therefore who deserves the praise for their victory. Whatever the truth of the situation was, it was only at the very last moment, after a campaign that was more bitterly fought and doubtful in terms of the likely results than any election since 1979, that the PSOE once again repeated its victory.

It did so thanks to the candidate who had not wanted to stand. González managed to give the impression that he was prepared to change his attitude and perform an act of contrition at the same time as he dismissed his adversary – Aznar – as lacking expertise and likely to become a danger to stable democracy. His cleverest bid, when it came to putting together the lists of candidates, was to offer the second position on the Madrid list to Judge Baltasar Garzón, who had led the investigations into drugs cases and the GAL murders.

This most recent socialist victory can be explained in part by the fact that the prime minister was still Spain's politician with the highest popularity ratings, but even more so by the sudden rise in the number of people voting due to widespread fear of the PP coming to power – a party that had not yet managed to give the impression that it would be capable of bringing about change responsibly. The PSOE won 38 percent of the vote and 159 seats, while the PP had 34 percent of votes and 141 seats. The United Left (IU) managed only 9.6 percent of votes and 18 seats, one more than it had gained in the previous election. Once again the opposition to the left of the PSOE was unsure on its feet at what seemed a perfect moment to snatch votes from the PSOE.

For the opposition, the results of the 1993 elections were very disappointing. This was the second occasion on which José María Aznar had headed the Popular Party, standing as its candidate for the post of prime minister (the first had been in 1989). Yet it was only in the 1990s that this alternative to the socialists, with Aznar as its leader, began to stand out on the political horizon. Its most distinctive trait was, from the very first moment, its youthfulness. By 1989 it was already the case that only 16 percent of AP candidates were standing for the second time. Their leader had moved ground from a right-wing position that had little sympathy for the Constitution to one where he identified more closely with the young liberals from the now extinct center party. His next step was to become the candidate for the presidency of Castilla-León despite competition from other far more experienced rivals, and he won the race for the candidacy for the regional presidency in 1987. He then managed at last to push for the national leadership at the very moment at which Fraga rejoined the party leadership in 1988. At the time, Aznar was the only young AP politician who had an important political and administrative post, but the fact that he was standing for the national leadership meant from the very start that he was bound to break with what had been usual right-wing policy up to that time. "I don't have any of the transition mannerisms," he went so far as to assure the very man who was the personification of the transition. Aznar's opposition style, which was systematically confrontational, did not follow the general consensus, even on the question of terrorism, though this was usually the case with Spanish democratic politics. The public's judgment was never very kind about the sort of politics practiced by the PP. At the start of the 1990s, 55 percent of the electorate thought that the PP could do nothing better than criticize.

This critical attitude was, however, very much in tune with the opposition to González's government in the press. A particular example of this was the daily newspaper *El Mundo* and its editor Pedro J. Ramírez. This newspaper had the undoubted merit of having brought to light many of the scandals that had emerged at this stage in the socialists' time in office (the GAL, FILESA . . . ), but at the same time, it is possible to point out some serious disadvantages in the stance it took, such as contact with self-confessed criminals, extremism in its criticism of supposed cases of immorality that turned out to be nothing of the sort, the way it used information like a battering-ram rather than with strict objectivity . . . The newspaper also actively encouraged the collaboration – the "pincer-movement" – which drew together the two political opposites of left and right in their fight against González. After the 1993 elections, despite the results, everything seemed to suggest that the PSOE was not going to find its new term of government at all easy. By the time of the European elections in June 1994, the PP was already ten points ahead of the PSOE, while the socialists lost their majority in Andalusia – their old feudal heartland.

The history of the other political parties of sufficient importance to offer alternatives to the PSOE can be summarized far more simply, given that their leaders had not changed as much as had been the case in the Popular Alliance–Popular Party. Adolfo Suárez's CDS, as we have already seen, reemerged in 1986 with a surprising and promising resurrection which, however, proved short-lived because of the party's uncertainty on strategy which led to oscillation between pacts with both the AP and the PSOE. In 1993, after Suárez had retired from politics, the CDS, with less than 2 percent of the vote and only a quarter of the share it had had in the previous general election, lost its last seats in the Congress of Deputies. Its end was made even more grotesque by the fact that its candidate for the post of prime minister in 1996 was the financier Mario Conde, who was already under police investigation and in prison.

For its part, the left, encouraged by the anti-government stance of the unions, saw some progress, though this was soon revealed as being limited. The name that it had taken – "United Left" – had been the result of an attempt to draw smaller groups in with the PCE, and a diffuse feeling that was critical of the PSOE, but despite all its efforts, initially there was no substantial change in its share of the vote. In 1986 it barely grew, with fewer than 50,000 new votes, despite the fact that the PSOE had outlined its policy on staying in NATO; it was only in 1989, after the general strike, that IU managed to double its percentage, which then remained unchanged in 1993. Anguita did manage to sketch out his own position. He deliberately distanced himself from agreements with the PSOE and he had no hesitation about working with the right on specific issues. However, all that this enabled him to do was to give advantages to the right without gaining anything in return.

## A Tense Term of Office (1993–6)

The results of the 1993 elections seemed at first to offer Spanish society a brief period of normality after what had in effect been an especially tense election campaign. The situation in Parliament forced González to seek the support of other groups in the *Cortes*, such as the centrists or the Basque and Catalan nationalists. In the medium term, however, Catalan support in Parliament, which presupposed substantial material gains in return as well as establishing a "bilateral" relationship, did much to poison political life because it drew attention in a very harsh manner to the relationship between the center of Spain and its periphery. González now found himself obliged to do something similar. He gained the support of Parliament and formed a government with a large number of independent members. It seemed for a moment that the Catalanist Miquel Roca might be made president of the Congress of Deputies and a Basque Minister for Industry, but both of these political groups ended up doing no more than offering support from outside the government itself. There were none of Guerra's supporters, despite the fact that González seems to have tried repeatedly to persuade Benegas to take on the Public Administration portfolio (he was a socialist who tended to have a good understanding with the PNV).

The most significant of the independent members of the government was Belloch, the Justice Minister, who had made a name for himself by defending the judiciary against the executive, and who had spent 2 years on the General Council of the Judiciary. For the very first time, there were three women in the government. As the man responsible for the fight against drugs, in the position of secretary of state, another member of the government was Judge Baltasar Garzón, with all the prestige from his past which included having pursued those responsible for the GAL. It appears that both Serra and Solana had important roles to play in the running of the new executive, and this seemed to open the way for a seamless handover of power by González. From 1993 on, Serra exercised in full his powers as deputy prime minister, taking charge of coordination, though there were some matters that remained the direct responsibility of the prime minister himself, such as foreign and home affairs. The prime minister also decided to take a firm hold on the reins of the party from the very start, or at least, he intervened in party affairs for the first time. He aimed to put Carlos Solchaga at the head of the parliamentary minority and made it perfectly clear that he was ready to resign if Solchaga were not elected.

The pro-Guerra faction complained that this decision split the party, but in practice, after 1993, the *guerristas* gradually lost all importance and support at the same time as the influence of the territorial "barons" was increasing. In March 1994, at the thirty-third party conference, González's triumph was clear for all to see, and this did not cause any increase in internal dissentions. It is very possible that the prime minister would have preferred a total victory, but he did not push for it. What is clear is that the way things appeared at the start gave little clue as to what would happen later as a result of the flood of scandals that erupted afterwards. Serra could state later that in actual fact "there was not even a parliamentary group" as such; such were the divisions at the heart of the PSOE.

Very few months had passed before the González government – which had, throughout the 1980s, enjoyed several years without having to do any penance at all – suddenly seemed sentenced to make up for the lack in a series of unfortunate events. Until this point, González had managed to show considerable "psychological fortitude" in the face of adversity. Now, however, there were aspects of the scandals revealed by the press that he could barely handle; he himself stated afterwards that "the level of corruption left me paralyzed, bemused."

Before we allude to this tidal-wave of scandals, however, we should ask if the period of government that began in 1993 was not simply a rather worse prolongation of the previous term of office, or whether, on the contrary, it showed a will to set matters to rights. Despite what might seem to be the case at first glance, the real answer is in fact the second. As the Minister for the Presidency at the time, Alfredo Pérez Rubalcaba, said, the government "never lost its sense of direction [but] it did lose touch with its agenda." The term "sense of direction" refers to its self-definition in terms of a program, while its "agenda" refers to its capacity to respond in the face of the successive scandals it had to confront.

Positive aspects of the program set out by González's last government include political reforms, measures to tackle the economic crisis, and the correction of errors in home affairs. The political reforms implemented were far-reaching, but only a very few of them were actually approved. The interpretation put forward by the Catalanist Miquel Roca during the investiture was probably right: the Spanish people had decided on what needed to be set to rights, but they wanted it done by those who had governed so far and not by the opposition. The measures that were implemented (the creation of an office to prosecute in case of corruption, new procedures on state contracts . . . ) were important, but they could achieve little in the face of a positive tidal-wave of political scandals relating to the past.

The economic crisis was brief and, besides, González was in no doubt about his basic policies. He did not put his European ambitions on hold (nor, therefore, his support for a single currency), nor did he compromise on a program that was in many ways liberalizing, though it was implemented at a different pace from the way the opposition wanted it to proceed. This explains – within the parameter of a tendency that is common in western economies – the Law on the Autonomy of the Bank of Spain (*Ley de Autonomía del Banco de España*) of 1994.

Spain's economic growth had increased since 1985 until in 1992–3 a crisis hit that affected the whole of Europe and was serious though not long-lasting, so that in 1992 the economy only grew 0.7 percent and in 1993 the figure was below zero. While it lasted, however, the limitations of Solchaga's economic management were particularly obvious. In the final phase of the socialist government, after the 1993 elections, the politician mainly responsible for its economic policy, Pedro Solbes, managed to channel expenditure by the ministries within acceptable limits. The failure of the general strike in 1994 helped him to do this – indeed, significantly so, since it allowed him to cut social spending. In any case, we have to take into account the fact that the need to rely on the minority Catalan vote forced the socialist government to keep to a strictly orthodox economic policy.

Setting matters to rights in the Interior Ministry was, quite clearly, essential. There was, for example, a need to regularize the handling of reserved funds, which had been managed without any form of control, or in ways that were manifestly fraudulent in the sense that they had been used for purposes for which they had not been intended. There was also the matter of what to do about the men who had held major positions of responsibility in the past (the Secretary of State, Rafael Vera, and the Director General of the Civil Guard, Luis Roldán), who considered themselves nothing less than indispensable in the fight against terrorism.

González appointed Antoni Asunción as Interior Minister, but Roldán's flight, amid a hail of accusations of embezzlement of public funds (April 1994), brought about his resignation. The prime minister decided, as the best possible solution, to give the Ministry of the Interior to Belloch, who was already Justice Minister and so collected two of the most important jobs in politics. Belloch did not want to follow Serra's advice when putting together his ministerial teams, which was clear evidence of dissention within the socialist party.

As for Garzón, who had been accorded some police powers along with his title, he thought (or chose to think) that González had intended him to take on powers both to fight terrorism and for the war on corruption as well. Belloch was not prepared to pass any powers over to him and González did not arbitrate between them, with the result that he kept avoiding the judge, who then resigned. He immediately returned to the judiciary and, as we shall see, in a legal but rather curious way, he reopened a law case that allowed him to put on trial a man who had for a few days held very high office at his side in the Interior Ministry (Vera). Both Garzón and Belloch were after the same areas of responsibility and both were indiscreet and exhibitionist, but in all probability they had the best intentions as they tried to impose a change in direction on the Ministry of the Interior. "What we did," Belloch has stated, "was to give the judges what they were asking for and tell the police to get on and do their duty."

On these three points – economic policy, political regeneration, and a change in direction in the Interior Ministry – there was, therefore, a real attempt to bring about "a change within the existing change." However, in the first two instances this did not do much to improve the government's image and, in the third case (because it was inevitable), the government was plunged into an even deeper pit. The string of scandals which followed hard on each other's heels in the last months of 1993 and, even more so, after the spring of 1994, caused profound social unrest with grave political repercussions.

Some events were nothing to do with the management of the Socialist Party. The economic crisis that Spain suffered around 1993 destroyed expectations that had been megalomaniac and were totally unjustified, but there had been a time when they had seemed quite serious. In December 1993, the paper producer Torras, which was controlled by the financier Javier de la Rosa, suspended all payments, while Banesto, one of Spain's traditional business enterprises, also came under investigation. Its chairman, Mario Conde, had not only become a key figure on the Spanish economic scene, but was also seen as a role-model by a section of Spain's young people. In November 1994, a complaint brought against him led to a demand for an enormously high sum as bail and he was put in prison the following month.

Yet it was not only big employers who suffered in the economic crisis. The PSV (*Promotora Social de la Vivienda*), a social housing cooperative set up in connection with the UGT at about the same time as Conde became chairman of Banesto, began to experience serious difficulties as a result of its megalomania and weak leadership. In 1994, when the PSV's economic situation was at its worst, relations between the government and the UGT were also very bad given the threat of another attempt to hold a general strike. This situation turned what was originally a problem of management into open conflict between the country's major trade union and the socialist government. Nonetheless, the government behaved in a far more sectarian way than it has been credited with doing and managed to sort the situation out.

In the space of only a very few months – April, May, and June 1994 – a succession of spectacular events occurred one after another. The first was the flight of the Director General of the Civil Guard, Luis Roldán. The arrest of the ex-Governor General of the Bank of Spain, Mariano Rubio, and of the former trustee of the Madrid Stock Exchange, Manuel de la Concha, was a result of irregularities in the handling of their own finances. From a political point of view, these arrests brought about the immediate resignation of Solchaga, who had vouched for Rubio in public in his role at the head of the socialist minority in the Congress of Deputies. As if this were not enough, the Agriculture Minister, Vicente Albero, also resigned because of tax problems.

Two further scandals should be added to those already mentioned. First, there was the sacking of the State Attorney General, Eligio Hernández, which took place before the Supreme Court declared his appointment illegal, which had always been perfectly evident. In addition, however, systematic fraud was uncovered in the awarding of public contracts in the autonomous community of Navarre, and those who would be found to be guilty were its foremost socialist leaders, including Gabriel Urralburu, who was a former priest who had been thought to be beyond reproach. Suddenly, the honest socialist leaders discovered that they had been trying to treat the illness of corruption with "drugs" rather than "surgery," but one can easily understand, too, the agonizing sense of disorientation that the party's top leadership experienced.

The upshot of all this was that in less than 2 years González, instead of regenerating the political scene, had been obliged to do away with no fewer than five of his original 17 ministers. The introduction of reformist measures had begun well, but in October 1994, two out of every three Spaniards did not trust González's word and by the end of the year more than a third believed that it was essential to hold another general election.

Yet the string of calamities suffered by the socialist government did not even end here. González had demonstrated on previous occasions that he was not prepared to move a finger on behalf of anybody, and he had looked in the other direction when these events had happened. He was especially angry at Rubio's behavior because it had involved a personal lie, and at Urralburu, because it caught him completely by surprise. Now, however, events that would implicate him personally and directly came to the fore once again.

Until that time, the two policemen, Amedo and Domínguez, had kept silent thanks to generous remuneration from reserved funds; however, when Belloch cut off this source of finance, they became very ready to talk. Thanks to their statements before Garzón, who was now back to practicing as a judge, they managed to obtain both their own release from prison at the end of 1994 and the trials of the Secretaries of State, Vera and Sancristóbal, and the ex-minister Barrionuevo, along with many other members of the police. There was even a possibility that González himself might be implicated. What happened in the case of these two policemen was complemented by the actions of Roldán after the start of 1995, who denounced his colleagues at the ministry to justify his sudden and spectacular wealth.

In March 1995 the Lasa-Zabala case was reopened. These were two *etarras* who had been among the first victims of the GAL who had been tortured first and then murdered. Somewhat more than a year later (in May 1996), the Civil Guard General, Enrique Rodríguez Galindo, was put in prison, having played a crucial part in the fight against terrorism (the forces under his command had suffered 10 percent of the casualties inflicted by ETA on the security forces). Galindo was finally sentenced in 2000 to more than 70 years in prison for having planned and directed anti-terrorist operations that had been manifestly illegal.

Like Amedo and Domínguez, Conde tried to practice a kind of blackmail using the information he had at his disposal. He was so daring that he went so far as to demand a huge sum of money as compensation for his bank being the subject of an investigation. The recording and storing of private conversations on mobile phones that were carried out by military intelligence (the CESID) and were then made available to Conde by an official source provided him with the necessary material to be in the strongest position for blackmail; even so he did not succeed. What the CESID had done was clearly against the spirit of the Constitution, thought there was no specific legislation on the subject. The political repercussions of the scandal surrounding the tapes not only brought about the resignation of the deputy prime minister Narcís Serra, of the Defense Minister, Julián García Vargas, and the director of the CESID, General Alonso Manglano, but they also, at least in part, contributed to the withdrawal of Catalanist support for the government in Parliament and, therefore, the dissolution of the *Cortes* and the calling of new elections.

The impact of the scandals was not so much due to the torrent of discoveries and revelations that took place as to the social climate which was close to hysteria and which lasted for several months. None of the information given by the accused, whose innocence seemed increasingly unlikely (from Amedo through to Roldán), was sufficient to stop the normal processes of justice or serious endanger the institutions themselves. It is true that some of the judgments raised doubts. The sentencing of Barrionuevo and Vera had no other basis than accusations by other guilty parties, though at the same time there are difficulties in believing that responsibility stopped with the latter and did not reach any further.

With hindsight we can see that none of the institutions acted entirely as it should have done, although the degrees to which that is true may vary. González was far from exercising any moral leadership. The government's attitude when faced with the successive scandals was, in the first instance, to deny them all, and then it had to admit that there was some truth in the accusations but it was not responsible, or at most, only to a limited extent. It never offered an overall explanation as to why there had been so many scandals and what its own share of the guilt was for allowing such a situation to arise. Nor did the opposition play a major part in exposing the scandals, preferring instead to sit back and watch them unfold and to take advantage of them, although it then turned the affair into a chance to pass judgment on socialism as a whole, rather than on a few socialists in particular. All in all, it seems hard to justify a situation in which a judge, on abandoning a political position and no doubt angry with the Executive to which he himself had once belonged, should be able to take charge of a case affecting that same government, and the ministry in which he himself had been working. Nor, indeed, does it seem admissible behavior for a man who reveals the crimes that he has committed (Amedo) to be rewarded by being released from prison. Nonetheless, the democratic state passed through a difficult time of trial and survived it by seeing that justice was done.

## The 1996 General Election. Drawing up the Balance on the Socialists' Time in Government

As the scandals multiplied, so the opposition prospects for an election improved. In the elections to the European Parliament in 1994, the PP won an almost universal victory; it was ahead in 13 of the 17 autonomous regions and in six of them it gained more than 50 percent of the vote. This trend could be seen even more clearly in the regional and municipal elections in 1995 which could even be said to have served as primaries for the electorate. In addition, just a few weeks earlier, Aznar had been the object of an assassination attempt on the part of ETA, and this aroused many people's sympathy towards him. The PP won a clear victory in terms of the urban vote; while it had been the party that had gained the highest vote in only 11 provincial capitals in 1987, and 21 in 1991, it was now the winner in 44 such cities. More significant still was the fact that in some of the towns in the industrial belt around Madrid (Alcorcón, Móstoles, and Alcalá) it was also out in front of the left-wing candidates. It had even made deep inroads into an electorate that had until now resisted its attempts at conversion: in Catalonia. The PP vote rose in this region from 7 to 12 percent, and in Barcelona and the Spanish-speaking outskirts of the capital the level actually reached 17 percent.

However, the election held in March 1996 gave the victory to the PP by a much narrower margin than expected, since they polled only 39 percent of the vote, going up by 4 points and having 156 deputies, while the PSOE barely went down by one point to 37.5 percent of the vote and still had 141 deputies. The difference between the two largest parties was, then, only around 300,000 votes. The very same tension that had made the removal of the socialists from power so urgent in fact ended up spoiling the chances of the right-wing opposition, which continued to cause concern because of its lack of experience and its excessive tendency to raise levels of tension. The other political groups did not see their position in Parliament change to any great extent. For example, the United Left managed to gain 21 deputies, but this was only three more than in the previous Parliament.

This meant, therefore, that the PP had to exercise its imagination in ways that could not have been anticipated only a few months earlier. For their part, the socialists could at least hope that what had happened in Greece would also happen in Spain – that is to say, that the socialists who had been ousted from power via the ballot-box would be returned very shortly afterwards thanks to the lack of experience and other limitations of the new governing party. This was the situation at the start of the new term of office.

José María Maravall, one of Felipe González's most influential ministers and advisers, has stated quite rightly that what went wrong during the socialists' time in power was not so much the government's "policies" as its "politics." If we extend the scope of what he was suggesting, we could say that the party's "politics" failed in three ways. First, some bad decisions were taken that were, paradoxically, the result of the huge amount of political capital that the socialists had accumulated by their sweeping victory in 1982. The consolidation of what was in effect a poor level of democracy can be explained in large measure by this reason alone, but the GAL and the dirty war were also products of the atmosphere that resulted from an overwhelming majority and the desire to solve problems quickly without letting any ethical barriers stand in the way.

Second, if the link between the party and the government did not work, it was not only because the party leaders tried to exert an influence that was not theirs to exert, or because theirs was a populist program that paid little attention to economic norms; it was also because González did not appear at all interested in what they were doing. In this sense it is not possible to exonerate him of all guilt concerning what went on in the party.

In terms of specific policies, the overall balance is much more positive. What is curious, though, is that the policies that were adopted in the majority of cases presupposed some fundamental continuity with the policies of the UCD, contrary to what one might have thought at first. In other words, the suggestion that this was a period that saw the "consolidation" of democracy is entirely correct. The socialists' political capital might indeed have induced them to make mistakes, but it also allowed them to make improvements in their foreign policy and, above all, it gave them the opportunity to enact a reform of the Armed Services that had not been possible until that time. Last but not least, they also made a Spanish state with autonomous regions a reality.

If we return for a moment to González's own assessment of the overall balance of his time in power once it was over, we find that modernization, the liberalization of the economy, and the increase in the actual physical capital in Spain were all indisputable realities. The degree of openness of the Spanish economy towards the outside world was much greater. For example, in 1994 half the cars registered in Spain had been manufactured abroad, while national production for export had doubled. Liberalization also increased where previously there had been state intervention, though not enough as yet. Nor was the dynamism of the business sector great enough yet. Of the 100 top firms in Europe in 1996 only 3 were Spanish. Spanish foreign investment was only an eighth of that of France, Germany, or Britain, and a third of the Italian level. In short, from an economic viewpoint, in 1990 the Spanish per capita income was 80 percent of the European average, which was identical to the percentage in 1975; when the Spanish socialists came to power the figure that measured this distance was 75 percent. There had been some closing of the gap after the economic crisis had made an impact, but Spain was still a long way behind Europe.

A considerable effort had also been made in relation to social spending, and this brought about an improvement in terms of human capital. Between 1980 and 1993, the volume of public spending in terms of the GDP rose from 33 to 49 percent, thanks mainly to increases in direct taxation. According to Maravall, in the period 1980–94, Spain managed to move from a level of social spending equivalent to 65 percent of the European average to 87 percent. The number of people benefiting from Spain's policy on unemployment went up by 1.5 million, the number of students by 2 million and those being cared for by the health service by 9.5 million. The huge transformation that had taken place in social spending was directed principally at education – a sphere where funding rose from 2.8 percent of GDP to 4.7 percent. The school age was raised to 16, the sum spent on grants was multiplied by 6 over the period 1982–1992, and the number of children benefiting from these changes went up from 500,000 to 800,000. All in all, in 10 years the number of student doing professional training courses doubled, and finally, it has been estimated that between 1980 and 1990 10 percent of the poorest Spaniards had seen their income rise by 17 percent, while 10 percent of the richest had seen theirs go down by 5 percent.

This commitment to increased social spending during the 1980s and the first half of the 1990s favored widespread changes in society. These had begun as soon as the transition was under way. A visitor who had known Spain in 1960 and came back in 1993 would think he was in a different country. In fact, the distance between Spain and Europe was much greater in 1960 than it had been in 1930, especially in terms of cultural habits, but a large part of the dynamism in Spanish society is, as is logical, a product of the changes that came about as a result of economic growth. After all, the per capita income had barely grown by 25 percent between 1930 and 1960, whereas by 1990 it was 12 times what it had been in 1960.

In the middle of the 1990s Spain was already the eighth country in the world in terms of gross domestic product and ninth in relation to its index of human development. By around 1995, 76 percent of the population lived in an urban environment and agriculture provided no more than 3.5 percent of GDP. Demographic data also show a society that was very similar to others in Western Europe. This meant a significant change in matters relating to the distribution of ages in the population. In 1995 there were in Spain some 5.5 million people over the age of 65 and more than 2 million over 75. The older population had increased; furthermore, there was a greater degree of mobility than ever. In the mid 1990s almost half of all Spaniards lived in a different place from where they had been born and a quarter lived in another province.

Perhaps the greatest change in the 1980s and early 1990s – which was a continuation of an earlier trend – concerned the growing role of women in Spanish society, and also the decisive change in forms of behavior and development. These were not the result of any political decision, but it would be appropriate to recall at this point that it was at the start of the 1980s that for the first time since the Civil War there was a woman appointed as a government minister. The percentage of Spanish women in work had risen during the 1980s from 27 to 33 percent despite the fact that in the first half of the decade the economic crisis did not make this change at all easy – quite the contrary. Nonetheless, the level was still well below the European average. Yet at the same time, and for the first time in Spanish history, in the academic year 1987–8 half of all university students were women. Linked to this phenomenon was that of the sharp decline in the birth rate, which went down from an average of 2.8 children per marriage to only 1.3. What was most significant about this was the speed with which it happened and the fact that it seems to have been irreversible, at least up to the present day.

One very characteristic trait of Spanish society in the 1980s and 1990s was also its secularization. At the start of the 1980s only a third of all Spaniards could be described at practicing Catholics, and this proportion went down to a fifth among the young. However, people still had a vague sense of being associated with Catholicism, and this was particularly so at certain key moments in life such as marriage, birth, and death. Yet a degree of respect for the Church, or a sense of the comfort to be derived from it, was limited to about 42 percent of the population, whereas in Italy the figure was 62 percent, and in Poland 69 percent.

In contrast, it was clear that family values persisted. In essence, this attitude was a result of a deeper sense of social cohesion which is characteristic of southern Europe as opposed to the individualism that typifies northern Europe. Eighty percent of Spaniards in the 1990s thought family values the most decisive and fundamental of all. In Spain, the number of people who lived alone was, relatively speaking, less than half the levels in the rest of the European Community. The figures on divorce were low compared with European figures, and although the number of illegitimate births was multiplied by six between 1970 and 1986, the levels remained low; the same can be said for cohabitation outside marriage, where again figures were low compared with other countries. The average age to marry in the 1990s was around 28 for men and 26 for women. What was considered most fundamental – cohesion, paternal authority, solidarity across the generations and in economic terms – remained. Of the 14 million families in Spain, only half a million were de facto couples.

One last characteristic that could be seen as typical of Spanish society at the start of the second half of the 1990s was a certain "anomia" – that is to say, a lack of fixed rules and deep-rooted values. The rules and values of previous generations had in large measure disappeared or were in the process of doing so. If post-materialist values are beginning to emerge in Spanish society today, a rather cynical materialism lacking any sense of solidarity is still to be found and it makes Spaniards feel uncomfortable, but deep down they adopt its values. As regards post-materialist values, there was clear evidence of their existence when nongovernmental organizations (NGOs) appeared on the scene, especially among the young. At the same time, "cynical democratism," which is yet another recipe for cynicism and a lack of solidarity in politics, meant that only 18 percent of Spaniards declared that they had any respect for professional politicians. In short, this kind of "anomic" attitude left Spanish society in difficulties when it came to facing up to the problems that would loom in the future. Spain was late in facing up to the problem of xenophobia because immigration to the Peninsula started late. In 1993 there were half a million legal foreign residents in Spain and about 200,000 or 300,000 illegal immigrants. Instances of xenophobia still tended to be directed at gypsies, but the panorama was about to change radically and very quickly in the years that followed.

―――――――　**Culture in the Post-Franco Period**　―――――――

It would be appropriate at this point to try to look at developments in Spanish culture in post-Franco Spain, for two fundamental reasons: first, because it was during the years when the socialists were in power, in the mid 1980s, that there were significant changes in Spanish culture, and second because, after all, that was the longest single chronological period since the advent of democracy.

One of the obvious signs of the consolidation of the new political system, when viewed from outside, was that Spain suddenly seemed to begin to export culture. Spanish culture was presented as a mixture of modernity, tradition, and uniqueness. Spanish culture "was no longer different, but at the same time, it was not the same" as in other countries. The problem facing the historian is in trying to define its uniqueness. In recent times, in fact, everything seems to be a symptom, though then it can be seen as merely anecdotal or even banal. Even so, we shall begin by trying to identify some of the essential characteristics of Spain's recent cultural development. Of course, freedom is the first of these defining characteristics. The final years of the Franco period witnessed at one and the same time an uprising and an obvious boldness on the part of the cultural media in relation to the regime. Freedom of expression then became a reality quickly yet step by step. Marías has written that there was in Spain a year and a half of liberalism without democracy and that produced "a kind of healthy de-politicization" of cultural life. His description is apt. What is important, in any case, is that there were unfortunate incidents but in the end complete freedom was achieved. There was an early proliferation of political texts, but in fact it only lasted until 1979.

Freedom was accompanied by an extreme diversification such that one can say without any doubt at all that it was greater than any that had ever been seen in the whole of Spanish history. It is important to bear in mind that the length of the lives of some of our great authors and the new opportunities open to young people, for example, allowed a literary society to evolve in which up to five generations of creative writers coincided. Muñoz Molina won the Critics' Prize (*Premio de la Crítica*) in 1987 and in 1995 he was made a member of the Royal Academy (*Real Academia*). An inter-generational coexistence such as this was not always without difficulties. Cela launched fierce and frequent attacks against all young writers, who were far from sharing his particular sensibilities, but so did

Francisco Umbral, who accused them of being "Anglo-bores." What happened in the literary world was repeated in other areas of the creative arts such as cinematography. Luis García Berlanga has produced much of his best work since 1975.

A third defining characteristic of post-Franco culture has without doubt been the conquest of a far bigger market than ever before. Democracy came hand-in-hand with the popularization of culture and a closer relationship with market forces. It was not for nothing that Spain went from having 16 to around 60 universities, and the Readers' Circle (*Círculo de Lectores*) has 1.5 million members. Arturo Pérez Reverte sold 3 million copies of his novels between 1992 and 1998. Like the new political era, the Spanish literary world has normalized. For example, it has seen the appearance of the literary agent and "writing schools" (*"escuelas de letras"*), though it still lacks a school of criticism respected by everyone outside Spain. Traditional bookshops may be experiencing times of crisis, but now there are books sold in hypermarkets. These characteristics are as applicable to the literary world as they are to the plastic arts. At the start of the 1980s more than 200,000 people attended an exhibition commemorating Picasso's centenary. The Velázquez exhibition was seen by 550,000 people and more than 300,000 catalogues were sold.

This positive scenario also has its disadvantages and weaknesses. The very fact that the commemorative exhibitions have taken place has, at times, rather trivialized the worlds of culture. Also, figures that appear to be brilliant can often hide realities that are less so. The publishing market produced 17,000 titles in 1975, 34,000 in 1985, and 38,000 in 1987, yet reading figures in Spain are less than half the European average, and in 1998 a half of all Spaniards said that they did not read books. The network of public libraries was not buying more than 2 percent of all books published in Spain, which is 10 times lower than the figure in the United Kingdom. Only 13 percent of Spaniards say that they have bought a book as often as about once a month.

A fourth important factor if we are to understand recent developments in Spanish culture is to be found in the rapid move towards an audio-visual culture. In around 10 million homes there were 11 million televisions in 1989, but in addition, unlike what had happened in other countries, the arrival of audio-visual technology in Spain had come about without there having been an earlier serious book culture. Reading, which was demanding, was abandoned in favor of audiovisual or cybernetic entertainment. The consequences of this may even have been fairly negative for the producers themselves, for a time at least; for example, the film-maker Andrés Vicente Gómez said on one occasion that young Spanish directors were very good visually but much less good in literary terms.

The attraction of audio-visual media should be linked to the break with traditional genres and fields of creativity as a more generalized phenomenon characteristic of the last quarter of the twentieth century. For some time now, narrative writers in Spain have worked as journalists at the same time. Two notable cases have been Francisco Umbral and Manuel Vicent. One can even go so far as to talk in the Spanish context of journalistic articles as a literary genre. Now, however, the phenomenon has become more widespread. In the immediate post-Franco years, up to 17 percent of films were based on works of literature, though in some years the figure went up to 42 percent (in 1991, for example). Indeed, this allowed Spanish cinema to reach some of its highest peaks of achievement. With Mario Camus's *La colmena* (*The Beehive*, 1982) and *Los santos inocentes* (*The Holy Innocents*, 1984), Spanish cinema reached levels of great brilliance by taking great literature as its starting-point.

A fifth factor to take into account is that in the cultural sphere the presence of women has been far more obvious, and also that of young people at a much earlier stage. An anthology of poetry published in 1985 was entitled *Las diosas blancas* (*The White Goddesses*), but a similar title could well have been given to the narrative writings of Adelaida García Morales or Soledad Puértolas, heirs of a group of Catalan women writers with links to the world of publishing who were already in evidence in the world of Spanish culture in the 1970s. The role of women in poetry is particularly significant, though from a sociological point of view it might be more interesting to draw attention to the fact that the novel is more especially aimed at a female readership. On the other hand, in the case of men and women, first novels are being published much earlier. Nowadays, it is possible for a novelist enjoying a certain degree of success to make a living from a literary career, though many are, at the same time, journalists.

What is characteristic of the recent generations in any of the creative arts is, in general, their cosmopolitanism. Muñoz Molina's novels show the influence of William Faulkner, and in the case of crime fiction and Javier Marías's narratives, the influence is that of British authors, while the film-maker Fernando Trueba is a great admirer of Billy Wilder. One can, however, detect the same phenomenon in the human and social sciences. Sociologists such as Manuel Castells and historians such as José Antonio Iglesias have made contributions of prime importance in their particular areas of specialty that are of universal worth. The presence of Spanish creative artists in all the most important international competitions, where they are accorded acclaim and applause from the public and the critics, cannot fail to impress. Barceló was hugely successful in Kassel in 1982 and since 1995 Javier Marías has been translated into 20 languages and has sold as many millions of copies of his books. The architect Rafael Moneo won the Pritzker Prize in 1996. Nobel Prizes for Literature were awarded to Vicente Aleixandre in 1977 and Camilo José Cela in 1989. The successive Oscars presented to José Luis Garci, Fernando Trueba, and Pedro Almodóvar were until very recently unthinkable.

Another aspect of Spanish culture is that there is increasing evidence of the plurality of the Iberian Peninsula which is already inscribed in our political and administrative life. Between 1975 and 1990, the number of books published in Catalan multiplied by a factor of five. However, it may be even more significant that there are writers who find themselves astride two cultural worlds, who enjoy success in both, as is the case with Bernardo Atxaga, Manuel Rivas, and Quim Monzó.

One last aspect of Spanish culture that should be noted is a characteristic that is more generalized, in other countries as well, and that is its postmodernism. This postmodern character can be seen in many different areas of artistic creativity that are all interrelated. First and foremost, the term postmodernity reminds us that the great period of modernism, which saw the rise of the scandals of the avant-garde, is not over. There is no longer any need to rise up in protests in aesthetic terms against the past; the time of collective demonstrations is now past. For its part, the avant-garde has now become a cosmopolitan form of classicism to which artists can return when they choose; so, for example, a young Spanish painter may feel an affinity with Cézanne or with the German Expressionists. The prescriptive tendencies of the avant-garde have now give way to a lack of any dominant aesthetic norms.

Another characteristic of postmodern times is a tendency to abandon any form of social or political commitment, along with a frank decline in intellectual involvement in the creative process. In Spain's case, the end of any such commitment can be set in 1987, when a conference was held to celebrate the man who had gathered anti-fascist writers together during the Civil War. This was the occasion on which Octavio Paz stated that intellectuals should not commit themselves to the passing interests of political parties. There is now no longer any prescribing of aesthetic norms and nor is there any real desire to transgress any norms; the same is true in politics where democracy means that the intellectual is no longer needed to legitimize any position at all. In relation to Francoism, there has been evidence of a certain "Stockholm Syndrome" – a mixture of aversion, nostalgia for lost youth when choices seemed easier to make, and a sarcastic distancing from the earlier period. An unexpected early inheritance from the dictatorship was a flowering of Marxism in the human and social sciences that was the antithesis not only of Francoist culture but of republican culture too (Salvador Giner). However, that only lasted for a very short time. It was, in fact, a liberal philosopher, Julián Marías, who stood out as the real intellectual standard-bearer in Spain during the transition. Then, at the start of the 1980s, José Luis López Aranguren's nonconformist stance made an increasing impact, though the work that made a yet more decisive mark on these modern times was Fernando Savater's *Panfleto contra todo* (*Pamphlet Against Everything*), which was written at the time that the Constitution was being drawn up and so seemed to be a general critique of any attempt to set up an ideal political system – or to put it another way, it offered a disenchanted version of democracy. There were artists, such as the singer-songwriter Lluís Llach, who declared "*No és això, companys*" ("*That's not it, my friends*"). Yet the most fundamental legacy of the transition was also a collection of disenchanted, stagnating cultural figures who were imaginative and knowledgeable about market forces, who used bizarre names and published botched but singable music (José Carlos Mainer). That is, in effect, what the so-called "movida" ("*movement*") actually was.

In other fields, postmodernity indicated a range of different notions. Ethics and aesthetics were particularly richly explored in essays and philosophical writings; there was, without doubt, a desire for practical reflection and a sense of immediate usefulness. There was, for example, no attempt to construct grand, complete philosophical systems. Philosophers (Xavier Rubert de Ventós, Fernando Savater, Eugenio Trías ... ) often took the masters of skepticism and criticism as the point of departure for their reflection, but they never intended to offer an exhaustive study and they focused on problems of everyday life. The most common characteristics of philosophical essays were that they were autobiographical, fragmentary, and impressionistic. There was a new reading of history put forward that set out to correct the notion that Spain had been exceptional which had obsessed thinkers in the past like a kind of enduring tragedy. Its chosen method was to compare it with what had happened in other countries, and in short it concluded that what had happened in Spain was no different from what had happened elsewhere. In the plastic arts, the notion that swept all before it was that of "art for art's sake" without any kind of commitment. It was possible to talk about the "color of democracy," in the sense that the stark, agonized palette of the past gave way to a far wider and more joyful range of colors.

Postmodernity also means a kind of new individualistic revolution that celebrates the intimate personal sphere. A form of literature devoted to the Self has emerged that was like a late normalization in Spain of a genre that already had faithful readerships in other countries. Diaries and accounts, autobiographies and memoirs, or, more generically, explorations of lived day-to-day experience have flooded the market of cultural creativity. The protagonist of these narratives is almost always a self-reflective voice pondering on the reality surrounding it. That novelists such as Soledad Puértolas and Antonio Muñoz Molina should have taken on the task of writing about their memories of life seems to suggest what they are doing might be compared to what would happen if, at a given moment, biographies were to be viewed as the supreme way of writing history.

The weakness of postmodernity has been its tendency to trivialize. The novel has gained a wider public but has lost prestige. The tendency to avoid grand systems has at times led to pure literary expressionism and, quite simply, an indulgence in ingenious creativity. Marías has said accusingly that "people talk endlessly about culture and at times they forget to create it"; there might also be a tendency to describe anything at all as culture – the simplest of activities, or even desires that are never realized because of the limits imposed by the difficulty of communication. This statement could well apply, for example, to the "*movida*," whose ephemeral nature has become evident with the passage of time. Furthermore, because trivializing has had as a corollary a proliferation of commemorative events (and of prizes), it is not surprising that it is hard to identify any real values.

## From a Time of Rediscovery to a State Culture

No parallels can be drawn between the political transition in Spain and any kind of substantial change in terms of its culture. The transition meant that there was now freedom in the world of cultural creativity. We shall now try to take it apart chronologically. At the very start, even as the political process was moving ahead, there was a rediscovery of an intellectual tradition that had been lost, or at least, not well enough known during the Franco period. In fact, the process of rediscovery had started earlier, in the 1950s and 1960s, but it only came into its own at this point. The political belligerence of the cultural world at the end of the Franco period did play quite a major part in driving political change.

In actual fact, Spain's cultural transition took place later and new political freedoms did not produce an immediate cultural flowering. Spanish culture was still for a time led principally by those who had begun to play a significant role in the mid 1960s – a time when not only major figures and trends but also a number of commercial networks and an albeit minimal infrastructure appeared and essentially remained active until well on into the 1980s.

The move towards greater freedom in cultural matters was rapid and, in general, did not present any great problems. In 1976 only two foreign films (by Oshima and Pasolini) were banned in Spain because of their sexual content; on the other hand, others such as Martín Patino's *Canciones para después de una guerra* (*Songs for after a war*) and Chaplin's *The Great Dictator* which had previously been banned were now shown. In November 1977 censorship of films ceased and one could at last see in Spanish cinemas examples of hitherto forbidden cinema, such as Buñuel's *Viridiana*. The case of Pilar Miró's *El crimen de Cuenca* (*The crime in Cuenca*), which could not be shown for a year and a half, was as unfortunate as it was unjustifiable and exceptional. This particular film, which should have been premiered at the end of 1979, was about the historic case when Civil Guards tortured people who had not committed a crime. The film was denounced by a military attorney and could only be shown after the attempted military coup of February 23, when it became the greatest box-office success in 1981. There was a similar incident involving the Catalan theater group *Els Joglars*, who were also denounced by a military attorney, supposedly for having criticized the Army. With the passage of time both questions were resolved as a result of the reform of the Armed Services.

In general, although there was evidence in the transition years of continuing leftist belligerence on the part of many intellectuals, it would not be true to say that either a radically aggressive attitude to the past or one that defended it was typical of the intellectual world or of any other area of Spanish life. Any reference to the past was made from a distance tinged with sarcasm. An exception to the rule was Jaime Camino's attempt at a documentary style in *La vieja memoria* (*Old memory*, 1977). In Berlanga's *La escopeta nacional* (*The nationalist shotgun*, 1977), the grotesquely distorted image of the passion for hunting in the Franco period, humor is used as a distancing device. In Fernando Fernán Gómez's *Las bicicletas son para el verano* (*Bicycles are for summertime*, 1982), what we see is not the tragic collective experience of the Civil War so much as the feelings of the individual, such as fear, privations, or the closeness of death.

One decisive aspect of Spanish culture during the transition was, without doubt, the distinctive trait of having rediscovered and recovered a liberal tradition from the past. In fact, this procedure was nothing other than a continuation of what had begun in the mid 1960s and was now moving ahead faster and more clearly towards completion. In 1976 Salvador de Madariaga had at last taken his seat in the Royal Academy of the Spanish Language (*Real Academia de la Lengua Española*) after being elected as far back as 1936. The awarding of the Nobel Prize for Literature to Vicente Aleixandre in 1977 can be seen as evidence of the recovery of the Spanish liberal tradition, and a similar process could be seen in other areas too. In the theater, for example, the works of Rafael Alberti, Federico García Lorca, and Ramón del Valle-Inclán were performed once more. In philosophy and the social sciences, two illustrious exiles, both representatives of the Generation of 1914 – Claudio Sánchez Albornoz and Salvador de Madariaga – returned to Spain in 1976, to be followed finally in 1984 by María Zambrano. In the plastic arts, the arrival of *Guernica* in Spain in September 1981, and in general the interest in Picasso, was another way in which the link with the past and with Spain's historic avant-garde was forged. It is also clear that the rediscovery of authors whose works had been banned or were little known, such as Max Aub, Ramón Sender, Rosa Chacel, and Fernando Arrabal, resulted in very different levels of popular appreciation in Spain.

Alongside rediscoveries such as these, one might also mention a desire for the government administration to acknowledge officially what was going on in the creative arts at the time. One example of this would be the awarding of a Fine Arts Gold Medal (*Medalla de Oro de Bellas Artes*) to people such as Antoni Tàpies and Eduardo Chillida, or the many exhibitions of their work organized by the state in their honor. The immediate precedent was the organizing of a great exhibition of the works of Joan Miró in 1978. The task of recovery and normalization was essential, but at times it seemed as though Spanish culture was looking back to the past far too much. In fact, the attraction of themes relating to times past continued to be felt not only at the time but for years to come; even in a film such as Garci's *Volver a empezar* (*Starting all over again*), which won an Oscar in 1982, the protagonist is an exile who comes back to Spain.

Trueba's *Belle époque*, too, which won a second Oscar for Spain, looks back to the past, albeit in a comic vein.

We have already spoken in previous pages of the popularization of culture, and now it is time to be more precise and add that this was a result of the society in Spain at the end of the 1970s. In contrast to what had usually happened shortly before this time, culture became an object that drew an almost reverential respect and, for the very first time, attracted consumers from all levels of the population. Some statistics, such as those relating to the number of books published (40,000 at the start of the 1980s), are significant. The increase in the music on offer, or the repercussions after a festival of modern art such as ARCO (*Arte Contemporáneo*), can also be seen as important indicators. Nor was this popularization of culture in general accompanied by a lessening of demands for excellence; even the films that proved most successful with the general public were notable for the quality of their production.

If the normalization and dissemination of cultural values can be seen as the most positive aspects of the transition, there were at the same time weaknesses in the legislation and structures that were being put in place. The existing legislation on cultural matters was clearly obsolete, and there were also new problems arising as a result of new cultural needs and in terms of relations with the state. The instability that was characteristic of the UCD (in 5 years there were six director generals in the film world), and the existence of other political priorities meant, for example, that it proved impossible to gain approval for new legislation that would allow cultural foundations to be set up and Spain's historic art heritage to be adequately protected. At the same time, there were demands being made for new conditions for cultural production. The lack of adequate protection for Spain's own film industry led to a decrease in the numbers of spectators watching Spanish films, which went down to a sixth in a very short space of time while costs rose by 66 percent. The theater was facing a similar problem, since it soon became a partly publicly funded activity which could barely survive without state support. As if this were not enough, Spain found itself facing a situation in which increasing cultural demands were not matched by a corresponding infrastructure capable of supporting them. For example, there were no concert-halls, and worse still, there was no musical education on offer to allow for the training of professional musicians.

It might also be useful to refer briefly to the part played by intellectuals in bringing about political change. In the first instance, it is not, of course, possible to make any comparison between the role played by intellectuals in 1931 and in the transition at present under discussion. The elections in 1982 saw a new surge of interest in politics among intellectuals, but then, as a direct result of the postmodern times that they lived through, the idea of any political commitment soon faded.

If we have spoken of a rediscovery of a liberal intellectual tradition that had been cut short as a consequence of the Civil War, our use of the term "rediscovery" could also be used in another sense. The interest in their own culture felt by ordinary Spanish citizens led to a deep concern over Spain's artistic and monumental heritage. Little by little, the capital invested in conservation of what was inherited from the past increased, and at the same time the techniques for preserving an artistic heritage became ever more refined. In due course, there was a realization that one could view "antiquity as the future" – that is to say, Spain's cultural heritage was now being viewed as an important attraction for cultural tourism. In the mid 1990s up to 25 percent of tourists were "intensive consumers" of this kind of attraction, while at least 20 percent were occasional consumers. What it is important to note is that democratic Spain was able to respond to this demand in ways that were appropriate, original, and brilliant from the perspective of the protection of the national heritage. In 1985, the year when a new national heritage law was passed, there was for the first time talk of a possible "Cathedrals Plan," which led to work beginning at the start of the 1980s, using the most advanced technology available.

If the popularization of culture can be seen as an outstanding value of the time – one that was positive and was quickly accepted during the transition – at the same time there was increasing evidence of legal and structural deficiencies in Spain's cultural administration. As was already the case in much of the world, in Spain at this time there were moves made towards a "state culture" – that is to say, to provide an array of legal measures and institutions that would establish a framework for the public administration to take responsibility in this area. The cultural policies of successive governments, whatever their politics, have been a response to a clear desire to create a "state culture," and this has meant that in the public sphere, in any action taken on the matter, there has in fact been a vital degree of continuity. Continuity has also been achieved in the way that there has been collaboration on the most important and decisive decisions concerning key legal measures, and also on the most crucial agreements on particular issues such as the Thyssen Collection and the Prado. The creation of a state culture was basically a task that faced the socialist governments, because it was while they were in power that there was enough stability to allow the process to move ahead.

The setting up of Spain's state culture has had two main aspects: the approval of new legislation and the creation of new permanent institutions aimed at satisfying demand. As we have noted, Spanish legislation on cultural matters was still manifestly obsolete at the start of the 1980s. The law on the national heritage dated back to the 1930s (1933), while the law on intellectual property was from the last quarter of the nineteenth century. Although in both of these areas the foundations for change were laid while the UCD was in power, it was in the PSOE years that the political situation was stable enough to allow laws to be passed and major projects to be undertaken.

Perhaps the most important of the new steps taken was the Historic Heritage Law (*Ley del Patrimonio Histórico*) of 1985 which allowed for extensive state intervention in the field and provided for the implementation of measures to foment culture such as the "cultural 1 percent." As time went by, what may perhaps have become a missed opportunity in relation to Spain's monumental past was encouraging private initiatives, though this would later play an increasing part in all areas of life. One should note, however, that according to estimates, if in 1990 private initiatives had in the previous few years provided investments in culture totaling thousands of millions of pesetas, 70 percent of the total had been spent on consumables – mainly on exhibitions of paintings and concerts – instead of on more lasting investments, such as the restoration of monuments. The second major legal provision on cultural matters was the Law on Intellectual Property (*Ley de Propiedad Intelectual*) of 1987, which could well be described as one of the laws that offers the best protection to authors of any in the entire world. That would seem to be borne out by the revenue earned by the General Society of Authors and Publishers (*Sociedad General the Autores y Editores* or SGAE), which grew six-fold in a decade to reach a total of 30,000 million pesetas.

Another supremely important aspect of state culture has been the codifying of honors for excellence and the creation of new institutions or locations in response to the demands of a society that has become increasingly interested in culture. The Cervantes Prize (*Premio Cervantes*), instituted in 1976 and presented to Jorge Guillén in 1977 by the king, has become the Spanish equivalent of the Nobel Prize for Literature and has acquired well-deserved prestige. Furthermore, the Spanish Literature Prize (*Premio de las Letras Españolas*) has encouraged literary creativity in

Spain's other official languages. As for the founding of cultural institutions, one need only mention that in all fields entities have appeared over time, with more or less success, which have specialized in particular areas. So, for example, to promote theater, both the National Center for New Trends in Stage Design (*Centro Nacional de Nuevas Tendencias Escénicas*, 1984) and the National Classical Theater Company (*Compañía Nacional de Teatro Clásico*, 1985) came into being during the time that the socialists were in power.

To gain a better sense of the changes that have taken place in Spain as a result of the birth of a state culture, it is interesting to refer briefly to museums and art galleries, and also concert-halls. As regards museums and art galleries, it has been said quite rightly that "never before have they been the object of so much attention, discussion, and debate." The changes that have occurred have been of the first magnitude and they represent the application in Spain of a phenomenon that is well known the world over. Museums, having been – as the etymology of the name suggests – temples of the Muses, have now become temples of the masses. In Spain the most important initiatives in this area have been the creation of the Queen Sofía National Art Museum (*Museo Nacional Centro de Arte Reina Sofía*) in 1986, the bringing of the Thyssen Bornemisza Collection to Spain in 1992, and the Guggenheim Museum in Bilbao, which opened its doors to the public in 1997. The *Reina Sofía* is a response to a passionate interest in contemporary art, which has also resulted in a proliferation of similar galleries in the autonomous communities. As for the Thyssen Collection, which cost the state many tens of thousands of millions of pesetas merely to bring it to Madrid, it not only represents Spain's acquisition and housing of one of the world's most important private collections, but it also completes the totality of the country's art collections because of the particular contribution it makes in terms of art from the start of the century. This collection, most of which has been hung in Madrid, though there is also a part of it in Barcelona, offers a general overview of the history of art, but the last of its owners placed special emphasis on areas that were very unlike the usual contents of Spanish art collections, such as the German Expressionists. Last but not least, the Guggenheim Museum in Bilbao has been a great success – at least as great as expected – and has transformed the image of the Basque city after the inevitable processes of urban redevelopment following the decline of heavy industry. What it has also achieved, exceeding all expectations, has been to attract more visitors than anticipated, of whom every other one has been from outside Spain.

The changes that have taken place in Spanish museums and art galleries have not only affected the great institutions such as those mentioned, but also many much smaller ones. Once the autonomous communities had been set up as part of the Spanish state, it was decided that the old provincial museums would be run according to a somewhat complex system. They would be state owned but management would be transferred to the autonomous communities, which has caused complications. However, what Spain has to offer in terms of its museums has now become quite spectacular thanks to the pooling of local, regional, and state resources.

Alongside all these positive achievements, there have also been less successful projects. The Prado Museum has been a constant cause of confrontation between political groups, and of scandal in the eyes of the general public in relation both to attempts to extend it and to the way it is run. In the short term, nothing changed effectively in terms of the buildings that it occupies except that one building that had housed administrative offices previously was now made part of the museum itself. There has also been debate on the matter of how this, Spain's foremost national art museum, should be run. Until the year 2000 a mixed system was in effect which was somewhere between the model used by the great American art museums, which are partly funded by contributions from patrons, and the European model, where the only kind of help from patrons takes the form of scientific expertise. That system did not work well. Furthermore, the reintroduction of entrance fees had a negative impact on the number of visitors to the museum, which went down from 2,600,000 in 1990 to 1,800,000 in 1999. Other disadvantages can be seen in other Spanish museums and galleries. If one thing is obvious, it is that Spanish museums lack adequately trained personnel, both to see to the day-to-day running of these institutions, but more importantly to research into what these collections contain and represent – in other words, to offer more specialist scientific study.

There have also been substantial changes in relation to the provision of concert-halls for orchestral performances. Since 1975 more than 20 concert-halls have been built, though many of them had been planned before then. This means that Spain may well have the best infrastructure of this kind in the whole of Europe. At the end of the same period, there are 10 times more music colleges, and for years Spain has had a reputation for offering foreign orchestras exorbitant fees to come and perform. The change that had taken place was spectacular by the start of the third millennium, especially when one realizes that in 1971 there was only one music college and that had been founded a century and a half before, and the only spaces created for musical performances were the *Palau de la Música* in Barcelona and the *Palacio de Congresos* in Mallorca. The first new auditorium, designed by José María García de Paredes, was inaugurated in Granada in 1978. Others who worked alongside García de Paredes on this project included some of the great architects from around Spain such as Francisco Javier Sáenz de Oiza (Santander), Juan Navarro Baldeweg (Salamanca), Óscar Tusquets (Las Palmas), Rafael Moneo (Barcelona and San Sebastián) . . . In addition, 43 theaters were restored, including the Theater Royal (*Teatro Real*) and Lyceum (*Liceo*) in Barcelona after the fire in 1994. Needless to say, after the building of the concert-halls came a proliferation of music festivals and – more importantly still – the founding of new orchestras. To the four that already existed in Spain were added more than 20, but already musical vocations had been encouraged at an early age by the National Youth Orchestra of Spain (*Joven Orquesta Nacional de España*), and other such orchestras had also been set up in the autonomous communities. The Achilles' heel of music-making in Spain was in the musical education on offer at the level of compulsory schooling.

The creation of so many institutions has often given rise to criticism concerning the excessive centralization of Spanish culture, focused on Madrid, which absorbs two-thirds of the total budget when, for example, until 1982 there was not a single orchestra or theater group with a permanent base anywhere in Andalusia. Nonetheless, as time has passed, the situation has changed. The overall panorama offered by the institutionalization of state culture has been completed as efforts have been made to export Spain's culture to other countries. After exhibitions in Brussels (Europalia, 1985) and in Paris (1987), 1991 saw at last the creation of the Cervantes Institute (*Instituto Cervantes*), very late in the day but holding much promise for the future given the fact that there are 300 million Spanish-speakers worldwide. The Institute may prove to be a key element in providing important opportunities to take Spanish culture out into the rest of the world.

Culture is based not only on the work of individual creative artists but also on the existence of industries, and if these experience crises, that affects any chances the artists might have of influencing society. Some such industries have suffered serious crises in recent times. That has been the case for the publishing industry, which has seen its markets in Latin America threatened, or even more so, in the film industry. The Spanish film industry reached its historic peak in terms of numbers of viewers in 1979 (24 million), but at the end of the decade it suffered a very acute crisis when barely 10 films were made in a quarter of a year, whereas at other times there had been almost 200 produced per year. The protective measures set in place by the socialist Administration, when Pilar Miró was director general of RTVE at the start of the 1980s, provided five times more state funding than before, which helped to create the phenomenon of the director who was also the producer of his own films. Even so, the level of protection in Spain was much less than in France and the film industry has made irregular progress. The theater, on the other hand, has suffered a constant deficit, so much so that it could not survive without public funding. Although the spread of musical culture has been greatly helped by the founding of new orchestras, some 70 percent of their members are from abroad. In contrast, the success of Spanish popular music abroad has been spectacular. In the 1990s, the totality of Spanish cultural industries provided between 2 and 4 percent of GDP – figures which put this industry above car manufacturing, for example, but below the construction industry. In Spain at the start of the third millennium some 45 million recordings were being produced and around 60 films a year.

The real changes in Spanish culture did not coincide with the key political changes but instead date from later, around 1985, more or less. The intellectual moved from being in the political vanguard to being a fellow-traveler, and today he has either turned away from any direct political responsibility or has taken on a socially responsible role as a kind of moral conscience. Threatened by increasing specialization in all areas of knowledge, the thinker who chooses to become a defender of fundamental values must be aware of the powerful role played by the media nowadays. At the end of the twentieth century, either the Spanish intellectual becomes a media personality or he cannot continue to exist as such. Fernando Savater is a good example to study, having become such a media personality in the 1980s, though many others have followed in his footsteps. Intellectuals, rather than defining themselves in relation to political parties, do so in terms of the media they work for.

It is not at all easy to define the common characteristics of Spain's new generations. One should, nonetheless, point out two traits that are clearly apparent in the generations that emerged onto the cultural scene after the middle of the 1980s. We are talking, in the first instance, of generations whose character was defined by their openness to the world outside Spain. The references made by the new novelists (Antonio Muñoz Molina, Javier Marías . . . ) or painters (Miquel Barceló, José María Sicilia, José Manuel

Broto . . . ) normally owe nothing to traditional notions of Spanishness – are not *casticistas*. Poets who have followed the line traced by Pere Gimferrer share their exoticism and French or Anglo-Saxon influences, their evocation of the 1920s avant-garde, and the emphasis they place on contemporary popular culture.

---

## Fields of Creativity

As we move on to discuss scientific culture, essays, and the humanities, we must be aware of fundamental changes that occurred around these areas. Research went from accounting for 0.37 percent of GDP to 0.48 percent in 1975–83; by 1989 it had reached 0.75 percent, and in 1996 the figure rose to 0.77 percent, which means that one could say that Spain had doubled its material commitment to research since the death of Franco. In what are called "pure sciences" – in other words, not the humanities or the social sciences – for which there are objective criteria by which to judge the quality of what each country produces, Spain's position is that of tenth in the world and sixth in the European Union, after both Holland and Italy. In the humanities and social sciences one cannot measure quality objectively in this way. Nonetheless, one can say that two basic traits that give an indication what has happened over the last quarter of a century would be a growing interest in matters of a general or even global nature affecting any society, and at the same time, the capacity shown by Spanish researchers to use new methods to address issues that were once left to specialists from other countries to investigate. In relation to history, the paradigm used to interpret the past, which for a few years was predominantly Marxist, changed, as did the center of gravity. Researchers stopped focusing all their attention on the 1930s and began to show more interest in the Franco years and the liberal revival. Perhaps the most decisive change of all was that Spanish historiography at last managed to take the place of the foreign colonizers of our historical past.

The art of essay-writing has in recent times shown several very significant characteristics. First of all, one should mention a style inherited from Nietzsche, which is highly relevant in the case of Trías and Savater. Essays by these two authors try above all to uncover absolute truths of all kinds; on the other hand, no attempt is made to construct a system. There is also a clear intention to avoid academic reflection and a preference for what is literary, which explains a certain fondness for accounts and aphorisms. A practical response to the more acute problems of today's world also lies at the heart of the work of José Antonio Marina and Victoria Camps.

Any journey through the different fields of creativity in the plastic arts would be incomplete without some reference to architecture. That is where not only the profound transformation of urban development within Spain, but also international acceptance of figures such as Rafael Moneo and Santiago Calatrava have been palpably obvious. As for the plastic arts themselves one must, of course, be constantly aware of the existence of a creative world "beyond the bounds of Spain" – that is to say, of "a generation of artists who now, for the very first time, do not live day by day tortured by the problem of Spain, nor do they have any inferiority complex about the fact that they are Spanish" (Francisco Calvo Serraller). This generation benefited from far greater opportunities than any available to previous generations when numerous public and private collections of the highest artistic quality were created. It would not be inappropriate to cite some of the names of those who could be termed "newest of the new" – "*novísimos*" – in the plastic arts. A selection that cannot but be incomplete might include, for example, Ferrán García Sevilla, who had started out as a conceptualist, and Guillermo Pérez Villalta, interested in a style of painting that is narrative, mythological, and centered on classical architecture. As for Miguel Ángel Campano, he offered good evidence of the climate of postmodernity at the time, declaring that his paintings are "in the style of" Poussin, Delacroix, and Cézanne. The multiplicity of aesthetic options becomes obvious when one contemplates two opposites: the different kinds of transparency achieved by José María Sicilia and the expressionism and density of different materials that are typical of Miquel Barceló. For her part, Susana Solano led in an area of a very personal and sensitive sculptural minimalism. Seeking new fields of expression, Miguel Navarro constructed what might be called city-scapes or urbanistic contexts, while Juan Muñoz presented scenic spaces occupied by anonymous figures.

If we move on from the plastic arts to literary creativity, we can consider the world of market forces and restricted initiatives. The world of poetry in Spain is made up of only about 500 people if one takes into account both producers and consumers, which means that a run of 400 copies of a book of poems is sizeable. When Luis Antonio de Villena has tried to characterize the "post-newest of the new" ("*posnovísimos*") poets, he has done so by referring back to a sensibility associated with rock music and an openness to new aesthetic possibilities. Whether or not this is so, any social or political commitment has almost completely disappeared, and a colloquial style and narrative approach have proved most successful in the period after 1984 in what has been called "post-newest of the new poetry."

Prose narrative, on the other hand, has very obviously had a totally different trajectory from that of poetry. The opening up of the market has made it possible for authors to live exclusively on what they earn from their writing, and this has allowed them to make an extraordinary impact on society, at the same time as multiplying their chances of seeing their work transferred to the screen. On the other hand, recent novels have been criticized for having lost the intellectual solidity that they had in the past. As we have already noted, it seems as though the novel has gained a wider public but has lost prestige.

Its starting-point was not very promising. In 1975 the novel did not seem to be in very good health because potential readers were bewildered by the experimentalism that was in vogue at the time. It has even been said that the most recent book praised by the critics "might be of interest to cultured readers much as poems of exercises in style would be, but not as narratives." In fact, much the same seemed to be happening everywhere, or at least in Europe. It was only some time later that there was once again evidence of "the pact with the reader based on a narrative style" being revived, in Spain as elsewhere.

According to Antonio Muñoz Molina, who quotes Borges, "literary historians enjoy long genealogies like those in the Bible," and indeed it is true that we often try to find in authors from the past the seeds of present-day writers. However, there can be no doubt at all that with hindsight the appearance of *La verdad sobre el caso Savolta* (*The Truth about the Savolta Case*, 1975) by Eduardo Mendoza signaled a marked change. Written while the author was in New York, this novel was a kind of collage, set at the start of the century, of a Barcelona that was entirely imagined but also convincing. It showed no signs of needing to try out daring experiments in form, and it appeared to take pleasure in narration for its own sake as it set out calmly and with considerable erudition to depict a past age. All of these elements also appeared on more than one occasion in the narratives that enjoyed the greatest success from this time on. The year 1976 saw the publication of Fernando Savater's *La infancia recuperada* (*Childhood rediscovered*), described as "a vindication of the power and magic of novels and short stories about adventures."

The masters of these new generations were easier to detect than one might think. What set these writers apart from Cela was his tone, the way that he looks down on his characters as though they were insects, and also his language, taken from the world of brothels, which was no longer in use. Towards Delibes young writers felt a "warm sense of closeness," as well as admiration for his "marvelous technique." Needless to say, they were also strongly attracted by the new Latin American novel because, in the words of one writer, "we had thought we were witnessing the twilight of the novel" and García Márquez and Vargas Llosa "took us almost as far back as its mythological beginnings." Doubtless Juan Benet exercised a very strongly personal kind of influence over some of the young writers such as Javier Marías, but "none of us really seemed to like what was going on around us," as one of them said. They preferred instead to draw their inspiration from intimate experience, or else they tended to look back to traditional literary genres such as the historical novel, romantic melo-drama, or mystery novel. As one would expect in such a cosmopolitan age, many of these writers have taken universal literature as their reference point, sometimes even using works that they themselves have translated (as has been the case with Marías). There has been a return to novels of intrigue and detective fiction, even when there is also a critical edge, as in the case of Manuel Vázquez Montalbán's *Los mares del sur* (*The southern seas*) and *Galíndez*. On the other hand, the working-class hero, who was so popular a figure in the novels of the end of the 1950s and start of the 1960s, has disappeared completely.

It is also important to bear in mind that there was also an overlap between generations. The realist generation, and more especially Carmen Martín Gaite and Juan Marsé, were constantly appearing on publishers' lists and critical writings, and the great postwar authors and those closer to the younger generation also continued writing. It is interesting that Cela and Benet both wrote about the Civil War: *Mazurca para dos muertos* (*Mazurka for two dead men*, 1984) and *Herrumbrosas lanzas* (*Rusting lances*, 1984–7) respectively.

It is hard to sum up in a few brief words the characteristics of some of the major authors who were part of the generation that emerged in the 1980s. The Javier Marías of *Todas las almas* (*All Souls*, 1986) was a complete novelty because he was dealing explicitly with unusual foreign literary worlds. In *El héroe de las mansardas de Mansard* (*The hero of the attics of Attic*, 19883), Álvaro Pombo describes worlds closed in on themselves that would become the central theme in all his work. Muñoz Molina tried to ensure that his books were "narratives that would entertain" in order to "save and invent memory." *Beatus ille* (*Blessed is he*, 1986) and *Un invierno en Lisboa* (*A winter in Lisbon*, 1987) were his first two successes and both showed foreign influences derived from films as well as literature. The *Historia abreviada de la literatura portátil* (*Abridged history of portable literature*, 1985) by Enrique Vila-Matas displays clear mastery of irony. Luis Landero's *Juegos de la edad tardía* (*Games of a late age*, 1989) revealed an early mastery of literary technique.

Recent years have confirmed many of the values that emerged in the 1980s. The Mendoza of *Una comedia ligera* (*A light comedy*, 1996) moves from modernist Barcelona to postwar summers on the coast. Clear cases of narrative progression and a debt to a literature shaped by very un-Spanish forms can be seen in the works of Marías and Pombo. Muñoz Molina is more committed and tense and gives unequivocal signs of maturity in *El jinete polaco* (*The Polish Horseman*, 1997). Meanwhile, a writer such as Arturo Pérez Reverte is a prime example of how to use the structure of detective fiction and the romantic melodrama combined with documentation of a sophisticated world of culture to conquer a wide readership. Writers such as Juan Madrid and Alfredo Mañas, who belong to the most recent generation of writers, explore irrationality, solitude, and boredom in their novels, or life "in the fast track," all of which are characteristics of a youth culture of which they are fairly much a part.

There was a time, at the start of the transition, when it seemed as though Spanish cinema might disappear completely as a result of the financial problems it faced. The policy adopted was erratic and the Cinema Congress (*Congreso del Cine*, 1978) expressed its indignation at the Administration's obvious apathy on the matter. In 1977–80, the quota set for screenings of Spanish films was reduced to 7 percent. When we take these figures into account, it is hard to understand how in later years the quota was raised again to16 percent and Spanish directors even managed to win four Oscars.

These results were achieved in part thanks to an official policy on pro-tection that took the French system as its model – that is to say, "prior subsidies" for productions. This was the policy followed by Pilar Miró, who was, as we have already mentioned, director general during the socialist years. Nonetheless, nothing would have been possible had this policy not coincided with the emergence of new creative talents in film. For a time there was insufficient literary skill in story-lines and scripts, though in the end we can see that "literature has given the cinema the very best it had, and in return the cinema gave literature its greatest ambitions." Halfway through the 1979s there were few film directors who dared to say, like Manuel Gutiérrez Aragón, that "what I really enjoy is writing," though the fact that, in time, Almodóvar won an Oscar for the best film script shows just how great a change has taken place.

A quick glance at Spanish film-making since 1975 requires the identification of certain themes and acknowledgment of a considerable diversity of genres. It is worth commenting on how often Spanish cinema has paid its debt to the past and how exactly this has been done. As we have already seen, it did so initially by choosing a documentary style (Martín Patino's *Canciones para después de una guerra* or Jaime Camino's *La vieja memoria*), but then it did so by using irony, distance, and a touch of personal nostalgia for the past. Luis García Berlanga's series of "choral *esperpentos*" – grotesquely distorted farces, which spanned a period from the last years of the Franco period up to the socialist years, were sarcastic but not hurtful. The past as a reference point has also been a fundamental theme in the work of Mario Camus, which has had especially close links with literature (*Los santos inocentes* and *La colmena* being based on novels by Miguel Delibes and Camilo José Cela respectively). Nonetheless, as time has passed these themes have in large part been abandoned. The new generation, from the 1990s onwards, with works such as Moncho Armendáriz's *Historias del Kronen* (*The Kronen Stories*, 1995), Alex de la Iglesia's *El día de la bestia* (*The Day of the Beast*, 1995), or Juanma Bajo Ulloa's *Airbag* (1997), are showing a preference for crazy stories linked to a childlike world. Other themes also turn away from the past, dealing with relationships across generations in a world plagued by difficulties, as in Benito Zambrano's *Solas* (*Women Alone*, 1999), or with the harshness of life in urban slums, as in Fernando León's *Barrio* (*The District*, 1998).

The success of a film industry such as the Spanish film industry is based on a combination of continuity, cosmopolitanism, and a capacity for bringing to the screen worlds that are unique and unrepeatable. Garci's *Volver a empezar*, which won Spain's first Oscar, was a kind of reworking and updating of the "third way" ("*tercer vía*") which, in the closing years of the Franco period, tried to offer products that would appeal to the masses, whose tone was melodramatic or humorous, and which also included food for thought. Essentially, the film was about an exile returning to Spain to relive a past love. Trueba's films are new versions of what were known in the theater as "*Opera prima*" – traditional comedies of manners – which he has blended with the film world of American high comedy. The peculiar world of Pedro Almodóvar can be seen as a kind of modern romantic melodrama which focuses on the peculiarities of the female soul and chronicles women's loves and emotional traumas.

In terms of literary creativity, the world of the theater has perhaps been the most open to international influences, although at the same time there has been a return to more traditional genres. Although, as we have already suggested, there was a time when it seemed as though the Spanish theater was destined to disappear and could only survive with public support, it has at last produced three separate, autonomous areas of activity: commercial theater, theater in other public spaces, and independent theater.

As in so many other areas of cultural creativity, a first step after Franco's death was to rediscover banned authors, and among those who saw their works performed for the first time were Manuel Martínez, author of *Las hermanas de Búfalo Bill* (*Buffalo Bill's Sisters*, 1975) and Martín Recuerda, who had written *Las arrecogías del Beaterio de Santa María Egipciaca* (*The orgiastic ecstasies of Blessedness of Saint Mary of Egypt*, 1977). Antonio Buero Vallejo was a particularly persistent presence on the Spanish stage at this time. Of the authors who had been in exile, Arrabal and Alberti, who had not made a name for themselves in Spanish theater until then, saw their works staged but without the success they had hoped for. In contrast, during the years of the transition proper, several figures who were already well known in the theatrical world but had as yet gained no recognition as authors enjoyed quite exceptional success. This was, for example, the case with Francisco Nieva, whose staging of plays had already made him famous. In those years too, two works by men who had already won names for themselves as some of Spain's greatest actors were immensely successful: Adolfo Marsillach's *Yo me bajo en la próxima, ¿y usted?* (*I'm getting off at the next stop. What about you?* 1981) and a work we have already mentioned, Fernando Fernán Gómez's *Las bicicletas son para el verano* (1982). Both works dealt with problems encountered in daily life in a traditional way, but also revealed a profound understanding of dramatic techniques.

Be that as it may, among the plays that have been performed there have been both a rebirth of tradition and a persistence of an avant-garde aesthetic. Typical of the first would be the use of the traditional light comedy or "*sainete costumbrista*" whose content is much more thought-provoking than its comic appearance would suggest. This vein has been mined by José Luis Alonso de los Santos in *Bajarse al moro* (*South to Morocco*, 1985) or, rather more incisively, by Fermín Cabal in *Vade retro* (*Get thee behind me!* 1982). Another playwright whose work is not far off this style is José Sanchis Sinisterra, though *Ay Carmela* (1986) does feature one scene depicting the Civil War. The degree of continuity in experimentation in the theater is especially evident in Catalan theater groups, from the late Franco period but also in what is known as *Teatre Lliure* (*Free Theater*) founded in 1976. Of such groups, *Els Joglars* (*The Troubadours*) is both the oldest and the one that has come closest to offering a critique of day-to-day life.

We have already spoken about the immense change that took place in Spain after 1975 in terms of musical infrastructure, and this reality coincided with changes in the areas of musical creativity. Those who had been innovators at the end of the 1950s became members of the Academy in the 1980s. This was the case, for example, for Ernesto Halffter, Antón García Abril, Luis de Pablo, and Carlos Alonso Bernaola. By 1995 there were signs that Spain was at last awakening out of its 40-year lethargy. One of the best-known figures at the time in this particular field of cultural creativity, Ernesto Halffter, could state that there was more music-making since 1985 than there had been at any previous time. As regards performance, although characters such as Montserrat Caballé, José Carreras, and Plácido Domingo could never be repeated, "the line of succession was now assured, though in very few cases with the brilliance that there had once been on the international stage" (Vicente Gallego). As for popular music, along with the apparently contradictory phenomena of increasing cosmopolitanism on the one hand and the survival of the traditional "*copla*" on the other, there were also new and very original musical forms emerging, such as flamenco-rock, whose best exponent is perhaps the group *Ketama*.

## Bibliography

Works of a general nature: Alfonso GUERRA and José Félix TEZANOS, *La década del cambio. Diez años de gobierno socialista, 1982–1992*, Sistema, Madrid, 1992; Javier TUSELL and Justino SINOVA (eds.), *La década socialista*, Espasa Calpe, Madrid, 1992; Javier TUSELL, Emilio LAMO DE ESPINOSA, and Rafael PARDO, *Entre dos siglos. Reflexiones sobre la democracia española*, Alianza, Madrid, 1996; Carlos ALONSO ZALDÍVAR and Manuel CASTELLS, *España, fin de siglo*, Alianza, Madrid, 1992.

Memoirs: Joaquín ALMUNIA, *Memorias políticas*, Aguilar, Madrid, 2001; José BARRIONUEVO, *2.001 días en Interior*, Ediciones B, Barcelona, 1997; Julio FEO, *Aquellos años*, Ediciones B, Barcelona, 1993; Alfonso GUERRA, *Cuando el tiempo nos alcanza. Memorias, 1940–1982*, Espasa Calpe, Madrid, 2004; María Antonia IGLESIAS, *La memoria recuperada*, Aguilar, Madrid, 2003; Fernando LÓPEZ AGUDÍN, *En el laberinto. Diario de Interior, 1994–1996*, Plaza y Janés, Barcelona,

1996; Fernando MORÁN, *España en su sitio*, Plaza y Janés, Barcelona, 1990; Gregorio PECES BARBA, *La democracia en España. Experiencias y reflexiones*, Temas de Hoy, Madrid, 1996; Jorge SEMPRÚN, *Federico Sánchez se despide de ustedes*, Tusquets, Barcelona, 1993; Carlos SOLCHAGA, *El final de la edad dorada*, Taurus, Madrid, 1997; Jorge VERSTRYNGE, *Memorias de un maldito*, Grijalbo, Barcelona, 1999.

Academic works and essays: Manuel GARCÍA FERRANDO, Eduardo LÓPEZ ARANGUREN, and Miguel BELTRÁN, *La conciencia nacional y regional en la España de las autonomías*, CIS, Madrid, 1994; Richard GUNTHER, *Politics, society and democracy: The case of Spain*, Westview, Boulder, CO, 1993; Justino SINOVA and Javier TUSELL, *El secuestro de la democracia. Cómo regenerar el sistema político español*, Plaza y Janés, Barcelona, 1990; Ignacio SÁNCHEZ CUENCA and Belén BARREIRO, *Los efectos de la acción de gobierno durante la etapa socialista (1982–1996)*, CIS, Madrid, 2000; Julián SANTAMARÍA and Mercedes ALCOVER, *Actitudes de los españoles ante la OTAN*, CIS, Madrid, 1987; Consuelo DEL VAL, *Opinión pública y opinión publicada. Los españoles y el referéndum de la OTAN*, Siglo XXI, Madrid, 1996.

Economic and social aspects: Amando DE MIGUEL, *La sociedad española*, Alianza, Madrid, several years; David S. REHER, *La familia en España. Pasado y presente*, Alianza, Madrid, 1996; Juan José TOHARIA, *Cambios recientes en la sociedad española*, Instituto de Estudios Económicos, Madrid, 1989.

Cultural aspects: Samuel AMELL and Salvador GARCÍA CASTAÑEDA, *La cultura española en el posfranquismo. Diez años de cine, cultura y literatura (1975–1985)*, Playor, Madrid, 1988; EQUIPO RESEÑA, *Doce años de cultura española (1976–1987)*, Ediciones Encuentro, Madrid, 1989; Jordi GRÀCIA, *Hijos de la razón. Contraluces de la libertad en las letras españolas de la democracia*, Edhasa, Barcelona, 2001; John HOPEWELL, *El cine español después de Franco*, Ediciones El Arquero, Madrid, 1989 (*Spanish cinema after Franco*, London, British Film Institute, 1986). National Heritage: *Foros Banesto sobre el Patrimonio Histórico*, Fundación Banesto, Madrid, 1994; Sergio VILA-SAN-JUAN, *Pasando página. Autores y editores en la España democrática*, Destino, Barcelona, 2003, and *Crónicas culturales*, Delibros, Barcelona, 2004. On the literary world: Darío VILLANUEVA (ed.), *Los nuevos nombres, 1975–1990* and Jordi GRÀCIA (ed.), *Los nuevos nombres, 1975–2000*, Crítica, Barcelona, 2000.

Memoirs by intellectuals: Francisco NIEVA, *Las cosas como fueron. Memorias*, Espasa Calpe, Madrid, 2000; Fernando SAVATER, *Mira por dónde. Autobiografía razonada*, Taurus, Madrid, 2003, and Eugenio TRÍAS, *El árbol de la vida. Memorias*, Destino, Barcelona, 2003.

Foreign policy: Robert P. CLARK and Michael H. HATZELL, *Spain in the 1980s. The democratic transition and a new international role*, Ballinger, Cambridge, 1987.

Works by journalists about those in power: Pilar CERNUDA, *El Presidente*, Temas de Hoy, Madrid, 1994; Miguel FERNÁNDEZ BRASO, *Conversaciones con*

*Alfonso Guerra*, Planeta, Barcelona, 1983; José Luis GUTIÉRREZ and Amando DE MIGUEL, *La ambición del César. Un retrato político y humano de Felipe González*, Temas de Hoy, Madrid, 1989; Manuel HERMÓGENES and Alfonso TORRES, *El agujero. PSV y los dineros de UGT*, Temas de Hoy, Madrid, 1995; Fernando JÁUREGUI, *La metamorfosis. Los últimos años de Felipe González*, Temas de Hoy, Madrid, 1993; Santos JULIÁ (ed.), *La desavenencia. Partidos, sindicatos y huelga general*, El País-Aguilar, Madrid, 1988; Juan Luis GALIACHO and Carlos BERBELL, *FILESA. Las tramas del dinero negro en al política*, Temas de Hoy, Madrid, 1995.

Journalistic works on the opposition: Tom BURNS, *Conversaciones sobre la derecha*, Plaza y Janés, Barcelona, 1997; Raimundo CASTRO, *El sucesor*, Espasa Calpe, Madrid, 1995; Pilar CERNUDA and Fernando JÁUREGUI, *Crónicas de la crispación*, Temas de Hoy, Madrid, 1996; Esther ESTEBAN, *El tercer hombre. PJ, la pesadilla de FG*, Espasa Calpe, Madrid, 1995; Federico JIMÉNEZ LOSANTOS, *La dictadura silenciosa*, Temas de Hoy, Madrid, 1993.

Other journalistic works: Jesús CACHO, *Asalto al poder. La revolución de Mario Conde*, Temas de Hoy, Madrid, 1988, and *MC. Un intruso en el laberinto de los elegidos*, Temas de Hoy, Madrid, 1994; Ernesto EKAIZER, *Banqueros de rapiña. Crónica secreta de Mario Conde*, Plaza y Janés, Barcelona, 1994; Melchor MIRALLES and Ricardo ARQUÉS, *Amedo: el Estado contra ETA*, Plaza y Janés, Barcelona, 1989; Manuel VÁZQUEZ MONTALBÁN, *Un polaco en la Corte del Rey Juan Carlos*, Alfaguara, Madrid, 1996, and *Mis almuerzos con gente inquietante*, Planeta, Barcelona, 1995.

The Basque Country: Francisco José LLERA, *Los vascos y la política*, Universidad del País Vasco, Bilbao, 1994; Paddy WOODWORTH, *Guerra sucia, manos limpias*, Crítica, Barcelona, 2002 (*Dirty war, clean hands: ETA, the GAL and Spanish democracy*, Cork, Cork University Press, 2001).

# 6

# The Turn of the Right (1996–2004)

Paradoxical though it may seem, the result of the 1996 elections was as "sweet a defeat" for the losers as it was a "bitter victory" for the winners. Even so, a new stage was opening up in Spanish politics; on the one hand the democratic requirement of peaceful change had been fulfilled and the right now had a chance to exercise power; on the other, this marked a significant break in relations within the governing class.

## The Popular Party in Power: José María Aznar

We have already given a brief outline of Aznar's political career. Now we should describe him in more detail as a political figure. It has been said that the PSOE made the mistake of underestimating him. If so, the mistake was more a matter of not placing him in the right context. Aznar represented a new generation in Spanish politics – one with life experience and a starting-point that were very different from those of the Spaniards who had been in politics during the transition. For his age-group the transition was not part of their life story; nor did it represent a shared striving. It was just plain reality: an accepted fact. The first key moment in their life story was when they were in opposition and were making no concessions to the socialists in power, for their arrival in politics caught the socialists just as their fortunes were declining, and it proved that they could be defeated. Most of Aznar's generation came from the traditional right wing with deeper roots in the Franco regime than in the opposition, and they then transformed and became ultra-liberal because that was the ideology that was most workable in the circumstances in which they found themselves. One of Aznar's most precise statements was that in his party "there were no social democrats." To put it another way, for this younger generation politics was not a more or less costly commitment so much as a profession for which they had been destined since their youth. There was a similar phenomenon in the PSOE.

Within this generation, Aznar stood out because of his ability to survive. Despite his opponents, he had had many successes thanks to his own efforts and also to his "patience, prudence, and perseverance," and he made this his motto. His "feeling for power" – that is to say, how to get it, how to store up as much of it as he could, and how not to lose it – was always very strong. The many objective difficulties that he faced in his political career developed in him a toughness that made him a formidable enemy; at the same time, these very same obstacles made him prone to the dangers of paranoia. There has been no man of the right in the whole of Spanish twentieth-century history who has kept such a firm grip on the reins of power in his party as Aznar. He always ruled the PP with satin gloves and an iron hand – exactly the opposite of what Manuel Fraga did but with infinitely better results. His "personnel politics" worked very well for him and he acted as both butcher and homeopath – two professions from which party leaders will always have something to learn (to destroy possible adversaries and divide the remaining power in such a way as to reward friends on all sides). Unlike his predecessors, the new prime minister listened carefully without always revealing his own position, and he asked others' opinions and knew how to achieve teamwork. He did not allow anyone to stray from the government's fundamental line of action, as had happened before, even during the socialist years. On other matters, such as terrorism, he accepted that there might be alternative ways to move ahead. Aznar's political strengths and weaknesses always seemed minor; in that sense he was more like Franco than like Fraga. Both strengths and weaknesses were no doubt a sign of normality in the political process. Every public figure is transfigured when they reach the pinnacle of their career, and although the transformation was more palpable in Aznar during his second term of office, when he had an absolute majority, it was already discernible in his first term. His most worrying trait was a megalomania that would increase to a dangerous extent as time went by.

In 1996, however, Aznar did not have a parliamentary majority. He believed that public opinion was against him making a pact with the Catalan nationalists, who were the only minority that would allow him to gain a parliamentary majority. Yet the Catalans were always ready to make pacts, and it seems frankly unlikely that they wanted to hold more elections. The difficulties that Aznar faced were a result of the position of the PP itself when it was in opposition and not of any conspiracy. It took almost 2 months of talks before an agreement was finally reached on April 26. A program was drawn up to deal with economic issues, and on other areas such as military service and the suppression of the post of civil governor. The agreement that was reached, in the negotiations in which Rodrigo Rato played a decisive role, aroused strong suspicion among those associated with the Catalan party *Convergència i Unió*. No doubt, although this was a result of mutual distrust, the fact that the agreement was written and not just verbal was a very positive step forward. For the very first time in its history, the Spanish center right showed that it was capable of joining together with nationalist groups from the periphery and finding a workable political solution. In fact, the PNV also supported Aznar's investiture as prime minister, but it did so leaving one essential aspect on one side: anti-terrorist policy. On the other hand, the pact did cover questions such as the returning to historic areas of parts of their cultural heritage.

Finally, on May 4, Aznar became prime minister of Spain. The composition of his new executive had been carefully thought out by the one who made the appointments. Seven of the ministers (and both deputy prime ministers) were from the Popular Alliance. The most notable appointments were Rodrigo Rato to the post of vice-president with responsibility for the economy, and Francisco Álvarez Cascos as political deputy prime minister. Only three ministers had been active members of the now extinct UCD (Jaime Mayor Oreja at the Home Office, Javier Arenas at the Labor Ministry, and Rafael Arias-Salgado Montalvo in charge of Promotion); there were also three independents. Aznar had formed a cabinet with the highest number of women ever in Spanish history. He gave his ministers one commission: simply "to last." One can well understand such a modest objective because the contention that the PP was centrist in 1996 was largely unjustified if one considers its antecedents. The suspicions of the other parties had not entirely been laid to rest. The stability of Parliament, though promising, was not completely assured.

## —————— Success in Economic and Social Policies ——————

The start of Spain's economic recovery must be set in 1994 – that is to say, during the last socialist government which should, therefore, be given due credit for what it did. In other words, the PP benefited from a reasonable start, though it is true that it then made good use of it. Together with Ireland, Spain was the western European country that grew most in the next few years.

With support from the Catalan nationalists, until 1998 Spain's economic policy followed an option set out in the Maastricht Treaty. Macroeconomic stability was maintained at all times, with its corresponding prices, lowering of interest rates, and decrease in the public deficit and debt. This helped to create a culture of stability which was destined to last. The decisive factors for growth were consumption and private investment, but greater openness to the outside world, both passive and active, also played a crucial role as Spain moved on from being on the receiving end of capital to exporting it, especially to Latin America, where it became the major European investor.

Liberalization and privatization had been vital components of the socialists' economic policy. What was new now was the emphasis that was placed on these two words, which came from the liberal ideology already mentioned. The result was massive disentailment of state-owned companies to a total of over 4 billion pesetas. Yet in actual fact this measure, which could equally have been adopted by their political opponents, had consequences that seemed to clash with the terms "liberalization" and "privatization." The way that party feeling had influenced the election of the chairmen of new companies had changed the center of gravity in Spanish economic life. In previous cases of privatization (or in other countries), those involved had not acted in this way. Furthermore, in the privatizations now taking place there was not sufficient care taken to guarantee "service to the public"; it was taken for granted that the simple fact of passing companies into private hands would guarantee efficiency. At the same time, little help was given early on to the organizations that were supposed to be regulating the market. One can therefore say that the era of public monopolies gave way to an era of private oligopolies. With privatization, and the reform of personal income tax (*Impuesto sobre la Renta de las Personas Físicas* or IRPF) in 1998, and also of company tax in 1996 – all measures aimed at reducing the burden of tax – the PP brought about a decisive change of direction in Spaniards' economic culture.

More surprising still is just how successful their social policy was. The right needed society's approval, given its forebears and its previous close association with employers. The approach adopted by the Labor Minister

Javier Arenas, who had been a member of the UCD, was prudent and opportune: it consisted of doing everything possible to ensure that agreements were signed by social agencies and then gained the appropriate support from the government. After the failure of the strike planned for 1994, the unions themselves needed to broker agreements. As had been the case with reforms enacted under the socialists, the labor reform of 1997 had as its main objective to make the labor market more flexible while also improving its quality. In contrast, the most obvious mistakes in social policy were to be found in health care, where there was no desire to reach agreements. There was also shortsightedness and a lack of coordination in dealing with the problem of immigration which, one might say, exploded onto the Spanish political scene in a way that was as unexpected as it was dramatic. The immigration question began to be viewed by the public as a serious problem towards the end of 1999 and on into the early months of 2000. By January 2000 a general agreement had been reached by all political parties and independent groups on passing a law, but it was then withdrawn because of disagreements within the government which were serious enough to lead to the resignation of the Labor Minister Manuel Ramón Pimentel. The weeks leading up to the 2000 elections saw the first incidents of xenophobic violence erupt, targeted against immigrants from the Magreb living in El Egido in Almería.

## The Dark Side of the Right

In other areas the PP's policies achieved good if not particularly spectacular results. There was, for example, a degree of continuity with what had gone on before. The government did not agree to the declassification of the CESID documents requested by a section of the press, arguing that they had been stolen and perhaps altered, and it ended up pardoning the Interior Minister José Barrionuevo. Both measures turned out well in that they did much to defuse political tensions.

In May 1998 approval was given to the "fully voluntary and professional nature of service in the armed forces," without any discrimination between the sexes, and attempts were soon made to put these principles into practice. They were the product of the extent of conscientious objection to military service, of a pact between the different parties, and of widespread agreement in Spanish society. The problem lay in how to implement the measures. It soon became obvious that recruits were now so few and so badly trained that it was only with the greatest of difficulty that Spain's basic needs were covered.

In terms of foreign policy too, one might say that there was continuity with the past. Full military integration into NATO had now been agreed by the PSOE, which also gave its consent on Spain's military contribution to the air strikes on Milosevic's Yugoslavia. As regards Europe, the balance of Aznar's government's policies was positive, and there was no evidence that they were ideologically biased. During its time in opposition, the PP had shown signs of Euro-skepticism but it had then abandoned this to implement in Spain a program that followed the objectives set out at Maastricht. It is only logical that this should have been the case because Spain would receive more aid from Europe in the next few years than it had done in the previous 5 years; having said that, the sums made available tended to decrease and were soon destined to disappear altogether.

In terms of Spain's foreign policy, however, there was an increasing emphasis on ideology which brought about slight alterations in certain tendencies. The element of discontinuity with previous policy on Europe was an immediate result of lining up with the United Kingdom, though in fact the real point of reference was the United States. Aznar had an idea of balancing up the driving forces in the European Union by linking up with another power that had always had a special relationship with the Americans. He was never a European federalist and in 2000 he, together with Blair, put forward a liberalizing economic and social policy (the Lisbon Agenda). Yet it was not easy to reconcile these new loyalties with Spain's traditional politics and interests. In fact, Latin America remained now, as it had been at the start of the transition, Spain's only possibility of rising above its present position as a middle-ranking regional power within Europe. Although over this period Spain increased both her investment in and her cooperation with Latin America, the Spanish presence was concentrated in certain sectors and was linked to cases of privatization that frequently brought very unpopular price rises in services, and this had contradictory effects on public opinion. As regards Cuba, there were difficult moments to be lived through in the PP's early years in government because of its confrontational politics, and these difficulties were never entirely resolved. For a year and a half, Spain had no ambassador in Cuba and Aznar vetoed a royal visit to the island. Relations with Chile were complicated by the trial of Pinochet over which Judge Baltasar Garzón presided, and by the subsequent detention of the Chilean ex-dictator in London.

As regards education, it is hard to find a single way in which, by the year 2000, the PP had provided any real cause for satisfaction shared by all relevant groups. An acute sense of uncertainty about the plans to be implemented, together with an agenda that was far too ideologically weighted, ended up increasing needless conflict to previously unimaginable levels, even in sectors that had never before experienced any such thing. Essential legislation at every level of education could not be altered because there was not a parliamentary consensus to do so. Yet a great opportunity to change legislation on universities by consensus was missed, and there were instances of serious conflict which could have been avoided. An attempt was made to bring about reform in the study of the humanities on the assumption that the teaching given in the autonomous communities was leading to the propagation of serious errors, though in the end the proposal was withdrawn. A demand by the Catalan Generalitat to have its Civil War documents returned, which could have been resolved easily, instead led to yet another needless confrontation.

Cultural policy was dogged by uncertainty about industries associated with culture, and also by a lack of respect for professionalism in cultural management. That, together with the aim of ensuring that the main responsibility in these matters should be determined according to models based on managing companies, led to a curious attempt to bring about changes in the running of the Prado, and unnecessary clashes with the film and book industries. As time passed, these attitudes were modified considerably, but only at the end of the government's term of office were there any budget increases. The Fund for the Protection of Cinematography (*Fondo de Protección a la Cinematografía*), for example, saw its budget increased from 3,500 million to 5,500 million in the period 1998–2000; nevertheless, these figures were well below funding in France, Germany, or Italy. To those in power, the demand for protection was seen as tantamount to a lack of creativity, and so conflict brewed that would explode in the course of the PP's second term in office.

The government's performance on justice was also poor. The year 1999 closed with what was virtually a strike by judges over pay, and with the prime minister almost resigning, together with the full General Council of the Judiciary because the government had failed to respond to its petitioning for reform. The problems in the Spanish justice system were only too evident by 1996. It was slow and there was political interference in judicial matters. Over the course of this period of government 3,400 new civil servants were added to the judicial administration, of whom more than 500 were judges and magistrates and rather fewer than 200 were public prosecutors, while about 14,500 million were spent on investments. The Organic Law of the Judiciary was passed which, among other measures, set the length of time after which judges and magistrates who wanted to enter politics could do so, and major steps were also taken towards passing a law on sentencing in civil justice. Yet if all this seems far too little, the government's attempts to depoliticize the processes of justice were even further from the mark. A new way of electing the Council of the Judiciary could have done much to create greater confidence, but the procedure by which it was done – through judges' associations – soon showed how inadequate it was. Even so, for as long as Javier Delgado was its president, the Council managed to avoid the most blatant examples of politicization, though however professional it was, the office of the State Public Prosecutor always acted with clear bias, especially after the first man to be appointed to the post was replaced in May 1997.

The Environment Ministry, which had been requested for a long time, was well received by the general public when it was at last set up. Nonetheless, the passivity of those in charge of it politically, who were either tangled up in senseless disputes with social organizations or incapable of setting up a team that would last, prevented any benefit being derived from the new institution. In a situation such as the one described here, it can come as no surprise that there was such a tardy response to an ecological disaster of the magnitude of Aznalcóllar – the worst of its kind in Europe to date.

If there was one policy where the contradictions between what was said in the manifesto presented at the 1996 elections and what the PP actually did between 1996 and 2000 were most obvious, it was the government's policy on the media. The resentful attitude displayed by Aznar's government towards certain of the media, the need it felt to ensure support for itself, and the demands from the opposition for there to be measures to counterbalance services rendered to the party in power are all factors that help to explain what happened after the PP's electoral victory.

What occurred can be described as both the result of a political strategy that in part tried to build on what had gone before, and a desire to break with the past and try to modify the existing situation in the media. The element of continuity can best be appreciated in the blatant use of the public media to benefit those in power, in just the same way as had happened with all previous governments. On the other hand, nothing whatever was done to try to control the level of debt, which therefore continued to rise. What was new was the idea of using the mechanisms of power to shape a new attitude in the media that would be kindly towards the government, and this can be seen as breaking with the most basic norms of democratic practice.

Confrontation continued in the form of a confused and bitter struggle both in law and directed at public opinion. It began in digital television but then spread to all other fields. Telefónica, whose chairman was a friend of Aznar's, bought the television channel *Antena 3*, whose news broadcasts began to follow the government line closely, and he also began to set up a multimedia group by acquiring radio stations (*Onda Cero*) and print publications (*Grupo Recoletos*). Yet the erosion of public confidence in the government forced it to step down, while the European Commission also told Spain to alter its law on digital television, which had been passed with support from both the PP and IU. When Aznar, who was now losing control of Telefónica, wanted to present a more centrist image of his politics, the first thing he did was take a less belligerent line on this issue.

No doubt the executive was satisfied when it saw the chairman of the foremost Spanish news broadcasting company taken to court. The accusation, which originated on the far right, was without any foundation, but its processing through the law-courts took 250 days; public television showed the chairman of the Prisa Group attending court on more than 60 occasions. The bias displayed in the case by the judge, Javier Gómez de Liaño, was such that all his sentences bar one were annulled by a higher court. In October 1998 the filing of what was known as the "*Sogecable* case," after the company taken to court, was decreed. Its directors responded by taking legal action against Judge Gómez de Liaño who, in October 1999, was found guilty of prevarication and lost his position in the judiciary. It is clear that the independence of judges, the increasingly important role of the European Union in matters of communications, and the pressure of the independent media forced Aznar's government to change direction, at least in part, in the area in which it had made the worst mistakes of its entire time in power.

## A Pluralistic Spain: Nationalities and Terrorism

In this section we shall try to give an account of the policy on the autonomous communities implemented during the Popular Party's first term of office. We shall also endeavor to offer a general overview of the historical development of those communities which lay claim to the status of "nationalities."

Keeping up a degree of continuity with the past, during the PP's first term in office the 1992 pacts on regional autonomy signed by the PP and the PSOE were fully implemented. The most significant handover, as one would expect, was that of non-university education, which involved 157,000 state employees and almost 900,000 million pesetas. By now the public spending controlled by the autonomous communities must have been rather more than 35 percent of the total, while the state still held on to more than 50 percent. There were, however, questions still to be resolved, for in spite of having tried out new solutions on financing, such situations were always thought of as emergency measures. At the same time the figure of assistant provincial delegate or "*subdelegado*," as a substitute for the civil governor, had the effect of establishing a dependency on the provincial delegate that had not existed previously, though it is very unlikely that the appearance of the post had the symbolic effect with which the Catalanists would have liked to endow it.

The political situation in Catalonia was not without its problematic elements. It soon became obvious that the fact of having signed a pact was not enough to keep the peace between the PP and CiU although, at the same time, "a lack of love does not make a marriage invalid." The problems became more acute as the nationalist vote fell away. In the elections in November 1995 Pujol, who had been in power for 15 years, lost the majority he had had in Catalonia and was forced to cling on to a difficult situation in which he depended on support from the ERC and PP alternately. Also, in 1996, Roca gave up his most important posts while Pere Esteve moved to being general secretary of *Convergència* with a more radical program that had as its pivotal point the notion of "shared sovereignty" and that was given more weight by support from other nationalist groups such as the PNV and the Galician Nationalist Block (*Bloque Nacionalista Galego* or BNG).

However, this more radical stance did nothing to improve the CiU's electoral chances. In the 1999 elections Pujol had already needed the support of the 12 PP deputies to be elected, and even with them he managed it by only one vote; he therefore went from having a decisive influence in Spanish politics to being a hostage of the right, though he was always a contentious one. The results of the elections in 2000 made Pujol much more dependent on the PP than ever before, to the extent that he had no alternative but to forget for the time being about any reform of the Catalan Statute and the Constitution.

In Galicia the PSOE had lost votes steadily after 1986, and in 1997 it finished as the third largest party in the Galician Parliament. In contrast, the Galician right was absorbing the nationalist sentiment of the center. The slow but steady progress towards the unification of left-wing nationalism in the BNG was not consolidated until 1996–7 and at the same time it was becoming more moderate. We can, nonetheless, still say that the political panorama did not change significantly.

In 1996 the government in Euzkadi was made up of the two nationalist parties and the PSOE. The pact between Aznar and the PNV on the formation of the government dealt with only minor matters and excluded from discussion the most important issue of all in Basque politics: terrorism. Yet for some months at least it seemed to have produced a new situation in which there was a previously unknown desire for collaboration. Alongside that, the efficiency of police action in fighting terrorism was increasing: in the early months of 1998 the number of *etarras* imprisoned equaled numbers in the period 1995 to 1997; in 1997 alone 67 members of the group were arrested. Advances were also made in terms of international collaboration and France finally ceased to be a "sanctuary" for terrorism.

There was also a judicial offensive against ETA. At the end of 1997 the members of the committee of HB were put in jail for having provided a space for ETA to broadcast a video during the 1996 election campaign. May 1998 saw the dismantling of a network of businesses that provided financial support for the terrorist organization and the following month the newspaper *Egin* was closed down after its editor – so it was said – was not only named by ETA but even found to have received instructions from the group via his computer. In 1996 ETA murdered five people and in 1997 there were 13 deaths; in fact these figures were evidence of the organization's impotence as the victims were PP councilors and therefore soft objectives for terrorist attacks. Yet their impotence tended to mean more barbaric acts rather than fewer. In July 1997, after being kidnapped and held for 532 days, the prison worker José Antonio Ortega Lara was released. Ten days later ETA captured Miguel Ángel Blanco, a PP councilor from Ermua, and threatened to kill him if ETA prisoners held outside the Basque Country were not brought closer to their families. The news affected all Spaniards deeply, even more so when the councilor was executed. At first the political parties were unanimous in their condemnation of the action but that situation did not last long.

The so-called Estella–Lizarra Pact signaled a break with the long period of collaboration between the PSOE and democratic nationalism

(1987–98). From 1995 on, meetings took place between the PNV, EA, and ETA. The events of the summer of 1997 and the increased PP vote meant that the Basque nationalists felt the need to take urgent and drastic initiatives to achieve peace by bringing together the entire nationalist vote. In March 1998 the *lehendakari* Ardanza published a document in which his starting-point was that the Basque conflict was a matter for the Basques themselves. He acknowledged the advances that had been made due to the Statute and he denied that there was a lesser degree of democracy in the Euzkadi than anywhere else. At the same time he also asked for an unlimited cessation of violence and for dialogue without conditions or limits in order to work towards a new institutional framework. This might have been a very worthwhile starting-point had it not been preceded by such high levels of tension.

Crucial meetings took place between ETA and the PNV at the start of 1998 and continued throughout the summer. They received new impetus when the PSOE abandoned the Basque government. ETA made a cessation of violence conditional upon the PNV and EA breaking with parties associated with Spain, and on the creation of an institution that would serve as a starting-point along the road to sovereignty for all territories of Euskal Herria. The final agreement was characterized by its ambiguity and lack of precision, no doubt because the moderate nationalists thought that after the truce violence would not be resumed. September 1998 saw the signing of the Estella Pact which laid down conditions for a "Basque area of decision-making," which it situated outside the Constitutional framework, thus arousing the indignation of the majority of political groups. The Estella Pact aimed to provide a "landing-strip" for ETA in the legal political arena, but it also allowed the PNV to take off in a new direction and forget its traditionally moderate approach to the question of autonomy.

In the autonomous elections in October 1998, the correlation between nationalist and non-nationalist seats remained the same but there was a definite tendency towards bipolarization that benefited HB and the PP. The Estella Pact established a truce during which the only meeting between the government and representatives of ETA took place in Switzerland, but no agreement was reached. The Congress of Deputies gave unanimous approval to a resolution which asked the government for "greater flexibility" in its policy on prisons and, though the news did not make much impact in the press, there were partial changes in government policy. Some 200 *etarras* were freed and 135 were moved to prisons nearer the Basque

Country, while 60 of the 150 members of the group who had emigrated to France now returned home. In addition – whether or not this was a political decision – in 1998 the Constitutional Court finally annulled the sentence it had pronounced on the HB committee. In June, European and municipal elections were held, and in the former the results were much the same as on previous occasions: PNV-EA won 34 percent of the vote and PP, PSOE, and EH 19 percent each.

This meant that the situation for the nationalists had become very complex, and that became even more so when ETA cut contact with the government, and especially after November 1999 when it announced its renewal of "armed action" and loudly reproached the democratic nationalists. EH (*Euskal Herritarrok*, the new name for HB) refused to cut its ties with ETA. Throughout 1999 there were no murders committed by the terrorists but it was later discovered that ETA had used this time to convert its *kale borroka* or "street fighting" commandos – which had meanwhile increased their activities – into full-blown terrorists. In January 2000 ETA once again killed a soldier in Madrid. There is not the slightest doubt that the guilty party in the breakdown of the peace process was ETA. There must have been sections of the group that wanted peace, but as ever it was hard-line elements who had their way. It is impossible to know the reasons behind the change in posture at the end of 1999, but in the months running up to that moment EH's attitude was a model of incoherence: at one and the same time it wanted the government to take the initiative and yet it also supported the *kale borroka*. For its part the PP government was always alert to the possibilities of immediate political profit. It entertained unrealistic hopes of being the one to solve the problem when it was in fact behind the times. The socialists did not outline their own position but instead moved from collaboration with the PNV and EA to joining forces with the PP. The democratic nationalists had told Aznar of their change of direction before making approaches to ETA, but they trusted too much in the chances of the peace process working. They forgot their traditionally moderate stance, they did not react quickly enough when ETA took up arms again, and they did not realize that an agreement such as the Estella Pact meant in effect an anti-nationalist front and a reduction of their own influence within the territory. Besides ETA's obvious culpability, there was then a collective failure on the part of all democrats. Bishop Juan María Uriarte of San Sebastián, who took part in the negotiations, attributes what happened to "the impatience of some and the immobility of others."

## Government and Opposition.
## The Elections in March 2000

In accordance with his policy of "lasting," Aznar only introduced political changes in his government halfway through its term in office. It was then, in 1998, that he replaced the controversial government spokesman Miguel Ángel Rodríguez, who had been one of the main protagonists in the PP's policy-making on the media and had made some totally inappropriate statements about the Catalanists. Aznar insisted on the need to reinforce the party's centrist tendencies, which he presented as a personal mission. He therefore went back to reaffirming what he had said during the 1996 campaign. At the end of the year, when the ETA truce had been declared, he once again re-stated the same position. Alvarez Cascos, another major player in the battle for the media, had by now lost any importance he had ever had in the front line of the party leadership. However, there was no doubt that he had had it in the early years when he had even tried to prolong the government's fragile collaboration with the PNV. At the start of 1999 he effected a government reshuffle which had consequences for the Labor portfolio: Javier Arenas was replaced by someone who appeared to be one of his closest collaborators so that he could become party general secretary.

Meanwhile, the results of the opinion polls were promising for the PP. After all, while they were in office between 1996 and 2000 Spain had reduced by three points the differential in income between it and the European Community average, and it had also achieved the highest level ever of real convergence: some 83 percent. Its economic success was becoming a "fine rain" which soaked everything and distracted attention from any less agreeable reality.

The opposition also helped the PP. The socialists, plagued for a long time by a conjunction of unfortunate circumstances that were largely the result of its own mistakes, remained in 1996 at a much reduced electoral distance. Felipe González, who was still an absolutely key figure in the party leadership, though he had had to face such harsh confrontation during his last years as leader, despised his successor. For months on end he gave the socialists the impression that Aznar's victory could be reversed in a short space of time.

At his party conference in June 1997, to the great surprise of the majority and even of the man who was to succeed him, González refused to stand for reelection as General Secretary; with this decision he took with him both Alfonso Guerra and José María Benegas, the two other survivors from the Suresnes Conference who were still in the Socialist leadership. The election of Joaquín Almunia as general secretary could have given the impression that it was a decision from the highest level of the PSOE leadership that had remained in power over the previous 14 years. In fact, it was a decision aimed at achieving continuity and it had a logical objective: Almunia was a leader of the "renewal" faction who had not been involved in the worst aspects of the socialist Administration.

Almunia took two decisions that soon proved to be far too risky: he called primaries within the party and proposed a pact with IU. Essentially, not only were both of these steps positive but they were probably also irreversible in the sense that one way or another they were bound to lead to important decisions being taken which would have a decisive impact. The majority of the socialist electorate thought that Almunia would win the primaries, but neither the candidate nor the party leadership as a whole took into account the fact that the primaries themselves would open the Pandora's box of increased conflict within the party at a time of internal disorientation and unease. Against all predictions, in April 1998 Almunia lost the primaries with only 44.5 percent of the vote against Josep Borrell's more than 55 percent.

Borrell emerged as the politician most highly rated by public opinion, ahead of Aznar, who had to be content with third place (González being in second place). Yet the "Borrell effect" proved to be a very ephemeral episode in Spanish politics. When the debate on the state of the nation had taken place 41 percent gave the victory to Aznar and only 14 percent to Borrell. Having two heads in the party (though some suggested that there was no head at all) very soon became problematic as Almunia stayed on as party's general secretary.

The decisions of the justice department on questions arising from cases as yet unresolved in the courts tarnished the PSOE's image still further. At the end of July 1998 sentencing in the Marey case meant that an ex-socialist minister, Barrionuevo, and a Secretary of State, Vera, both went to prison. Socialist party members found that they were obliged to choose between a shameful solidarity and the shame of not supporting their fellow socialists who had held such important posts. It was only in December that a pardon was granted – a wise and even admirable decision on the part of the government in terms of easing relations between the constitutional parties.

Borrell was finally induced to step down. Probably he himself realized that he was too weak and inadequate and gradually he forgot the reproaches that he had initially leveled at the other party leaders. In the end, in May 1999 he resigned as a candidate for the Presidency when it became obvious that a scandal involving two men who had worked closely with him, concerning illegal activities in the Ministry of Finance, might affect the party as a whole.

All these goings-on did not mean that IU was helped in any way by the situation inside the PSOE. There was instead such a slow but evident leakage of support from those who had till now been IU voters that in 1997, from an electoral point of view, their share of the vote was now half what it had been in the 1996 elections. The proposal on collaboration put forward by the PSOE caused a complete turnaround in Anguita's policy so far. Almunia had thought that he could only galvanize his electorate by making a pact with IU. As a result he had put forward a program that was too far to the left, offering more radical action on the Welfare State, and using a more emotive style of language. This meant losing the centrist vote.

In contrast, at the end of its term in office Aznar's government had cause to be pleased with its performance. This had been a time when economic results had been genuinely good; the numbers in employment had risen and the pressure of direct taxation had decreased, though there had been a rise in indirect taxation. The sense of prosperity and optimism regarding the future were now part of the way that Spanish society felt. Aznar's government was also the first Spanish executive since 1982 which had not had to face the threat of a general strike.

From the summer of 1998 on, opinion polls suggested that a victory for the Popular Party was probable, though the situation had not always been so clear. After a brief initial advantage for the PP, from the autumn of 1996 until the summer of 1997 (that is to say, three consecutive terms) the PSOE remained in front in terms of electoral expectations, and it found itself in this position once again in the spring of 1998. Compared with these four terms, for 14 other terms the PP was in the lead, sometimes with substantial margins (of up to 8 percentage points). Now, facing new elections, the number of Spaniards who saw the situation as positive ("good" or "very good") was over 40 percent – a figure that had never been reached before in democratic Spain. Even so, winning an absolute majority seemed inconceivable, even to the leaders of the right. That was the opinion of almost all analysts too. One more piece of information should be taken into account: the high level of uncertainty among electors. In October

1999, more that 25 percent of voters did not know how they were going to vote – a figure that went above 34 percent before the election campaign and only went down to 28 percent once the campaign was under way. All in all, never before had any government come to the end of its term of office with such good economic and political indicators and yet such uncertainty over the possible election results.

The PSOE's intention of maximizing the electoral turn-out on the left was a great surprise. Having been decided on in January 2000, it was made easier by Anguita's withdrawal as a candidate for the leadership on health grounds. It was not in fact in response to any discernible demand from Spanish society, and it actually triggered a reaction and mobilization among right-wing voters. The kind of partial coalition that had existed was absurd because it could only succeed where it did not really exist, and it by no means won all the votes that might have come its way. It was only effective in small right-wing areas.

In the end the campaign did much to ensure bad results for the Left. The PP campaign was based on identifying the party firstly with what had been achieved so far ("Action") and also with the possibility of achieving as much again in the future ("We're going on to do even more"). One aspect of the campaign that had very positive results for the PP was the "sequencing" of its political program – that is to say, the gradual revelation over time of the precise content of its manifesto. In contrast, the left's campaign, along with its unrealistic claims, gave an impression of general uncertainty. The two campaigns resulted in a difference in the level of turnout of voters on the two sides. The PP did much to maximize turnout and its voters stayed loyal, while in the case of the PSOE and IU, the turnout was much lower with less focus and conviction.

The PP, with 44.5 percent of the vote, won 183 seats – 8 more than it needed for an absolute majority; it had moved up almost 5 percentage points. For its part, the PSOE won 34.1 percent of the vote and 125 seats, which meant that it had gone down by 3.5 points and had lost 16 seats. Yet this defeat was nothing compared to that of IU which, confirming its relentless decline, was left with only 5.5 percent of the vote and 8 seats, compared with a figure of almost double that in 1996 (10.6 percent of the vote) with almost triple the number of seats (21). The nationalist vote remained overall as stable as is usual in Spain but there were also some differences. EH's call to voters to abstain failed, as the decrease in votes in the Basque Country was no more than 7 percent between the earlier and later elections – a figure lower than that over Spain as a whole. All of this leads one to conclude that a part of the radical vote had gone over to the PNV.

The overall impression that we gain is that a part of the left-wing electorate decided to "let the PP win with my abstention counting against it." They therefore chose abstention and passive acceptance of a result that did not seem all that bad given the success already achieved by the economic policies of the party in power. All in all, the PSOE lost 3 million votes compared to 1996 and its weakness was evident in the low percentage of those who turned out to vote.

On this basis of this data it is possible to offer two contradictory interpretations of these election results. The first would be most favorable to the PP. It would suggest that Aznar's absolute majority in 2000 was a "universal majority" like that of the PSOE in 1982, even if the level of abstention was higher. It could now be said to be true that "votes belong to nobody," in the sense that party allegiances were not as fixed as they had been in the past. Moving from one party to another could mean stability. As Aznar stated, this could at last be "the end of the Civil War." There is no doubt whatever that his opinion on this matter had a decisive impact on his subsequent time in office.

However, while the victory in the year 2000 was undoubtedly a victory for the right, it was nonetheless won with help, because if Aznar gained, Almunia lost. In 2000 the PSOE had a starting position that was undoubtedly much better than the one that the right had had in 1982, and the PP could not be as sure that it would have two terms of office as its political opponent had no doubt been after the earlier elections. What is certain is that the right now had a party that was as firmly established and disciplined as the PSOE had been in 1982 and, furthermore, everything had worked in its favor (even Anguita's illness). Spain's experience was similar to what had happened in Portugal, when in 1985 the center-right leader Anibal Cavaco won elections that had seemed uncertain in prospect, though after his victory and the implementation of an economic plan, he was able to win a crushing majority in 1987 and confirm his position again in 1991.

On the basis of this interpretation of the election results we can try to draw up a balance and evaluate the right-wing government's actions during its first term in power. As we attempt a summary and consider how the future looked for the PP in 2000, if we want to take positive achievements into account first we should look at its economic record. The way the Spanish economy had developed over the previous 4 years had been so positive that we can even talk in certain areas, such as foreign investment, of a genuine historic peak. This cycle of stability and increased employment, which can be traced back to the socialist years, allowed considerable annual growth accompanied – and this was crucial – by macroeconomic stability. Among the aspects of the government's administration most deserving of praise were its ability to control public sector spending and the reliability of its anti-inflation policy despite difficulties towards the end. The way in which it carried out privatization counterbalances these positive aspects. Nevertheless, 1,800,000 new jobs were created and the level of unemployment was cut by 7 percent, though it still remained above the European average. At the same time unemployment benefit decreased but social benefits rose overall.

This brilliant management of the economy became more erratic in other areas of public life, and there is even some doubt as to whether in some of these the essential rules of peaceful coexistence were not broken. It is virtually only in the Interior ministry's policies on policing that praise can be given to the same extent as on economic affairs. What is clear is that there was continuity in some areas (foreign policy, defense . . . ), but management in matters such as education, culture, justice, and the environment was deficient and there was no question of even hoping for an absolute majority. The question of the media was dealt with in a way that was frankly abusive and unacceptable. Other crucial matters were simply set aside, such as the raising of expectations on the quality of Spain's democracy, or else matters took rather a dangerous direction. This was the case for Spain's different regions, with their cultural diversity, all living together. Nonetheless, the results that Aznar obtained by the year 2000 seemed far better than his own objective merits would have suggested.

Yet Aznar's government also left a legacy of an important change in Spanish political life in the medium and long term. There is no doubt at all that the balance was positive in economic affairs, but it is also possible that the stamp left by the right-wing government on Spain's politics would prove to be reasonably long-lasting. Privatizations had begun in the socialist years, which means that one cannot say that there were in this area any really radical new moves. On the other hand, it is possible to say that there was genuine innovation in terms of taxation. It is unlikely that in the future tax increases will continue to be seen as inevitable as happened in the past over so many years.

One might also say that by the year 2000 there was one element of what was going on in Spain that had become clear over recent months, that was destined to last, and that meant a change of primary importance in Spanish life, though it should not be attributed exclusively to political management: at the end of a century and of a millennium, Spaniards' assessment of themselves was now clearly positive. The sequence of events over the course of the transition, the socialist years, and the PP's time in power had had this final result, and it greatly benefited the PP at this time.

The last consideration to be put in the balance when evaluating this first term in office for the right has to do with the future prospects offered by PP policy after winning an absolute majority in the elections in the year 2000. This unexpected result drastically changed its possibilities and way of governing and posed the question – always present in PP politics – of whether to opt for its usual component of classic right-wing policies or adopt a more centrist position.

## The Style of Government with an Absolute Majority

On this occasion, after the elections in 2000, nobody could talk about "bitter victories or sweet defeat" as had happened in 1996. The year 2000, to everyone's surprise and without the sense of a miracle having taken place as had been the case in the earlier elections, seemed to be the 1982 of the Spanish right. Indeed, in Parliament, the PP found itself with a desert stretching out in front of it: the PSOE did not seem to present any kind of a viable political alternative because it had not yet come to terms with its electoral defeat. IU was crippled with debts and had to dismiss a number of its workers. Also, unlike the Basque Country, the governments of Catalonia and the Canary Islands depended for stability on PP support. Yet at the same time, in the year 2000, 56 percent of voters chose to tick the box for parties other than the PP; it was only thanks to CiU and the Canary Island Coalition (*Coalición Canaria* or CC), who supported Aznar's candidacy, that the right-wing vote could reach 50 percent. The PP's absolute majority was not, then, a blank check, though it could be seen as such. Aznar himself could indeed go on and do even more: victory, as Churchill reminded us, can and should result in a generous attitude. That in itself can bring numerous benefits, but Aznar did not act generously.

What did happen was that he struck a conciliatory note at the start. When he formed his new government at the end of April, a key post went to Mariano Rajoy who had acted as a fire-break during a crisis in the Ministry of Education. A very temperate politician, Rajoy was made deputy prime minister with responsibility for political matters at a moment when the PP did not have to fill a quota of posts from the traditional center. Two excellent moves in Aznar's personal political game were to make Federico Trillo – a potential rival who had kept his distance somewhat as president of the Congress of Deputies during the PP's previous time in office – Minister of Defense and not of Justice as Trillo would have preferred, and to put Álvarez Cascos – a representative of the party's old guard – in a job involving investment, in the Ministry of Promotion, which was in no way to be despised but was, politically speaking, fairly irrelevant. Both men had in effect been demoted. One could view Rajoy's ascent as running parallel to Rodrigo Rato's decline, but that would be an exaggeration since Rato was after all doubling in his ministerial post as a person of political influence, while also holding on to his position as deputy prime minister with responsibility for economic matters. Aznar personally took responsibility for ministerial changes and he also played an important part in lower-level changes. The government that was sworn in at the end of April could count on the support of 202 deputies: the same number as the PSOE members of parliament in 1982.

Within a very few weeks this government forgot that it had talked of dialogue and instead displayed all the disadvantages that can come with an absolute majority. Spanish nationalist ambitions, a growing self-satisfaction, and scorn of the opposition – especially the nationalist opposition – were characteristics that shaped its fundamental position. Aznar had no hesitation in stating that Spain should aim to "take a huge leap forward in the first decade of the 21st century" and join the G8, and he assured the nation that they should "not feel any shame" in saying as much. Spain was not a problem but a world power. The prime minister said of himself: "I am like those poets who have no biography because their works are their biography." Speaking in a most forthright manner, he said accusingly of the Basque nationalists that "every time ETA had had its back against the ropes they had stepped in to save it." Other ministers charged the PNV with having been a perpetual "traitor" to democracy. The impression was given that the work that the government undertook would be "vital for making a mark on the next decade." Aznar became a kind of dogmatic, even prophetic moral reformer. He acted entirely independently of existing social circumstances, and of the consensus that it would have been necessary to build up if the decisions to be taken were to have any real chance of lasting any length of time.

This situation produced a flood of new-style reforms, accompanied by a growing sense of tension arising from the government's aggressive manner towards its opponents, and by an attitude that swung from being defensive to throwing its weight around. That became particularly so after the summer of 2001. It was all entirely unnecessary and even counter-productive in terms of the government's aims. At the end of the year, the *Centro de Investigaciones Sociológicas* or CIS published a survey in which 26 percent of those questioned declared that the political situation was bad or very bad compared with 22 percent who described it as good or very good. This was a situation that was almost unimaginable with an absolute majority in parliament. It was written of Margaret Thatcher – idol of the PP leadership – that at the end of her time in power she lay back in her chair and her behavior, like that of the French king on his throne in 1789, seemed aimed at provoking revolution. The same could be said of Aznar around this time.

## The Limits of PSOE Renewal

There is no doubt at all that the government could afford to adopt this stance because of the apparent lack of any effective opposition. Although for a very short time, and after its electoral defeat, the PSOE seemed to take a new direction, this did not make any notable impact on the way people intended to vote.

Alongside other representatives of political groups with a personal style of leadership the two main candidates for the post of party general secretary had very distinct political profiles. José Bono was an old-style territorial baron who could count on solid absolute majorities supporting him in the regional elections, and this offered a certain continuity with the past. However, although he doubtless enjoyed the support of those who had led his party, he always seemed too closely tied to the previous government to lead a party that now wanted change. He was also rather too provincial to become prime minister of the Spanish state. No doubt some of his greatest virtues came to the fore in the way he received the news that he had been defeated by a mere nine votes: he immediately congratulated his opponent. José Luis Rodríguez Zapatero's victory was to a great extent a surprise. The desire for change made it easier to vote in a little-known candidate without having too clear an idea of what views he represented, though the statements he made were sensible and he was in just the right position astride continuity and change.

Zapatero's biography reveals curious similarities and differences when compared with Aznar's. They had their youthfulness in common: the new socialist general secretary was only 25 years old when he joined the Congress of Deputies in 1988. University had played a more important role for him than for Aznar: he had taught constitutional law in León. The two politicians' family backgrounds were diametrically opposed: the young Aznar was of a family that had been important within the Franco regime; Zapatero was the grandson of an Army captain who had refused to join the 1936 military uprising and had been executed for it. Aznar had been trained in administration. Zapatero had devoted himself to party politics and had managed to tame a socialist provincial group such as the group in León which had devoured many general secretaries but reelected him at four consecutive party conferences without the slightest difficulty. He was a peace-maker, not an advocate of the sharp break, and he could appear somewhat lack-luster.

The *guerrista* tendency within the PSOE attributed Zapatero's victory to the "renewal of the renewal," and to an extent they were right. Thanks not so much to an overwhelming victory as to its element of surprise, the new socialist leader could embark on a decisive and rapid period of generational change. The party militants from the postwar or transition years vanished from his team and those from the democratic years began to take their place. What Aznar had done slowly and carefully in opposition, Zapatero was able to do suddenly, though not always with sufficient transparency. Later, in the final run-up to the elections, he would try – successfully – to attract back those of the party's leadership team who had drifted away.

From the end of July 2001 on, the PSOE's election hopes rose once more but without ever becoming entirely convincing. Alfonso Guerra was said to have nicknamed the new general secretary "Bambi" because of his softness. Other leaders called those who had replaced them "the kinder-garten." The weakness of the party's program on economic matters seemed obvious to all. In June 2001, Santos Juliá declared that Zapatero's socialism was characterized by good manners but gave the impression of having to improvise when devising policies. Josep Ramoneda criticized Zapatero for "making an ideology out of making pacts" at a time when the PP's renewal of government posts was continuing uninterrupted and giving the impression that it was grabbing any part of the cake it could lay its hands on. A journalist heard the PNV leader Xabier Arzalluz express an opinion that was not far off those mentioned: in his view the new socialists lacked "any real backbone." In matters where his message was clearest, such as the organization of the territory of the Spanish state, Zapatero's stance conflicted with that of a section of socialist organizations. At an early stage (in June 2000) the PSOE leader took as his own the model of the PSC – that is to say, of Maragall and the Catalan Socialists – for drawing the different elements of Spain together and opening up a way ahead for possible reforms of the Statutes of the autonomous communities and of the Constitution. Nonetheless, little by little Zapatero was settling in as leader due to his own good sense and the mistakes of his opponents.

By the time of the debate on the state of the nation in June 2001 Zapatero was able to defeat Aznar. Throughout 2002 the socialist leader made more and more proposals for "political regeneration" – a field in which his suggestions seemed fair enough, especially taking into account the overwhelming hegemony of the government in power. The socialist leader was almost always right in his criticism of the measures taken by the government and in many cases – such as the pact on justice or the Law on Political Parties – the socialist opposition did much to improve texts that had either not been viable or whose content was initially very questionable. Nonetheless, the overall socialist program still had to be outlined. Its ideas on tax reform were not clearly defined and did not convince experts; even the make-up of the team in charge of the PSOE's economic policy remained controversial and subject to change. The proposals put forward by the opposition, which suggested that the solution might be increased spending (on housing and security), did not seem problematic but equally did not give the impression that they were part of a global plan. On many occasions, socialist programs of action seemed little thought out.

In the debate on the state of the nation in mid July 2002, Zapatero argued once again that "Spain had a social deficit that was unbearable for society's weakest members" and he added this new issue to the political agenda. In October he caught the government by surprise when he defended his own alternative budget proposals against those of the Finance Minister. Although it could still be described as feeble, the opposition was gradually gaining in popularity. By November 2002, opinion polls all showed something that looked like a technical draw between the PP and the PSOE, with Aznar half a point below Zapatero.

## Dramatic Basque Elections

In the year after the general election the question that was most often tabled in discussions on Spanish politics was the situation in the Basque Country where, on the one hand, Juan José Ibarretxe's government lacked a parliamentary majority without the support of the radical nationalists (*abertzales*) and, on the other hand, terrorism was on the increase after a truce that many had thought would never be broken.

Terrorist incidents made the summer of 2000 the bloodiest for several years, with 11 deaths by August 21 (in comparison to 15 deaths in 1996, 13 in 1997, 6 in 1998, and none at all in 1999). What was most conclusive, however, was that whereas towards the end of the 1970s there were up to 100 people dying per year, now, despite much lower figures in this area, the number of those living under permanent threat was incalculably higher. Indeed, among those killed there were not only leaders or active members of the PP and people associated with right-wing elements of society but also members of the left whose attitude was often typically one of radical opposition to collaboration with moderate Basque nationalists.

When faced with such murderous barbarity, what possible explanation can there be for the PNV taking so long to change its position on terrorism? The Lizarra program was still in force, but it was by now little more than a useless "fetish" since a section of those who had signed up to it did not condemn the daily acts of violence that were being committed. In October 2000 the political situation in the Basque Country took a new turn which was not entirely unexpected. The nationalist government needed confirmation of its support, while the policy of the PP consisted of reaching a more or less explicit pre-election agreement with the PSOE to get rid of the PNV. Opinion polls painted a contradictory picture. On the one hand the *lehendakari* was the institution that was most widely accepted, while on the other a rejection of violence was the most widespread sentiment in the region. "What the Basques seem to be asking for," it was suggested, "is an iron hand against ETA (which is what the PP is offering but not the PNV), together with an understanding of the nationalist option (which is what the PNV is offering but not the PP)." There was much speculation about the possible outcome of the elections, and the opinion polls indicated for the first time that there was a possibility of a new government that would not be nationalist.

The campaign began in February, though in reality it had continued unobtrusively since the previous general election. In May Mayor Oreja left his post as Interior Minister. According to general opinion, the combination of his calm discussion, his underlying firmness, and good information on policy had made him the best non-nationalist candidate imaginable. He also began his campaign with moderation; in fact, Ibarretxe did the same. Ibarretxe benefited from his position within the government and from the fact that his electorate were not slow to show their support. Also, he did not provoke reactions of rejection. Thirty-four percent of electors wanted Ibarretxe as *lehendakari* whereas only 6 percent said that they preferred Mayor Oreja. Carlos Garaicoechea, for his part, declared in the daily newspaper *ABC*: "EH has not managed to dissociate itself from ETA and it will have to pay for the broken china of the failure of the truce"; his statement proved to be closer to the truth than speculation by anti-nationalist intellectuals who saw the formation of a government without the PNV as imminent.

On polling-day (in May 2001) there was the highest turnout of any Basque autonomous elections ever, at only one point below the level for the general election in 1982. The nationalists won a clear victory but the specific weight of each electoral block was seen to be similar. At the same time it was evident that there was very little porosity between the two blocks. PNV-EA, with 33 seats, fulfilled all its imaginable objectives: a good turnout of nationalist voters, a percentage improvement of 6.5 percent, and seven more parliamentary seats. In contrast, as Garaicoechea had predicted, EH suffered the consequences of the broken truce, losing half its seats to end up with only seven. For its part, in the non-nationalist block, the PP was confirmed as the second largest political force with 19 seats (three more than before, but two of them came from the Alavese Unity Party (*Unidad Alavesa*)). If in this case it was a question of a pause in the PP's rise, in the case of the socialists, who went down from 14 to 13 seats, it was a pause on their way down. Ibarretxe had won thanks to his centrist strategy based on making the most of the strengths in his personality, the national identity vote, and good results during his period of government so far. For its part, the joint strategy of the PP–PSOE ended up frightening the electors. It was not clearly understood what was actually going to happen: a typical reaction from a society endowed with a strong sense of national identity facing what it considered an unfair and insulting judgment (which equated nationalism with terrorism).

These election results, which allowed a government to be formed with nationalist and communist members, eased the tension caused by the politics of two opposing blocks but only for a short time. Mayor Oreja declared immediately that he was ready for talks between all parties to get rid of ETA. Acting on an initiative from Zapatero, Nicolás Redondo, the socialist leader, tried to carve out a space for the Basque PSOE that would allow it to be less dependent on the PP. Hopes dawned that Ibarretxe's prominence in the PNV might mean a new stage in Basque politics based on dialogue. At first only a few pens linked to the right were discouraging; Alonso de los Ríos stated that he looked "with fear" on the PSOE as though anticipating betrayal by them. All that was really clear was that confrontation would not end in victory for anybody.

## The Policy of Making Pacts and Breaking with Consensus

The policy of making pacts which began to take shape towards the end of 2000 should be seen to a great extent as evidence of the determination on the part of the new PSOE leadership to constitute a "useful opposition." The PP accepted this, conscious that it would be the major beneficiary, but it did so in such a way as to spoil any chances it might have had of maximizing its advantages.

From the outset, in the "pact for civil liberties and against terrorism" there was a clear discrepancy between the points of view of the only two parties who finally signed up to it. At the end of November 2000, the PSOE was still insisting that the PNV must also sign up, but the pact was published on December 9 and demanded that the nationalists abandon the Estella Pact as an "obvious and necessary prerequisite" for reestablishing unity on the issues of the Basque Statute and the Constitution. It also provided the groundwork to allow special attention to be paid to the victims of terrorism and for a series of basic principles to prevent the fight against terrorism becoming a site of confrontation between the different political parties. The nationalist parties, including the Catalans, were never prepared to sign up to this pact. In fact it was given undue importance if one takes into account that it was not strictly adhered to, and in government hands it served to measure the supposed anti-terrorist sentiments of social and political players in public positions. However, it did no more than allow the leaders of the respective parties to exchange information about action taken by the police.

If we are to understand how it was that a pact on justice was made (in early May 2001), we must start by mentioning the widespread dissatisfaction in society with this area of the Administration. At the point where views differed most radically, the agreement offered at least a partial solution. On the one hand it meant that the Congress of Deputies kept the election of the 12 members who would represent the judiciary on the General Council of the Judiciary in its own hands, but the judges' associations were to propose three times the number of candidates needed and the final choice would be made by Parliament on the basis of a three-fifths majority. The result was a mixed system. The pact on justice, which set out the groundwork for promoting legislative changes and provided additional means for organization within the judicial system, was received with general satisfaction. Neither in the press nor within the parties was any mention made of a problem area that was later seen to have remained unresolved: the Office of the State Public Prosecutor.

In one sense there was a third pact made. In the second week of July 2001 the PP's and PSOE's aim of reaching an agreement on reappointments to various posts in state institutions, notably in the judiciary, seemed in danger of making no further progress. The debate to decide on nominations had brought together the members of the General Council of the Judiciary, the magistrates of the Constitutional Court, the members of the Audit Tribunal (*Tribunal de Cuentas*), and other dignitaries. Agreement was finally reached at the start of October, but this late decision did not prove satisfactory either. When the press published the names of the candidates, who had been voted in without any difficulties, it also noted each one's party membership. It became clear that this had counted for far more than any consideration of the candidates' own personal worth. The consequences were even clearer in 2003. The PSOE accused the government of understanding the pact in terms of party allegiance and filling all the posts with the most conservative elements of the judiciary. What had been promised was inter-party collaboration in the drawing up of new legislation but this soon deteriorated, especially when the PP tried to solve any problems that arose by passing new laws, notably on penal matters. If the Office of the State Public Prosecutor had already shown its political bias by this time, with the passage of time its party allegiance would in due course become even more blatantly obvious.

The government's policy of making pacts was, on the other hand, compatible with its desire to introduce profound legislative changes counting entirely on its absolute majority. The Universities Act (*Ley Universitaria* or LOU) was its first measure on education as well as being the most controversial, and it provoked the strongest protests. In May 2001 the vice-chancellors of 61 of Spain's 68 universities rejected the bill. They argued that it was not based on any consensus as it should be, and nor did it pay due attention to the European model. Nonetheless, the new law was passed in July 2001. Although the issues raised could not easily be understood by the public at large, it was clear that the law was unacceptable to those most directly affected by it. There was an awareness that reform was needed, but not of the kind that the government had chosen to impose. The government's defiant stance, which was very evident after the summer, meant that the argument became fiercer still. The law did not provide for an increase in public spending on universities, which in Spain had gone down from 0.96 percent of GDP in 1998 to 0.84 percent in 2001, despite the fact that the growth in wealth had been far higher. In the countries of the OECD the level was at around 1.3 percent.

The Law on the Quality of Education (*Ley de Calidad de Enseñanza*), which had first been proposed at the end of 2001 and would remain under discussion throughout 2002, was also exclusively a consequence of the government's absolute majority in Parliament. As had happened on issues such as universities or immigration, in this case, too, no kind of green paper was issued outlining a starting position. Similarly, there was no prior consultation either on a matter that had very direct implications for the organization of the autonomies within the Spanish state. Once again no budgetary commitment was made. The designation of religion as an examinable subject within the curriculum was highly contentious, as was the proposal of an alternative along the lines of "religious studies." This and other measures were in danger of reopening conflict on religion that had so far been avoided thanks to the 1978 Constitution and agreements made in 1979.

As far as other cultural matters are concerned, there was new evidence of shortcomings in the government's management, while at the same time it made a discernible shift towards the right. The attempt to privatize the Prado ended at the close of 2001 with a clash between the museum director and the president of the Trust, and this dispute resulted in the director's post becoming vacant. Although there was a coherent policy on the conservation of Spain's historic heritage, there was particular conflict over cultural matters relating to the autonomous communities. There was once again an attempt made to bring about changes in the study of the humanities and this time it succeeded, though they were not very far-reaching. Nonetheless, in ways that were quite clear for all to see, the PP's second term in office saw a distinct move away from a so-called liberal position to one that was distinctly neo-conservative. The intellectual world closest to government circles often consisted of former left-wingers, the marginalized, the exaggeratedly heterodox, or the unclassifiable. A large number of them lacked the prestige needed for the roles to which they laid claim, and which they sometimes played. What is important, however, is that they insisted on adding to the political agenda a number of subjects that once again broke with the consensus that had existed from the transition on. Their distinguishing features were a Spanish neo-nationalism that rejected any alternative pluralistic vision of Spain, a very clear-cut sense of the role Spain could play in the world, excessive pride over its recent development, and a certain historical revisionism which was not at all consistent with a more scientific viewpoint on the past.

## ——— The PP: Idyllic Peace and Neo-conservatism ———

Before discussing this neo-conservatism we should first of all mention the total unity – only occasionally marred by some minor passing matter – that the PP experienced during its second term in office. As early as August 2000, Arenas announced that "the PP will elect Aznar's successor in autumn 2003." It is remarkable with what watch-maker's precision the prime minister planned, from November 2001 onwards, the party conference that was to take place and to debate the issue in 2002. In fact, the amount of his life spent in a position of political power was greater than that of Felipe González. It was because of a mere promise that had perhaps not been very well thought out that he decided not to stand again for reelection. On successive occasions the prime minister tried to prevent the leaders of his own party speculating on the succession but inevitably they continued to do so.

Rodrigo Rato was "number two" in the party and therefore looked like the obvious successor. However, in January 2001, perhaps for personal reasons, he seemed less likely to stand for the post of prime minister. Mayor Oreja was ahead of him in the opinion polls and his lead grew over subsequent months. Nonetheless, the succession did not appear particularly problematic. In the elections in Galicia the PP, with 51 percent of the vote, held on to its majority with the loss of only one seat. The slight slump for the nationalists of the BNG and the rise of the socialists at the start of 2002 showed that in this autonomous community there were swings at the opposite end of the political spectrum to the PP, but not in the PP itself. For its part, the PP party conference did nothing important apart from confirming that Aznar would not stand again, while those who would put themselves forward as candidates made themselves much more visible. Three deputy general secretaries were appointed: Mayor, Rato, and Rajoy, but in July 2002, when there was a ministerial reshuffle, it became clearer which direction events were going to take: Rajoy returned to the Prime Minister's Office and was made government spokesman, while a new rising star, Eduardo Zaplana, became Labor Minister. The entire crisis was very well handled by Aznar: even his offer to Roca of the Foreign Office portfolio was part of a sophisticated strategy linked to Catalan nationalism. When Alberto Ruiz Gallardón – one of the few conservatives with his own votes – stood for the post of Mayor of Madrid, this did much to reinforce his links with the pinnacle of power once again, while the addition to the list of the prime minister's wife, Ana Botella, apart from soothing personal wounds, also reinforced an image of party unity. In the final months of 2002, the clockwork mechanism that Aznar had put in place to deal with the succession marked time passing inexorably. Halfway through November, the new Foundation for Sociological Analysis and Study (*Fundación de Análisis y Estudios Sociológicos*) came into being, over which Aznar himself was due to preside once he had ceased to be prime minister. Its motto – "think Spain and preserve what works" – was consistent with neo-conservative ideas, and that was the line along which Aznar doubtless intended his party to continue.

As regards the candidates, their different positions were by now fairly plain to see. Ruiz Gallardón looked like a candidate who would only be acceptable to the PP if there were a crisis, or if the socialists seemed likely to have a clear advantage in the opinion polls. Mayor Oreja had faded gradually from the scene because of his total absorption in what was going on in the Basque Country and his scant interest in other aspects of Spanish national life. Rato had come much more to the fore, but he still seemed an unlikely candidate because of his more exposed position in relation to possible scandals arising from the latest case of financial corruption, the Gescartera affair. Zapatero had no hesitation in commenting that from his point of view Rajoy was the best candidate. Rajoy's response was typical of the man: when any question was asked about his candidacy, confounding journalists, he always replied with another question in return.

Nonetheless, despite the idyllic peace within the PP on the matter of Aznar's successor, other kinds of problems did arise, especially between the government and Spain's historic national entities. It soon became clear that there was a fundamental and almost total lack of understanding between the two major players on the political stage at the time: Aznar and Pujol. It appears that Pujol told the Basques that Aznar "despises us and is to be despised." In the summer of 2000 Pujol had outlined his position, which consisted of not allowing himself to be displaced from the center politically while at the same time proclaiming loudly his dissatisfaction with the attitudes of Spain's central government. Aznar's response was politically astute and, at the same time, tortuous, unsympathetic, and difficult to combat. In March 2001, the PP and CiU had diverged over the matter of the National Hydrological Plan (*Plan Hidrológico Nacional*). This was the PP's major project in terms of its environmental policy. It was soundly based on objective needs and it shows how vital it is that the Spanish autonomous communities establish a forum for discussion on matters of common interest. However, because the idea of a pact was rejected at the start, the project was simply not viable. In spring 2001, the PP government outlined a program on autonomy that it tried to push through in the months that followed. From its content one can deduce that what Aznar wanted was what we might call a "closure" on the issue of the Spanish state of autonomous regions. In the future there would be no further transfers of powers. Spain would have reached the "furthest point" in terms of such transfers and it was now time to stop the process. The right-wing media accused the nationalists of pushing for a "brutal process of de-nationalization of Spain" against which it was now time to react.

Other causes of confrontation between the PP and CiU arose as a consequence of the king's speech on the occasion of the awarding of the prestigious literary prize, the *Premio Cervantes*, because one phrase he used suggested that Castilian Spanish had never been imposed. CiU had managed to avoid the Republican Left (*Esquerra Republicana*) coming to prominence after its role had been reduced to a mere token appearance thanks to Pujol's cleverness in the 1980s. Now it came to life once more, though its reemergence did not prevent a degree of radicalization in CiU such that the general secretary, Pere Esteve, left the party, accusing it of being too close to the pro-Spanish right. In March 2003 the Catalanists voted with the Catalan left in Parliament when they pushed for an increase in the level of self-government for their autonomous community.

If there was now a deep divide between the government and the Catalanists on the matter of their different concepts of Spain, in the case of the Basque Country it would be more appropriate to talk of a yawning gulf. The language used by the Basque parliamentary majority was ambiguous to say the least on the matter of sovereignty: "On the basis of the present statutory framework," they claimed "recognition of Basque society's right to decide on its own future." In addition to this, the crisis in the Basque socialist party helped to complicate matters further. The results of the last elections had left Redondo's leadership in a poor state because of its relations with the PP. In March 2002, the winner at the Basque socialist party conference was Patxi López who, in the end, carried with him almost two-thirds of the votes in favor of an executive capable of bringing about a greater degree of political self-determination for the Basques.

However, in the PP's second term of office, the main issue under debate was new legislation on political parties that would allow Batasuna to be outlawed. In March the Council of Ministers approved a bill, and in the third week in May the Congress of Deputies passed the law with a large majority of no less than 95 percent of the House. The law gained the support of PP, PSOE, CiU, CC, and the pro-Andalusia lobby. PNV, EA, and BNG together totaled 16 votes against. As for the Basque Country itself, at whom the law was directed, 11 Basque deputies voted for it and 8 against; had Navarre been included there would have been 16 votes in favor.

Nevertheless, legislation that affected political parties always raised serious issues of principle, and even some doubts as to whether it was in effect practicable. In all probability the new legislation could never have been as effective as it was said to be, or as counterproductive as the nationalist lobby thought it was. The nationalists showed that in practice they were generally in favor of the measure despite the fact that they had clearly voted against it. At the start of August 2002, there was a terrorist incident on the coast of Alicante which was especially detestable because the victims were children and elderly people. The actual outlawing of EH was approved by 313 votes in favor (PP, PSOE, CC, and PA), only 10 against (PNV, EA ERC ... ) and 27 abstentions (CiU, IU, BNG ... ). This decision was reached because there seemed no other means of combating the legal wing of ETA.

Meanwhile, on the other side, Ibarretxe's proposal for solving the political problems of the Basque Country was made public in September 2002. The *lehendakari* suggested a free associated state whose existence should be voted on in a referendum that would take place without the use of violence. This state would have the right to merge with Navarre and Iparralde (the French Basque Country), to an autonomous Basque judicial power, and to exclusive control over matters such as security, language, culture, and international representation. The contents of the plan went beyond the provision made by the 1978 Spanish Constitution and were also unlikely to be politically viable. Not only could the plan not gain the necessary majority in the Spanish *Cortes*, but in principle it would fail to do so too in the Basque Parliament as well. Furthermore, it was quite likely that in a future referendum the percentage of votes might be far lower than for the Guernica Statute which had won above half of the votes polled.

From October 2002 until the end of the year, the PP's position on the plan was perfectly clearly defined and was presented incisively. This was, in any case, part and parcel of the party's neo-conservative and pro-Spanish program. Basque Nationalism was increasingly equated with ETA, and in speeches by PP politicians Catalan nationalism was presented more and more as being identical to Basque nationalism. "Reinforcing Spanishness" also had turned to traditional symbols – for example, flying a 249-square-meter national flag in the Plaza de Colón in Madrid. The term "constitutional patriotism," coined by Jurgen Habermas, became in the hands of the ideologues a strong element to support a notion of the fatherland that had by this time faded and become meaningless. However, an even more powerful means of sparking a reaction was the immediate imposition of a "compulsory nationalism" that brought crowds out to march against Ibarretxe's plan and support Spain and the Constitution. It seemed, then, that there was once again to be blind confrontation in the Basque Country without any possibility of a solution.

There were, at the same time, improved results in the struggle against terrorism. At the end of 2002, pressure by the Spanish and French security forces had once again decapitated ETA, capturing its third leadership since the truce. Despite bad omens concerning the effects of outlawing Batasuna, that year ended with fewer dead (5), fewer terrorist attacks, and more terrorists in prison (140). The number of incidents of *kale borroka* also dwindled, and in 2002 there were only 190, compared to 490 in 2001 and 630 in 2000.

## From More to Less: Government Policy in the Second Four-year Term

This political situation was played out against a background of the judgment of ordinary Spaniards on the government's handling of affairs which, if positive in some ways, in others was far from being so.

Economic growth continued to be at between 3.1 and 2.3 percent per year between 2000 and 2003. These figures were above the Spanish average for the twentieth century and, moreover, above the most recent European figure of 0.4 percent. Within the European Union only Greece grew more than Spain. Furthermore, the increase in levels of employment between 1996 and 2002 had benefited 3 million people, reducing the level of unemployment by 10 percentage points and coming more closely in line with the rest of Europe (at 11 percent in comparison to 9 percent in Germany and France). The balance of public spending was perhaps the government's best and least disputed asset during this second 4 years in office, and Social Security was also far healthier, allowing for a surplus of 1 percent of GDP over the last few years.

It has to be said that towards the end of 2003 a more thorough examination of what was going on revealed undoubted weaknesses in the overall panorama of the Spanish economy. First of all, it is obvious enough that continued economic growth in Spain was not possible without European funding, which was the equivalent of about 1 percent of GDP. On the other hand, no substantial changes had been made in either Social Security or the state broadcasting network RTVE. A third factor was that since 1998 Spain's macroeconomic policy had been aimed at increasing internal demand by pushing up families' disposable income. This meant that the construction industry became the motor driving the economy, growing at a rate of more than 4 percent per year and representing 40 percent of the European total. In 2003 Spain consumed more cement than Germany, which has twice the number of inhabitants and is still facing the consequences of reunification. Another additional problem was the slump in competitiveness and productivity and the increasing deficit in the balance of payments. If the increase in jobs was a sign of hope, at the same time it also presented evident weaknesses (the jobs were of low quality, the percentage of short-term contracts being over 30 percent, which was the highest in Europe), and there was a very high level of work-related accidents. The particular form of "capitalism among friends" that came into being after 1996 has not gained sufficient advantages from the possible economic effects of liberalization.

If Spain's economic policy seen from this angle offers a less optimistic picture, the PP government's social policies in the second term in office were even less promising in many respects. As had happened to the socialist government in 1988, Aznar's government also acted absolutely blindly when it believed that the support afforded by a parliamentary majority was going to allow it to confront the trade unions. The reform of labor relations was attempted by means of a decree-law which then had to be convalidated in the *Cortes*. The way the measure was presented illustrates very well the typical manner in which the government behaved: imposing the bulk of the proposal and only rectifying specific, not very decisive points later.

The *decretazo*, as it came to be known,[1] was given government approval in the *Cortes* on June 14, 2002 and the resulting strike took place on June 20. As was predictable from the start, there were bitter discussions over the results of the strike. Electricity consumption was reduced to 20 percent as if it were a non-working day, but the level of participation varied widely between 20 and 80 percent, depending on the kind of work. Even so, the government – caught entirely by surprise, especially the prime minister – was forced to change tack. The PP, which was supposed to show at least a semblance of unity, ended up committing itself – in Aznar's own words – to "being prepared to shake hands" with the union leaders. At the start of July, Aznar gave Rato the task of speaking to the trade unions, and Rato passed the job on to three ministers. In practice, although it was made to look like hard negotiation that lasted quite some time, the government in effect did nothing other than back down from its initial position. By the start of October, the government suggested to the unions that it was prepared to modify the harshest terms of the *decretazo*. Zaplana, the new Labor Minister, was ultimately put in charge of negotiating with them.

As regards immigration, government policy was once again disconcerting and contradictory, though one might well say that this sums up generally the attitude of the Spanish ruling classes as a whole. However, after seemingly endless discussions, it did at least seem as though there was a desire for a consensus which took shape finally in September 2003. At a time of widespread sullenness in politics, agreement on an issue that was to be crucial for the future was good news. By this time, a survey conducted by the CIS revealed that for 59 percent of those questioned there was a link between immigration and crime in Spain's cities.

Agreement had been reached after a period of several months in which the government had been notable for its bad management of the crisis. From October 2003 on, the PP found itself facing circumstances that were as unexpected as they were negative and its response was extreme, confused, and inefficient at one and the same time.

Reducing crime levels in cities had been one of the major promises it had made, but from 2000 onwards the number of robberies rose by 10 percent a year. The only reason why crime figures were rising was a reduction in police on the job, but instead of addressing this issue, there was an attempt to limit crime by means of successive poorly thought-out reforms to penal legislation. Imitating John Wayne, always ready to draw his gun in his films, the government proposed measures that were exorbitant and extravagant (Javier Pradera).

As for the sinking of the oil-tanker *Prestige*, the events can be summed up very briefly. In a coastal area where, over a century, there had been about 150 shipwrecks, a violent storm threatened to wreck an oil-tanker which, being old, had been repaired not long before. The ship was captained by a man of experience but he was now quite old and the crew had been recruited from all over the world. The owner and the person responsible for the ship's state of repair were hidden behind several layers of companies. The tanker, which received instructions to move away from the coast, finally sank on November 19. The decision taken by the Spanish authorities – to move it away from the coast – was wrong, hurried, and absurd. However, what was even more absurd was the fact that they appeared to be entirely unaware of the ecological disaster that was bound to occur and tried to divert attention away from the Spanish coastline. Under attack, a sulky Aznar did not go to Galicia for a month and a day.

Nor should the accident that cost the lives of more than 70 Spanish soldiers in Turkey on a flight back from Afghanistan be seen as the direct responsibility of the Spanish authorities. They were, however, not wise to hire Ukrainian planes, and they then tried so hard to avoid being implicated in the affair that the funerals were performed in haste and some of the victims were wrongly identified. It is worth noting that the Americans lost 37 men in their action in Afghanistan while Spain – which did not fight there – lost double the number. On this matter Aznar's policy diverged from that of the other European countries in that he offered to send troops without informing the Spanish general public, political parties, or Spain's European allies.

Morocco's decision to withdraw its ambassador from Madrid at the end of October 2001 came as a total surprise. The decision was taken by one of Morocco's so-called "sovereign" ministers – that is to say, one appointed by the king himself – and this means that it cannot be seen as purely circumstantial. It is highly likely that the crisis might have lasted for months, fed by Spanish demands for Morocco to control illegal emigration, until it reached its unfortunate conclusion. The occupation of Parsley Island by a Moroccan patrol in July 2002 shone a spotlight on a controversial issue of which the Spanish public was not even aware. There followed a clearly exaggerated rhetorical performance by the Minister of Defense, and in the end the question remained unresolved. Something similar happened as regards Gibraltar. In April 2002 it was stated that the Spanish and British Foreign Ministers were putting the final touches in secret to a pact which would lead to shared sovereignty along much the same lines as had happened in the case of Hong Kong. Yet this supposed good news went quiet and nothing came of it – proof that it had been the product of unfounded optimism.

The second Iraq war hit Spanish politics like a meteor. From January 2003 on, opinion polls gave storm warnings in the event of Spain taking part in a war that it now seemed hard to avoid. Sixty-one percent of Spaniards expressed their total rejection of the idea of taking part and 24 percent expressed support on the condition that intervention was approved by the United Nations. From very early on it was clear that Aznar, despite everything, was ready to commit Spain fully. His attitude was born of a nationalism that saw as its ideal a "Great Spain" that depended on its cohesion as a nation and needed to overcome "a certain complex about its history," or even "a new legend." One should also add to these factors his total admiration for the American Republican Party. While for the European communities Aznar became an uncomfortable and unpopular associate, in official documents what was spoken of was "a special relationship" with the United States, and the pacts of 1953 were now described as "the start of Spain's opening out to the rest of the world." A parallel can be drawn between Aznar and Thatcher, who suggested that the British should recover their self-esteem by means of the Falklands War.

Acting as though he was the true and only Foreign Minister, hoping that French objections in the Security Council would be short-lived, believing that the war would not last long and that an American victory would be swift and decisive, Aznar convinced himself that Spain could make a huge leap forward if it took advantage of the situation with United States backing. His analysis was wrong and it broke sharply and unequivocally with traditional Spanish foreign policy. He could have shifted his position to one that was more moderately Euro-centered, or that favored transatlantic relations and was not so flamboyant. However, he acted like an "embittered falcon," not only aligning himself closely with the American position but even on occasion running ahead of it or speaking about it in yet more drastic terms. This led to him making even worse errors in his diagnosis. He saw the meeting in the Azores as a great personal triumph when for the American Secretary of State it was an outright failure. On the other hand, he gave himself only a tiny role in the military operations, which were later given the dubious label "humanitarian."

The result was a public reaction that was entirely unexpected in terms of its magnitude. In mid February 2003 some 3 million Spaniards joined in a demonstration against the war: an appreciable percentage of them were PP voters. However, we must remember that it was not just Aznar who was wrong at this time. The same could be said about those who thought this was a kind of "citizens' revolt" against the government. In the opinion of the actors and actresses who marched at the head of the demonstrations, the accusations against Saddam's Iraq were "false" and they insisted that there was "no moral imperative at all" that would allow intervention in that land. It was likely that the war would be long and bloody for the Americans too, but the speed of the campaign seemed to belie that, and although barely 10 percent of Spaniards agreed with the government's actions, foreign policy has never been a decisive element in Spanish election campaigns (as was demonstrated in the 1986 campaign following the referendum on NATO).

## The Final Straight

At a time when new elections were on the horizon, 53 percent of voters disapproved of Aznar's recent performance, but the government was still scoring higher than the prime minister and only a third of PP voters thought that it would be a positive step for another party to govern Spain. One in ten people who voted for the PP and two in ten young people said that they had taken part in the demonstrations against the war. Nonetheless, the PSOE did not manage to capitalize on a rejection of the war of such magnitude that it brought people out onto the streets all over Spain.

The 2003 municipal and regional elections allowed the PSOE in opposition to increase its quota of political power but did not cause the upheaval that had seemed conceivable if one looked only at the anti-war demonstrations. The Iraq war had much less of an impact than anticipated, at least from the left's point of view. In contrast, the *Prestige* affair undoubtedly affected election results in Galicia, though not throughout the region. The National Hydrological Plan, which had disappeared below the horizon of what was thought immediately important, had more of an effect, though once again it depended on the region.

The PSOE won between 100,000 and 200,000 votes more in the national arena (the municipal elections), but where autonomous elections were being held – and that was only in some communities – the PP won. Aznar considered it a personal victory, given what had gone on in previous months, but in reality 2 million PP votes (or 10 percentage points) had vanished into thin air.

During its first term in office the PP had given no sign at all of attempting to bring about any political regeneration by means of approving new legal measures. During the second term there were only the most timid attempts as early on as September 2000, and then later in the summer of 2003 after the municipal elections and those in the autonomous regions. On many other matters such as the Gescartera Affair, the far from impartial behavior of the State Public Prosecutor's Office and the government's policies on the public information media reached hitherto unknown levels in terms of the use of political power for the benefit of those in government. In the end, Telefónica reached the point where it seemed unable to control its own media and it finally abandoned that sphere of activity. Aznar, who went so far as to put his trust in four successive teams to direct the media that he had provided to promote his own position, ended up turning his back on the matter. "Those are the oxen one has to plow with," was his final reflection. Of course the very same oxen were handed over to a publishing company which had shown its support for the government.

In case this evidence of the very low quality of democracy in Spain was not enough, we also have the indisputable testimony of what happened after the 2003 elections at two very different points on the Spanish map: Madrid and Marbella. By their absence, two socialist deputies from Madrid allowed a Popular Party candidate to be elected President of the Madrid Assembly. It soon came to light that the Madrid socialist organization was made up of a collection of clans that fought for nothing but power and were capable of hurling the most serious accusations at each other. It is highly likely that the start of the conflict was nothing other than the disillusionment experienced by one sector of the party, but the party leadership took several wrong turns when it tried to shift the blame onto a supposed property scam linked to the conservative party. The mistakes made by the PP were also huge and shameless, beginning with their attempt to take advantage of a situation that they knew only too well was manifestly immoral. The Marbella case is barely worth a paragraph. It involved not parties but interest groups who pulled the strings to make the mayor's office dance to the rhythm of the benefits derived from their property deals.

In circumstances such as these, the political climate seemed to become more favorable towards the government once again. It had lost the autonomous community of Madrid but it won it back in October 2003 after new elections. Aznar's last debate on the state of the nation (July 2003) produced a very different result from its predecessors: 52 percent of those questioned in a CIS survey declared that Aznar had won the debate and only 15 percent gave the victory to Zapatero. However, the central issue in Spanish politics was still the debate on the organization of the territory of the Spanish state, permeated throughout by the Basque problem in an atmosphere of ever-increasing tension.

The ruling majority in the Basque Parliament had refused to dissolve the Batasuna group and had used legal arguments that were in part understandable. However, the resulting confrontation was a response to political realities and was irresponsible on the part of both sides. If the Basque government left no loophole for dialogue, Aznar's language, which had always been harsh, sometimes disagreeable, and on occasion even intolerable, now bordered on the ridiculous. He gave the distinct impression that apart from the PP everyone else in Spanish politics was a gang of idiots. Adenauer retired without ever having been defeated in elections, and he could say that he did so "serenely and without resentment." Aznar could never have used those words.

In another respect, on the other hand, he was very successful. The handing-over of the leadership of a party often gives rise to moments of tension that are not easily resolved. Aznar managed to make the handover to another leader in a manner that was not only very professional but also had a certain grandeur about it. We cannot know the thought processes which led to his decision not to stand for office a third time, but he had lived through the experience of the long-drawn-out death of the Popular Alliance in the second half of the 1980s (in which he himself had initially been a loser) and he did not want to repeat it.

Extremely confident about his control of the party, he was also able to pick the right political moment and then he acted fast. He could have delayed his decision until the end of 2003 had only an election campaign in Catalonia been on the horizon, but the repeat of the elections in Madrid forced him to move faster. He no doubt showed great magnanimity as he handed over power, and this had been sadly lacking previously. However, he also chose his successor well. Mariano Rajoy had not been a close member of his team, but he did have a more moderate and balanced temperament and had shown himself to be a politician capable of solving problems.

Rajoy's arrival at the pinnacle of power in the PP meant that Aznar was sentenced to at least partial relegation, which allows us to offer here an overall assessment of him as a political figure. Aznar was not a Maura[2] to whom several right-wing political families owed their existence – a man whose stature, even in areas as far-removed from politics as culture, was accepted by all; a man who was called on automatically when the time came to form a national government. Nor was he a Gil Robles – a skilled tactician whose complex strategy during part of his life remains indecipherable up to the present day, a great speaker in Parliament with considerable popular appeal but condemned to only the briefest time as a political leader: as brief as the party that he led. The historical figure with whom we could compare Aznar is not Fraga either, whose behavior was always exaggerated but who was, nonetheless, capable of making crucial decisions for the benefit of everyone (winning agreement on the text of the Constitution from many who had had no intention of accepting it). Even less was he an Areilza, who was in essence a refined loner who found intellectual pursuits attractive but lacked that vital tool for democratic political action: a party. Fundamentally, Aznar's abilities – if one sets the question of the dictatorship aside – meant that he most closely resembled Franco. Because of his closed nature, his coldness, his sense of timing, and his ability to arbitrate between his followers, and because of his apparent inanity, which led to him being despised by his opponents but which hid a powerful sense of ambition, and his unbeatable skill at the cut and thrust of political life within the party, the parallels between these two figures is much greater than it might at first seem.

In preceding pages we have used a distinction from Maravall which is useful when passing judgment on the socialist years. During that period "politics" was a failure while "policies" had brought success. "Politics (the party–government relationship, the leadership . . . ) had worked well for the PP, but what about specific policies?

During its first term of office, when it had an absolute majority, the PSOE made some of its worst mistakes, which made the illegal fight against terrorism and political corruption possible. Yet it also carried out political maneuvers that were of benefit to the country as a whole, such as an orthodox policy of economic adjustment and placing Spain in the position that it was to occupy in the international context.

What will remain as an inheritance from the period of government by the PP will above all be what it achieved in its first 4-year term. One might think that the second term was when the party was most truly itself, while in the first it was forced by circumstances not to reveal its true intentions. Be that as it may, the greatest asset the PP government has had throughout its time in power has been economic prosperity. However, alongside that, deep cracks have appeared in fundamental aspects of its politics that have been unnecessary and counterproductive. The PP's foreign policy has led to undoubted inflexibility, particularly in its relations with Europe and the United States. On education there has been a break not only with the other political forces in Spain but also at the heart of society itself. Last but not least, once of the most serious problems facing Spain today concerns its pluralistic nature and the possibility of translating that nature into political and institutional terms. The PP, which has been a major player in all the agreements on autonomy, closed its mind to any kind of change to the Constitution. This has not been by chance but is rather more a result of its gradual drift away from defining itself as liberal to adopting a neo-conservative ideology.

It has been possible to describe the most recent elections held in Spain in March 2004 as the most dramatic ever in our country in the wake of the most brutal terrorist attack ever to take place in Europe. They were not the first elections to take place under the sign of terrorism, since terrorists have often struck at such crucial moments, but the equivalent of one in five of the total number of those murdered by ETA died in just one day. Until that moment it had been believed that Islamic terrorism saw Spain as nothing more than a kind of logistical base, not a place in which to carry out attacks. In this matter the conservative government was wrong and so was the left-wing press. There is no doubt, however, that the 192 deaths on Madrid's local train network left a deep and lasting impression.

Yet it should not be thought that the Atocha bombings alone can explain what happened in the ensuing elections; instead, one must also take into account what had gone on before this event. According to the opinion polls, between April 2000 and January 2004 the PP had lost 8 percentage points in popular acceptance, while the PSOE had risen by 7. The succession of badly managed crises (the *decretazo*, the *Prestige*, the air accident in Turkey . . . ) and the party's displays of dominance had damaged its credibility in government. In a very particular way, Spain's participation in the Iraq war was neither understood not accepted by the immense majority of the population, including most of the right-wing factions. Also, the points awarded to ministers were, in all cases, very low. There was not, however, any great enthusiasm felt towards the opposition either, especially after the crisis in Madrid and the level of inefficiency shown by the PSOE leadership in dealing with it. Even so, the socialist candidate, Rodríguez Zapatero, was slightly ahead of the prime minister and the PP candidate, Rajoy, at the start of the year.

The campaign proper consistently gave a certain advantage to the PP but also noticeably raised opposition expectations. The PP campaign was atrocious in that it seemed to be no more than a projection of bureaucratic expectations, it focused on an exasperatingly unitarian view of Spain, and, at the same time, it avoided direct confrontation with its opponents to prevent any unwelcome surprises. The PSOE was unequivocal in its support of its candidate, who was presented for the first time surrounded by figures who could be described as representing solid, objective values from the party's previous time in office. The campaign also placed special emphasis on the problems faced by ordinary citizens. It promised a fresh political climate based on dialogue and not on confrontation. It also called for strategic voting, stating that it would not be able to govern without gaining more votes than the PP.

There was no reason why the Atocha bombings should have favored the opposition as no one blamed the government for what had happened. Nonetheless, the government did display a kind of behavior that many found intolerable, either concealing or not knowing the truth about what had happened, reacting ridiculously forcefully against its political adversaries, and proving unable to draw on a consensus at such a crucial time. Just as in 1996 the PSOE had been brought down not by the corruption of some of its members but by the fact that the problem persisted and the government seemed unable to solve it, so too in this case it was not the terrorist attack itself but the government's reaction to it that was so disastrous for the PP. For a start, there was an 8.5 percent increase in voting in the elections when in Spain abstention is traditionally a left-wing characteristic. Fewer voted than in 1977 and 1982, but numbers were close to those of 1993 and 1996.

The PSOE won 42.6 percent of the vote and 164 seats – a total of 3 million votes and 39 seats more than before. The Popular Party managed a mere 9.6 million, with a loss of 7 percent of the vote and 35 seats, which left it with 148 seats. Generally speaking, there was a concentration of strategic voting with exceptions in the case of Navarre and Catalonia. In Catalonia, circumstances gave Esquerra 450,000 votes and 8 seats (7 more than on the previous occasion) while CiU, thanks to its relationship with the PP, lost 140,000 votes and 5 seats, being left with only 10. The IU vote only went down by 1 percent, but because of the electoral law it lost seats, going down from 9 to 5. CC, BNG, and PA each lost one seat. Over the entire electoral map of Spain there were some significant occurrences to be seen, such as the collapse of the conservative vote in towns and the historical national entities, and also in those regions that had been adversely affected by the National Hydrological Plan. As well as considering all that happened during the campaign and in the months running up to it, it is worth asking who the new PSOE voters were. Apart from abstentionists and strategic voters, we should bear very much in mind those who were using their right to vote for the first time, and the undecided from the center-ground of Spanish politics.

The political situation that emerged as a result of these elections was not comparable with any of the previous occasions on which the PSOE had won at the polls. In fact the closest parallel was with the UCD's experience in 1977 and 1979, which had meant an outcome in parliament that allowed a government to be formed with sufficient support but a minority nonetheless. In this way, via consensus guaranteed by an atmosphere of dialogue, it was possible to initiate important political changes based on raising the standard of democracy as demands were heard for institutions such as the law courts and public television to be independent of the government, and for adjustments to be made to the Constitution on the matter of the organization of territory within the Spanish state.

## Bibliography

General works: Joaquín ALMUNIA, Los puntos negros del PP. La cara oscura de sus ocho años de gobierno, Aguilar, Madrid, 2004; Pilar CERNUDA and Fernando JÁUREGUI, El sequerón. Ocho años de aznarato, Planeta, Barcelona, 2004; Victoria PREGO, Presidentes. Veinticinco años de Historia narrada por los cuatro jefes de gobierno de la democracia, Plaza y Janés, Barcelona, 2000; Javier TUSELL (ed.), El gobierno de Aznar. Balance de una gestión, Crítica, Barcelona, 2000, and El aznarato, Aguilar, Madrid, 2004.

About Aznar: Amando DE MIGUEL, Retrato de Aznar, Planeta, Barcelona, 2002; José DÍAZ HERRERA and Isabel DURÁN, Aznar. La vida desconocida de un presidente, Planeta, Barcelona, 1999; Graciano PALOMO, El vuelo del halcón. José María Aznar y la aventura de la derecha española, Temas de Hoy, Madrid, 1990, and El túnel. La larga marcha de José María Aznar y la derecha española hacia el poder, Temas de Hoy, Madrid, 1993; Graciano PALOMO and J. A. MARTÍNEZ VEGA, La tierra prometida. Todas las claves del nuevo poder en España, Javier Vergara, Madrid, 1996.

Memoirs: Iñaki ANASAGASTI, Agur Aznar. Memorias de un vasco en Madrid, Temas de Hoy, Madrid, 2004; José María AZNAR, Ocho años de gobierno. Una *visión personal de España*, Planeta, Barcelona, 2004; Pedro J. RAMÍREZ, *El desquite. Los años de Aznar*, La Esfera de los Libros, Madrid, 2004.

Economic and social policy: José Luis GARCÍA DELGADO (ed.), *España, economía: ante el siglo XXI*, Espasa Calpe, Madrid, 1999; Jesús MOTA, *La gran expropriación. Las privatizaciones y el nacimiento de una clase empresarial al servicio del PP*, Temas de Hoy, Madrid, 1998, and *Aves de rapiña*, Temas de Hoy, Madrid, 2001; Pedro SCHWARTZ, *Queda mucho por hacer. Conversaciones con cuatro ministros del PP*, Marcial Pons, Madrid, 2000.

The question of regional autonomy and Basque and Catalan nationalism: Eliseo AJA, *El estado autonómico. Federalismo y hechos diferenciales*, Alianza, Madrid, 1999. On terrorism: Fernando REINARES, *Terrorismo y antiterrorismo*, Paidós, Barcelona, 1998, and *Patriotas de la muerte. Quiénes han militado en ETA y por qué*, Taurus, Madrid, 2001; Isabel SAN SEBASTIÁN, *Mayor Oreja. Una victoria contra el miedo*, La Esfera de los Libros, Madrid, 2001.

The opposition: Gonzalo LÓPEZ ALBA, *El relevo. Crónica viva del camino hacia el II Suresnes del PSOE*, Taurus, Madrid, 2002; Luis YÁÑEZ, *La soledad del ganador. La verdad sobre el efecto Borrell*, Temas de Hoy, Madrid, 2001.

Journalistic accounts: Jesús CACHO, *El negocio de la libertad*, Foca, Madrid, 1999; Ernesto EKAIZER, *El farol. La primera condena de Mario Conde*, Temas de Hoy, Madrid, 1997; Mariano SÁNCHEZ SOLER, *Las sotanas del PP. El pacto entre la Iglesia y la derecha española*, Temas de Hoy, Madrid, 2002; Pilar URBANO, *Garzón. El hombre que veía amanecer*, Plaza y Janés, Barcelona, 2000.

The media: José Antonio MARTÍNEZ SOLER, *Jaque a Palanco*, Temas de Hoy, Madrid, 1998.

Foreign policy: Carlos ELORDI, *El amigo americano*, Temas de Hoy, Madrid, 2003; Charles POWELL in Nigel Townson, *Historia virtual de España*, Taurus, Madrid, 2004.

The final stage and the elections: Belén BARREIRO, "14-M: elecciones a la sombra del terrorismo," *Claves*, no. 141 (April 2004); Magis IGLESIAS, *La sucesión. La historia de cómo Aznar eligió a Mariano Rajoy*, Temas de Hoy, Madrid, 2003.

## Notes

1   The suffix *-azo*, used to denote a blow being delivered (*puño*, fist; *puñetazo*, punch), suggests that the decree was used as a weapon.
2   Antonio Maura played an important and contentious role in late nineteenth/ early twentieth-century politics.

# Index

CPSIA information can be obtained
at www.ICGtesting.com
Printed in the USA
FSOW03n0237080717
36066FS